NEW DIRECT

MW00808055

Series Editor:

Imke Meyer

Editorial Board:

Katherine Arens, Roswitha Burwick, Richard Eldridge, Erika Fischer-Lichte, Catriona MacLeod, Stephan Schindler, Heidi Schlipphacke, Ulrich Schönherr, James A. Schultz, Silke-Maria Weineck, David Wellbery, Sabine Wilke, John Zilcosky.

Volumes in the series:

Ghostwriting

W. G. Sebald's Poetics of History

Richard T. Gray

BLOOMSBURY ACADEMIC
NEW YORK • LONDON • OXFORD • NEW DELHI • SYDNEY

BLOOMSBURY ACADEMIC
Bloomsbury Publishing Inc
1385 Broadway, New York, NY 10018, USA
50 Bedford Square, London, WC1B 3DP, UK

BLOOMSBURY, BLOOMSBURY ACADEMIC and the Diana logo are trademarks
of Bloomsbury Publishing Plc

First published 2017
Paperback edition first published 2019

Copyright © Richard T. Gray, 2017

For legal purposes the Acknowledgments on p. ix constitute an
extension of this copyright page.

Archival Materials © 2017, The Estate of W. G. Sebald. All Rights Reserved.

Cover design: Andrea Federle-Bucsi
Cover image © Scala/Art Resources, NY

All rights reserved. No part of this publication may be reproduced or
transmitted in any form or by any means, electronic or mechanical, including
photocopying, recording, or any information storage or retrieval system,
without prior permission in writing from the publishers.

Bloomsbury Publishing Inc does not have any control over, or responsibility for,
any third-party websites referred to or in this book. All internet addresses given
in this book were correct at the time of going to press. The author and publisher
regret any inconvenience caused if addresses have changed or sites have
ceased to exist, but can accept no responsibility for any such changes.

Library of Congress Cataloging-in-Publication Data
Names: Gray, Richard T., author.
Title: Ghostwriting : W. G. Sebald's poetics of history / Richard T. Gray.
Other titles: W. G. Sebald's poetics of history
Description: New York : Bloomsbury Academic, 2017. | Series: New directions
in German studies ; 19 | Includes bibliographical references and index.
Identifiers: LCCN 2017018313 (print) | LCCN 2017034122 (ebook) | ISBN
9781501330001 (ePub) | ISBN 9781501330018 (ePDF) | ISBN 9781501329999
(hardback)
Subjects: LCSH: Sebald, W. G. (Winfried Georg), 1944-2001–Criticism and
interpretation. | Literature and history. | Memory in literature. | Exiles
in literature. | Collective memory and literature. | BISAC: LITERARY
CRITICISM / European / German. | LITERARY CRITICISM / Semiotics & Theory.
Classification: LCC PT2681.E18 (ebook) | LCC PT2681.E18 Z6345 2017 (print) |
DDC 833/.914–dc23
LC record available at https://lccn.loc.gov/2017018313

ISBN: HB: 978-1-5013-2999-9
PB: 978-1-5013-5261-4
ePDF: 978-1-5013-3001-8
eBook: 978-1-5013-3000-1

Series: New Directions in German Studies

Typeset by Fakenham Prepress Solutions, Fakenham, Norfolk NR21 8NN

To find out more about our authors and books visit
www.bloomsbury.com and sign up for our newsletters.

Contents

List of Illustrations

Acknowledgments

The research and writing of this book were promoted by the generous support of numerous individuals and institutions. I owe infinite gratitude to the Byron W. and Alice L. Lockwood Foundation for its sustained and sustaining commitment to my scholarly endeavors since 2003. Resources from the Lockwood Professorship helped to fund two extended stays at the Deutsches Literaturarchiv in Marbach, where I was able to peruse books from Sebald's working library and study the manuscripts and materials in his literary estate. One of these research visits also benefited from travel funding provided by the Center for West European Studies at the University of Washington. My research into the ecocritical and ecopsychological aspects of Sebald's Corsica project was made possible by a Renewed Research Prize Award (*Forschungspreis Wiederaufnahme*) from the Alexander von Humboldt Foundation, which funded a three-month research leave at the Rachel Carson Center for Environment and Society at the Ludwigs-Maximilian-Universität Munich. Special thanks are due to Professor Christof Mauch, the Director of the Carson Center, for his support, and for placing the manifold resources of the Center at my disposal. I profited greatly from the interactive atmosphere among the fellows and the Center staff.

I am particularly grateful to Dr. Ulrich von Bülow, director of the manuscript division at the Deutsches Literaturarchiv in Marbach, for providing me with an opportunity to study Sebald's manuscripts and for sharing with me his own considerable expertise about Sebald's writing strategies and compositional practices. The staff and librarians at the archive also warrant thanks for their untiring assistance and consistently friendly demeanor during my research stays. In addition to Dr. von Bülow, special mention is owed to Katharina von Wilucki and Susanne Rößler, the librarians in the Reading Room whose help in locating and recovering items was instrumental for my research.

Some parts of this book have previously been published in preliminary form. An earlier version of Chapter 3 appeared under the title

"Sebald's Pretexts: 'Dr. Henry Selwyn' and its Textual Predecessor" in *Seminar* 45 (2009): 387–406; Chapter 4 appeared in abbreviated form in the volume *Literatur im Zeitalter des Totalitarismus: Festschrift für Dieter Sevin*, edited by Elke Gilson, Barbara Hahn, and Holly Liu (Hildesheim: Georg Olms, 2008), 209–26; Chapter 6, "Fabulation and Metahistory," was first delivered as a Solomon Katz Distinguished Lecture at the University of Washington, and a preliminary version appeared in the collection *Literarische Experimente*, edited by Christoph Zeller (Heidelberg: Carl Winter Verlag, 2012), 271–301; an early rendition of Chapter 7 was printed in *The Germanic Review* 84 (2009): 26–58; and finally, sections of Chapter 8 appeared in provisional form as "Writing at the Roche Limit: Order and Entropy in W. G. Sebald's *Die Ringe des Saturn*" in *The German Quarterly* 83, no. 1 (Winter 2010): 38–57, and "From Grids to Vanishing Points: W. G. Sebald's Critique of Visual-Representational Orders in *Die Ringe des Saturn*," in *German Studies Review* 32 (2009): 495–526, © 2009 Johns Hopkins University Press, reprinted with permission by Johns Hopkins University Press. I want to express my thanks to all these journals and publishers for permission to reprint these essays in revised form.

Special gratitude is due to the Estate of W. G. Sebald for permission to cite from Sebald's published works and unpublished archival materials, as well as to reprint illustrations from published works and manuscripts. These materials are used by permission of the Wylie Agency, LLC on behalf of the estate of W. G. Sebald. I benefitted from the kind interventions of Savannah Lake from Wylie's New York office, whose charitable attitude, understanding, and responsiveness served as a lifeline in an otherwise often suffocating process. To her I owe an endless debt of gratitude. I also want to express my special appreciation to my editor at Bloomsbury Academic, Haaris Naqvi, and to his assistant Katherine De Chant, for standing by and assisting me along the often arduous path of obtaining the necessary permissions, as well as for shepherding the book through to publication.

Many other individuals have supported the research for this project in diverse ways. Among these, I want to single out the students in my graduate seminars on Sebald at the University of Washington in 2007 and 2015, and at the University of Tübingen in 2013. Their enthusiasm and creative engagement with Sebald was infectious, and it helped stimulate my own constant rethinking and re-engagement with his texts and his thought. I also want to thank my colleagues in the Department of Germanics at the University of Washington for maintaining a collaborative intellectual community in which scholarly and pedagogical pursuits can thrive. Finally, this project could never have been realized without the boundless patience, emotional support, and intellectual companionship of my wife, Sabine Wilke, and the willingness of my daughter, Cora Wilke-Gray, to endure my paternal bumbling. I dedicate this book to them with enduring love.

RTG
Seattle/Winthrop, 2017

List of Abbreviations

Throughout this book Sebald's works are cited by their German titles, followed by the page reference to the German original and, after the slash, the reference to the published English translation. Sebald's works of prose fiction are cited from the first, hardbound German editions. Since subsequent paperback German editions commonly follow the same page format, although the specific page numbers may differ, those using these versions should be able to locate citations without difficulty. The one exception is *Schwindel. Gefühle*, where the formatting and page numbers of the first edition and the later paperback editions vary enormously. Here I have elected to reference the more commonly available German paperback version. English renditions follow the standard published translations. English versions of untranslated works are my own.

"Auf ungeheuer dünnem Eis" = *"Auf ungeheuer dünnem Eis"*: *Gespräche 1971 bis 2001*. Edited by Torsten Hoffmann. Frankfurt am Main: Fischer, 2011.

"Aufzeichnungen" = "Aufzeichnungen aus Korsika: Zur Natur- und Menschenkunde." In *Wandernde Schatten: W. G. Sebalds Unterwelt*, edited by Ulrich von Bülow, 129–209. Marbach am Neckar: Deutsche Schillergesellschaft, 2008.

Ausgewanderten = *Die Ausgewanderten: Vier lange Erzählungen*. Frankfurt am Main: Eichborn, 1992 (*The Emigrants*. Translated by Michael Hulse. New York: New Directions, 1997).

Austerlitz = *Austerlitz*. Munich: Hanser, 2001 (*Austerlitz*. Translated by Anthea Bell. New York: Modern Library, 2001).

Beschreibung = *Die Beschreibung des Unglücks: Zur österreichischen*

Literatur von Stifter bis Handke. 1985; rpt. Frankfurt am Main: Fischer Taschenbuch Verlag, 1994.

Campo Santo = *Campo Santo*. Edited by Sven Meyer. Munich: Hanser, 2003 (*Campo Santo*. Translated by Anthea Bell. New York: Random House, 2005).

"Leben Ws" = "Leben Ws: Skizze einer möglichen Szenenreihe für einen nichtrealisierten Film." In *Saturn's Moons: W. G. Sebald—A Handbook*, edited by Jo Catling and Richard Hibbitt, 324–33. London: Modern Humanities Research Association, 2011.

"Literaturfonds" = Typescript of an application to the *Deutscher Literaturfonds*. Konvolut: Unterlagen für die Bewerbung um ein Werkstipendium des Deutschen Literaturfonds, Deutsches Literaturarchiv Marbach, inventory number HS.2004.0001.00011.

Logis = *Logis in einem Landhaus: Über Gottfried Keller, Johann Peter Hebel, Robert Walser und andere*. 1998; rpt. Frankfurt am Main: Fischer, 2000 (*A Place in the Country*. Translated by Jo Catling. New York: Random House, 2013).

Luftkrieg = *Luftkrieg und Literatur*. 1999; rpt. Frankfurt am Main: Fischer, 2001 (*On the Natural History of Destruction*. Translated by Anthea Bell. New York: Modern Library, 2003).

"Projekt Wittgenstein" = Konvolut: Leben Ws: Skizze einer möglichen Szenenreihe für einen nichtrealisierten Film, Deutsches Literaturarchiv Marbach, inventory number HS.2004.0001.00007.

Ringe = *Die Ringe des Saturn: Eine englische Wallfahrt*. Frankfurt am Main: Eichborn, 1995 (*The Rings of Saturn*. Translated by Michael Hulse. New York: New Directions, 1997).

Schwartz = Lynne Sharon Schwartz, ed. *The Emergence of Memory: Conversations with W. G. Sebald*. New York: Seven Stories Press, 2007.

Schwindel = *Schwindel. Gefühle*. 1990; rpt. Frankfurt am Main: Fischer Taschenbuch Verlag, 1994 (*Vertigo*. Translated by Michael Hulse. New York: New Directions, 2000).

Unheimliche Heimat = *Unheimliche Heimat: Essays zur österreichischen Literatur*. 1991; rpt. Frankfurt am Main: Fischer, 1995.

Introduction: Sebald's Literary Séance

"The past is never dead. It's not even past."

William Faulkner[1]

"In der Beschäftigung mit der Vergangenheit, der eigenen und der ihrer einstmaligen Lieben, treffen Gespenster und Schriftsteller einander."
["Ghosts and writers meet in their concern for the past—their own and that of those who were once dear to them."]

W. G. Sebald (*Campo Santo* 187/144)

In a 1998 interview with Sarah Kafatou, the German émigré writer W. G. Sebald (1944–2001) articulated succinctly what might be considered the program of his literary endeavor. "Works of literature, like the crystallized twigs, are the hardened remains of former lives." He went on to remark that "behind all of us who are living there are the dead."[2] Those familiar with Sebald's work will recognize the metaphor of the crystallized twig as a common leitmotif, one that first appeared ten years earlier in the short story "Beyle oder das merckwürdige Faktum der Liebe" ("Beyle, or Love is a Madness Most Discreet") from his inaugural collection of fictional prose, *Schwindel. Gefühle* (*Vertigo*). The persistence of this image for Sebald's thought is exemplified by the fact that it resurfaces in the final story of his second collection of tales, *Die Ausgewanderten* (*The Emigrants*), titled "Max Aurach" in the German original and "Max Ferber" in the English translation. As in the 1998 interview, this metaphor alludes to issues of natural creation and, obliquely, to artistic production. In this tale, Sebald's characteristic first-person narrator spends an entire afternoon in the saline works of Bad Kissingen, watching and listening to the play of water in the

---

1   William Faulkner, *Requiem for a Nun* (New York: Vintage, 2001), 73.
2   Sarah Kafatou, "An Interview with W. G. Sebald," *Harvard Review* 15 (1998): 32, 33.

mines, caught up, as he remarks, in "ruminations about the long-term and (I believe) impenetrable process which, as the concentration of salts increases in the water, produces the very strangest of petrified or crystallized forms, imitating the growth patterns of Nature even as it is being dissolved" ("Nachdenken über die langwierigen und, wie ich glaube, unergründlichen Vorgänge, die beim Höhergradieren der Salzlösung die seltsamsten Versteinerungs- und Kristallisationsformen hervorbringen, Nachahmungen gewissermaßen und Aufhebungen der Natur" [*Ausgewanderten* 344/230]). This remark is immediately followed by an illustration of a crystallized bough (see Figure I.1), depicting the results of this simultaneously generative and degenerative process.

Beyond simply providing visual documentation of the crystallization process, this illustration serves as a pictorial transition to the deliberations that follow, which deal specifically with the narrator's difficulties in adequately recording his protagonist's life:

> Über die Wintermonate 1990/91 arbeitete ich in der wenigen mir zur freien Verfügung stehenden Zeit ... an der im Vorhergehenden erzählten Geschichte Max Aurachs. Es war ein äußerst mühevolles, oft stunden- und tagelang nicht vom Fleck kommendes und nicht selten sogar rückläufiges Unternehmen, bei dem ich fortwährend geplagt wurde von einem immer nachhaltiger sich bemerkbar machenden und mehr und mehr mich lähmenden Skrupulantismus. (*Ausgewanderten* 344)
> [During the winter of 1990/91, in the little free time I had ... I was working on the account of Max Ferber given above. It was an arduous task. Often I could not get on for hours or days at a time,

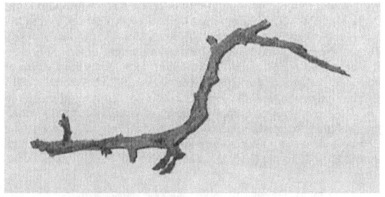

Figure I.1: Crystallized Twig, "Max Aurach"/"Max Ferber" (*Ausgewanderten* 344/230).

and not infrequently I unravelled what I had done, continuously tormented by scruples that were taking tighter hold and steadily paralysing me. (*Emigrants* 230)]

The illustration of the crystallized twig plays a metafictional role: by linking these two passages, it suggests that the natural process of crystallization and the reiterative process of life writing are analogous. And indeed, they are. For just as the salt crystals are conceived both as imitations—*Nachahmungen*—of nature, they simultaneously mark its dissolution—*Aufhebungen*. This German word is especially rife with meaning, since it refers both to dissolution, as indicated by the English translation, but also suggests elevation. The German philosopher Georg Friedrich Wilhelm Hegel (1770–1831) employed this term to designate the complex relationships of abrogation and preservation inherent in the dialectical resolution of opposites, and the German word unavoidably calls up this historical allusion. Crystallization as a creative process manifests this paradoxical tension between creating and dissolving, imitating and supplanting, doing and undoing. The illustration of the petrified bough, with its bends and shifts in direction, as well as its myriad offshoots and unrealized buds, concretizes both the tortured and twisted path of Aurach's life, but also the fits and false starts, the abandoned pathways toward a reconstitution of his existence that plague the narrator, for whom writing inherently implies unwriting and rewriting, a deliberative and corrective process in which various possibilities are played out, tested, and variants rejected and rewritten.[3] Moreover, as a mineralized agglutination that grows on the surface of the bough, crystallization emblematizes a dynamic of simultaneous imitation and fictionalization: the crystals grow along the contours preordained by the shape of the twig, and thereby "imitate" it; but they also represent accretions, supplements that transfigure the substance on which they emerge. In that sense, crystallization is an emblem for Sebald's poetics of history: the creative,

---

3   Sebald returns throughout his works to similar metafictional and self-reflexive models that comment on his own creative processes. One thinks of the textiles produced by the Ashbury sisters in *Die Ringe des Saturn* (264–5/212) or, in the same text, of the miniature temple of Jerusalem created by Alec Garrard/Thomas Abrams (303–5/243–5). For a related exploration of the metaphor of crystallization in Sebald, see Claudia Öhlschläger, "Kristallisation als kulturelle Transformation: Stendhal, W. G. Sebald und das Problem der Wirklichkeitstreue," in *Verschiebebahnhöfe der Erinnerung: Zum Werk W. G. Sebalds*, ed. Sigurd Martin and Ingo Wintermeyer (Würzburg: Königshausen & Neumann, 2007), 105–18. Öhlschläger explicates this image in terms of the limitations of mimetic art, but this unduly restricts the reach of this metaphor and forecloses the richness with which Sebald invests it.

fictional elaboration on patterns proffered by historical models, with the purpose of enhancing what Sebald liked to call the *effect* of the real.[4] One of the defining features of Sebald's literary artistry is the subtle and allusive character by which, as in the example from "Max Aurach," this association of crystallization and life writing is made: his readers are asked to build transitions that will lend coherence to these loosely connected fragments, and in so doing they also are encouraged to engage in this process of creative crystallization themselves. However, this passage also indicates how images in Sebald's works, far from being merely illustrative, often serve strategic functions: in this case, forming a connective bridge between two seemingly unrelated textual segments, and simultaneously providing a visual supplement that elaborates on the problematic discussed in the text.

When Sebald first explores the metaphor of the crystallized twig in the story "Beyle," it does not stand for the general process of creativity, nor as an analogy for adequate representation in life writing; instead it refers to the imaginative process by which lovers project surplus value onto the objects of their desire. The protagonist of this story, the French writer Henri Beyle, better known by his pen name Stendhal, visits the Hallein salt mines with his then-lover Mme. Gherardi and presents her with just such a crystallized twig as an emblem of his devotion. Sebald's narrator summarizes: "The protracted crystallisation process, which had transformed the dead twig into a truly miraculous object, appeared to Beyle, by his own account, as an allegory for the growth of love in the salt mines of the soul" ("Der langwierige Prozeß der Kristallisation, der den toten Zweig in ein wahres Wunderwerk verwandelt hatte, schien Beyle, wie er eigens ausführt, eine Allegorie für das Wachstum der Liebe in den Salzbergwerken unserer Seelen"; *Schwindel* 31/26). What is remarkable about this transformative process, regardless of the metaphorical tenor to which it is applied, is its uncanny ability to transmogrify something "dead" into something "truly miraculous." This formula might stand as a watchword for the power of Sebald's fiction, its capacity to reanimate what is dead, be that a deceased person, a historical event, or even a forgotten narrative account. "And so they are ever returning to us, the dead"—"So also kehren sie wieder, die Toten" (*Ausgewanderten* 36/23): this statement from the concluding paragraph of "Henry Selwyn," the first tale in *Die Ausgewanderten*, articulates a succinct metacommentary on Sebald's literary project, which is persistently occupied with staging precisely such (narrative) returns. What

---

4   In an interview with Carole Angier, Sebald admits that he falsified—that is fictionalized—parts of the diary of his uncle Ambros Adelwarth, in the story of that name, in order "to provide *l'effet de réel*," a phrase he borrows from Roland Barthes (Schwartz 72).

the metaphor of crystallization in "Beyle" suggests, however, is that this process of reanimating the dead as enervated and vital "ghosts" of themselves relies on the creative implementation of imaginative embellishment. Inspired recreation of the past—in the literal sense of breathing life back into it—is only possible through the employment of animating fictions: fact and fiction enter into a cooperative project, just as do salt water and twig in the creative process of crystallization. My title "Ghostwriting" is intended to invoke this notion of revitalized return of what was once dead, while the subtitle "poetics of history" suggests the paradox that the process of reconstructing dead lives in all their authenticity depends precisely on the strategies of creative fiction.

There is one further dimension that lends emblematic significance to Sebald's employment of the crystallization metaphor: his tendency to latch onto prominent motifs and return to them in varied contexts and with divergent functions and meanings. Thus in the 1998 interview, crystallization is linked directly with that aspect of his own literary project that presents "former lives" in the "hardened remains" of the literary text, whereas in the tale of Max Aurach the very dynamism of the crystallizing process suggests an analogy between petrification and writing. Moreover, in its initial adaptation in "Beyle," the metaphor is simply borrowed from Stendhal as a representation for the creative, elaborative fictions wrought on an object by the loving—and desiring— imagination. The metaphor itself, significantly, is not Sebald's creative invention, but represents an appropriation, something he lifts in scarcely modified form from its source in Stendhal's *Love*. But when he later revisits this allegory, he transmutes and adapts it to new contexts. This is another dimension of the phenomenon of return and reiteration that is typical of Sebald's prose fictions: the recurrent resurfacing of certain salient images—one thinks, for example, of walking, of travel by water, of fire, of dust, or of ash—that re-emerge throughout his works like the underlying drone of a thoroughbass, but which are constantly refunctionalized, refurbished, and recontextualized in their multiple recurrences. In this regard Sebald is a ghostwriter of himself, since this network of motivic lines, which emerge along the pattern of theme and variation, establish a discursive common ground that links one work with another based on *intra*textual echoes. Sebald's privileged motifs and metaphors themselves undergo a process of crystallizing accretion as they develop throughout his oeuvre. This reflex of self-reference is closely allied with Sebald's recognized practice of intertextual allusion and citation, as evidenced in his adaptation of Stendhal. These modified repetitions lend Sebald's works an enticing ring of the familiar, while simultaneously avoiding the static mundaneness of the same. Sebald's readers are frequently haunted by a pervasive sense of discursive déjà vu, or more precisely déjà entendu or déjà lu, of having already *heard* or *read* these words before. The reiteration of motifs on the *intratextual* level of Sebald's oeuvre, and the allusion to the words and texts of others in their *intertextual* dimension, replicate in the domain of discursive practice the narrative and memorial return of what is "dead," lost, or forgotten. Inter- and intratextual practices, as repetitions, are thus fundamental to Sebald's ghostwriting, as a *poetics* of history.

Sebald's fiction does not simply enact discursive returns in the intricacies of its textual networking, or deal with fictionalized, animated returns of the dead protagonists on the diegetic level of his storylines; rather, his writing performs this gesture of return in the superimpositions of narrative voices it practices in its narrative texture. We witness this overlay of voices in simplified form in the cited passage from "Beyle," which embodies that typical Sebaldian moment in which the voice of his narrator communes with a distinct voice from the past, recounting in its own recognizable diction Stendhal's historical account of his visit to the Salzburg saline works, his love for Mme. Gherardi, and his elaboration on the process of crystallization as a metaphor for the lover's imaginative investments. Sebald's narrator summarizes, with scant divergence, the portrayal Stendhal offers in his treatise *Love*.[5] Thus Sebald's fictional endeavor does not merely represent a form of ghostwriting in the sense that it resuscitates the dead on the diegetic level of the story itself, but also insofar as it practices in its own narrative discourse a kind of literary séance in which the narrator functions as a medium who invokes the presence of other narrators through whom he speaks, and who ventriloquizes their voices in his own speech and literary diction. The metaphor of crystallization is appropriate for this configuration as well, because it captures both the layering of diverse voices and the temporal accretion inherent in this voiceover. The living voice of his narrator is indeed one that instantiates and practices the dictum that "behind all of us who are living there are the dead," to return to the comment from Sebald's interview with Sarah Kafatou. His literary undertaking constitutes a form of "ghostwriting" in the concrete sense that his narrator speaks, and hence Sebald as author writes, in the voices and in the names of those others whose stories he recounts and reshapes.

The spiritualist séance represents an especially fitting allegory for this narrative situation. It is easy to imagine Sebald's narrator sitting at a table in a darkened room, lit perhaps only by candlelight, holding hands with a series of informants who wish to communicate with a deceased or lost figure from the historical past. The experiences and words of this

---

5   See the section "The Salzburg Bough" in Stendhal's *Love*, trans. Gilbert and Suzanne Sale (London: Penguin, 2004), 284–92, where this episode and the metaphor of crystallization are elaborated.

recaptured "ghost" are intoned by this narrator in his role as a spiritual medium, who relies on the input of the informants at the table to facilitate this spectral return.[6] Moreover, we should imagine ourselves, as Sebald's readers, sitting at this same table, holding hands with the narrator and his informants in an extended chain of communication in which the past comes to life and what is "dead" is transformed into "a truly miraculous object"—into the literary work of art that, like the crystallized bough, refracts the light of the present through the petrified accretions of the past. Sebald's narrative practice is also distinctive due to the insistence with which he calls attention to the presence of his narrator as medium and mediator of these past voices, persons, experiences, and events. In his texts the diegesis never emerges transparently, as pure story decoupled from the "lens" or the framing perspective of this narrating presence. On the contrary, the intermediated moment of retelling is continually highlighted by reference to the narrator's performance of indirect speech acts, his narrative recounting of the speech of others in his own words. In this sense Sebald's narrator functions quite literally as a "ghostwriter," as someone who speaks or writes in the name of and on behalf of someone else.[7] Sebald liked to refer to this highly mediated, or Chinese-box, structure for recounting the past as "periscopic" narration, a technique whose development he attributed to the Austrian writer Thomas Bernhard. He explained the strategic purpose of this narration-at-a-distance in an interview with Kenneth Baker, published just two months before his death:

> I've always felt that the traditional novel doesn't give you enough information about the narrator, and I think it's important to know the point of view from which these tales are told, the moral makeup of the teller. That's why my narrator has such a presence. I intimate that the narrator doesn't know more about the lives of other characters than they've told him. So you have this periscopic point of view through layers of hearsay.[8]

---

6   Thomas Kastura, "Geheimnisvolle Fähigkeit zur Transmigration: W. G. Sebalds interkulturelle Wallfahrten in die Leere," *Arcadia* 31 (1996): 199, identifies the process of transmigration as the signature feature of Sebald's writing. Uwe Schütte, *W. G. Sebald: Einführung in Leben und Werk* (Göttingen: Vandenhoeck & Ruprecht, 2011), 13, also emphasizes the ghost-like presence of the undead in Sebald's works.

7   See Arthur Williams's "W. G. Sebald," in *The Literary Encyclopedia*, http://www.litencyc.com/php/speople.php?rec=true&UID=4961 (accessed March 17, 2017). Williams designates Sebald's narrators as facilitators for those whose voices have been silenced.

8   Kenneth Baker, "W. G. Sebald: Up Against Historical Amnesia," *San Francisco Chronicle*, October 7, 2001, R2. On the model of this technique in the literary

Expressed in a different metaphorical register, Sebald's narratives insistently foreground the act of narration as a kind of echo chamber in which the voices of the past are reconstituted through the monolithic voice of the present-day narrator. As a result, Sebald's narrator takes on a concrete presence in his own right, assuming the pseudo-autobiographical traits of the author W. G. Sebald. The narrative frame of his works thereby assumes the status of an independent diegesis that has a life of its own. Moreover, this narrator shares certain features and experiences—most explicitly, the fate of the expatriate or the exile—with those figures whose stories he recounts and whose voices he ventriloquizes. This shared emotional and experiential register is arguably what makes Sebald's narrator into a successful spiritual "medium" for those whose lives he reconstructs. The adumbration of this narrator's past and present hence assumes a significant role in Sebald's fictions, precisely because it legitimates his function as an intermediary instrument with enough sympathetic resonance—to employ another metaphor from the realm of sound—to guarantee the requisite consonance and empathy between narrator and protagonist, medium and mediated.

In a handwritten note found among Sebald's posthumous papers, he elaborates explicitly on the importance of this parallel between the lives of his protagonists and that of his narrator. Found among the documents related to *Die Ausgewanderten*, this exposé represents an early attempt to summarize the aims of this work in the form of a jacket note:

> In diesem Buch werden die Lebens- und Todesgeschichten von vier Auswanderern erzählt. Es sind vornehmlich jüdische Geschichten, aber auch deutsche. Genau genommen geht es darum, wie aus einer jüdischen Geschichte eine deutsche, bzw. aus einer deutschen eine jüdische wird. Die Wege der mit dem Lebenslauf des Erzählers eng verbundenen Figuren führen aus der süddeutschen Provinz hinaus in die Schweiz, nach Frankreich & England & bis in die fernen Wunderstädte New York & Jerusalem. Da auch der Erzähler im Ausland auf Wanderschaft

---

practice of Thomas Bernhard, see Sebald's interview with Martin Doerry and Volker Hage (*"Auf ungeheuer dünnem Eis"* 204), as well as James Wood's "An Interview with W. G. Sebald," *Brick* 59 (1998): 28, and Sebald's late radio interview with Michael Silverblatt, where he praises Bernhard for deviating radically from the standard form of the modern novel. In Sebald's estimation, Bernhard "only tells you in his books what he learned from others. So he invented, as it were, a kind of periscopic form of narrative. You're always sure that what he tells you is related, at one remove, at two removes, at two or three" (Schwartz 83).

ist, ergibt sich eine doppelte Verfremdung. Ein Ausgewanderter blickt mit den Augen eines anderen auf die Heimat zurück. Verluste und Einbußen beginnen je länger, desto schwerer zu wiegen. In allem rumort der Phantomschmerz der Erinnerung, & wer sich davongekommen wähnte, wird eingeholt von der Vergangenheit.[9] [This book tells the stories of the lives and deaths of four emigrants. They are predominantly Jewish stories, but also German ones. More precisely, it is a matter of how a Jewish story becomes a German one, or how a German one becomes Jewish. The paths of these figures, who are intimately connected with the narrator's life story, lead out of provincial Southern Germany to Switzerland, France, & England & on into the distant fabled cities of New York & Jerusalem. Since the narrator also lives abroad as a wanderer, this produces a double alienation. One exile looks back on the homeland with the eyes of another. Losses and sacrifices assume greater weight with the length of the interval. Everything is suffused with the phantom pain of memory, & those who thought they escaped the past are overtaken by it.]

What Sebald articulates here for the four protagonists of *Die Ausgewanderten* applies equally to the characters, and the narrators, of his other works: Henri Beyle and Franz Kafka in the two biograph-ically-inflected tales from *Schwindel. Gefühle*; Jacques Austerlitz in his eponymously named last work of prose fiction; and numerous characters, such as Roger Casement, Joseph Conrad, or even the Ashbury family in the travelogue *Die Ringe des Saturn* (*The Rings of Saturn*). Expressed in the broadest terms, Sebald's fictional narratives tell the stories of outsiders from the perspective of a narrator who defines himself as an outsider, and this position of shared marginality underwrites an empathetic consonance that links the teller and the told.[10] Sebald emphasizes precisely that his narrator, like his protago-nists, is a peripatetic wanderer in foreign lands, involved in a search for orientation. That he highlights the German-Jewish nature of the characters from *Die Ausgewanderten*, and the manner in which German and Jewish self-understandings merge with one another, bespeaks his

9   This note is the first item contained in folder 6, titled "Adelwarth, Manuskript Teil 1," of the file *Die Ausgewanderten*, which bears the inventory number HS.2004.0001.00009 at the Deutsches Literaturarchiv.

10 Eric Santner, *On Creaturely Life: Rilke, Benjamin, Sebald* (Chicago: University of Chicago Press, 2006), 51–8, expresses this empathetic affinity in terms of one wounded interiority, that of the narrator, who communicates with another, that of the protagonist, emphasizing that empathy in Sebald's works is figured as the narrator's participation in the spiritual world of another.

fascination with a German-Jewish symbiosis whose potentials were radically snuffed out by the rise of fascism and World War II.

Nostalgia for a lost or voluntarily abandoned homeland represents another theme that pervades Sebald's literary works. In the cited exposé, alienation as diegetic theme is replicated in the stance of the narrator, so that the very idea of "home" is subject to a "double alienation," distorted by the parallel displacements of the protagonists and the narrator. More noteworthy still is the implied reversal of perspective this doubling suggests. For if Sebald's narrator serves as a "ghostwriting" medium that resuscitates the story behind the lives and deaths of his protagonists, these figures, in turn, become lenses through which this narrator reflects his own sense of alienated distance from the security and comfort of "home." In keeping with this reversible perspective, the final statement of this note leaves the subject position tantalizingly open, so that the "losses and sacrifices," the "phantom pain of memory," and the tragic irony of being "overtaken" by a past that one has tried to outrun could apply equally to the four protagonists or the narrator. This passage thus provides a rudimentary inventory of those shared features that define the solidarity felt between Sebald's narrator and his protagonists, and that complicate their communal perspective on that illusory place, that literal utopia or "no place" that goes by the designation of "home."[11]

At the time Sebald was conceiving and composing the stories of *Die Ausgewanderten*, he was also completing a literary-critical project that focused on the uncanny alienation Austrian writers felt toward their alpine homeland. Titled *Unheimliche Heimat* (Uncanny homeland), this essay collection first appeared in 1991, just one year prior to the publication of *Die Ausgewanderten*. The story Sebald tells in these essays closely parallels the motifs he identifies in this jacket note as constitutive of the historical fictions assembled in his second collection of stories. His central theme is the pervasive alienation from their native country experienced by a wide range of Austrian writers from the middle of the nineteenth century into the post-war years of the twentieth. In Sebald's diagnosis, this alienation derived from the tendency of this homeland to assume a perverse and ideologically distorted guise, one that elevated narrow-mindedness to a political program, strove to eliminate all differences, and stamped as traitors those who deviated from this mainstream political program (*Unheimliche Heimat* 14). The writers he examines distinguish themselves by their radical critique of this *false*

---

11 See Sebald's assertion in the essay on the Austrian-Jewish writer Joseph Roth that for such figures "homeland [is] nowhere and hence the quintessence of pure utopia" ("die Heimat [ist] nirgendwo und somit der Inbegriff der reinen Utopie"; *Unheimliche Heimat* 110).

definition of the homeland, and their oppositional stance positions them as "potential refugees and exiles" ("potentielle Heimatlose und Exilanten"; *Unheimliche Heimat* 15), even if they never leave their country of origin. One of the central traits Sebald identifies with this ideological alienation from one's native land is especially germane for the theme of ghostwriting: these Austrian writers experience this alienation as the resurgence of ghosts, revenants who return from a more idyllic past to haunt the aberrant present. Insofar as their literature voices a critique of this ideologically-tainted vision of the homeland, these writers themselves serve as ghostwriters who reanimate these figures from the past, in implicit parallel to the role Sebald and his narrator play in his own prose fictions. "It is obviously still not easy," Sebald the literary critic remarks, "to feel at home in Austria, especially if the uncanny quality of the homeland, as was not infrequently true in recent years, is called to mind more often than is expedient due to the various appearances of revenants and ghosts of the past" ("Es ist offenbar immer noch nicht leicht, sich in Österreich zu Hause zu fühlen, insbesondere wenn einem, wie in den letzten Jahren nicht selten, die Unheimlichkeit der Heimat durch das verschiedentliche Auftreten von Wiedergängern und Vergangenheitsgespenstern öfter als lieb ins Bewußtsein gerufen wird"; *Unheimliche Heimat* 15–16). Sebald, the German living in voluntary English exile, surely identified closely with this critical perspective. He figures his own literary endeavors, which are haunted by "revenants and ghosts of the past," as critical expressions of his own alienation from a homeland whose image has been irrevocably distorted by a perverse and pervasive political ideology.[12]

Sebald's uniqueness on the contemporary German literary scene is defined not only by his status as an emigrant, writing about Germany and things German from the perspective of his self-imposed English exile, but also by the fact that his path to creative writing passed through his lifelong activity as a critic of German-language literature. As the temporal and thematic proximity of critical works like *Unheimliche Heimat* with literary projects such as *Die Ausgewanderten* indicates, there is a great deal of continuity between Sebald's work as a literary scholar and the explicitly fictional texts he produced in

---

12 For Sebald's critical take on his German homeland, see his references to the so-called "conspiracy of silence" that suppressed all critical discussion of the Nazi past during the immediate post-war era (Schwartz 44, 84–5). In his interview with Michael Silverblatt, Sebald emphasizes that this silence created an "emptiness" that "needs to be filled by accounts from witnesses one can trust" (Schwartz 85). Sebald believed his narratives could help fill that void. In his interview with Joseph Cuomo, Sebald also cites the persistence of a starkly authoritarian proclivity in post-war Germany, against which his own inherent "anarchist streak" caused him to protest (Schwartz 107).

the final twelve years of his life. He distinguished himself as a critic of German and Austrian literature above all by his biographically-oriented approach, which sought to understand the literary expression of the writers he examined in the context of their life experiences and life writings. Reiner Stach, the author of a monumental and authoritative three-volume biography of the writer Franz Kafka, recently pointed to the necessary limitations of literary biography, emphasizing that biographical reconstruction is inherently restricted by the serendipity of the amount and kind of information and documentation that survives. Stach is refreshingly open in admitting that in many instances "biographers have nothing to go on but scattered hints in the extant documentation. There are contours, shadows, and mute gestures; the rest is reconstruction." He goes on to voice the suspicion that those junctures where documentation is absent or faulty "might represent the most interesting and even crucial episodes," precisely because they are most dependent on the biographer's art of speculative reconstruction.[13] Sebald, who completed several literary-critical essays on Kafka from a biographical perspective, would certainly have been fascinated by Stach's biographical project, had he lived to witness it. He would have affirmed Stach's assertion that biographical criticism reaches its apogee where documentation fails and interpretive reconstruction begins; and this gray area between documentable fact and interpretive speculation forms the terrain that preoccupied Sebald both in his literary-critical endeavors and in his biographically-inflected works of prose fiction. The borderlines between Sebald's scholarship and his works of fictional prose are thus extremely fluid. Indeed, one can easily imagine his turn away from literary criticism and toward biographical fictions as a strategy for creatively exploring that territory left uncharted by extant documentation, and hence generally viewed as off-limits to the academic scholar.

Sebald was aware that his fictional writing represented a supplementary activity that allowed him to move beyond the acceptable boundaries of the literary critic. In a 1996 radio interview with Walther Krause, he acknowledged that even his critical endeavors had always been somewhat unorthodox, largely because of his loose, essayistic approach. But he also admits that this attitude helped him gravitate fluidly toward fictionalized takes on similar problems. "This rather essayistic procedure," he comments, "then moved, I believe, more or less naturally in this direction of the fictional. I simply had the feeling that there are things at the limits of what is absolutely provable, provable in a scholarly sense, about which one would simply have to

---

13 Reiner Stach, *Kafka: The Years of Insight*, trans. Shelley Frisch (Princeton, NJ: Princeton University Press, 2013), 83.

speculate" ("Diese eher essayistische Verfahrensweise hat sich dann, glaube ich, mehr oder weniger natürlich in diese Richtung des Fiktiven bewegt. Ich hatte einfach das Gefühl, daß es an der Grenze des absolut Nachweisbaren, wissenschaftlich Nachweisbaren, Dinge gibt, über die man sehr wohl spekulieren müßte"; "*Auf ungeheuer dünnem Eis*" 147). Fictional biography—as practiced above all in the Stendhal and Kafka pieces in *Schwindel. Gefühle*, the four stories of *Die Ausgewanderten*, and the extended narrative *Austerlitz*—thus represented a liberation from the constraints of what is "provable in a scholarly sense" and allowed Sebald to explore more creatively that historical and biographical space where documentary evidence is absent. Sebald's characteristic proclivity for subsuming marked and unmarked intertextual allusions in his fictional works—most prominently practiced in his travelogue *Die Ringe des Saturn* and the Corsica project—similarly represents an extension of the scholarly procedure of quotation and documentation, but one that radically transgresses the allowable boundaries of accepted scholarly practice. Whereas in academic discourse the lines between the scholar's thought and language must be clearly demarcated from those of the primary and secondary sources by such diacritics as quotation marks and footnotes, Sebald's intertextuality consciously blurs these boundaries and thereby creates a literary discourse constituted as an amalgam of disparate voices. This inherent uncertainty about who is speaking at any given moment represents one of the principal authenticating devices of Sebald's fictions; it allows him to conjure up a collective historical perspective, a chorus, so to speak, that makes pretense to greater validity because it represents a multiplicity rather than a singularity. One is reminded of the conclusion to one of Franz Kafka's well-known aphorisms about the problematic of truth and lie: "Only in the chorus may there exist a certain kind of truth" ("Erst im Chor mag eine gewisse Wahrheit liegen").[14]

Like Kafka, Sebald was fundamentally skeptical about the possibility of articulating absolute "truths." In the same radio interview with Walther Krause he maintained that "discovery of truth" ("Wahrheitsfindung"), as critical aim, should be replaced by the more creative "invention of truth" ("Erfindung der Wahrheit"), whereby he acknowledges that any such inventive approach is both paradoxical and fraught with peril ("*Auf ungeheuer dünnem Eis*" 147–8). One of the distinguishing traits of Sebald's fiction is that he managed

---

14 Franz Kafka, *Nachgelassene Schriften und Fragmente II*, ed. Jost Schillemeit (Frankfurt am Main: Fischer, 1992), 348. Stanley Corngold, "Sebald's Tragedy," in *Rethinking Tragedy*, ed. Rita Felski (Baltimore, MD: Johns Hopkins University Press, 2008), 234–5, makes a similar claim. Not surprisingly, Corngold the Kafka scholar also notes the relevance of Kafka's metaphor about the chorus of lies.

to successfully navigate these difficult seas between the Scylla of documentary truth and the Charybdis of fictional elaboration. This is the liminal space in which his poetics of history emerges and flourishes. This problem is also clearly relevant for the most recognizable and characteristic dimension of Sebald's fictions, his patented play with the juxtaposition of text and visual documentation of various sorts, a gesture that constitutes his fictions as "iconotexts," forms of writing that integrate visual material in quirky and unpredictable ways. Sebald notoriously explores this text–image relationship in order to problematize the purported authenticating, "documentary" function of "illustrations." But more importantly, this visual component adds another layer to the complex "chorus" of voices or perspectives that are critically overlain in Sebald's fictions.

This leads directly to the fundamental problematic of memory in Sebald's fictional works. If written records serve primarily as expedients that support and help preserve memory, then intertexts in Sebald's work function largely as media that open up avenues to history, to experiences and events from the past. They can be considered as bridges across which information traffic moves between the past, the present time of narration, and the "future" time of reading. Intertexts appear in Sebald's works in a wide array of manifestations: as allusions to works of literature, to historical documents, to archives such as museums and libraries; as tourist brochures; and even as visual documents in the form of historical postcards or family photographs. Sebald has come to be seen, for good reason, as a leading proponent of that highly mediated form of memory that Marianne Hirsch has called "postmemory." Without rehearsing once more the vast and varied critical literature on the relationship between Sebald and postmemory,[15] suffice it to say that Hirsch's term designates precisely the problematic relationship that those living in the present have with a past with which they experience a powerful emotional bond, but to which they can only secure access in mediated form: through the stories of others; via photos and family albums; by means of literary reconstructions; or through

---

15 On the problematic of postmemory in Sebald's fiction, see Mark M. Anderson, "*Tristes Tropes*: W. G. Sebald und die Melancholie der deutsch-jüdischen Vergangenheit," in *Gedächtnis und Identität: Die deutsche Literatur nach der Vereinigung*, ed. Fabrizio Cambi (Würzburg: Königshausen & Neumann, 2008), 232–4; Murray Baumgarten, "'Not Knowing What I Should Think': The Landscape of Postmemory in W. G. Sebald's *The Emigrants*," *Partial Answers* 5, no. 2 (2007): 267–87; Richard Crownshaw, "Reconsidering Postmemory: Photography, the Archive, and Post-Holocaust Memory in W. G. Sebald's *Austerlitz*," *Mosaic* 37 (2004): 215–36; and Anne Fuchs, *Die Schmerzensspuren der Geschichte: Zur Poetik der Erinnerung in W. G. Sebalds Prosa* (Cologne: Böhlau, 2004), 12–17.

historical documentations.[16] Hirsch herself focuses on the role of photographs and other visual materials in the constitution of postmemory, and this is reflected in Sebald scholarship by a concentration on discussions of postmemory in relation to his use of illustrations.

What sets Sebald's works apart is their integration of a wide cross-section of historical materials as the mediators of the past, so that issues of postmemory extend well beyond his use of visual materials. Moreover, Hirsch focuses on questions of postmemory in its relationship to personal, individual memory, hence her preoccupation with remembrance as a procedure for working through trauma and her insistence on the context of the "family frame." Sebald, by contrast, is concerned with *collective* forms of memory, or processes of remembrance that emerge in a larger social framework, at the level of community, nation, or historical generation. His emphasis on social memory received major impetus from the French philosopher and sociologist Maurice Halbwachs (1877–1945), whose 1925 treatise on collective memory, *Les cadres sociaux de la mémoire* (*On Collective Memory*), Sebald owned and read in its German translation. It is not possible to date precisely Sebald's preoccupation with Halbwachs's theories, but his intensive engagement with this work is documented in the dense annotations and marginal notes he left in his working copy of the book. Halbwachs argues that memory is always bound up with a social context, and indeed, that individuals who are radically isolated from a defining social framework would by necessity lose all memory of that period of their lives, and he insists on the relevance of the dialogic situation for the stimulation of memory recall. His operative statement, "when I remember, it is others who spur me on; their memory comes to the aid of mine and mine to theirs,"[17] succinctly pinpoints the narrative dynamic operative in all of Sebald's prose fictions. We only need add that the dialogic partner must not be a living individual, but could be represented by a text, an intertext, a document, or an archive. In this regard, Sebald's fictions constitute collective stories that emerge at that memorial interface between his narrator and his various informants, be these people, other texts, historical documents, or visual memorabilia. This conception of his works as multilayered memories reflects on a different level the principal theme of Sebald's literary séance as an accretion of voices that superimposes past stories and lived experiences, that comprises a form of "ghostwriting" grounded in a poetics of history.

---

16 Marianne Hirsch, *Family Frames: Photography, Narrative, and Postmemory* (Cambridge, MA: Harvard University Press, 1997), 22–3.

17 Maurice Halbwachs, *On Collective Memory*, ed. and trans. Lewis A. Coser (Chicago: University of Chicago Press, 1992), 38.

Memory, remembrance, and recall are never straightforward in Sebald's works—not merely because they are multiply mediated and arise in a context of social and interpersonal dependence. Halbwachs documents various situations in which memories undergo distortion and displacement, such as dreams that assume the character of real memories, the replacement of original memories by artificial reproductions, recollections that are removed from their chronological context, and the adjustment of remembered events to fit the judgments and prejudices of our social context. In his German translation of Halbwachs's book, Sebald highlights and annotates these various examples of problematic memory recall.[18] The Italian philosopher Giambattista Vico (1668–1744) articulated this problem of memory's fallibility, as well as its inherent *creativity*, in his 1725 treatise *New Science*. In that section of this work dealing with the age of Homer and the role of the ancient poets as cultural historians, Vico delineates three distinct functions of memory:

> Thus memory has three distinct aspects: memory [*memoria*] when it recalls things; imagination [*fantasia*] when it alters or recreates them; and ingenuity or invention [*ingegno*] when it orders them in a suitable arrangement or context. For these reasons the theological poets called Memory the mother of the Muses. Poets were thus the first historians of their nations.[19]

The three features Vico associates with the faculty of memory are relevant not only for Sebald's conception of history and remembrance, but also suggest the inherent correlation between the processes of historical recall and the structures that guide poetic recreation of the past.[20] Memory itself, as a turning of one's attention to events from the past, is but one reflex of a much more complex mental attitude for Vico. *Memoria* as simple recall must be allied with two further functions if it is to assume the character of a genuine narrative of the past. These are imagination, as a creative embellishment or alteration of recalled events, and invention as their reordering, recombination, or emplotment. It is no coincidence that Sebald's own inaugural narrative fiction, "Beyle," deals explicitly with the distortions and potential disingenuousness of

---

18   Maurice Halbwachs, *Das Gedächtnis und seine sozialen Bedingungen*, trans. Lutz Geldsetzer (Frankfurt am Main: Suhrkamp, 1985), 45, 58, 30, 153.

19   Giambattista Vico, *New Science*, trans. David Marsh (London: Penguin, 1999), 369.

20   James Olney, *Memory and Narrative: The Weave of Life-Writing* (Chicago: University of Chicago Press, 1998), 91–8, explores the relevance of Vico's multifaceted conception of memory for narratives of the past, especially for autobiography and autofiction.

memory. Indeed, Sebald embraces there a thematic that underpins his entire literary oeuvre. But more importantly, the functions Vico lays out as mechanisms of memory adequately describe the fundamental operations at work in the mnemonic poetic practice I have designated as Sebald's literary séances: *memoria* as the invocation of the ghosts of the past; *fantasia* as a creative fictional elaboration or embroidery on these historically-grounded figures, as exemplified in the process of "crystallization"; and *ingegno* as the recombinatory practice by which familiar elements are reshuffled, remixed, and replotted so that they reveal hitherto unrecognized meanings. These three dimensions constitute Sebald's poetics of history; they are the foundational principles of his metafictional literary aesthetics. The investigations contained in the following chapters attempt to unveil the detailed workings of these aesthetic principles on the basis of close readings and structural analyses of key works in Sebald's literary oeuvre.

*

My approach in the chapters that follow is philologically oriented, which means that the focus is on Sebald's texts at the level of structure, pattern, and narrative technique, but also on the micro-level of sentence, word, and diction. This explains why my analyses rely on Sebald's German-language originals, rather than on the published English translations—although these are cited for the benefit of a wider academic and non-academic readership. But these analyses are also embedded in what might be called a historical-critical context, a wider purview distinguished by a genetic interest: a concern with the emergence, growth, development, and historical maturation of Sebald's most common and characteristic literary techniques, and their relationships with his broader intellectual pursuits. This explains why the interpretive chapters dedicated to Sebald's published works are framed by examinations of two of his unfinished artistic projects: his fragmentary film script on the life of the philosopher Ludwig Wittgenstein (1889–1951), and the incomplete Corsica travelogue. My examinations therefore devote considerable attention to Sebald's literary coming-out, his evolution from an academic critic into one of the major representatives of contemporary German historical fiction, and his maturation as a creative writer; but they also attempt to interrogate poetic roads not taken, or only inadequately realized, prior to Sebald's untimely death in 2001. It is consistent with this historical-critical approach that I discuss relevant textual variants, and that my project is frequently informed by Sebald's annotations to books in his working library as well as by his manuscripts and papers. The hope is that these studies will shed new light on Sebald's published works by viewing them against the backdrop of unpublished and largely unknown materials.

Chapter 1, "Wittgenstein's Ghost," begins before the beginning of Sebald's emergence as a creative writer, examining his first attempt to formulate a creative project that pushes off against his professional activity as a literary scholar. This occurs already in 1986, when Sebald composes a screenplay on the life of Ludwig Wittgenstein, titled "Leben Ws" (W's life), and submits an application for project funding to the Filmförderungsanstalt, the German institute for the promotion of film housed in Berlin. Although this project does not yet explicitly take the form of prose fiction, it displays many affinities with the literary works that will emerge just a few years later, and it reveals in inchoate and rudimentary form many of the principles that will guide Sebald's poetics of history. Most prominently, this screenplay follows a biographical orientation, while straddling the line between factual information about Wittgenstein's life, derived from scholarly sources, and fictional, anecdotal embellishment. Conceived as a loosely joined concatenation of individual cinematic scenes, this enterprise already anticipates the significance images will have in Sebald's future works of fiction, and the manuscript is interspersed with images Sebald borrowed from one of his sources, an illustrated life of Wittgenstein. Significantly, this screenplay shuns chronological development in favor of a scattershot approach that juxtaposes pregnant events from diverse periods of Wittgenstein's life, thereby suggesting leitmotifs that underlie his existence and opening up provocative questions about personal motivations. Already in this first take on fictional biography, Sebald experiments with that recombinatory practice so characteristic of his later fictions, and he begins to hone his skill at building creative narrative transitions that compensate for lack of chronological sequence. Finally, Wittgenstein represents a touchstone in Sebald's own life, the model of a German-Austrian intellectual who emigrates to England and cultivates the existence of a homeless expatriate. Wittgenstein haunts Sebald's later prose fictions as a persistent revenant, and my analysis traces these manifestations of Wittgenstein's "ghost" and its significance for Sebald's literary project.

Chapter 2, "The Birth of the Prose Fictionalizer from the Spirit of Biographical Criticism," investigates Sebald's first collection of shorter fictional pieces, *Schwindel. Gefühle*, as a manifestation of his transformation from a biographically-minded literary critic into a fiction writer who laminates fictional life writing with a narrative approach that relies on autobiographical allusion. I examine the works in this collection not in the order of their eventual publication, but instead in the sequence of their composition. The texts on Stendhal and Kafka, as the first two pieces written, betray their origins in Sebald's literary-critical practices.

Both rely heavily on primary and secondary source materials treating the lives of their respective authors, but the traces of these critical resources are largely effaced. We witness the birth of Sebald's inter-textual literary technique out of the citation practices of the scholarly critic. In these early works Sebald also initiates his experiments in the creative possibilities of the text–image relationship. But only in the more autobiographically-tinged texts of this collection, "All'estero" and "Il ritorno in patria," does he begin to develop that character-istic language, style, narrative voice, and tone that have come to be associated with his fictions. Finally, the leitmotivic interweaving of these extremely diverse texts—around themes like travel, coincidental correspondence, repetition, and suicide—exhibits Sebald's incipient skill as an artistic manager or impresario who exploits these struc-tural patterns to impose a sense of consonance onto a hodge-podge of enormously diverse textual and visual materials. He accomplishes this largely through the clever expedient of exploiting the figure of Kafka's undead Hunter Gracchus as a thematic ghost whose constant reappearance stitches together these textual remnants, shaping them into a brilliantly faceted literary-artistic quilt.

Chapter 3, "Sebald's Literary Refinement," continues this emphati-cally philological and historical-critical investigation into Sebald's development as a writer by examining the first tale in the collection *Die Ausgewanderten*, "Henry Selwyn," with reference to an earlier version Sebald published in the Austrian literary journal *Manuskripte*. This chapter shows how by the early 1990s Sebald was refining both his language and his tactical deployment of visual materials. Examinations of significant textual variants and the replacement of illustrations disclose how Sebald tightens the weave of his themes and leitmotif-like patterns, and enhances their resonance by means of suggestive allusion and eerie, spectral interconnection. Most significantly, Sebald's process of revision reveals how the sometimes playfully ironic, self-reflexive, and at times even jocular tone of this story in its initial published form is transmuted into a text that carries that more ominous, melancholic tenor we have come to associate with his prose fictions.

The next two chapters, "Neither Here nor There" and "Sebald's Ectopia," offer interpretive analyses of the first and final texts in *Die Ausgewanderten*, "Henry Selwyn" and "Max Aurach" ("Max Ferber"). These interpretations share a focus on the central theme of exile that shapes all the narratives in this collection. Chapter 4 reads images of façades and nature's resurgence as emblematic for how the renascent memories of Selwyn's childhood in a Lithuanian *shtetl* resurface, overtake, and ultimately shatter the inauthentic existence he assumes after his family emigrates to England. Like so many of Sebald's protag-onists, Selwyn is haunted by a ghost from his past. But unlike the other characters in the stories of this collection, Selwyn is not spooked by the specters of others, by lost friends, family, or parents, but by the ghost of his own former self. In this story, Sebald's marquee theme of the uncanny return of the past thus takes on a peculiar inflection, since it calls into question this figure's strategic acts of assimilation. When his past reawakens, it does so with the violence of the Freudian return of the repressed, resulting in Selwyn's late-life suicide.

The eponymous protagonist of "Max Aurach"/"Max Ferber," by contrast, lacks any well-defined past self whose resurgence might invade and disrupt his present. Indeed, if Selwyn succeeds in recapturing his past, with fatal consequences, Aurach struggles to piece together a heritage, a line of inheritance and descent, that might give his life meaning and provide the existential orientation he longs for. My analysis demonstrates how Aurach's visual art, which is predicated on shadowy reiteration and recomposition, reflects his own futile quest to reconstruct a personal history and heritage. This diegetic quest is recapitulated at the level of narrative reconstruction in the first-person narrator's search for facts and information that will allow him to reassemble and retell Aurach's story. The text constructs this narrator explicitly as an exile whose existence parallels that of Aurach, and it figures him as a Parsifal-like character who, after initially failing to inquire into the causes of his interlocutor's emotional suffering, ultimately becomes a facilitator who aids the protagonist in uncovering the roots of his personal trauma. In a curious twist, this story portrays Sebald's narrator as haunted by the specter of the informant whose life he seeks to reconstruct, and his own redemption is mysteriously tied to his capacity to mediate Aurach's search for his own vital heritage. This interpretive juxtaposition of the first and final tales in *Die Ausgewanderten* helps us understand how Sebald's typical first-person narrator is fleshed out and gains increasingly in prominence over the course of this volume, culminating in the striking parallels between narrator and protagonist characteristic of the final story.

Chapter 6, "Fabulation and Metahistory," marks a radical change of critical perspective in several respects. It steps back from the close-up view on individual texts, the examination of compositional techniques, and the development of detailed interpretive readings that define the previous chapters, assuming instead a wide-angle perspective that positions Sebald and his works in the broader context of Holocaust fiction more generally, and in that of German-language Holocaust fiction of the 1990s more particularly. This retreat out of focused interpretive involvement to a bird's-eye historical perspective is consistent with the dynamic Sebald himself practices in his best fictions. Some readers may be surprised that what is commonly recognized as Sebald's *magnum opus, Austerlitz,* receives such cursory interpretive treatment, whereas unpublished works and less acclaimed texts like *Schwindel. Gefühle* are afforded detailed critical examination. Yet this is consistent with one of the primary thrusts of this book: the desire to give center stage to what are often seen as Sebald's more marginal or less known literary fictions, and shift *Austerlitz* more to the periphery, by revealing it as an extension—as a perfection, if you will—of the strategies already practiced in the narratives of *Die Ausgewanderten*. This chapter compensates for the absence of a detailed interpretive reading by outlining Sebald's provocative contributions to the genre of Holocaust fiction, describing his narrative innovations and metafictional tactics and mapping them onto the traditional controversies surrounding Holocaust literature in general, and German-language Holocaust fiction more particularly. The second major deviation arises out of this chapter's divergence from the chronological trajectory otherwise adhered to throughout this book. The reason for this is that this final work coheres thematically, structurally, and aesthetically with the texts of *Die Ausgewanderten*; indeed, it represents the culmination of that direction in Sebald's literary production that emphasizes themes of exile, displacement, historical trauma, and recovery of the past. This chapter attempts to show how Sebald departs from, and creatively intervenes in, the tradition of Holocaust literature by ignoring the unspoken code of this genre, which ties Holocaust remembrance to authentic testimony by the victims and eschews most forms of aesthetic enhancement. My analysis documents how Sebald succeeds in wedding Holocaust history with the implementation of metafictional literary devices. It examines Sebald's technique of creating an individualized protagonist composed as a fictional composite of several historical personages. This fictionalized agglomeration creates a more generalized and representative life story, thereby increasing the potential for empathetic identification on the part of Sebald's readers. This composite quality of Sebald's historical-fictional protagonists represents another fundamental dimension of his poetics of history. Further, this investigation establishes how Sebald's complex Chinese-box strategy of narrative layering positions multiple figures as both testifiers and witnesses, thereby modeling on the level of narrative structure the uneasy, unsettled empathetic communion that theorists of Holocaust literature propose as its most effective communicative strategy. Finally, by exhibiting how Sebald consciously disrupts the texture and trajectory of his narrative through the implementation of metafictional tactics, this chapter proposes that his characteristic innovation goes beyond mere "documentary fiction" and instead deserves the more precise appellation of "documentary metafiction."

The remaining chapters are dedicated to two texts from what I designate as the intermediary period of Sebald's literary production, the years from 1993 through 1998 that are devoted predominantly to *Die Ringe des Saturn* and the unfinished Corsica project. These works mark a distinct direction in Sebald's creative life, one in which the loose genre of the literary travelogue becomes a capacious vehicle for the expansion and further development of selected themes and problems. Most significant is the ecocritical turn Sebald's fiction takes in these two narrative works, a gradual shift in emphasis from the catastrophes of human social history to an interest in the natural and environmental disasters that are promoted by modern civilization and its industrial history. Chapter 7, "Sebald's Segues," extends this book's deliberations on the structural, narrative, and aesthetic strategies that distinguish Sebald's prose fictions by focusing on the art of narrative transition he perfects in *Die Ringe des Saturn*. This investigation makes evident how this more multifarious work—which, unlike his other fictional texts, lacks the unifying thread of a recovered life story—evolves via impromptu resolutions of narrative problems that arise from the patchwork diversity of its themes and ideas. It concludes by highlighting the encyclopedic structure of this work, as modeled in several of its most significant intertexts. Chapter 8, "Writing at the Roche Limit," extends the analysis of the aesthetic and literary parameters of this travelogue by demonstrating how centrifugal tendencies toward fragmentation, disintegration, and disaggregation are countered by centripetal forces that foster defragmentation and the resurrection of a gravitational center or unifying position. The rings of Saturn in Sebald's title represent constructs that emerge at the Roche limit: at the place of balance between disintegrative and integrative gravitational forces. The rings of Saturn thereby become an allegory for the travels of Sebald's narrator, which lend unifying contours to the diversity of places and the disparity of historical times and themes to which his journey gives rise. This chapter depicts Sebald's text as a work of literary art that emerges precisely at the intersection of the forces of dissipation and coalescence, entropy and order—as a literary network of loosely connected and interrelated fragments that are always on the verge of falling into disintegration, but are ultimately pulled together by the unifying strategies of an authorial manager. Finally, this chapter examines the implicit critique of enlightened rationality articulated in this text, exhibiting not only how it impugns the discursive strategies typical of instrumental reason, but simultaneously demonstrating how its own textual practices model an alternative form of reasoned discourse, a new variation on the poetics of history. This chapter also shows how this critique of enlightened thought is transferred to an interrogation of reasoned technologies for organizing the field of vision, specifically taxonomic grids and the vanishing point, exposing these techniques as ideological constructs that skew perception and the discovery of knowledge. This final argument marks a return to considerations of Sebald's use of visual materials for strategic ends that complement the artistic and thematic components of his fictions.

My study concludes with a chapter titled "Narrating Environmental Catastrophe," which offers a detailed examination of Sebald's fragmentary manuscript based on his travels to the island of Corsica. Like the Wittgenstein screenplay, with whose analysis my investigation begins, the Corsica project is currently only accessible in its original German and hence has remained largely on the margins of mainstream Sebald scholarship. Yet despite the fact that Sebald broke off work on this project in favor of extending his acknowledged success as a German writer of exile and Holocaust fiction, with the composition of his final work *Austerlitz*, the Corsica manuscripts represent a significantly innovative if not (yet) definitively developed aspect of his oeuvre. This work constitutes an experimental etude in which Sebald searches for a narrative voice that can effectively relate the stories of human-caused environmental catastrophes. If as a writer of Holocaust and exile literature Sebald succeeded in implementing fictional and metafictional strategies that fostered a sensitive engagement with historical and sociopolitical cataclysms, the challenge he faced in the Corsica project was the development of an aesthetic stance and narrative technique adequate to dealing with tales of environmental destruction and human-caused natural-historical devastation. The environmental history of the island of Corsica serves as a microcosm for European environmental decline more specifically, and more generally for the global environmental conundrum that confronts humanity today. Sebald's contribution to this problematic is his discernment of the complex psychological dynamics that prevent humans from acknowledging, embracing, and acting upon the insight that our own actions are responsible for a debilitating spiral of environmental degradation. He fictionally enacts a problematic that is theorized by the recently developed field of ecopsychology, a branch of contemporary psychological science dedicated to understanding the complex relationships between humans and their environment. Peculiar to Sebald's approach is that his critique of destructive human environmental interventions is not launched from a self-righteous perspective that exempts the teller from the story he is telling. On the contrary, he self-consciously demonstrates how his own narrator is entangled in those same disastrous mindsets that promulgate the wanton extermination of plant and animal species across the globe. His narrator plays the dual role of critical protagonist who lashes out against environmental decline, and antagonist whose own unthinking actions further the very decimation he laments. This narrator thereby becomes an emblem for that pressing paradox of contemporary human existence, namely the awareness that the technological innovations we deploy as a means for enhancing life ultimately strip away the very preconditions for that life itself. Sebald was on the verge of discovering a novel narrative approach for the literary representation of this endemic ecopsychological paradox. Given his penchant for returning to problems and projects that proved especially challenging and fascinating, I am inclined to believe that although he aborted the Corsica project, he might have subsequently returned to it and brought it to fruition if his sudden death in December 2001 had not intervened. The Corsica project remains significant to the extent that it suggests the unrealized artistic potential of one of the great prose writers of recent European literature.

Perhaps I may be excused for committing the rhetorical faux pas of concluding this Introduction by pointing to those works by Sebald that may seem conspicuously absent in what otherwise purports to be a comprehensive study: the early "elemental poem" *Nach der Natur* (*After Nature*) and the Zurich lecture series *Luftkrieg und Literatur* (*On the Natural History of Destruction*). The exclusion of these works is motivated by the simple fact that this book is framed explicitly as an investigation into Sebald's *prose* fictions, and more specifically into the narrative and aesthetic innovations he introduced into contemporary German documentary and biographical fiction. The essays in *Luftkrieg und Literatur* do not qualify for examination in this context for the simple reason that they represent a fallback into the tenor, attitude, and approach that characterized Sebald's literary-critical studies. Indeed, these essays can be disqualified since they are decidedly not works mediated by a narrative voice or narrative strategies, but instead are articulated from the standpoint of the biographical persona W. G. Sebald himself. Moreover, the theme of these essays marks a return to a critical project that occupied Sebald in the early 1980s, well before his emergence as an author of creative literature. The Zurich lectures thus provide him with a more general and popular forum for revisiting a problem of perennial concern to Sebald the literary critic: the failure of post-war German literature to engage with the total destruction wrought by the Allied air war. The situation is not as clear in the case of the poem *Nach der Natur*, which anticipates in rudimentary fashion some of the themes and preoccupations of Sebald's prose fictions. Most importantly, this poem rehearses that intertwining of biographical and autobiographical modes that reached its most mature realization in the collection *Schwindel. Gefühle.* However, this "elemental poem" merits exclusion not only because it is written in verse, but also because, in my estimation, Sebald is at best a mediocre poet. This work constitutes an immature concretization of those artistic practices and techniques that would only reach full maturation in his later prose fictions. The halting tempo of free verse does not provide Sebald with the necessary latitude to develop the elaborate and complex periods, with their characteristic tempos, rhythms, and antiquated neo-Baroque tone, that would eventually become the hallmark of his fully-fledged prose style. His enduring artistic and literary achievement is represented above all in the exemplary works of narrative prose fiction he produced in the dozen or so years from the late 1980s until his death in 2001. As my study attempts to demonstrate, these works poignantly embody Sebald's mastery in the genre of documentary prose (meta)fiction. My hope is that the analyses and interpretations presented here will foster increased appreciation of the literary and aesthetic achievements Sebald realized in this unique series of prose-fictional masterpieces.

One Wittgenstein's Ghost: Toward Understanding Sebald's Literary Turn

"Man bezeichnet die Erinnerung als ein Bild. Das Bild kann ich mit dem Original vergleichen, aber nicht die Erinnerung. Die Erlebnisse der Vergangenheit sind ja nicht wie die Gegenstände im Zimmer nebenan: Jetzt sehe ich sie zwar nicht, aber ich kann hinübergehen. Aber kann ich in die Vergangenheit gehen?"
["Memory is called a picture. I can compare a picture with the original, but this is not true for memory. The experiences of the past are not like the objects in the room next door: I do not see them at the moment, to be sure, but I can go over there. But can I go back into the past?"]

Ludwig Wittgenstein[1]

More than almost any other contemporary prose fictionalist of international repute, W. G. Sebald is a critic's author. Long before he emerged in the early 1990s as an acclaimed writer of prose fictions, Sebald had enjoyed a nearly twenty-year career as teacher, researcher, and widely published scholar engaged primarily with German and Austrian literature. Not surprisingly, Sebald's fictions are haunted by the presence of intellectual sages whose guiding spirits—whose ghosts—lend shape and thematic unity to his fictional endeavors. Intertextuality is the name now commonly associated with this heteroglossic aspect of Sebald's fictions, in which the voices of older authors and intellectual mentors rise up to speak through the diction of Sebald's first-person, pseudo-autobiographical narrator. This gesture of speaking through

---

1   Quoted in Michael Nedo and Michele Ranchetti, *Ludwig Wittgenstein: Sein Leben in Bildern und Texten* (Frankfurt am Main: Suhrkamp, 1983), 7.

or speaking with named or unnamed intellectual companions is also one of the defining features of critical writing on literature, and this is what often relegates criticism to the potentially demeaning status of "secondary" literature. This term implies that "critical" elaboration is derivative of another form of writing, relying on the so-called "primary" works whose sense, meaning, and structure the critical work investigates and purports to explain. However, Sebald's "primary" works of fiction are *consciously* and *deliberatively* "secondary" and derivative in a manner very similar to critical explorations. The major difference is that once one abandons the pretense to reasoned interpretive analysis, one can also jettison the rhetoric of persuasion, including the detritus of the scholarly apparatus, such as references, footnotes, and quotation marks.

Sebald spoke eloquently about this turn from the objectivity of scholarly investigation to the subjective, emotional engagement with the thought and words of others in an interview with Uwe Pralle, given just prior to the life-ending heart attack at the wheel of his car in December 2001. He remarks that the scholarly ideal with which he and his generation of students in Germany had been imbued demanded that the critic never use the pronoun "I," that all subjective moments be banished, and scholarship reduced to the abstract gathering of factual information. While admitting that such a collection of objective materials has its significance, Sebald insists that this accumulation of prima facie information only becomes productive when it is infused with subjective experience: "To be sure, this type of material-gathering is not entirely useless, but I believe it only becomes productive for us in that moment when we project our own subjective experience into the area we are researching" ("Nun ist diese Form der Materialsammlung natürlich nicht vollkommen unnütz, aber ich glaube, sie wird für uns produktiv erst in dem Augenblick, in dem wir unsere subjektive Erfahrung hineindenken in das von uns erforschte Umfeld"). He goes on to specify that we must "interpolate" into the discourse of evidence the radically subjective color provided by our personal psychology, our own melancholy, hopes, and desires ("*Auf ungeheuer dünnem Eis*" 255). This is precisely what Sebald's shift from a biographically-inflected form of literary criticism to a mode of fictional discourse, haunted by the voices of his intellectual and literary mentors, allowed him to accomplish.[2]

---

2   Sebald never shied away from championing that form of biographical literary criticism he self-consciously practiced as a literary scholar. See his interview with Volker Hage, in which he asserted that biographical criticism constitutes fundamental research ("Grundlagenforschung"), but bemoans what he sees as a scholarly climate in which such scholarship is demeaned as "unserious" ("*Auf ungeheuer dünnem Eis*" 183).

Among the myriad forebears on whose life, works, and insights
Sebald drew, three figures assume peculiar significance and prominence. At the top of the list stands, without question, the Prague
German-Jewish writer Franz Kafka, with whom Sebald engaged
throughout his career as a literary scholar,[3] and whose shadow falls in
some way on every fictional work he created. Another guiding figure
for Sebald's creative texts is Vladimir Nabokov, the Russian-born
émigré writer whose life and works held special fascination for
Sebald.[4] If Kafka and his works, especially the figure of his revenant
Jäger Gracchus (Hunter Gracchus), supply the stitching that weaves
the disparate texts of *Schwindel. Gefühle* into a coherent whole, then
Nabokov, about whom Sebald also wrote a critical study,[5] plays a
similar role in *Die Ausgewanderten*, where he appears as the recurrent
figure of the Butterfly Man. Cast as the prototypical ever-wandering
emigrant, Nabokov binds together on a motivic level the stories of
the four emigrants retold in this work.[6] The third primary predecessor does not appear on the surface to have the same prominence
and formative influence on Sebald's fictional works; and yet his
life, thought, and language haunt Sebald's prose fictions on a more
subliminal, if equally pervasive level. This is the early-twentieth
century Austrian philosopher Ludwig Wittgenstein, whose life and
work course through Sebald's fictions like a rhythmic thorough-bass.[7]

---

3   See Sebald's early critical essays on Kafka, "The Law of Ignominy: Authority,
    Messianism and Exile in The Castle," in *On Kafka: Semi-Centenary Perspectives*
    (New York: Barnes & Noble, 1976), 42–58; "Thanatos: Zur Motivstruktur in
    Kafkas *Schloss*," *Literatur und Kritik* 66–7 (1972): 399–411; "The Undiscover'd
    Country: The Death Motif in Kafka's *Castle*," *Journal of European Studies* 2 (1972):
    22–34; and "Tiere, Menschen, Maschinen—Zu Kafkas Evolutionsgeschichten,"
    Literatur und Kritik 205–6 (July/August 1986): 194–201.

4   For a detailed study of the breadth and depth of Nabokov's reach in Sebald's
    prose fictions, see Verena Schowengerdt-Kuzmany, "Into the Funhouse: Modes
    of Intertextuality in the Works of W. G. Sebald" (Ph.D. diss., University of
    Washington, 2014).

5   See Sebald's essay "Traumtexturen" ("Dream Textures"), republished in *Campo
    Santo*, 184–92/141–9.

6   On the constitutive role Kafka and Nabokov play in Sebald's first two books of
    prose fiction, see Oliver Sill, "Aus dem Jäger ist ein Schmetterling geworden:
    Textbeziehungen zwischen den Werken von W. G. Sebald, Franz Kafka und
    Vladimir Nabokov," *Poetica* 29 (1997): 596–623. Adrian Curtin and Maxim M.
    Shrayer, "Netting the Butterfly Man: The Significance of Vladimir Nabokov in
    W. G. Sebald's *The Emigrants*," *Religion and the Arts* 9 (2005): 258–83, elaborate
    on Nabokov's function as a unifying figure in *Die Ausgewanderten*.

7   Martin Klebes, "W. G. Sebald: Family Resemblances and the Blurred Images of
    History," in *Wittgenstein's Novels* (New York: Routledge, 2006), 87–130, is the
    only scholar who has investigated the impact of Wittgenstein's life and thought
    on Sebald's fictions.

Wittgenstein stands out in this group for several reasons. First, he is a philosopher rather than an author of literary texts, although, as David Edmonds and John Eidinow point out, in his popular reception he has gained the quasi-mythical status of such Modernist authors as Kafka, Proust, Eliot, or Beckett.[8] Second, unlike Kafka and Nabokov, he was never the subject of a critical study by the scholar Sebald. Third and finally, Wittgenstein figures in Sebald's fictions less on the level of intertextual resonance—although this dimension is not completely absent—than as an iconic figure whose life and lifestyle serve a paradigmatic function for the types of biographies that especially fascinated Sebald. Wittgenstein represents the classical voluntary émigré, someone who leaves his native Austria by choice, but who nevertheless remains emotionally attached to this homeland not as a political entity, nor for reasons of national or ethnic identity, but instead because of an intimacy with its landscapes and its natural environment. Wittgenstein thus reflects the ambivalent love–hate relationship Sebald himself harbored toward his native post-war Germany, reviling its cultural-political backwardness while relishing the magnificent alpine panoramas of the Allgäu region in which he grew up. Wittgenstein the émigré thereby models the same liberation from the habituation and constraint of one's native circumstances that motivated Sebald's own life of voluntary exile. According to his friend David Pinsent, Wittgenstein cultivated the state of exile as the condition of possibility for his intellectual productivity,[9] and this also captures Sebald's motivation to emigrate. Wittgenstein's biography further parallels Sebald's in remarkable ways: both spent their self-willed emigrations in England, and they shared the city of Manchester as their introduction to Britain and the British lifestyle. Wittgenstein lived in Manchester from 1908 through 1911, where he was enrolled as an engineering student at the College of Technology. Only later would he take up permanent residence in Cambridge, where he earned academic degrees and eventually assumed the post of professor of philosophy. Sebald, similarly, lived from summer 1966 through autumn 1968, and autumn 1969 through summer 1970, as a lecturer at the University of Manchester, before eventually moving to Norwich and the University of East Anglia, first as a Ph.D. student and then as a member of the teaching staff.

---

8   David Edmonds and John Eidinow, *Wittgenstein's Poker: The Story of a Ten-Minute Argument Between Two Great Philosophers* (New York: Ecco/HarperCollins, 2001), 22. For a wide-ranging study of Wittgenstein's influence on creative writers and artists more generally, see Marjorie Perloff, *Wittgenstein's Ladder* (Chicago: University of Chicago Press, 1996). A desideratum to her investigation would be the inclusion of Sebald in this extensive catalogue.

9   Edmonds and Eidinow, *Wittgenstein's Poker*, 196.

In an interview for Austrian television broadcast just before his death, Sebald addressed the close affinity he felt throughout his life for Wittgenstein, grounded, as he admits, more in his fascination with the person than with any inherent sympathy for or profound understanding of his philosophy. Sebald emphasizes that what intrigues him about Wittgenstein is "the history of his personality, how it developed ... with all the pathological facets that were part of it" ("die Geschichte seiner Persönlichkeit, wie sie sich entwickelt hat ... mit all den pathologischen Facetten, die dazu gehörten"; *"Auf ungeheuer dünnem Eis"* 229). What drew him to this figure was the peculiar combination of analytical genius and critical insight, coupled with a penchant for pathological brooding, insecurity, and morose isolation. These are personality traits Wittgenstein shared with Kafka, that towering presence in Sebald's intellectual biography. In the cited interview, Sebald continues by specifying how he felt peculiarly mesmerized by photographs of Wittgenstein and his social milieu, coming to identify him as a life companion: "I just simply cannot get enough of looking at ... the existing photographs of him [Wittgenstein]; not only pictures of the person, but also those of his entire social milieu. This somehow meshes in such a manifold way with my own interests that he has become, so to speak, a companion for me, a secret companion" ("Ich kann mich einfach nicht satt sehen ... an den Bildern, die es von ihm [Wittgenstein] gibt; nicht nur den Bildern seiner Person, sondern dem ganzen sozialen Umfeld. Das verzahnt sich irgendwie auf so eine vielfältige Weise mit meinen Interessen, daß er sozusagen zu einem Kompagnon, einem insgeheimen Kompagnon geworden ist für mich"; *"Auf ungeheuer dünnem Eis"* 229). Sebald tellingly emphasizes the *visual* engagement he entertains with Wittgenstein the person and his life surroundings. This is consistent with Sebald's special fondness for illustrated biographies, concretized most poignantly in his propensity for the Rowohlt collection of biographical monographs that formed one anchor of his own personal library.[10] Not surprisingly, the volume in this series treating Wittgenstein's life and works is among Sebald's extensive collection of books by and about the Viennese philosopher.[11] But most indicative of Wittgenstein's significance for Sebald's intellectual trajectory is that in the mid-1980s, around the time of his life-changing transition from a literary critic to an author of creative fictions, Sebald developed an inchoate project centered on this

10 Jo Catling, "Bibliotheca abscondita: On W. G. Sebald's Library," in *Saturn's Moons: W. G. Sebald—A Handbook*, ed. Jo Catling and Richard Hibbitt (London: Modern Humanities Research Association, 2011), 283.
11 Kurt Wuchterl and Adolf Hübner, *Ludwig Wittgenstein mit Selbstzeugnissen und Bilddokumenten*, Rowohlt Monographien 275 (Reinbek: Rowohlt, 1979).

philosopher, conceived as a film that would recreate his life in a series
of images and dramatic scenes. He referred to this endeavor as his
"Projekt Wittgenstein," and the work on this cinematic documentary,
which bore the title "Leben Ws" (W's life), served as an incubator for
many of the ideas, aesthetic strategies, and narrative innovations that
inform his prose fictions.

Among Sebald's literary remains and posthumous papers is a folder
containing application materials to the Filmförderungsanstalt in Berlin,
the German institution charged with promoting the development and
production of independent cinema. In this application, Sebald requests
financial support for the creation of the Wittgenstein film script. This
file contains a completed application form, a narrative description
and justification of the project, and an outline of sixty-four scenes that
constitute the bulk of the film.[12] The signed application form is dated
August 25, 1986, and these materials represent photocopies of the
original application Sebald submitted to the Filmförderungsanstalt on
or around that date. Although the file contains no letter of response,
we must assume that Sebald's application was rejected. The application
cover letter requests salary replacement for four months, allowing
Sebald to devote himself to fleshing out the film script, a small
sum to fund research and materials, and costs for producing the
final screenplay in the thirteen copies required by the foundation. In
addition to the completed project description, this file contains twelve
pages of handwritten notes that record Sebald's ideas for elaborating
individual scenes. The sketchiness of these amplifications suggests that
Sebald broke off detailed work on this project at an early stage.

"Leben Ws" is not entirely unknown to Sebald scholars. Sebald
himself published this proposal on April 22, 1989, under the title
"Leben Ws: Skizze einer möglichen Szenenreihe für einen nichtrealisierten Film" (W's life: Sketch of a possible series of scenes for an
unrealized film), in the cultural segment of the *Frankfurter Rundschau*.
The piece was meant to commemorate, as was the film itself, the
hundredth anniversary of Wittgenstein's birth on April 26, 1989.[13]
Nonetheless, this project has received surprisingly little attention in the

12 Deutsches Literaturarchiv Marbach, file "Leben Ws: Skizze einer möglichen
    Szenenreihe für einen nichtrealisierten Film" (W's life: Sketch of a possible
    series of scenes for an unrealized film), archive number HS.2004.0001.00007.
13 The project description has been published as "Leben Ws: Skizze einer
    möglichen Szenenreihe für einen nichtrealisierten Film," in *Saturn's Moons:
    W. G. Sebald—A Handbook*, ed. Jo Catling and Richard Hibbitt (London: Modern
    Humanities Research Association, 2011), 324–33. Citations to "Leben Ws"
    reference page numbers from this more accessible reprint. Currently no English
    translation is available. For the sake of clarity, references to the documents in
    the file at the Deutsches Literaturarchiv will be cited as "Projekt Wittgenstein."

relevant critical literature.[14] Already in the project description Sebald cited the Wittgenstein anniversary as the immediate trigger behind this endeavor ("Leben Ws" 324). In the unpublished version of this proposal Sebald adds further justifications that explain his personal motivations. One of these is the "enigmatic quality" ("Rätselhaftigkeit") of Wittgenstein's personality ("Projekt Wittgenstein" 1), and this underwrites, he explains, the non-discursive exploration of his life in a desultory series of scenes and images. But Sebald also stresses his own personal motivation, noting that "a whole series of specific points of identification" ("eine ganze Reihe spezifischer Identifikationspunkte") yoke his existence to the life of the philosopher. As examples he names the geographical places at which they spent significant parts of their lives: Manchester, Cambridge, Vienna, and the rural Austrian (or South German) provinces ("Projekt Wittgenstein" 1). Thus the affinity Sebald feels for Wittgenstein is based on the inexplicable and serendipitous intersection of their lifelines. Whether the poet Michael Hamburger, the philosopher Ludwig Wittgenstein, or the writer Franz Kafka, Sebald exhibited a curious penchant for identifying "affiliated souls," individuals whose attitudes, fates, and proclivities uncannily replicated those of "Sebald" in his own self-understanding. In the section of *Die Ringe des Saturn* in which he reflects on the ties between himself and his friend Hamburger, Sebald's narrator deliberates about these "elective affinities and correspondences" ("Wahlverwandtschaften und Korrespondenzen") that mysteriously link our lives to those of other human beings, so that these others take on the character of enigmatic predecessors who have pre-lived our own experiences (*Ringe* 227–8/182).[15] In the story "Max Aurach"/"Max Ferber," Sebald transferred his own personal identification with Wittgenstein to his eponymous protagonist. As an art student in Manchester in the early 1940s, Aurach lives in the same building in which the Viennese philosopher dwelled during his engineering studies. And although Aurach admits that the connection he feels with Wittgenstein is "purely illusory" ("rein illusionär"), he nevertheless insists that it occasions a "sense of brotherhood" ("Gefühl der Brüderlichkeit") that lends Aurach a feeling of companionship with this historical predecessor (*Ausgewanderten* 248/166–7). Wittgenstein is but one in a long line of such "ghosts" who

---

14 The one exception is Richard Weihe's essay, "Wittgensteins Augen: W. G. Sebalds Film-Szenario 'Leben Ws,'" *Fair: Zeitung für Kunst und Ästhetik* 7, no. 4 (2009): 11–12, which offers a brief summary of the project and documents how its visual character found resonance in *Austerlitz*.

15 See also Sebald's admission, in a 1992 interview with Piet de Moor, that he believes such coincidences are metaphysical remnants of experiences and events that transcend the limits of rational life (*"Auf ungeheuer dünnem Eis"* 74).

haunt Sebald's self-understanding and who manifest objective, out-of-body representatives and historical antecedents of the subjective self. Sebald's exploration of these "doubles" is always simultaneously an investigation of the self, its own motivations, and its foibles.

Before launching into a more detailed interpretive investigation of Sebald's Wittgenstein screenplay and how it prefigures the ideas, concerns, and aesthetic approach of his narrative fictions, we need to locate this project chronologically in Sebald's overarching intellectual trajectory. He began his life as a public intellectual by playing the role of a renegade literary critic who did not shy away from articulating views that ran counter to the contemporary critical mainstream. He wrote his MA thesis at the University of Manchester on the German-Jewish playwright Carl Sternheim, and a revised and expanded version of this thesis appeared one year later.[16] If Sternheim had been a darling of post-war German literary critics, in large part because of his audacious satires on social life prior to the rise of National Socialism, Sebald relativized Sternheim's satirical clout by focusing on the contradictions that emerged from his Jewish heritage and his drive to assimilate into mainstream Wilhelmine society. He continued with this counter-establishment approach when he moved from Manchester to the University of East Anglia, where he completed a doctoral thesis on the author Alfred Döblin that once again questioned the literary-aesthetic status of a post-war German literary icon.[17] During his professional life at the University of East Anglia, Sebald's renegade critical stance began to mellow, especially as he discovered his interest in modern Austrian literature.[18] Yet he continued to distinguish himself as an independently-minded critic with influential essays on, among other topics, the mainstream writer Franz Kafka. By the mid-1980s, Sebald's academic career was approaching its zenith: in 1985 he published his

16 W. G. Sebald, *Carl Sternheim: Kritiker und Opfer der Wilhelminischen Ära* (Stuttgart: Kohlhammer, 1969). This first literary-critical book was based on work Sebald completed while attending the University of Fribourg, Switzerland, from 1965 to 1966. See Richard Sheppard, "The Sternheim Years: W. G. Sebald's Lehrjahre and Theatralische Sendung 1963–75," in *Saturn's Moons: W. G. Sebald—A Handbook*, ed. Jo Catling and Richard Hibbitt (London: Modern Humanities Research Association, 2011), 56–64, 75–9.

17 The dissertation appeared as *Der Mythos der Zerstörung im Werk Döblins* (Stuttgart: Klett, 1980). Uwe Schütte, *Interventionen: Literaturkritik als Widerspruch bei W. G. Sebald* (Munich: edition text + kritik, 2014), 65–157, provides a detailed investigation of Sebald's resistant and non-conventional positions as an emerging literary critic.

18 For more detailed information about Sebald's scholarly research into Austrian literature, see Ritchie Robinson, "W. G. Sebald as a Critic of Austrian Literature," *Journal of European Studies* 41, no. 3–4 (2011): 305–22, and Schütte, *Interventionen*, 199–340.

first collection of critical essays on Austrian literature, *Die Beschreibung des Unglücks* (The description of misfortune), and this work was accepted in April 1986—around the time of the application requesting funding for the Wittgenstein project—as Sebald's *Habilitationsschrift* at the University of Hamburg, a scholarly and academic achievement that would qualify him for a professorial-level appointment at a German university. Curiously, it was precisely when he had reached full stride in his scholarly accomplishments that Sebald made his first attempts to establish himself as a creative writer. The three parts of the "elementary poem" *Nach der Natur* (*After Nature*) appeared in separate installments in the Austrian literary journal *Manuskripte* between October 1984 and March 1987, and in March and June of 1988 the same journal published Sebald's first two pieces of prose fiction, "Berge oder das ..." (Mountains or the ...), an early version of "Beyle oder das merckwürdige Faktum der Liebe" ("Beyle, or Love is a Madness Most Discreet"), and "Verzehret das letzte selbst die Erinnerung nicht?" (Does not the last thing even consume memory?), an early rendition of "Henry Selwyn." The mid-1980s thus mark years of upheaval in Sebald's life, as manifest most prominently in a shift away from his successful scholarly studies to diverse forms of creative writing.

When asked in a 1998 interview about what motivated the sea change from literary critic to creative writer when in his forties, Sebald pointed to the example of the German writer Theodor Fontane, who began a highly successful writing career relatively late in life. But Sebald went on to cite changing conditions and educational reforms at British universities as the immediate impulse behind this shift in emphasis.[19] Sebald was increasingly troubled by the trying professional circumstances at British universities in the wake of the reforms implemented by Margaret Thatcher and her Conservative government, which came to power in May 1979. Among the new measures introduced by the Conservatives were increased standards of accountability and performance, and keener scrutiny into the role research played in the teaching mission of the universities. All of this will sound familiar to those acquainted with the situation at North American universities in recent decades. But according to Richard Sheppard, Sebald's colleague at the University of East Anglia, their institution went through an especially challenging period from 1983 through 1986, when it was operating under a severe financial deficit.[20] This

19 See the interview "'Characters, plot, dialogue? That's not really my style ...',"
Observer Review (June 7, 1998): 17.
20 Richard Sheppard, "W. G. Sebald: A Chronology," in *Saturn's Moons: W. G. Sebald—A Handbook*, ed. Jo Catling and Richard Hibbitt (London: Modern Humanities Research Association, 2011), 631.

brought the university under increased governmental scrutiny and led to intense criticism, due to low completion rates for students seeking higher degrees. The university also came under attack on political grounds, since it was thought to favor liberal political views and quash conservative perspectives. This turmoil came to a head in spring 1986, when Sebald developed his application for the Wittgenstein project. Although this screenplay still represents a crossover work between scholarly research and creative initiative, Sebald clearly felt pressure to pursue funding resources outside of Great Britain and beyond the British university system.

The opening paragraph of Sebald's project description provides a compact summary of the thematic substance, aesthetic intention, and narrative structure of this proposed cinematic representation of Wittgenstein's life:

> Der Film LEBEN Ws soll die Geschichte einer solitären Figur, diejenige des Philosophen Ludwig Wittgenstein erzählen und zwar nicht in der Form einer Dokumentation oder bebilderten Biographie, sondern in der reinen Form von Bildern, aus denen sich das Leben Ws zusammengesetzt hat. Der Natur reiner Bilder entsprechend, geht es also um die Konstruktion eines achronologischen, asyntaktischen "Satzes," in welchem "ausgesprochen" werden soll, worüber W. zeit seines Lebens sich weitgehend ausgeschwiegen hat. Der Kontrapunkt, nach dem verfahren werden könnte, ist der Todesbegriff, wie ihn Wittgenstein andeutungsweise hier und da entwickelt hat. ("Leben Ws" 324)
> [The film W'S LIFE is intended to tell the story of a solitary figure, that of the philosopher Ludwig Wittgenstein; however, not in the form of a documentary or illustrated biography, but rather in the pure form of pictures that constituted W's life. Consistent with the nature of pure pictures, the aim is the construction of an a-chronological, a-syntactical "sentence" that is intended to "express" all those things about which W. largely remained silent throughout his life. The counterpoint according to which one might proceed is the conception of death, as Wittgenstein developed it in an indirect manner here and there.]

The project Sebald envisions is particularly rife with tensions. Although he denies that this film would be a simple documentary or assume the form of an illustrated biography, his primary resource is just such a pictorial documentation of Wittgenstein's life history: Michael Nedo and Michele Ranchetti's quarto volume *Wittgenstein: Sein Leben in Bildern und Texten* (Wittgenstein: His life in images and texts). What is peculiar about this book is that, aside from the brief introduction by Brian

McGuinness, a leading Wittgenstein scholar, its meager textual material is drawn from authentic sources written by Wittgenstein, his family, and his acquaintances. The editors thus largely restrict themselves to the selection and arrangement of materials, with only minimal interpretive commentary. This book is dominated, moreover, by images and illustrations that document the milieus in which Wittgenstein lived, along with his interactions with friends and colleagues. Many of the pictures are taken directly from Wittgenstein's own photo album, so that the assemblage reflects those images the philosopher collected for his own personal reasons. This work thus enacts exactly that frameless representation in images, lacking documentary explication, that Sebald envisioned for his film. Sebald's application includes eleven photocopied images, interspersed irregularly throughout the draft, taken directly from Nedo and Ranchetti's book. These range from portrait photographs of the philosopher, pictures of him together with family members, friends, or collaborators, illustrations of the important places he lived and worked, and of course the mandatory photograph of the house he designed for his sister in Vienna.[21] Although Sebald claims to be diverging from the illustrated biography, he has in fact employed just such a work as the model for this project. However, what distinguishes Sebald's approach is the change of medium from print book to film. Nonetheless, in its emphasis on a series of still images, Sebald's project replicates the "pure series" of pictures provided in this textual prototype. The major divergence Sebald introduces is a radical disruption of the chronological sequence of Wittgenstein's life, whereas Nedo and Ranchetti structure their book according to the sequential unfolding of his biography.

This relates to another defining tension in Sebald's formulation of this project. On the one hand, the objective is to tell the story or history of a specific individual's existence, and the words "Geschichte" ("story"/"history") and "erzählen" ("tell," or "narrate") emphasize

---

21 These images are found in Nedo and Ranchetti, *Ludwig Wittgenstein*, and are listed here in the order of occurrence in Sebald's manuscript: 176–7 (Wittgenstein with his elementary school class in the Austrian village of Puchberg); 209 (together with the builder of the house he designed); 220–1 (the house he designed); 93 (Wittgenstein's father hunting on horseback); 264–5 (an impromptu street photograph of Wittgenstein with Francis Skinner in Cambridge); 33 (a childhood portrait of Ludwig with his brother Paul and their sisters); 291 (a portrait from Wittgenstein's own photo album); 317 (a portrait photo taken by his friend Ben Richards); 324 (photographed on a London street with Ben Richards); 334 (one of the last portrait photos taken before Wittgenstein's death); 30–1 (a landscape photograph, taken by his brother Rudi, of a lightning storm over the Hochreith area of Austria, where the Wittgenstein family had an estate).

this narrative aspect. But on the other hand, this narrative is supposed to defy both chronological order and syntactical logic. We might imagine the film's structure as a visually translated replication of the aphoristic model Wittgenstein himself employed in his first philosophical work, the *Tractatus Logico-Philosophicus,* or even of the fragmentary, notebook-like character of his later *Philosophische Untersuchungen* (*Philosophical Investigations*). To be sure, the *Tractatus* provides a numerical system of interrelated and hierarchically ordered propositions as a substitute for discursive linkage. This is no longer the case in Wittgenstein's later works, which operate more like notebooks where individual entries commune in implicit ways with their textual surroundings or thematically with other reflections scattered throughout the work. Sebald's film script thus more closely approximates the aphorism-like quality of Wittgenstein's later notebooks, since the absence of explicit discursive or logical connections between scenic images opens up a wider range of *implicit* meanings that might fill the "a-syntactical" void. This greater flexibility in meaning also implies heightened interpretive labor on the part of the reader, in Wittgenstein's case, or of the viewer, in the instance of Sebald's film. In both interpretive scenarios, the recipient is invited not simply to fill in the gaps between adjacent statements or scenes, but also to construct meaningful bridges between elements that may not be immediately proximate. Thus the structure absent from the aesthetic construction of the text or film must be creatively interpolated during the process of reception.

This hypothesis that Sebald intends his film to imitate the pattern of Wittgenstein's philosophical thought and aphoristic discourse is supported by the words Sebald places in quotation marks, which invoke principles central to Wittgenstein's philosophy. The term "Satz" refers not only to the linguistic entity of the "sentence," but also alludes to the more philosophical rendering of "proposition," a term that is of special significance in Wittgenstein's *Tractatus.* Here he famously argues that all propositional logic can be reduced to the two fundamental forms of tautology and contradiction, and that these two propositional forms mark the limits of what can be sensibly and meaningfully articulated in language.[22] The second word, "ausgesprochen," meaning what is "expressed" or "openly stated," reinforces this logical divide, central to the argument of the *Tractatus,* between what is meaningfully expressible and what must be relegated to the inexpressible domain of metaphysics

---

22   Ludwig Wittgenstein, *Tractatus Logico-Philosophicus,* trans. C. K. Ogden (London: Routledge, 1981), proposition 4.46. I follow the convention of citing this work by the proposition number. The referenced edition provides both the German and English texts.

and hence must remain unsayable.[23] Especially telling in Sebald's exposition is that he extracts this dichotomy from Wittgenstein's philosophical vocabulary and applies it instead to his approach to his own life. Thus the word "ausgesprochen" stands in conscious opposition to the term "ausgeschwiegen," meaning "to be silent about," as applied to Wittgenstein's secrecy regarding his personal life. This semantic tension is crucial for the conception of the film project—and it embodies a dynamic that is central to Sebald's prose fictions. In the case of the film "Leben Ws," Sebald suggests that the a-syntactical and a-chronological ordering of scenes and images performs a revelatory function, expressing indirectly and hence alluding to those intimate secrets of Wittgenstein's life about which he remained stubbornly mute. Appropriating the language Wittgenstein himself employs in the *Tractatus*, we can say that Sebald's film is strategically constructed to *show*—Wittgenstein's verb is "zeigen," which has the deictic implication of pointing at—what Wittgenstein himself was never willing to openly *say* about himself.[24] Sebald's insistence on reducing this film to pure or uncontaminated pictures ("Natur reiner Bilder") is consistent with the thrust of Wittgenstein's showing/saying distinction, as well as with Wittgenstein's reliance throughout the *Tractatus* on the metaphor of the "Bild," the picture or image, as model for our perceptual comprehension of the empirical world. Wittgenstein's ultimate insight in the *Tractatus* is the apparent paradox that the only possibility for articulating what is fundamentally ineffable is by limiting oneself to expressing the effable. As he argues, it is precisely by limiting oneself to this act of saying the sayable that one simultaneously also *shows* what is unsayable, *ex negativo*.[25] Sebald transposes the logic of Wittgenstein's argument from the domain of philosophical speech and written expression, where "saying" and "expressing" are discursively dominant, to the realm of images and representative scenarios, which by their very nature are less governed by the discourse of saying than they are by the immediacy of showing. However, this may ultimately "say" something about Sebald's understanding of how images operate, especially when they are intended as illustrative. And indeed, "illustration" in the medium of images might be taken as parallel in expressive function to the role of "saying" in the medium of discursive language. Sebald's implicit extension of Wittgenstein's saying–showing distinction from verbal language to the domain of images thereby suggests that pictures also function as a "language" for which the divide between the expressible and the inexpressible is equally germane. The theory of images Sebald

---

23 Wittgenstein, *Tractatus*, 6.522–6.54.
24 Ibid., 6.522.
25 Ibid., 4.113–4.1212.

develops in his engagement with this film project thus anticipates the peculiarly suggestive employment of illustrations in his literary iconotexts. These images often radically shun the illustrative gesture of "saying" something about the text, the plot, or the characters, opting instead to "show," suggest, or imply things about the story that operate below or beyond the level of textual expression. Formulated as a hypothetical proposition, Wittgenstein's theory about the limits of the expressible, and his insistence on a dichotomy between what can legitimately be said and what can be shown, informs the cinematic practice Sebald implements in "Leben Ws" and applies *mutatis mutandis* to his employment of visual material in his subsequent fictional narratives.

Sebald's concerted occupation with Wittgenstein in 1986 pre-dates his reception of Roland Barthes's book on photography, *Camera lucida*, whose significance for Sebald's conception of photographic images the writer himself acknowledged, and whose impact on Sebald's use of visual materials has been widely recognized.[26] One of the miscellaneous notes Sebald kept in conjunction with the Wittgenstein project indicates that he only became familiar with Barthes subsequently. A page with scattered remarks has the imperative "Read" written and circled in the upper left-hand corner, and among the titles Sebald names in this to-read list is "Barthes—Chambre claire."[27] Thus when he was working on the Wittgenstein project in April 1986, Sebald was not yet familiar with Barthes's famous thesis about how photographic images document the living "past" of what is now non-existent.[28]

The relevance of Wittgenstein's silence/expression and saying/ showing dichotomies for Sebald's use of visual images has hitherto gone unnoticed. Yet these same dichotomies play a fundamental role in the thematic issues central to Sebald's fictional texts. Silence, for example, constitutes one of the reigning pathologies in the life of Henry Selwyn, the eponymous protagonist of the first story in

26 Sebald affirms his debt to Barthes in his interviews with Kenneth Baker, "W. G. Sebald," R2, and with Christian Scholz (*"Auf ungeheuer dünnem Eis"* 165–8). For a critical examination of Sebald's use of photographs and its relation to Barthes, see Carolin Duttlinger, "Traumatic Photographs: Remembrance and the Technical Media in W. G. Sebald's *Austerlitz*," in *W. G. Sebald: A Critical Companion*, ed. J. J. Long and Anne Whitehead (Seattle: University of Washington Press, 2004), 155–71, and Lise Patt, "Searching for Sebald: What I Know for Sure," in *Searching for Sebald: Photography After W. G. Sebald*, ed. Lise Patt (Los Angeles: Institute of Cultural Inquiry, 2007), 16–101.

27 This sheet is the tenth of the twelve pages of notes in the file "Projekt Wittgenstein" at the Deutsches Literaturarchiv.

28 Roland Barthes, *Camera Lucida: Reflections on Photography*, trans. Richard Howard (New York: Hill and Wang, 1981), 78–9, 82–4. In his copy of this text, Sebald highlights these passages where Barthes stresses the photograph's role of documenting what is past and dead.

Die Ausgewanderten. Ashamed of his heritage as a Jewish immigrant from Lithuania, Selwyn not only represses the memories of his own childhood, but remains silent about his ethnicity even to his wife Hedi (Elli in the English translation); moreover, he speculates that the revelation of this secret might have caused the alienation that has disrupted their relationship (*Ausgewanderten* 34–5/21). In contrast, Selwyn's interaction with Sebald's first-person narrator emerges as a long, if discontinuous verbalization of those things about which he has remained silent, including his deteriorating relationship with Hedi, his fascination with the disappeared mountain guide Johannes Naegeli, and his reminiscences about his childhood in a Lithuanian *shtetl*. For Selwyn, as for all of Sebald's "emigrants," recollection of the past and its verbal expression go hand in hand. When Sebald's narrator has immediate contact with his protagonists, as in "Henry Selwyn," "Max Aurach," and *Austerlitz*, this encounter both stimulates the recollection of lost memories and marks their verbalized liberation from confining silence. In those cases where Sebald's narrator is communing with the dead, as in "Paul Bereyter" and "Ambros Adelwarth," the narrative still unfolds as a process in which what is hidden is brought to light; but in these cases this knowledge is facilitated by third-party informants, such as Lucy Landau and Aunt Fini. This process of narrative revelation is arguably what makes Sebald's texts so engaging, since they develop like detective stories in which the investigative narrator gradually reveals the knowledge and insights he has acquired over the course of his inquiries. Indeed, Sebald's approach in the Wittgenstein project reveals precisely the intimate manner in which the dynamic of forgetting and remembering is intertwined with the dichotomy of silence and verbal expression. This is a motif Sigmund Freud also highlighted in his psychoanalytic theory, and this connection is likewise relevant for Sebald. But contrary to Freud, Sebald is not as sanguine about the therapeutic relief afforded by remembrance or the articulation of what has been kept secret. Henry Selwyn commits suicide either *despite* his recollections and their articulation, or—in the worst case scenario—precisely *because* of them; and the same might be said of Paul Bereyter. For these two individuals, increased self-awareness leads to self-indictment and suicide. Aurach, by contrast, survives, but the recovery of his memories and his confession to the narrator do not provide him with emotional relief or promise therapeutic recovery. Adelwarth ultimately flees from the confessional situation in which he recalls his past to Aunt Fini, seeking instead imposed forgetfulness in shock therapy. Only the example of Austerlitz holds out hope that the recapture of his past might offer therapeutic release and allow more complete engagement with life, as he looks ahead to uncovering the truth about his father's disappearance and possibly rekindling the lost relationship with Marie de Verneuil (*Austerlitz* 410/292). What is true about all of Sebald's protagonists is that they live at the cusp between life and death, like Kafka's Hunter Gracchus. Their existences are persistently haunted by the shadow, but also by the *possibility* of death. This brings us back to Sebald's description of the Wittgenstein project, where he comments that this screenplay's unifying thematic is the philosopher's conception of death, his "Todesbegriff." Sebald's wording is as evocative as it is enigmatic: "The counterpoint according to which one might proceed is the conception of death, as Wittgenstein developed it in an indirect manner here and there" ("Der Kontrapunkt, nach dem verfahren werden könnte, ist der Todesbegriff, wie ihn Wittgenstein andeutungsweise hier und da entwickelt hat"; "Leben Ws" 324). The noun "Kontrapunkt" implies that a contrapuntal structure operating with or around Wittgenstein's notion of death will compensate for the lack of syntactical or chronological coherence. If Wittgenstein is said to have articulated this notion of death only suggestively and somewhat sporadically—"andeutungsweise hier und da"—then the contrapuntal pattern Sebald identifies for his film imitates the sporadic recurrence of this death theme in Wittgenstein's thought. Curiously, Sebald's exposé nowhere cites directly Wittgenstein's reflections on the idea of death. But death is a frequent topic in the screenplay, as in the death of Wittgenstein's father (324), the funeral of his friend Francis Skinner (329), the suicides of his three older brothers Hans, Rudi, and Kurt (327), and finally an allusion to Wittgenstein's own death, concretized in the last photographic portraits (332). The reference to Francis Skinner's funeral in particular contains an indirect allusion to Wittgenstein's thoughts about death, and in Brian McGuinness's essay, printed as foreword to Nedo and Ranchetti's illustrated biography, Sebald surely was struck by the philosopher's reaction to his friend's death. McGuinness quotes the philosopher as lamenting "Skinner has abandoned me" ("Skinner hat mich verlassen"), and he remarks that Wittgenstein conceives death as afflicting less the dying themselves than the living who witness their passing.[29] The implication is that the pain of death only affects the survivors, those who, as Wittgenstein asserts, feel "abandoned" by the departed. Sebald reflects this attitude in the language of his screenplay when describing Wittgenstein's attitude at Skinner's funeral: "W. looking more desperate than usual" and "W. auf einem Spaziergang. Quite wild" ("W. on a walk, quite wild"; "Leben Ws" 329). These

29   Brian F. McGuinness, "Wittgensteins Persönlichkeit," in *Ludwig Wittgenstein: Sein Leben in Bildern und Texten*, ed. Michael Nedo and Michele Ranchetti (Frankfurt am Main: Suhrkamp, 1983), xi.

words are adopted directly from the passages describing this event in Nedo and Ranchetti's biography.[30]

This perspective on death from the point of view of the "abandoned" survivor runs like a leitmotif through Sebald's fictional works. One thinks of the interminable grief experienced by Henry Selwyn at the disappearance of his companion Johannes Naegeli (*Ausgewanderten* 24/14), of the loneliness Ambros Adelwarth experiences upon the passing of his lifelong partner Cosmo Solomon (*Ausgewanderten* 128–9/88), or of the long-term repercussions for Paul Bereyter's life caused by the deportation of Helen Hollaender (*Ausgewanderten* 73/49–50). This list could be extended to include the lost parents of Max Aurach and Jacques Austerlitz, as well as the latter's friend Gerald, who dies prematurely in a plane crash. This latter episode replicates the death of Wittgenstein's friend David Pinsent, who perished on May 8, 1918 during a test flight.[31] Wittgenstein's response to the death of Francis Skinner can be viewed as a paradigm for this inextinguishable grief experienced by the survivors of intimate friends or relatives.

In the notes accompanying his screenplay, Sebald alludes to Wittgenstein's idea that death is not a part of life itself, but that the two are separated by an absolute divide and exist in mutual exclusion. On a sheet of notes with the heading "Gespräche und Gesprächsthemen" ("Conversations and discussion themes"), in which he outlines various motifs he wants to include in the film, Sebald notes, "death & meaning of the world, which must lie outside of it" ("Tod & Sinn der Welt, der außerhalb liegen muß"; "Projekt Wittgenstein" notes, sheet 8). The allusion is to two propositions from the conclusion of Wittgenstein's *Tractatus*, in which he asserts that one can only make sense of the world from a perspective that lies outside of it, that life can only be understood from the point of view of death.[32] Wittgenstein associates death with the realm of the metaphysical, with that domain about which one cannot meaningfully speak and whose significance can hence only be shown. But in this conception, death assumes the status of an enhanced insight, a privileged meta-empirical perspective from which the underlying sense of empirical existence is ultimately revealed. In his foreword to Nedo and Ranchetti's biography, McGuinness concludes by stressing Wittgenstein's obsession with the notion of death and with thoughts of suicide: "Depression and a death wish were nothing uncommon during certain periods of his life; yet Wittgenstein's affirmation of

---

30 Nedo and Ranchetti, *Ludwig Wittgenstein*, 311.

31 Justus Noll, *Ludwig Wittgenstein und David Pinsent: Die andere Liebe der Philosophen* (Berlin: Rowohlt, 1998), 137. This book was part of Sebald's library, and in his copy Sebald highlighted this passage.

32 *Tractatus* 6.4311–6.4312.

death went far beyond this. It was typical that, when someone spoke about how sad the death of a friend had been, he responded: 'Why? Nothing better could have happened to him'" ("Niedergeschlagenheit und Todeswunsch sind während bestimmter Lebensperioden durchaus nichts Ungewöhnliches, doch Wittgensteins Bejahung des Todes ging weit darüber hinaus. Typisch war, daß er, als jemand davon sprach, wie traurig der Tod eines Freundes gewesen sei, sagte: 'Wieso? Ihm hätte gar nichts Besseres geschehen können'").[33] When Sebald refers to Wittgenstein's conception of death as the "counterpoint" that will pull together the divergent scenes of his film, he is alluding to this affirmation of death not only as a form of relief from life but also as the metaphysical key to understanding it.

Wittgenstein's belief that death was not horrible for those who experienced it, but rather only for those left behind to grieve, is closely related, as McGuinness indicates,[34] to his lifelong thoughts of suicide as ultimate relief from his persistent feelings of guilt, inadequacy, and hopelessness. Sebald emphasizes this motif, tying it to the central theme of Wittgenstein's solitude, when he devotes one of the longest scenes of his screenplay to the suicides of Wittgenstein's three older brothers: Hans in 1902 on his boat in Havana; Rudi in 1904 in Berlin by poisoning; and Kurt by self-inflicted gunshot at the end of World War I to avoid suffering the humiliation of surrender. In Sebald's portrayal, Ludwig castigates himself for not having the courage to follow his brothers' model, and he condemns himself as an "Übrigbleiber," as someone who has remained behind. This word, significantly, also carries the implication of being extraneous. Sebald summarizes this problematic by having Wittgenstein formulate the following idea: "Whoever lacks the courage to abandon the others would be abandoned by them" ("Wer den Mut nicht habe, die anderen zu verlassen, würde von den anderen verlassen werden"; "Leben Ws" 327). Thus the theme of Wittgenstein's solitude is closely imbricated with the problematic of death and the inability to embrace suicide. Sebald reinforces this thematic in a purely visual manner just a few scenes later, when he focuses on the death of Ludwig's brother Hans by invoking the boat that was the vehicle for his suicide: "His brother Hans's boat. Apparently rudderless" ("Das Boot des Bruders Hans. Anscheinend steuerlos"; "Leben Ws" 328). These brief remarks constitute this scene in its entirety; yet in its brevity, its concentration on a single image, and its evocativeness, it is representative of many episodes Sebald sketched for this film. It emblematizes what Sebald meant when he maintained that the film should emerge in the pure form of loosely

33 McGuinness, "Wittgensteins Persönlichkeit," xv.
34 Ibid., xiv–xv.

concatenated images. The suggestion that this boat is "steuerlos" implies not only that it is "rudderless" or lacks a helmsman, but also conjures up a lack of orientation, the impossibility of finding one's bearings as a motive for Hans's self-willed exit from life. The image of the brother's boat alone on the open sea also relates to Sebald's central theme of isolation and solitude, so that the picture of this unmanned ship becomes a cipher for Wittgenstein's life: the emptiness felt by the person left behind. This simple scene also provides a telling example of the allusive approach Sebald seeks to exploit in this film. This is just one of the ways in which this screenplay functions as an etude in which he can fine-tune the art of intimation that will become a hallmark of his later prose fictions. Expressed in Wittgenstein's terminology, Sebald is honing the art of allusively *showing* something whose expression would be immeasurably impoverished by any simple and immediate act of *saying*. This obliquely suggestive technique represents one of the hallmarks of Sebald's poetics of history, which approaches purported historical "facts" via a practiced art of evocative circumscription.

This minute, but deeply allusive scene portraying Hans Wittgenstein's aimlessly drifting boat also forges a link between this film script and *Schwindel. Gefühle*, on which Sebald was working during and immediately subsequent to his occupation with the Wittgenstein project. If the theme of death is the "counterpoint" intended to hold together the disparate scenes of the film "Leben Ws," then a similar claim might be made for the texts of *Schwindel. Gefühle*; for it is the dead—or, to be more precise, the undead—figure of Kafka's Hunter Gracchus that binds together the four very different narratives assembled in this volume. Gracchus has perished in a hunting accident; but during his journey from the realm of the living to that of the dead, a supposed error by the ship's helmsman has left him lost in the netherworld between these two domains. The image of Hans Wittgenstein's drifting, unguided boat prefigures the Gracchus motif. Sebald himself reinforces this connection in his notes for this screenplay, the last page of which bears the heading "Motiv" and encompasses one single entry: "Death motif—the sail boat[.] My brothers have been my forerunners" ("Todesmotiv—Das Segelschiffbild[.] Die Brüder sind meine Vorgänger gewesen"; "Projekt Wittgenstein" notes, sheet 12). The image of Hans's sailboat serves as the single example for the motif of death that Sebald names as the thematic anchor of this project. This reinforces the emblematic character of this image. The interpolation of Wittgenstein's thought that his brothers are his forerunners encapsulates Ludwig's sense that he is summoned to follow their example. But especially striking is the association of the death motif with the image of the sailboat, for this suggests the linkage to Kafka's Gracchus and his representation in *Schwindel. Gefühle*. When Kafka's story is

Figure 1.1: Sailboat from "Dr. K." (*Schwindel* 178/163).

invoked in "Dr. K.s Badereise nach Riva" ("Dr. K. Takes the Waters at Riva") and his story retold, Sebald includes a grainy reproduction of a sailboat on open waters (*Schwindel* 178/163) (see Figure 1.1). Gracchus represents much more than the motif of death, or the liminal existence of the undead who have lost their worldly home but are unable to settle in the land of Hades. As we will see in our analysis of this story, Sebald's narrator implies that Gracchus's fate may have resulted from suicide, a hypothesis supported by the prominence of the suicide motif throughout these stories.

It is easy to see Wittgenstein's life of solitude, his existence as an "Übrigbleiber," as someone abandoned not only by his suicidal brothers but also by deceased friends, as closely akin to the liminal existence of Kafka's Hunter Gracchus. Both Wittgenstein and Gracchus course through the world of the living as solitary outcasts, condemned to the existence of restless and homeless wanderers. Wittgenstein, like Gracchus, lives as a ghost in the world of the living. But he is also a ghost who insistently haunts the world of Sebald's fictions. As a figure dogged by the contemplation of suicide, Wittgenstein can be viewed as a prototype for all of Sebald's emigrants, some of whom, like Selwyn, Bereyter, or Adelwarth, dare to take the leap into voluntary death for which Wittgenstein, in his own estimation, lacked the courage. Others, like Aurach and Austerlitz, are driven to the verge of suicide, but ultimately manage to find a purpose that keeps them alive. Regardless of the choices they make, all these figures live their lives, like Kafka's Gracchus, in the liminal space between life and death, defined by the freedom to either affirm or renounce their own existence.

Turning now to an examination of the thematic dimensions that Sebald envisioned as constitutive of the Wittgenstein project, we get a sense of the germinal role this work played in the development of the concerns that would become foundational for his prose fictions. In the penultimate paragraph of his exposé, Sebald articulates the range of themes the film will encompass and discusses the problem of selecting from among the myriad images available for documenting Wittgenstein's life:

Zu den Themenbereichen gehören in erster Linie "widersprüch-liche Paarungen" wie Kindheit/Alter, Lehren/Lernen, Natur/Technik, Isolation/Gesellschaft, Juden/Deutsche, Heimat/Exil, Männerfreundschaft/Frauenliebe und umgekehrt, Reichtum/Armut. Was das Bildmaterial betrifft, so ist die hauptsächliche Schwierigkeit die eines embarras de richesse, denn das Leben Ws spielte sich ja immer an Orten und in Umgebungen und Milieus ab, die an Bildern weit mehr hergeben würden, als sich ohne weiteres bewältigen ließe. Es wird nicht leicht sein, die dem

Subjekt angemessene Disziplin bei der Auswahl der *richtigen* Bilder zu wahren. ("Leben Ws" 324)

[The thematic scope encompasses above all "contradictory pairings" such as childhood/old age, teaching/learning, nature/ technology, isolation/society, Jews/Germans, homeland/exile, male friendship/love of women and vice versa, wealth/poverty. With regard to the visual material, the primary difficulty is an embarrassment of riches, for W's life constantly played out at places and in settings and milieus that would provide much more visual material than could possibly be managed. It will not be easy to exercise the kind of discipline in the choice of the *proper* images that is appropriate for this subject matter.]

What Sebald offers as a list of thematic interests for this film reads like a veritable inventory of the major themes that undergird his prose fictions in their entirety. Perusing the secondary works about Wittgenstein that were part of Sebald's personal library, one is struck by the close overlap between this handful of themes and the marginal highlights and notes Sebald made in his copies of these books. On the motif of Jews and Germans, for example, which is so central to Sebald's later prose fictions, he repeatedly marks references to the so-called "confession" Wittgenstein made to his friends and colleagues in 1937 that he is three-quarters Jewish and only one-quarter German. Regarding the motif of wealth and poverty, Sebald marks passages that refer to Wittgenstein's transferal to his siblings of the fortune he inherited from his father, the modest circumstances in which he voluntarily lived, his enjoyment of a life of relative poverty, and his negotiations with the Nazi government for reclassification of his sisters as "mixed race" rather than Jewish, so they could continue to live in Nazi-ruled Vienna unmolested.[35] In reference to the theme of homeland and exile, Sebald notes Wittgenstein's sense of feeling alien even after living in England for many years, his early thoughts about emigrating to the Soviet Union, and his predilection for travel and extended stays abroad. Sebald pursues the dichotomy of nature/ technology by emphasizing Wittgenstein's penchant for retreating into and enjoying natural settings, his early training as an engineer, and his skill as a mechanic, able to repair engines and machines. In this vein

---

35 According to Edmonds and Eidinow, *Wittgenstein's Poker*, 132–8, the amount of the Wittgenstein family fortune transferred to the Nazis was the equivalent of 1.7 tons of gold. They provide a detailed discussion of Wittgenstein's participation in this process that in Nazi lingo was termed "Befreiung," "dispensation" or "liberation," and that allowed Jews to renegotiate their racial makeup to a less threatening status in accordance with the Nuremberg racial laws.

he also highlights one of Wittgenstein's aphoristic remarks, in which he suggests that the advent of the age of science and technology marks the decline of humanity: "It is, for example, not senseless to believe that the scientific and technological age marks the beginning of the end for humanity; that the idea of great progress is a deception, as is that of the ultimate recognition of truth; that there is nothing good or desirable in scientific knowledge and that humanity, which strives for it, is running into a trap" ("Es ist z. B. nicht unsinnig, zu glauben, daß das wissenschaftliche und technische Zeitalter der Anfang vom Ende der Menschheit ist; daß die Idee vom großen Fortschritt eine Verblendung ist, wie auch von der endlichen Erkenntnis der Wahrheit; daß an der wissenschaftlichen Erkenntnis nichts Gutes oder Wünschenswertes ist und daß die Menschheit, die nach ihr strebt, in eine Falle läuft").[36] This remark could stand as a motto for that strain of Sebald's work, manifest above all in *Die Ringe des Saturn* and the Corsica project, in which he exposes the dialectic that ties advances in human civilization to the decimation of the natural world. With regard to the theme of teaching/ learning, we can trace throughout Sebald's marginalia his interest in the philosopher's decision to become an elementary schoolteacher, the impatience he exhibited at the stupidity of his pupils and later of his university students, and the violent outbreaks that such incidents often called forth. Finally, concerning the theme of male friendship and love of women, Sebald exhibits a special interest in allusions to the homosexual relationships Wittgenstein may have entertained with friends such as Pinsent, Skinner, and Ben Richards, and also to his failed love relationship with Marguerite Respinger. All of these themes find resonance in Sebald's draft screenplay, and in most instances the scenes Sebald chooses have direct corollaries with passages he highlighted in the works he consulted. In this respect Sebald was still working under the modus operandi of the literary critic: drawing on secondary sources to identify and bring evidentiary support for those themes he sought to highlight in the life and works of the individual under investigation. To be sure, his borrowings from secondary resources remain unmarked in the creative project itself, and in this sense they are indicative of Sebald's shift away from formal documentation and toward an unacknowledged integration of references as intertextual allusions.

When Sebald refers to the "embarrassment of riches" one faces when confronting the visual materials available about Wittgenstein's life, he places emphasis on the importance of careful selection among these photographs, and above all on the strict discipline such choices require. Although, in keeping with the cinematic nature of this project, he is speaking specifically of visual images, this caveat applies generally

36 Wuchterl and Hübner, *Ludwig Wittgenstein*, 129–30.

to the creative process he deploys in his works of prose fiction. Throughout Sebald's creative endeavors, the role of the "author" is less that of a font of imagination, a creative source for inventive ideas, characters, plots, or dramatic situations, and more one of a painstaking culler from a broad body of available material and a careful organizer of the elements he selects. This role as the reorganizer, shaper, or rearranger of "found," historically or textually given "evidence" constitutes another fundamental feature of Sebald's poetics of history. It is closely related to the pseudo-documentary nature of his texts. Much like the Wittgenstein film project, Sebald's fictional works rely on available lives, extant information about those people, and the discriminating judgment of the authorial presence in selecting and ordering the primary textual building blocks. The aim is to assemble them in such a way that they evoke not simply what Sebald liked to call, following Roland Barthes, the "effet de réel,"[37] but also so that the assemblage itself, like a provocative collection of aphorisms or a notebook full of engaging fragments, throws open intractable questions and problems. Sebald's poetics is predicated above all on an ingenious combinatorial practice; and his procedure in the Wittgenstein project already reflects, in its explicitly a-chronological and a-syntactical concatenation of images, this drive toward the creative recombination of "found" material. It aims to invoke Wittgenstein's "ghost" by means of these creatively combinatory acts.

This characteristic also helps explain the intense engagement with which readers approach Sebald's fictions. He purchases this receptive buy-in by bringing together those structural elements foregrounded in his summary of the Wittgenstein screenplay: a thoughtful and discriminating selection among available materials; a-chronological and a-syntactical ordering of the chosen elements; and motivic interweaving of these elements so that they take on the guise of a coherent, carefully or even beautifully constructed whole. One of the images Sebald copied from Nedo and Ranchetti's biography and included as the final illustration for his draft screenplay might be viewed as a pictorial metacommentary on this aesthetic structure (see Figure 1.2). It is a photograph, taken by Wittgenstein's brother Rudi, of a lightning storm over the Hochreith region of Austria, where the Wittgenstein family maintained a rural estate. This image stands out among those Sebald selected because it is the only one that does not depict the philosopher himself or one of his friends or relatives. It documents both the overweening power of nature, as the storm explodes over the

37 Roland Barthes, "The Reality Effect," in *The Rustle of Language*, trans. Richard Howard (Berkeley: University of California Press, 1989), 141–8. For Sebald's use of this phrase, see, for example, his interview with Carole Angier (Schwartz 72).

Figure 1.2: Lightning Storm over the Hochreith; Sebald's photocopy from Nedo and Ranchetti (30–1), File HS.2004.0001.00007, Deutsches Literaturarchiv Marbach.

mountainous landscape, and the inherent beauty of this show of force. Indeed, this photograph might be taken as an example of the sublime in nature. But in its depiction of chaotic strikes, its stark contrast between light and dark, and the sudden emergence of arabesques of lightning out of the monolithic background, this image visually performs the a-syntactical logic of a film in which a jumbled sequence of pictures flash across the screen in an attempt to illuminate the silent secrets of Wittgenstein's life. It is as though Sebald included this image as a graphic depiction for the loose but evocative structure he envisioned for this cinematic biography. In its capturing of the momentary flashes of light, of apparitions that appear against a historical landscape, this image might serve as an emblematic allegory for the "ghostwriting" Sebald practices throughout his creative works.

Sebald's most poignant self-reflection on this creative ideal, in which "found" material is woven together in a seemingly random manner, but where its recombination ultimately achieves an unexpected aesthetic perfection, is the wedding dress created by the Ashbury sisters in *Die Ringe des Saturn*. Composed of disparate swaths of silk fabric and sewn together in a network-like manner with silk thread, this patchwork concoction strikes Sebald's narrator as a quintessential work of art (*Ringe* 264–5/211–12). We will return to this example in our subsequent analysis; for now, it suffices simply to point out that Sebald's narrator recognizes in this creative fusion of found and carefully selected fragments a work of art so compelling and complete that it even surpasses one's most fantastic imaginings (*Ringe* 265/212). To emphasize this combinatory aspect of Sebald's art is not to diminish the inventiveness that enters his fictional creations on other levels: in his characteristically archaic yet compelling diction, for example; in his ability to generate depth of vision out of what seem like passing remarks by his narrator or his characters; or in his skill at building smooth transitions between the various elements of his richly diverse conglomerate. All of these represent salient aspects of Sebald's poetics of history. Above all, despite the fact that his works are reducible to a handful of repeating themes—they are, in large part, the themes he articulates in the proposal for the Wittgenstein project—he manages continually to present them so that they never feel tired, tarnished, or recycled. Sebald is, in short, a kind of literary Johann Sebastian Bach, a master in the art of stating, restating, and regenerating innovative and surprising variations on a finite set of themes. Perhaps it is no coincidence that in his description of the Wittgenstein project he employs the metaphor of the contrapuntal pattern perfected by Bach.

Although composed in response to a period of personal and profession crisis in Sebald's life, and as an occasional piece intended to commemorate the philosopher's hundredth birthday, Sebald's Wittgenstein project is anything but "occasional" in the narrow sense. It bundles in rudimentary fashion the central themes that will occupy him in his second career as creative writer. The aesthetic strategies he first articulates here, along with his demonstrated fascination with narratives assembled around carefully selected visual materials, are the same practices he subsequently develops in his fictional prose writings. To be sure, the film about Wittgenstein's life never materializes as a set of recorded images; it exists merely as a text, as the film *script* Sebald assembled for the application to the Filmförderungsanstalt. But due to its inherently visual character, this screenplay also figures as a warm-up for that ekphrastic technique that later becomes another hallmark of Sebald's fictions. The primary difference is that in this case his text does not merely extrapolate from the images culled from Nedo and Ranchetti's biography, but also writes *toward* those images that he *imagines* as elements in a discrete cinematic sequence.

If in his later creative work Sebald continued to draw on the themes, techniques, and aesthetic practices he first began to develop in the Wittgenstein project, he also repeatedly borrowed from the raw materials of his intensive occupation with the life and thought of the Viennese philosopher. One striking feature of Sebald's intellectual profile is that he rarely regarded topics that vigorously engaged him as ever being laid to rest, even when they had developed into published works. The best example of this is his early critical occupation with the presumed refusal of German literature to respond effectively to the devastating air campaign the Allies conducted against German cities during World War II, arguments he had developed already in the early 1980s in the essay "Zwischen Geschichte und Naturgeschichte" (Between history and natural history) and then readdressed more controversially in the 1998 Zurich lectures that eventually became the book *Luftkrieg und Literatur* (*On the Natural History of Destruction*). The same can be said about the abandoned Corsica project, from which Sebald rescued themes and plot elements that were later integrated into *Austerlitz*.[38] An even stronger case can be made for the "ghostly" afterlife of the themes and motifs that occupied Sebald in the Wittgenstein screenplay, which find their way in most concentrated form into the short story "Paul Bereyter" and the extended prose fiction *Austerlitz*. In both of these cases the protagonists are identified with Wittgenstein, through their association with symbols, motifs, or episodes characteristic of the latter's life, and which Sebald already highlighted in his film project. These elements are clearly marked in the case of Austerlitz, whose exile in England and ever-present knapsack are aligned specifically with the life of Wittgenstein (*Austerlitz* 58–9/40). In addition, when the narrator refers to the discerning eyes of certain artists and philosophers, he includes cropped images of two sets of eyes (7/5), one pair taken from a Wittgenstein portrait Sebald copied from Nedo and Ranchetti's illustrated biography.[39]

The situation is far more complicated, and the connections between the protagonist and Wittgenstein more masked, in the example of Paul Bereyter, where allusions to Wittgenstein and his life form a significant, if obscure, subtext. In interviews Sebald acknowledged that he had transcribed aspects of Wittgenstein's life onto this character (Schwartz 46, 72–3). But one reason for the less overt treatment of these connections might lie in the fact that Sebald was reconstructing the life of a personal acquaintance, his former elementary schoolteacher Armin Müller, news of whose suicide reached him in January 1984—as reported by the narrator of "Paul Bereyter" (*Ausgewanderten* 41/27). But Bereyter, as his fictional name indicates—a name borrowed from one of Stendhal's lovers, Angela Bereyter, with which Sebald was familiar from his work on "Beyle"—is a largely conglomerate figure, assembled out of knowledge Sebald either possessed or gathered regarding the life of his former teacher, but overlain with a series of

---

38 See Ulrich von Bülow, "Sebalds Korsika-Projekt," in *Wandernde Schatten: W. G. Sebalds Unterwelt*, ed. Ulrich von Bülow, Heike Gfrereis, and Ellen Strittmatter (Marbach am Neckar: Deutsche Schillergesellschaft, 2008), 220–1. Bülow argues that the Corsica project forms the missing link between *Die Ringe des Saturn* and *Austerlitz*.

39 Richard Weihe, "Wittgensteins Augen," 11–12, focuses on the linkages between the visual aspects of Sebald's Wittgenstein project and their resonances in *Austerlitz*.

elements borrowed from Wittgenstein's biography. In short, Bereyter represents one of the first instances in Sebald's work of a composite character who is constructed out of information drawn from a personal acquaintance and facts taken from the life of a well-known historical personage. It is difficult to discern exactly what motivated Sebald to lend his teacher some features of the historical Wittgenstein. One reason is surely the family resemblance—to appropriate Wittgenstein's term—between these two men, concretized most emphatically in their common choice of occupation as village schoolteachers. One of the motifs that particularly fascinates Sebald about Wittgenstein's life is the decision of the trained engineer and philosopher to abandon his more discerning intellectual pursuits in favor of the vocation of an elementary schoolteacher in a rural setting. His sister Hermine famously remarked that applying his talents in this rudimentary fashion was like using a precision instrument to open a cabinet,[40] an anecdote Sebald integrates into his Wittgenstein screenplay ("Leben Ws" 330). But Sebald also likely believed the amalgamation of Müller's life with Wittgenstein's would lend a more universal, prototypical cast to the individual existence of an otherwise unremarkable village school-teacher. Sebald's aim clearly goes beyond simply lending this character a more generally approachable *effet de* réel; he implicitly ascribes to this teacher the quirks and foibles of the acknowledged genius Wittgenstein, thereby elevating the common personal acquaintance to the status of a famous, even infamous, personality. Sebald therewith enacts a fictional enhancement of the potentially mundane character whom he experienced during his childhood. In fictionalizing Armin Müller's life through the prism of Wittgenstein's personality, Sebald pays belated homage to this highly respected teacher, effectively eulogizing him in the form of a literary-fictional monument. This composite technique becomes one of the mainstays of Sebald's "ghostwriting" strategy; it allows him to allude to verifiable historical facts and personalities, while simultaneously refracting this historical picture through the lens of combinatory fictions.

   Wittgenstein is only directly named at one single point in the narrative about Paul Bereyter, when his late-life companion Lucy Landau reports that Paul kept notebooks with excerpts from books he had read, most of which had been written by authors who either committed suicide or who seriously contemplated it. Wittgenstein is named here along with figures like Walter Benjamin, Klaus Mann, and Stefan Zweig (*Ausgewanderten* 86/58). The central theme of death and suicide, which motivated Sebald's composition of this story in the first place, thus

---

40   This remark is cited by Konrad Wünsche, *Der Volksschullehrer Ludwig Wittgenstein* (Frankfurt: Suhrkamp, 1985), 40, a book contained in Sebald's library.

forms one of the mainline connections to the Wittgenstein project. The other central thematic motivating the association of these two figures is their mixed heritage as Germans or Austrians of partial Jewish descent, and their own ambivalent response to this in the context of anti-Semitic attitudes during the early decades of the twentieth century. Sebald's film script plays up the philosopher's widely discussed "confession" that he was three-quarters Jewish ("Leben Ws" 329), a theme Sebald follows in the secondary literature on Wittgenstein's life.[41] Paul Bereyter has the presumed advantage of being three-quarters Aryan; but in the context of Nazi racial laws this nevertheless caused him to lose his teaching position. Moreover, the truth about his heritage is something that Bereyter, like Wittgenstein, largely keeps under wraps, even after the end of the war (*Ausgewanderten* 74/50). Bereyter, the victim of National Socialist racial politics, hence participates in the "conspiracy of silence" about the wartime years that, in Sebald's view, characterizes post-war German and Austrian society more generally. We recall that Sebald articulated this same dichotomy between silence and revelation as one of the underlying themes of the Wittgenstein screenplay.

There are many more minor features that Sebald extracted from Wittgenstein's life and grafted onto the character of Paul Bereyter. When reference is made to Paul's uncommon skill at whistling classical music (*Ausgewanderten* 61/40–1), this quality is borrowed directly from information Sebald had noted about Wittgenstein's proficiency as a whistler,[42] reference to which he also incorporates into his film script ("Leben Ws" 326). The joy and solace Bereyter takes in cultivating Lucy Landau's garden (*Ausgewanderten* 85/57–8) represents another theme from Wittgenstein's life, with which Sebald was familiar from the resources in his library.[43] More closely related to Bereyter's and Wittgenstein's occupation as elementary schoolteachers, Sebald attributes to his fictionalized character an episode from Wittgenstein's

41 Sebald was familiar with this episode from McGuinness's "Wittgensteins Persönlichkeit," xiii, and from the report on this event by Fanja Pascal, quoted at length in Nedo and Ranchetti, *Ludwig Wittgenstein*, 302. References to this confession can also be found in the edition of Wittgenstein's correspondence contained in Sebald's library, *Briefe: Briefwechsel mit B. Russell, G. E. Moore, J. M. Keynes, F. P. Ramsey, W. Eccles, P. Engelmann und L. von Ficker*, ed. Brian F. McGuinness and Georg Henrik von Wright (Frankfurt am Main: Suhrkamp. 1980), 13, 204, where Sebald duly highlights them.

42 Sebald marks the passages in the biographies by Wünsche, *Der Volksschullehrer Ludwig Wittgenstein*, 112, and by Wuchterl and Hübner, *Ludwig Wittgenstein*, 62, where reference is made to the philosopher's talent for whistling.

43 Sebald, himself an avid gardener, marks the passages in Wittgenstein's *Briefe*, 114, and Wünsche, *Der Volksschullehrer Ludwig Wittgenstein*, 44, 168, 280, where reference is made to the philosopher's activities as a gardener.

life in which he prepared a fox skeleton he found in the woods so it could be used as an educational prop in the classroom (*Ausgewanderten* 56/37)—a tale with which Sebald was familiar from the detailed description provided by Wünsche and highlighted in Sebald's copy.[44] One symptom of Bereyter's devotion to his students, and its expression in anti-institutional educational practices, is his rejection of the prescribed reading materials in favor of a compilation of stories excerpted largely from Johann Peter Hebel's *Rheinischer Hausfreund* (Rhineland household friend; *Ausgewanderten* 56–7/37–8). This episode is also filched, down to the reference to Hebel, from Wittgenstein's life.[45] Sebald appropriates a plethora of concrete details familiar to him from his study of Wittgenstein's biography to lend vivacity to his own faded memories of his elementary schoolteacher. The result is the fictional persona Paul Bereyter, a character assembled, via Sebald's combinatorial poetics of history, out of elements of at least two different lives.

Sebald does not shy away from altering or playing down aspects of Wittgenstein's life that might detract from the more positive image he seeks to paint here. Wittgenstein was infamous for the impatience he showed toward his pupils, and this quality is evident in Paul Bereyter as well, where it serves as an indication of the educator's feverish investment in his students' learning (*Ausgewanderten* 53/35, 65/43–4). However, in Wittgenstein's case this impatience could manifest itself as outright physical violence, and just such an incident caused him to be relieved of his teaching post in 1926, when he hit a student, rendering him unconscious.[46] Sebald overlooks this more aggressive aspect of Wittgenstein's pedagogy when he transfers its principles to Bereyter.

One final point is worth mentioning, since it involves a detail that can easily pass unnoticed, but which reinforces how Sebald choreographs the life of his teacher to make it reflect that of the philosopher: this is the wind jacket Paul takes from the closet and dons, after having disregarded it for almost forty years, on the evening of his suicide. For Lucy Landau, the absence of this jacket constitutes a foreboding sign, indicating that she will never again see Paul alive (*Ausgewanderten* 90/61). As Sebald noted in his copies of Wittgenstein's biographies,[47] Wittgenstein was known for always wearing an identical outfit: leather boots, flannel pants, and a characteristic wind jacket. When Paul

44   Wünsche, *Der Volksschullehrer Ludwig Wittgenstein*, 264.

45   Ibid., 81, 209.

46   Camillo Schaefer, *Wittgensteins Größenwahn: Begegnungen mit Paul Wittgenstein* (Vienna: Jugend und Volk, 1986), 61. In his copy of Schaefer's text, Sebald places double bars in the margin next to the passage that reports this incident.

47   Wünsche, *Der Volksschullehrer Ludwig Wittgenstein*, 115; Wuchterl and Hübner, *Ludwig Wittgenstein*, 98.

Bereyter dons the wind jacket he has neglected for forty years and lies down on the tracks in anticipation of the approaching train, he is symbolically also assuming the character of Ludwig Wittgenstein. After all, it was the theme of death and suicide that Sebald saw as the red thread for his screenplay about the philosopher's life, and Bereyter enacts in effigy the suicide that Wittgenstein himself could never commit. Of course, the fact that Bereyter has not touched this jacket for almost forty years indicates—since his suicide takes place in December 1983—that it is a remainder from, and reminder of, the pre-war and war years when he was openly persecuted for his Jewish heritage. The obvious implication is that Bereyter is carrying out, in radical time lag, the act of self-destruction to which he was driven by Nazi politics and their subliminal after-life in post-war Germany. This is a fate, Sebald suggests, that might also have overwhelmed the three-quarter Jew Ludwig Wittgenstein, had he not lived in English exile.

The life and thought of Ludwig Wittgenstein pervades the works of W. G. Sebald on several levels, and the Wittgenstein project he actively pursued in the mid-1980s constitutes a quarry of material that he subsequently mined over the remainder of his creative life. This applies not simply to motifs, episodes, or anecdotes borrowed from the philosopher's life and appropriated for Sebald's fictional protagonists, but also to central themes and problems Sebald persistently pursued and first articulated in the proposal he developed for the Wittgenstein screenplay. This project constituted a testing ground for many of the aesthetic strategies that typify Sebald's subsequent narratives, such as the refusal of chronologically ordered plots, the pleasure in assembling a-syntactically associated fragments and episodes, and above all the subtle art of motivic networking that supplies a subliminal structure for a surface text that appears to be a mere conglomerate of randomly collected incidents. If Wittgenstein is an all-pervasive ghost in Sebald's creative fictions, then he is a ghost who comes alive once more. And in this regard he represents those many other ghosts and those many other lives—Kafka, Stendhal, Armin Müller, Selwyn, and the various living people who make up the composite figures of Max Aurach and Austerlitz, to name just a few—without whose ghostly presence Sebald's fictions would be unimaginable. At its very heart, Sebald's creative work is a form of writing about lives as a writing about ghosts. His literature is incessantly haunted by the lives of others, and in this sense his fiction is constituted foremost as a form of ghostwriting. Sebald's poetics of history brings these ghosts back to life: his fictions are *vivifying* reconstructions and re-presentations that, unlike vampires that suck the life out of the characters they embrace, breathe life back into them. This reinvigorating moment explains the engagement and attentiveness Sebald's readers invest in his fictionalized revenants.

Two The Birth of the Prose Fictionalizer from the Spirit of Biographical Criticism: *Schwindel. Gefühle*

"The biographer has little choice but to forge ahead stoically
... yet unable to shake the nagging suspicion that the very
point at which the documentation breaks off might represent
the most interesting and even crucial episodes."

Reiner Stach[1]

Envisioning Fiction(s)

In addition to the application for the Wittgenstein film project, Sebald's posthumous papers contain another application for financial support from about the same time, addressed to the German Literaturfonds (Foundation for literature), the primary institution providing fellowship support for creative writers. In this draft application Sebald sought relief from his teaching and administrative duties in order to pursue his early forays into the composition of prose fictions.[2] While the typescript of this draft proposal is undated, its composition can

---

1 Reiner Stach, *Kafka: The Years of Insight*, trans. Shelley Frisch (Princeton, NJ: Princeton University Press, 2013), 83.
2 This application is found in folder 11 under the heading "Konvolut Prosa, Sammlung *Ausgewanderten*," with the file name "Konvolut: Unterlagen für die Bewerbung um ein Werkstipendium des Deutschen Literaturfonds" and the inventory number HS.2004.0001.00011. The primary documents in this file are the application materials Sebald submitted to the Foundation in 1991 for completion of the stories for *Die Ausgewanderten*. Included, however, is also the earlier draft project proposal discussed here, which was never submitted and which describes Sebald's writing project in very different terms from the 1991 application. This five-page typescript will henceforth be cited as "Literaturfonds," with the relevant manuscript page.

be most likely situated in the first quarter of 1988, based on temporal indicators related to Sebald's professional background as provided in the description itself.[3] This exposé is of special significance because it documents Sebald's self-understanding of his literary undertakings at a time when his conceptions for these fictional prose narratives were just beginning to germinate. When he wrote this application, the three sections of the prose poem *Nach der Natur* (*After Nature*) had already appeared in the literary magazine *Manuskripte*, and the first segment was about to be published in Dutch translation. Sebald also indicates that he expects to find a book publisher for this poem, and this information serves to establish Sebald's credentials as an already published author of literary works, not simply as a scholar of literary criticism. Yet Sebald takes pains to emphasize that the poetic excursions of *Nach der Natur* are nothing but etudes, "a preliminary exercise and practice piece" ("eine Vorübung und ein Probestück"), preparing the way for the much more comprehensive prose fictions for whose composition he is requesting financial support ("Literaturfonds" 1). Thus in Sebald's self-understanding in early 1988, *Nach der Natur* represents a transitional work that rehearses the themes, ideas, and literary structures that will mature and culminate in the fictional prose narratives he has just begun to envision and draft.

Sebald's detailed description of this literary undertaking begins by characterizing it vaguely as "a work of prose that operates with pictures" ("eine Prosaarbeit mit Bildern"), going on to stress that the images are not mere illustrations, but instead constitute an integral part of the text itself ("Literaturfonds" 2). The formative character of the image–text relation is indicated by the priority lent this feature. This dimension was not yet represented in *Nach der Natur*, although, as we have seen, images figured prominently in the Wittgenstein screenplay. He also specifically identifies the problem of visual representation as an issue with which his prose narratives will engage thematically. In order to document the nature of this text–image relation, he refers to two stories he plans to include with his application materials. These tales treat "the attempts by two writers, Stendhal (*1783) and Kafka (*1883), to gain happiness, that is, their misfortunes, both of whom spent time at Lake Garda, the first in September 1813, the second in September

---

3   Sebald remarks that an edited volume on "Contemporary German Theatre" will appear in the coming autumn, a reference to the collection *A Radical Stage: Theatre in Germany in the 1970s and 1980s* (Oxford: Berg, 1988). He also notes that he has not yet found a publisher for the book version of *Nach der Natur*, although he indicates that negotiations are underway. Since he signed a contract for that work with Greno Verlag on April 5, 1988, the draft proposal must have been written earlier, or between January and the end of March 1988.

1913" ("die Glücksversuche bzw. das Unglück zweier Schriftsteller: Stendhal (*1783) und Kafka (*1883), von denen sich der eine im September 1813, der andere im September 1913 eine Zeit am Gardasee aufgehalten hat"; "Literaturfonds" 2). Sebald is describing what will become the first and third stories in *Schwindel. Gefühle*, "Beyle oder das merckwürdige Faktum der Liebe" ("Beyle, or Love Is a Madness Most Discreet") and "Dr. K.s Badereise nach Riva" ("Dr. K. Takes the Waters in Riva"). An early version of the Stendhal piece appeared in the March 1988 issue of the literary magazine *Manuskripte* under the title "Berge oder das ..." (Mountains or the ...), and since the draft proposal makes no mention of this work having been published, this provides another clue for dating this draft application. That Sebald intended to include the Kafka text as part of the application suggests that this piece was close to completion at this time.

Sebald's application indicates that he already envisioned questions of temporal and geographical coincidence as playing "a central, although not a dominant role" ("eine zentrale, wenn auch nicht dominante Rolle") in the makeup of this work ("Literaturfonds" 2), exemplified by the serendipitous connections between Stendhal's and Kafka's biographies, the century that separates both their years of birth and their stays in Riva.[4] After referencing these two largely finished stories and elaborating on the themes of image–text relations and coincidence as fundamental motivations and structural aspects of this project, Sebald then shifts to a wide-ranging inventory of the interests that outline his eventual trajectory as an author of narrative fictions. He notes briefly that the Stendhal and Kafka pieces will be followed by two autobiographical works: one in which the first-person narrator recapitulates the trip from Vienna, via Venice and Verona to Riva that these literary predecessors took; another that takes the narrator from Riva to the village of W. on the northern edge of the Alps ("Literaturfonds" 2). These are clear references to the other two texts that round out *Schwindel. Gefühle*, "All'estero" and "Il ritorno in patria." But from this point onward Sebald's exposé opens onto a stunning diversity of topics that look ahead to the primary concerns we now associate with his later prose fictions. Citing references to Kafka's story about the Hunter Gracchus in the tale about the return to the village W., he explains how this theme of the eternal wanderer will be developed in texts that examine biographies from the Seelos family—Sebald's own ancestors—who were born in this village. He

---

4   In an interview with Piet de Moor from 1992, Sebald explained how the coincidences he discovered between the lives of these writers provided one of the primary motivations for the composition of *Schwindel. Gefühle* (*"Auf ungeheuer dünnem Eis"* 71).

stresses that these life stories will be treated in a synoptic manner, whereby the very problematic of the bird's-eye view will become a recurrent motif. He is clearly looking ahead to later works, such as *Die Ringe des Saturn*, in which this thematic plays a significant role. Sebald goes on to maintain that the representational strategies pursued on the level of literary practice will be self-reflexively thematized in the narrative substance of these works. But he also elucidates how, via the history of the family Seelos, the theme of exile and "emigration" ("Auswanderung") will assume center stage, and he concludes this exposition with the pointed question, "How did the Seelos siblings get to New York?" ("Wie sind die Geschwister Seelos nach New York gekommen?"; "Literaturfonds" 3). Thus this project description contains the rudiments of ideas and figures that will populate Sebald's second collection of prose fictional narratives, *Die Ausgewanderten* (*The Emigrants*), in particular the family stories built around his great-uncle Wilhelm Seelos, who appears in that text under the pseudonym Ambros Adelwarth. Sebald refers explicitly to this great-uncle toward the end of this draft proposal, and he includes a photograph of him, taken in Jerusalem in 1906, in Arab costume, an image that is ultimately reproduced in "Ambros Adelwarth" (*Ausgewanderten* 137/94) (see Figure 2.1).

Another aspect of this project is coherent with the so-called "Weltkrieg," or "World War" endeavor that Sebald had begun to pursue in the months just before his death—and for which he received a prestigious National Endowment for Science, Technology and the Arts (NESTA) fellowship for research and writing from the British government.[5] In the Literaturfonds application he outlines his plans to investigate the life of his ancestor Mathild Seelos, who was suffused in the mysticism of Jakob Böhme (1575–1624) and Emmanuel Swedenborg (1688–1772), but who was also devoted to the work of socialist-feminists like Clara Zetkin (1857–1933) and Lily Braun (1865–1916). He also voices his intention to complete research on Rudolf Egelhofer (1896–1919), whom Sebald identifies as the nephew of his maternal grandfather Josef Egelhofer (1872–1956). Rudolf figured as a commander in the Red Army that briefly took control of Munich at the end of World War I, and he died in this political struggle in 1919 ("Literaturfonds" 3). In January 1988, Sebald spent several days working in the Bavarian State Library in Munich, where, among other things, he likely pursued research on this figure.

---

5   The most detailed knowledge we have about this project is contained in the application materials Sebald composed for the NESTA grant, cataloged under the name "Weltkrieg Bewerbung" among Sebald's papers at the Deutsches Literaturarchiv. This file bears the inventory number HS.2004.0001.00660.

Figure 2.1: Wilhelm Seelos ("Adelwarth") in Arab garb in Jerusalem (*Ausgewanderten* 137/94).

The branches of this loosely conceived literary endeavor multiply even further. Sebald cites "teaching and learning" as a prominent theme, and under this rubric he describes the character and professional life of his elementary schoolteacher Armin Müller, here already christened with the surname "Bereyter," in anticipation of the pseudonym he will receive in the story "Paul Bereyter." Sebald emphasizes how during his exile in France, Müller became a fan of Stendhal's writing, and with this we begin to see how he imagines that these diverse stories will be unified based on interwoven thematic or motivic networks. The name "Bereyter" itself reinforces the connection to Stendhal, since it is derived from one of the French writer's many lovers, Angéline Bereyter, whom Sebald mentions by name in the first text of *Schwindel. Gefühle* (26/22). He also remarks that the life of this former teacher motivated him to explore the phenomenon of "Altersselbstmord," late-life suicide ("Literaturfonds" 3). This proposal also includes paragraphs that describe the problem of memory as one of the project's principal preoccupations, whereby reference is made to a mountain climber whose body is freed from a glacier seventy years after his disappearance ("Literaturfonds" 3–4). This is none other than the climber Johannes Naegeli in "Dr. Henry Selwyn," who is already associated with the theme of return from the dead. Thus this project description from March 1988 embodies a comprehensive sketch of the central ideas, aesthetic practices, themes, and characters that would eventually constitute Sebald's first two major collections of prose fiction. Significantly, at this early stage they are conceived as parts of a *single* literary endeavor.

Sebald openly acknowledges the extreme heterogeneity of this project. Indeed, he admits that the outlined plan could potentially "develop, or even proliferate, in many different directions" ("dass ein Projekt dieser Art in viele Richtungen wachsen, ja auswachsen kann"; "Literaturfonds" 4). In addition, he notes that the very diversity of this material demands that these narratives be stitched together via motivic connections, a shared topography, and a series of what he calls "Gedenktage" or commemorative days ("Literaturfonds" 4). He thereby anticipates the strategy of motivic interweaving he will employ throughout his book-length narratives in order to lend them structural coherence. One thinks of Kafka's Hunter Gracchus as an intertext for the stories in *Schwindel. Gefühle*, of Nabokov the "Butterfly Man" as the thread that links together the four very different tales of *Die Ausgewanderten*, or of the motif of silk and silkworms that joins the various episodes of *Die Ringe des Saturn*. Sebald was already cognizant at this early stage that the type of work he imagined required a high degree of managerial oversight, a supervisory will to order and structure that would ensure a semblance of integrity, unity, and coherence. In an interview published in the *Observer Review* in June 1998, he acknowledged the significance of these secondary, managerial interventions for his prose fictions, calling these works "artifacts" that require conscious retrospective shaping by the author.[6] If in his Literaturfonds application Sebald emphasizes that coincidence and serendipitous return constitute central concerns, he also understands that motivic interweaving, or a pattern of textual return and reiteration, is the structural device most coherent with this thematic interest. He understood early on that much of the artistry in his prose fictions would derive from the structural organizing these works received through the conscious textual choreography imposed by the author.

When towards the conclusion of this project description Sebald addresses questions of possible predecessors or generic models, he names the *Kalendergeschichte* (Almanac story), a non-specific form of prose writing that includes manifold text types, such as story, anecdote, historical report, and didactic example: "I prefer not to speak of models. Ideally what would emerge would be something like almanac stories, which I or someone else could later continue writing ad libitum" ("Von Vorbildern will ich nicht reden. Am liebsten wäre es mir, es würden sich sowas wie Kalendergeschichten ergeben, an denen ich, oder auch sonst wer, später nach Belieben fortschreiben kann"; "Literaturfonds" 4). Sebald has in mind the loosely-organized collection of narratives with which he was familiar from the folk almanacs his beloved maternal grandfather Josef Egelhofer read, and more specifically its more formalized literary manifestation in Johann Peter Hebel's *Der rheinländische Hausfreund* (Rhineland household friend), one of Sebald's favorite works of literature, about which he later wrote a critical essay.[7] Sebald imagines something like a serial or periodical publication, whereby he identifies his own narrative voice with that of a quasi-anonymous storyteller or editor; this allows him to envision this project as infinitely extendable by someone other than himself. Thus he understands his narrator as speaking in a communal voice, through whom others with shared interests and investments might also speak. Moreover, he also defends the idea that a network of subliminal interconnections runs throughout the real world, and that his narratives would simply replicate in their own texture the

---

6 "'Characters, plot, dialogue? That's not really my style ...'," *Observer Review* (June 7, 1998): 17.

7 "Es steht ein Komet am Himmel" ("A Comet in the Heavens"), from *Logis in einem Landhaus* (*A Place in the Country*). Sebald relates here how he constantly felt driven to reread Hebel's stories, and how his grandfather's use of language was reminiscent of this historical predecessor. He also notes that his grandfather purchased an almanac of this sort at the beginning of every new year (*Logis* 12–14/10–12).

inherent interrelatedness of worldly events. "The ultimate logic is that when one looks at things minutely, everything is truly connected with everything else, and if one pulls on just a single thread, soon an entire blanket comes unraveled" ("Die Logik ist zuletzt die, dass, wenn man nur genau hinschaut, wirklich alles mit allem verbunden ist, und dass man, wenn man nur an einem Faden zieht, bald schon eine ganze Decke aufgedröselt hat"; "Literaturfonds" 4). This inherent interdependence among things in the real world, and its quasi mimetic reflection in the motivic interlacing constitutive of the literary text, resonates with Sebald's understanding of Hebel and the genre of the *Kalendergeschichte*. This genre is similarly characterized by tremendous heterogeneity, but also by a democratizing quality that shuns hierarchies in favor of a one-dimensional aggregation of elements that stand on an equal footing. A comment from Sebald's essay on Hebel reads like a retrospective reiteration of what he foresaw already in 1988 as the structure of this multifaceted collection of prose narratives. Remarking on Hebel's proclivity for paratactic structures, as signaled by his frequent use of conjunctions such as "and," "or," and "but," he observes, "Opposed to any hierarchy or subordination, they [these conjunctions] suggest to the reader in the most unobtrusive way that in the world created and administered by this narrator, everything has an equal right to coexist alongside everything else" ("Gegen jede Über- und Unterordnung gerichtet, legen sie [diese Konjunktionen] dem Leser auf die unaufdringlichste Weise nahe, daß in der von diesem Erzähler geschaffenen und verwalteten Welt alles nebeneinander bestehen soll mit gleichem Recht"; *Logis* 21–2/19). The narrative world of Hebel's *Kalendergeschichten*, like the sweeping work of narrative fiction Sebald conceptualizes in this project summary, is not "created" spontaneously through the labor of the imagination, but carefully "administered"—actively managed and painstakingly structured—by a quasi-depersonalized authorial consciousness. Sebald thus attributes to Hebel and his characteristic genre of the *Kalendergeschichte* the same kind of self-reflexive deliberation and aesthetic ordering that he deems necessary for his own prose narratives. The ultimate purpose of this careful patterning is the suspension of temporality, the eradication of time as a succession of moments or a developmental process. The fictional world he associates with Hebel, like the one proposed in the project description, stresses spatial juxtaposition or proximity— "nebeneinander"—as opposed to temporal succession. This is a fictional world in which historical time has been suspended and all things are created equal; every form of hierarchical ordering is rejected in favor of placing historically disparate episodes on a single temporal plane.[8]

---

8   Jonathan Long, *W. G. Sebald: Image, Archive, Modernity* (New York: Columbia

This shunning of temporal sequence and logical connection recapitulates, in more sophisticated form, the a-chronological and a-syntactical structure Sebald envisioned for the Wittgenstein screenplay just two years earlier.

This 1988 project statement leaves the impression that what will emerge as Sebald's individual works of prose fiction are cut more or less arbitrarily from a single textual cloth: that they are iterations of a handful of repeating ideas, themes, and motifs, administered by a coherent authorial perspective. Those critics who have emphasized the consistencies in voice, tone, narrative approach, and emotional tenor across all of Sebald's works will surely find confirmation in the comprehensive manner in which, in this early formulation, he envisions a single narrative project that bundles together these diverse ideas and problems.[9] However, if this draft proposal reads like a programmatic statement about Sebald's enduring literary and aesthetic ideology, certain fundamental elements are nonetheless missing. To be sure, he touches obliquely on some of those central pursuits with which his work has come to be associated, such as memory, emigration, pedagogy, suicide, the return of the dead, and the investigation of personal biographies. But there is little in this exposé that suggests its author might later be identified as a Holocaust writer. Indeed, the word "Holocaust" does not appear anywhere in this typescript, and the one place its role could be emphasized—in the elaboration of the life of the partial-Jew Armin Müller, whom the Nazis prevented from pursuing his calling as an educator—the wording is especially cautious and circumspect, emphasizing this teacher's bonds with the natural environment and his idealism. Sebald's summary largely circumvents the political implications of Nazism by generalizing this figure's fate as an example of late-life suicide.

Especially noteworthy is that this application gathers together the individual texts of Sebald's first two books of prose fiction, *Schwindel. Gefühle* and *Die Ausgewanderten*, into one and the same project.[10]

University Press, 2007), 106, is correct in associating the dense texture of motivic repetitions in Sebald's works with the material world as a site of wonder and metaphysics.

9   It has become common to understand Sebald's fictions as interlocking pieces of a singular, monolithic narrative puzzle. John Wylie, "The Spectral Geographies of W. G. Sebald," *Cultural Geographies* 14 (2007): 174, argues that Sebald's texts constitute "a single body of writing" unified by "tone, mood, form and theme." Gray Kochhar-Lindgren, "Charcoal: The Phantom Traces of W. G. Sebald's Novel-Memoirs," *Monatshefte* 94 (2002): 370, similarly believes all of Sebald's works are unified by their style and thematic.

10 Jo Catling, "Bibliotheca abscondita: On W. G. Sebald's Library," in *Saturn's Moons: W. G. Sebald—A Handbook*, ed. Jo Catling and Richard Hibbitt (London:

Additionally, it looks ahead to the personal histories that would inform the "Weltkrieg" project that captured Sebald's attention at the end of his life. Thus these application materials sketch a trajectory that betrays an abiding interest in how individual life stories intersect with world-historical events, a thematic that is central for the Beyle and Kafka pieces. Yet there are also aspects of Sebald's later work that fall conspicuously outside of this early vision of his narrative project. There is, for example, no mention of those sociopolitical and environmental interests that inform *Die Ringe des Saturn* and the Corsica project, which dominate his creative energies from 1993 through 1997. This provides one of the strongest indications that these works mark a distinctly different phase in the realization of Sebald's narrative artistry, whereas his final work, *Austerlitz*, represents a return and extension of the larger narrative project he formulated already in early 1988. As a significant interlude that interrupts this trajectory, Sebald's historical-environmental travelogues deserve separate treatment, and this justifies my decision to handle them at the end of this study, out of line with the chronological order of their composition.

There is one other significant point of divergence between the works Sebald ultimately completed and this early outline: the plan to address individual life stories in a fleeting, "synoptic," and rudimentary manner—"as if in over-flight" ("wie im Überflug"), as he writes ("Literaturfonds" 2)—ultimately gives way to a much more thorough, involved, and elaborate engagement with the lives and incidents on which he focuses, culminating in the novel-like exposition of his final work, *Austerlitz*. This is the only one of Sebald's prose narratives held together entirely by the internal coherence of a unitary plot, structured around the process of discovery by which the eponymous protagonist recalls, pieces together, and relates to Sebald's first-person narrator the submerged memories of his former life. In this text the consciousness, emotional attitudes, and probing curiosity of the narrating instance, which lend the earlier texts their semblance of unity, recedes into the background and functions more like a simple sounding-board.[11] By contrast, the earliest texts Sebald composes for his first two collections

---

Modern Humanities Research Association, 2011), 279, notes that Sebald was working on the composition of the texts from *Schwindel. Gefühle* and *Die Ausgewanderten* simultaneously, but she does not recognize that he initially conceived them as parts of a single project.

11 Markus R. Weber, "Bilder erzählen den Erzähler: Zur Bedeutung der Abbildungen für die Herausbildung von Erzählerrollen in den Werken W. G. Sebalds," in *W. G. Sebald: Mémoire. Transferts. Images. Erinnerung. Übertragungen. Bilder*, special issue of *Recherches Germaniques* 2 (2005): 44, is correct to maintain that Sebald's narrators tend to fade into the background in his later works, when they assume the roles of researchers into the lives of others.

of stories, the Stendhal and Kafka pieces and the "Selwyn" and
"Bereyter" texts, tend more toward this synoptic treatment, as reflected
in the less sustained exposition of the characters, the sketchy outline
of the narrator, and the relative brevity of the texts themselves. This
begins to change with the last two tales in *Die Ausgewanderten*, "Ambros
Adelwarth" and "Max Aurach," which develop as longer expositions
in which the narrator figures more prominently as a character in the
diegesis.

Although Sebald's 1988 draft project description holds important
implications for his emergence as a writer of prose fictions in general,
the ideas formulated there have the greatest relevance for the texts
collected in *Schwindel. Gefühle*, if only because this work is conceived
and written in close temporal proximity with the ideas first laid out
in this application. This exposé thus provides important clues about
Sebald's beginnings as a prose writer, and these can serve as guideposts
that help us trace, through an analysis of his texts in the chronological
order of their composition, the genesis of what we now recognize as
Sebald's unique narrative voice and posture. If my exposition of this
project description has emphasized how it embryonically prefigures
many of Sebald's abiding concerns and aesthetic strategies, it is also
important to keep in mind that it marks a moment of transition in
Sebald's life and in his development as a writer. The opening paragraph
of this application, which he dubs a "preamble," emphasizes that the
majority of Sebald's previous publications are in the field of literary
criticism, but that since composing the prose poem *Nach der Natur* he
finds himself at a new threshold in his writing career. He stresses in
particular the therapeutic aspect of creative writing, noting that he is
eager to unburden himself of the mental baggage that has bedeviled
him for many years. The language in which Sebald, the Kafka scholar,
formulates this motivation echoes one of Kafka's famous statements
about the need to relieve himself, via writing, of the incredible world
in his head.[12] Like Kafka, Sebald articulates this urge to attain relief via
literary expression as a necessity:

Ich trage schon lange Zeit vieles im Kopf herum, was ich
aufschreiben möchte und müsste, wußte aber nie ... ob ich mich

---

12 See Kafka's diary entry from June 21, 1913: "The tremendous world I have
in my head. But how free myself and free it without being torn to pieces?,"
The Diaries, 1910–1923, trans. Joseph Kresh and Martin Greenberg (New York:
Schocken, 1988), 222; "Die ungeheure Welt, die ich im Kopfe habe. Aber wie
mich befreien und sie befreien ohne zu zerreißen?," *Tagebücher*, ed. Hans-Gerd
Koch, Michael Müller, and Malcolm Pasley (Frankfurt am Main: Fischer, 1990),
562.

auf dieses Geschäft [des Literaturschreibens] einlassen soll, vor
allem deshalb nicht, weil ich mir über die Anforderungen, die es
an einen stellt, keine Illusionen mache. ("Literaturfonds" 1–2).
[I have been carrying many things around in my head for a long
time now, things I wanted, even needed to write down, but I
never knew ... if I should really get into this business [of writing
literature], above all because I am under no illusions about the
kinds of demands it makes on one.]

When Sebald acknowledges the demands the "business" of literature
imposes on an author, this can be read as another nod to Kafka, who
wavered throughout his mature life between a sense of his innate
literary calling and a profound diffidence regarding the quality of the
artistic works he produced. Coherent with this is Sebald's assertion that
his own inaugural forays into the world of narrative fiction deal with
the misfortune ("Unglück") and fortune-seeking ("Glücksversuche")
of two writers, Stendhal and Kafka ("Literaturfonds" 2). In the first
two narratives he composes, Sebald engages with and self-reflexively
deliberates on the pursuit of writing as therapeutic activity and the
potential personal repercussions—increased misfortune—that might
ensue from this endeavor. The significance of this set of ideas for
Sebald's intellectual profile is reflected in the fact that three years
prior to formulating this draft application, he published a major
work of criticism on Austrian literature with the noteworthy title
Die Beschreibung des Unglücks (The description of misfortune). In the
introduction to that volume he programmatically argues that "The
description of misfortune inherently subsumes the possibility of its
overcoming" ("Die Beschreibung des Unglücks schließt in sich die
Möglichkeit zu einer Überwindung ein"; *Beschreibung* 12), and he goes
on to name Thomas Bernhard and Peter Handke as two contemporary
authors who exemplify this overcoming of misfortune via the medium
of the artistic word:

Wo zeigte sich das deutlicher als an den beiden anscheinend so
gegensätzlichen Autoren Bernhard und Handke: sie sind, ein jeder
auf seine Art, guten Muts, trotz der genauesten Einsicht in die
historia calimatatum. Weder der seltsame Humorismus Bernhards
noch die Feierlichkeit Handkes wären als Gegengewichte zur
Erfahrung des Unglücks zu erreichen ohne das Medium der
Schrift. (*Beschreibung* 12)
[Where has this made itself more clearly evident than in the
works of those two seemingly so contrary authors Bernhard
and Handke: both of them, each in his own way, are of good
cheer, in spite of the most intimate insight into the historia

calimatatum [history of calamities]. Neither Bernhard's peculiar humor nor Handke's solemnity could serve as counterweights to their experience of misfortune without the medium of writing.]

Sebald concludes this argument in defense of the therapeutic effect of fiction writing by citing the story of Rabbi Chanouch, who tells a crying child that the best way to end his misery is to open a book—a tale Sebald pointedly dubs a "parable about the bridge made of letters between misfortune and solace" ("Parabel von der Buchstabenbrücke zwischen Unglück und Trost"; *Beschreibung* 13).

This metaphor of a bridge of letters tying misfortune with emotional comfort could stand as a watchword for Sebald's venture into the domain of prose fictions at the end of the 1980s. When asked by Piet de Moor, shortly after the publication of *Schwindel. Gefühle*, about what animated his turn from literary criticism to the creation of literature proper, Sebald cites a personal midlife crisis—emotional misfortune— as the instigator and emphasizes how the autobiographical texts in this collection represent life-historical excavations in the service of self-understanding (*"Auf ungeheuer dünnem Eis"* 71). Self-discovery is one of the persistent motives Sebald names when asked about the reasons for his turn to the composition of prose fictions so late in life. About *Schwindel. Gefühle* he confesses in an interview with Andreas Isenschmid,

> Es ist so eine Art fiktiver Text, teils biographisch, teils autobiographisch, teils essayistisch, teils handelt es sich um Bildbeschreibungen, teils handelt es sich um Reiseberichte und zum Teil auch um Versuche psychogrammatischer Art, also daß man schreibend sich bemüht, hinter Dinge zu kommen, hinter die man sonst nicht ohne weiteres kommt. (*"Auf ungeheuer dünnem Eis"* 50–1)
> [It is a kind of fictional text, part biography, part autobiography, part essayistic; in part it is a matter of describing images, in part it is a writing of travelogues, and in part it also embodies experiments of a psychogrammatic character—that is, that in the act of writing one is making an effort to understand things that one cannot otherwise understand.]

Sebald is explicit about how this looser, less academically and institutionally constrained form of writing provides a form of psychological self-therapy. It is as though the very heterogeneity of these fictional texts were responsible for the sense of liberation he feels from the limitations of scholarly exposition. And yet his language harks back precisely to those traits that already distinguished his literary criticism:

the focus on *biographical* study, on the one hand, and the tendency to approach his critical objects with *essayistic* verve rather than with the analytical rigor characteristic of mainstream, institutionally-mandated scholarship, on the other. Concerning the latter point, Sebald remarked in a 1996 interview with Walther Krause that his loose, essayistic approach to criticism relegated him to the status of an outsider among literary scholars. But he also noted that this helped pave the way for his transition to prose fiction (*"Auf ungeheuer dünnem Eis"* 147).[13] But Sebald is often much less apologetic when it comes to the biographical emphasis that informed his literary scholarship. In a discussion with Volker Hage from the year 2000, he defends literary biographers as the practitioners of "fundamental research" ("Grundlagenforschung") and lodges a complaint against those institutional parameters that cause literary scholarship to downplay the importance of such work: "If as a university professor you write a biography, then it might happen that you are disdained, above all by your colleagues. Such things are thought to lack seriousness. And yet such works are much more important than a new theory of the novel or of narrative" ("Wenn Sie als Universitätsprofessor eine Biographie schreiben, dann kann es passieren, daß Sie verachtet werden, vor allem von Ihren Kollegen. Das gilt als unseriös. Dabei wären solche Arbeiten viel wichtiger als noch eine neue Roman- oder Erzähltheorie"; *"Auf ungeheuer dünnem Eis"* 183). If formal literary criticism demands, as Sebald remarks elsewhere, that critical writers banish everything subjective from their approach (*"Auf ungeheuer dünnem Eis"* 254–5), then in the first two texts written for *Schwindel. Gefühle*, "Beyle" and "Dr. K.," Sebald gives free reign to those subjectivist proclivities that threatened to compromise his scholarly endeavors. These two texts are decidedly transitional pieces, marking his passage from literary criticism to historically-oriented, but imaginatively embroidered prose fictions. Sebald openly acknowledged the hybrid status of the Kafka piece specifically, which he claimed marked a shift from a "description of literature to the writing of literature itself" ("Beschreibung der Literatur zur Literatur selbst"; *"Auf ungeheuer dünnem Eis"* 97).

Sebald was most explicit about the significance of the Stendhal and Kafka texts as transitional works in the detailed interview he gave to Andreas Isenschmid immediately after the publication of *Schwindel. Gefühle* in 1990. When he admits that these "descriptive"

---

13 See Manfred Jurgensen, "Creative Reflection: W. G. Sebald's Critical Essays and Literary Fiction," in *W. G. Sebald: Schreiben ex patria / Expatriate Writing*, ed. Gerhard Fischer (Amsterdam: Rodopi, 2009), 422, who makes the case that Sebald's prose fictions and his affirmative literary-critical essays share essential qualities, including a similar voice.

("beschreibende") narratives were the first ones composed for the collection, Isenschmid reacts with surprise, declaring that he had assumed them to be the last (*"Auf ungeheuer dünnem Eis"* 63–4). Sebald responds by emphasizing the necessary priority of these works as mediators between literary criticism and creative writing:

> So habe ich also zunächst diese beiden ersten Texte, also Kafka und Stendhal, geschrieben, in dem Gefühl, daß es sich da noch um etwas sehr Distanziertes handelt, wo ich aber bestimmte Dinge entwickeln kann, die ich in einem literaturkritischen Essay nicht entwickeln kann. Das war also der erste Schritt … Und ich habe gemerkt, daß also der Impetus bei mir dann dahin geht, daß ich also wirklich etwas über mich selbst auch herausfinden will und nicht nur über diese beiden anderen Figuren, daß diese beiden anderen Figuren also wirklich im Grunde für mich Folien waren, um hinter meine eigenen, von mir unerkannten Gedanken zu kommen. (*"Auf ungeheuer dünnem Eis"* 64)
> [I initially wrote these first two texts, that is Kafka and Stendhal, with the sense that they represent something very distant, but where I can develop certain things that cannot be developed in a literary-critical essay. That was thus the first step … And then I realized that the impetus behind this is that I really want to find out something about myself and not about these two other figures; that in principal these two other figures are really nothing but foils that serve as a way to discover my own, unknown thoughts.]

We are back at the theme of fictional writing as a mode of self-discovery, as a way of coming to terms with thoughts and ideas that have long occupied the author subliminally, but that require a liberating act of writing in order to be processed. Sebald identifies the Stendhal and Kafka pieces as threshold works that mark his transition from literary criticism to literature by pointing to the shift from a distanced, quasi-objective treatment to a form of emotional self-involvement in which an exploration of the writer's own subjectivity, as refracted through deliberations on the writing of others, becomes paramount.

If Kafka and Stendhal play the roles of "foils" that help promote this shift from objective criticism to subjective narrative exposition, then this is because these authors model exactly this kind of self-exploration in their own literary undertakings. They also exemplify a reflex that transforms autobiographical deliberations into literary self-mystifications, and hence they model the pseudo-autobiographical focus characteristic of the other two narratives included in *Schwindel.*

Gefühle, "All'estero" and "Il ritorno in patria."[14] What Stendhal and
Kafka share with Sebald, and what lends their own literary undertakings significance as paradigms for his emerging literary endeavor, is
their tendency to generate prose fictions as conscious self-stylizations.
As authors, they are exemplary for the intimate intertwining of literature and life that Sebald admired and studied in the writers whose
works he valued as a literary critic, and this reflex informs the pseudo-
autobiographical dimension of his own first-person narrators. When
investigated according to the order of their composition—rather than
following the order in which Sebald retrospectively assembled them in
Schwindel. Gefühle—it becomes apparent how these texts perform this
transition from critical biography to fictional autobiography. "Beyle"
and "Dr. K." are decidedly hybrid works that manifest Sebald's shift
from literary criticism to pseudo-documentary prose fictions. This
transitional character is signaled by the adherence to a third-person
narrative stance—an anomaly in Sebald's fictional texts—that imitates
the objective, external perspective of the critical scholarly observer,
even though this voice already tends to identify with its objects of
study and to merge subjectively, via the citing of life documents, with
the personal perspective of the writers under examination. Only in the
last two pieces composed for this volume, "All'estero" and "Il ritorno
in patria," does Sebald begin to speak in his own peculiar narrative
voice. This chapter will highlight the crossover texts "Beyle" and "Dr.
K.," whose character as hybrids between literary criticism and fictional
prose has largely escaped critical attention.

A Text with a View: Imaginative and Visual Experiments in "Beyle oder das merckwürdige Faktum der Liebe"

The inaugural text of *Schwindel. Gefühle*, "Beyle oder das merckwürdige
Faktum der Liebe," opens not with text but with an illustration (7/3),
a black-and-white reproduction of Carle Vernet's (1758–1836) etching
Passage du Grand Saint-Bernard from 1806 (see Figure 2.2). The image
emphasizes the grandeur of the mountain itself, which literally dwarfs
Napoleon and his army as they move through the lower foreground,
and in Sebald's reproduction the snaking line of soldiers ascending the
pass is virtually indistinguishable. His source was Victor Del Litto's
Album Stendhal, a profusely illustrated biography of the French writer
that appeared in the renowned series "Bibliothèque de la Pléiade" of
the Paris publisher Gallimard.[15] Del Litto's work serves as the source

---

14 Sebald employs the term "pseudobiographical" when referring to "Il ritorno" in
    a 2001 interview with Arthur Lubow (Schwartz 168). As the context indicates,
    he likely meant pseudo-*auto*biographical.
15 Victor Del Litto, *Album Stendhal, Iconographie* (Paris: Gallimard, 1966).

Figure 2.2: Napoleon crossing the St. Bernard Pass (*Schwindel* 7/3).

for the vast majority of images Sebald includes in "Beyle," and if this text had been presented as a critical work rather than as documentary fiction, Sebald might have been accused of plagiarism, since this source is never named.[16] The image itself represents a cross between landscape and historical painting, and its position at the outset of the narrative gives a first clue that "Beyle" is a text with a view: a piece of narrative prose in which the integration of illustrations is of central importance. This is the first work of this sort in Sebald's oeuvre, and the fact that the image precedes any text, thereby playing the traditional role of a frontispiece, sets this story apart from the other three narratives in this volume. Sebald would subsequently employ this same strategy to great effect in the first two stories of *Die Ausgewanderten*. In the case of "Henry Selwyn," the photograph depicts a large tree in the midst of a cemetery, and its relationship to the story itself remains unarticulated and mysterious (7/3). Its function is to evoke a somber and melancholy mood and thereby set the emotional stage for all the biographies that

---

16 For this reason, it is necessary to contradict Michael Niehaus, "Ikonotext. Bastelei: *Schwindel. Gefühle* von W. G. Sebald," in *Lesen ist wie Sehen: Intermediale Zitate in Bild und Text*, ed. Silke Horstkotte and Karin Leonhard (Cologne: Böhlau, 2006), 161, when he claims that the majority of illustrations in *Schwindel. Gefühle* fall into the category of "found objects." The illustrations for "Beyle" and "Dr. K." explicitly go against this hypothesis, since the majority are drawn from targeted sources.

follow. The image that inaugurates "Paul Bereyter" imitates the osten-
sible perspective this figure himself may have had as he lay down on
the railroad tracks to await his own death (*Ausgewanderten* 41/27). It
thus is illustrative in the literal sense, since it connects directly with
the opening lines of text describing how the narrator's former teacher
stretched himself out "where the railway track curves out of a willow
copse into the open fields" ("wo die Bahnlinie in einem Bogen aus
dem kleinen Weidengehölz herausführt und das offene Feld gewinnt";
41/27). These words coordinate closely with the scene presented in
the reproduced photograph, so that text and image communicate in a
mutually supportive dialogue (see Figure 2.3).

The same can be said for the relationship between text and image
at the inception of "Beyle": the illustration sets the tone and gives a
first impression of the historical event, while the opening lines provide
explanatory detail. The text replaces the missing title of Vernet's
etching by emphasizing the monumental challenge Napoleon and his
army overcame. "In mid-May of the year 1800 Napoleon and a force of
36,000 men crossed the Great St Bernard pass, an undertaking that had
been regarded until that time as next to impossible" ("Mitte des Jahres
1800 zog Napoleon mit 36 000 Mann über den Großen St. Bernhard,
ein Unternehmen, das bis zu diesem Zeitpunkt für so gut wie ausge-
schlossen gegolten hatte"; *Schwindel* 7/3). Noteworthy about this

Figure 2.3: Paul Bereyter's perspective upon his suicide (*Ausgewanderten*
41/27).

textual opening is the quasi-objective stance of the largely omniscient narrator, who makes his presence known only by means of vocabulary that suggests amazement at Napoleon's feat. This narrative stance copies the distance and wide-angle view present in Vernet's etching, and only with the second paragraph does this perspective narrow, focusing on the life of Henri Beyle, who experienced Napoleon's Italian campaign as an insider among his military ranks. Sebald copies the traditional gestures of realistic, historical storytelling: he begins by setting the scene, painting it in broad narrative brushstrokes, facilitated by the initial illustration, only to shift abruptly to the personal perspective of the participant in these events as provided by Beyle's point of view.

The narrative diction throughout this piece underscores this traditional mode of storytelling, since Beyle's experiences are consistently portrayed from the third-person perspective of an unnamed outsider, who relies exclusively on textual sources composed by Beyle himself in order to gain access to his thoughts, emotions, and responses. This work thereby poses as a piece of biographical criticism that exploits visual and textual documents to make pretense to historical accuracy. In keeping with this, the narrator's primary resources, aside from Del Litto's biography, are texts authored by Stendhal himself, namely his fictionalized autobiography, *The Life of Henry Brulard*, and the treatise *Love*. But references to these works remain unmarked, although the narrator makes no effort to disguise that he is drawing on Beyle's self-representations. Sebald capitalizes on his previous writing experience as a biographically-oriented literary critic, and unlike his later fictional prose pieces, "Beyle" is structured predominantly according to the paradigm of a critical engagement with the life and works of the historical figure Stendhal.

The major difference between this work and Sebald's earlier critical writings, aside from issues of scholarly mechanics and critical apparatus, is that in "Beyle" Stendhal serves as the vehicle for exploring the author's and biographer's own intellectual preoccupations. This is not to say that this was not true for Sebald's literary scholarship—indeed, it is surely a motivating factor behind many scholarly and academic pursuits—but only that this authorial self-focalization comes into greater prominence. "Beyle" also reflects the attitude and stance Sebald typically represented in his critical writings insofar as it reads Stendhal's literary works and life documents in tandem, as mutually-informing resources. Moreover, this story is strongly essayistic in character, and Sebald's experiments with embellishing his text through the use of illustrations—far from lending it greater documentary value—tend to highlight those acts of subjective fashioning and craftsmanship characteristic of essayistic prose. This marks the text as a transitional stage to Sebald's more emphatically fictionalized works that will follow. Of principal importance is that in "Beyle" and "Dr. K.,"[17] in contrast to Sebald's later biographical fictions, the voices of his informants are mediated by *textual* rather than by *verbal* communications. Intertexts still function as primary resources, much as they do in literary-critical scholarship.

The principal focus of my analysis will be on questions of perspective and point of view, but I will also examine the innovative experiments with illustrations that Sebald introduces in "Beyle," and that arguably constitute much of the writerly craft and literary creativity manifest in this work. But before engaging in this investigation it makes sense to catalogue the intellectual issues and conceptual problems that motivate Sebald's engagement with Stendhal, and that inform the thematic interests of this text. Not coincidentally, one of the first questions Sebald poses upon introducing Beyle as a witness to Napoleon's campaign is the problematical veracity of autobiographical reflections that recount events from which the self-reflecting narrator is separated by a significant temporal gulf. This is the perennial conundrum of autobiography, in which the supposed identity of character is ruptured by the temporal divide between the narrating and the narrated self. Thus in the same sentence that names Beyle's notes as the narrator's resource, the evidentiary value of these notes is simultaneously undercut: "The notes in which the 53-year-old Beyle ... attempted to relive the tribulations of those days [during the crossing of the St. Bernhard] afford eloquent proof of the various difficulties entailed in the act of recollection" ("Die Notizen, in denen Beyle im Alter von dreiundfünfzig Jahren ... die Strapazen jener Tage [beim Ersteigen des Großen St. Bernhards] aus dem Gedächtnis heraufzuholen versucht, demonstrieren eindringlich verschiedene Schwierigkeiten der Erinnerung"; *Schwindel* 8/5). Sebald announces not only the central theme of this story—the complex dialectic between remembering and forgetting, between factual recording of and fictional embellishment on past experiences—but of his narrative prose works more generally. He emphasizes the thirty-six-year span that separates Beyle's act of remembering and writing about his life—in *The Life of Henry Brulard*, which was composed between 1835 and 1836—and his crossing of the Alps as part of Napoleon's military campaign in 1800. This probing question about the validity of memories across a remarkable temporal gulf is relevant not only for Stendhal's autobiography, but for the subsequent autobiographical texts that Sebald includes in *Schwindel. Gefühle*. Yet in "Beyle" Sebald

---

17   Most of the claims made here about "Beyle" as a narrative form marking the transition between Sebald's literary criticism and his more mature fictionalized prose narratives apply *mutatis mutandis* to "Dr. K.s Badereise nach Riva."

does not simply highlight the problematic of mnemonic accuracy, but also explores the creative and imaginative productivity that arises from this temporal divergence. This is why Stendhal represents the perfect choice of subject to facilitate these deliberations; for whereas in *Brulard* he problematizes issues of mnemonic accuracy and treats invention as a potential distortion of historical facts, in *Love* he is concerned with the creative illusions one forms so as to valorize people, objects, and events in which one has significant emotional investment. Autobiography always entails this process of imaginative "crystallization," whereby the embellished object is no longer the lover, but the self. Stendhal's double-take on this problem instantiates the dialectic embodied in the ambiguity of the word *Schwindel*, meaning both the vertiginous disorientation that arises from the discrepancy between memory and factual experience, and the "swindle" of fictional and imaginative embellishment.[18] If Ambros Adelwarth is purported to suffer from Korsakov's syndrome, an illness "which causes lost memories to be replaced by fantastic inventions" ("bei dem ... der Erinnerungsverlust durch phantastische Erfindungen ausgeglichen wird"; *Ausgewanderten* 149/102), then both Beyle and Sebald's narrator, who operate in this gray area between factual recall and fictional invention, are afflicted by this disorder.

Sebald's proclivity for exploring matters of memory through metaphors drawn from the fields of vision and optics is inaugurated in "Beyle," where the protagonist is credited with the insight that his memories fall into two contrasting categories: "At times his view of the past consists of nothing but grey patches, then at others images appear of such extraordinary clarity he feels he can scarce credit them" ("Einmal besteht seine Vorstellung von der Vergangenheit aus nichts als grauen Feldern, dann wieder stößt er auf Bilder von solch ungewöhnlicher Deutlichkeit, daß er ihnen nicht glaubt trauen zu dürfen"; *Schwindel* 8–9/5). On one side he discovers fuzziness, obscurity, and indistinct grayness; on the other a precision so crystal

---

18 See Dieter Wrobel, *Postmodernes Chaos—Chaotische Postmoderne: Eine Studie zu Analogien zwischen Chaostheorie und deutschsprachiger Prosa der Postmoderne* (Bielefeld: Aisthesis, 1997), 307–8, who appropriately notes that the title *Schwindel. Gefühle* offers a pregnant formula for characterizing insecurities in perception and self-orientation, as is characteristic of Post-Modernism more generally. Doren Wohlleben, "Poetik des Schwindelns und Verschwindens bei Hartmut Lange, W. G. Sebald und Horst Stern," in *Differenzerfahrung und Selbst: Bewußtsein und Wahrnehmung in Literatur und Geschichte des 20. Jahrhunderts*, ed. Bettina von Jagow and Florian Steger (Heidelberg: Winter, 2003), 336, stresses that the "vertigo" referred to in Sebald's title derives from the differential between imagination ("Einbildung") and mimetic representation ("Abbildung").

clear that it seems almost hyperreal. The paradox is that precisely this stark contrast throws the veracity of the seemingly precise images into question, and as an example Sebald's narrator cites Beyle's memory of seeing General Marmont on the battlefield in his royal blue robes of the State Councilor, whereas in fact he must have been wearing his general's uniform (*Schwindel* 9/5). This episode is taken directly from Stendhal's *Life of Henry Brulard*, where it likewise serves to undermine the validity of ostensibly exact memories.[19] The subsequent examples of deficient or inaccurate memory Sebald's narrator catalogues also derive from this source: Beyle claims to have been so emotionally overwhelmed by the dead horses and military debris strewn along the army's course that the impression was wiped completely from his memory (*Schwindel* 9/5-6);[20] or he discovers that his memory image of first viewing the city of Ivrea at sunset derives from an etching he once saw of a similar scene (*Schwindel* 11–12/8);[21] he reinforces this tendency of the copy to replace the original by explaining how Johann Friedrich Wilhelm Müller's engraving of the San Sisto Madonna in Dresden has completely supplanted his memory of Raphael's original statue (*Schwindel* 12/8);[22] and finally, in an example that anticipates the theory of crystallization in *Love*, Beyle relates how he fell madly in love with the actress he saw playing in Cimarosa's *Il Matrimonio Segreto*, despite her obvious aesthetic defects, such as a missing tooth (*Schwindel* 13–14/9–10).[23] In order to provide this diverse inventory of memory effects that document the divergence between image and historical event, Sebald's narrator, like the literary critic, only needs to follow the incidents Stendhal provides in his autobiography. These examples offer an exhaustive catalogue: some memories can be *eradicated* by especially traumatic experiences; or they can be *replaced* by images that are aesthetically more appealing; good images are capable of being *supplanted* by inferior images—a kind of transference of Gresham's Law, which asserts that bad money displaces good money, to the realm of visual images; and an inherently ugly reality can be *adorned* by desire and imaginative fantasy. Consistent throughout these examples is the stress Stendhal places on the distortion of memory and its ties to visual reproductions.

There are other, unnamed sources that extend the penumbra of the image–memory dynamics drawn from Stendhal. In *Camera lucida*, a

---

19 Stendhal, *The Life of Henry Brulard*, trans. John Sturrock (New York: New York Review of Books, 2002), 463.
20 Ibid., 478–9.
21 Ibid., 468.
22 Ibid.
23 Ibid., 479.

work Sebald closely studied, Roland Barthes reflects on the capacity of the photograph to block out the memory of the event it records, allowing it to attain the status of a counter-memory.[24] And surely it is no coincidence—or if so, then a coincidence of the Sebaldian sort— that Barthes claims he experiences "a kind of vertigo, something of a 'detective' anguish" when he sees a photograph of himself but cannot remember the historical event it purportedly documents.[25] Similarly, in another work that held special importance for Sebald's intellectual profile, Primo Levi's *The Drowned and the Saved*, the Holocaust survivor devotes the entire first chapter of his camp memoire to an exploration of the difficulties of exact remembrance.[26] Emphasizing the "scant relia- bility of our memories," Levi examines in particular how the genuine memory of an event can be displaced by the invented story through which one repeatedly recounts it: "it is also true that a memory evoked too often, and expressed in the form of a story, tends to become fixed in a stereotype, in a form tested by experience, crystalized, perfected, adorned, installing itself in the place of the raw memory and growing at its expense."[27] What Barthes and Stendhal treat in terms of how *images* substitute for remembrance, Levi approaches as the tendency of *story* or *narrative* to take the place of "raw" memory. This point is relevant for Sebald, the incipient author of historically- and memory-oriented iconotexts that explore the tensions between image and word. When in his first work of prose fiction Sebald focuses explicitly on Stendhal's critical reflections regarding the frailty and distortions of memory, the French author serves as a stand-in for a larger set of intellectual influences. The intertextual references to Stendhal's reflections about remembrance form a nodal point at which intertextual allusions to other thinkers concerned with similar problems converge by way of associ- ation. Levi's *The Drowned and the Saved* provides a further interesting example of this typically Sebaldian phenomenon: when Levi asserts that the horrors of one's experiences in the camps entails the *necessity* of forgetting, he turns to a metaphor that must have resonated with Sebald, referring to the "attic of memory where all the clutter of stuff that is no longer useful in everyday life is stored."[28] Sebald literalizes this metaphor in "Il ritorno in patria" when his first-person narrator visits the attic that was off-limits in his childhood and discovers the

---

24 Roland Barthes, *Camera Lucida: Reflections on Photography*, trans. Richard Howard (New York: Hill and Wang, 1981), 91.

25 Ibid., 85.

26 Primo Levi, *The Drowned and the Saved*, trans. Raymond Rosenthal (New York: Random House/Vintage, 1989), 23–35.

27 Ibid., 23–4.

28 Ibid., 142.

horrible memories of the past (*Schwindel* 243–50/223–9). This episode represents a threefold intertextual convergence, since it alludes not only to Levi, but draws explicitly on Kafka's fragmentary story "Auf dem Dachboden" (Up in the attic) and also points to the place of childhood refuge and "exile" the German post-war author Peter Weiss (1916–82) describes in his own fictionalized memoire, *Abschied von den Eltern* (*The Leavetaking*).[29] The thematic thread that runs through the examples of problematic memories and their visual representation, borrowed from Stendhal's *Life of Henry Brulard*, thus resonates with a handful of other intertextual sources that are significant for Sebald's intellectual profile. These themes are explicitly reflected in Sebald's own inclusion of "illustrations" in this story. I place this word in quotation marks because it is precisely this referential or deictic gesture linking image and memory-event that Sebald problematizes.

The *Life of Henry Brulard* also stands as a literary model for Sebald and his narrator insofar as Stendhal inserts his own illustrative drawings as enhancements to his textual depictions. In Stendhal's fictionalized autobiography, text and image already enter into a communicative relationship. Sebald pays homage to this by including several reproductions of Stendhal's sketches in his own work. He thereby self-consciously entangles his own compositional practice with the problematic dialectic of reproduction and original articulated in and performed by Stendhal's work. But Sebald further complicates this relationship between original and reproduction insofar as the images he borrows are not drawn directly from Stendhal's *Life*, but instead are mediated through reproductions printed in Del Litto's biography. Sebald's reproductions are already at least twice removed from Stendhal's "originals."

If Stendhal's *Life of Henry Brulard* largely explores dilemmas about point of view, remembrance, self-observation, and self-narration, these are precisely the themes Sebald pursues and further problematizes in his own retelling of Beyle's story. In order to highlight these questions, he borrows a relevant example from Stendhal's *Life*. Following up on the anecdote of how the horror of the Battle of Bard wiped out all Beyle's memories of this event, Sebald's narrator, speaking through the voice of Beyle, refers to a drawing Stendhal made of this scene as a graphic aid for recall (*Schwindel* 10/6) (see Figure 2.4). He follows

---

29 Peter Weiss, *Abschied von den Eltern* (Frankfurt am Main: Suhrkamp, 1961), 43–4; *The Leavetaking*, trans. Christopher Levenson (New York: Harcourt, 1962), 32–3. Almut Laufer, "Unheimliche Heimat: Kafka, Freud und die Frage der Rückkehr in W. G. Sebalds *Schwindel. Gefühle*," *Naharaim* 4, no. 2 (2010): 254, identifies the intertextual relationship between Weiss's text and the attic episode in "Il ritorno in patria."

Stendhal's commentary by identifying each significant point on this pictorial rendering of the battle scene: the position Stendhal himself occupied as observer; the canons on the opposite cliff, in whose fire he was engulfed; the horses that leapt to their deaths in fear of the explosions around them; and the pathway the canons were attacking.[30] But Sebald's narrator adds a commentary that focuses on the paradox that this illustration, which depicts Beyle as both participant in the battle and its distant observer, can only represent a falsified and imaginary view of the experienced scene: "Yet, of course, when Beyle was in actual fact standing at that spot, he will not have been viewing the scene in this precise way, for in reality, as we know, everything is always quite different" ("Freilich wird Beyle, als er sich auf diesem Punkt befand, die Sache so nicht gesehen haben, denn in Wirklichkeit ist, wie wir wissen, alles immer ganz anders"; *Schwindel* 10/6–7). Sebald's narrator puts his finger on the paradoxical problematic of self-representation, or of autobiography as autofiction more generally. But more significantly, he exposes the problematic of this dynamic in the instance of an attempt at accurate *graphic* illustration. Stendhal must imaginatively transport himself to a fictional point *outside* the action in order to portray his own experiences *inside* this event. This is the very dynamic Sebald tries to explore throughout his fictional texts, and it constitutes one of the most compelling features of his poetics of history.

It is no coincidence that the two authors on whom *Schwindel. Gefühle* focuses, Stendhal and Kafka, are among the most notoriously obsessed and critical self-observers in the Western literary canon. Stendhal's *Life of Henry Brulard* can be read as a sustained deliberation on the aporias of autobiography and the (im)possibility of accurate self-representation. Sebald's narrator stresses the point that the very act of self-observation, whether through textual, visual, or any other medium, entails the assumption of a perspective that necessarily diverges from the one the self occupied when these experiences were digested: an unavoidable displacement, alienation, and falsification are figured as the very condition of possibility of self-observation and self-narration. This theme of difference at the heart of identity is precisely what this collection's title, *Schwindel. Gefühle*, invokes: the vertigo that emerges out of the difference between original and copy, lived experience and memory, thought-image and its narrative or illustrative reproduction.[31] Accordingly, Sebald's narrator first alludes to

---

30 Stendhal, *The Life of Henry Brulard*, 478.
31 Numerous critics have deliberated on how Sebald's title invokes issues of discrepancy or dichotomy. Ben Hutchinson comes closest to the position I am advocating, in "'Umgekehrt wird man leicht selbst zum Verfolgten': The Structure of the Double-Bind in W. G. Sebald," *Revista de Filología Alemana* 14

Figure 2.4: Beyle's drawing of the Battle of Bard (*Schwindel* 10/6).

the vertiginous sensations named in this book's title when he describes
the discrepancy Beyle experiences between his memories of the Battle
of Marengo and the reality of the battlefield itself when he revisits it
fifteen months later: this difference "occasioned in him a vertiginous
sense of confusion such as he had never previously experienced"
("verursachte ihm ein noch niemals gespürtes, schwindelartiges Gefühl
der Irritation"; *Schwindel* 21/17). In *The Life of Henry Brulard*, Stendhal
repeatedly thematizes this "irritating" or "confusing" divergence in
terms of the transformation of life into literature. Just as his absorption
in events during the Battle of Bard prevents him from forming any
lasting memory, he forgets, then invents his first sexual encounter with
his mistress Giulia, claiming "My memory is only a novel fabricated
on that occasion."[32]

This statement precisely articulates Sebald's theme in this, his
first work of prose fiction: the transformation of life into literature,
the fictive fabrication that commonly passes as memory, and the

---

(2006): 103, when he claims that vertigo is associated with differences between
past and present, imagination and reality. Wrobel, *Postmodernes Chaos*, 207–8,
reads the title as a formula for insecurities in perception and self-orientation,
whereas Laufer, "Unheimliche Heimat," 273, emphasizes the combinatory
possibilities opened up when Sebald joins two nouns without any specified
semantic connectors. Markus Zisselsberger, "The Afterlife of Literature: Sebald,
Blanchot, and Kafka's Hunter Gracchus," *Journal of the Kafka Society of America*
31–2, no. 1–2 (June 2007–December 2008): 116, offers a discerning interpretation
when he claims that vertigo refers to the gap between the subject's inner constitution and the outside world. He further maintains that this gap is graphically
marked by the period separating the words *Schwindel* and *Gefühle* in Sebald's
title. I will return subsequently to the significance of this graphic mark.
32 Stendhal, *The Life of Henry Brulard*, 479.

resurgence of memories as inventions. Similarly, what occupies him in "Dr. K.s Badereise" is how Kafka transposed his experiences in Riva in autumn 1913 into the fragmentary story "Der Jäger Gracchus" ("The Hunter Gracchus") some three years later. Literary fiction becomes for Kafka—as it was for Stendhal—a way to come to terms with lived experience, often well after the fact. This is the very same problematic with which Sebald engages in the pseudo-autobiographical texts in this collection, "All'estero" and "Il ritorno in patria"; and one might speculate that the foreign-language titles of these two pieces encapsulate the dilemma, concretized in the episode from Stendhal, that self-observation always implies a view of the self that is distorted by an alien perspective.[33] Sebald discovers in this illustration by Stendhal an emblem for the set of issues that will take center stage throughout his prose fictions: the quandary associated with all forms of representing the past, and especially with representing one's *own* past. The past is never one's own, and hence one cannot properly "own" it. This dilemma returns in the well-known passage from *Die Ringe des Saturn* in which the narrator visits the memorial to the Battle of Waterloo and remarks, in reference to the panorama painting of that event, that the "representation of history ... requires a falsification of perspective" ("Kunst der Repräsentation der Geschichte ... beruht auf einer Fälschung der Perspektive"; *Ringe* 158/125). Notably, this episode from Sebald's travelogue is loosely associated with the earlier one from "Beyle" through the unifying thread of the Napoleonic Wars. But there is also a much closer connection, for when the narrator of *Ringe* seeks an alternate perspective, one that depicts the battle from the inside, from the perspective of a participant, he turns to the experience of Stendhal's hero Fabrizio from *The Charterhouse of Parma*, embellishing his own narrative by means of a marked intertextual import from this work (*Ringe* 158–9/126). Literary representation, as the passage from "Beyle" suggests, may indeed be based on falsifications; but at the same time, as the episode in *Ringe des Saturn* counters, literary transmission might provide the most "authentic" approximation of real events by invoking the intimate experience of participants in these occurrences, in all their emotional entanglement. Once again, history can be represented most accurately and intimately by poetic means. What informs all the passages analyzed here is not only a set of deliberations on the

---

33 Primo Levi mocks the Italian word "patria," *The Drowned and the Saved*, 162, as artificial, claiming "no Italian, except for a joke, would ever say, 'I'll take the train and return to the fatherland.'" Sebald's use of this term in his own story about a "return to the fatherland" is likely informed by the ironic undercurrent Levi emphasizes. Sebald's title thus resonates with more than simply Monteverdi's opera *Il ritorno d'Ulisse in patria*.

very possibility of accurately representing past experience, but also reflections on the *medium* by which such representation occurs. Beyle's sketch, which serves as a graphic aid for *picturing* the experience he is struggling to describe in *words*, ultimately also misses the mark of accurate depiction, but for very different reasons. What Sebald explores in "Beyle," his first "iconotext" that self-consciously explores the inter-medial dynamic of image and text, is the productive but problematic tensions that emerge at the intersection of these media.

One thing that sets "Beyle" apart from the other texts in *Schwindel. Gefühle*, as well as from Sebald's later works, is the experimental verve with which it probes this image–text imbrication. Sebald's text practices, in this regard, in its own aesthetic constitution the problems it addresses in its primary themes. One can conceive "Beyle" as an experimental etude in which Sebald consciously plays with text–image conjugations, thereby paving the way for a trademark feature of his fictions.[34] My analysis has already discussed two strikingly divergent examples. The illustration with which "Beyle" opens serves an expos-itory function, establishing scene and situation, and providing an introductory snapshot around which the subsequent text can emerge as elucidating description and as textual embellishment. The traditional hierarchy in the text–image relation, in which visual illustration concre-tizes a verbal depiction, has been reversed, so that the subsequent text literally builds a frame for the picture, providing it with the context necessary for the narrative development. By contrast, Stendhal's sketch of the battlefield at Bard provides a vehicle for the narrator's metacom-mentary, raising central questions about the illustrative capacity of images and self-representations as such. By means of a metafictional turn, this image is staged so that it presents a self-reflexive deliberation on the representational aporias of self-observation across a temporal divide and via acts of remembrance. Sebald's narrator gives and takes away with the very same gesture, in that he both presents this image— as does Stendhal—as an elucidatory illustration, but also undercuts its value *qua* illustration by pointing to the performative contradiction at its core: the fact that Stendhal could not have perceived the scene in the

---

34   Niehaus, "Ikonotext. Bastelei," 157, also views this work as an experimental
     platform in text–image relationships, but he associates this too loosely
     with the playfulness of Lévi-Strauss's *bricolage*. Maria Zinfert, "Grauzonen:
     Das Schreiben von W. G. Sebald: Versuchsanordnung mit schwarzweissen
     Fotografien," in *"Ein in der Phantasie durchgeführtes Experiment": Literatur und
     Wissenschaft nach Neunzehnhundert*, ed. Raul Calzoni and Massimo Salgaro
     (Göttingen: Vandenhoeck & Ruprecht, 2010), 322–3, maintains that Sebald
     engages in an experiment with black-and-white photography, but she identifies
     this too monolithically as invoking the "gray zone" between life and death that
     Sebald associated with photography.

way he portrays it, which renders it as an imaginative (and imaginary) construction.

In between these two illustrations, Sebald includes juxtaposed self-portraits of Stendhal, one of the child, the other of the adult, which underscore the thematic of self-representation that lies at the heart of *The Life of Henry Brulard*. However, they invoke this theme via visual rather than textual signs. Both self-portraits raise questions about the possibility of accurate visual portrayal insofar as they depict the face in partial obscurity: in the first image hidden by the figure's own hand, in the second by a blot of ink. This second portrait calls attention to the act of representation as potentially distorted by the manipulation of the very tools that make such recording possible, pen and ink. But more relevant for a discussion of Sebald's experiments in text–image juxtapositions is the fact that this passage betrays a conscious attempt to coordinate verbal and visual media: the word "Kindheit" ("childhood") is printed below the picture of Beyle as a child, the term "Jugend" ("adolescence") placed below his self-portrait as a youth, with the conjunction "und" ("and") centered between the two words and associated with the gap between the two portraits (*Schwindel* 8/4).[35] This insistence on spatial coordination of image and text is even more prominent in the preliminary publication of "Beyle" in the journal *Manuskripte*, where it appeared under the title "Berge oder das …". Here the text is printed throughout in double columns on each page, and each of Stendhal's self-portraits is aligned with one of these two columns, with the word "und" set perfectly in the gap between the two rows of text[36] (see Figure 2.5). Image and text are coordinated so closely that their relationship approaches redundancy. Playing on a visual metaphor, we might say that image and text mirror one another, while at the same time insisting on the difference and independence of each medium. As with most of the illustrations in this story, Sebald borrows these images from Del Litto;[37] but in the first case he manipulates his source by cropping the image so that face and hand are centered, and both images are reduced in size so as to fit side by side on a single printed page.

In a further, well-known instance, Sebald includes a cropped picture of Beyle's eyes in order to demonstrate the unusual distance between them that earned him the hated nickname "*Le Chinois*" (*Schwindel*

---

35 This self-reflective text–image configuration is unfortunately not retained in the English translation, where these images stand above and below one another, separated by the text, rather than side by side with the text aligned under the portraits.

36 W. G. Sebald, "Berge oder das …," *Manuskripte* 28, no. 99 (March 1988): 71.

37 Del Litto, *Album Stendhal*, 42, 43.

unabsehbarer Zug von Menschen, Tieren und Material von Martigny aus über Orsières durch das Tal von Entremont und sodann in endlos scheinenden Serpentinen hinauf auf die zweieinhalbtausend Meter über dem Spiegel

Zu den wenigen nicht namenlos gebliebenen Teilnehmern an dieser legendären Alpenüberquerung gehörte Henri Beyle. Er war damals siebzehn Jahre alt, sah das Ende seiner von ihm auf das Tiefste verhaßten

Kindheit   und   Jugend

gekommen und stand mit einiger Begeisterung im Begriff, seine Laufbahn im Dienste des Heeres anzutreten, die ihn, wie wir wissen, noch weit in Europa herumführen sollte. Die Notizen, in denen Beyle im Alter von dreiundfünfzig Jahren – er hielt sich zur Zeit ihrer Niederschrift in Civita Vecchia auf – die Strapazen jener Tage aus dem Gedächtnis heraufzuholen versucht, demonstrieren eindringlich verschiedene Schwierigkeiten der Erinnerung. Einmal besteht seine Vorstellung von der Vergangenheit aus nichts als grauen Feldern, dann wieder stößt er auf Bilder von solch ungewöhnlicher Deutlichkeit, daß er ihnen nicht glaubt trauen zu dürfen, beispielsweise auf dasjenige des

Generals Marmont, den er in Martigny zur Linken des Wegs, auf welchem sich der Troß voranbewegte, in dem himmel- und königsblauen Kleide eines Staatsrats gesehen zu haben meint, und das er genauso, wie er uns versichert, immer noch sieht, wenn er, die Augen schließend, sich diese Szene in Erinnerung ruft, obschon Marmont damals, wie Beyle sehr wohl weiß, seine Generalsuniform und nicht das blaue Staatskleid getragen haben muß.

Beyle, der behauptet, um diese Zeit, aufgrund einer völlig verkehrten, allein auf die Ausbildung bürgerlicher Fertigkeiten ausgerichteten Erziehung, die Konstitution eines vierzehnjährigen Mädchens gehabt zu haben, schreibt

Figure 2.5: Coordinated portraits and text in "Berge oder das …" (71), an earlier version of "Beyle."

15/11).[38] This image plays a traditional illustrative role, offering concrete visual evidence for a claim made by the text. But Sebald ironically reflects on this evidentiary function by leaving the word "Augen" ("eyes") out of the text completely and putting the cropped image in its place. Image and text thereby enter into a substitutive relationship.[39] The cropping of the image also calls attention to the editorial manipulation to which pictures can be subjected in order to enhance their role as supporting evidence.[40] This isolation of the eyes as emblematic of character points ahead to later examples in Sebald's work. One thinks of the eyes cropped from Pisanello's St. George fresco and reprinted in

---

38   For critical reflections on this particular illustration, see Gerhard Fischer, "W. G. Sebald," in *Praktizierte Intermedialität: Deutsch-französische Porträts von Schiller bis Goscinny/Uderzo*, ed. Fernand Hörner, Harald Neumeyer, and Bernd Stiegler (Bielefeld: Transcript, 2010), 270; Niehaus, "Ikonotext. Bastelei," 169; and Susanne Schedel, *Wer weiß, wie es vor Zeiten wirklich gewesen ist? Textbeziehungen als Mittel der Geschichtsdarstellung bei W. G. Sebald* (Würzburg: Königshausen & Neumann, 2004), 74.

39   This is another text–image effect that is not reproduced in the English version of this story. Niehaus, "Ikonotext. Bastelei," 169, discusses this example, inexplicably categorizing it as a "disruptive" image, rather than in terms of a substitutive relationship.

40   See Del Litto, *Album Stendhal*, 68, for the full version of this image.

"All'estero" (*Schwindel* 87/75–6), or of the eyes of owls, philosophers, and artists discussed and depicted in the opening section of *Austerlitz* (7/4–5), or of the series of eyes for which Sebald composed textual subscripts in *Unerzählt* (*Unrecounted*), his collaborative project with Jan Peter Tripp.

The next visual component of "Beyle" calls attention to this gesture of intervention by the narrator/editor who selects, adjusts, and alters his source illustrations. It presents a portrait of one of Beyle's lovers, Angela Pietragrua, in which her face is overlain with a grid, like the *lucida* that artists commonly employ as a device to foster accurate mimetic representation (*Schwindel* 16/12).[41] Interestingly, the only difference between the earlier version of this text published in *Manuskripte* and the final version in *Schwindel. Gefühle* is the addition of this overlain grid, which is lacking in its first printing.[42] This late intervention transforms this image from a mere illustration of the object Beyle adored into a metafictional or meta-medial reflection on the process of mimetic representation itself, as well as on the interventions imposed by the managerial presence that administers Sebald's texts. This supplemented grid anticipates a series of images in *Die Ringe des Saturn* that play on grids as artificial devices for mapping and rationally ordering an otherwise indiscriminate visual space, and in a subsequent chapter we will examine how Sebald's use of images in this later text implicitly interrogates ideologies of visual representation. In "Beyle," this gridded image presents a self-reflexive metacommentary on questions of mimetic visual representations and their questionable use as documentary evidence.

The next set of images in "Beyle," depicting in threefold iteration an examination of the oral cavity, reinforces the textual comment that Beyle repeatedly examines the sores in his mouth caused by his syphilitic infection: "over and over again, with the aid of a mirror, he examined the inflammations and ulcers in his mouth and at the back of his throat" ("immer wieder untersuchte er mit einem Spiegel die Entzündungen und Geschwüre in seiner Mundhöhle und in der Tiefe seines Rachens"; *Schwindel* 18/14). On the simplest level this image is nothing but an illustrative reinforcement of what the text states. But on a deeper level the repetition of the selfsame image serves a performative function by imitating Beyle's iterative act, expressed in the adverbial phrase "over and over again" ("immer wieder"), of *repeatedly* examining his oral

41 Claudia Öhlschläger, *"Cristallisation, c'est l'opération de l'esprit": Stendhals Theorie der Liebe und ihre Bedeutung für W. G. Sebalds Poetik der Einbildung*, Paderborner Universitätsreden 98 (Paderborn: Universität Paderborn, 2005), 23, also views the added grid as a self-reflexive reference to the means of representation.
42 Sebald, "Berge oder das ...," 73.

cavity. Repetitive action is imitated in the repetition of the image. This is
a technique Sebald employs once more in *Schwindel. Gefühle*, when the
narrator in "Il ritorno in patria" describes how the statue of St. George
at the church in W. penetrates "forever" ("ohne Unterlaß") the "throat"
("Rachen") of the dragon with his spear. The substance of this statement
and the pattern of iteration is reinforced by a threefold depiction of this
statue (264–5/242).[43] The allusion to the parallel illustration in "Beyle"
is signaled not only by the performance in multiple images of the repetitive action expressed by the adverbial phrase, but also by their shared
depiction of a mouth probed by an instrument. Their linkage is further
underscored by the occurrence of the word "Rachen" ("throat") in
both examples (18/14, 265/242). This type of communication between
disparate images and across divergent texts will take on greater significance in subsequent works. On the level of visual representations, this
technique parallels the intratextual linkages or cross-references by
which Sebald lends cohesion to his book-length narratives.

Two further examples of text–image conjunctions in "Beyle" merit
closer examination, since they extend the catalogue of practices with
which Sebald is experimenting in this early iconotext. At the thematic
highpoint of the story, where Sebald's narrator anticipates the title
of this collection and discusses the "vertiginous sense of confusion"
("schwindelartiges Gefühl der Irritation") Beyle experiences when
he becomes aware of the "difference between the images of the battle
[of Marengo] which he had in his head and what he now saw before
him as evidence that the battle had in fact taken place" ("Differenz
zwischen den Bildern der Schlacht [von Marengo], die er in seinem
Kopf trug, und dem, was er als Beweis dessen, daß die Schlacht sich
wahrhaftig ereignet hatte, nun vor sich ausgebreitet sah"; 21/17),
Sebald includes a carefully cropped fragment from Louis-François
Lejeune's (1775–1848) painting *The Battle of Marengo* (*Schwindel* 22/18).
The originals of this image among Sebald's posthumous papers indicate
that he deliberated intensively about the form this illustration should
take. The prototype he used was a set of colored photographs of the
painting, and this in itself is unusual since color images are rare among
the sources Sebald employed. Aside from two copies of this image
cut into an elongated strip depicting the monument, the battlefield,
and an individual soldier caught expiring, as reproduced in faded
black and white in "Beyle," Sebald's folder contains two other, very
differently cropped fragments.[44] These unused images concentrate on

43 Niehaus, "Ikonotext. Bastelei," 172–3, makes a similar argument about the
    repetitive character of these two images and remarks on their parallels.
44 These images are found in the first folder of the file *Schwindel. Gefühle*, inventory
    number HS.2004.0001.00019, at the Deutsches Literaturarchiv.

different aspects of the battle scene, highlighting the active fighting and the dead and wounded who lie strewn across the battlefield. This provides a salient example of how Sebald deliberated about the effects that different out-takes of this painting might have, before deciding on the one he could integrate most effectively into the text. The fragment he selected has the virtue not only of succinctly depicting the central features of this historical scene, but that the individual soldier in the foreground, who is literally disappearing into the smoke that spreads across the battlefield, replicates the emotions Beyle himself feels as he identifies with those who "sank" or "perished" in this fight. The words printed under this image, centered on the page as if they were a subscript, are "wie ein Untergehender" (*Schwindel* 22), inadequately rendered in the English translation as "like one meeting his doom" (*Vertigo* 18). The German phrase points to the veritable disappearance and "submerging" (German: *untergehen*) of the painfully gesticulating soldier, caught by this image as he both disappears from life and into the billowing smoke. The gaze of the reader, who follows the narrowly cropped image as it moves down the page, reiteratively performs this act of "going under" or "going down." Sebald thus crops and prints this picture not only so as to maximize the complexities of its inter-action with the surrounding text, but also to reflect meta-critically on the reader's engagement with the printed page. This example reveals especially well the kind of thoughtful reflection Sebald invested in the selection, alteration, and embedding of illustrative material already in this first work of prose fiction.[45]

The final example worthy of discussion is the purported illustration of the plaster cast that Beyle had made of his lover Métilde's hand, and which serves as his source of inspiration during the composition of *Love* (*Schwindel* 25/20–1). In this instance the printed image and the descriptive text are marked by discrepancies that highlight tensions in the text–image relationship. According to the narrator's report, this hand serves as a metonymic representation of Métilde, who had broken off the relationship with Beyle. The narrator insists that this artificial embodiment is capable of evoking emotions more violent than any Beyle has ever known before. The substitute thereby more

45 Lise Patt, "Searching for Sebald: What I Know for Sure," in *Searching for Sebald: Photography After W. G. Sebald*, ed. Lise Patt (Los Angeles: Institute of Cultural Inquiry, 2007), 39–45, extends these questions about Sebald's integration of images in *Schwindel. Gefühle* to the nitty-gritty of the position of the image on the page, describing how his decisions vary across different editions of this work. She emphasizes that layout in Sebald always bears the fingerprints of the manipulator, the "trickster at play," 43, who is constantly refashioning his books. The image discussed here exhibits marked variations not only in the English translation, but also in the hardbound and paperback German editions.

than compensates for the absence of the original. This can again be read as a metacommentary about the relationship between original and copy more generally, and hence as a deliberation on the value of reproductions, even in the highly degraded form in which they appear in Sebald's texts. But additionally, the narrator's reference to the "slight crookedness of the ring finger" ("leichte Krümmung des Ringfingers"; 26/21), which is said to provoke Beyle's emotions, is so subtle and commonplace as to defy its association with such a visceral response. This image problematizes not only the relationship between original and copy, and between image and textual environment, but also calls into question the passion invested in "graven images" as fetish-like placeholders. When we compare Sebald's printing of this image to the source,[46] we recognize just how actively Sebald, as editorial manipulator, intervenes. In Del Litto's reproduction, this hand occupies an entire page and is printed so as to highlight the magnified details of the knuckles and the texture of the skin. In Sebald's miniaturized reproduction, all these details are lost. Moreover, in Del Litto's printing, this hand is oriented with the fingers pointing downward, whereas in Sebald's rendering, the picture is rotated 90 degrees clockwise, so that the fingers point to the left. But this example also contains a hidden allusion to just such acts of manipulation: for this hand is not only the concrete symbol of Beyle's Métilde, but also an allusive cipher for the authorial *manipulator*, whose *manis*—Latin for "hand"—operates behind the scenes to doctor, distort, and refashion this very image.

This particular illustration forms a powerful nodal point in this text, a place where a series of themes, ideas, and problems converge. On the most basic level it calls attention to a motif that runs not only through "Beyle," but throughout this collection as a whole: the expressive character of hands. This idea is already suggested in Stendhal's self-portrait as a child, where his hand covers the lower half of the face—everything below the eyes (8/4). These two illustrations link up as an intercommunicating pair. But an important illustration highlighting the hand is also found near the beginning of "All'estero," ostensibly portraying how the narrator's grandfather held his hat at his side while walking, of which he is reminded by the similar pose struck by his friend Ernst Herbeck (46/39). As we know, the illustration printed here is of the writer Robert Walser; but it is above all his left hand—like the left hand of Beyle's Métilde—that occupies the center of the cropped image. Hands form a leitmotif on the textual plane of these narratives as well, appearing as the hand that Grillparzer lays on K.'s knee, or that Gracchus places on the knee of the mayor of Riva

---

46 Del Litto, *Album Stendhal*, 185.

(158/142, 183/167); or as the gesture by which the narrator, in imitation of Kafka, places his hands behind his head (72/63, 106/93, 126/111, 161/145). One is also reminded of the episode in "Il ritorno in patria" in which the narrator recalls an incident from his childhood where in the delirium of a fever he places his hand into a vat of pickled eggs and is suddenly gripped by the overwhelming sensation that these eggs are eyes (273–4/250–1)—a clear allusion to the loss of a hand or an eye as a symbolic rendering of the fear of castration, as outlined in Sigmund Freud's essay "Das Unheimliche" ("The Uncanny"), another significant intertext for *Schwindel. Gefühle.*[47] Thus this illustration of Métilde's hand alludes to Sebald's conscious manipulations of his visual materials, but also constitutes an emblematic knot that binds together a series of leitmotivic threads that wind their way throughout this entire volume.

If "Beyle" demarcates Sebald's beginnings as a creative writer of evocative iconotexts, then this beginning is energized by a concerted set of reflections on, and experiments with, the text–image relationship. The creative work of fashioning, which Sebald, as the textual impresario, choreographs in terms of pattern, structure, and networking, stands in stark contrast to the derivative character of the textual matter itself, which is rewritten with minor variations directly from Stendhal. For this reason one might claim that "Beyle" is the least "original" of Sebald's fictions, since it draws so heavily on its intertextual pretexts and relies on information and images culled from Del Litto's illustrated biography. Sebald's narrator merely ventriloquizes the voice of his literary precursor. Indeed, he exploits those dilemmas, expressed so eloquently by this predecessor, regarding the problematic accuracy of self-representation and the undecidable intertwining of memory and imaginative invention, as jumping-off places for articulating the central concerns of his own fiction. In doing so, Sebald's narrator replicates the stance and attitude typical of the literary critic. To be sure, the narrative voice of this text liberates itself from direct quotations, footnotes, and explicit references to primary and secondary materials; but it never abandons the ostensibly objective perspective of the independent, third-person investigator. If the composition of this text allows Sebald to probe some of his signature themes, they are still clearly marked as purloined from Stendhal. That said, Sebald demonstrates his incipient creativity and originality in his deliberate and deliberative experimentation with the dynamic interaction of text and image, as well as in the managerial interventions that shape this text and stitch it together

---

47 On Freud as intertext, see especially Laufer, "Unheimliche Heimat," 221, who uses the allusion to castration to portray the father as a disciplinarian who threatens the narrator with unmanning (248–9).

with the others in this collection. "Beyle" affords us a privileged glance
into the workshop of the emerging artist W. G. Sebald, allowing us to
observe how he develops a repertoire of intermedial and intertextual
practices that will be creatively reimplemented in his subsequent prose
fictions.

After Kafka: The Transition from Literary Criticism to Literature in "Dr. K.s Badereise nach Riva"

The spring 1983 issue of the literary-cultural journal *Freibeuter* contained
a special section dedicated to the theme "Franz Kafka, nachgestellt"
(Franz Kafka, pursued). The timing of this publication was significant
in several respects, not least of which was its celebration of the 100th
anniversary of Kafka's birth in July of 1983. For the perennial Kafka
scholar Sebald, this year and this particular publication held special
significance, and an annotated copy of this issue exists in Sebald's
personal library.[48] Even a cursory perusal of the essays in this special
issue suggests that it constitutes one of a handful of critical sources that
inform the thematic Sebald pursues in "Dr. K.s Badereise nach Riva."
The Kafka section begins with an essay by the actor Hanns Zischler
that documents Kafka's responses to early cinema.[49] This piece represents Zischler's initial research into Kafka's responses to the modern
art of moving pictures, which would culminate thirteen years later in
his book *Kafka geht ins Kino* (*Kafka Goes to the Movies*). Sebald published
a glowing review of Zischler's book in the *Frankfurter Rundschau* in
1997, and the full text of this review appeared several years later in the
posthumous volume *Campo Santo* (193–209/151–67). When Sebald's
narrator in "All'estero" re-enacts his Italian journey in Kafka's (and
Stendhal's) footsteps, he is also retracing Zischler's visit to the Verona
public library to peruse newspapers from the period Kafka spent in
that city in August and September 1913 (*Schwindel* 133–8/117–23).
The narrator of "Dr. K.s Badereise" refers to these researches, and also
indirectly to Zischler's findings, when he identifies *La lezione dell'abisso*
(The lesson of the abyss) as one of the films that played in Verona on
September 20, 1913, the day on which Kafka, as he reported in a letter
to Felice, cried during a visit to a Verona cinema.[50]

   The title of this film is clearly important for Sebald and his narrator;
"the lesson of the abyss" could serve as an appropriate subtitle for all

---

48 Catling, "Bibliotheca abscondita," 280.
49 Hanns Zischler, "Maßlose Unterhaltung: Franz Kafka geht ins Kino," *Freibeuter*
    16 (1983): 33–47.
50 Franz Kafka, *Briefe 1913–1914*, ed. Hans-Gerd Koch (Frankfurt am Main:
    Fischer, 1999), 295; *Letters to Felice*, ed. Erich Heller and Jürgen Born, trans.
    James Stern and Elisabeth Duckworth (New York: Schocken, 1973), 326.

the narratives collected in *Schwindel. Gefühle*. Kafka's Hunter Gracchus perishes when he falls into an abyss, and his counterpart Hans Schlag from "Il ritorno in patria" also dies from a similarly inexplicable plunge. Standing on a precipice, or at the edge of an abyss, constitutes a fundamental situation in which one experiences vertigo, and Sebald's text is peppered with metaphorical and semantic abysses, from the discrepancies between memory and image recounted in "Beyle" to the gulfs that separate past and present experience in the narrator's return home in "Il ritorno." The very text of *Schwindel. Gefühle* is engineered to maneuver readers into a series of semantic and conceptual abysses, whose negotiation they must master in order to avoid the fates of Gracchus and Hans Schlag. In accordance with this, the descent of Sebald's narrator into the "gorge" ("Tobel") of the Krummenbach, as he hikes from Oberjoch to "W." in "Il ritorno," is staged as a *Katabasis*, a descent into the underworld (*Schwindel* 193–5/177–80). Moreover, the "warning" ("überdeutlich hörbare Warnung") the narrator hears as he stands before the open door of a train in a London subway station, "*Mind the Gap*" (283/259), could stand as a motto for this entire text and as admonition to its readers. Notably, Sebald's narrator ultimately decides not to venture into this train, but instead remains "for a considerable time on the brink, so to speak" ("eine beträchtliche Zeit sogar auf der Schwelle"), without daring to take "the final step" ("den entscheidenden Schritt"; 284/259).

Schwindel. Gefühle is a text about thresholds, gaps, abysses, discrepancies, gulfs, and fateful—sometimes *fatal*—descents. This problematic is thematized in the work's German title, where the full stop placed between the two nouns "Schwindel" and "Gefühle" graphically marks the abyss before which Sebald's narrator, characters, and readers stand. An early manuscript page held among Sebald's posthumous papers, on which he writes in a fair hand this work's collective title as well as that of the first story, indicates that initially Sebald punctuated the division between these two words as a hyphen, and only later transformed this hyphen, by circling it, into a period[51] (see Figure 2.6). This bulky period occupies the middle of the line, where a hyphen would normally stand. The hyphen, Sebald probably realized, does not adequately render the tension his title is intended to invoke, because although separating and marking divergence, it also joins. This second implication is what Sebald sought to avoid when he transformed this hyphen into the full stop—the abyss—of a period. This period also challenges the reader to enter into a semantic and cognitive game that liberates both terms and

51 This sheet is found in the second folder of the "Konvolut Sammlung *Schwindel. Gefühle*," inventory no. HS.2004.0001.00019, in the Deutsches Literaturarchiv.

transforms their conjunction into a free-ranging combinatory exercise.[52] Recalling that the German word "Schwindel" is a pun meaning both "dizziness" and "swindle," we are forced to ask: Are we dealing with feelings of vertigo, with the swindle of feelings, with the feelings generated by swindle or vertigo, or just with the very dizziness we experience when we try to "mind the gap" and make sense of this title? The phrase *Schwindel. Gefühle* economically exploits the simple graphic sign of the period as shorthand for indicating that these words cannot simply be read as an utterance *about* feelings of vertigo or about the swindle of feelings, but that instead they instantiate a *performative* act of writing, a *swindle*, that graphically depicts a vertiginous abyss. This period thereby marks that moment when feelings of vertigo and the sense of being swindled are cognitively transferred to the text's readers as they negotiate this title's semantic tensions.

Returning to the 1983 issue of *Freibeuter*, we note that Zischler's article is but one of several impulses from this special issue that resonates through "Dr. K.s Badereise" and has larger implications for all the texts in *Schwindel. Gefühle*. Zischler's essay ends by invoking a scene from the Danish film *Die weiße Sklavin* (The white slave-woman), which Kafka describes in unusually precise detail in the fragmentary joint novel he composed with his friend Max Brod during their trip to Paris in August and September 1911. Kafka's text describes in a single, visually precise sentence the arrival of the "innocent heroine" ("unschuldige Heldin") at the train station and her abduction by two men.[53] Zischler documents the precision of this recollection by pairing each descriptive segment with stills from the film.[54] What is relevant from the perspective of Sebald's reception of this essay is the atmosphere of paranoia, the fear of abduction, and Zischler's emphasis on the two mysterious men who perpetrate this kidnapping. These two men find their analogues in the two strangers Sebald's narrator first becomes aware of in the Venice train station (*Schwindel* 79/68), whom he subsequently sees again in the Verona amphitheater (83–4/72), and who eventually motivate his premature flight from Italy. Compared to two "watchmen" ("Wächtern"; 83/72), these mysterious figures invoke the myriad doubles that haunt this text, as well as alluding to the warders who announce Josef K.'s arrest in Kafka's *Der Proceß* (*The Trial*). Sebald's narrator is gripped by the fear of being shadowed, pursued, or even stalked by these men, and his growing sense of

---

52 Laufer, "Unheimliche Heimat," 273, similarly emphasizes the combinatory possibilities signaled by the period in Sebald's title.
53 Franz Kafka, *Drucke zu Lebzeiten*, ed. Wolf Kittler, Hans-Gerd Koch, and Gerhard Neumann (Frankfurt am Main: Fischer, 1994), 428.
54 Zischler, "Maßlose Unterhaltung," 43–5.

Figure 2.6: Manuscript page, Konvolut Sammlung *Schwindel. Gefühle,* file HS.2004.0001.00019, Deutsches Literaturarchiv Marbach.

paranoia dominates this section of "All'estero." Notions of pursuit and stalking are intoned in the very title under which the special Kafka segment of *Freibeuter* appeared: "Franz Kafka, nachgestellt." The verb *nachstellen* suggests clandestine pursuit, secret and unobtrusive observation, as though Kafka were the investigative object for a group of literary-critical detectives or spies. This idea of obsessive pursuit, of tracking, stalking, and tailing, assumes central importance in an episode Sebald's narrator cites from Kafka's diaries, and the semantics of this verb inform Sebald's own approach to "Kafka" in "Dr. K.s Badereise," whom the narrator is figuratively stalking.

Aside from Zischler's essay on Kafka and cinema, the Kafka special section of *Freibeuter* also includes an essay by Michael Müller on "Kafka and Casanova," whose relevance for *Schwindel. Gefühle* scarcely requires elaboration. Müller documents in Kafka's letters a persistent fascination with Casanova's autobiography, in particular the account of his imprisonment and escape from the Doge's palace in Venice. The thrust of Müller's argument is that Kafka's reading of Casanova had a formative impact on the "punishment fantasies" recorded in *The Trial.*[55] In a manner that Sebald the literary critic was sure to admire, Müller provides detailed analysis of the concrete points of intersection between

---

55 Michael Müller, "Kafka und Casanova," *Freibeuter* 16 (1983): 68.

Casanova's and Kafka's texts. He duly notes that unlike Casanova, Josef K. does not manage a successful flight from his persecutors.[56] As if in response to this, Sebald's narrator focuses in "All'estero" on a retelling of Casanova's suffering under the brutal penal conditions and his daring escape (*Schwindel* 63–9/54–60). This account concludes with an ironic parallel between the narrator and Casanova, when the former discovers that his own visit to Venice took place on October 31, the anniversary of Casanova's flight (68–9/60). More compelling as evidence of the impact Müller's article had on Sebald is the reference in "Dr. K.s Badereise" to Kafka's stay in Venice in autumn of 1913, and the astonishment registered by Sebald's narrator that this city leaves so few traces in Kafka's letters and diaries:

> Über Einzelheiten aber schweigt Dr. K. sich aus. Wir wissen also, wie gesagt, nicht, was er in Wirklichkeit alles gesehen hat. Es gibt nicht einmal einen Hinweis darauf, daß er den Dogenpalast besucht hätte, dessen Bleikammern in der Entwicklung seiner Prozeß- und Strafphantasien einige Monate später einen so wichtigen Platz einnehmen sollte. (*Schwindel* 164)
> [But more precise details Dr. K. does not disclose. We know, as I have said, nothing of what he really saw. There is not even a reference to the Doge's Palace, the prison chambers of which were to play so prominent a part in the evolution of his own fantasies of trial and punishment some months later. (*Vertigo* 148)]

Aside from reinforcing one of the prominent themes of this story collection—the discrepancies between life experience, the memory of these experiences, and their reconstruction by subsequent investigators—this passage alludes unmistakably to Müller's thesis that Casanova's tale informed Kafka's punishment fantasies more generally, and his novel *Der Proceß* specifically. In his role as literary critic, Sebald would have needed to cite Müller and his essay at this juncture; in his guise as travel writer who is re-enacting Kafka's 1913 journey, however, he can remain silent about this source and couch Müller's conclusion as his own speculative deliberation. Sebald and his narrator can express this opinion as though it were a matter of general agreement or uncontested fact, rather than as a scholarly hypothesis.

The final essay in the *Freibeuter* issue on Kafka was contributed by the pre-eminent Kafka biographer Klaus Wagenbach.[57] In this piece, "Drei Sanatorien Kafkas" (Three of Kafka's sanatoria), Wagenbach

---

56 Ibid., 76.
57 Klaus Wagenbach, "Drei Sanatorien Kafkas: Ihre Bauten und Gebräuche," *Freibeuter* 16 (1983): 77–90.

documents Kafka's trips to health spas and summarizes documents that relate the ideological and medical practices of these institutions. The final section deals with the sanatorium run by Dr. von Hartungen in Riva, where Kafka spent three weeks in September and October 1913, and several of Wagenbach's observations—including the diagnosis that Kafka was suffering from neurosis, his brief love affair at the sanatorium with a young Swiss woman, and the theme that only love helps one resist the desire to perish—find echoes in Sebald's treatment of this episode in "Dr. K.s Badereise." More significant is Wagenbach's primary thesis that Kafka's story "Der Jäger Gracchus" represents a transmutation of his experiences in Riva into literary-fictional form. Both Kafka and the Hunter Gracchus, Wagenbach notes, arrive in Riva by ship from Desenzano; and both enjoy the knowledge that they are completely cut off from the world, with their whereabouts unknown. Wagenbach quotes from a letter Kafka wrote to his fiancée Felice, in which he remarks, "The fact that no one knows where I am is my only happiness" ("Mein einziges Glücksgefühl besteht darin, daß niemand weiß, wo ich bin").[58] He goes on to emphasize the parallel with Kafka's Hunter Gracchus, who explicitly maintains, "No one knows about me, and if he did know about me, he would not know where I reside" ("niemand weiß von mir, und wüßte er von mir, so wüßte er meinen Aufenthalt nicht").[59] Moreover, throughout his essay Wagenbach documents in word and image the details of hydrotherapy, which Sebald and his narrator also follow in "Dr. K." and which resonates in the story's title.

Wagenbach's influence also enters this story from another avenue: his illustrated biography, *Franz Kafka: Bilder aus seinem Leben* (*Franz Kafka: Pictures of a Life*), which appeared in the same year as the *Freibeuter* collection. This book plays a role in "Dr. K." similar to that of Del Litto's *Album Stendhal* for "Beyle." Several of the images with which Sebald documents Kafka's journey are drawn directly from Wagenbach's book. The picture of Kafka with his traveling companions in a mock airplane at the Vienna Prater, for example (*Schwindel* 160/144), is a cropped copy of an illustration found in Wagenbach's collection.[60] Similarly, Sebald prints an iris-cropped image of the letterhead of the Hotel Sandwirth (163/147), where Kafka stayed in

58 Ibid., 87; cf. Kafka, *Briefe 1913–1914*, 295; *Letters to Felice*, 326.
59 Wagenbach, "Drei Sanatorien," 87; cf. Franz Kafka, "Der Jäger Gracchus," in *Nachgelassene Schriften und Fragmente I*, ed. Malcolm Pasley (Frankfurt am Main: Fischer, 1993), 311. This segment of Kafka's story, which was recorded in fragmentary form in one of his notebooks, is not included in the English translation.
60 Klaus Wagenbach, *Franz Kafka: Bilder aus seinem Leben* (Berlin: Wagenbach, 1983), 150.

Venice, that is derived from the facsimile of a letter Kafka wrote to Felice reproduced by Wagenbach.[61] Finally, the two images of a crowd in the city of Desenzano, waiting for the arrival of Dr. K. in his role as Vice-Secretary of the Workers Accident Insurance Institute, are drawn from Wagenbach's book.[62] Moreover, both Wagenbach and Sebald embed these images in text that cites—in Wagenbach's case explicitly, in Sebald's only implicitly as unmarked intertexts—Kafka's own reflections from letters he wrote during his stay in Riva.

Sebald's approach is more subjective and manipulative than Wagenbach's, as indicated by this refusal to mark quotations and by the alterations he imposes on the images to bring them into relation with his textual exposition. The first two pictures are cropped so as to emphasize the details Sebald's narrator highlights: the smile Kafka musters in the first photo, and the uncanny similarity of his companions Otto Pick and Albert Ehrenstein, whom the narrator casts as another of the myriad twins who haunt these narratives (*Schwindel* 158–60/143–4); in the facsimile letterhead the steamships and gondolas on the Venetian lagoon, which invoke the motif of Kafka's Hunter Gracchus and his bark. In the final example, Sebald exploits the practice of doubling by printing the image in a format identical to its rendering by Wagenbach (168/153), as well as in the magnified excerpt of a specific detail, highlighting the gestures of those people waiting in vain for Dr. K.'s arrival (169/154). In the foreground of this picture stands a woman holding her hand above her eyes, as if shielding them from the sunlight so that she might see better. Sebald's text plays on this woman's gesture by commenting on how the villagers "continued their watch for" the elusive Dr. K. ("noch Ausschau gehalten haben"; 169/154). Sebald's narrator goes on to relate how the crowd eventually dispersed after it became clear that they would be disappointed. Sebald and his narrator further embellish this episode by adding the invented verbal reaction of one of these frustrated villagers: "One of them is reported to have observed that those in whom we invest our hopes only ever make their appearance when they are no longer needed" ("Einer von ihnen soll die Äußerung getan haben, daß diejenigen, in die wir unsere Hoffnungen setzen, immer dann erst kommen, wenn sie keiner mehr braucht"; 170/154). Kafka scholars will recognize this statement as a bowdlerized version of a famous Kafka aphorism about how, if the Messiah should ever arrive, his appearance will come too late for human salvation: "The Messiah will come only when he is no longer necessary, he will come only one day after his arrival, he will not come on the last day, but on the last day of all" ("Der Messias

---

61 Ibid., 151.
62 Ibid., 152.

wird erst kommen, wenn er nicht mehr nötig sein wird, er wird erst nach seiner Ankunft kommen, er wird nicht am letzten Tag kommen, sondern am allerletzten").[63] This example provides an especially telling inventory of the metafictional practices that Sebald, already at this early stage of his career as a fiction writer, employs to manipulate the text–image dialectic: images are imported into the text as pseudo-documentary evidence, but they are freely doctored to coordinate with their textual environment, and, more importantly, they can give rise to textual inventions that lend fictional accounts a guise of verisimilitude by allowing them to resonate in an intertextual echo chamber. We can still perceive the rudimentary practices of Sebald the literary critic, in his reliance on critical perspectives and on visual resources like Wagenbach's biography; but any critical apparatus is abandoned and interpretive points are embellished by fictionalizing addenda and other intertextual resonances.

Sebald's "Dr. K." also relies heavily on another literary-critical resource: an essay by Anthony Northey titled "Kafka in Riva, 1913" that appeared around the time Sebald was composing "Dr. K."[64] Added value accrues to Northey's contribution since he is among that handful of scholars Sebald praises, in his review of Zischler's *Kafka geht ins Kino*, for following the same painstaking biographical approach that Zischler practices (*Campo Santo* 195–6/153–4). By contrast, Sebald shows nothing but disdain for those hermeneutical and textual analysts—he derisively calls them "the general run of German critics, whose plodding studies regularly become a travesty of scholarship" ("die zünftigen Germanisten, deren verbohrte Untersuchungen regelmäßig umschlagen in eine Travestie von Wissenschaft"; *Campo Santo* 195/153)—who merely muck around in Kafka's literary texts and appeal to ethereal theoretical perspectives.[65] Seen from Sebald's

---

63 Franz Kafka, *Nachgelassene Schriften und Fragmente II*, ed. Jost Schillemeit (Frankfurt am Main: Fischer, 1992), 57; *The Blue Octavo Notebooks*, ed. Max Brod, trans. Ernst Kaiser and Eithne Wilkins (Cambridge, MA: Exact Change, 1991), 28.

64 Anthony Northey, "Kafka in Riva, 1913," *Neue Zürcher Zeitung*, Fernausgabe No. 93 (April 24, 1987): 37–8. Jo Catling, "Bibliotheca abscondita," 280, points to the relevance of this essay for Sebald's story, indicating that copies of the article were found among Sebald's teaching materials. A copy of the essay is also contained in Sebald's background materials for *Schwindel. Gefühle*, folder 2 of the file "Konvolut Sammlung *Schwindel. Gefühle*" (HS.2004.0001.00019) in the Deutsches Literaturarchiv.

65 One of the ironies of Sebald scholarship is that most of it is perpetrated in the very hermeneutical and text-analytical spirit for which Sebald expressed such disdain. Pressed to name an exception to this in mainstream Sebald criticism, one thinks of Mark Anderson, whose biographical approach emulates the best aspects of Sebald's own critical methodology.

perspective, Northey's critical credentials could scarcely be more solid. The thrust of Northey's essay is to link Kafka's composition of "Der Jäger Gracchus" in 1917 with his experiences at the sanatorium in Riva in 1913. This general idea that fiction represents a retrospective refashioning of lived experience is fundamental to the mode of writing Sebald himself is trying to practice in the stories of this collection: he, too, is reflecting retrospectively, in particular in "All'estero" and "Il ritorno in patria," on his own past experiences, transforming them in the process of remembrance into pseudo-autobiographical works of (auto)fiction. The argument Northey makes about the creative process that produced Kafka's "Der Jäger Gracchus" thus applies *mutatis mutandis* to Sebald's own transformation from literary critic to a fictionalizer of his own lived experiences. One of the central themes of Northey's essay, moreover, is that Kafka's Italian journey represented a strategic attempt to create those conditions that would jumpstart his creative productivity. In a letter to Max Brod from this time—Northey cites it as one of his sources—Kafka emphasizes his absolute need for isolation, what he calls "Alleinsein" ("solitude"), and he uses that word in this letter no fewer than four times.[66] The Italian journey marks for him a flight from the engagement with Felice Bauer, which he had sought to dissolve just prior to his departure. When in this letter Kafka expresses his dilemma as a catch-22—"I cannot live with her and I cannot live without her" ("Ich kann mit ihr nicht leben und ich kann ohne sie nicht leben")[67]—he formulates that paradoxical neither-nor that determines the fate of his Hunter Gracchus, who is neither dead nor alive, but instead exists in a nether world between the realms of the living and the dead. Northey casts this dilemma largely as one of writing, emphasizing that Kafka goes to Riva on the one-year anniversary of composing the short story "Das Urteil" ("The Judgment"), which he held up throughout his life as a model of inspired creativity. The implicit irony of Northey's argument was surely not lost on Sebald: Kafka failed during this trip to discover the creative spark he so desperately sought, but it would emerge several years later in his concentrated *recollection* of this experience, giving rise to "The Hunter Gracchus." Sebald surely viewed his own Italian journeys as prompts for his creative production; and like Kafka he was only able to realize this creative impulse in retrospect, in the act of *recalling* these experiences. This explains why the narrator of "All'estero" claims that his first Italian journey was motivated by the need to get over an emotionally troubling and unstable period in his life (*Schwindel* 39/33). Sebald figures the journey that marks his productive

---

66 Kafka, *Briefe 1913–14*, 285–6; *Letters to Friends, Family, and Editors* (New York: Schocken, 1990), 101–2; cf. Northey, "Kafka in Riva," 37.

67 Kafka, *Briefe 1913–14*, 286; *Letters to Friends*, 102.

shift from literary critic to creative writer as a flight from personal crisis that emulates Kafka's motivations to travel to Italy in 1913.

Northey's take on Kafka's trip emphasizes the role of one of Kafka's tablemates at the sanatorium as the trigger for the subsequent creative translation of this experience into literature. Northey is the first to identify this figure by name as *Generalmajor* Ludwig von Koch. During Kafka's stay at the sanatorium, von Koch commits suicide by shooting himself with his own pistol. Northey's archival research turns up the report on his death written by the head of the sanatorium, and he emphasizes that the general succeeded in shooting himself "both in the heart and in the head" ("sowohl durch das Herz als auch durch den Kopf").[68] This phrase reappears word for word in Sebald's retelling of this incident in "Dr. K." (*Schwindel* 177/162). Similarly, Sebald culls from Northey's essay the information about von Koch's funeral, and the idea that the laying out of Gracchus's corpse copies this memorial ceremony.[69] More importantly, Northey calls attention to the general's act of suicide, duly noting that although Kafka's Hunter is not said to be a suicide victim, he shares the legendary fate traditionally associated with them: the condemnation to eternal wandering.[70] Paradoxically, von Koch, despite being a suicide, was buried in a cemetery in Riva—in hallowed ground. Sebald alludes to this paradox in his version of this incident when the priest attending Koch's burial prays for "everlasting peace" ("die ewige Ruhe"), but suddenly opens his eyes widely "with a reproachful expression" ("mit vorwurfsvollem Augenaufschlag"; *Schwindel* 178/162). The words Sebald's priest gives as an excuse for the general's behavior, "*quest'uomo più taciturno e mesto*" (178/162), are taken directly from Northey's account, who also quotes this in the original Italian.[71] Sebald clearly lent credence to Northey's belief that Gracchus's fate is tied to his death as a suicide victim. This explains why his narrator, after describing Gracchus's history in words that retell the opening section of Kafka's story, calls his death, which purportedly occurred during his pursuit of a chamois, "one of the strangest items of misinformation in all the tales that have ever been told" ("eine der eigenartigsten Falschmeldungen aller Erzählungen, die je erzählt worden sind"; 180/165). Literature is free to perpetrate hoaxes, to advance "misinformation," to embellish real events with invented fictions, to *swindle*; but Sebald's narrator suggests that such fictions must nevertheless retain some semblance of verisimilitude, and

---

68 Northey, "Kafka in Riva," 37.
69 Ibid.; see Kafka, "Jäger Gracchus," 306–7; "The Hunter Gracchus," in *The Complete Stories*, ed. Nahum Glatzer (New York: Schocken, 1971), 226–7.
70 Northey, "Kafka in Riva," 37.
71 Ibid.

in his view the cause of Gracchus's death lacks even that credibility necessary for a coherent fiction. Sebald's fictional works are replete with characters who either commit suicide or narrowly escape it. Henry Selwyn shoots himself with the elephant gun from India he had otherwise never used (*Ausgewanderten* 35/22–3); Paul Bereyter lays down on the railroad tracks in his home town and awaits the train's arrival (41/27); Ambros Adelwarth submits to electroshock treatments that he knows will be the death of him (163/111); and even Max Aurach only narrowly escapes a leap off the Grammont when he is rescued by the mysterious Butterfly Man (259/174). But suicide is also an undercurrent that runs throughout the texts of *Schwindel. Gefühle.* In "Dr. K." this theme is reinforced in that round-about, circumspect, and allusive manner that will become typical of Sebald's prose fictions. In the travel diary he begins during his stay in Vienna, Kafka writes about the uneasy relationships he entertains with his acquaintances Otto Pick and Albert Ehrenstein. These are, we recall, the "twins" depicted alongside Kafka in the staged photograph in an airplane fuselage at the Prater, which Sebald reproduces from Wagenbach's illustrated Kafka biography (*Schwindel* 160/144). Kafka refers here to his inability to engage sympathetically with Ehrenstein's poetry. Sebald picks up on this allusion and supplements it with lines printed in italic type to indicate their intertextual nature: "*You, however, take delight in the ship, despoiling the lake with sails. I will go down to the deep. Plunge, thaw, go blind, become ice*" ("*Ihr aber freut euch des Schiffs, verekelt mit Segeln den See. Ich will zur Tiefe. Stürzen, schmelzen, erblinden zu Eis*"; 159/143). These words are taken from an Ehrenstein poem with the title "Der Selbstmörder" (The suicide victim).[72] The lines Sebald cites, with their references to a ship, sails, and a lake, resonate with allusions to Kafka's "Jäger Gracchus" and his stay in Riva on Lake Garda. The connection between Gracchus and suicide is further reinforced by the words "deep" ("Tiefe") and "Plunge" ("Stürzen"), which connect directly with Gracchus's fall into the abyss. This same motif arises in "Il ritorno in patria," where the narrator ekphrastically describes a painting that hangs in the Café Alpenrose, run by his aunts Bina and Babette. This image portrays "two lovers in the act of committing suicide" ("der Selbstmord eines Liebespaares") as they stand at the edge of a precipice prepared to jump to their deaths (238/218).[73] In his recollection of this painting, the

---

72 Albert Ehrenstein, "Der Selbstmörder," in *Gedichte und Prosa* (Neuwied: Luchterhand, 1961), 95.

73 This ekphrastic description represents an unmarked, word-for-word intertextual borrowing from a letter Kafka wrote to Felice Bauer, *Briefe 1913–1914*, 110; *Letters to Felice*, 205. There are several other allusions to death by suicide, or

narrator highlights how the viewer vicariously experiences the gravitational pull felt by this pair: they have given in to the power of vertigo, succumbed to their "Schwindelgefühle," and they seem to call for him to follow their lead.

Sebald's narrator is constantly enticed by the draw of the abyss and of suicide. This is indicated in a self-reflective passage from "All'estero," where he deliberates on the emptiness he felt during his journey in November 1980 and reflects on his own tendency to brood and record his ruminations in occasional jottings, figuring them as activities that bring him to the verge of death: "It seemed to me then that one could well end one's life simply through thinking and retreating into one's mind" ("es schien mir damals, als könne man sich tatsächlich ohne weiteres durch Nachdenken und Sinnieren allein ums Leben bringen"; 74–5/65). Suicide by intensive or exaggerated rumination, contemplation, or pondering: this seems to be the characteristic that aligns Sebald's narrator most intimately with the brooding artist Kafka, and with his fictional Hunter Gracchus who plummets to his death—overwrought by indecision? Sebald's narrator takes pains to emphasize his own connection with Kafka's Gracchus when he notes that when he formulated this reflection, his body became cold and stiff, and he appeared to himself as someone who "had already been interred or laid out for burial" ("wie ein Bestatteter oder doch zumindest wie ein Aufgebahrter"; 75/65). The narrator literally adopts the role and pose of Kafka's Hunter Gracchus, complete with the allusion to suicide that is mediated by Northey's critical interpretation of how Kafka translated his personal experiences in Riva into a fictional account about an ever-wandering revenant. Throughout the texts of *Schwindel. Gefühle*, Sebald's narrator figures himself as a character who "follows" both Kafka and Gracchus.[74]

---

from a fall into a precipice, in this story of belated homecoming. Dr. Rambousek, the outsider from Moravia whose medical practice is shunned by the natives, dies from an overdose of morphine (*Schwindel* 256/234). Cousin Lena and her husband mysteriously perish in an automobile accident when their Oldsmobile plunges into the depths (230–1/211). Even the death of Benedikt Ambroser in May 1933 alludes to suicide due to the transformed political situation after Hitler's assumption of power (217–18/200).

74 Wouter Dehairs, "Literatur im Kontext? Kontext als Intertext: Analyse von W. G. Sebalds *Schwindel. Gefühle* und dessen Ethik des Erinnerns," in *Rezeption, Interaktion und Integration: Niederländischsprachige und deutschsprachige Literatur im Kontext*, ed. Leopold Decloedt, Herbert Van Uffelen, and M. Elisabeth Weissenböck (Vienna: Praesens, 2004), 277, similarly notes that Sebald's narrator represents a fictional incarnation of Kafka's Hunter Gracchus, without recognizing the significance of the suicide theme.

This assumption of the role of the double-figure Kafka/Gracchus represents one of the primary metafictional strategies Sebald's narrator adopts throughout the four texts of *Schwindel. Gefühle*, and it parallels, on the level of form and narrative stance, the leitmotif-like references to Kafka's "Gracchus" that stitch this work into a coherent whole. When the narrator lies on a bed resting his head in his hands (72/63, 106/93, 126/111, 161/145), he is imitating a gesture common to Kafka;[75] and when he imagines himself crossing bodies of water, has feelings of seasickness, or actually rides in a boat, he is re-enacting Gracchus's journey (44/37–8, 75–6/65–6, 88–9/77, 283/258). More pointedly, when in "All'estero" the narrator meets an acquaintance named Salvatore Altamura in Verona (140/124), he is repeating the rendezvous between Salvatore, the mayor of Riva, and Gracchus in Kafka's story. Already typical of Sebald's artistry as a narrator is this playful texture of cross-references or *intra*-textual networks, and the provocative equivocality of individual words or phrases. These lend this text a semantic depth into which its readers peer and from which they experience a conceptual or linguistic vertigo of their own.

The title of the special Kafka section of *Freibeuter*, "Franz Kafka, nachgestellt," emphasizes this aspect of pursuing, following in the footsteps of, and/or stalking this author. We now have a better sense of how the diverse nuances of the verb *nachstellen* apply not only to the articles in this special issue and to Sebald's interest in just such a critical approach, but also the extent to which Sebald's narrator himself is pursuing Kafka, "following" in his forerunner's literary footsteps. Throughout these texts Sebald's narrator acts out Kafka's/Gracchus's role, obsessively stalking him—as a hunter stalks game. It is thus fitting that "Dr. K." concludes with an episode from Kafka's life that stresses precisely such an act of obsessive stalking. In a letter to Felice Bauer from February 23–24, 1913—seven months prior to Kafka's trip to Riva, and before their engagement, when his relationship with her was at the height of its passion—Kafka reports about a strange episode that befell him on the previous day. In order to exemplify the seemingly perverse manner in which he takes pleasure from situations that are by nature not pleasant, he describes how he obsessively followed the son of a Jewish bookstore owner through the streets of Prague, until his quarry disappeared behind the door of the "Deutsches Haus," the local German Club, where this man regularly went after taking his evening meal.[76] Kafka employs the sexually charged adverb "lüstern"

---

75   In the copy of Kafka's *Nachgelassene Schriften und Fragmente II* contained in his library, Sebald marks with a double line the passage on page 16 where Kafka describes himself sitting at his desk with his hands folded behind his head.

76   Kafka, *Briefe 1913–1914*, 107; *Letters to Felice*, 203–4.

("aroused"), which means lustfully or lasciviously, to describe the intensity of his inexplicable emotional investment in this figure. In the lead-up to this story he explains how on that evening he was absorbed in his own misfortune, as he caught sight of this figure with whom he and his family had been acquainted for years. He goes on to catalogue the many misfortunes this man had experienced in his life, including an engagement that failed due to a lack of financial resources and a subsequent marriage in which his wife went insane and had to be committed after only a few weeks, resulting in a divorce and, according to Kafka, the man's ultimate liberation. Here we should call to mind Sebald's claim in the project description for the Deutscher Literaturfonds that his fictions would investigate the misfortune of two writers, Stendhal and Kafka, or their attempts to gain happiness ("Literaturfonds" 2), for this episode from Kafka's life fits this theme exactly. It documents the subtle manner in which misfortune can be mysteriously transmogrified into good fortune. Kafka notes that this man is now once again "free" ("frei"), even though his life is confined to working day in and day out in his father's bookstore.[77]

The tale Kafka tells represents an allegory for his own situation: the fate of this pursued character is marked by a perverse dialectic of misfortune—his failed attempts at marriage—reverting to unexpected good fortune—his "liberation" to a life surrounded by nothing but books. What Kafka projects onto the life of this Jewish acquaintance is a wish-fulfillment fantasy of his own: his emancipation from the emotional relationship with Felice and his "condemnation" to a life surrounded by nothing but printed words. The fact that this man visits the German Club every evening contributes a second, ethnic-national aspect to Kafka's projection; for he explicitly relates that this Jewish man "considers himself a German, is a member of the local German Casino which, though open to all, is considered among the local Germans the most exclusive club" ("fühlt sich als Deutscher, ist Mitglied des hiesigen deutschen Casinos, einer zwar allgemeinen, aber unter den hiesigen Deutschen doch vornehmsten Vereinigung").[78] The surprising subsidiary fortune of this man, born of great personal *mis*fortune, is marked not simply in terms of successful assimilation into the local German community, but also by his uncanny ability to rise into its higher echelons—as an honored member of its "most exclusive" organization, suggesting Kafka's own acceptance in the canon of "German" writers. When he concludes his story by asking Felice if she has any idea why he stalked this man so "lasciviously" through the streets, or why he experienced such pleasure as he

---

77 Kafka, *Briefe 1913–1914*, 107; *Letters to Felice*, 203.
78 Kafka, *Briefe 1913–1914*, 108; *Letters to Felice*, 204.

watched this Jew disappear behind the door of the German House, his question seems purely rhetorical. For Kafka, this man obviously represents the transmogrification of misfortune into fortune: a "liberation" from confining personal relationships and social reintegration at a higher level through unencumbered assimilation into a dominant and representative national-ethnic community; and a fulfillment of his secret wish to sacrifice his relationship with Felice for a life dedicated to "books," to literature alone, and to be himself enshrined as a "German" writer.

In Sebald's retelling of this episode most of the background information suggesting Kafka's subliminal motivations is elided, and the Jewish man whom Kafka obsessively pursues is reduced to a "focus of the illicit emotion" ("Kristallisationsfigur der illegitimen Ergriffenheit"; 181/166) described in this letter. The term "Kristallisationsfigur" is central for Sebald, since it returns to the thematic dealt with in the opening piece of *Schwindel. Gefühle* on Stendhal, alluding to the French author's theory of crystallization as the imaginary embellishment of any person who has won our love or our fascination—an allusion lost in the English translation of this passage. The implication is that this son of the Jewish bookstore owner has become the object of Kafka's own imaginary embellishments, a figure onto which he projects his secret wishes. Yet this is also precisely what Sebald's narrator has done in this story: pursued, shadowed, and stalked a figure, "Dr. K.," who mesmerizes him. In addition, he has imaginatively enhanced this figure, to the point that he thinks he sees him in the flesh—and doubled, to boot—on a bus traveling from Verona to Limone (*Schwindel* 101/88–9). Thus if Kafka's letter to Felice recounts his fascination and pursuit of this son of a Jewish bookstore owner as an allegory for his desire ("lüstern"/"lasciviously") to replicate this man's ability to grab fortune from the jaws of misfortune, Sebald pursues Kafka through Italy, through the tale of "Dr. K.," and, indeed, throughout the narratives of *Schwindel. Gefühle* out of his own obsessive desire to emulate this admired writer. Similar to Kafka, Sebald's narrator is struggling to overcome a "particularly difficult period" in his life ("eine besonders ungute Zeit"; 39/33), and he tries to resolve these difficulties by following the solution Kafka envisioned, transforming his own lived experience into literature. Sebald is especially taken by the gesture with which Kafka's Gracchus acknowledges his "savior," the burgomaster of Riva, Salvatore—whose name, of course, means redeemer—by placing his hand on his knee (*Schwindel* 158/142).[79] "Dr. K." ends with a reference to this gesture (182–3/167). Might we not suppose that Sebald himself is striving to fictionally redeem Kafka and

---

79 Kafka, "Gracchus," 311; "Hunter Gracchus," 230.

his Hunter Gracchus, thereby accomplishing something in the medium of prose fiction that he could never have hoped to achieve in the genre of literary criticism?

Sebald launches his career as a writer of creative prose fictions by imaginatively and "lasciviously" stalking two literary figures, Stendhal and Kafka, whom as a literary critic he could only have pursued in the dry and objective manner of plodding academic scholarship. This explains why the texts devoted to Stendhal and Kafka still operate predominantly with the voice and stance of a third-person narrator, only slipping occasionally—as at the end of "Dr. K.," when the narrator briefly assumes the perspective of his subject (181–2/166–7)—into the internal view of the figure whose life he is recounting. This also explains why the predominant intertexts of "Beyle" and "Dr. K." are extracts from primary sources by these authors themselves—*The Life of Henri Brulard* and *Love* in the case of Stendhal; the fragment "Der Jäger Gracchus" and select letters and diary entries in the case of Kafka. We have also documented the extent to which critical sources on Kafka— Wagenbach's illustrated biography, the essays in the special issue of *Freibeuter*, and Anthony Northey's piece on Kafka's stay in Riva—form a supplementary intertextual layer that serves an implicit evidentiary function. If Sebald had toned down the ironic playfulness of "Dr. K." a few notches and added quotation marks, footnotes, and references, this text might pass as a piece of criticism in that essayistic-biographical mode Sebald liked to practice. In this regard the Stendhal and Kafka texts look ahead to future projects that Sebald the literary critic will pursue. These early fictional works anticipate the brand of literary criticism Sebald will accomplish in the essays from the volume *Logis in einem Landhaus* (*A Place in the Country*), first published in 1998, well after he had promoted his once subsidiary occupation as a writer of prose fictions to his primary profession. These later critical essays—although they do at times use quotation marks and even cite, albeit without references or footnotes, other scholars—are largely essayistic and subjective and read like literary-critical "pursuits" that "crystallize" and imaginatively embellish their object of study. Unlike Sebald's earlier critical studies, they are also "iconotexts" that exploit juxtapositions between expository text and illustrative or suggestive images.[80] "Beyle" and "Dr. K." are thus bridge pieces that allow Sebald to expand creatively on practices he implemented as a literary critic, but that initiate a search for his own creative voice and for the fictional, metafictional, and

---

80 In *Sebald's Vision* (New York: Columbia University Press, 2015), 148–63, Carol Jacobs emphasizes how Sebald's essay on Jan Peter Tripp shifts between critical (descriptive) and fictional (narrative) perspectives, and she identifies this as a culmination in Sebald's artistry.

intermedial tactics that would inform his more mature literary works.[81]
It is important to acknowledge and analyze these pieces as transitional
works, as literary etudes whose value resides precisely in their experimental character. They are decidedly not of a piece with the other two
narratives, "All'estero" and "Il ritorno in patria," that make up the
collection *Schwindel. Gefühle.* Chronologically speaking, "Beyle" and
"Dr. K." are the first texts composed for this volume, as Sebald readily
acknowledged,[82] and exhibit a close proximity to his literary-critical
scholarship. But only in the two later works, written in the first-person
form and in the mediated, ventriloquized voice of the narrator who
has come to be identified as "Sebald" (in quotation marks, to denote
that he is at best an alter ego of the author W. G. Sebald), does Sebald
begin to discover his authentic fictional voice.[83] It is as though this
could only happen after Sebald self-reflexively "worked through" his
fascination with figures like Stendhal and Kafka, creating "Sebald"
as a vehicle for pursuing *Sebald* in his pursuit of Stendhal and Kafka.
This self-reflection on his journey in the tracks of Stendhal and Kafka
through Italy is ultimately what empowers Sebald's creative voice in
"All'estero." This leads directly to the final, strictly autobiographical
text of this collection, in which "Sebald" literally pursues Sebald back
to the village in which he spent his childhood.

Sebald acknowledges in a 1992 interview that the autobiographical
segments of *Schwindel. Gefühle.* amount to a "search for my own self"
("Suche nach meinem Ich";"*Auf ungeheuer dünnem Eis*" 71). When
viewed in their order of composition, these texts reveal a trajectory
that moves from the pursuit of others (Stendhal, Kafka, and the Hunter
Gracchus) to the pursuit of self in the fictionalizing medium of creative
writing. Sebald imitates that process by which Stendhal transforms

81 The claim that Sebald's literary fictions emerge from a transformation of
    the analytical-interpretive methods of the literary critic into poetic practices
    has been asserted more generally by Heike Gfrereis and Ellen Strittmatter,
    "Wandernde Schatten: W. G. Sebald's Unterwelt," in *Wandernde Schatten: W. G.
    Sebalds Unterwelt*, ed. Ulrich von Bülow, Heike Gfrereis, and Ellen Strittmatter
    (Marbach: Deutsche Schillergesellschaft, 2008), 7. My analyses in this chapter
    lend critical flesh to the bare bones of their hypothesis.

82 Sebald remarks in his interview with Piet de Moor on the chronological
    emergence of these stories and how the autobiographical tales grew out of the
    literary-biographical essays on Stendhal and Kafka ("*Auf ungeheuer dünnem
    Eis*" 71).

83 One might approach the difference in voice between the literary-biographical
    texts "Beyle" and "Dr. K." and the autobiographical stories "All'estero" and
    "Il ritorno" by maintaining that in the former the narrator still speaks through
    the personae and the intertexts of Stendhal and Kafka, while in the latter the
    reverse is true: his informants speak through the unitary and dominant voice of
    the first-person narrator.

himself into a literary figure in his autobiography *The Life of Henry Brulard*, or by which Kafka fictionalizes his own life experience in Riva in the story "Der Jäger Gracchus." Literature, or the literary rendering of one's lived experience, takes the form of what Sigmund Freud called a substitutive satisfaction: a form of compensatory fulfillment that stands in for more deep-seated pursuits that cannot, or can no longer, be achieved. Expressed as Kafka might have put it, Sebald discovers a form of fortune that miraculously emerges from the deliberation upon his own *mis*fortune. We recall once more the claim Sebald made in the preface to his essay collection *Die Beschreibung des Unglücks*: "The description of misfortune inherently subsumes the possibility of its overcoming" ("Die Beschreibung des Unglücks schließt in sich die Möglichkeit zu seiner Überwindung ein"; 12). But more apropos are surely Sebald's deliberations in the preface to *Logis in einem Landhaus*, where he describes the occupation of writing as a "peculiar behavioral disturbance which causes every emotion to be transformed into letters on the page and which bypasses life with such extraordinary precision" ("jener sonderbaren Verhaltensstörung, die jedes Gefühl in Buchstaben verwandeln muß und mit erstaunlicher Präzision vorbeizielt am Leben"; *Logis* 6/*Place* 4). It is hard to imagine a more concise statement about the misfortune of writing as a largely inferior substitute for living. But Sebald goes on to describe the subsidiary fortune that emerges from the writer's self-sacrifice when he argues that the *readers* of literature profit from the writer's behavioral disorder: "the hapless writers trapped in their web of words sometimes succeed in opening up vistas of such beauty and intensity [for their readers] as life itself is scarcely able to provide" ("die in ihrer Wörterwelt gefangenen Schriftsteller eröffnen ihr [der Leserschaft] doch manchmal Ausblicke von solcher Schönheit und Intensität, wie sie das Leben selber kaum liefern kann"; 7/5). Inciting this uncommon pleasure in their readers ultimately affords the authors of literary fictions a second-order pleasure of their own, one that compensates for the self-sacrifice they make by *writing* about life instead of *living* it.[84] As with Kafka's pursuit of the son of the Jewish bookstore owner, literature manifests a strategy for drawing fortune out of misfortune. This is precisely what Sebald accomplishes when he transforms himself from an author of literary-biographical criticism

---

84 This pattern of second-order compensation derived from the pleasure others take in one's sacrifices parallels the structure Sigmund Freud identifies as the subsidiary pleasure joke-tellers derive from the laughter they incite in their audience. See *Der Witz und seine Beziehung zum Unbewußten*, vol. 6 of *Gesammelte Werke*, ed. Anna Freud (London: Imago, 1940), 174; *Jokes and Their Relation to the Unconscious*, vol. 8 of *The Standard Edition of the Complete Psychological Works of Sigmund Freud*, ed. and trans. James Strachey (London: Hogarth, 1960), 155–6.

into the composer of (pseudo)autobiographical prose fictions while
writing the stories of *Schwindel. Gefühle.*

Gracchus/Sebald: The Undead Revenant as Ghostly Writer

Sebald once remarked that *Schwindel. Gefühle* could be read as one grand
homage to Kafka (*"Auf ungeheuer dünnem Eis"* 77). But we should also
not sell short the importance of Stendhal, especially Stendhal's essay
Love, which serves as a prominent intertext for the motif of "crystallization." This imaginary amplification of a loved object's traits, due
to the refracting lens of desire (*Schwindel* 30–3/25–8), informs not only
the love motif so prominent in this work, but underwrites the general
theme of fictionalization as an imaginary enhancement of past personal
experience,[85] as a poetics of history in the sense of the transformative
embellishment of real-life experience. But the significance of Stendhal's
treatise on love also has implications for the narrative constitution
of *Schwindel. Gefühle. Love* is composed in the personal, subjective
form of the first-person, and although it makes pretense to being an
objectively valid statement about the nature of this emotion, it never
tries to camouflage its own semi-autobiographical perspective. On
the contrary, Stendhal makes a point of defending his use of the first-
person against any possible charges of bias and egocentrism. "I may be
charged with egotism for the form I have adopted," he apologetically
suggests; but he justifies this point of view as the only one appropriate
to the mode of writing he is practicing here: "But a traveler is allowed
to say: 'I embarked at New York for South America' ... The traveler is
not accused of being too fond of the first person singular; all these *I*'s
and *me*'s are forgiven him because to use them is the clearest and most
interesting way of relating what he has seen." Stendhal positions this
work explicitly as a form of travel literature, going on to specify that his
text documents what he terms a "moral journey ... through Italy and
Germany," in which he not only describes what he has seen and experienced, but also gives an account of "that disease of the soul called
love."[86] Stendhal's words are germane for the two texts in *Schwindel.
Gefühle* in which Sebald adopts a first-person, pseudo-autobiographical
perspective, and in which he relates his travels through Italy and
Germany, "All'estero" and "Il ritorno in patria." Even more fitting is
that Stendhal, in a subsequent footnote, highlights the irony that this
first-person form, far from bearing testimony to the author's authentic
emotional experiences, represents an expedient convention that allows
him to bundle together a plethora of alien experiences under a single

---

85 See Öhlschläger, *Cristallisation*, 175, regarding the relevance of this natural
    process for Sebald's aesthetics of fictionalization.
86 Stendhal, *Love*, trans. Gilbert and Suzanne Sale (London: Penguin, 2004), 25–6.

unified frame: "It is for the sake of *brevity*, and in order to depict experience from the inside, that the author, by using the first person singular, brings together a number of feelings quite alien to him. He has had none of his own which are worth mentioning."[87]

The paradox of this passage goes to the heart of the "swindle" inherent in the kind of self-representation Stendhal purports to be practicing. How is one able to "depict experience from the inside" if one has not enjoyed these experiences oneself, and if one denies that the writer has ever had experiences worthy of sharing? Indeed, if these feelings are fundamentally "alien" to the writer, how can he make pretense to portray them "from the inside" at all? Stendhal is ironically playing on the dialectic between personal authentication and a rendering of the experience of the "other" as if it were one's own, thereby articulating a problematic that is germane for Sebald's biographical fictions. Perhaps he is also alluding to the gulf that separates the narrated I of autobiography, the experiencing self, from the narrating I, who as the recorder of this experience is alienated from that past self by the medium of memory and the process of written recording. Regardless of how one assesses the ironic discrepancies voiced in Stendhal's self-reflection, Sebald replicates this gesture of asserting the veracity of his representations while simultaneously questioning their very possibility. One could make the case that precisely this problematic of discrepancy—between past and present, the memory of an event and its real experience, fact and fiction, literary criticism and literature—forms the crux of what occupies Sebald in the texts of *Schwindel. Gefühle*,[88] and we have already noted that the period separating the words in this title constitutes the graphic marker of discrepancy.

One of the elements that links Stendhal's *Love* and Kafka's "Jäger Gracchus," as affiliated intertexts, is their common emphasis on travel. "Gracchus" is not a travelogue in any ordinary sense; but then neither is Stendhal's *Love*. Whereas the latter makes pretense, in its narrative voice, to adhering to the conventions of travel literature, "Gracchus" simply intones the theme of infinite travel, or of a journey whose aim has been thwarted. Stendhal and Kafka are brought together in Sebald's imagination by their embarkation on trips with very similar itineraries, separated by exactly 100 years. In this sense they represent a further

---

87 Ibid., 49.

88 Carol Jacobs, *Sebald's Vision*, 175, elevates these "unsystematic permutations of many voices: critic, scholar, fiction writer, recorder of citations" to the essence of Sebald's fictions. My point is that the texts of *Schwindel. Gefühle* rehearse the possibilities of such blending, which will become the hallmark of Sebald's mature prose fictions.

set of those uncanny doubles who spook throughout *Schwindel. Gefühle*. If Kafka constitutes the overriding literary presence in this collection, this is largely because his own literary ghost, the Hunter Gracchus, haunts the pages of every story. Sebald sees Gracchus as Kafka's own double, a representation of this writer's diffidence and indecision in all significant existential matters, above all in his relationship with his on-again-off-again fiancée Felice Bauer. But above all, his ghostly recurrence throughout the tales of *Schwindel. Gefühle* allows Gracchus to function as the unifying thread that weaves these diverse stories into a larger unity.[89] Gracchus is especially suitable for this role due to his status as a liminal figure inhabiting the space of the in between, the neither-here-nor-there, the nether world between life and death. He thus not only *represents* the fate of the revenant, but also *performs* this role throughout Sebald's text, as the ghostly textual presence who constantly returns and recurs. As a wanderer in a domain that is neither alien nor domestic, but that represents a peculiar hybrid between the homeland and the foreign, we can imagine Gracchus navigating that space marked by the full stop in Sebald's title: the breach, rupture, or the line of discrepancy that generates the semantic richness of Sebald's title and this work. The sense of vertigo itself, of *Schwindel* in the common sense of that word, results from the experience of spatial discrepancy: it emerges from the visual contrast between the proximity of the stable ground on which one stands and the distance of that miniature world below. Sebald translates this radical contrast between near and far from spatial into temporal terms, as well as from the realm of perceptual experience to its representation in word and image. We can conceive Gracchus as the unwilling explorer of this intermediary realm of rupture and discrepancy that lies at the core of *Schwindel*, of vertigo or "swindle" ("Schwindel").

In his deliberations on Kafka's story, the narrator of "Dr. K.s Badereise" stresses that no cause is given for Gracchus's misfortune, and that questions of guilt and responsibility remain unanswerable. When the mayor of Riva asks Gracchus to recount how his unimaginable fate has come about, Gracchus tells how, occupied as a wolf hunter in the Black Forest, he fell to his death while in pursuit of a chamois. Sebald's narrator displays open skepticism about this explanation, calling it one of the most blatant examples of "misinformation" ("Falschmeldungen") in all of literature (*Schwindel* 180/165). In lieu of

---

89 In his interview with Andreas Isenschmid, Sebald calls Gracchus "one of the seams in this text, where the fictional more or less zips together with the documentary or the quoted material" ("eine der Nahtstellen im Text, wo sich das Fiktive mit dem Dokumentarischen oder mit dem Zitierten mehr oder weniger reißverschlußartig zusammensetzt"; "*Auf ungeheuer dünnem Eis*" 56).

causal explanation, Gracchus creates a narrative composed of nothing but a series of improbabilities: the improbability that a hunter who knows this terrain so well would fall to his death; the improbability that a wolf hunter would take any interest in pursuing a chamois; and the factual improbability that a chamois, an animal that inhabits high mountain peaks, might even be sighted at the relatively low altitudes of the Black Forest. Called to account for the unanticipated turn in his own life, Gracchus can only fall back on threadbare excuses or outright lies. What makes his "misinformation" or hoax so "peculiar" is its very preposterousness, which marks it indelibly as a flight into fiction, a "swindle." Yet the theme of sudden diversion, an unantici-pated "wrong turn of the tiller" ("falsche Drehung des Steuers"; *Schwindel* 180/165) applies not only to Gracchus and his condemnation to sailing the "seas of the world" ("irdischen Wassern") without ever being able to "make land" ("an Land zu gelangen"; 180/165), but can also be read as a cipher for Sebald's own surprising turn from the objectivity of literary criticism to an occupation with the fictional embellishment made possible by literature. And is this not also one of the most peculiar hoaxes of all storytelling, that a literary scholar would feel impelled to make the transition from writing criticism to the composition of prose fiction? The implication of this parallel is that as the author of literary prose, Sebald himself is living and writing on a threshold between self and other, past and present, experiential fact and fictional elaboration—as was true not only for Kafka and his figure Gracchus, but also for Henri Beyle, alias Stendhal, alias Henry Brulard. Sebald tellingly remarks in an interview that the return to his childhood home, experiencing first-hand the discrepancy between his own memories and the reality with which this visit confronted him, put him in a position analogous to that of Kafka's Hunter Gracchus: he found himself caught "in a no-man's land between not here and not there, between not entirely living and not entirely dead" ("in einem Niemandsland zwischen nicht hier und nicht dort, zwischen nicht ganz lebendig und nicht ganz tot"; *"Auf ungeheuer dünnen Eis"* 60). This parallel between the liminality of Kafka's Gracchus and of Sebald, as the emerging author of prose fiction, underpins the iconotexts of *Schwindel. Gefühle* on multiple levels. In his guise as writer of prose fiction, Sebald figures himself as a ghostwriter, a ghostly revenant similar to Kafka and his Hunter Gracchus.

The most poignant parallel occurs at the very inception of "All'estero," when the first-person narrator describes his aimless wanderings through a closely circumscribed section of Vienna at the beginning of his 1980 journey in Kafka's footsteps. This text introduces the common incipit formula that would become a hallmark of Sebald's fictions: the narrator begins by explaining how his trip to Vienna was motivated by the need to escape a particularly difficult period in his life and the perennial cloudy ambience of his English residence (39/33). But the narrator explicitly describes the repetitive city walks that filled his first days in Vienna as substitutes for his daily work of writing and gardening at home, so that his perambulations are presented as an *alternative* to those activities. His aimless wandering through Vienna is figured as a symbolic rendering of precisely that *new* form of writing activity marked by the composition of the prose narratives contained in *Schwindel. Gefühle.* And as with Stendhal in his treatise on love, the very genre of the travelogue justifies the use of the first-person form. Yet as the narrator later discovers to his own surprise, his perambulations are subject to unacknowledged restrictions and never cross the limits of a narrowly circumscribed terrain.

Das oft stundenlang fortgesetzte Kreuzundquergehen in der Stadt hatte dergestalt die eindeutigste Eingrenzung, ohne daß es mir je klargeworden wäre, was das eigentlich Unbegreifliche an meinem damaligen Verhalten gewesen ist, das ständige Gehen oder die Unfähigkeit, die unsichtbaren und, wie ich auch jetzt noch annehmen muß, völlig willkürlichen Grenzlinien zu überschreiten. (*Schwindel* 40)
[My traversing of the city, often continuing for hours, thus had very clear bounds, and yet at no point did my incomprehensible behaviour become apparent to me: that is to say, my continual walking and my reluctance to cross certain lines which were both invisible and, I presume, wholly arbitrary. (*Vertigo* 34)]

The narrator reflects that if one were to map out these traverses, they would leave the impression of someone constantly trying, and failing, to transgress the limits of his "reason, imagination or will-power" ("am Rand seiner Vernunft, Vorstellungs- oder Willenskraft"; 40/34). The upshot is that Sebald's newly-initiated writing practice, like these meanderings, develops without a carefully laid-out plan and emerges almost as an unconscious force that guides the author and holds him within a specifically bounded terrain, an unwittingly ordered motivic field, as it were. The model for this kind of unconscious, but ultimately meaningful and necessary literary activity is Kafka, who throughout his life longed wistfully for periods of such unconscious, mysteriously directed creativity as he had experienced when writing his masterpiece story "Das Urteil" ("The Judgment").[90]

---

90 See Kafka, *Tagebücher*, 461; *The Diaries*, 213, where he remarks after composing this short story, "Only *in this way* can writing be done, only with such coherence, with such a complete opening of the body and the soul" ("Nur so

Sebald associates such moments of unconscious artistic production with the accidental, involuntary, and endless voyage of the Hunter Gracchus, so that this figure becomes a veritable symbolic rendering of the Kafka-like literary author. Like Gracchus, creative writers are the undead: they no longer *live* life, because instead of living it they *write* about it; but at the same time, they have not passed out of life itself. As Sebald would later propose in the preface to *Logis in einem Landhaus*, fiction writers get trapped in the netherworld of their own language, what he calls their "Wörterwelt," their "web of words," and hence continually confront the impossible choice of laying down their pens (*Logis* 7/5). This "web of words" is the literary rendition of Gracchus's no-man's land between the living and the dead, or the network of the narrator's meanderings in Vienna, and this parallel is already touched on in Kafka's short story, where Gracchus identifies himself as a writer, but laments that no one will read what he has put down on paper.[91]

The passage at the beginning of "All'estero" describing the narrator's ramblings through Vienna constitutes a significant nodal point in Sebald's emergence as a creative writer, not simply because it stands at the threshold of his transition from academic to creative writing, but also because it self-reflexively deliberates on the paradox of the unwittingly constrained spontaneity that Sebald associates with the process of composing prose fiction. It presents Sebald's first iteration of the identification between walking/traveling and writing, an association that will recur in the second pseudo-autobiographical text of this collection when the narrator makes the descent into his childhood village of W., but simultaneously into his own past. The monumental travelogue *Die Ringe des Saturn* represents the expansion of this linkage between walking and writing as the structuring principle for a book-length narrative. But the depth and significance of the description from "All'estero" are intensified by the fact that it is underwritten by two influential intertexts, one borrowed from Sigmund Freud, the other from Ludwig Wittgenstein. Sebald's narrator experiences his mysterious peregrinations explicitly in Vienna, the native city of these two intellectual giants. The most obvious intertextual allusion is to the section in Freud's essay on the uncanny where the psychoanalyst describes an experience of his own while walking through an unfamiliar Italian city. Although these wanderings have no defined aim, Freud discovers to his surprise that he keeps returning to a particular quarter in the city. He is dismayed—but also, ultimately, enlightened—when he recognizes

---

kann geschrieben werden, nur in einem solchen Zusammenhang, mit solcher vollständigen Öffnung des Leibes und der Seele").

91 Kafka, "Gracchus," 311. This passage is not included in the English translation.

that his ramblings keep returning him to the red-light district.[92] The erotic aspect of this episode is secondary, although it links up with the overall theme of love that, according to Sebald, interconnects the individual tales in this volume.[93] More pronounced is the theme of unconscious guidance.[94] By citing this personal episode, Freud seeks to illuminate how human actions are involuntarily steered by subliminal drives, impulses, or unacknowledged aims. He uses this experience to demonstrate how patterns of repetition, which he associates with the very nature of the uncanny—and which Sebald aligns with the structure of historical coincidence—lend pattern and sense to our lives. Sebald suggests that a reflex allied to this *Wiederholungszwang*, this compulsion to repeat, operates behind the back of the successful writer of literary fictions, constantly bringing authors back to certain themes, motifs, structures, or ideas that lend their work coherence, unity, and a characteristic signature.[95]

The intertext from Wittgenstein derives from the *Philosophische Untersuchungen* (*Philosophical Investigations*) and draws an analogy between the organization of an ancient city and the structure of language. The thrust of Wittgenstein's argument is that language evolves over time, just as a municipality grows and changes sporadically, without an overriding plan that imposes order or organic coherence. This explains, according to Wittgenstein, why language, like such a disordered cityscape, fails to provide the person negotiating its

---

92 Sigmund Freud, "Das Unheimliche," in *Gesammelte Werke*, ed. Anna Freud et al., 18 vols (London: Imago, 1940–87), 12:249; "The Uncanny," in *The Standard Edition of the Complete Psychological Works of Sigmund Freud*, ed. and trans. James Strachey, 24 vols (London: Hogarth, 1953–74), 17:237.

93 In a 2001 interview with Maya Jaggi, "Recovered Memories," *Guardian*, September 22, 2001, 6, Sebald claimed all the texts in *Schwindel. Gefühle* deal with "the problem of love," without treating it "in the standard way."

94 I am inclined to question John Zilcosky's insistence, "Sebald's Uncanny Travels: The Impossibility of Getting Lost," in *W. G. Sebald: A Critical Companion*, ed. J. J. Long and Anne Whitehead (Seattle: University of Washington Press, 2004), 107, on the sexual implications of this intertextual connection to Freud. Although Sebald made the case that love was one of the overriding themes linking these texts, this concept should not be reduced to sexuality and the erotic. Love of home, intoned in the notion of the "patria" and the return home in the final story, represents a significant offshoot of this topic, as does the imaginary enhancement Stendhal associates with love, or Kafka's explicitly non-sexual theory of "disembodied love," invoked by the narrator of "Dr. K." (*Schwindel* 173/158).

95 Only with regard to this implicit and unconscious sense of form and aesthetic reiteration can one properly speak of Sebald's inability to get lost as a structuring principle of his texts. I thus am skeptical about Zilcosky's view, "Sebald's Uncanny Travels," 105–6, that Sebald feels unconsciously constrained by his literary predecessors and by the conventions of the travel writing genre.

streets, alleys, or squares any points of orientation.[96] The crux of the problem, as Wittgenstein later writes, is that users of language, like those who try to familiarize themselves with a chaotically assembled city simply by walking through it, lack any overview that could supply the needed bearings.[97] As indicated by markings and marginal notes in his personal copy of Wittgenstein's text, Sebald not only registered these reflections but actively deliberated on their reach and their relevance. He highlights this passage by drawing two vertical lines in the margin next to it. Moreover, he exploits this same passage over a decade later, in *Austerlitz*, when his protagonist describes the persistent confusion he experiences while reading and writing by comparing it to the lack of orientation one senses in an old city, whereby his words are drawn almost directly from Wittgenstein (*Austerlitz* 178–9/123–4). At the top of the page in his personal copy of Wittgenstein's text, where the philosopher bemoans our inability to have any overview over the use of words, Sebald writes, "Sprache & Stadt nicht zu erfassen" ("language & city defy comprehension"), thereby drawing an explicit connection to the previous passage comparing our unguided peregrinations through language with our ramblings in an unknown city. The adoption of Wittgenstein's position by Austerlitz, as a way of articulating the depth of his own linguistic pathology, suggests that this view marks a debilitating extreme that Sebald and his characters seek to avoid. Indeed, one could surmise that Austerlitz circumvents this very problem in the moment when he turns to Wittgenstein to find an appropriate model for describing it. This points to the underlying significance inherent in Sebald's subtle linkage of these intertexts from Freud and Wittgenstein in the description of his own circuitous meanderings. The allusion to Wittgenstein emphasizes that walking through the city is a metaphor for the negotiation and traversal of language in the act of writing. But what Wittgenstein portrays as the absolute inability to get one's bearings or gain orientation undergoes critical revision through the alignment with Freud, who insists that even when we lack overview, we are yet subject to an internal, unconscious steering mechanism that provides unanticipated guidance. There is a ghost in the (writing) machine, or perhaps better, a ghost*writer* who imposes aesthetic direction behind the back of the author. When read in conjunction with the intertexts it invokes, this passage from "All'estero" coalesces into an early programmatic statement about the process of writing and the aesthetic attributes of Sebald's prose

---

96 Ludwig Wittgenstein, *Philosophische Untersuchungen*, in *Schriften* (Frankfurt am Main: Suhrkamp, 1963), 296; *Philosophical Investigations*, trans. G. E. M. Anscombe (Oxford: Blackwell, 2001), 7.

97 Wittgenstein, *Philosophische Untersuchungen*, 345; *Philosophical Investigations*, 42.

fictions. The inherent irony is that what is portrayed as an unconscious and spontaneous act is in fact the product of conscious and deliberate construction, exploiting the managerial skill of the authorial impresario who carefully interweaves these intertextual allusions. The creative spontaneity invoked here is decidedly a *staged* spontaneity.

In the preface to *Logis in einem Landhaus*, Sebald identifies the act of fiction writing as a "behavioral disturbance" ("Verhaltensstörung"; *Logis* 6/4), and throughout his work artistic activity tends to be aligned with pathologies. Whether in the case of Austerlitz, or in the pilgrimage recounted in *Die Ringe des Saturn*, which ends with physical laming and the need for a corrective operation, or even in the repetitive process of creation, destruction, and recreation modeled in the artistic activity of the painter Max Aurach and the narrator who records his story, artistic activity, and creative writing in particular, tend to be collated with psychological or physical debilities that are invariably linked to issues of repetition. In "All'estero" this connection is drawn in multiple ways, but it is indicated most immediately by the veritable physical and psychological deterioration the narrator undergoes during his ramblings in Vienna. In these ten days filled almost solely with walking, he exists in a state of utter speechlessness, has no contact with other human beings, devolves into a tramp-like figure with worn, dirty clothes and tattered shoes, hallucinates the ghostly presence of long-dead relatives—in anticipation of the return home that will be narrated in the final story of this collection—and even conjures up the ambulating spirit of the poet Dante (*Schwindel* 40–1/35–7). When the narrator begins to harbor vague concerns about his own psychic and physical health, he is overcome by "a feeling of vertigo" ("ein Gefühl der Übelkeit und des Schwindels"; 42/35) that results not only in the dissolution of images in his mind but of his thoughts altogether. Although he begins to suspect that he is suffering from a "mental paralysis" ("Lähmung oder Krankheit des Kopfes"; 42/36), his only response is to go on walking until he collapses from exhaustion on his hotel bed. Ultimately this apparent free fall of psychic "decline" ("Niedergang"; 43/37) is interrupted by a jarring, disruptive, and disturbing experience he has on the Ruprechtsplatz in Vienna's inner city. On this square stands a building that houses a synagogue, a kosher restaurant, and the Jewish community center, and the narrator is thrown into total disorientation when he hears the voices of Jewish children singing the Christmas songs "Jingle Bells" and "Silent Night" in English (44/37). This experience of cultural discrepancy is heightened by an atmospheric contrast between the summer-like temperatures of the day and the themes of winter and snow intoned in these songs. The narrator awakens the next morning with memories of this disjunctive experience, intent on the impression that during the night he crossed a vast waterway. He imagines himself on the gangway of a ship, and he resolves to spend the day visiting the poet Ernst Herbeck in Klosterneuburg, before taking the night train to Venice (44/37–8). The motifs of water and ship travel invoke themes from Kafka's "Gracchus," but also allude to the unconscious prods that motivate Gustav von Aschenbach, in Thomas Mann's novella *Der Tod in Venedig* (*Death in Venice*)—a further significant intertext for "All'estero"—to travel to Venice.[98]

Both Herbeck and Aschenbach reinforce the association of creative authorship, pathology, and perambulation. Mann's Aschenbach encounters the mysterious man at the cemetery who incites his sudden wish to travel when wandering through the streets of Munich after spending the morning sitting at his desk writing. Like Sebald's narrator, he too is a character for whom wandering on foot figures as a substitute for the labor of writing. Moreover, his travels lead to emotional, mental, and physical debilitation. The physical and psychological decline that Sebald's first-person narrator experiences in Vienna replicates in many respects the degradation Aschenbach undergoes as he pursues the beautiful youth Tazio through the streets of Venice. When Sebald's narrator travels to the town of Klosterneuburg just outside of Vienna, he is also enacting a many-faceted return: renewing, first of all, his acquaintance with the schizophrenic poet Ernst Herbeck; returning to a place he visited with his friend Olga, just two years earlier; and visiting the locale of Kafka's death. As the Kafka scholar Sebald well knew, the Prague writer spent the final days of his life at a clinic for tuberculosis patients near this town. This episode not only permits Sebald to reinforce the connections between pathology and literary authorship— Herbeck, we are told, has "been afflicted with mental disorders ever since his twentieth year" ("leidet seit seinem zwanzigsten Lebensjahr an seelischen Störungen"; *Schwindel* 44/38)—but also to elaborate on the theme of Jewish abjection and oppression in the Christian world of Central Europe, which is announced by the emanation of English-language Christmas songs from the Jewish community center in the heart of Vienna.

Herbeck is associated with the writer as wanderer by the subtle detail that he wears a "hiking badge" ("Wanderabzeichen") on the lapel of his coat (46/39). But this parallel is underscored when we learn that his institutionalization occurred just a year after the end of World War II, when he was found aimlessly wandering the streets of Vienna and was unable to provide the police with a clear explanation

---

98 Thomas Mann, "Der Tod in Venedig," in *Gesammelte Werke*, 12 vols (Frankfurt am Main: Fischer, 1960), 8:446–7; *Death in Venice*, trans. Michael Henry Heim (New York: HarperCollins, 2004), 5–6.

of his activities (45/38). The proximity of his bout with insanity to the end of the war suggests that it is a response to the trauma of war itself and the post-war period. Although Herbeck himself is not an immediate victim of the Nazis, and hence may not suffer from what Dominick LaCapra calls "historical trauma" in relation to the political oppression of this period, he is figured as an individual particularly susceptible to what LaCapra dubs "structural trauma," which marks the resonance of traumatizing historical events in those who are only indirectly affected.[99] In this respect, Herbeck shares a central trait that distinguishes many of Sebald's first-person narrators: he exhibits an especially acute empathetic sensitivity to the historical trauma suffered by others, to the point that it leaves a lasting psychic imprint on his life. This connection between Herbeck's psychological fragility and his personal experiences during the war is hinted at in the brief biographical sketch Sebald's narrator provides. Already in 1940 Herbeck entered a clinic, due to an eating and sleep disorder precipitated by his work as an apprentice in a munitions factory. What Herbeck designates as the most oppressive feature of his family life is his father's severe or caustic rationalizing (45/38), which was "corroding his nerves" ("zersetzte ihm … die Nerven"; 45/38).

Precisely this vague, scarcely articulable interconnection of the political oppression characteristic of the Nazi and post-war era with the rigorous rationality and discipline of the father constitutes a further leitmotif in Sebald's oeuvre. It resurfaces in a childhood recollection recorded in "Il ritorno in patria," where the castration anxieties the young boy experiences in face of the all-powerful father are mingled with the figure of the barber the father insists he visit every month, and whose name, "Köpf," is etymologically related to the German verb for beheading, "köpfen" (266/243).[100] A structurally and thematically parallel episode occurs near the beginning of *Austerlitz*, when the unnamed first-person narrator visits the fortress of Breendonk and associates the torture chamber used by the SS with the butcher shop in his hometown of W., the washroom in his home, and the "scrubbing brush" ("Wurzelbürste") wielded by his father as a "cleansing" tool or an instrument of punishment (*Austerlitz* 37/25). The experience of Breendonk catapults Sebald's narrator back to the horrors of his

---

99 Dominick LaCapra, *Writing History, Writing Trauma* (Baltimore, MD: Johns Hopkins University Press, 2001), 76–9.
100 Laufer, "Unheimliche Heimat," 248–9, stresses the castration anxiety inherent in this scene. See also Mark M. Anderson, "Wo die Schrecken der Kindheit verborgen sind: W. G. Sebalds Dilemma der zwei Väter," *Literaturen* 7/8 (2006): 35, who reads this episode as an autobiographical allusion to the difficult relationship Sebald had with his father.

childhood, which are evocatively associated with the father and this bristly brush.[101] In a gesture typical of Sebald's fictions, personal and universal history are co-mingled.

These allusions to the war, to oppressive father figures, and to the Holocaust as an undercurrent still extant in daily life in post-war Austria come to a head when Herbeck and the narrator return to Klosterneuburg and are confronted with the sight of an especially decrepit concrete-block building, with boarded-up windows on the ground floor and an absent roof marked by scattered iron reinforcement bars. As if to prove that such a dilapidated edifice could still be standing in Klosterneuburg, a tightly cropped illustration of this building's facade interrupts the narrative (see Figure 2.7). The ominous aura of destruction and decay that surrounds this structure is made palpable by the reactions it evokes in the narrator and Herbeck. On the former it leaves an impression of "witnessing a hideous crime" ("den Eindruck eines schweren Verbrechens"), while the latter averts his gaze and accelerates his gait (51/43–4). When the narrator refers to it as a "fearful monument" ("das furchtbare Denkmal"; 51/44), we are left to wonder exactly what it memorializes. Is it a remnant of the war's destruction? An edifice that played a role in the politics of Nazi oppression? Or simply a condemned structure whose state of disrepair represents a symbolic "monument" to the "hideous crime" of the past?[102] While prompting such suggestive questions, the text leaves them provocatively open. Only the children's voices emanating from the nearby school can suspend the stupor into which Herbeck and the narrator have fallen (51/44).

Yet these singing voices do not bring genuine relief—certainly not for the readers of Sebald's text, nor for its narrator, who are reminded of the voices of the children intoning Christmas songs at the Jewish community center, an experience the narrator had recounted just prior to his visit with Herbeck (44/37). Although brief and seemingly insignificant, the disruption created by this second set of children's voices becomes burdened with ominous meaning: "A little further on, the children inside the primary school were singing, the most appealing sounds coming from those who could not quite manage to hit the right notes" ("Ein paar Häuser weiter sangen die Kinder in der Volksschule. Am schönsten die, denen es nicht recht gelang, den Bogen der Melodie einzuhalten"; 51/44). The staccato-like character of these sentences is consistent with the broken, paratactic style that

---

101 On Sebald's persistent association of the father with the pain of childhood, see Anderson, "Wo die Schrecken," 35.

102 Niehaus, "Ikonotext. Bastelei," 165, also reads this illustration as an image of trauma.

Figure 2.7: Dilapidated building in Klosterneuburg (*Schwindel* 51/44).

dominates this episode. The word "Volksschule," which designates
a primary school, but which literally means "school for the *Volk*,"
invokes the discourse of National Socialism, with its proclivity for
compound words containing the ideologically-charged element *Volk*,
such as *Volksgenosse* ("compatriot"), *Volksgericht* ("people's court")
or *Volksschädling* ("national pest"), to cite just a few examples. These
implications are reinforced by the tacit contrast with the voices from
the Jewish community center. Moreover, the semantic tension between
the Jewish "community" ("Gemeinde") and a racially defined nation
("Volk") stands emblematically for larger political tensions. But the
narrator's sense that the voices of those children who can't quite

follow the melody—the subtlety of Sebald's German is lacking in the English translation—are ultimately the most beautiful ones is also rife with deeper implications: beauty is equated with nonconformity, with deviance from the "party line," or with divergence from the lock-step of social demands.

The episode relating the narrator's visit with Herbeck, which itself constitutes a break in the overall narrative trajectory, is itself breached at this juncture by an analepsis that recounts how the narrator stood in front of this very school two years earlier. On that occasion he was accompanying his acquaintance Olga (Clara in the English translation) to Klosterneuburg so that she could visit her grandmother, who lived there in a home for the aged (52–4/44–6). This subplot is marked by the same kind of foreboding historical-political innuendo that characterizes the Herbeck episode more generally. After visiting her grandmother, Olga pays a visit to this same school building, which she had attended as a child. To her own surprise, this simple act of nostalgia results in a fit of tears and a state of emotional distress:

> In einem der Klassenzimmer, ebendem, in dem sie zu Beginn der fünfziger Jahre gesessen hatte, unterrichtete, fast dreißig Jahre darauf, mit unveränderter Stimme dieselbe Lehrerin und ermahnte die Kinder nicht anders als damals, bei der Arbeit zu bleiben und nicht zu tuscheln. Allein in dem großen Vorraum, umgeben von den geschlossenen Türen, die ihr seinerzeit wie hohe Pforten erschienen waren, wurde Olga, wie sie mir später erzählte, von einem Weinkrampf ergriffen. Jedenfalls befand sie sich, als sie wieder auf die Albrechtstraße herauskam, wo ich auf sie wartete, in einem Zustand der Erschütterung, wie ich ihn noch nicht bemerkt hatte an ihr. (*Schwindel* 52)
> [In one of the classrooms, the very one where she had been taught in the early 1950s, the selfsame schoolmistress was still teaching, almost thirty years later, her voice quite unchanged—still warning the children to keep at their work, as she had done then, and also not to chatter. Alone in the entrance hall, surrounded by closed doors that had seemed at one time like mighty portals, Clara was overcome by tears, as she later told me. At all events, when she came out she was in such a state of distress as I had never seen her in before. (*Vertigo* 44–5)]

Stylistically this account develops with a syntax that is more labyrinthine and convoluted than the staccato-like parataxis in which the narrator's and Herbeck's encounter with the uncanny, dilapidated building is related. It is as though in its continual interruption of the main clause by subclauses, the language of this passage were attempting to imitate how the primary plot line has been broken by a subplot, a set of recollections on the part of the narrator and the emotional response by his friend Olga to the unanticipated and unpleasant return to her childhood. The thrust of the scenario clearly links up with the themes of involuntary memory and the haunting of the present by the political and emotional past. In both examples, moreover, the import of these experiences is made manifest solely in the emotional reactions of the characters, without any explanatory commentary. The common denominator is a theme that lies at the heart of Sebald's work more generally: the continuity of the past in the present, or as the narrator formulates it here, Olga's "unexpected encounter with her past" ("die unversehene Wiederkunft der Vergangenheit"; 52/45).

We recall that in his application to the German Literaturfonds, Sebald had announced this very problematic as one of his most pressing themes: "Memory as such. How everything is buried and yet still comes to light again" ("Überhaupt das Gedächtnis. Wie alles verschüttet wird und dann doch wieder zutag kommt"; "Literaturfonds" 3). In that respect this episode looks ahead to the stories of *Die Ausgewanderten*, especially its inaugural tale, "Dr. Henry Selwyn," which articulates this fusion of the return of memory with the return of the dead in the summary statement at its conclusion: "And so they are ever returning to us, the dead" ("So also kehren sie wieder, die Toten"; *Ausgewanderten* 36/23). We are reminded once again how in Sebald's application materials his first two literary projects coalesce into a single work in which diverse storylines would be loosely bound together under the framing device of the literary almanac. The striking concatenation of subplots that characterizes this section of "All'estero" represents an instantiation of this almanac-like structure.

The episode in which Sebald's narrator reminisces about his earlier encounter with Olga has deeper implications, for the name of this woman's grandmother, Anna Goldsteiner, as well as the specific ailment from which she suffers, chronic memory loss, suggest that she may have been a Jewish victim of Nazi persecution. Her forgetfulness has reached such extremes that she no longer remembers the names of her three deceased husbands, and she must be institutionalized because she is unable to perform the simple tasks of daily life. The Nazi past, the destruction of the war, the political persecution of the Jews, and the continuity into the present time of narration of those mentalities that generated these problems: these are the themes that are craftily—and with narrative craft—intertwined in this excursus relating the narrator's visit to Klosterneuburg. After pursuing these narrative "tangents," the narrator returns to the ideational frame that unifies this collection through an account of the narrator's fantasies as he looks out of the window of Anna Goldsteiner's room. In his imagination, the landscape surrounding the building is transmogrified into a turbulent sea. As though lost in a daydream, the narrator envisions himself aboard a ship, the mainland gradually receding, and with the sound of a foghorn in his ears. As his phantasmagoric ship journey develops it is contrapuntally interwoven with the activities going on in Anna Goldsteiner's room, the attentions of her granddaughter, and the sounds and actions of the other residents in the hallway (53–4/45–6). This fantasy resonates with the motivic thread of Gracchus's sea journey, and the specter of this ghostly revenant is relevant to the narrated situation itself. Anna Goldsteiner will perish just three weeks hence, as the narrator reveals (54/46), and she exists quite literally in that nether realm between life and death to which Gracchus is condemned. The sailor the narrator imagines on the deck of a steamer, "signaling in semaphore with two colourful flags" ("machte mit zwei bunten Flaggen komplizierte semaphorische Zeichen"; 54/46), constitutes a mirrored reflection of the narrator himself, who throughout this excursus has been sending out a plethora of subtle semiotic hints. But the narrator's recollection of this episode culminates in an imaginative "crystallization," to borrow Stendhal's metaphor once more, that analogizes this act of mnemonic reconstruction with the infinite journey of Kafka's undead Gracchus.

I have devoted such detailed attention to an analysis of the Herbeck episode and its concatenation of sub-stories because it exemplifies many of the techniques that will eventually evolve into staple components of Sebald's mature narrative style. The close scrutiny of how this narrative passage—and it is indeed a *passage*—evolves provides us with a glimpse into Sebald's workshop as the emerging writer of prose fictions. The digressive, literally ex-cursive character of this section of "All'estero" is in itself significant. Insofar as this episode deviates from the general flow of Sebald's overriding narrative, it resembles the voices of the children singing songs at the primary school, who either cannot, or who refuse to follow the dictates of the melody. Moreover, if this divarication from the prescribed tune is what strikes the narrator as most appealing about this performance (51/44), then by analogy we are encouraged to ascribe the most aesthetic significance to those passages in Sebald's text(s) that appear to be most marginal, divergent, and disjunctive—the ones that highlight discrepancies and invoke sensations of vertigo. Put differently, Sebald's narratives are most engrossing and most meaningful where they are most nomadic, where they stray and wander, and yet where—like the peregrinations of the narrator in Vienna, which are mysteriously restricted to a closely circumscribed terrain—they nevertheless return to a defined set of themes and motifs. This segment also anticipates the complex pattern of narrative sequencing and transitioning that will become typical of Sebald's later texts. What we witness here is a preliminary, if yet immature form of that narrative nesting, a Chinese-box or Russian-doll structure, that will become a defining feature of Sebald's most mature texts. Embedded in the overall frame relating the narrator's trip to Vienna and Italy we have the episode of the narrator's visit to Herbeck, which itself becomes a narrative frame for the analepsis recounting the previous trip to Klosterneuburg with Olga, which in turn contains this acquaintance's experience of the traumatic return of her childhood past and the story of her grandmother's death from advanced Alzheimer's disease. What we do not yet witness is the passing of the narrative baton, the first-person pronoun, from one character to another, as we find in later texts such as the stories in *Die Ausgewanderten* or, in strategically exaggerated form, in *Austerlitz*. In "All'estero," only Sebald's first-person narrator has the privilege of saying "I," and to that extent Sebald's "periscopic" narrative technique is not yet fully developed.

There are further features of the analyzed passage from "All'estero" that mark it as a developmental station, a kind of narrative training ground that betrays Sebald's efforts at honing some of his more characteristic narrative, fictional, and metafictional practices. We have noted how the diverse threads of the various subplots converge around themes that become mainstays in Sebald's fictions, such as the traumatic return of the past, the continuity of past and present, the persistence of anti-Semitism and its psychological repercussions, the questionable momentum of conformity, and the persistent dynamic of remembrance and forgetting. But similarly representative of Sebald's approach is his roundabout, suggestive, or oblique take on these issues. Already in this episode we experience the compelling allusiveness of his style, his ability to invoke powerful implications on the basis of simple, seemingly marginal observations, and to document the impact of events mediately via the psychological responses of the participants or witnesses. Sebald is sharpening his skill for depicting events, personal experiences, and perceptions that seem to hover in an interpretive vacuum, while simultaneously drawing out the common thread that ties them together. At the same time, his first-person narrator liberates himself from the reliance on textual resources like Stendhal's *Life of Henry Brulard* or Kafka's letters and diaries. As a result, he can invest more fully in the memories and fantasies generated by this narrator himself, as the reflex of the imaginative and invented. This does not mean that the narrator's intertextual allusions disappear, but only that they become less clearly marked and are gradually subsumed into the dominant consciousness of the narrating voice itself. Thus whereas in "Beyle" and "Dr. K." the intertexts serve above all to document the states of mind of these two historical figures, the intertextual allusions to Freud and Wittgenstein in "All'estero" function so as to characterize the psychology, attitudes, and activities of this *narrator* himself. We witness how the transition from biographic criticism to autobiographic storytelling manifests itself in a transformation of Sebald's intertextual practices.

The examination of an episode from "Il ritorno in patria" can serve as further evidence that the texts of *Schwindel. Gefühle* should be considered transitional works in which Sebald is experimenting with narrative, fictional, textual, linguistic, stylistic, and visual strategies that will mature in his later prose narratives. This passage anticipates in salient ways the relationship between first-person narrator and informant that becomes a hallmark of Sebald's subsequent works. The episode in question occupies more or less the middle section of this story, after the narrator hikes to the village, takes up residence in the Engelwirt where his family lived during his childhood, and reflects on the anxiety the frescoes of the local painter Hengge have invoked in him. In his first days in W., the narrator is overcome by a veritable fit of paralysis, rendering him unable to leave the confines of the hotel (223/204). Only after ten days can he bring himself to seek out his childhood acquaintance Lukas Seelos, whom he meets several times to share stories about the past and discover the fate of the members of Lukas's family and other villagers (229/210). Over the next twenty or so pages, Lukas's reminiscences about the past, his stories about his family, and his reflections about the vagueness of memories mingle with the narrator's own recollections, his tales about the Café Alpenrose run by aunts Bina and Babette, and his childhood visits with his grandfather who played cards with these two spinsters (229–50/210–29). This textual segment culminates in the visit to the attic in Lukas's house, where the narrator encounters the gray hunter he was taught to fear as a child. In this episode his reminiscences are intertextually interwoven with elements drawn from Kafka's short story "Auf dem Dachboden" (Up in the attic). This larger episode is remarkable insofar as it represents the first sustained encounter of Sebald's first-person narrator with an informant who shares stories about the past. Throughout this section the narrator relates Lukas's speech in indirect discourse, clearly marked in the German text by the use of the subjunctive voice. The narrator is careful to remind us at strategic junctures that it is Lukas whose speech and thoughts are being reported, and phrases such as "he observed" or "Lukas said" are strategically interspersed throughout this report. Only after their first meeting and exchange of initial reminiscences does the narrator begin to generate his own detailed recollections about his childhood experiences in W. (235/215). With the assistance of clues supplied by Lukas, he now can recount in detail the lives of Bina and Babette (235–43/215–23), including precise descriptions of the two paintings that adorn the walls of the Café and memories about the atlas he was given as a child to keep him occupied while the adults interacted. These ekphrastically described paintings themselves are significant for the narrative: one depicts the pair of lovers who leap from an abyss (238/218), and whose relevance for the theme of suicide was discussed earlier; the other portrays a wild boar disrupting a hunter at his breakfast and bears the ominous title "*Im Ardennerwald*," an allusion not only to the Hunter Gracchus motif, but also invoking horrors like the ominous Battle of the Ardennes Forest (242/222).[103] Sebald's readers begin to wonder where the narrator's memories end and his imaginative fictions about this past begin, since these recollections seem both too fantastic and simultaneously too appropriate to the story's overriding themes to be matters of simple fact.

One could go on at length about the importance of this episode as a thematic nodal point for this text in particular, and for *Schwindel. Gefühle* more generally. But what interests us here is the status of this episode as prototype for those encounters between Sebald's first-person narrator and his central informants that become mainstays of his later work, culminating in the final story of *Die Ausgewanderten*, "Max Aurach," and the extended interchange between the narrator and Jacques Austerlitz that structures Sebald's last and most extensive prose narrative. Many of the traits of Sebald's more mature narrative style, to be sure, are not yet apparent in the encounter between the narrator and Lukas Seelos in "Il ritorno." For example, the indirect speech of the narrator's informant is consistently marked here through the use of the subjunctive, whereas in Sebald's later fictions a subtle shift from subjunctive to indicative voice throws open questions about whose thoughts are being related. Closely aligned with this, Lukas is always referred to in the third person and never takes over the first-person voice, which is reserved for the perspective of Sebald's autobiographical narrator. Nor do we encounter any of the Chinese-box patterns that distinguish Sebald's later narratives, where one informant recounts the discourse of another informant who recounts the discourse of another, as is especially characteristic of the narrative structure of *Austerlitz*. As a result, this episode also lacks those complex attributions of person, such as "said Vera, said Austerlitz," which Sebald copied from the narrative style of his beloved Thomas Bernhard. In "Il ritorno," Sebald is experimentally probing this narrative configuration in which first-person narrator and informant exchange information, reconstruct memories, and share stories; but what distinguishes the structure of this configuration in the

---

103 Both paintings represent unmarked intertextual borrowings from a letter Franz Kafka wrote to his fiancée Felice Bauer. See *Briefe 1913–1914*, 110; *Letters to Felice*, 205–6.

encounter between Lukas and the first-person narrator is that the roles of memory-stimulator and memory-recoverer are largely reversed. In Sebald's mature fictions it is the probing research, the questions, and—above all—the attentive and patient listening of the first-person narrator that tease out memories and information from his interlocutors and informants. By contrast, in this episode from "Il ritorno" the informant Lukas and his recollections serve as the catalyst for the narrator's own childhood memories. Hence it is only after meeting Lukas that the narrator can recreate his most intimate recollections about his childhood and the individuals in W. Aside from the extended exposition of the lives of Bina and Babette, the narrator now can reconstruct an entire series of childhood events: the life and death—by apparent suicide, naturally—of Dr. Rambousek (250–6/229–34); the story of the Engelwirt waitress Romana and her liaison with the hunter Hans Schlag (256–61/234–40)—himself a figure imported from Kafka's story "Auf dem Dachboden"; the tale of the narrator's childhood love for the schoolteacher Fräulein Rauch—whose family name means "smoke," *nomen est omen*—and who functions as chronicler of all the catastrophes that have shaped the village's history (262–4/240–1); the story about the death of Hans Schlag himself, who turns out to be the living avatar of Kafka's Hunter Gracchus (268–72/245–9); and even the severe illness he experienced shortly after learning of Hunter Schlag's mysterious fall to his death (272–5/249–52). Only once these memories have been recollected and duly recorded can Sebald's narrator, who reflects self-consciously about being bent over his papers and working tirelessly on his "writing" ("Aufzeichnungen"; 276/252), complete his "return home" and commence his journey through the wasteland of modern Germany back to his place of residence in England.

If the pseudo-autobiographical texts from *Schwindel. Gefühle* describe a journey that traverses a geographical circle, Sebald's travels across the terrain of fictional prose narratives also follow a circle of sorts, manifesting in the reminiscences that constitute the last half of "Il ritorno in patria" precisely that kind of literary endeavor Sebald envisioned in the March 1988 project description for the German Literaturfonds, with whose analysis this chapter began. Starting with the narrator's encounter with Lukas Seelos, through to his departure from the village, Sebald's narrator has produced precisely that type of literary almanac, modeled on Johann Peter Hebel's *Kalendergeschichten*, that he described in his application prospectus. He has not only produced "a prose work with illustrations" ("eine Prosaarbeit mit Bildern") that deals, among other things, with the misfortune of the writers Stendhal and Kafka ("Literaturfonds" 2), but has also created a literary topography that, as he says in his prospectus, "can develop, or even proliferate, in many different directions" ("in viele Richtungen wachsen, ja auswachsen kann"), forcing him to unify this diversity on the basis of "motivic connections" ("motivische Verbindungen"; "Literaturfonds" 4). Sebald also expressed in this exposé his desire to focus on the "retelling of diverse lives from the Seelos family, that are supposed somehow to be depicted synoptically, as if in over-flight" ("Erzählung verschiedener Lebensläufe der Familie Seelos, die irgendwie synoptisch, wie im Überflug erfasst werden sollen"; "Literaturfonds" 2), and precisely this quick, episodic concatenation of individual histories is what his narrator accomplishes in the concluding segments of "Il ritorno." This reinforces the hypothesis that in the texts of *Schwindel. Gefühle*, Sebald is experimenting with those literary possibilities that he envisioned in the 1988 application to the German Literary Foundation. This collection of stories represents the testing- and proving-ground of the peculiar strategies that inform and shape his later, more mature prose fictions. *Schwindel. Gefühle* manifests Sebald's narrative beginnings, not only in terms of his prototypical themes and interests, but also with regard to his exploitation of inter-medial text–image dynamics, experiments with narrative voice, plays with intertextual resonances, and above all exercises in coherent literary fashioning. What Sebald accomplishes with this work is the meaningful concatenation of disparate and widely diverse materials into something that approaches a cohesive and intelligible whole, despite the fact that it largely displays what Jonathan Long calls weak narrative cohesion.[104] He accomplishes this in part by disguising the process of generative emergence these texts betray when examined in the chronological order of their composition, arranging them in a counterpoint that alternates the pseudo-biographical literary deliberations in "Beyle" and "Dr. K." with pseudo-autobiographical reminiscences that replicate that very trans-formation of life into literature that the models of Stendhal and Kafka instantiate. If these works testify to the birth of the prose fictionalizer out of the spirit of literary criticism, they also bring evidence for the incipient emergence of the aesthetic craftsperson who can fashion unity out of the most scattered diversity. What Sebald learns in the composition of *Schwindel. Gefühle* is the art of stringing individual narrative pearls on the leitmotivic strand provided by the story of Kafka's infinite wanderer, the Hunter Gracchus. Surely it is significant that Gracchus is figured as the ghostly writer, the *ghostwriter*, suspended between the immediacy of lived experience and its literary transubstantiation. In this respect he stands as a symbol for the maturation of the prose fictionalist that is in evidence in this, Sebald's first work of literary-fictional narratives. But he also represents Sebald's own suspension between the disparate roles of literary scholar and creative writer, a hybrid position out of which the texts of *Schwindel. Gefühle* emerge.

---

104 Long, *W. G. Sebald*, 91.

Three Sebald's Literary Refinement: "Dr. Henry Selwyn" and Its Textual Predecessor

"My texts are written like palimpsests. They are written over and over again, until I feel that a kind of metaphysical meaning can be read through the writing."

W. G. Sebald[1]

Philological and historical-critical investigations into the works of W. G. Sebald are still in their infancy. This situation is destined to change, given the acquisition of Sebald's literary estate and his private library by the Deutsches Literaturarchiv in Marbach. The Archive itself presented a major exhibition on Sebald and his works from September 2008 through January 2009, titled "Das Leben der Anderen: W. G. Sebald" (The life of others: W. G. Sebald), which highlighted the relationship between materials from Sebald's posthumous papers and central themes of his fictional works. It represented one of the first attempts to shed light on the working method of a writer notorious for his creative use of images and documents, as well as for the frequent incorporation of intertextual citations and allusions.

Sebald is also known for the meditative and self-reflexive character of his writing, and his prose fictions often include metafictional passages that refer to the process of their own composition. One thinks of the narrator's deliberations in "All'estero," as he sits on the terrace of a hotel in Limone, his papers and notes spread around him, attempting to draw "connections between events that lay far apart but which seemed to me to be of the same order" ("Verbindungslinien

---

1   Kenneth Baker, "W. G. Sebald: Up Against Historical Amnesia," *San Francisco Chronicle*, October 7, 2001, R2.

zwischen weit auseinanderliegenden Ereignissen, die mir derselben Ordnung anzugehören schienen"; *Schwindel* 107/94). It is easy to read this passage as a self-commentary on the *Beziehungswahn*, the mania for connections and coincidences, that forms one of the central impulses of Sebald's writing.[2] This self-reflection also highlights the role of the authorial impresario, who manages the creative work by staging motivic patterns and drawing connective threads. More common than such immediate self-reflections, however, are descriptions of the artistic practices of third parties, whose details invoke Sebald's own style and method. The first chapter of *Die Ringe des Saturn*, for example, contains a series of such seemingly digressive episodes in which the narrator exposes his own writing practice: the longer passage on Thomas Browne's use of metaphors and his labyrinthine sentence structure (*Ringe* 28/18); the narrator's discussions with his colleague Janine Dakyns about Flaubert's literary scruples and philosophy of writing (14–16/7–9); or even his thoughts about Rembrandt's painting *The Anatomy Lesson of Dr. Nicolaes Tulp*, where the apparent anatomical error incorporated in the painting is interpreted as a subversive gesture on the part of the artist (25/17). The best known and most widely affirmed self-commentary on Sebald's method and practice of writing is found in the story "Max Aurach," where the narrator explicitly compares the obsessive revisions this artist undertakes in his paintings to his own "Skrupulantismus," the constant and deliberate correcting and rewriting of the manuscript of this very piece:

> Dieser Skrupulantismus bezog sich sowohl auf den Gegenstand meiner Erzählung, dem ich, wie ich es auch anstellte, nicht gerecht zu werden glaubte, als auch auf die Fragwürdigkeit der Schriftstellerei überhaupt. Hunderte von Seiten hatte ich bedeckt mit meinem Bleistift- und Kugelschreibergekritzel. Weitaus das meiste davon war durchgestrichen, verworfen oder bis zur Unleserlichkeit mit Zusätzen überschmiert. Selbst das, was ich schließlich für die "endgültige" Fassung retten konnte, erschien mir als ein mißratenes Stückwerk. (*Ausgewanderten* 344–5)
> [These scruples concerned not only the subject of my narrative, which I felt I could not do justice to, no matter what approach

---

2   See Marcel Atze, "Koinzidenz und Intertextualität: Der Einsatz von Prätexten in W. G. Sebalds Erzählung 'All'estero'," in *W. G. Sebald*, ed. Franz Loquai (Eggingen: Edition Isele, 1997), 152–3, who explores this mania for connections and its tendency to stimulate a similar drive in Sebald's readers. Bianca Theisen, "Prose of the World: W. G. Sebald's Literary Travels," *Germanic Review* 79, no. 3 (2004): 168, calls this reflex a "referential mania" and relates it to a "paranoia of misguided semiosis."

I tried, but also the entire questionable business of writing. I had covered hundreds of pages with my scribble, in pencil and ballpoint. By far the greater part had been crossed out, discarded, or obliterated by additions. Even what I ultimately salvaged as a "final" version seemed to me a thing of shreds and patches, utterly botched. (*Emigrants* 230–1)]

This passage provides a salient description of what Sebald called the palimpsest-like quality of his writing, his proclivity for near-obsessive reformulation, until the proper tone, atmosphere, or resonance could be achieved—as he notes in the interview with Kenneth Baker cited in the epigraph to this chapter. This diffidence toward his own ability to "capture" his subject in writing—a diffidence with which Sebald was intimately familiar from the critical self-reflections of such admired writers as Kafka and Flaubert—leads to a seemingly never-ending process of revisions and rewriting. Even the most fleeting glance at Sebald's manuscripts indicate that this represents an accurate account of the painstakingly deliberate and self-critical manner with which he approached the writing process. In the early stages of a project he concentrated on smaller segments of text, subjecting these passages to frequent and minute rewriting. One thing that stands out at this point is that, instead of correcting earlier versions on the manuscript pages themselves, Sebald frequently reworked an entire passage, even when making only minor stylistic changes. His method is generally characterized by a pronounced pattern of repetition, so that the only way to "get it right" was by continued reformulation and reiteration. This is indicative of Sebald's keen stylistic sensitivity, his awareness that the alteration of a single word can profoundly influence its immediate textual environment. It is also symptomatic of a kind of writing whose aim, as Sebald remarks in the cited interview, is to hone the text in such a manner that its "metaphysical meaning" increasingly shines through. Given this "hands-on" approach to the process of rewriting, one can also better understand Sebald's notorious rejection of computers and text-processing software: such mechanical tools caused disruptions of the physical flow of language from head to hand, to pen or pencil, and to paper.[3]

---

3   One is reminded of the description of the bent posture of the writer, accompanied by a photograph of a child hunched over a writing desk, pencil in hand, that Sebald included in the story "Max Aurach" (*Ausgewanderten* 255–6/171–2). Sebald was also familiar with Vladimir Nabokov's *Speak, Memory: An Autobiography Revisited*, Penguin Classics (London: Penguin, 2000), which includes in the unpaginated illustrative section a photograph depicting Nabokov at his writing table. Given the role Nabokov and his memoir play in

The purpose of the present chapter is to provide some insights into Sebald's "revisionist" writing practice by examining some of the transformations he undertook between the penultimate and the final versions of the story "Dr. Henry Selwyn." This analysis is possible because Sebald published a substantially different earlier version of this story prior to its final printing as the introductory tale of *Die Ausgewanderten*. Since Sebald tended either to destroy or reuse his manuscript pages once a work had attained definitive published form, in many cases the archival materials provide only a limited view into the writer's workshop.[4] The earlier rendition of this tale appeared in the influential literary journal *Manuskripte* in 1988, a full four years before its ultimate printing in the first edition of *Die Ausgewanderten*. Generally speaking, the divergences between these two texts are few enough to supply a manageably limited set of examples. At the same time, the changes Sebald introduced sometimes shift the significance of central passages, and they also shed light on the ways he sought to steer the thematic emphasis and the "metaphysical meaning" of this work. This comparative, historical-critical analysis is intended to provide some insight into our as yet rudimentary knowledge about Sebald's practice of writing; but it also supplies clues as to how, at this relatively early stage of his creative writing career, Sebald's method of composition was evolving and maturing. This investigation demonstrates that at the later stages of revision, Sebald was concerned primarily with strategies of refinement that highlight and underscore central ideas, but that also enhance the rhizomatic character of the text. Yet in rewriting he was not only occupied with marking out "connective lines," but also with obscuring some of those lines that may have seemed either too obvious or textually out of place. This process of revision turns on a dialectical balance between honing for precision and clarity, and loosening the textual threads so as to create openings for interpretive speculation and engagement on the part of the reader.

The first published version of "Dr. Henry Selwyn" appeared under the title "Vezehret das letzte selbst die Erinnerung nicht?" (Does not the last thing even consume memory?). These words are drawn from Friedrich Hölderlin's (1770–1843) poem "Elegie," written in 1800, a sustained melancholic deliberation on the experience of loss and

Die Ausgewanderten, the illustration in "Max Aurach" likely contains an intertextual allusion to this photograph.

4   The materials related to "Dr. Henry Selwyn" in the Marbach archive do not contain any handwritten manuscripts, but only a typescript of the original printing from the journal *Manuskripte* that was modified for the final version. See folder 1 of the file "*Die Ausgewanderten*," inventory number HS.2004.0001.00009. The archived materials do include, in a second folder, the documentary and illustrative materials Sebald collected for this story.

its emotional consequences. The environment in which these words appear in Hölderlin's elegy suggests their relevance for the thematic Sebald pursues in this text and the stories of *Die Ausgewanderten* more generally.

> Darum irr' ich umher, und wohl, wie die Schatten, so muß ich
> Leben und sinnlos dünkt lange das Übrige mir.
> Danken möcht' ich, aber wofür? verzehret das Lezte [*sic*]
> Selbst die Erinnerung nicht?[5]
> [Thus I wander aimlessly about, like the shades; this is how I must live, and everything else has long struck me as senseless. I would like to express my gratitude, but for what? Does not the final thing even consume memory?]

Like the lyrical I of Hölderlin's poem, Henry Selwyn—in this regard similar to Sebald's other exiles—lives like a shade, his existence rendered meaningless by a past he can scarcely grasp or even recall. Sebald's choice of title thus reflects on the central themes of the story. In the text printed in *Die Ausgewanderten*, Sebald displaces Hölderlin's words from the title to the status of an epigraph. Curiously, whereas in the initial publication he accurately renders Hölderlin's words and his somewhat idiosyncratic punctuation, when rendered as an epigraph for "Dr. Henry Selwyn" these words undergo a marked transformation:

> Zerstöret das Letzte
> die Erinnerung nicht (*Ausgewanderten* 5)
> [And the last remnants
> memory destroys (*Emigrants* 1)]

By printing the motto as two lines, Sebald retains the allusion to the verse form they had in Hölderlin's "Elegie"; however, by dropping the original punctuation, in particular the question mark, he renders the statement radically equivocal. In the context of Hölderlin's poem, despite a principal grammatical ambiguity, the abstract noun "das Lezte" ("the last/final thing") is the subject of the sentence and "Erinnerung" ("memory") the direct object, implying that temporally (or qualitatively?) "final" or more "recent" things possess the capacity to eradicate memory. When Sebald quotes Hölderlin in his epigraph, the grammatical ambiguity is unresolved: "das Letzte" could be the subject and "Erinnerung" the direct object, but the reverse

---

5   Friedrich Hölderlin, *Sämtliche Werke, Briefe und Dokumente in zeitlicher Folge*, ed. D. E. Sattler, 12 vols (Darmstadt: Wissenschaftliche Buchgesellschaft, 2004), 9:44.

could also be true, so that memory would be that active force that is destroying or consuming the last or final things. Moreover, the elimination of the question mark adds a possible new reading as an imperative. When interpreted in this manner, this statement could be rendered in English as "Destroy the final (or ultimate) thing(s), just not memory." This has proven to be the rendering commonly preferred by interpreters.[6] Sebald encourages this interpretation by means of another revision, his elimination of the emphasizing particle "selbst" ("even"). In Hölderlin's text, this particle not only helps suggest that "Erinnerung," memory, is the direct object of the sentence, but also reinforces the statement's interrogative character. However, the most drastic alteration Sebald introduces is the intensification of Hölderlin's verb "verzehret" ("consume") to the much more drastic "zerstöret" ("destroy").[7] A metaphor of laborious digestion, in which the more positive implication of incorporation is at least potentially suggested, is replaced by the far more absolute idea of violent annihilation. This latter significance is more in keeping with the motifs of destruction and decline that dominate the stories of *Die Ausgewanderten*, themes that will assume special prominence in Sebald's next major prose work, *Die Ringe des Saturn*. If the humorous, more playful tone characteristic of *Schwindel. Gefühle* is still in evidence in the first published version of the Henry Selwyn story, by the final version it has been displaced by the more ominous undertone contained in the verb "zerstöret."

A similar transformation can be witnessed in the changes that take place in Sebald's use of illustrations in the two published versions of this story. "Dr. Henry Selwyn" (and thus *Die Ausgewanderten*) opens, after its ambiguous but menacing epigraph, with the image of a cemetery in which the worn, sometimes precariously leaning tombstones are overshadowed by a tree with a lavish crown (*Ausgewanderten* 7/3) (see Figure 3.1). This illustration sets a tone of mourning and melancholy already before the reader has encountered the narrator's introductory words: it invokes death, the passing of time, forgetfulness, and decline (the dilapidation of the headstones), but also, in a curious dialectic, the vitality of life as manifest in the lush branches of the tree. It also assumes an inner-connective structural function in the collection as a whole, since it forms an intratextual or intramedial linkage with the

---

6   Both Carol Jacobs, *Sebald's Vision* (New York: Columbia University Press, 2015), 22, and Silke Horstkotte, "Pictorial and Verbal Discourse in W. G. Sebald's *The Emigrants*," *Iowa Journal of Cultural Studies* 2 (2002): 38, explicitly maintain that this epigraph should be read as an imperative rather than as a question.

7   This change is noted by Richard Sheppard, "Dexter—Sinister: Some Observations on Decrypting the Mors Code in the Work of W. G. Sebald," *Journal of European Studies* 35, no. 4 (December 2005): 452.

Figure 3.1: Opening illustration of "Dr. Henry Selwyn" (*Ausgewanderten* 7/3).

illustration of Gustave Courbet's *The Oak of Vercingetorix* included in the story "Max Aurach" (*Ausgewanderten* 268/180). By contrast, the illustration with which "Verzehret das Letzte die Erinnerung nicht?" opens has a markedly different tone and function: it presents a youthful image of the author, Max Sebald, riding a bicycle in front of a high stone wall. This photograph includes a caption—this alone is an anomaly in the context of Sebald's later use of illustrations— that reads "Fotografiert von O. im Frühjahr 1971 vor der Mauer von Prior's Gate" ("Photographed by O. in spring 1971 in front of the wall of Prior's Gate"; "Verzehret" 150)[8] (see Figure 3.2). Prior's Gate is the estate at which the narrator first meets the protagonist Henry Selwyn, and at which he and his wife—in this early version she is designated simply as "O.," whereas the final text refers to her by her given name "Clara"—will take up temporary residence. The wall before which the author/narrator rides is identified in the opening lines of each version

---

8   Sheppard, "Dexter–Sinister," 427, has noted this variance in the illustrations, without going into details about the implications.

Fotografiert von O. im Frühjahr 1971 vor der Mauer von Prior's Gate

Figure 3.2: Opening illustration of "Verzehret" (150).

as the "two-metre wall" ("mannshohen Mauer") behind which the manor house lies hidden ("Verzehret" 151; *Ausgewanderten* 8/3). Far from invoking gloom, melancholy, and a dialectic of life and death, this photograph functions more as a tool of documentary verification. By exhibiting the convergence of visual evidence and textual description, it encourages the reader to accept the empirical existence of Prior's Gate and its stone wall. This lends weight to the "factual" and documentary dimension of the story, restricting the play between fact and fiction that is otherwise so characteristic of Sebald's mature writing style, and for which Peter Craven has employed the felicitous descriptor "faction."[9] If in discussions with James Atlas, Sebald baldly asserted, "Facts are troublesome. The idea is to make it seem factual, though some of it might be invented,"[10] then the image Sebald initially used to open this story proved troublesome precisely *because of* its insistence on factuality.

But there is more to it than this. Since this image recognizably depicts the author Sebald himself, it threatens to undercut the strategy by which he keeps the possible identification of author and narrator in suspense. This has the detrimental effect of shifting the weight of Sebald's narrative in the direction of genuine autobiography and

9   Peter Craven, "W. G. Sebald: Anatomy of Faction," *HEAT* 13 (1999): 224.
10 James Atlas, "W. G. Sebald: A Profile," *Paris Review* 41, no. 151 (Summer 1999): 282.

documentary, dispelling at the outset the possibility that it is fiction written through the pose of documentary (auto)biography. In the final version, Sebald is careful to reduce the interventionist presence of his narrator as an empirical subject, highlighting instead a more neutral, functional, and ethereal narrative voice. This depersonalization becomes especially important in the final version, when the text is incorporated into the collection *Die Ausgewanderten*, since this establishes the parameters for a unitary narrative voice that is consistent throughout all these stories, without it being identified narrowly with the empirical author.[11] Finally, the opening illustration in the first rendition manifests a self-reflective playfulness that is more in line with the pseudo-autobiographical tone of *Schwindel. Gefühle*, on which Sebald was working at approximately the same time.[12] Such tricksterlike metafictional reflections become much more muted—although they never disappear—in Sebald's later, more mature works.

Both published renditions of this text contain approximately the same number of images, six in the first and seven in the final version. The placement of the illustrations is also for the most part identical within the textual environment. The one picture that is strikingly absent in "Verzehrt das Letzte selbst die Erinnerung nicht?" is the depiction of Vladimir Nabokov with his butterfly net in an alpine landscape (*Ausgewanderten* 27/16). Its addition in the final version might be related to pragmatic considerations, such as the previous unavailability of the image. But its inclusion is important for the final constitution of *Die Ausgewanderten* if only because the motif of Nabokov as the "Butterfly Man" becomes the unifying thread that links the various stories of this collection into a unified whole. We have already seen how the image of the tree in a cemetery that is the inaugural image of *Die Ausgewanderten* performs a similar function, pointing ahead to the illustration of Courbet's oak in the last story. To understand how important this gesture of motivic interweaving ultimately was for Sebald, we only need refer to one emendation he introduced to the second narrative, "Paul Bereyter," for its final

---

11 On this unitary narrative voice that is maintained throughout Sebald's prose fictions, see E. L. Doctorow, "W. G. Sebald," in *Creationists: Selected Essays, 1993–2006* (New York: Random House, 2006), 147, and also Adam Zachary Newton, "Place from Place, and Place from Flight: W. G. Sebald's *The Emigrants* and Aharon Appelfeld's *The Iron Tracks*," in *The Elsewhere: On Belonging at a Near Distance: Reading Literary Memoir from Europe and the Levant* (Madison: University of Wisconsin Press, 2005), 43, who conceives Sebald's narrator structurally as an "organizing presence."

12 One thinks, in particular, of the parallel image in the story "All'estero" that presents a copy of Sebald's passport photo with a dark bar running perpendicular through his face (*Schwindel* 129/114).

publication. Sebald initially submitted this story, under the title "Und manche Nebelflecken löset kein Auge auf" (There is a mist that no eye can dissolve),[13] when he entered the competition for the Ingeborg Bachmann Prize in 1990, for which he was eventually honored as the runner-up. Aside from differences in paragraphing and the fact that it contains no illustrations, this earlier text is largely identical with the one published in *Die Ausgewanderten*, with one especially notable exception. In "Paul Bereyter" the eponymous protagonist introduces himself to Lucy Landau in Salins-les-Bains when he discovers her sitting on a park bench reading Nabokov's autobiography *Speak, Memory* (*Ausgewanderten* 65/43); in the earlier version the book Lucy is reading, and that causes Paul to notice her and strike up a conversation, is Flaubert's *Education Sentimentale*.[14] Flaubert's novel alludes to the educational and pedagogical themes that play such a prominent role in Paul Bereyter's story, and it thereby served as a thematic nodal point in the earlier version of this tale. In the rendition for *Die Ausgewanderten*, Sebald made the strategic decision to sacrifice this function as *thematic* cornerstone in Bereyter's story for the greater *intra-textual*, cross-referential linkage with the other stories in this collection, formed by the allusion to Nabokov.

Of the remaining images included in this story, the first three in "Dr. Henry Selwyn" are added for the book publication, while of the final four, one is included here for the first time (the picture of Nabokov) and the other three—the picture of Selwyn's "folly," the depiction of the glacial moraine, and the clipping from the Lausanne newspaper reporting on the rediscovery of Johannes Naegeli's body— are employed in both renditions and located at identical places in the text.[15] The three opening illustrations thus display the greatest variance, and we have already examined the significance of the first substitution, the image of the cemetery and tree for the depiction of Sebald on his bicycle. In the narrative as published in *Die Ausgewanderten*, the second and third illustrations evoke the struggle between nature and culture, a theme that dominates this tale. This problematic is addressed early on through the reference to the vines covering the façade of the mansion at Prior's Gate: "the front of the large, neoclassical house

---

13   W. G. Sebald, "Und manche Nebelflecken löset kein Auge auf," in *Klagenfurter Texte: Ingeborg–Bachmann–Wettbewerb 1990*, ed. Heinz Felbsch and Siegbert Metelko (Munich: Piper, 1990), 111–37. In the final version, this title is once again displaced to the position of epigraph when the story assumes the name of its protagonist.

14   Ibid., 124.

15   If it is true, as Newton, "Place from Place," 52–3, has argued, that the order of illustrations in "Dr. Henry Selwyn" tells its own story, then this is a strikingly different tale in the first published version.

was overgrown with Virginia creeper" ("Die Fassade des breit hingelagerten klassizistischen Hauses war überwachsen von wildem Wein";
"Verzehret" 151; *Ausgewanderten* 8/4). The second and third images
in "Dr. Henry Selwyn" underscore how nature is gradually reoccu-
pying the ground that culture had appropriated. The first shows the
grass tennis court that has fallen into a state of disrepair, while the
second portrays the result of leaving "the once well-tended garden
to its own devices" ("Die Verwilderung des einstmals vorbildlichen
Gartens"; "Verzehret" 152; *Ausgewanderten* 14/7), representing decrepit
outbuildings and hothouses that are partially hidden behind an unruly
growth of brush. These illustrations play an important role in the final
version of the text, since they reiterate and metaphorically reflect the
gradual collapse of Henry Selwyn's assumed, highly cultivated, and
assimilative character, indicating how it is being atavistically overtaken
by a natural self, of humble origins, that violently returns out of his
repressed past. The initial victory of artifice over nature is marked
by the protagonist's change of name, from Hersch Seweryn to Henry
Selwyn, which seals his transformation from an anonymous Jewish
refugee from a Lithuanian *shtetl* to a surgeon and social high-roller
married to a wealthy Swiss factory-owner's daughter ("Verzehret" 157;
Ausgewanderten 33–4/20–1).

The first version does not profit from the inclusion of these illustrations that so powerfully invoke this principal problematic in Selwyn's
life. In their place we find two rather nondescript photographs whose
function is more difficult to discern. The first portrays, as its caption
indicates, "Dr. Selwyn" toiling in his garden ("Verzehret" 152). But is it
really Dr. Selwyn? The image plays a cat-and-mouse game with identification, portraying this figure kneeling among the flowers, bent forward
toward the camera, his head and face entirely hidden by a wide-
brimmed gardening hat (see Figure 3.3). The next image appears at first
entirely superfluous, since it simply provides another perspective on
what seems to be the same location in the garden at Prior's Gate, with
an explosion of blossoming anemones, and is appropriately captioned
"Unter den Anemonen" ("Among the anemones"; 152) (see Figure 3.4).
Instead of providing a visual demonstration of the struggle between
nature and culture, and of Selwyn's comment, reported by the narrator,
that "Nature itself was groaning and collapsing beneath the burden we
placed upon it" ("die unbeaufsichtigte Natur … stöhne und sinke in
sich zusammen unter dem Gewicht dessen, was ihr aufgeladen werde
von uns"; "Verzehret" 152; *Ausgewanderten* 13/7), the first picture
shows Selwyn actively *cultivating* nature, and in both photographs
nature appears to be flourishing, unencumbered by the effects of
human civilization. Far from contributing to the thematic texture of the
story, these images are disruptive and strangely out of place. In the first

Figure 3.3: "Dr. Selwyn" from "Verzehret" (152).

Figure 3.4: "Unter den Anemonen" ("Verzehret" 152).

version Sebald apparently sensed the need to incorporate images that documented the state of nature at Prior's Gate, without yet being able to select photographs that both accomplished this and aligned better with the thematic of the struggle between nature and artifice.

A final point should be made about the illustration depicting Henry Selwyn at work in his garden. By including a human character and naming this figure as the story's protagonist, this photograph fulfills a documentary function similar to that identified for the first illustration in this earlier version. If that opening photograph insisted on the empirical existence of the author and narrator, the one depicting and naming Selwyn confirms the existence of his primary interlocutor and the narrative's protagonist. But like the opening illustration, this second one also ironically plays with and makes light of this drive for documentary confirmation: it shows us someone who is purported to be Henry Selwyn, but it conceals him behind his bent posture and the hat that obscures his face. This image hence reinforces the tension between fact and fiction that is operative in Sebald's prose narratives in general, suggesting that there "really" is a Henry Selwyn, but preventing the possibility of definitive identification. Although this photograph fails to invoke the struggle between nature and culture and the "burden" civilization places on the natural world, the cramped posture of the human figure suggests that *Selwyn himself* is crushed by the burden of nature. This interpretation is able to make thematic sense of the image, where such a connection is not otherwise obvious. This is not the case, however, for the comparable illustrations in the version of this story published in *Die Ausgewanderten*, where the images appropriately underwrite the text and its central themes. What we witness in the transformations Sebald enacts in terms of visual material from the earlier to the final version is a general refinement of his skill in exploiting the subtle dialectic between image and text.

I have concentrated thus far on the differences in illustrations because they constitute one of the most obvious transformations Sebald introduces into this story. But there are also a large number of revisions to the text itself, some more extensive, some relatively minor, many of which are significant when viewed with an eye for their impact on thematic consistency and interpretive significance. I will begin with a textual emendation that was likely occasioned by a substitution of illustrations. In "Verzehret" the tennis court is described as being surrounded by a rusty wire-net fence: "The hazel walk led to a tennis court whose wire-net fence had become rough with rust" ("Der Haselgang endete bei einem Tennisplatz, dessen Maschendrahtgitter vom Rost rauh geworden war"; 152). In *Die Ausgewanderten* the complementary sentence reads, "The hazel walk led to a tennis court bounded by a whitewashed brick wall" ("Der Haselgang endete bei einem

Tennisplatz, an dem eine geweißelte Ziegelmauer entlanglief"; 13/7).
This sentence is followed by the picture of the tennis court itself, with
the white brick wall clearly visible, while the rusty fence can barely be
discerned in the background. The text in the final version is altered so
as to better reflect the accompanying illustration. The initial description
of the rust-encrusted fence may have been intended to reinforce the
state of decline governing the manor of Prior's Gate. However, the
tennis court and its fence might also contain an intertextual allusion to
Nabokov's *Speak, Memory*, the very text that eventually dominates the
intertextual dimension of *Die Ausgewanderten*. The second chapter of
that memoir, relating Nabokov's childhood experiences on his family's
country estate Vyra, invokes its dilapidated and "obsolete" tennis
court, which is described as "now a region of moss, mole-heaps, and
mushrooms," and which is separated from the adjoining meadow by
the "wire mesh of an ample enclosure."[16] In the preliminary version the
motif of the dilapidated tennis court thus constitutes one of those intertextual coincidences in which Sebald took particular delight, causing
the decrepit court at Prior's Gate to resonate with the one described
in *Speak, Memory*. In the final version, however, the rusty mesh fence,
which enhances the intertextual connection to Nabokov's work, gives
way to the whitewashed wall whose presence is predominant in the
incorporated illustration.

The kinds of textual alterations Sebald undertook to arrive at the
final form of "Dr. Henry Selwyn" range from substitutions of single
words, through deletions and additions, to heavily reformulated and
rewritten passages. Beginning with the replacement of a simple word,
we can document the complex deliberations and sensitivity to textual
resonance that frequently motivated Sebald's transformations. In the
Manuskripte printing of the story, the opening paragraph describes
how the manor house of Prior's Gate is hidden not merely by a high
wall, but also "behind ... a thick shrubbery of hollies and Portuguese
laurel" ("hinter ... einem dicht ineinandergewachsenenen Gebüsch
aus Stechholder und portugiesischem Lorbeer"; 151). In the final
text, this line is the same except that the adjective "lusitanischem"
replaces "portugiesischem" as a descriptive modifier of the laurel
(*Ausgewanderten* 8). Sebald's translator Michael Hulse apparently did
not know what to make of this adjective, and his English translation,
instead of using the neologism "Lusitanian," employs the same word
as in Sebald's first version, "Portuguese" (*Emigrants* 3). At first glance,
the alteration Sebald introduces appears to be a minimal change.
Geographically speaking, Lusitania is the name of the one-time Roman
province that approximately overlaps with present-day Portugal.

16 Nabokov, *Speak, Memory*, 33–4.

However, for modern readers Lusitania is associated with the British ocean liner of that name sunk by a German U-boat in May 1915, a malicious and brutal attack on a civilian ship that turned worldwide public opinion against the German war effort. Sebald's use of this adjective conjures up this catastrophe. But it also does much more, since it indirectly alludes to the flight of Henry Selwyn and his family by ship from Lithuania—we should note the alliteration (and in English the assonance) that connects Lithuania and Lusitania (in their German adjectival forms, *lusitanisch* and *litauisch*)—to London (although, as we know, their actual destination was New York). Moreover, by invoking one of the principal incidents of World War I, this adjective draws a motivic line to that phase in Selwyn's life that brings about a fundamental transformation: his leave-taking from the mountain climber Johannes Naegeli, to whom he feels powerful emotional attachments, when Selwyn is called up to serve in the English military. Naegeli disappears on the Aar glacier during the war, and news of this death sends Selwyn into a depression of such magnitude that it nearly causes his discharge from the service ("Verzehret" 155; *Ausgewanderten* 24–5/14–15). The adjective "lusitanisch" serves, as the adjective "portugiesisch" could not, as an allusive nodal point that yokes the opening description of Prior's Gate with central events in Selwyn's life and the primary motifs of his story. This move provides evidence of the clever and subtle refinement with which Sebald went about revising this work. By pulling on this one thread, he is able to tighten the weave of the entire text, drawing together its motivic and thematic network into a denser mesh. The semantics of this passage can also be read as an allegorically enciphered reflection on precisely this manner of textual construction: the text is just as densely interwoven as are the laurel bushes this passage describes. It is hard to imagine an example that could better document how Sebald's literary handiwork and artistry are informed by flashes of stylistic brilliance.

If in this instance Sebald's emendation is motivated by a wish to call attention to certain themes and problems, there are also cases where the opposite is true, where he is at pains to cover his tracks and expunge a connection that may appear too obvious or seem stylistically clumsy. An appropriate instance can be found in the second sentence of the text. The *Manuskripte* version reads, "Über Felder, an Hecken entlang, unter ausladenden Eichen hindurch, vorbei an einigen zerstreuten Ansiedlungen, *dort, wo früher Wegkehren gewesen sind*, geht die Straße an die fünfzehn Meilen durchs Land, bis endlich Hingham auftaucht ..." ("for some 25 kilometres the road runs amidst fields and hedgerows, beneath spreading oak trees, past a few scattered hamlets, *at the place where once there were serpentines*, till at length Hingham appears"; 151; emphasis added). The commensurate sentence in the version from *Die

Ausgewanderten is identical, except that the phrase I italicized has been deleted (7–8/3). Why? Probably because the reference to "Wegkehren," to serpentine paths or switch-backs, anticipates too abruptly several of the story's themes, such as the "serpentine" and laborious path Selwyn has traversed in his life. On a semantic and even a semiotic level, this word also contains the root *Kehre*, "turn" or "turning-point," as well as alluding to the prominent motif of *Wiederkehr*, of return, that is manifest most poignantly in the narrator's commentary on the resurfacing of Naegeli's body: "So also kehren sie wieder, die Toten" ("And so they are ever returning to us, the dead"; "Verzehret" 158; *Ausgewanderten* 36/23). This story is replete with returns, most of them unhappy: the return of Selwyn to his past, which ultimately incites him to suicide; the return of the narrator to his memories of Selwyn; the return of Selwyn himself, in spirit if not in flesh, by means of the narrator's recollection of his life. But this is also a tale of difficult turns and turning-points, the most significant of which is Selwyn's abandonment of his past as a Jewish exile and his assumption of an entirely assimilated persona, marked by his change of name. This *Wegkehre*, this switch-back or change in (life's) course, lies at the root of Selwyn's melancholy, and his story relates how he gradually maneuvers a new turn later in life, a *Wegkehre* of another sort, by acknowledging—and bemoaning—this initial change in course. Sebald likely felt that presaging these ideas in the second sentence of the narrative, by referring to *Wegkehren*, was either too precipitous and premature, or too heavy-handed. He may also have been bothered by the adverb "früher" ("once") in the deleted phrase, which highlights the temporal discrepancy between the narrated time and the time of narration by suggesting that these serpentines had existed when the narrator first went to Hingham, but have been removed by the time he begins relating Henry Selwyn's story.[17] Sebald elevates this gesture of removal to a higher level—namely to the dimension of his own editorial practice—when he deletes the passage that describes the eliminated serpentines.

---

17 In one other instance Sebald deletes a temporal marker that alludes too directly to the discrepancy between past and present in Selwyn's life. The narrator and his wife decide to rent rooms in the manor at Prior's Gate because the view through the windows easily compensates for the dank and gloomy interior. In the earlier version, the description of how this interior "versank hinter einem" ("ceased to exist") when one took in the natural surroundings afforded by the view through the windows includes the temporal simile "wie in die Vorzeit" ("as if into prehistoric times"; "Verzehret" 153; cf. *Ausgewanderten* 15/8). In the final version, this temporal comparison is deleted, probably because it too clearly prefigures the temporal discrepancy in Selwyn's life that separates his "dark" and obscure "prehistoric" past from the relative light of his assimilated lifestyle.

A similar, even more significant deletion occurs at the very conclusion of the narrative. The text as printed in *Manuskripte* appends a gnomic utterance at the end of the short, final paragraph.

So also kehren sie wieder, die Toten. Manchmal nach mehr als sieben Jahrzehnten kommen sie heraus aus dem Eis und liegen am Rand der Moräne, ein Häufchen geschliffener Knochen und ein Paar genagelte Schuhe. Denn was Genügen gibt, endet dort, wo es genügt, und wo es endet, genügt es nicht mehr. (158) [And so they are ever returning to us, the dead. At times they come back from the ice more than seven decades later and are found at the edge of the moraine, a few polished bones and a pair of hobnailed boots. For whatever provides satisfaction ends at the moment it satisfies, and when it ends, it no longer satisfies.]

In the final version, the text ends after the word "Schuhe" ("boots"; *Ausgewanderten* 37/23), without any further commentary by the narrator. What are we to make of this curiously paradoxical, structurally chiastic statement with which the earlier version ends? Its logic is circular, since it maintains that the power to satisfy ceases once satisfaction has been granted, but that once this power is suspended it also ceases to satisfy. No doubt, this remark offers a telling commentary on Selwyn's life story, on the impossibility of achieving satisfaction even in the face of social advancement, acquisition of wealth, and successful assimilation. The upshot of this commentary might thus be that even accomplished assimilation fails to bring satisfaction, and that the end of the process of assimilation opens up new needs and desires, such as those for the recovery of the pre-assimilated self. This represents an obvious case where the remark is simply too heavy-handed, intrusive, and ineffectively clumsy, thereby calling for its deletion in the final rendition of the story. In addition, this statement is out of character with the pose the narrator maintains throughout this text, as well as with his language. Nowhere else do we find such objective, gnomic commentary. Indeed, when he utters this aphorism-like conclusion—if it can even be attributed to Sebald's intra-diegetic narrator at all, and not rather to an extra-diegetic, quasi-omniscient commentator—the narrator seems to fall out of his role as empathetic but non-judgmental witness to Selwyn's life and fate. Just as such utterances are out of place in most (but not all) of Kafka's stories and novels, they are also disruptive in Sebald's narratives, since his narrating persona rarely assumes the degree of distanced objectivity that would allow for such a broad-ranging generalization. When he does, these commonly take the form of self-reflections on his own condition or his act of writing. Sebald was following his best instincts when he chose to expunge this sentence for the final text of "Dr. Henry Selwyn."

One of the most important changes that distinguishes the earlier version of this story from the text in *Die Ausgewanderten* relates to the subtle differences in the relationships among the three principal male characters: the protagonist Selwyn, the narrator, and Selwyn's sole visitor, the botanist and entomologist Edward Ellis (whose family name in the earlier rendition of the story is Evans, and who is called Edwin Elliot in the English translation). Ellis is the primary figure in this narrative who has a close, positive connection with Selwyn's past. As we know, Selwyn is alienated from his wife Hedi (Elli in the English translation), and the only other figure with emotional significance in his life, Johannes Naegeli, is long dead. When Selwyn tells the narrator of Ellis's impending visit, he emphasizes the bond they share from past times: this character is described as a "friend with whom he [Selwyn] had been close for many years" ("Freund, mit dem ihn [Selwyn] von früher her vieles verbinde"; "Verzehret" 154; *Ausgewanderten* 20/12). The slides presented during the dinner party, which depict Selwyn and Ellis on a joint trip to Crete that took place ten years previously, develop more fully the nature of their friendship. This friend's visit represents a seminal scene, since this encounter is what induces Selwyn to begin recounting his past. Ellis's appearance functions as a psychic trigger that stimulates the recollection of related but repressed past experiences. The fact that during their visit to Crete the two men were active hiking and mountain climbing suggests that Ellis is a substitute for the deceased mountain guide Naegeli, and hence that the deep emotional bond Selwyn once felt for the Swiss mountaineer has been transferred to this entomologist. The narrator's report on this evening concentrates almost completely on a description of the dinner and the images depicted on the photographic slides, and he gives us little information about the precise relationship between Selwyn and his friend, aside from his impression that the two men viewed the slides from their trip with a certain emotional responsiveness ("nicht ohne eine gewisse Rührung" ("an occasion for some emotion") "Verzehret" 156; *Ausgewanderten* 28/17). This remark supplies the only hint at a possible emotional intimacy in their relationship, and it is important that it arises through the nostalgic connection to a shared past experience.

The earlier version of the text, however, suggests on several levels a greater closeness between these two characters. First of all, Ellis, who is addressed by his first name Edward in the text published in *Die Ausgewanderten*, is consistently referred to by his nickname Ted in the earlier rendition. This implies a greater degree of familiarity than is ever conjured up in the final version of the story. The use of this nickname stands out in a story in which the narrator consistently addresses his primary informant and the tale's protagonist with the extremely formal "Dr. Selwyn." One of the qualities that particularly distinguishes Sebald's narrator as witness is his capacity to fall into the role of his informants. "Verzehret" exaggerates this overlap in perspective when it allows the narrator to refer consistently to Edward with the familiar "Ted," thereby not merely stressing the greater intimacy between Selwyn and his friend, but also indicating that the narrator shares this personal proximity. By eliminating the use of the nickname in the final version, substituting for it instead the use of the full first name Edward, Sebald softens the contrast between the formal and informal means of address and also infuses more distance into the relationship between the two old friends.

The alterations Sebald made to one specific passage underscore how in the shift from the earlier to the later version he is careful to ensure that the bond between Selwyn and Ellis gravitates toward a balance between intimacy and the distance of social propriety. The critical passage immediately follows Selwyn's reminiscence about his leave-taking from Naegeli at the station in Meiringen and the profound suffering this separation caused him. In the final version of the story the narrative continues:

> Aber vielleicht bilde ich mir das nur ein, sagte Dr. Selwyn etwas leiser für sich, weil mir die Hedi die Jahre über in zunehmendem Maße fremd geworden ist, während mir Naegeli, jedesmal, wenn er auftaucht in meinen Gedanken, vertrauter geworden scheint. (*Ausgewanderten* 24)
> [But I may only be imagining it, Dr. Selwyn went on in a lower tone, to himself, since Elli has come to seem a stranger to me over the years, whereas Naegeli seems closer whenever he comes to my mind. (*Emigrants* 14–15)]

The complementary passage in "Verzehret" reads much differently and emphasizes how the narrator and his wife, on the one hand, and Ted Evans, on the other, have become aware of the alienation that increasingly characterizes Selwyn's relationship with his wife:

> Es mag dies natürlich auch damit zu tun haben, daß Hedi mir die Jahre über, wie [S]ie,[18] sagte er zu Ted, ja wissen, und [S]ie, gegen uns gewendet, vielleicht bemerkt haben, in zunehmendem Maße

---

18 The *Manuskripte* text prints a lower-case "s" in the word "sie," an obvious typographical error, since Selwyn is using the formal form of address ("Sie") for Ted Evans.

fremd geworden ist, während mir Nägeli [sic], jedesmal wenn er auftaucht in meinen Gedanken, vertrauter geworden scheint. (155) [This may, of course, be tied to the fact that Hedi has come to seem a stranger to me over the years, as you well know, he said to Ted, and you will have perhaps noticed, he addressed to us, whereas Nägeli seems closer whenever he comes to my mind.]

Several things are striking about these changes. First, Selwyn explicitly points out that his friend Ted is well aware of his growing alienation from his wife, and this suggests an almost substitutive relationship between her and Ted. This might be taken as evidence corroborating the suggestion that the relationship between Selwyn and Ellis, as between Selwyn and Naegeli, is tinged by latent homoeroticism.[19] The alterations Sebald undertook seem to be aimed at playing down such an implication. This is marked in the earlier version by Selwyn's use of the formal mode of address, "Sie," instead of the more intimate "Du," when he speaks directly to Ted. Especially when employed in conjunction with the familiar use of this nickname, the formal "Sie" creates a tension between intimacy and distance. This is what Sebald sought to achieve in this passage, as in the characterization of the relationship between Selwyn and Ellis in general. However, he surely noticed that the contrast between the formal "Sie" and the familiar nickname seemed anomalous, and this likely motivated his revisions. Moreover, in this initial version Selwyn alternately addresses his friend and the relative strangers, the narrator and his wife, and emphasizes the discrepancies in their knowledge about him. Aside from the general unwieldiness of the language, what also militates against the inclusion of this passage is the implication that the narrator, who after all is telling Selwyn's story, is reduced to speculation about this figure, since he clearly does not know him as well as does his long-time friend Ellis.

---

19 For reflections on the possible homosexual implications of the relationship between Selwyn and Naegeli, see Eric Santner, *On Creaturely Life: Rilke, Benjamin, Sebald* (Chicago: University of Chicago Press, 2006), 171. Jörg Drews, "Wie eines jener bösen deutschen Märchen," *Süddeutsche Zeitung* (October 2–4, 1992): x, attributes both Selwyn's and Ambos Adelwarth's sufferings to repressed homosexuality. Maya Barzilai, "Facing the Past and the Female Spectator in W. G. Sebald's *The Emigrants*," in *W. G. Sebald: A Critical Companion*, ed. J. J. Long and Anne Whitehead (Seattle: University of Washington Press, 2004), 203, views the intimate interactions between Sebald's narrator and his informants as highlighting a more general process of male bonding. Helen Finch, *Sebald's Bachelors: Queer Resistance and the Unconforming Life* (Oxford: Legenda, 2013), 3–7, makes the most detailed case for the relationship between Naegeli and Selwyn as inherently homoerotic, reading it as a paradigm for homosexual interactions throughout Sebald's texts.

An equally important alteration in this passage, however, is the qualifying addition that Selwyn's deep pain at the leave-taking from Naegeli might just be a figment of his imagination ("vielleicht bilde ich mir das nur ein"; "But I may only be imagining it"), which constitutes a retrospective projection on Selwyn's part. This idea emerges only in the final version of the text, and it is significant because it opens up questions about the true nature of Selwyn's relationship with Naegeli. Was it really so intimate? Or does Selwyn merely mystify and exaggerate this emotional attachment when he views it through the lens of his nostalgia for the past? Why does Sebald take care to introduce this uncertainty into the final text? The answer is related to the symbolic function both Naegeli and, to a lesser degree, Ellis perform as links to Selwyn's repressed past. If the slideshow from their travels to Crete, depicting the plateau of Lasithi and the mountain Spathi, conjures up mere screen memories, related to the pre-war experiences Selwyn enjoyed with Naegeli in the Swiss Alps, then Naegeli, in turn, might also represent a screen memory for a prior, more fundamental experience of bonding and its tragic loss: for none other than the enigmatic and repressed loss of Selwyn's Lithuanian homeland, which lies at the root of Selwyn's melancholy demeanor.[20] The revisions to this passage play down the emotional bond that links Selwyn to Naegeli and to Ellis so as to emphasize their *symbolic* function as harbingers of the intimacy and emotional security associated with the hominess of Selwyn's lost childhood. This is reinforced by the single positive memory Selwyn is able to recount about life in the Lithuanian *shtetl* into which he was born: the memory of his *cheder* teacher fondly placing his hand on his pupil's head. "I can still see the teacher who taught the children in the *cheder*, where I had been going for two years by then, placing his hand on my parting" ("Ich sehe, sagte er [Selwyn], wie mir der Kinderlehrer im Cheder, den ich zwei Jahre schon besucht hatte, die Hand auf den Scheitel legt"; "Verzehret" 156; *Ausgewanderten* 31/19). His only other memories from this time are of the process of

---

20 See Sigmund Freud, "Über Deckerinnerungen," in *Gesammelte Werke: Chronologisch geordnet*, ed. Anna Freud et al., 18 vols (London: Imago, 1940–87), 1:529–54; "Screen Memories," in *The Standard Edition of the Complete Psychological Works of Sigmund Freud*, ed. and trans. James Strachey, 24 vols (London: Hogarth, 1953–74), 3:301–22. Here Freud describes how more recent memories can substitute for, and thereby conceal (or screen), more primordial, still unconscious, repressed memories that are linked to traumatic experiences. For critical reflections on Sebald's use of screen memories in the construction of his fiction, see Todd Presner, "Vienna–Rome–Prague–Antwerp–Paris, The Railway Ruins of Modernity: Freud and Sebald on the Narration of German/Jewish Remains," in *Mobile Modernity: Germans, Jews, Trains* (New York: Columbia University Press, 2007), 249, 267–8.

emigration itself: the empty rooms of the house prior to departure; the wagon ride to Grodno; the train trip to Riga; and the ship voyage. For Selwyn, *Heimat* is attached to two things: to the intimacy of his male teacher in the *cheder*; and to the experience of departure and loss. These are the very same issues that link him emotionally with Naegeli. We recall that at the time of their friendship, the mountaineer was sixty-five years old while Selwyn was a mere twenty-one ("Verzehret" 155; *Ausgewanderten* 23/13). Sebald's final version emphasizes how Selwyn's relationship with Edward Ellis replicates the mentorship with his *cheder* teacher and the mountain guide Naegeli.

Sebald makes a further emendation that highlights this attempt to stress the manner in which Selwyn's relationship with Ellis repeats his friendship with Naegeli and links up with the central theme of the return of the past. Of course, the entire evening of Ellis's visit, centered on the slide presentation of their trip to Crete, is choreographed so as to stage precisely such a resurgence of the past. Already in "Verzehret," when describing the two men's emotional response upon viewing these slides, the narrator stresses how they silently reconnect with their past experience: "I sensed that, for both of them, the images, in which they resurfaced from their past, provided an occasion for some emotion" ("Ich spürte, daß sie beide die Bilder, auf denen sie aus der Vergangenheit auftauchten, nicht ohne eine gewisse Rührung betrachteten"; 156). The text of the final version retains the idea of their resurfacing out of the past, but it reformulates it in words calculated to highlight the notion of repetition and to anticipate the story's final event, the return of Naegeli's corpse from the Aar glacier. The parallel passage reads, "I sensed that, for both of them, this *return of their past selves* was an occasion for some emotion" ("Ich spürte, daß sie beide ihrer *Rückkehr aus der Vergangenheit* nicht ohne eine gewisse Rührung beiwohnten"; *Ausgewanderten* 28/16–17; emphasis added). The phrase "Rückkehr aus der Vergangenheit" clearly alludes on its semiotic and semantic levels to the "Wiederkehr," the uncanny return of Naegeli's body, as well as to the more general problematic of the return and resurgence of the past and of memory. Sebald's language highlights this linkage, placing Naegeli and Ellis, as *Wiederkehrer*—returners, ghosts, or revenants—in a lineage that is inseparably yoked to Selwyn's attempts to return to his past more generally, including to his memories of the *cheder* teacher identified with his Lithuanian homeland and eventual exile. This lineage suggests that the relationship binding Selwyn to these male figures is best characterized as caring mentorship, rather than as latent homoeroticism. A Freudian reading might interpret all three figures as distorted displacements of the father, himself serving as a symbolic connection to the lost fatherland. The emendations Sebald makes in the language of the earlier printed text foreground such symbolic linkages and marginalize more emotional, potentially homoerotic implications.

I will conclude this investigation with one final example that treats a typical form of Sebaldian symbolism and the way revisions to the final text render this symbol more enigmatic, mysterious, and multivalent. It occurs in one of the most evocative scenes in this text, the description of the noise and light produced by the slide projector prior to viewing the pictures from Crete. The ultimate rendering of this passage is predominantly descriptive, with a symbolism of translucent transcendentalism hinted at by some of the individual words. "The low whirr of the projector began, and the dust in the room, normally invisible, glittered and danced in the beam of light by way of a prelude to the pictures themselves" ("Das leise Surren des Projektors setzte ein, und der sonst unsichtbare Zimmerstaub erglänzte zitternd im Kegel des Lichts als Vorspiel vor dem Erscheinen der Bilder"; *Ausgewanderten* 26/15). The luminous, wavering glow of the dust, rendered visible by the light of the projector, is the primary indicator that this passage should be read as symbolically invoking a metaphysical horizon. The transition of the dust particles from invisibility to visibility parallels the themes of return and the recollection of forgotten memories. Sebald frequently draws the analogy between such returns and the appearance of revenants, as he does in this text by associating remembrance with the reappearance of Naegeli's corpse. He also commonly attributes to the undead a strangely flickering image, similar to the wavering quality of the dust particles in this scene. In the prose fragment "Campo Santo," for example, he maintains that when one looks closely at such revenants, their faces blur and their images "flickered at the edges, just like the faces of actors in an old movie" ("flackerten an den Rändern, gerade wie die Gesichter der Schauspieler in einem alten Film"; *Campo Santo* 34/29). Characteristically Sebaldian is the way this tremulous quality is connected to mechanical means of visual reproduction, such as the slide projector, old films, or older forms of still photography. Those readers who know Sebald well, and who are aware that in his works dust functions metaphorically as a kind of "redeemed substance,"[21] will piece together this network of connections that point to the metaphysical implications of this passage.

The earlier printed version is vastly different in this regard: "The low noise of the projector, the mumbling monologue of the machine began, glittering dust, an entire starry firmament from God's box of blotting sand, danced in the beam of light by way of a prelude to the pictures themselves" ("Das leise Geräusch des Projektors, das murmelnde Selbstgespräch der Maschine, setzte ein, glänzender Staub, ein ganzes

21 Santner, *On Creaturely Life*, 102.

Sternengefild aus der Streusandbüchse Gottes, zitterte im Kegel des Lichts als Vorspiel vor dem Erscheinen der Bilder"; "Verzehret" 155). The projector is personified when the narrator imagines it voicing a mumbled monologue. The temptation to read this as an allegorical commentary on Selwyn's own confessions, which begin in earnest during the dinner and slideshow that evening, might be the reason why this phrase was eventually expunged. Mumbled monologue would be a rather negative characterization of the empathetic interaction between Selwyn and Sebald's narrator, even though the latter may serve more as a passive sounding board than as a genuine interlocutor—as is true for Sebald's narrators in general. The characterization of an informant's confessions as mumbled monologues is a suggestion Sebald surely wanted to avoid. More significant is how this earlier rendition makes explicit the metaphysical undertones that are only implicit in the final text. The luminosity of the dust is already mentioned, as is its wavering quality in the projector's light; but the metaphorical association of these dust particles with a star-filled firmament, on the one hand, and with God's blotting sand, on the other, not only makes the metaphysical dimension too obvious, but also verges dangerously on kitsch. The identification of dust and sand reinforces—through a connection with the proverbial sands of time—the nostalgic sense of passing time and times past. But such a direct statement about the metaphysical significance of this scene is out of keeping with Sebald's more subtle and allusive approach to such issues, and that is surely the reason why these descriptive metaphors were ultimately—and justifiably—eliminated. It is, after all, his light touch when it comes to metaphysical matters that is one of the distinguishing and appealing traits of Sebald's mature fictions.

The analyses provided here are admittedly provisional and of largely local significance, confined to the illumination of a single creative phase and based on the example of one short work. General scholarly access to the materials and manuscripts in Sebald's literary estate are likely to engender more detailed studies that will draw more wide-ranging conclusions about the procedures he followed in the composition and refinement of his texts. My investigation is of necessity restricted to the latter phase of production in which the text undergoes critical honing. It can say little about the earlier processes of creation, invention, inspiration, and initial composition. Nevertheless, we can extrapolate more general insights into Sebald's method and practice of writing, as well as into his style and his thematic concerns, from the conclusions drawn here based on the examination of a single short text and the final revisions it underwent. The stylistic transformation of this text occurs at a transitional phase in Sebald's development as a composer of prose fictions, the years 1988 to 1992, when he is discovering his creative voice and refining the skills of his narrative and rhetorical artistry. In that regard the alterations he undertook for the final version of "Dr. Henry Selwyn" can be viewed as emblematic for his incipient genesis into a creative writer of great skill and stylistic subtlety. The analyses provided here are intended to demonstrate that a close philological, historical-critical examination of Sebald's works can shed considerable light on the nuances of his central themes and the manner of their exposition. They also provide some fundamental hermeneutical guidance for the engagement with his fiction. In the instance of "Dr. Henry Selwyn," a text-historical analysis that deals with the nitty-gritty of editorial emendations turns up considerable information that carries critical weight for the interpretive understanding of this text. Some of this evidence will be brought to bear in the analysis of this story that is the subject of the next chapter.

Four Neither Here Nor There: Exile as Dis-Placement in "Dr. Henry Selwyn"

"The less we are free to decide who we are or to live as we like, the more we try to put up a front, to hide the facts, and to play roles."

Hannah Arendt[1]

An anecdote in Thomas Bernhard's collection of mixed prose pieces *Der Stimmenimitator* (*The Voice Imitator*) bears the telling title "Ausgewandert" ("Emigrated"). The narrator of this short piece relates the story of a former schoolmate who emigrated to Australia, subsequently returned to his home in the Austrian region of Styria, emigrated again to Australia, returned to Styria, and who continues to shuttle back and forth between these two places. The narrator speculates that this behavior will go on until his acquaintance finds "Ruhe," suggesting both peace and stasis, in one place or the other.[2] If this allegory of exile as suspended in the periodicity of eternal departure and return were not ironic enough, Bernhard turns the screw even tighter by relating the similar fate of this schoolmate's father, who likewise lived a life of perpetual transit between his home and a place of exile. The narrator thereby suggests that the proclivity for exile, defined as back-and-forth between emigration and homecoming, is a hereditary trait. However, this story explodes into parody when we learn that the two localities between which the

1   Hannah Arendt, "We Refugees," in *Hitler's Exiles: Personal Stories of the Flight from Nazi Germany to America*, ed. Mark A. Anderson (New York: Norton, 1998), 258.

2   Thomas Bernhard, *Der Stimmenimitator* (Frankfurt am Main: Suhrkamp, 1978), 62; *The Voice Imitator*, trans. Kenneth J. Northcott (Chicago: University of Chicago Press, 1997), 37.

father oscillates are the neighboring Austrian regions of Carinthia and Styria: born in the former, he "emigrates" to the latter, but keeps returning "home" to Carinthia and re-emigrating to Styria, as his son will do on a grander scale. Aside from poking fun at Austrian conceptions of home as the circumscribed "soil" of one's birthplace, Bernhard also parodies the idea of exile by identifying it with a figure who moves just a short way down the road to an environment that is closely related to his indigenous homeland. This mocking undertone rises to the surface when we are told, in a final *pointe*, that the father ultimately finds "peace," "Ruhe," in his native Carinthia only by hanging himself from an iron hook "because he was homesick for Styria" ("aus Heimweh nach der Steiermark").[3] The object of his homesickness has changed from Carinthia, his true *Heimat* in the sense of his birthplace, to Styria, the elected homeland of his "exile." Ultimately this figure—like his son—is destined to perish from homesickness; for no matter where he goes, he will be gripped by longing for the place where he is *not*. Perpetual motion, or a kind of suspended animation between two geographical poles, manifests the inescapability of homesickness and the nostalgia for always being somewhere else.

It comes as no surprise that in Sebald's copy of Bernhard's *Stimmenimitator* the pages of this anecdote are flagged by a prominent dog-ear. Bernhard's "Ausgewandert" can be seen as a condensed prototype for the themes and structures characteristic of many of Sebald's stories. The issue of exile itself is one of the cornerstones of Sebald's life work, not only of the fictional texts produced in the final years of his life, but of his literary scholarship as well.[4] It is further noteworthy that in Bernhard's tale, exile culminates in suicide, a pattern frequently repeated by Sebald's emigrants, for whom, as in Bernhard's anecdote, only death provides a final resting place and a "home." But beyond these thematic similarities, Bernhard's text shares certain paradigmatic structural features with Sebald's works. Most prominent is the pattern of repetition, concretized in the obsessive oscillation between emigration and homecoming practiced by the classmate and his father. Then there is the parallelism marked by the fact that both these figures are locked into the same repetitive behavior. On a more profound level, the very structure of Bernhard's text, in which a first-person narrator relates the story of a second person (the classmate) and subsequently that of a third (the father), prefigures the first-person nesting-box structure typical of Sebald's fictional

---

3   Bernhard, *Der Stimmenimitator*, 62; *The Voice Imitator*, 37.
4   One of Sebald's most widely received collections of literary essays bears the salient title *Unheimliche Heimat*, "Uncanny [or Unhomely] Homeland."

technique. Sebald frequently admitted his debt to Bernhard with regard to this narrative strategy, for which he commonly employed the term "periscopic narration."[5] Given Sebald's acknowledgment that Bernhard exerted substantial influence on his writing, we can speculate that the very title of this anecdote resonates in Sebald's *Die Ausgewanderten*, the heading under which he compiled four tales of twentieth-century exiles. This helps explain Sebald's choice of the less familiar form *Die Ausgewanderten*—which could be translated as "The Exiled" or "The Emigrated"—over the more common *Die Auswanderer* ("The Exiles" or "The Emigrants"). The allusion to Goethe's novella collection *Unterhaltungen deutscher Ausgewanderten* (Conversations of German emigrants) may also be operative behind this choice of title,[6] whereby one should note that the "exiled" people named in Goethe's work are refugees from the Napoleonic invasions, and that they enjoy the comfort of taking refuge in other German-speaking lands. In that respect, they are similar to the father in Bernhard's tale, minus the parody, of course. As Oliver Sill has noted,[7] the German past participle "ausgewandert" signals grammatically an action completed in the past that continues to influence the present, and this suggests that for Sebald's (as for Bernhard's) emigrants, the condition of exile is a never-ending state of affairs. The resonance between Bernhard's and Sebald's titles points toward the more specific affinity that characterizes their conceptions of exile as such: its status as a condition of constant oscillation, of absolute disquiet and an inability to find a place of permanent repose except in death. Sebald's emigrants, even when they settle geographically in a stable place—one thinks of Max Aurach's life in Manchester—are never really mentally or emotionally at home. As is true for the former schoolmate in Bernhard's anecdote, Sebald's exiles are always spiritually on the move, like ghosts, and for them exile is not defined so much by their being "strangers," aliens forced to live in

5   Sebald commented in his 2001 interview with Martin Doerry and Volker Hage on Thomas Bernhard's narrative approach, "Ich würde sein [Bernhards] Verfahren als periskopisch bezeichnen, als Erzählen um ein, zwei Ecken herum—eine sehr wichtige Erfindung für die epische Literatur dieser Zeit" ("I would call his [Bernhard's] procedure periscopic, narrating around one or two corners—an extremely important invention for the epic literature of this period"; *"Auf ungeheuer dünnem Eis"* 204). See also James Wood, "An Interview with W. G. Sebald," *Brick* 59 (1998): 28, as well as the radio interview with Michael Silverblatt (Schwartz 82–3).
6   Rüdiger Görner, "Los der Ausgewanderten: Literarische Umsetzungen der Exilproblematik," *Neue Zürcher Zeitung*, April 29, 1994, 38, points to this connection to Goethe's title.
7   Oliver Sill, "Migration als Gegenstand der Literatur: W. G. Sebalds *Die Ausgewanderten*," in *Nation, Ethnie, Minderheit: Beiträge zur Aktualität ethnischer Konflikte*, ed. Armin Nassehi (Cologne: Bölau, 1997), 313.

a foreign context, as it is by their provisional status as figures caught in a condition of in-between-ness.[8] Throughout Sebald's works, exile designates a state of perpetual disorientation, of sustained mental and geographical displacement, in the literal sense of that term. Sebald's exiles are trapped in an elsewhere that is a nowhere; but the "no place" of exile is no utopia.

When the eponymous protagonist of the story "Paul Bereyter" voices the paradoxical assertion that he is "as the crow flies, about 2,000 km away—but from where?" ("zirka 2000 km Luftlinie weit entfernt—aber von wo?"; *Ausgewanderten* 83/56), he expresses the fundamental geographical and mental disorientation Sebald associates with the condition of exile. Another immigrant, the narrator's Uncle Kasimir in the story "Ambros Adelwarth," echoes these words when meditating on his attraction to the "edge of darkness" ("Rand der Finsternis"; 129/88) he discovers on the New Jersey coast, and the resonance of these two remarks constitutes a Sebaldian "coincidence" insofar as it is orchestrated to *appear* as such. "I often come out here, … it makes me feel that I am a long way away, though I never quite know from where" (129/89). Always being a long way away from any discernible fixed point, no matter how far or where one travels, or even if one is running in place: that is the meaning of exile in Sebald's works. Nowhere is this condition of displacement, understood as a disorienting liminality and a state of perpetual non-belonging, explored more subtly and in such detail as in "Dr. Henry Selwyn." This story justifiably assumes the privileged position of inaugural piece among these tales of "Ausgewanderten," for it introduces, defines, and elaborates the peculiar condition of exile, played out in all these stories, as a state of permanent displacement and disorientation.

Although Henry Selwyn maintains, in the "confession" that he

---

8   Philip Schlesinger, "W. G. Sebald and the Condition of Exile," *Theory, Culture and Society* 21, no. 2 (2004): 47, has come closest to capturing this unstable quality of exile in Sebald's works, identifying it with anthropologist Victor Turner's concept of "liminality" as "social limbo" (47). He goes on to claim that Sebald's exiles remain "trapped in a state of perpetual liminality," 62, a condition he exemplifies with reference to *Austerlitz*. Christopher Gregory-Guider, "The 'Sixth' Emigrant: Traveling Places in the Works of W. G. Sebald," *Contemporary Literature* 46 (2005): 428, also remarks that Sebald's emigrants are "caught in an interstitial no-man's land." Jo Catling, "Gratwanderungen bis an den Rand der Natur: W. G. Sebald's Landscapes of Memory," in *The Anatomist of Melancholy: Essays in Memory of W. G. Sebald*, ed. Rüdiger Görner (Munich: Iudicum, 2003), 41, similarly describes exile as a "limbo" to which Sebald's characters are "condemned." For more general reflections on the status of exile as a "third" realm located "between" an originary and an acquired place, see Elisabeth Bronfen, "Exil in der Literatur: Zwischen Metapher und Realität," *Arcadia* 28 (1993): 171.

makes in one of his last meetings with the first-person narrator, "that in recent years he had been beset with homesickness more and more" ("daß ihn das Heimweh im Verlauf der letzten Jahre mehr und mehr angekommen sei"; *Ausgewanderten* 30/18), homesickness is not really an accurate designation for the nostalgia this character experiences. When his memories of Lithuania, his native village outside of Grodno, and the ambience of his childhood finally return, we get sparse details of what life in the homeland was truly like. In fact, Selwyn's memories are concerned almost exclusively with the act of departure itself: the empty rooms of his former household, the wagon on which he rides to Grodno, the train station from which he departs, the train ride to Riga, the harbor, and the space on the deck of the ship where his family tries to define its personal domain (31/18–19). For this reason, it is inaccurate to claim that Sebald's characters suffer from chronic *Heimweh*, "homesickness," as critics are wont to do;[9] their nostalgia is directed not so much toward some lost "home" as toward the act of leave-taking itself, and as such it expresses a covert longing for the adventure of travel and the experience of being dislodged. Even under the oppressive conditions of life on the deck of the freighter, Selwyn's family manages to make themselves "at home." In his recollection Selwyn comments, "I see ... the dark corner on deck where we did our best to make ourselves *at home* in such confined circumstances" ("Ich sehe ... die dunkle Ecke des Decks, in der wir, soweit es anging unter den gedrängten Verhältnissen, *häuslich* uns einrichteten"; 31/19, emphasis added). The "home" for which Selwyn pines, then, is none other—and this is only seemingly paradoxical—than the home manifest in the act of flight itself, the provisional home established on the deck of the vessel that carries him from one place to another. Like Sebald's exiles in general, Selwyn suffers from melancholy in the specific sense defined by Slavoj Žižek: he confuses *lack* with *loss*, and assumes that because he experiences the lack of homeland, this homeland must have existed at some time but has somehow gone missing.[10] Exile in Sebald's works is not so much marked by the *loss* of home as by its utter *absence*, by an enduring condition of non-belonging. In this sense, Mark Anderson is correct when he insists that Sebald should not be viewed

---

9   See, for example, Noam M. Elcott, "Tattered Snapshots and Castaway Tongues: An Essay at Layout and Translation with W. G. Sebald," *Germanic Review* 79 (2004): 204; and Markus R. Weber, "Phantomschmerz Heimweh: Denkfiguren der Erinnerung im literarischen Werk W. G. Sebalds," in *Neue Generation—Neues Erzählen: Deutsche Prosaliteratur der achtziger Jahre*, ed. Walter Delabar, Werner Jung, and Ingrid Pergand (Opladen: Westdeutscher Verlag, 1993), 58.

10 Slavoj Žižek, "Melancholy and the Act," *Critical Inquiry* 26, no. 4 (Summer 2000): 659–60.

narrowly as a Holocaust writer, since his works deal more universally
with the problem of "existential exile."[11]

Selwyn's exile as an interstitial space between a vague place of
departure and a sketchy destination is captured allegorically in the
course of the voyage he and his family undertake. Although they have
booked a passage from Riga to, as Selwyn calls it, "Amerikum" (32/19),
they mistakenly leave the ship at the first port of call, which happens
to be London, unaware that they have not yet arrived at their intended
destination.[12] Or have they? Insofar as the "destination" of exile is the
state of suspension between two places, Selwyn and his family have
indeed "arrived." In a story replete with the motif of the "gap," "crack,"
or "rift"—the crack in the glass of the slide depicting Selwyn's trip to
Crete (28–9/17), and the crevasse into which the mountaineer Johannes
Naegeli disappears (24/15)—Selwyn and his family symbolically fall
into the rift of exile. Having departed, but without ever reaching his
"true" destination, Henry Selwyn will remain a dis-placed person—a
person without a place of his own—his entire life.[13] This suspension
in a geographical gap between departure and destination has its
counterpart in a spiritual or mental rupture: the discrepancy between
reality and belief, a syndrome Selwyn diagnoses as typical of those
exiles who have gotten off the boat too soon: "But in fact ... we had
gone ashore in London. Most of the emigrants, of necessity, adjusted to
the situation, but some, in the teeth of all the evidence to the contrary,
persisted for a long time in the belief that they were in America" ("In
Wirklichkeit aber waren wir ... in London gelandet. Die meisten der
Auswanderer fanden sich notgedrungen in ihre Lage, einige freilich
hielten, allen gegenteiligen Beweisen zum Trotz, lange an dem Glauben
fest, in Amerika zu sein"; 32/19). The either/or Selwyn presents here—
either making concessions to reality or holding fast to the mirage of
a mistaken belief—does not fully account for his own situation. He

---

11 Mark M. Anderson, "The Edge of Darkness: On W. G. Sebald," *October* 106
    (2003): 104.
12 Sebald first employed this motif of emigrants who erroneously disembark in
    London, mistaking it for New York City, in his screenplay "Leben Ws" (330),
    where Wittgenstein tells this anecdote to his friend Ben Richards. The reference
    in "Selwyn" thus likely represents an intertextual allusion to information
    Sebald gained while researching the Wittgenstein project.
13 Gray Kochhar-Lindgren, "Charcoal: The Phantom Traces of W. G. Sebald's
    Novel-Memoirs," *Monatshefte* 94 (2002): 372–3, also emphasizes that Sebald's
    narratives are peopled by displaced persons; but rather than associating
    displacement with exile, he identifies it with the motifs of walking, writing, and
    traveling, which characterize Sebald's narrators as well as his characters. See
    also Gabriele Annan, "Ghosts," *New York Review of Books*, September 25, 1997,
    29, who suggests that the term "displaced persons" provides the most accurate
    description for Sebald's protagonists.

will remain suspended *between* reality and a false belief, permanently underway, a kind of Wandering Jew who is not at rest even when he is ostensibly residing in Hingham on the estate at Prior's Gate—an estate owned, notably, not by Selwyn himself, but by his wife. He conforms perfectly with what Mary McCarthy has called the "archetypal exile": "The Wandering Jew is the archetypal exile, sentenced to trail about the earth until the Second Coming."[14] In this regard Henry Selwyn and the other exiles of Sebald's fiction are manifestations of the ghosts, the "undead," who populate Sebald's fictional world, represented most concretely by the figure of the Hunter Gracchus Sebald borrows from Kafka as the touchstone character for *Schwindel. Gefühle*.[15] Sebald becomes a ghostwriter in the literal sense when he records the stories of these ghost-like exiles.

In the instance of Dr. Henry Selwyn, the physical dis-placement of exile expresses itself psychologically as a split personality, as the rift between the superficiality and pose of an assumed persona and the gloom of a cordoned-off, inaccessible, but purportedly authentic "self." When Selwyn introduces himself to the narrator and his wife as "a kind of ornamental hermit" (11/5), this phrase succinctly identifies this dualistic aspect of his character: he is "ornamental" to the extent that his life has consisted of putting up a front—the guise of a high-roller living, through the graces of his wealthy wife Hedi, in the upper echelons of society (34/21)—and his existence as a "hermit," withdrawn from the world of human interactions and isolated at the walled-off estate of Prior's Gate. The name of this retreat already indicates its function in Selwyn's life: it demarcates a gateway to the prior,[16] and as threshold it identifies the liminal space that must be traversed if Selwyn hopes to re-enter the forgotten, repressed interior of his past. The name "Prior's Gate" thus already anticipates the theme of return that is so central to this narrative. It is not only the dead, like the corpse of Johannes Naegeli, who will return, but also seemingly dead memories and superseded versions of the self. Indeed, the communicative interaction between Sebald's narrator and his informant Henry Selwyn functions as just such a gateway to the prior, an avenue for the return of the past to conscious awareness.[17]

---

14 Mary McCarthy, "A Guide to Exiles, Expatriates, and Internal Émigrés," in *Altogether Elsewhere: Writers on Exile*, ed. Marc Robinson (Boston: Faber & Faber, 1994), 49.

15 Mark McCulloh, *Understanding W. G. Sebald* (Columbia: University of South Carolina Press, 2003), 100, has pointed out that the Hunter Gracchus illustrates the condition of complete or absolute exile.

16 Claudia Öhlschläger, *Beschädigtes Leben. Erzählte Risse: W. G. Sebalds poetische Ordnung des Unglücks* (Freiburg im Breisgau: Rombach, 2006), 39.

17 The psychoanalytic "talking cure" suggests itself here as a model for the narrative interaction typical of Sebald's texts. However, the narrowly therapeutic

The thematic of redemption from the past is articulated most poignantly in Selwyn's story about the three horses he has rescued from the knacker's yard:

Um ein kleines Erlengehölz herum kamen drei schwere Schimmel, schnabend und in Trab Wasen aufwerfend ... Ich habe sie im vorigen Jahr für ein paar Pfund auf der Pferdeauktion gekauft, von der sie bestimmt in die Abdeckerei geraten wären. Sie heißen Herschel, Humphrey und Hippolytus. Über ihr Vorleben ist mir nichts bekannt, aber sie haben, als ich sie erstand, arg ausgesehen. (*Ausgewanderten* 11–12)
[Three heavy greys were rounding a little clump of alders, snorting and throwing up clods of turf as they trotted ... I bought them at an auction last year for a few pounds. Otherwise they would doubtless have gone straight to the knacker's yard. They're called Herschel, Humphrey and Hippolytus. I know nothing about their earlier life, but when I bought them they were in a sorry state. (*Emigrants* 6)]

On the most superficial level these horses are connected to Henry Selwyn through the alliterative first letter of their names. Moreover, Selwyn's given name of Hersch, before he changed it to Henry, resonates in the name of the first horse, Herschel. There are other, more subtle traits, however, that align these creatures with their new owner. We are introduced to them as they are in motion, trotting around and throwing up clods of turf, actions that symbolize their condition of unrest. Selwyn also acknowledges his total ignorance about their prior existence, and their lack of a "Vorleben," an "earlier life," reflects Selwyn's own inhibited access to his prior life. Yet their rescue at Prior's Gate alludes to the rescue of his own past, as well as its retribution. As is typical of Sebald's fiction, these ideas are suggested at a semiotic and textual level. The German word for knacker's yard, "Abdeckerei," alludes to a process of recovery and un-covering (*ab-decken*). For the knacker this refers to the removal of animal hides, and this signification applies by extension to the dismantling of Selwyn's "ornamental" façade-self. But in the context of Selwyn's life, this word also invokes the Freudian theme of the recovery of repressed memories and experiences. Selwyn

---

aim of Freudian practice is only of marginal relevance for Sebald's narrative interactions, as indicated by the fact that his characters, even when they gain knowledge of the past, never find salvation. Eric Santner, *On Creaturely Life: Rilke, Benjamin, Sebald* (Chicago: University of Chicago Press, 2006), 58–61, comes closest to identifying the empathetic but not necessarily therapeutic quality of Sebald's narrative interchanges.

rescues the horses (and himself) both literally from "skinning" and figuratively from this process of revelation. The redemption of the horses is a significant episode because it circumscribes the complex dialectic characteristic of Selwyn's life. On the one hand, he is concerned with revitalizing and refurbishing these animals' worn-out exterior and improving their appearance; on the other hand, their salvation marks the stripping down of this façade, its un-covering, and the unveiling of the insular interiority of the exile.

Sebald's fascination with architectural metaphors as allegories for the constitution of the human subject forms a dominant theme in *Austerlitz*, where fortresses-turned-prisons symbolize the psychological dialectic of defense against the outside world and containment of the threats that well up out of the interiority of the self (*Austerlitz* 21–37/14–25). Similar architectural images figure prominently in *Die Ausgewanderten*, in particular in this first story. This motif is introduced when the narrator and his wife first encounter the marketplace of Hingham, surrounded by "silent façades" ("schweigenden Fassaden"; 8/3). The very personification of these inanimate façades as "silent"— the German word *schweigend* actually highlights the active quality of *keeping* silent—hints at their symbolic character. The narrator's task will be to penetrate these façades and transform their silence into language by recreating the life and history of what transpires behind them. This façade motif is reiterated when the narrator encounters the mansion at Prior's Gate: "The front of the large, neoclassical house was overgrown with Virginia creeper"[18] ("Die Fassade des breit hingelagerten klassizistischen Hauses war überwachsen von wildem Wein"; 8/4). In addition, its windows appear to be made of "dark mirror glass" ("dunklem Spiegelglas"; 8–9/4) that prevents outsiders from peering into its interior. The mansion thereby allegorizes the character of its inhabitant, Henry Selwyn. Its façade is not simply classical, but explicitly classicistic or neoclassical—that is, it is an *imitation* of the classical and as such something inherently artificial, if no less imposing. In this regard the house prefigures the artifice of Selwyn's assumed life: the energies he invests in learning English quickly and becoming a model student (32–3/20); his marriage to the wealthy Swiss factory-owner's daughter Hedi (15/8); the exuberant lifestyle they enjoyed while squandering a large part of her fortune (34/21); and even his extended stay in India (20/11). Selwyn's forgetfulness of his past, and his compensatory investment in an invented, façade-like self, culminates when he jettisons his original name, Hersch Seweryn, and adopts the name Henry Selwyn (33/20). When

---

18 The English translation obscures this connection by rendering the German term "Fassade" as "front," rather than as "façade."

he maintains that the assumption of this name coincided with a peculiar reduction in his ability to learn, his "Lernfähigkeit" (33/20), the implication is that assimilation, as a process of adaptive learning, has reached its zenith. All the elements of this development, from the quick learning of English out of love for his teacher Lisa Owen (32/20), to the exaggerated drive for success at school, through finally to the change of names, are consistent with the erection of a "classicistic" façade with blind windows that block any access to Selwyn's shrouded interior. Ironically, Selwyn even acquires the weapon with which he ultimately puts an end to his own life, the double-barreled big-game rifle he purchased in India, simply because owning such a rifle was "obligatory" for men of his ilk (20/11). Radical conformity to the expectations of a "man of his caste," as this etiology suggests, will eventually be the death of Henry Selwyn. This is consistent with Selwyn's identification of the force of this weapon's recoil as its primary characteristic: "the recoil alone," he remarks, "was enough to kill one" ("einen allein ihr [der Büchse] Rückschlag schon ums Leben bringen könne"; 20/11). The gun's recoil alludes metaphorically to the psychological reflex of the violent return of the repressed. The increasingly haunting past that slowly asserts itself behind the façade of Selwyn's assumed existence will ultimately cause him to take his own life.[19] Selwyn's death thus is predicated on the implosion of his façade-like persona and a resurgent identification with the "self" that lies buried in the past. Existential authenticity, in Sebald's fictional world as in the philosophy of Martin Heidegger, is often achieved only in death.[20]

Sebald calls attention to the theme of the façade when his narrator describes how viewing the manor at Prior's Gate triggers a recollection of a country house in France, remarkable for its false façade replicating the palace of Versailles:

---

19 In his interview with James Wood, 25, Sebald refers explicitly to the return of a dormant past as what caught his attention in the biographies related in *Die Ausgewanderten*: "What particularly interested me, as I began to think about these lives, was the time delay between a vicariously experienced catastrophe and the point at which it overtook these people, very late in life." See Sebald's similar comment in his 1993 interview with Marco Poltronieri (*"Auf ungeheuer dünnem Eis"* 94).

20 We should not be surprised by this Heideggerean motif in Sebald's writing. His library contains a heavily annotated copy of Heidegger's *Einführung in die Metaphysik* (*Introduction to Metaphysics*)—purchased already in 1964, as his ex libris indicates—in which Sebald has underlined the passages dealing with the inescapability of death and its intimate connection to human *Dasein*. The next chapter will deal more explicitly with the Heideggerean implications surrounding Sebald's conception of exile.

Und mir kam das Landhaus in der Charente in den Sinn, das ich von Angoulême aus einmal besucht hatte und vor dem zwei verrückte Brüder, der eine Deputierter, der andere Architekt, in jahrzehntelanger Planungs- und Konstruktionsarbeit die Vorderfront des Schlosses von Versailles errichtet hatten, eine ganz und gar zwecklose, aus der Entfernung allerdings sehr eindrucksvolle Kulisse, deren Fenster geradeso glänzend und blind gewesen waren wie die des Hauses, vor welchem wir jetzt standen. (*Ausgewanderten* 9)
[And I recalled the château in the Charente that I had once visited from Angoulême. In front of it, two crazy brothers—one a parliamentarian, the other an architect—had built a replica of the façade of the palace of Versailles, an utterly pointless counterfeit, though one which made a powerful impression from a distance. The windows of that house had been just as gleaming and blind as those of the house we now stood before. (*Emigrants* 4)]

The details of this architectural construction metaphorically anticipate the assimilated lifestyle Henry Selwyn assumes. Like this façade, his persona is carefully orchestrated and assembled over a period of many years, and although from a distance it appears grandiose and impressive, Selwyn gradually recognizes it as ultimately senseless and without purpose. Henry's life, like this French country estate, is occupied—metaphorically, in this case—by "two crazy brothers," a roundabout allusion to the duplicity of Selwyn's self, split between the lost existence of Hersch Seweryn and the assumed life of Henry Selwyn. Although at this point in the narrator's exposition we are not yet cognizant of Selwyn's biography, this passage provides an anticipatory commentary on the imposing façade of his assimilated existence. Sebald's narrator highlights the parallel of this architectural description with the characterological realm when he applies the theatrical term "Kulisse," "backdrop," to describe this façade, an allusion that gets lost in the English translation. As the backdrop or barrier that separates the semblance of the onstage actions from the mechanisms operating behind the scene, this "Kulisse" presents an illustrative image for the self-division that rends Selwyn's existence. The word itself invokes the common German phrase "hinter den Kulissen," "behind the scenes," suggesting a secretive realm that cannot be exposed to the public eye. If the windows of this French country estate, like that of the house at Prior's Gate, both "gleam" and are "blind," then they reiterate on a symbolic level the dynamic of the façade itself, which both impresses, due to its architectural pomposity, and conceals an inaccessible interior. Blindness—in particular blindness for his own self and his past—is a trait that characterizes Henry Selwyn in particular. Sebald's narrative

Figure 4.1: Henry Selwyn's "Folly" (*Ausgewanderten* 19/11).

charts the slow but systematic dismantling of Selwyn's personal façade and the concomitant illumination of his dark and mysterious interior.

Selwyn's identity as an "ornamental hermit" is manifest most concretely in his voluntary displacement from the main residence at Prior's Gate to the so-called "folly," the ornamental garden house that serves as his place of refuge (18/10). The image of this folly, included as an illustration, depicts an imposing stone-walled, round structure reminiscent of the turret of a medieval fortress, with Gothic windows and a zigzag parapet (19/11) (see Figure 4.1) The windows are just as "blind" as those of the mansion itself. More curious, but perhaps more significant, is that in this illustration the building has no doorway for ingress and egress. If we read the name of this structure as a double entendre, then it provides a critical commentary on the "folly" of Selwyn's life: the senselessness of a self that is constructed as an elaborate façade, erected both as a defense against incursions from the outside world and as an enclosure that confines the self, as "hermit," within its imposing walls. Follies, of course, were traditionally built to serve purely ornamental functions, not to be personal residences. One can presume that they generally do not benefit from the typical infrastructure of a residential building, things like interior plumbing and even reliable sources of heat and power. Surely it is "folly" in the more common sense to live in such an edifice. By choosing to do so, Selwyn affirms his own self-image as "ornamental hermit." Taking up residence in his "folly" suggests Selwyn's refusal to negotiate the conflict between surface and depth, exterior and interior, façade persona and authentic self. Indeed, it symbolizes his insistence on *dwelling* in this rift, perpetually dis-placed in a continuous state of (self-)exile.

As indicated by the architectural metaphors that dominate its opening pages, the juxtaposition of inside and outside is fundamental to the theme and structure of Sebald's story. The narrator plays out this dichotomy when he describes his and his wife's reactions to the manor house and the motivation behind their decision to spend several months in residence there. They are genuinely enticed by this prospect,

denn der Ausblick von den hohen Fenstern auf den Garten, den Park und die Wolkenbänke am Himmel war weit mehr als nur ein Ausgleich für das düstere Interieur. Man brauchte nur hinauszuschauen, und schon versank hinter einem die gigantische, in ihrer Häßlichkeit nur mit dem Wort *altdeutsch* annähernd richtig bezeichnete Kredenz, löste der erbsfarbene Anstrich der Küche sich auf, entschwebte, wie durch ein Wunder, der türkisgrüne und vielleicht gar nicht ganz ungefährliche Gaskühlschrank. (*Ausgewanderten* 15) [since the view from the high windows across the garden, the park and the massed cloud in the sky was more than ample recompense for the gloomy interior. One only needed to look out, and the gigantic and startlingly ugly sideboard ceased to exist, the mustard yellow paintwork in the kitchen vanished, and the turquoise refrigerator, gas-powered and possibly not without its dangers, seemed to dissolve into nowhere, as if by a miracle. (*Emigrants* 8)]

The logic of this justification is grounded in the idea of sufficient or even excessive compensation. The gloomy interior of the manor's rooms is heightened by the gaudy and antiquated nature of its furnishings, as well as by the garishness of its interior colors. However, the expansive view from the windows, which takes in the gardens and the park, but also affords an encompassing view of the sky with its sublime cloud formations, more than makes up for the depressing atmosphere of the interior.

Several dichotomies are operative in this passage, and they are instrumental for the refinement of this inside–outside dichotomy. One is the prominent artifice–nature opposition. The interior of the house replicates its façade in at least this one respect: it is highly constructed, and it exudes anything but a sense of comfort, coziness, and livability. The disparate and desultory elements that make up its furnishings lend it more the ambience of a dusty museum than of a place where human beings live and interact. By contrast, when looking through the windows the narrator experiences a consolingly beautiful view of nature. To be sure, this is a nature that is cultivated—the park and the gardens of the estate; but it also encompasses the unconfined expanse of sky and clouds. Such juxtapositions of nature and artifice run in leitmotivic fashion throughout this story. One thinks of the wild Virginia creeper that overgrows the manor house's façade (8/4), the tennis court that can no longer completely withstand the encroachments of nature (12–13/6–7), and the "tumble-down Victorian greenhouses" ("halbverfallenen viktorianischen Glashäusern"; 13/7) that, despite their decrepit state, produce vegetables of diminutive size but of exceptionally refined flavor (14/8). Each of these images emphasizes the intertwining of nature and culture, the slow but incessant process by which nature retakes the terrain that was once its own but which has been—temporarily—occupied by cultured artifice. The house and grounds of Prior's Gate thereby reflect the process of renaturalization that is beginning to take hold in the existence of Henry Selwyn, as well: "Leaving the once well-tended garden to its own devices" ("Die Verwilderung des einstmals vorbildlichen Gartens"; 14/7) has its parallel in the explosion of unchecked inclinations that now invade the placid edifice of Selwyn's assumed persona. Moreover, just as the garden's lack of cultivation produces especially tasty fruits, Selwyn's relapse into a state of dis-cultivation generates a particularly refined human being, characterized by a "courtesy … of a style that had long fallen into disuse" ("längst außer Gebrauch gekommenen Verbindlichkeit"; 11/5). The irony of this process of renaturalization is that it will culminate in Selwyn's death at his own hands.

A further reflex of this inside–outside polarity is the juxtaposition between two contrasting modes of perception, a close-up view that homes in on details but loses sight of the larger picture—a myopia born of excess proximity—and a panoramic perspective that encompasses a wide field of vision—an overarching but inherently alienated perspective. In the narrator's experience of Prior's Gate, this near-sighted view is confined largely to the interior of the house, whereas the far-sighted panorama is offered as soon as the house's inhabitants peer through the windows—the same windows that when seen from the outside appear to be blind mirrors rather than translucent panes of glass. The narrative alternately positions Selwyn in each of these modes of observing. When we first encounter him he is lying motionless on the ground, "counting the blades of grass" (10–11/5), as he remarks to the understandably astonished narrator and his wife. This focus on the proximate, which has the subsidiary effect of blocking from view what is distant, accurately describes the perspective that underwrites assimilation as Selwyn's strategy for personal development and social accommodation. The basement apartment in Whitechapel, which his family occupied immediately upon settling in London (32/20), is the architectural and residential symbol of this myopia, and it anticipates the dark interior of the manor house at Prior's Gate. The detail that Selwyn's father is a "Linsenschleifer," a lens-grinder by profession (32/20), suggests that there are artificial means for correcting even the most debilitating visual handicaps. But Selwyn's historical development is marked by the repression of all that is distant and past in favor of the immediacy of his present environment and the pleasures of spontaneity. His personality is predicated on this near-sightedness, and on the chameleon-like manner in which he adapts to this immediate environment, denying even to his wife—as he does to himself—his origins as a *shtetl* Jew from Lithuania (34/20–1).

One character in this narrative symbolically represents Hersch Seweryn, the repressed or abandoned self of Selwyn's past who languishes in the dark confines of his unconscious mind: the servant Aileen (Elaine in the English translation), who haunts the interior of the manor house at Prior's Gate. The narrator presents her as a largely nondescript individual, her cropped hair, gray apron, and agitated personal demeanor all reminiscent of "inmates of asylums"

("Anstaltsinsassen"; 16/9). The nature of the institution in which she might be confined—insane asylum, prison, or even concentration camp—remains tantalizingly open. Aileen's most distinguishing trait is her strangely whinnying laughter, which erupts out of the blue and sends chills down the spines of the narrator and his wife (18/10). This horse-like laugh positions her as an analogue to the three iron-grays Selwyn rescued from the knacker's yard, and the fact that she rarely seems to be occupied with meaningful duties suggests that she may be another creature who was rescued as a charity case. But her significance in the narrative derives largely from a close association with the inner depths of the mansion: she is the only person who moves about the hidden passageways constructed for the purpose of allowing servants to perform their duties without disturbing the mansion's residents and guests (16–17/9–10). Her identification with these mysterious pathways, behind the walls and deep within the interior of the house, suggests that she serves as a reminder of Henry Selwyn's suppressed past, the shadowy, indistinct figure who moves about behind the elaborate façade of his public pose.

The narrator reinforces this association between this servant's position in the internal depths of the manor and Selwyn's psychic interior when he asks explicitly about the psychological constitution of those wealthy mansion dwellers who live with an awareness of the invisible specters that haunt the hidden passageways of their private quarters:

> Ich versuchte mir oft auszudenken, wie das Innere der Köpfe der Leute beschaffen gewesen sein mußte, die mit der Vorstellung leben konnten, daß hinter den Wänden der Zimmer, in denen sie sich aufhielten, irgendwo immer die Schatten der Dienerschaft am Huschen waren, und ich bildete mir ein, daß sie Angst hätten haben müssen vor dem gespenstischen Wesen derer, die für ein geringes Geld rastlos die vielen alltäglich anfallenden Arbeiten verrichteten. (*Ausgewanderten* 17)
> [Often I tried to imagine what went on inside the heads of people who led their lives knowing that, behind the walls of the rooms they were in, the shadows of the servants were perpetually flitting past. I fancied they ought to have been afraid of those ghostly creatures who, for scant wages, dealt with the tedious tasks that had to be performed daily. (*Emigrants* 9–10)]

The fear the narrator assumes the lords of such manors must have felt toward the incessantly laboring but invisible servants derives in part from an anxiety harbored by the upper classes toward the subaltern. The narrator's rhetoric reveals that he identifies these shadowy and unseen servants with ghosts or the undead: they are "Schatten," shadows that are like the shades of the living; their domain is dark and Hades-like; they have a "ghostly" presence; and they move about with that restlessness ("rastlos"; "Huschen") traditionally associated with revenants. Aileen, in short, functions as Selwyn's own ghost, presenting him with a constant reminder of his status as an exile, as someone ceaselessly on the move, and as a reminiscence of the "shade" Hersch Seweryn who disappears behind the façade of the courteous and prosperous Henry Selwyn. She recalls his own humble origins as a subaltern Other from a Lithuanian village. Perhaps her presence is what motivates him to move into the folly, where he is not continually reminded of his own past by the specter of this alter-ego? At any rate, she embodies the fate that might have befallen Henry Selwyn had he remained Hersch Seweryn: if he had not imposed upon himself a strict regimen of repressive sublimation and opportunistic assimilation so as to become a wealthy surgeon, marry a Swiss factory-owner's daughter, and lead a life of superficial luxury and "ornamental" splendor.

There are other, more subtle textual indicators that point to the association between Aileen and Henry Selwyn's pre-assimilated persona. The most obvious is her child-like character, brought out not merely by her unselfconscious and penetrating laugh and her companionship with a young girl with whom she leaves the house hand in hand (18/10), but also by her preoccupation with the innumerable dolls that crowd her bedroom:

> Eine Unzahl von Puppen, sorgsam herausgeputzt und die meisten mit Kopfbedeckung, standen und saßen überall in dem kleinen Raum herum und lagen auch in dem Bett, in dem Aileen selbst schlief, wenn sie überhaupt schlief und nicht nur die ganze Nacht leise singend mit ihren Puppen spielte. (*Ausgewanderten* 17–18)
> [[H]er small room was full of countless dolls, meticulously dressed, most of them wearing something on their heads, standing or sitting around or lying on the bed where Elaine herself slept—if, that is, she ever slept at all, and did not spend the entire night crooning softly as she played with her dolls. (*Emigrants* 10)]

In the narrator's imagination, the sleepless Aileen is aligned with the restless ghosts of the undead. Her childlike personality is emphasized not merely by the presence of these countless dolls, but also by his vision of her playing with and singing to these figures throughout the night. Yet what are we to make of the details of this scene, the peculiarity that most of the dolls are wearing "Kopfbedeckung," which we presume to be scarves, and that they are crowded together in this confined space? Is this an allusion to conditions in the Eastern

European *shtetl* from which Henry Selwyn and his family fled when he was a child? If so, then Aileen and her living quarters become place-holders for the *Heimat* Selwyn left behind, a *Heimat* whose amorphous absence calls forth his melancholic demeanor. We recall that when Selwyn speaks to the narrator of his homesickness, his memories attach solely to the act of departure and the reality of exile, rather than being directed at the homeland as a place of residence, of social interaction, or of emotional bonds. These are reserved for Aileen's overpopulated bedroom. This suggests that she represents Selwyn's *doppelgänger*, the "prior" self that exists behind the façade of the assimilated Henry Selwyn, and that haunts the internal depths of his unconscious as a latent memory. Through her connection to an interior space associated with myopia and an obscuring darkness, she symbolizes Selwyn's refusal to penetrate the barriers that separate him from his past, and his decision to focus instead on his constructed, façade-like self. But the short story "Dr. Henry Selwyn" has the trajectory of a fractured and truncated *Bildungsroman*: as it develops, its eponymous protagonist also progressively changes. His past increasingly comes into focus, while his present loses contour.

In one of the central scenes of this story, in which Selwyn finally conjures up memories from his past—the dinner and slide presen-tation on the occasion of Edward Ellis's/Edwin Elliot's visit—Aileen is the person charged with setting up the projector and screen, thereby providing the mechanism that will stimulate Selwyn's memories. In this pivotal episode, we are introduced to the only wholly positive characters attached to Selwyn's past, the mountain guide Johannes Naegeli, with whom he struck up an intimate friendship in the summer of 1913, and Edward Ellis, the botanist and entomologist who accompanied Selwyn on the trip to Crete that is the subject of the slide presentation. Naegeli and Ellis are significant as representatives of a positive and emotionally uplifting attachment to the past. They are therefore counter-models to Aileen's representation of repressed and unacknowledged memories. Furthermore, whereas the servant is persistently identified with the dark interior of the house, with the gloom, distortion, and myopia consistent with a focus on the spatially and temporally proximate, Naegeli and Ellis are aligned with distance, with that bright, panoramic vision the narrator and his wife enjoy when they look out through the windows of the house at Prior's Gate. Naegeli has escorted Selwyn to remarkable panoramic heights in the Swiss Alps (23–4/14), and the slides taken on the trip with Ellis portray the panoramic view from a mountain pass onto the plateau of Lasithi (28/17). Both of these characters are identified with an encompassing, panoramic perspective that stands opposed to a myopic obsession with the proximate.

The emotional bond that joins Selwyn and Naegeli is, on the surface, highly enigmatic, since it is difficult to discern anything about the nature of this relationship that justifies the profound feelings Selwyn harbors toward this individual and the pain of his loss. In this respect, however, Selwyn's relationship with Naegeli mirrors the one he has with his Lithuanian homeland: both attain significance due more to their *absence* than because of any specific features they possess. This explains why in his revelations about the pain he suffers upon his separation from Naegeli, Selwyn concentrates solely on the moment of departure and subsequent absence. Reflecting on his leave-taking when forced to join the Allied war effort, Selwyn remarks:

> [W]ie ich jetzt erst in der Rückschau vollends begreife, [ist mir] nichts so schwergefallen wie der Abschied von Johannes Naegeli. Selbst die Trennung von Hedi, die ich in Bern kennengelernt hatte um die Weihnachtszeit und die ich dann nach dem Krieg geheiratet habe, hat mir nicht annähernd denselben Schmerz bereitet wie die Trennung von Naegeli, den ich noch immer auf dem Bahnhof von Meiringen stehen und winken sehe. (*Ausgewanderten* 24)
>
> [[N]othing felt as hard, as I realize now looking back, as saying goodbye to Johannes Naegeli. Even the separation from Elli, whom I had met at Christmas in Berne and married after the war, did not cause me remotely as much pain as the separation from Naegeli. I can still see him standing at the station at Meiringen, waving. (*Emigrants* 14)]

The parallel between this leave-taking and the departure from his Lithuanian home is suggested by the motif of the train station, which is central to each recollection. Additionally, the absolute presence of this memory, marked by the manner in which Selwyn can conjure up Naegeli as though he still sees him ("den ich noch immer … sehe"; "I can still see him"), replicates the act of seeing and the anaphoric repetitions of the phrase "Ich sehe," "I see," that punctuate the rhetoric in which Selwyn catalogues his memories of departure from his native Lithuanian village (31/19). These scenes of departure constitute those moments of the past that are most present and alive in Selwyn's memories. The intensity of his pain at the separation from Naegeli derives from the fact that it unconsciously invokes this earlier separation from his homeland. Why this departure from Naegeli should be more difficult and traumatic than the separation from Hedi, who will later become his bride, remains mysterious if one insists on comprehending these relationships in emotional rather than in symbolic terms. When Selwyn first meets Naegeli he is a mere twenty-one years old, whereas the mountain guide is over three times his age, a rarefied sixty-five. Given this age discrepancy, an erotic bond seems less than likely, and an attachment to Naegeli as a symbolic father-figure suggests itself as an alternative explanation. Or perhaps Naegeli is the symbolic reincarnation of the schoolteacher in Selwyn's *cheder*, whose fond gesture of placing his hand on the child's head is the sole memory Selwyn recaptures from his childhood home (31/19), as I suggested in the previous chapter? At any rate, the intensity of Selwyn's suffering at the loss of Naegeli only makes sense when this figure is viewed as a symbolic parallel for the lost homeland. In a text that operates so fundamentally with the structure of return and reiteration, the departure from (and loss of) Naegeli represents the uncanny repetition of Selwyn's departure from and loss (or lack) of *Heimat*.

Selwyn's reaction upon the news of Naegeli's death confirms the symbolism of this attachment: he falls into a depression so deep that it nearly causes his discharge from the military, and he describes his emotional state in terms that emblematically revisit the physical death of Naegeli on the Aare glacier: he felt "as if I was buried under snow and ice" ("als sei ich begraben unter Schnee und Eis"; 25/15). Only with the death of Naegeli is Selwyn's past irretrievably "buried"; this is the second key experience of loss and lack in his life, and he compensates for it via the union with Hedi and the construction of the façade persona this marriage promotes. Sebald's German text is more emphatic about this connection, since it prints the illustration of the Aare glacier immediately after this remark about Selwyn's feeling of being emotionally buried, thereby making the parallel between these acts of physical and emotional burying more explicit (see Figure 4.2).

Whereas Naegeli is the symbolic representative of Selwyn's past, of Hersch Seweryn, Hedi is the figure around which the new life of Henry Selwyn crystallizes. When Naegeli disappears into the crevasse, so does Hersch Seweryn. The same symbolic logic demands, however, that when the body of Naegeli resurfaces, so must the memory of Selwyn's repressed identity as Hersch Seweryn. This symbolic configuration also explains why Selwyn interprets his emotional bonds to his wife and Naegeli in terms of a relationship of inverse proportion: as the ties to Hedi/Elli diminish over the years, the fondness he feels for Naegeli increases. Selwyn even formulates this shift of emotional allegiances as a kind of cause-and-effect relationship: "since Elli has come to seem a stranger to me over the years, whereas Naegeli seems closer whenever he comes to my mind" ("weil mir die Hedi die Jahre über in zunehmendem Maße fremd geworden ist, während mir Naegeli, jedesmal, wenn er auftaucht in meinen Gedanken, vertrauter geworden scheint"; 24/15). We recall that Selwyn consciously hid his *shtetl* origins from his wife, and that he interprets their ultimate

Figure 4.2: Illustration of a glacial field (*Ausgewanderten* 25/14).

revelation as a possible cause for the alienation in their marriage (34–5/20–1). The confession of his Jewish ancestry becomes the fissure that ruptures his relationship with her. Selwyn, like Naegeli, will fall into this "crevasse"; but it is a rift of his own making, one that mirrors the divide that traverses his own being and his self-understanding. By contrast, Selwyn's growing affection for Naegeli represents his gradual remembering and embracing of this lost past and his pre-assimilation self: it marks the attempt to heal or repair this rift—to return the body and spirit of Hersch Seweryn from the glacial crevasse in which it lies buried.

Henry Selwyn's life story is a tale about the return of the repressed; his past returns violently, symbolized by the recoil of the big-game rifle he uses to take his own life. Sebald is particularly fond of describing the processes of memory, forgetfulness, and recollection by drawing on metaphors from the domains of vision and photography. One of the most memorable examples of this can be found in *Austerlitz*, whose eponymous hero compares the act of remembering to the slow emergence of photographic images in the chemical bath during the process of development (*Austerlitz* 113/77). In the case of Henry Selwyn, life in his hermitage is marked by a dialectical process in which his thoughts both become more hazy, and, in a seeming paradox, simultaneously assume greater refinement and clarity.

> Er [Selwyn] lebte in seiner Eremitage und gab sich ganz seinen, wie er mir gegenüber gelegentlich konstatierte, einerseits Tag für Tag verschwommener, andererseits einsinniger und genauer werdenden Gedanken hin. (*Ausgewanderten* 20)
> [He [Selwyn] lived in his hermitage, giving his entire attention, as he occasionally told me, to thoughts which on the one hand grew vaguer day by day, and, on the other, grew more precise and unambiguous. (*Emigrants* 11)]

How can we explain the contradiction that Selwyn's thoughts become both more blurry and more precise at the same time? Sebald seems to be alluding to a common visual experience, one that can be paradigmatically recreated by a cinematic camera. If the eye/camera focuses on an object in the foreground of the field of vision, the background blurs into a haze; if we alter our visual orientation and make the background the object of our gaze, the objects in the foreground lose focus and become fuzzy.[21] This inverse structure has two analogues that we have already examined. One is the relation between Selwyn's affections for his wife and Naegeli, and the relationship to the present and the past they represent. The other is the dialectic between the restricted myopic concentration on the proximate and the expansive panoramic overview. This latter pattern is similarly drawn from the realm of visual perception, and it closely parallels the dynamic interaction of clarity and fogginess that Selwyn attributes to his reminiscences. Seen in the context of Selwyn's development during the diegesis itself, this dynamic describes the shifting relationship between present and past, proximate and distant, in his own self-understanding. As his thoughts and memories of his pre-assimilated self gradually return and come into greater focus, the thoughts concerned with his existence as the assimilated Henry Selwyn dissipate and become more vague. When

---

21 See Heiner Boehncke, "Clair obscur: W. G. Sebalds Bilder," *W. G. Sebald*, Special Issue of *Text + Kritik* 158 (April 2003): 48, who argues that this dialectic of light and dark, clarity and obscurity, which he refers to as a "Manichäismus der Wahrnehmung" (Manichaeism of perception), structures Sebald's entire aesthetic.

he sits down on his bed, places his chin on the muzzle of the big-game rifle, and fires this weapon—as the narrator remarks, for the first time "with intent to kill" ("mit tödlicher Absicht"; 35/23)—this act represents the elimination of the façade-like Henry Selwyn and the return—unfortunately, only in death, as is true of Johannes Naegeli as well—of Hersch Seweryn, the ghost of the absent homeland.

In order to better understand the implied relationship between a panoramic overview and the return of a repressed and abandoned past, we need to examine more closely the episode of the dinner and slideshow during the visit of Selwyn's friend Ellis/Elliot. On both a structural and thematic level, an image that unifies this text in leitmotivic fashion is a vision of a mountainous, alpine landscape. The very name Hersch Seweryn assumes in his act of assimilation hints at this, since the word "Selwyn" doubles as the appellation of two mountain ranges, one in British Columbia and the other in Australia. This motif is present in the text as *photographic* representation in three separate instances: in the depiction of a glacier field (see Figure 4.2) like that on which Naegeli disappeared (25/14); as background for the picture of Nabokov/Selwyn as butterfly catcher (27/16); and finally, in the photograph of the Aare glacier from the clipping of the Lausanne newspaper that reports on the "return" of Naegeli's corpse (37/22). Not coincidentally, the evening dinner party is introduced by the narrator's experience of looking out of the windows of the dining room and witnessing how the clouds are shaped as snow-white formations that remind him of massive alpine peaks:

Es war nun schon nahezu dunkel geworden im Innern des Hauses, und auch draußen begann das Grün blauschattiger und tiefer zu werden. Am Horizont aber war noch das westliche Licht und stand ein Wolkengebirge, dessen im Einnachten noch schneeweiße Formationen mich an die höchsten Massive der Alpen erinnerten. (*Ausgewanderten* 22)
[By now it was almost dark inside the house, and outside, too, the greenery was thickening with deep, blue shadows. The light of the west still lay on the horizon, though, with mountains of cloud whose snowy formations reminded me of the loftiest alpine massifs, as the night descended. (*Emigrants* 12–13)]

Contrasting the dark interior of the house with the waning evening light and bright horizon outside, this passage refers back to the earlier scene in which the narrator and his wife sense that the view of the bright natural world outside the manor's windows compensates for its gloomy interior (15/8). What has been added to the picture are the mirage-like mountain formations assumed by the clouds, which anticipate Selwyn's tale of his mountain-climbing adventures with Naegeli and the photographs of the mountain landscape taken during the trip to Crete.[22] The motif of return dominates the last half of this text. Just as, while viewing the slides of their trip that took place ten years ago, Selwyn and Ellis experience a "return of their past selves" ("Rückkehr aus der Vergangenheit"; 28/17), Selwyn is now able for the first time to access memories of his past. The most poignant return is that of the body of Johannes Naegeli, with which this narrative concludes; and this theme of return and the recall of past memories is closely intertwined, in the episode of the dinner party, with the panoramic picture of the Lasithi plateau and Spathi mountain depicted on the final slide.

In the narrator's ekphrastic recounting of this image, what stands out is the abundance or over-profusion of light:

> Auf dem letzten der Bilder breitete sich vor uns die von einer nördlichen Paßhöhe herab aufgenommene Hochebene von Lasithi aus. Die Aufnahme mußte um die Mittagszeit gemacht worden sein, denn die Strahlen der Sonne kamen dem Beschauer entgegen. Der im Süden die Ebene überragende, über zwei-tausend Meter hohe Berg Spathi wirkte wie eine Luftspiegelung hinter der Flut des Lichts. (*Ausgewanderten* 28)
> [In the last of the pictures we saw the expanse of the Lasithi plateau outspread before us, taken from the heights of one of the northern passes. The shot must have been taken around midday, since the sun was shining into our line of vision. To the south, lofty Mount Spathi, two thousand metres high, towered above the plateau, like a mirage beyond the flood of light. (*Emigrants* 17)]

The dinner guests sit silently gazing at this image until the glass frame of the slide breaks and a dark crack ("ein dunkler Riß") cuts through the picture on the screen (28–9/17). Just as the slide *depicts* an excess of light, it is also a surfeit of light and its concomitant heat that causes the slide to break. This crack symbolically invokes the rupture that rends the surface of Selwyn's façade-self and opens up a breach through which his repressed past gains access to consciousness. Only subse-quent to this episode is Selwyn able to relate the long-lost memories of his childhood departure from his native village in Lithuania and

---

22   Carol Jacobs, *Sebald's Vision* (New York: Columbia University Press, 2015), 32, notes that the mountainous terrain of Crete and the alpine tours with Naegeli are interrelated; but she does not draw the connection to the mountain-like cloud formations and the intratextual linkage that ties this episode to the dichotomies of interior–exterior, dark–light, and myopia–far-sightedness.

be slowly revisited by "homesickness," "Heimweh" (30–1/18). The intense light-effects and this panoramic overview stand in for the illumination of the past via an encompassing perspective. The narrator addresses the connection between the light-flooded view of the Lasithi plateau, the mountain Spathi, and the revitalization of memory when he relates how *his own* recollection of this picture and this evening at Prior's Gate is invoked when he screens Werner Herzog's film *The Enigma of Kaspar Hauser* in a London cinema:

> Der so lange, bis zum Zerspringen festgehaltene Anblick der Hochebene von Lasithi hat sich mir damals tief eingeprägt, und dennoch hatte ich ihn geraume Zeit vergessen gehabt. Wiederbelebt ist er worden erst ein paar Jahre darauf, als ich in einem Londoner Kino das Traumgespräch sah, das Kaspar Hauser mit seinem Lehrer Daumer im Küchengarten des Daumerschen Hauses führt. (*Ausgewanderten* 29)
> [That view of the Lasithi plateau, held so long till it shattered, made a deep impression on me at the time, yet it later vanished from my mind almost completely. It was not until a few years afterwards that it returned to me, in a London cinema, as I followed a conversation between Kaspar Hauser and his teacher, Daumer, in the kitchen garden at Daumer's home. (*Emigrants* 17)]

Significant in this episode from Herzog's film, according to Sebald's narrator, is that Hauser for the first time is able to distinguish between dream and reality. But is he? The language with which Hauser introduces his recapitulation of the dream is grammatically ambiguous: "Ja, es hat *mich* geträumt. *Mich* hat vom Kaukasus geträumt" ("I was in a dream, and in my dream I saw the Caucasus"; 29/17; emphasis added). Incorrectly using the accusative personal preposition "mich" instead of the dative "mir" opens up a curious ambiguity about whether Hauser is *having* this dream or if he himself is its product or inhabits it,[23] as the English translation struggles to suggest. Is Hauser dreaming, or is he *being* dreamed? This moment of undecidability represents a significant dimension in the life of the historical Kaspar Hauser: he is the paradigmatic exile, cut off completely from an obscure and vague past—one spent confined, no less, in a prison-like cellar—and whose emergence as individual is predicated upon a set of learned behaviors that slowly fashion him into a social, linguistically-competent being. But which of these existences is real and which is dream, the imprisonment in the cellar or the entrance into language—into the Lacanian symbolic order? The same question is relevant for Henry Selwyn, who is symbolically

---

23 Jacobs, *Sebald's Vision*, 33, points to this linguistic anomaly.

personified in the figure of Kaspar Hauser: both are exiles, separated by a deep rupture from a vague and darkly haunting past; and both must set out on a crash course of assimilation in order to adapt to their new social environment. Hauser's dream vision of the Caucasus Mountains is the analogue of Selwyn's photograph of the Lasithi plateau, and both images serve as summons to recollect a past engulfed in darkness. We hardly need remind ourselves that the "enigma" named in the English title of Herzog's film is nothing other than the enigma of Hauser's *origin*. This enigmatic origin is what he shares with Selwyn, and Herzog's film, like Sebald's narrative, depicts the halting attempts of certain individuals—Hauser's guardian Daumer in the film, and the witnessing narrator in Sebald's story—to aid the protagonist in recovering this shrouded past.

Sebald's narrator emphasizes this parallel between Hauser and Selwyn when he describes how Herzog's film cuts from Hauser as narrator of his dream vision to a panning panoramic shot of the landscape he has imagined:

> Die Kamera bewegt sich dann von rechts nach links in einem weiten Bogen und zeigt uns das Panorama einer von Bergzügen umgebenen, sehr indisch aussehenden Hochebene, auf der zwischen grünem Gebüsch und Waldungen pagodenartige Turm- oder Tempelbauten mit seltsam dreieckigen Fassaden aufragen, Follies, die in dem pulsierend das Bild überblendenden Licht mich stets von neuem erinnern an die Segel der Windpumpen von Lasithi, die ich in Wirklichkeit noch gar nicht gesehen habe. (*Ausgewanderten* 29)
> [The camera then moved from right to left, in a sweeping arc, offering a panoramic view of a plateau ringed by mountains, a plateau with a distinctly Indian look to it, with pagoda-like towers and temples with strange triangular façades amidst the green undergrowth and woodland: follies, in a pulsing dazzle of light, that kept reminding me of the sails of those wind pumps of Lasithi, which in reality I have still not seen to this day. (*Emigrants* 17–18)]

Although the narrator gives an accurate account of the images in Herzog's film, including their overexposed lighting effects—similar to the flood of light on the slide of Lasithi—and their curiously pulsating quality, he obliquely connects this vision with the life of Selwyn by means of his intratextual reference to façades and follies—to the architectural motifs that ruled the first half of this narrative and that represent Selwyn's assimilated persona. In this instance these architectural edifices have been infected by an Orientalizing tinge: the plateau strikes the narrator as somehow "Indian," the buildings are "pagoda-like," and they are no longer simple towers, as in the illustration of Selwyn's folly, but also temples. This hint of the Orient is justified by the fact that Hauser's dream is of the Caucasus Mountains, the symbolic geographical divide between Europe and Asia. As perceived by Sebald's narrator, Hauser has already been transported beyond the Caucasus, and it is tempting to read this insistence on the "Oriental" as an allusion to Selwyn's own Jewish, in the metaphorical sense "Oriental," origins. What this sequence calls to mind is the reality of the Jewish diaspora, and of Hersch Seweryn as a victim and Henry Selwyn as the product of this diasporic experience.

Sebald's intertextual and intermedial references are sometimes just as significant for what they leave out as for what they include. The connection to Herzog's *Kaspar Hauser* provides a telling case in point. At the very end of this film, just prior to his death, Hauser has another vision, which he relates not as a dream, but as a story whose conclusion eludes him.[24] This story tells of a blind Berber who leads a caravan across the desert. At one point the caravan participants perceive a mountain range on the horizon and believe they have lost their way. The caravan halts and tries unsuccessfully to find orientation with a compass. Finally, the blind Berber takes some sand into his mouth and tastes it, whereupon he announces the mountains are an illusion and the caravan is on the proper course. In Hauser's telling, the caravan arrives safely in an unnamed city to the north, but he confesses that the "true" story only begins at this point, and that he unfortunately is not familiar with it.

The relevance of this sequence for Sebald's story of Henry Selwyn is many-faceted. First, in the movie Hauser's internal narrative about the caravan is shot using the same technique of overexposed, pulsating images that he employed for the Caucasus dream, thereby linking these sequences. Moreover, the image of a caravan crossing the desert forms a recurrent motif in Sebald's works, one that ties together the diverse narratives of *Die Ausgewanderten*. In "Max Aurach" it surfaces as a fresco on the wall of the Café Wadi Halfa where the narrator and Aurach meet (243/164). In "Ambros Adelwarth" its manifestation is once again

---

24 Jacobs, *Sebald's Vision*, 33–5, identifies the relevance of this episode from Herzog's film and analyzes its significance for the stories in *Die Ausgewanderten*. She interprets it in the context of photographic phenomena, whereas my analysis focuses on the Orientalist allusions as the connective tissue to Selwyn's lost Jewish origins. For an especially penetrating examination of Herzog's film and its relevance for Sebald's story, see the chapter "Remembering and Re-visioning in W. G. Sebald's *Die Ausgewanderten* and Werner Herzog's *Jeder für sich und Gott gegen alle*" in Sabina Pasic, "W. G. Sebald and the Cinematic Imagination," Ph.D. diss., University of Washington, 2014, 79–131.

cinematic, occurring as the caravan conjured up by the magician
Sandor Weltmann in the film *Dr. Mabuse der Spieler* (Dr. Mabuse the
gambler; 141/97). In this story the hallucinatory caravan that Cosmo
Solomon sees invokes the past idyllic journey he undertook with
Ambros to the Orient. The psychological impact of this revisitation of
the past has such severe consequences that it leads to Cosmo's eventual
disappearance. The caravan scene from *Kaspar Hauser* condenses into
a single example many of the motifs and themes central to "Dr. Henry
Selwyn": a loss of orientation; the caravan as embodiment of the
nomadism of exile; the image of mountains as visionary illusion; the
Berber's mystical tasting of desert sand as the clue to orientation and as
an allusion to the irrational sense of belonging associated with *Heimat*.
Perhaps it is indicative of Sebald's narrative technique, especially of his
strategy for intertextual and intermedial references, that he leaves it to
his readers to reconstruct this network of subtle structural and thematic
allusions. By doing so he forces us to engage in precisely that activity of
interpretive reconstruction and recollection in which both his fictional
character, Henry Selwyn, and his narrator are involved. We must
retrieve and reconstruct memories, images, or experiences that, once
assembled and networked, allow us to connect the dots of Selwyn's
history, even if the picture that emerges is blurry, sketchy, and rent with
gaps and fissures. In our hermeneutical engagement with Sebald's text
we re-enact not only Selwyn's encounter with the fragmentary threads
of his own past, but also the narrator's attempts to draw connections
between Selwyn's life and his own experiences. What stands out about
the empathetic interactions that Sebald stages between his narrator
and his informant-character Henry Selwyn is the way in which their
experiences mutually illuminate each other. Sebald further develops
this technique of narrative empathy in the final story of this collection,
"Max Aurach," and brings it to fruition in his last completed narrative,
Austerlitz.

   There is a further cinematic lineage worth pursuing here, one
with which Sebald was intimately familiar, and which reinforces the
mysterious manner in which the panoramic view over the plateau of
Lasithi calls forth reminiscences of Selwyn's earlier life in the Jewish
diaspora. In his review of Hanns Zischler's *Kafka geht ins Kino* (*Kafka
Goes to the Movies*), published as "Kafka im Kino" ("Kafka Goes to
the Movies"),[25] Sebald refers to a sequence from Leni Riefenstahl's
Triumph des Willens (*Triumph of the Will*) that depicts a tent city strikingly reminiscent of the sails and the wind pumps on the Lasithi
plateau in "Henry Selwyn." He notes that the viewers partake in

25 This essay was first published in the *Frankfurter Rundschau* on January 18, 1997
    and later reprinted in the posthumously published volume *Campo Santo*.

this "strange, enormously evocative series of pictures" ("seltsame, ungeheuer suggestive Folge von Bildern"; *Campo Santo* 208/166) from a perspective high above the scenario. Sebald's ekphrastic description highlights the details perceived from this panoramic viewpoint (see Figure 4.3):

> Soweit das Auge reicht, sieht man weiße, pyramidenförmige Gebilde. Man erkennt aufgrund der ungewohnten Perspektive zunächst gar nicht, was es ist. Der Tag bricht gerade an, und nach und nach, auf dem noch halbdunklen Gelände, kommen aus den Zelten die Menschen heraus … Die erhabene Wirkung wird dann etwas zerstört, als man die deutschen Männer aus der Nähe sieht bei ihrer Morgenwäsche mit freiem Oberkörper, diesem Hauptemblem nationalsozialistischer Hygiene. Nichtsdestoweniger bleibt einem das magische Bild von den weißen Zelten in der Erinnerung. Ein Volk zieht durch die Wüste. Am Horizont erscheint schon das gelobte Land. (*Campo Santo* 208)
> [There they are, stretching as far as the eye can see: white pyramidal structures. At first, because of the unusual perspective, you do not see exactly what they are. Day is just dawning, and gradually, in the still twilit landscape, people come out of the tents … The edifying effect is rather reduced when you see the men in close-up performing their morning ablutions bare-chested, a frequent emblem of National Socialist hygiene. Nonetheless, a magical picture of those white tents lingers in the mind. A people traveling through the desert. The Promised Land appears on the horizon. (*Campo Santo* 166)]

In Sebald's interpretation, Riefenstahl stages the ideological occupation by Hitler's Brownshirts of the mythological exodus of the Jewish people through the desert to the Promised Land: exile culminates in the utopian dream of regained and purified *Heimat*. Several thematic and structural elements connect this scene to the slide of the Lasithi plateau. The panoramic perspective so central to the motivic structure of this episode in "Dr. Henry Selwyn" is replicated in the scene from *Triumph des Willens*, whereby the white tents scattered across the meadow are the visual replication of the white sails on the wind pumps of Lasithi. The "pyramidal structures" of the tents have their analogue in the "pagoda-like towers and temples with strange *triangular* façades" ("pagodenartige Turm- oder Tempelbauten mit seltsam *dreieckigen* Fassaden") in the Lasithi photograph (*Ausgewanderten* 29/18; emphasis added). Consistent in this series of images—the photograph of Lasithi, the Caucasus dream and caravan story in *Kaspar Hauser*, and the Nazi encampment in *Triumph des Willens*—is their suggestive invocation

Figure 4.3: Nazi encampment, Riefenstahl, *Triumph des Willens*.

of an Oriental atmosphere and the narrative of the "chosen people" traveling through the desert. In the essay "Kafka im Kino," Sebald reflects more generally on the power of photographic images to evoke peculiar feelings: "We are so moved by photographic images because of the curious aura of another world that sometimes emanates from them" ("Was einen an fotografischen Bildern so rührt, das ist das eigenartig jenseitige, das uns manchmal anweht aus ihnen"; *Campo Santo* 198/156). This precisely describes the effect the photograph of the Lasithi plateau has on Henry Selwyn, Ellis, and the narrator. It conjures up oddly "transcendental" impressions of another place, just out of reach of their conscious awareness, a place whose status exists at the boundary, in the liminal space between dream and reality, the noumenal and the phenomenal. This is Henry Selwyn's *Heimat*: the desert, the caravan, the Orient, the diaspora. And just as the Caucasus sequence in Herzog's *Kaspar Hauser* summons up the wind pumps of Lasithi—which, as the narrator admits, he has actually never seen "in reality"—the photograph of Lasithi invokes for Selwyn that mythological place of the Jewish homeland.

Henry Selwyn's home is located, paradoxically, in the diaspora. Its representative image is the caravan, the symbol of nomadism, of constant travel, of being on the move between two (or more) fixed points. The curse of his existence is that he is condemned to be neither here nor there, neither Henry Selwyn nor Hersch Seweryn, living neither in the myopia of the proximate nor in the panorama of far-sighted memory. Exile is not identifiable with either one of these poles; it is the condition of being caught between them, always dis-placed and dis-oriented, always just removed from somewhere—but never quite sure of where and what that somewhere actually is. We will further explore this state of what I call "ectopic" existence in the next chapter, dedicated to the tale of the exiled painter Max Aurach/Max Ferber. In this culminating story of *Die Ausgewanderten*, this ectopic state of being neither here nor there, of life in an unidentifiable no-place, conditions not only the existence of the eponymous protagonist but also Sebald's first-person narrator. Moreover, this sense of homelessness becomes the condition of possibility for the empathetic relationship between this narrator as voluntary exile and his exiled informant.

Five Sebald's Ectopia: Homelessness and Alienated Heritage in "Max Aurach"/"Max Ferber"

"Heimat ist das Entronnensein."
["Homeland is the state of having escaped."]
Horkheimer and Adorno[1]

Contemplating Heritage as Hidden History

In a central passage from his influential 1935 lectures *Einführung in die Metaphysik* (*Introduction to Metaphysics*), Martin Heidegger (1889–1976) exploits his characteristic etymological deliberations in order to explore the fundamental concept of *Sein* or Being. His ruminations culminate in the assertion that the search to determine the meaning of this word emerges as "Besinnung auf die Herkunft unserer *verborgenen Geschichte*" ("meditation on the provenance of our *concealed history*").[2] As is typical of Heidegger's language, the primary words in this statement have a provocative depth and demand individual explication. *Besinnung*, based on the root noun *Sinn*, which translates as "sense" in both the literal connotation of sensual perception and the figurative signification of "meaning," suggests concentrated contemplation, reflection, meditation, or heightened awareness. As a reflexive verb, *sich besinnen*, it implies directing one's attention to something and is often synonymous with the verb for remembering, *sich erinnern*. *Besinnung* thus describes an attitude of mind in which one focuses attention on something that is lost and hence must be recovered, and for Heidegger

1 Max Horkheimer and Theodor Adorno, *Dialektik der Aufklärung: Philosophische Fragmente* (Frankfurt am Main: Fischer Taschenbuch Verlag, 1988), 86; *Dialectic of Enlightenment*, trans. John Cumming (New York: Continuum, 1993), 78.

2 Martin Heidegger, *Einführung in die Metaphysik*, 2nd ed. (Tübingen: Niemeyer, 1958), 70; *Introduction to Metaphysics*, trans. Gregory Fried and Richard Polt (New Haven, CT: Yale University Press, 2000), 97.

this nuance of recuperation is especially important. The adjective *besinnungslos* describes a loss of consciousness, but also implies a thoughtlessness or ignorance that stems from neglect. In Heidegger's existential framework, the cognitive operation of *Besinnung* is fundamental precisely because it names the effort to regain awareness of something that has been forgotten, lost, misplaced, or neglected.

For Heidegger the specified object of this concerted recollection is *Herkunft*, a common noun signifying heritage, ancestry, lineage, provenance, or origin. This word derives from the verb *herkommen*, meaning to descend from, or to approach or arrive somewhere from a certain place. The term suggests connectedness, in the sense of an evolutionary development out of a specific source, or continuity with a certain tradition or set of customs. The need to take cognizance of this hereditary linkage implies that a rupture has occurred, an alienation from the human being's own existential origin. This loss is captured by the next term in Heidegger's statement, the adjective *verborgen*, which means hidden, secret, or concealed. What is it that, for Heidegger, has remained concealed and hence must become the object of concerted contemplation and thereby recovered? It is our *Geschichte*, the history, story, or narrative of our *Herkunft*, of human emergence, how we have arrived at our current state of being. Heidegger defines the human ontological task in terms of a meditative recuperation of the heritage manifest in our obscured history. His proposition, although syntactically uncomplicated and semantically lucid, defies any simple translation. In an attempt to invoke its various significations, we might render it in the following complex form: our search for the meaning of Being takes shape as "contemplation (remembrance; recovery) of the origin (lineage; heritage; derivation) of our hidden (concealed; forgotten; repressed) history (story; narrative; tradition)."

The multiple meanings of this proposition and its central concepts display a peculiar relevance for the project W. G. Sebald embraced in his prose fictions. Hence it comes as no surprise that in the copy of Heidegger's text contained in his personal library, Sebald placed two exclamatory bars in the margin opposite this passage. He is less interested in the broader ontological and philosophical implications of Heidegger's statement than in the application of this dictum to more pragmatic questions related to the interrogation of the historical past. The investigative process by which Sebald's first-person narrator reconstructs the past and the *Herkunft* of the four emigrants in *Die Ausgewanderten* and of the eponymous protagonist of *Austerlitz* —a process I designate throughout as "ghostwriting"—instantiates precisely the kind of "Besinnung auf die Herkunft unserer *verborgenen Geschichte*" that Heidegger champions.

The stories in Sebald's second collection of fictional narratives comprise contemplations about how the Being of four individuals emerges out of the hidden histories that these narratives uncover. Each of these stories' protagonists is engaged in an act of critical *Besinnung*, a recollection of his own heritage and his obscured or partially repressed history. Henry Selwyn experiences exile as a vague sense of displacement from a lost origin; Paul Bereyter is thrown off his life trajectory when Nazi racial policies force him to abandon his personal and professional calling as a teacher and lead to the deportation and presumed murder of his lover Helen Hollaender; Ambros Adelwarth's utopian existence as a stateless wanderer who frequents the gaming casinos peopled by an international elite is interrupted first by the intervention of World War I, and subsequently by the resulting insanity and death of his partner, Cosmo Solomon. All three of these figures end their own lives, but for different reasons. Selwyn kills himself because remembrance of his origins reveals his adult existence as an empty façade. Bereyter lies down on the railroad tracks because he embraces the fate of his partial Jewish heritage, which dictates that he, as his uncle once remarked, is fated to "end up on the railways" ("werde ... bei der Eisenbahn enden"; *Ausgewanderten* 92/62), suggesting he should have shared the destiny of Holocaust victims. Adelwarth, finally, opts for death by shock "therapy" precisely because it replicates the upheavals of his life, but provides the ultimate form of forgetfulness as the forced eradication of memory.

By contrast, Max Aurach, the protagonist in the final story of this collection—the last in the order of presentation, although the third in the order of composition[3]—avoids the temptation of suicide and, arguably, models most consistently a concerted effort toward that contemplation on heritage and his concealed history that Heidegger views as essential to the human ontological task. This is one reason why this story represents an especially appropriate object for examining how problems of heritage, homelessness, and exile develop in Sebald's oeuvre. In addition, it constitutes the most narratively complex of these four stories, and it marks an important station in the trajectory toward *Austerlitz*, Sebald's final work of prose fiction. In "Max Aurach,"

---

3   The materials in the files for the "Aurach" story at the Deutsches Literaturarchiv indicate that Sebald first intended to publish these stories in the chronological order of their composition, but that he later chose to print "Aurach" as the fourth and final piece. The photographs for this story initially bear the inscription "Teil III" (part III) with the relevant manuscript page, and only those images added toward the end of the editorial process are designated "Teil IV" (part IV). The photographic materials for "Adelwarth," *mutatis mutandi*, are originally marked "Teil IV" and corrected to "Teil III." See folders 10 and 15 in the file "*Die Ausgewanderten*," with the inventory number HS.2004.0001.00009.

problems of exile, emigration, and rootlessness are developed not only in the diegesis itself, in the life of the protagonist, but also in the framing narrative, in the life-situation of Sebald's first-person narrator, whose own status as an émigré is highlighted. This pronounced parallelism between narrator and protagonist distinguishes this story and justifies its status as the culminating tale of this collection. It raises questions about the narrator's own imbrication in the problematic of emigration as displacement and explores echoes between this autobiographical dimension and the biographical history of the protagonist. The extended frame of this text goes well beyond Sebald's typically brief incipit about the narrator's motivations. It emerges as a narrative in its own right, a story complete with a life-transforming insight. This narrator is figured as having elected to sever himself from his own heritage, lineage, descent, and personal history; empathetic investigation into the life of the exile painter Aurach provides a substitute for critical reflections about his own decision to abandon his past and indigenous home.

In "Max Aurach," readers learn much more about the past existence and motivations of Sebald's characteristic first-person narrator than in those stories where he is primarily concerned with reconstructing the life of an Other, such as the "Stendhal" and "Kafka" texts of *Schwindel. Gefühle*, the other three stories in *Die Ausgewanderten*, and even the more extended prose fiction *Austerlitz*. The more emphatically autobiographical texts of *Schwindel. Gefühle*, as well as *Die Ringe des Saturn* and the fragmentary Corsica project, stand apart because they explore the life of the first-person narrator more explicitly. "Aurach" is the one text in which autobiography and biography not only run parallel, but actively co-mingle. The central point is that the attitude of *Besinnung*, in the sense of contemplation and recovery of a *lost, forgotten*, or *hidden* history and heritage, is something that Sebald's narrator shares with each of his protagonists, but more emphatically with Aurach. The narrative texture of this tale is further complicated by the inclusion of a metadiegetic narrative that again reflects on problems of exile and displacement. This is the embedded story of Luisa Lanzberg and her family's exchange of an idyllic life in rural Steinach for a more metropolitan and, for her, alienated existence in Bad Kissingen. Narratively speaking, "Max Aurach" is constructed as a threefold cabinet of mirrors in which the lives of three émigrés, of different generations, and whose exiles have vastly different motivations, resonate with one another in multifarious ways. It is one of Sebald's most intricately structured narratives and arguably constitutes his most carefully crafted work of fiction.

Heidegger's statement about the search for Being as "Besinnung auf die Herkunft unserer *verborgenen Geschichte*" betrays a relevance for

the characteristic literary aesthetics Sebald implemented in his prose
fictions more generally. In terms of his aesthetic practice, it is germane to
consider Sebald's myriad intertextual allusions as an active integration of
his literary predecessors into the texture of his own writing. Intertextual
invocations are markers of an otherwise forgotten *literary* heritage, a
heritage that is recovered on the level of *language* in the heteroglossia of
Sebald's texts. In a 1993 interview with Ralph Schock, Sebald maintained
that the books one has read and the authors by whom one has been
influenced are as much a part of one's personal background as are social
context, country of origin, region of birth, and the places to which one
has travelled (*"Auf ungeheuer dünnem Eis"* 97). Sebald's readers might
be imagined as participants who are invited to engage with their own
form of *Besinnung*, of meditation on the lineage and descent of Sebald's
own texts, based on how they inflect these marked and unmarked
predecessor-texts. His intertextual practice can be regarded as a kind of
literary reconstruction of an intellectual lineage—one that marks out,
or perhaps substitutes for, the personal, familial, and national descent
of the narrator, and perhaps even of the author himself. Intertextuality
in Sebald represents an alternative heritage, one that manifests itself
in the linguistic dimension of his prose fictions, where "ghosts" from
the literary past are allowed to speak, and where Sebald's own texts
acknowledge their place in an obliquely charted literary-historical
lineage. In that regard, Sebald's poetics of history is also a history-
oriented poetics.

Modernity and the Breach with Heritage

One of Sebald's most intensive deliberations on the inter-human
alienation symptomatic of the modern world is voiced in the short,
posthumously published essay "Campo Santo" excerpted from his
incomplete Corsica project. Focusing on the culture of death rites
on the island of Corsica, Sebald emphasizes how community and
familial bonds among the Corsicans extended beyond the domain
of the living. Symptomatic of this heightened sense of kinship was
not only its negative inflection in the bloody tradition of feuding
clans, but also the more affirmative Corsican practice of burying
their dead in the hallowed ground of the home estate, where the
deceased remained in fellowship with the living. When describing
these family burial plots, Sebald invokes a dialectic of homeland and
exile, suggesting that the Corsicans do not banish their dead to an
otherworldly beyond, but instead let them continue to participate in
the community of the living.

Die in Korsika Jahrhunderte hindurch übliche Bestattung
auf dem von den Vorvätern ererbten Land glich einem die

Unveräußerlichkeit dieses Landes betreffenden Kontrakt, der
von Generation zu Generation stillschweigend erneuert wurde
zwischen jedem Verstorbenen und seiner Nachkommenschaft
... An solchen nicht selten besonders schönen und einen guten
Überblick über das Territorium der Familie, das Dorf und das
weitere Gelände gewährenden Plätzen waren die Verstorbenen
sozusagen ständig bei sich, waren nicht verbannt ins Exil und
konnten nach wie vor wachen über die Grenzen ihres Gebiets.
(*Campo Santo* 26–7)
[For centuries, the usual form of Corsican burial, on land inherited
from the forefathers of the dead, was like a contract affirming
inalienable rights to that land, a contract between every dead man
and his progeny and tacitly renewed from generation to generation ... In such places, which are often particularly beautiful and
have a good view over the family's territory, the village, and the
rest of the local land, the dead were always in a way at home,
were not sent into exile, and could continue to watch over the
boundaries of their property. (*Campo Santo* 22–3)]

These burial rituals provide evidence for a sense of heritage across
generations, beyond the borderline between life and death, that
cements a continuity of community and family. The grave site not
only exists on the ancestral territory, but overlooks the village and
the wider surroundings in which the lives of the deceased transpired.
At the close of this essay, Sebald contrasts this older, pre-modern
practice of incorporating the dead into the present-day community
with the modern, metropolitan proclivity for shunting them from
the circle of life and exiling them, as the forgotten, to the domain of
Lethe. In the modern world we not only clear the dead "out of the
way as quickly and comprehensively as possible" ("so schnell und
gründlich beiseite geräumt werden wie möglich"; *Campo Santo* 36/31);
they are also relegated to an ever-diminishing space, culminating
in the disappearance of their corpses in the crematorium (36–7/32).
Sebald implicitly contrasts the traditional death rituals of Corsica with
the technical processes of remainderless extermination practiced in
the Nazi death camps, which mark the culmination of this modern
alienation from death and from the dead, their consignment to a forgetfulness outside of history. Not surprisingly, Sebald aligns this increased
banishment of the departed with a refusal of remembrance that he
views as symptomatic of modernity. Citing the French Germanist
Pierre Bertaux on this mutation that defines modern humanity, he
remarks that "[t]o remember, to retain and to preserve" ("Erinnerung,
Aufbewahrung und Erhaltung"; 37/32) are only existential necessities
at times and places where population density is minimal. In densely

populated urban areas like Buenos Aires, Mexico City, or Bombay, both the dead and their memory must be obliterated as speedily and effortlessly as possible. He accuses modern human beings of responding to life in an overpopulated world by jettisoning their own childhood and youth, and goes on to indict them for the systematic and total eradication of their heritage, ancestry, and predecessors:

In den Stadtschaften des ausgehenden zwanzigsten Jahrhunderts hingegen, in denen jeder, von einer Stunde zur andern, ersetzbar und eigentlich bereits von Geburt an überzählig ist, kommt es darauf an, dauernd Ballast über Bord zu werfen, alles, woran man sich erinnern könnte, die Jugend, die Kindheit, die Herkunft, die Vorväter und Ahnen restlos zu vergessen … Und aus seiner gedächtnislosen Gegenwart heraus und angesichts einer vom Verstand keines einzelnen mehr zu erfassenden Zukunft werden wir am Ende selber das Leben lassen ohne das Bedürfnis, eine Weile wenigstens noch bleiben oder gelegentlich zurückkehren zu dürfen. (*Campo Santo* 37–8)
[In the urban societies of the late twentieth century, on the other hand, where everyone is instantly replaceable and is really superfluous from birth, we have to keep throwing ballast overboard, forgetting everything that we might otherwise remember: youth, childhood, our origins, our forebears and ancestors … And leaving a present without memory, in the face of a future that no individual mind can now envisage, in the end we shall ourselves relinquish life without feeling any need to linger at least for a while, nor shall we be impelled to pay return visits from time to time. (*Campo Santo* 32–3)]

An age devoid of all memory, one that has cut itself off completely from the past—an age of alienation from *Being*, in Heidegger's sense—is also an age that has no collective future. But more importantly, it is an age that has no ghosts, no voices that speak to it and "haunt" it from the past, and whose living members, by extension, can never hold out hope of being memorialized as revenants in the time beyond their own passing. The modern world is marked by radical isolation and individualism; all human beings are emphatically ectopic, in the literal sense of the Greek word *ek-topos*, meaning "out of place" or lacking any "home" of their own. The universal state of existence in modernity is one of homelessness, lack of heritage, and permanent exile. All of us live as émigrés or refugees, in a state of perennial banishment from our own pasts, our traditions, our heritage, our families.

In this context it is easier to understand Sebald's fascination with ghosts more generally, and with liminal figures such as Kafka's Hunter

Gracchus more specifically: they defy the modern banishment of
death as non-remembrance, and as revenants they function not only
as *reminders* of the past, but also as *remainders*, as the last vestiges of a
pre-modern world in which memory, heritage, descent, and the continuity of past and present were fundamental. Insofar as they struggle
with the dynamic of memory and forgetting, all of Sebald's protagonists represent such liminal, Gracchus-like figures. They exist at the
threshold between willful forgetting and effortful remembering, the
rejection of the past and its laborious recovery, the denial of heritage
and its oftentimes distorted return as the repressed. This claim can
be made not only for the "emigrants" whose stories are told in *Die
Ausgewanderten* and their spiritual compatriot Jacques Austerlitz, but
also for the autobiographical narrators of texts like "All'estero" and
"Il ritorno in patria," as well as for the perambulating narrators of *Die
Ringe des Saturn* and the aborted Corsica project, whose excursions
through present-day geographical spaces are motivated by a drive to
uncover the remnants of the past. This helps explain why archives of all
sorts, be they museums, libraries, zoos, or simple repositories of information and artifacts, figure so centrally in Sebald's texts and in the lives
of his protagonists.[4] What stands out about the reflections on death,
remembering, and the modern human being's forgetfulness of heritage,
as voiced in "Campo Santo," is the universality of this diagnosis and
its tone of condemnation. The forgetfulness of Holocaust victims like
Max Aurach, or of economic émigrés such as Henry Selwyn, or even
of German perpetrators of Nazi crimes against humanity, are of a piece
and represent a larger ideological puzzle: the monadic isolationism and
rootless existential condition of modern metropolitan humanity. This
historical and existential "homelessness" is a trait Sebald's protagonists
share with his first-person narrator, whose rejection of his past heritage
stems from his status as a second-generation German who is implicated
in the collective responsibility for the Nazi war crimes.[5]

---

4   On the significance of archives in Sebald's works, see especially Jonathan J.
    Long, W. G. *Sebald: Image, Archive, Modernity* (New York: Columbia University
    Press, 2007), 8–11, where Sebald's obsession with archives is associated with a
    criticism of modernity that follows in the footsteps of Michel Foucault.
5   Sebald comments on his shared responsibility for the crimes committed in the
    name of Germany during World War II in his 1993 interview with Ralph Schock:
    "Und insofern habe ich das, was in diesem Land geschehen ist und durch
    dieses Land geschehen ist, natürlich auch als Teil meines eigenen Gepäcks,
    ganz gleich, wo ich hingehe. Da kommt man also so leicht nicht raus" ("And
    to this extent what happened in this country [Germany] and through this
    country is, of course, also part of my own baggage, regardless of where I go.
    One cannot escape it so easily"; "*Auf ungeheuer dünnem Eis*" 101). See also the
    related comments in his 1997 interview with Eleanor Wachtel, where he says he

Exploring *Herkunft* in "Max Aurach"

"Max Aurach" is a text that displays in an especially forceful yet subtle manner how Sebald, even when explicitly interrogating a Holocaust thematic, conceives the problematic of memory and forgetting in the larger existential context so eloquently articulated in the "Campo Santo" excerpt. If questions of *Herkunft*, of heritage, ancestry, and our inherent connectedness with the past, form the fundamental thematic of this story, then the text itself operates as a textual reconstruction of a virtual heritage that not only reforges the lineage between Aurach, his familial forebears, and the Jewish traditions they once shared and celebrated, but also extends to the narrator, who experiences empathetic participation in this heritage through his retelling of this family's history. Far from evincing a simple, mono-directional plot, this narrative is constituted as three separate but parallel tales of alienation: that of the eponymous protagonist; the embedded story of his mother Luisa Lanzberg; and the history of Sebald's narrator himself, who records the experience of his own self-exile to Manchester. This mutual sense of rootlessness forms the basis for the empathetic resonance among these figures, and it accounts for the narrator's ability to feel his way into their experiences and their fates. The invitation to participate emotionally in this heritage, and thereby acknowledge one's own position in this lineage, is also extended to the readers of Sebald's text. The story "Max Aurach" not only manifests the recovery and reconstruction of heritage, but becomes the means for transmitting it into the future as a kind of lifeline against the otherwise universal ectopic experience of modern humanity. This text encourages us to practice the Heideggerean admonishment of meditation on the heritage of our hidden common history.

Several motifs in "Max Aurach" hark back to the more general problematic of heritage, forgetting, and the hallowed ground of the homestead burial plot that Sebald articulates in "Campo Santo." On the most obvious level, the narrator's research into Aurach's ancestors instigates his own trip to Bad Kissingen, where the family lived prior to the expropriation of their estate and their deportation by the Nazis. The centerpiece of this inquiry is his visit to the Jewish cemetery, which is gated and locked, presumably so as to prevent desecration. But since neither of the keys the narrator retrieves at the city hall actually fits the lock, he must gain entry by climbing the wall (*Ausgewanderten* 332–3/222–3).[6] This cemetery with the tombs commemorating the

has "inherited the backpack" of recent German history and is forced to "carry it whether I like it or not" (Schwartz 51).

6   This act of climbing the cemetery wall contains an intertextual allusion to a scene from Franz Kafka's *Das Schloß* (*The Castle*), a work about which Sebald

former Jewish citizens of Bad Kissingen is quite literally a lock-box: not only are the corpses and the memorial stones vaulted away, but so are the memories of individual Jews and of the Jewish heritage that once permeated the city. The state in which the narrator finds the cemetery testifies to its abandonment: it is "a wilderness of graves, neglected for years, crumbling and gradually sinking into the ground" ("ein seit langen Jahren verlassen daliegendes, allmählich in sich zerfallendes und versinkendes Gräberfeld"; 334/223). The most telling symptom of the decimation of the Jews and their traditions is the fact that very few graves show evidence of those stones traditionally placed by a visitor, in Jewish practice, as a symbol of remembrance (334–5/223–4). When he discovers the grave of Lily and Lazarus Lanzberg, Aurach's maternal grandparents, and of his parents Fritz and Luisa, Sebald's narrator places a stone of remembrance on the headstone (337/225)—a symptom of his empathetic identification with this lost community and an attempt to renew its traditions. Like the bodies and memories of these deceased individuals, the Jewish cemetery has been cordoned off as a place outside of time and heritage. It represents not merely the "mental impoverishment and lack of memory" of which the narrator accuses his fellow Germans ("Geistesverarmung und Erinnerungslosigkeit"; 338/225), but also a more widespread disregard for ancestry and heritage.

The decrepit condition of the cemetery reflects on a smaller scale the wider theme of decay, dilapidation, and deterioration that characterizes the post-industrial city of Manchester, Aurach's chosen place of residence and exile. The narrator emphasizes this parallel between the story's protagonist and his surroundings when he personifies this locale and its run-down buildings as "verwaist" (231/156), "orphaned" in much the same way that Aurach lives without any family ties.[7] The narrator further highlights this characterization of Manchester as a city endemically subject to decomposition when, upon his return twenty years later, he remarks that even the new buildings, intended to counteract this deterioration, now evince signs of decline (267/179). Manchester shares with the Jewish cemetery in Bad Kissingen this

---

the literary critic had written. In an early episode, Kafka's protagonist K. sees a church that is surrounded by a cemetery with a high wall. This reminds him of his childhood village and leads to an analepsis in which K. recalls the feeling of success he experienced as a child when he managed to scramble to the top of this wall. See *Das Schloß*, ed. Malcolm Pasley (Frankfurt am Main: Fischer, 1982), 49–50; *The Castle*, trans. Mark Harman (New York: Schocken, 1998), 28–9. This episode connects the motif of the cemetery with reminiscences of the indigenous home.

7   The English translation elides this metaphorical personification when it renders the term "verwaist" as "abandoned" (*Emigrants* 156).

quality of perennial deterioration and increased desolation, with the difference that the former reflects this on the plane of human civilization, while the latter manifests the degeneration of rituals of remembrance. More importantly, Manchester embodies an ongoing dialectical *process* of regeneration and subsequent decay, construction, and deterioration, and thus emblematically mirrors the dynamic characteristic of Aurach's works of art, which emerge from a repeated procedure of drawing and erasure, creation and dissolution (238–9/161–2).

The narrator's identification with the former Jewish inhabitants of Bad Kissingen is intensified when he discovers the grave of a certain Meier Stern, who shares a birth date, May 18, with both the narrator and Sebald himself. He is also affected by the symbol of the writing quill he discovers on the gravestone of Friederike Halbleib, in whom he takes a peculiar interest, sensing his own personal connection to this forgotten fellow writer, whose life he imitates and revivifies through his own acts of (ghost)writing:

Ich dachte sie mir als Schriftstellerin, allein und atemlos über ihre Arbeit gebeugt, und jetzt, wo ich dies schreibe, kommt es mir vor, als hätte *ich* sie verloren und als könne ich sie nicht mehr verschmerzen trotz der langen, seit ihrem Ableben verflossenen Zeit. (*Ausgewanderten* 336–7)
[I imagined her pen in hand, all by herself, bent with bated breath over her work; and now, as I write these lines, it feels as if *I* had lost her, and as if *I* could not get over the loss, despite the many years that have passed since her departure. (*Emigrants* 224–5)]

The loss of this unknown predecessor assumes a personal significance for him, as he inserts himself into a lineage of descent and heritage defined by shared acts of composition. The image of the writer bent over her desk, engrossed in the act of inscription, invokes an earlier passage in which Aurach describes the paroxysm of pain and the near paralysis he suffered after his visit to Colmar and his study of the Isenheim altar by Mathias Grünewald (252–4/170–2). These episodes are further linked by Aurach's and the narrator's shared visceral particip-ation in the suffering of an Other. The significance of this episode is bound up with the association of physical pain tied to Aurach's epiphany of remembrance:

Ich habe damals in Colmar, so sagte Aurach, alles auf das genaueste vor mir gesehen, wie eines zum andern gekommen und wie es nachher gewesen war. Der Erinnerungsstrom, von dem mir heute nur weniges mehr gegenwärtig ist, setzte damit ein, daß ich mich entsann, wie ich an einem Freitagmorgen

vor einigen Jahren überwältigt worden war von dem mir bis
dahin völlig unbekannten Schmerzensparoxysmus, den ein
Bandscheibenvorfall auslösen kann. (*Ausgewanderten* 254)
[When I was in Colmar, said Ferber, I beheld all of this in precise
detail, how one thing had led to another and how it had been
afterwards. The flood of memory, little of which remains with
me now, began with my recalling a Friday morning some years
ago when I was suddenly struck by the paroxysm of pain that a
slipped disc can occasion, pain of a kind I had never experienced
before. (*Emigrants* 171)]

The experiences in Colmar give rise to a stream of memories in which
Aurach, for the first time, is able to perceive his own life experience
in a historical continuity, in a causal sequence that makes him aware
of how past and present fit together in a meaningful succession. But
this moment of insight is linked to a memory of overwhelming pain
and physical paralysis. Symptomatic of Aurach's debilitating situation
is that he can recall *events* of remembrance, although the specific
memories that imbue these events fall victim to repressive forgetting.
Incidents of recall remain in his memory as epiphanic moments devoid
of actual content, made manifest in an emotional trauma so severe that
it is indistinguishable from excruciating physical pain.

The connection to the narrator's response at the gravestone of
Friederike Halbleib runs not only along this track of remembrance and
the individual's place in a lineage and historical continuity, but also via
the specific reference to the writers' cramped position, as they sit bent
over their writing desk. The bent posture Aurach assumes in response
to the pain of his slipped disc reminds him of a photograph of himself
in second grade, hunched over his desk and absorbed in his writing.
Sebald's narrator interpolates into this passage a relevant photograph
(*Ausgewanderten* 255–6/171–2)[8] (see Figure 5.1). The implication is
that the act of writing is inherently intertwined with the moment of
epiphanic remembrance Aurach documents here, and with the almost
unbearable physical and emotional pain that result from such recall
and insight. Sebald tellingly marks this *intra*textual connection, linking
Aurach's moment of epiphanic remembrance with his narrator's

---

8   In an interview, Sebald admits that this photograph depicts neither the
    individual who served as a model for Max Aurach, his acquaintance Peter
    Jordan, nor Sebald himself. He goes on to claim that ninety percent of his illus-
    trations are authentic, even if this one is not (Schwartz 73). Sebald frequently
    associates this posture with the emotional pain and sacrifice made by writers.
    Toward the conclusion of *Die Ringe des Saturn* he connects the cramped posture
    of weavers, toiling at their looms, with that of writers and scholars sitting at
    their desks (350–1/282–3).

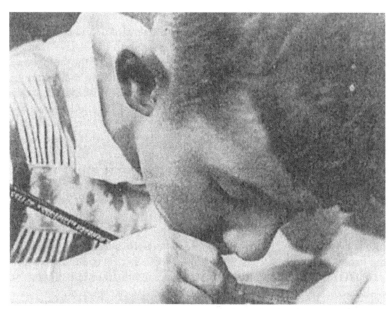

Figure 5.1: Aurach as a child bent over his desk (*Ausgewanderten* 255–6/171–2).

empathetic identification with the Jews of Bad Kissingen via a cross-reference to this earlier illustration. Notably, the episode describing the narrator's visit to the cemetery is more densely illustrated than any other in this story, condensing five images into a mere four pages of text. This drive for illustrative affirmation suggests that the "facts" Sebald's narrator discovers at the Bad Kissingen cemetery are stranger than fiction and hence require concrete documentation.[9] In keeping with this evidentiary function, the illustrations of the Bad Kissingen cemetery are photographs taken by the narrator/author himself, rather than found photos whose relevance is purely associative.[10]

9 Sebald remarks in his interview with Gordon Turner, "Introduction and Transcript of an Interview Given by Max Sebald," in *W. G. Sebald: History, Memory, Trauma*, ed. Scott Denham and Mark McCulloh (Berlin: De Gruyter, 2006), 27, on the role the camera plays in capturing evidence of events that no one would believe could really have happened. In a 1993 interview with Sven Boedecker he likewise stresses the legitimation function of images in his prose fictions, relating them to the importance of the found manuscript in the realistic literature of the nineteenth century (*"Auf ungeheuer dünnem Eis"* 110).

10 This distinction between evidentiary images, on the one hand, and those whose connection to the text is merely associative, on the other, lines up more or less with Long's assertion, *W. G. Sebald*, 124, that there are two fundamental types of

There is one further moment in "Max Aurach" when the narrator cleverly invokes the central themes of heritage, ritual, and community as a continuity across time and generations. As in the essay "Campo Santo," issues of burial in the "hallowed" ground of the homeland, of reunion with family and ancestors, and of death as a kind of homecoming are invoked as a contrast to the radical isolation experienced by modern human beings in general, and people like Aurach in particular. Near the conclusion of his tale, the narrator relates his final trip to Manchester upon receiving news that Aurach has been hospitalized with a severe case of emphysema. This respiratory illness is etiologically linked both to the production of dust resulting from Aurach's artistic procedure (238–9/161–2)[11] and to his existence in the dusty, decaying quarters of the dilapidated Midland Hotel (348–50/232–3), which itself stands as a microcosm for the dust-filled city of Manchester.[12] Taking a room in this hotel, the narrator finds himself transported, in a kind of phantasmagoric daydream, back to his first winter in Manchester in 1966–7 (350–2/233–5). In the silences that interrupt the noisy murmur of the city, he imagines ethereal music wafting to him from afar, and he recalls a karaoke performance in a wine bar in which a woman dressed in pink tulle—a double of his former landlady Gracie Irlam, who dresses in a pink candlewick robe (223–4/152)—plays a Wurlitzer in accompaniment to the guests who sing the hits of the day. The favorite of that season was the sentimental ballad with the opening lines "The old town looks the same as I step down from the train," a reference to Tom Jones's hit single "Green, Green Grass of Home." Indeed, this song topped the charts in England shortly after its release in November 1966. Although Sebald's narrator demeans this popular song as a maudlin piece of kitsch, the lyrics constitute a suggestive intertext that gathers together many of the

---

illustration in *Die Ausgewanderten*: those that index the real, and those that are vague and avoid specific reference.

11   Anne Whitehead, "The Butterfly Man: Trauma and Repetition in the Writing of W. G. Sebald," in *Trauma Fiction* (Edinburgh: Edinburgh University Press, 2004), 118, draws this connection between Aurach's respiratory illness and his dust-generating artistry. However, she overstates this relationship by lending it intentionality and interpreting Aurach's artistic method as evidence of his suicidal tendencies.

12   I agree with Christopher Gregory-Guider, "Memorial Sights/Sites: Sebald, Photography, and the Art of Autobiogeography in *The Emigrants*," in *Searching for Sebald: Photography after W. G. Sebald*, ed. Lise Patt (Los Angeles: Institute of Cultural Inquiry, 2007), 518, that crumbling buildings mirror the psychic unraveling of characters in *Die Ausgewanderten* generally; however, in Aurach's case the identification between place, decrepit buildings, decomposition, and decline are overdetermined by the connection with his deconstructive artistic method.

cardinal motifs of this story. It is uncommon for a pop song to serve in such a suggestive intertextual capacity in Sebald's works; the only other obvious examples are the allusions to Procul Harum's "Whiter Shade of Pale" and Marianne Faithfull's hit rendition of the Rolling Stones' "As Tears Go By," performed in the strikingly parallel context of a hotel dive bar in "Ambros Adelwarth" (*Ausgewanderten* 178–9/121).

As a song about the paradoxical homecoming of a man on death row who envisions his impending reunion with his family and his former lover when he is buried in the family plot, "Green, Green Grass of Home" provides an ironic commentary on the isolation and exile of the protagonist Aurach and of Sebald's exiled narrator. The song's refrain, "It's good to touch the green, green grass of home," gradually undergoes transformation as the prisoner invokes how he will touch this grass only in that moment when "they lay me 'neath the green, green grass of home." Homecoming can only occur in the moment of death. The theme of reconciliation and reunion is intoned in another recurring line of the song, "Yes, they'll all come to meet me, arms reaching, smiling sweetly," in which the singer imagines his parents and his golden-haired, cherry-lipped lover "sweet Mary" embracing him and welcoming him back.[13] This is an image of historical and ancestral continuity, in which the parents' generation is superseded by the union between the lyrical I and Mary. But this utopian vision is undone by the knowledge that this reunion only occurs upon the dreamer's death. Aurach himself, of course, can never entertain such a reunion, even as fantasy. His confinement to a hospital bed prefigures his own death; but as the locked gate of the cemetery in Bad Kissingen indicates, he has no hope of reintegration with his ancestry.

One further motif from this popular song suggests its relevance for the story of Aurach and his family: the reference to the "old oak tree" on which the lyrical I played as a child, and in whose shade he will be visited by "all" who come to see him ("Yes, they'll all come to see me in the shade of that old oak tree"). There are three analogues for this stately oak in "Max Aurach," and all stand as symbolic markers of home and community-belonging. The first, most obvious one is the reproduction of Courbet's painting *The Oak of Vercingetorix* that stands on an easel in Aurach's/Ferber's studio (268–9/179–80). This picture functioned as "the model that had served Ferber for this exercise in destruction" ("zum Ausgangspunkt für seine [Aurachs] Zerstörungsstudie"; 269/179–80): that is, as the artistic prototype for the bleak, constantly reworked and veritably indecipherable canvas on which he is working (268/179). Sebald's narrator includes as

13 Tom Jones, "Green, Green Grass of Home," by Curly Putnam, Decca Records, 1966.

documentary evidence a reproduction of Courbet's image, and as we noted previously, this illustration resonates with the photograph of a tree standing among the chaotic stones of a graveyard that opens "Dr. Henry Selwyn" (7/3).[14] If Aurach's painting deconstructs the Courbet oak that serves as its model, then it symbolically problematizes this tree's rootedness, along with the traditional association of the oak with Germanic blood. Aurach's art represents precisely the disquieting interrogation of heritage, homeland, and ancestry that is emblematically embodied in the oak, both in Courbet's painting and in the lyrics of the popular song to which Sebald's narrator alludes.

This episode in "Max Aurach" draws explicitly on a reference in Robert Hughes's art-historical monograph about the painter Frank Auerbach, acknowledged by Sebald as one of the people on whom the figure of Aurach was patterned (Schwartz 38–9, 73). Hughes's work served Sebald as a primary resource for information about Auerbach's life and art.[15] Hughes relates how on a visit to Tretire in Herefordshire in 1975, Auerbach became especially fascinated with the image of a solitary tree, of which he made several drawings. This image continued to occupy him after his return to London, evolving into a series of works depicting a lone hawthorn tree on Primrose Hill. Hughes comments on this motif, "This not quite central structure seems to surge out of the earth, spreading a canopy that holds up the wild sky; in its materiality and protectiveness it bears a distant resemblance to Courbet's 'historic tree,' *The Oak of Vercingetorix*, 1864." His language invokes not only the rootedness of this tree, its intense connection to the earth, and its role as a pillar that prevents the sky from collapsing, but also the security and "protectiveness" it provides. It represents the entwinement of the solitary individual with a stabilizing home. Hughes documents this interconnection by juxtaposing several of Auerbach's renditions of this solitary tree with a reproduction of Courbet's painting, thereby reinforcing the historical heritage that manifests itself in what he terms the "family resemblance" among these images.[16]

This issue of artistic heritage as a substitute for lost familial and parental ties forms one of the central themes of Hughes's take on Auerbach's life and art, and was surely an idea that caught Sebald's

---

14 On the implicit intratextual linkage between these two images, see Long, *W. G. Sebald*, 125–7, who employs Joseph Frank's conception of "reflexive reference" to describe those connective associations that run through Sebald's texts, and which I designate as *intra*textual links or associative cross-references.

15 Irene Heidelberger-Leonard, "Zwischen Aneignung und Restitution: Die Beschreibung des Unglücks von W. G. Sebald. Versuch einer Annäherung," in *W. G. Sebald: Intertextualität und Topographie*, ed. Irene Heidelberger-Leonard and Mireille Tabah (Berlin: LIT Verlag, 2008), 14–15.

16 Robert Hughes, *Frank Auerbach* (London: Thames & Hudson, 1990), 212.

attention. Hughes casts Auerbach as someone who, because he was exiled as a child from his native Germany and lost his parents to the Holocaust, was "possessed by filiation." In his view, Auerbach "transposed the wound of parental loss into the realm of art-making" by experimenting with techniques gauged to demonstrate "how past art might speak to, and through, images made in the present." The claim Hughes makes for Auerbach can be applied *mutatis mutandi* to the intertextual artistry of W. G. Sebald, who creates a *literary* art in which ghostly voices from the past continue to speak through the texture of the present work. Hughes lays particular stress on the construction of an alternate ancestry when discussing Auerbach's relationship to the past: artists do not "choose" their "parents," but instead are "drawn to their ancestors by a homing impulse"; and the essence of their art resides in knowing "one's heritage, its limits, the challenges these present."[17] He thus foregrounds in Auerbach's art the problematic recuperation of a lost heritage, and in his reading of this biography Sebald assimilated this theme and transposed it to the life of the fictional Max Aurach. The motif of the solitary tree instantiates this search for a lineage that provides stability even in the face of homelessness and permanent exile.

In the middle of the paved courtyard that forms the entryway to Aurach's studio stands a symbolic contrast to his artistic deconstruction of Courbet's oak: an almond tree, planted in a small patch of grass, which grabs the narrator's attention when he first discovers this studio (*Ausgewanderten* 236/160). This almond tree is blossoming when the narrator first encounters it in 1966; but it is also on the verge of blooming upon his return visit in 1989 (268/179), and this highlights its contrastive pairing with the deconstructive oak Aurach creates. A process of organic generation, "blooming," stands against the degenerative and regenerative artistic method Aurach practices. This almond tree thus assumes a hopeful aura, and due to its association with the painter at least two more times (271/181, 289/193), it takes on the character of a leitmotif that marks a rootedness in place, homeland, ancestry, and tradition that clashes with Aurach's existence and his predominant mental attitude. This blossoming almond tree represents the unconscious wish for reintegration with his lost heritage that Aurach never dares to articulate, but that nevertheless stands as a kind of symbolic sentinel outside his studio.

The third motivic analogue of this tree arises in the diary of Aurach's mother, Luisa Lanzberg, where it represents the home in Steinach with which she identifies the utopian, if idealized life of integration in family and community experienced in her childhood: the giant

---

17 Ibid., 9.

chestnut that overshadows the square across from her home. As Luisa emphasizes, she was born and raised in this house until her sixteenth year, when her father bought a mansion in Bad Kissingen and moved the family to the city (291/194). Chestnut trees are mentioned on two further occasions in association with her life in Steinach (293/196, 297/198). In her reminiscences, Steinach is invoked as a kind of paradise of family intimacy, community belonging, and celebration of the rituals of heritage. Insofar as it invokes the chestnut Luisa identifies with this idyllic childhood, the almond tree in the courtyard in front of Aurach's studio embodies an unconscious reminiscence of the rooted, "blooming" life Luisa experienced in this rural community.

Exile and Loss of Home in the Embedded Story of Luisa Lanzberg

Luisa Lanzberg's diary relates this fall from paradise in terms of the loss of rootedness associated with the rural lifestyle of the village of Steinach after her family, precipitated by her father's economic ascent, moves to Bad Kissingen. At the beginning of her reminiscences she reports that she and her brother Leo, as well as her father Lazarus and her grandfather Löb, were born in Steinach, and that their descendants had resided there since the end of the seventeenth century (289/193). She also maintains that at that time the population of the village was one-third Jewish, and given her nostalgic valorization of life there at the turn of the nineteenth century, it serves as an embodiment of the successful German-Jewish symbiosis prior to the rise of rabid racial nationalism and anti-Semitism.[18] She is quick to point out that at the time of her writing—Aurach locates these notes' composition in the years 1939 to 1941, the period of the unremitting German advance during World War II—Steinach is completely devoid of Jews and that the native German population has expropriated their homes and possessions. She also remarks that the memory of their former Jewish neighbors, where not totally eradicated, can only be summoned up with great effort (290/193–4). Invocations of the Holocaust and the banishing of the Jews from their centuries-old homeland form the introductory context in which Luisa's memoirs are situated.

---

18 Allusions to this German-Jewish symbiosis form a prominent leitmotif in the reconstruction of Luisa Lanzberg's diary. See her comment that the Jewish writer Heinrich Heine is the favorite poet of Luisa's mother and the Empress Elisabeth (292/195); the reference to Luisa's Jewish teacher as a "loyal servant of the state" ("treuer Diener des Staates"; 304/202–3); this same teacher's riddle about the three things that continually give and take, mother earth, the sea, and the German Reich (306/204); and the connection of the upswing in her father's horse-dealing business with sales to the German military (311–12/208).

Yet this political displacement, while representative of the terror of the Holocaust, also reflects the more intimate, personal displacement Luisa experienced when her family moved, in January 1905, from this village to the more metropolitan residence. Although her parents promise that this move will provide entry into "a completely new world, even lovelier than that of childhood" ("eine vollkommen neue Welt, schöner noch als die der Kindheit"; 312/208), for Luisa the opposite is true, and her life in Kissingen represents the narrowing of her possibilities, prefiguring the isolation she and her family experience when Nazi Germany has achieved its pinnacle of power and influence (312/208). The family mansion remains for her a "strange place" ("unvertraut"; 313/208), exuding an uncanny and unhomely atmosphere: "there was something distinctly creepy about all of it" ("etwas ausgesprochen Unheimliches ging von alledem aus"; 314/210). This disorienting atmosphere slowly infects and poisons her life. The oppressive impact of this city and especially of the Lanzberg mansion on the teenager Luisa is captured visually and provocatively by the image Sebald inserts into the text at this juncture: it depicts a young girl completely dwarfed by the spires of the multi-storied villa (313/209) (see Figure 5.2).

The very *manner* in which Luisa narrates these two very different phases of her life is indicative of the divergent sentiments she attaches to them. Her description of the years in Steinach is consistently related in the present tense, as though the experiences of this lost past were vividly present as she writes (291–310/195–207). When she describes the interior of the house in Steinach, she stresses how this act of recollection transports her back to this place: "Jetzt stehe ich wieder, schreibt Luisa, in der Wohnstube" ("Now I am standing in the living room once again, writes Luisa"; 291/195). She confirms this infusion of her paradisiac past into her present-time moment of remembrance when she notes that it seems to her as though this idyllic childhood has expanded into an infinite time that extends up to the very moment of composing her memoirs:

Denke ich heute ... an unsere Steinacher Kindheit zurück, so kommt mir oft vor, als hätte sie sich ausgedehnt über eine nach allen Richtungen unbegrenzte Zeit, ja, als währte sie weiter, bis in diese Zeilen, die ich jetzt schreibe, hinein. (*Ausgewanderten* 311) [If I think back nowadays to our childhood in Steinach ... it often seems as if it had been open-ended in time, in every direction—indeed, as if it were still going on, right into these lines I am now writing. (*Emigrants* 207)]

This past flows immediately into the present with the ink in which she records her recollections. Her narration also follows the cycles of the

Figure 5.2: Luisa Lanzberg dwarfed by the villa in Bad Kissingen (*Ausgewanderten* 313/209).

seasons, beginning in summer, moving through autumn and winter to spring, then back to summer and autumn, in a circle of repetition that replicates the integrity and continuity of village life. In this cyclical temporality, all moments of the past also exist in the present, and otherwise discriminate temporal layers lose their distinction and give way to an eternal recurrence that signals the continuity of history. This sense of invariance is underscored by the exaggerated repetition of names beginning with the letter "L" in Luisa's reminiscences: the bonds that tie together the family and the villagers into a single amicable community are represented graphically in the alliterative repetition of the first letter of their names. This is a technique Sebald would perfect in the novel *Austerlitz*, where the letter "A" from the protagonist's name also becomes a motivic cipher linking him to divergent people and places from his past.[19] It is testimony to Sebald's artistry that the style and tone of the Steinach reminiscences so subliminally and yet so effectively invoke the peace, harmony, and integration into life, community, and the past that is Luisa's central theme.

By contrast, Luisa has only "fragmentary memories" ("nur mehr bruchstückhafte Erinnerungen"; 312/208) of the years in Bad Kissingen. Fittingly, the passages related to this phase of her life are retold predominantly in the preterit, marking them as part of a historically distant past from which she stands apart, only occasionally giving way to present-perfect forms—which in German still emphasize past time. In this section of her diary, Luisa communicates her own coming of age, her various love relationships, including her engagement to the musician Fritz Waldhof that ends with his unexpected death, her loving investments in the convalescence of the wounded and blind soldier Friedrich Frohmann, who also dies of his wounds, and finally the happy if muted marriage to Fritz Aurach (318–25/213–18). Paradoxically, this is the part of her life from which she feels most alienated, as her diction itself reveals. Perhaps this is because death overshadows all of these love relationships, just as shadows and half-darkness constitute one of the reigning metaphorical registers in this part of her memoirs.[20] This is coherent with the signature event that characterizes this segment of her life: experiencing a total eclipse of the sun. She relates this episode in a

19 In Luisa Lanzberg's story, this symptom of inheritance and lineage across family lines is also embodied in the similar names of her three lovers, Fritz, Friedrich, and Fritz, suggesting once more a kind of symbolic continuity.

20 For allusions to shadows, half-shadows, and twilight in this section of Luisa's reminiscences, see 317/311, 318/212, 327/218. Shadow and twilight are also prominent motifs in the narrator's retelling of Aurach's life in Manchester, and the motif is prefigured in the epigraph to this story, "Im Abenddämmer kommen sie / und suchen nach dem Leben" ("They come when night falls / to search for life"; 217/147).

disconsolate and inauspicious way: "It was dreadful to see the shadow of the moon slowly blotting out the sun, the leaves of the rambling rose on the balcony (where we stood with our soot-darkened pieces of glass) seeming to wither, and the birds flapping around in a panic" ("Es war mir ungeheuer, wie der Mondschatten langsam die Sonne verdunkelte, wie die Blätter der Kletterrosen an dem Altan, auf dem wir mit unseren rußigen Glasscherben standen, zu welken schienen und die Vögel verscheucht und angstvoll herumflatterten"; 316/211). This episode summarizes metaphorically the radical reversal that has transpired in Luisa's life: shadows have darkened, even eradicated the sunshine of her childhood; vegetative nature wilts away, as do the bonds that join people into an ancestral community; even animal life takes fright at the dark premonition of the extinguished sun. This passage prefigures the loss of life that awaits Luisa and her husband when they are deported by the Nazis, just subsequent to her recording these memoirs.

Sebald's Narrator as Parsifal Figure

Aside from the meaningful reference to the popular song "Green, Green Grass of Home," the dream memory that wells up in Sebald's narrator during his stay at the Midland Hotel when he returns to Manchester in 1991 contains another significant musical allusion: to Richard Wagner's opera *Parsifal*. The first sounds that emerge as the narrator daydreams in his room in the Midland are the voice of a diminutive opera singer who, as he remarks, used to appear regularly in Liston's Music Hall and sang excerpts from *Parsifal* in the original German (351/234). After segueing into the diversion about the karaoke performance in the wine bar, Sebald's narrator returns to a description of the twice-weekly performances of this operatic tenor, whose voice stands out in the cacophony that wafts into his room and into his memory:

Mitten in dem zu fortgeschrittener Stunde meist chaotischen Menschen- und Stimmengewoge trat damals mindestens zweimal in der Woche der unter dem Namen Siegfried bekannte, wohl nicht viel mehr als fünf Fuß große Heldentenor auf. Er war Ende vierzig, trug einen fast bis auf den Boden reichenden Fischgratmantel, hatte einen nach hinten gekippten Borsalino auf dem Kopf und sang *O weh, des Höchsten Schmerzenstag* oder *Wie dünkt mich doch die Aue heut so schön* oder sonst irgendein eindrückliches Arioso, wobei er nicht zögerte, Regieanweisungen wie *Parsifal droht ohnmächtig niederzusinken* entsprechend schauspielerisch zu untermalen. Und jetzt hörte ich ihn, im fünften Stockwerk des *Midland* in einer Art Glaskanzel über dem Abgrund sitzend, zum erstenmal seit jener Zeit wieder. So sehr aus der Entfernung kam sein Ton, daß es war, als irre er hinter den Seitenprospekten einer in die unendliche Tiefe sich fortsetzenden Bühne herum. Auf diesen in Wahrheit gar nicht vorhandenen Seitenprospekten aber erschienen eines ums andere die Bilder einer Ausstellung, die ich im Vorjahr in Frankfurt gesehen hatte. (*Ausgewanderten* 351–2) [Twice a week, at a late hour when the heaving mass of people and voices verged on the infernal, the heroic tenor known as Siegfried, who cannot have been more than one metre fifty tall, would take the stage. He was in his late forties, wore a herringbone coat that reached almost to the floor and on his head a Homburg tilted back. He would sing *O weh, des Höchsten Schmerzenstag* or *Wie dünkt mich doch die Aue heut so schön* or some other impressive arioso, not hesitating to act out stage directions such as "Parsifal is on the point of fainting" with the required theatricality. And now, sitting in the Midland's turret room above the abyss on the fifth floor, I heard him again for the first time since those days. The sound came from so far away that it was as if he were walking about behind the wing flats of an infinitely deep stage. On those flats, which in truth did not exist, I saw, one by one, pictures from an exhibition that I had seen in Frankfurt the year before. (*Emigrants* 234–5)]

This passage is worthy of lengthy citation because it provides a trenchant example of the subtleties of Sebald's narrative artistry. Structured around a then/now ("damals"/"jetzt") dynamic that is typical of how Sebald's fictions meld past and present experience into a temporal continuity, it builds an organic bridge between the diegesis and the narrative frame. This memory of the opera singer's performance gives way to the narrator reliving it in his fantasy; he imagines himself transported back to the theater, recreating this singer's performance in all its dramaturgical immediacy. The italicized lines are drawn from the final act of Wagner's opera, when Parsifal returns on Good Friday with the holy spear and uses it to cure Amfortas's suffering.[21] This entire reminiscence has a functional role in preparing the shift to the final segment of Sebald's story, the description of the photographs from the Lodz ghetto, taken by the Nazi finance bureaucrat Walter Genewein, which the narrator saw the previous year at a Frankfurt exhibition.

This is a stunning example of Sebald's poetics of history, the seamless agglomeration of diverse temporal dimensions and historical episodes, as his narrative moves fluidly from the aural clues of the opera singer's performance, to the visual dimension of his theatrical rendering of the role of Parsifal, to the glass capsule or "turret room"

---

21 Richard Wagner, *Parsifal*, in *The Authentic Librettos of the Wagner Operas, Complete with English and German Parallel Texts* (New York: Crown, 1938), 467.

in which the narrator himself sits in the dilapidated Midland Hotel—
itself suggesting a kind of cinematic space or projection booth—to the
side-screens of the theater onto which he projects the memory-images
of the pictures from the Lodz ghetto. This surprisingly compact set
of transitions allows the narrator to tie his present-day existence
back to his youthful experiences in Manchester, reinvoke the theme
of Manchester's industrial past and its current state of deterioration,
connect it to the Polish city of Lodz—which due to its industrial base
was known as the Polish Manchester—and frame all of this in one
sweeping gesture by referencing the Jewish ghetto in Lodz as representative for the history of the Holocaust. The narrator has moved
from his own personal past, via this memory and the fantasies it
engenders, into the universal realm of grand history. At the same time,
he obliquely connects the trauma suffered by his protagonist Aurach in
Manchester with the suffering and labors of the ghetto inhabitants in
Lodz, thereby pointing to the events of the Holocaust as the mediated
source of Aurach's emotional distress. But he also aligns these with the
debilitating suffering of Amfortas in Wagner's opera and in its literary
model, Wolfram von Eschenbach's (1170–1220) courtly epic *Parzival*.
In a round-about way, the narrator has exploited his own personal
memories as a vehicle for articulating the reasons why, as Aurach
once said to him, the painter discovered in Manchester the place of
his "destiny" ("Ort meiner Bestimmung"; 251/169). For if Lodz, as a
stand-in for the Holocaust more generally, represents the repressed
source and causal event underlying his suffering, Manchester is his
destiny—his "Bestimmung"—because it provides a constant, if unconscious reminder of this symbolic origin of his torment. The narrator
enacts, on the level of his own storytelling, precisely that re-embedding
of personal reminiscence in the broader context of universal, historical
memory—a problem with which Aurach has struggled throughout his
life. Sebald's narrator has learned from Aurach's problems: he demonstrates his own capacity to integrate his life events into the history of
this traumatic past, at least in terms of emotional identification with
the victims.

The question this analysis has thus far left unaddressed relates
to the precise significance of the allusion to *Parsifal*. But in avoiding
this question we have also *performed* the very problem around which
the meaning of this reference turns: the *failure* to ask the pertinent
question. The story of *Parsifal*, after all, is more than a tale about the
quest for the Holy Grail and for redemption; it is also a narrative about
the incapacity to demonstrate due compassion at the proper time
and pose the pressing question into the *cause* of Amfortas's suffering.
This is a question that, quite literally, interrogates issues of *Herkunft*,
asking how something came to be, pursuing the *etiology* of an observed

phenomenon. The dwarf opera singer "Siegfried," whose name invokes the prototypical Germanic and Wagnerian hero, not only sings arias from Wagner's opera, but dramatically acts out the part of its hero. There is good reason for Sebald's narrator to latch onto this figure as a representative memory of his youthful days in Manchester: in retrospect, he recognizes that the role he played vis-à-vis his informant Max Aurach perfectly parallels the part Parsifal plays with respect to Amfortas. Both initially fail to ask the pertinent question about *Herkunft*, about origins, causes, and ancestry that underpin Aurach's and Amfortas's suffering. In his early life in Manchester, Sebald's narrator replicates the situation of Parsifal: although the latter *feels* Amfortas's pain, he does not make any effort to uncover its causes. He must depart for many years, before returning with the spear that will heal Amfortas's suffering and his own shame. The refrain Wagner's opera associates with Parsifal in the first act, "Durch Mitleid wissend, / der reine Thor" ("By pity enlightened, / The guileless Fool"),[22] also suits Sebald's narrator. If in the "first act" of his encounter with Aurach he, like Parsifal, is filled with compassion but remains a fool, by the "third act" he has attained enlightenment and returns holding the key to redemption—not a spear, in this case, but the instigation to recollect the past. In its overall structure, Sebald's story is thus modeled on the literary-operatic predecessor of the *Parsifal* legend.

Further parallels suggest an alignment of Sebald's narrator with this figure. Wagner's hero is ignorant of his own heritage and descent, which must be revealed to him by the witch Kundry,[23] and he thus shares with Sebald's narrator a feeling of liberated homelessness. If *Parsifal* is a tale about learning to ask the right question and pursuing the causes of another's suffering, then that is true of Sebald's story as well, and his narrator undergoes a fundamental transformation over the course of his narration. This tale of transformation, performed in the very act of narration, indicates that Sebald's narrator is not *born* into his role of the "good German"[24]—the compassionate German witness to the testimony of Jewish exile and suffering. This is a role into which he, like Parsifal, must grow over the course of his encounter

---

22 Ibid., 447.
23 Ibid., 442–3.
24 Brad Prager, "The Good German as Narrator: On W. G. Sebald and the Risks of Holocaust Writing," *New German Critique* 96 (Fall 2005): 101, expresses skepticism about the ability of Sebald's narrator to enact this role of the empathetic listener, suggesting that it may be a pose or even an imposition. The question is whether genuine empathy does not demand precisely such blurring, and whether empathy always entails an act of appropriation. This is a problem we will address more fully in our discussion of Sebald's relationship to Holocaust literature and the narrative structure of *Austerlitz*.

with the suffering protagonist and through the development of his own narrative adventure. The episode we have been explicating both comments self-reflexively on the narrator's role as a Parsifal-like figure, who must learn to empathize and ask the right questions about the origins of suffering, and demonstrates that this narrator has success-fully undergone such a metamorphosis. The narrator puts into practice the dictum that only the spear that smote the wound can also heal it: "die Wunde schließt / der Speer nur, der sie schlug" ("The one [weapon] that struck / Can staunch thy wounded side").[25] To be sure, Aurach never attains the kind of redemption that Parsifal can provide Amfortas. But Sebald's narrator does instigate Aurach to recreate his own *Herkunft* in his act of retelling his life experience, and in this regard the narrative interaction between informant and narrator establishes prerequisites for the *possibility* of such redemption.

The (Self-)Transformation of Sebald's Narrator

The engagement of Sebald's narrator with Max Aurach breaks down into two distinct periods. The first encompasses the three years he spent in Manchester as a young man, from autumn 1966 through summer 1969; the second recounts his rediscovery of Aurach, when he sees one of his paintings in the London Tate Gallery in 1989 and stumbles upon a magazine article that documents the painter's recent artistic successes. This article includes a thumbnail sketch of his life, detailing his German-Jewish roots and the deportation of his parents, and it stimulates Sebald's narrator to take the train to Manchester, where he spends three days interviewing his former acquaintance. Their interactions circle around the changes in Manchester over the preceding twenty years, but above all around Aurach's heritage, family, and the events surrounding his exile and their deaths. These two encounters are separated by an interim period in which the narrator—like Parsifal—not only lost all contact with Aurach, but in which the painter was extinguished from his thoughts and memory. He comments that the very face of the painter, whose art of portraiture renders faces as shadowy traces, had itself been reduced to a schematic shadow: "His face had become a mere shadow" ("Sein [Aurachs] Gesicht war zu einem Schemen geworden"; 264/177). He continues by providing a flimsy self-justification for this loss of contact and for his own failure to inquire into the artist's development: "I assumed that Ferber had been drowned in his labours, but avoided making any closer enquiries" ("Ich nahm an, Aurach sei untergegangen in seiner Arbeit, wußte es jedoch zu vermeiden, genauere Erkundigungen einzuziehen"; 264/177). The wording of the German original is telling:

---

25   Wagner, *Parsifal*, 470.

Sebald's narrator did not simply avoid making enquiries, he *knew how to avoid* procuring relevant information, a turn of phrase that suggests not simply passive forgetting, but active resistance to remembrance. If in the first phase of their relationship the narrator resists asking questions about Aurach's past out of negligence, this omission becomes purposeful avoidance during the twenty-year hiatus in their relationship. Only after he discovers "by sheer chance" ("durch Zufall"; 264/177) Aurach's German-Jewish heritage does Sebald's narrator begin to ask himself why he never posed the obvious questions about the painter's origins.

The repeated and intensive study of Aurach's eye, printed in the cited magazine article and duly reproduced in Sebald's German text (265), but not in the English translation, is what stimulates the narrator's curiosity:

> Wochenlang trug ich das Magazin mit mir herum, überlas den Artikel, der in mir, wie ich spürte, ein Verlies aufgetan hatte, immer wieder von neuem, studierte das dunkle Auge Aurachs, das aus einer der dem Text beigegebenen Fotografien ins Abseits blickte, und versuchte wenigstens im Nachhinein zu begreifen, aufgrund welcher Hemmungen und Scheu wir es seinerzeit vermieden hatten, das Gespräch auf die Herkunft Aurachs zu bringen, obgleich ein solches Gespräch, wie es sich jetzt herausstellte, eigentlich das Allernaheliegendste gewesen wäre. (*Ausgewanderten* 265)
> [For weeks I carried the magazine around with me, glancing time and again at the article, which, I sensed, had unlocked in me a sort of gaol or oubliette. I studied Ferber's dark eye, looking sideways out of a photograph that accompanied the text, and tried, at least with hindsight, to understand what inhibitions or wariness there had been on his part that had kept our conversations away from his origins, despite the fact that such a talk, as I now realized, would have been the obvious thing. (*Emigrants* 177–8)][26]

The subterranean dungeon ("Verlies") that opens up for the narrator as he makes this recognition is an especially telling metaphor: it suggests not only the darkness of ignorance, but also the artificial confinement

---

26 The English translation incorrectly renders the adverb "seinerzeit," meaning "at that time," as though it read "seinerseits," meaning "on his part" (178), which attributes the blame for these inhibitions solely to Aurach. This is a crucial error, since Sebald's German text carefully avoids attributing these inhibitions to one or other of the men, suggesting that it was a kind of silent agreement or compact.

prompted by the narrator's own inhibitions. The discovery of this article thus stimulates the narrator's moment of *anagnorisis*, since he now feels liberated from the emotional shackles that once bound him. There are numerous reasons why a discussion of Aurach's heritage and personal history, his *Herkunft*, seems in retrospect to have been an obvious topic passed over in their earlier conversations. Most prominent is the simple fact that both men, although of different generations, had to be aware of their shared German roots. The narrator points out that during this period Aurach was especially careful to relate only that part of his past that transpired after 1943, when he moved to Manchester to begin his art studies; and the narrator explicitly *believes* he recalls, in a typical Sebaldian qualification of memory that the English translation elides ("glaube mich jedoch zu entsinnen"; "though I do remember"; 247/166), that Aurach "was loath to answer any questions about his story and his early years" ("daß er nur ungern auf meine an diese Lebensbeschreibung sich anschließenden und seine Vorgeschichte betreffenden Fragen einging"; 247/166). The failure to address issues of *Herkunft* can hence be set down both to Aurach's purported resistance, and to the narrator's willing agreement to avoid potentially sensitive topics.

If we examine the precise place where the narrative of their first encounter, and of Aurach's retelling of his life story, breaks off, we recognize how forced and intentional the avoidance of this issue appears. After relating his visit to Grünewald's Isenheim altar, his second ascent of the Grammont, his encounter with the Butterfly Man who rescues him, and his failed attempt to capture the image of this peculiar character in a painting (258–60/173–5), Aurach recounts a phantasmagoric dream in which he visits an art exhibition where his own paintings are displayed side by side with works traded by his father, who pursued the profession of an art dealer prior to the war. Among the works in this exhibition, Aurach discovers an especially effective *trompe l'oeil* of a doorway that affords a view of the living room of his parent's home in Munich. On an ottoman sits a strange man with a miniature model of Solomon's Temple on his lap. Introducing himself as "Frohmann, from Drohobycz" ("Frohmann, aus Drohobycz gebürtig"; 262/176), he explains that he has reconstructed this temple accurately from the descriptions provided in the Bible, and that he travels from ghetto to ghetto in order to show it to the dispersed Jewish community. Aurach responds by declaring this temple to be the first "true work of art" ("ein wahres Kunstwerk") he has ever encountered (263/176). It is precisely at this point that the narrator's account of the two men's initial relationship precipitously ends.

In Sebald's works, dreams—as we saw in our foregoing analysis of the narrator's fantasy in the Midland Hotel—often enact narrative transitions. Significantly, Aurach's extended recounting of this dream of homecoming does *not* build a segue, but instead leads to a radical rupture and temporal break in the narrative. Yet this dream incorporates manifold *invitations* to meaningful transitions. It raises, first of all, central questions about Aurach's relationship with his father, and even suggests, through the juxtaposition of paintings in a single exhibition, that Aurach's art is an offshoot of his father's profession as an art dealer. Aurach thus comes close to touching on some of the more intimate details of his heritage. Additionally, the invocation of his parent's living room begs questions about place, the status of the family, and their fates. This is, after all, as close to a virtual homecoming that Aurach will ever get. But the reference to Frohmann and Solomon's Temple also gives a first indication of Aurach's Jewish heritage. Sebald's narrator is invited to pursue any and all of these pathways toward further illumination of Aurach's past, his family, his heritage, and, above all, the cause of his suffering; but he shuns them all. This is a particularly dense and rich passage in Sebald's text, not only because of this compact confluence of themes, but also because, as scholars have pointed out,[27] the reference to Frohmann and his reconstructed temple represents an intertextual allusion to a 1927 essay by the Austrian writer Joseph Roth (1894–1939), evocatively titled *Juden auf Wanderschaft* (Wandering Jews). In his role as literary critic, Sebald refers to this episode in the essay on Roth included in his book *Unheimliche Heimat* (117), so that the reference in "Max Aurach" constitutes an intertextual double-exposure: Roth, cited through Sebald the literary critic, cited through Sebald's fictional narrator. But the true significance of this figure only comes to the fore if we return to the summary provided by the scholar Sebald, who explains why Frohmann has made this temple and transports it from village to village: "Herr Frohmann, who travels with his work of art from one ghetto to another, and from time to time comes to Berlin, sees himself as the guardian of tradition" ("Herr Frohmann, der mit seinem Kunstwerk von einem Ghetto zum andern fährt und gelegentlich nach Berlin kommt, versteht sich als Hüter der Tradition"; *Unheimliche Heimat* 117). Aurach and Frohmann are Jewish artists who stand at opposite ends of the ideological spectrum: Frohmann is the *guardian* of tradition, who creates a work figured as the paragon of Jewish creativity, an exact replica of Solomon's Temple, and who, moreover, exploits this work of art as a reminder to the Jews living in the diaspora that they share a common, unifying heritage. This theme of community-belonging in

---

27 See Peter C. Pfeiffer, "Korrespondenz und Wahlverwandtschaft: W. G. Sebalds *Die Ringe des Saturn*," *Gegenwartsliteratur* 2 (2003): 234–5, and Uwe Schütte, *W. G. Sebald: Einführung in Leben und Werk* (Göttingen: Vandenhoeck & Ruprecht, 2011), 113–14.

the face of diasporic exile is highlighted even more emphatically in Roth's essay, where an older Jew standing before the miniature temple imitates his "brothers" in the Holy Land who cry and pray at the remaining wall of the original temple: "I saw an elderly Jew standing in front of the miniature temple. He resembled his brothers who stand, cry, and pray at the only remaining wall of the destroyed temple in Jerusalem" ("Ich habe einen alten Juden vor dem Miniaturtempel stehen gesehen. Er glich seinen Brüdern, die an der einzig übriggebliebenen heiligen Mauer des zerstörten Tempels in Jerusalem stehen, weinen und beten").[28] Frohmann's temple possesses the quasi-magical power of representing perfectly the shrine it imitates, to the extent that those who experience this reproduction are directly affiliated with those worshipping at the original. Aurach's art is incapable of approximating this magical effect; it can only invoke heritage in the hesitant form of those shadowy figures that flit across his canvases.

We will investigate subsequently the extent to which Aurach's artistry reflects a problematized version of the heritage that is represented positively in the allusion to Frohmann's temple. For the present, we simply need to emphasize that the dream Aurach recounts, and in which the narrator's story about the first phase of their relationship culminates, offers a wide set of inroads into questions about Aurach's past, his origins, and his heritage. But they remain roads not taken. It is only after he accidentally acquires more information about Aurach, specifically the details of his exile from Germany in 1939 and the deportation of his parents in November 1941, that Sebald's narrator falls into self-accusations, wondering how he could have been so remiss as to fail to ask Aurach the relevant questions about his past:

> Unverzeihlich erschien es mir nun im Nachdenken, daß ich es damals in Manchester entweder verabsäumt oder nicht fertiggebracht hatte, Aurach jene Fragen zu stellen, die er erwartet haben mußte von mir; und also fuhr ich zum erstenmal seit sehr langer Zeit wieder nach Manchester. (*Ausgewanderten* 266)
> [As I now thought back, it seemed unforgivable that I should have omitted, or failed, in those Manchester times, to ask Ferber the questions he must surely have expected from me; and so, for the first time in a very long while, I went to Manchester once again. (*Emigrants* 178)]

This passage alludes to the narrator's role as Parsifal, experiencing that moment of *anagnorisis*, of recognition and self-recognition, about

---

28 Joseph Roth, *Juden auf Wanderschaft*, in *Werke*, ed. Klaus Westermann, 6 vols (Cologne: Kiepenheuer & Witsch, 1990), 2:868–9.

his own resistance to asking questions about Aurach's origins and the source of his suffering. He expresses a certain ambivalence about his own motivations, wondering whether this failure was a naïve omission, or if he actually lacked the gumption to pose the hard questions—hard not only for Aurach, the victim who tries to repress the Holocaust as the font of his personal misery, but also for the narrator, who as a non-Jewish German stands in the lineage of Nazi perpetrators. Quite similar to Aurach himself, Sebald's narrator seeks to deny, ignore, or at least refuse to acknowledge his own heritage as a post-war, post-Holocaust German. One of the many things that Aurach and Sebald's narrator share is this desire to distance themselves from their ancestry and its history.[29] Regardless of how we evaluate these underlying motivations, Sebald's narrator is clearly portrayed as a Parsifal-like character who gains insight into his failure to ask questions about the origin and cause of the suffering he witnesses. When after a twenty-year hiatus he re-establishes contact with Aurach, he compensates for the failure, neglect, and omission characteristic of his earlier encounter with the painter. He now asks Aurach to explain the cause of his emotional distress, thereby inviting him to participate in a therapeutic encounter with his own repressed past.[30] But this dialogue not only demands an act of self-overcoming on Aurach's part; Sebald's

---

29 Prager, "The Good German as Narrator," 97, similarly notes that Sebald's narrator and Aurach are doubles, but he does not point to their shared existence as exiles as a significant point of contact. Irene Heidelberger-Leonard, "Zwischen Aneignung und Restitution," 20, maintains that the narrator's and Aurach's perspectives tend to merge into identification. However, she also ignores their common status as ectopic exiles and how this forms a basis for identity. For more general reflections on the tendency of Sebald's narrator to assume a position of empathy or identification vis-à-vis his informants, see Judith Kaspar, "Intertextualitäten als Gedächtniskonstellationen im Zeichen der Vernichtung: Überlegungen zu W. G. Sebalds *Die Ausgewanderten*," in *Wende des Erinnerns? Geschichtskonstruktionen in der deutschen Literatur nach 1989*, ed. Barbara Beßlich, Katharina Grätz, and Olaf Hildebrand (Berlin: Erich Schmidt, 2006), 89, who associates this capacity with Walter Benjamin's concept of "mimetisches Vermögen," an inherent mimetic ability; or Tanja van Hoorn, "Erinnerungspoetiken der Gegenwart: Christoph Ransmayr, Reinhard Jirgl, W. G. Sebald," *Der Deutschunterricht* 57, no. 6 (2005): 62, who maintains that Sebald choreographs a classical narrative situation in which an outsider finds his way into the reported memories of his interlocutors by participating in the history they unveil.

30 Jonathan Long, "Disziplin und Geständnis: Ansätze zu einer Foucaultschen Sebald-Lektüre," in *W. G. Sebald: Politische Archäologie und melancholische Bastelei*, ed. Michael Niehaus and Claudia Öhlschläger (Berlin: Erich Schmidt, 2006), 235, recognizes that Sebald's narrator serves as a therapist for Aurach, but he views this in terms of the former's imbrication in a Foucauldian complex of power-knowledge, rather than due to empathetic facilitation.

German narrator must also overcome his own "Hemmungen und Scheu" ("inhibitions or wariness"; 265/178), the reticence and shame he experiences due to his own German ancestry, when confronting this German-Jewish victim of the Nazi Holocaust.[31]

It falls to one of the more enigmatic figures in Sebald's text, his narrator's Manchester landlady Gracie Irlam, to voice the crucial question about heritage and origin when the narrator appears unexpectedly at her door on a Friday morning in autumn 1966. Surprised that someone is ringing at such an early hour, and taken aback by the appearance of this young student—her usual roomers are traveling businessmen—her opening question is, "And where have you sprung from?" (224/152). Her query is one about origin, but her vocabulary and diction lend what would otherwise be a mundane question—Where do you hail from?—a mysterious, even metaphysical aura. Her verb "sprung" resonates with the German word *Ursprung*, meaning source, origin, or font, which is itself a cardinal term of German metaphysical thought, especially in the work of Martin Heidegger. Immediately upon the narrator's arrival, Gracie articulates the very question vis-à-vis the narrator that he will *fail* to ask Max Aurach during his three-year stay in Manchester. Her question is not out of place; for in his retrospective account of his decision as a twenty-two-year-old to "move to" England—he specifically uses the more technical verb "übersiedeln" (219/149), which suggests a permanent form of migration, not a temporary relocation— Sebald's narrator highlights the independence, isolation, and absolute autonomy that this status as an emigrant affords him. He enjoys the feeling of being wholly self-reliant, "thrown back entirely on my own resources" ("ganz nur auf mich gestellt"; 219/149); and he remarks on how he approaches existence in this alien world with wonder and amazement, and with what in retrospect seems like a false sense of security (220/149). Even his description of the plane flight from Kloten airport to Manchester emphasizes these qualities of separation and an insular encapsulation in the self: "There were only a very few passengers on board, and, as I recall, they sat wrapped up in their coats, far apart in the half-darkness of the cold body of the aircraft" ("Es befanden sich nur wenige Passagiere an Bord, die, in ihre Mäntel gehüllt, weit voneinander entfernt in dem halbdunklen und, wie ich mich zu erinnern

---

31   In an interview with Carole Angier, Sebald addressed this problem of his own "paralysis," as he calls it, when speaking with German-Jewish émigrés about their heritage: "There was a sort of shyness, a sort of paralysis on both sides. It has taken all these twenty or thirty years for the paralysis to fade. In one sense I regret it, because Withington and Didsbury were full of German and Austrian Jews, whom I could have talked to. But in another sense I don't, because I would certainly have said all the wrong things then. I think I might even say all the wrong things now" (Schwartz 65–6).

glaube, ziemlich kalten Gehäuse saßen"; 219/149). The narrator finds comfort in the distance that separates him from the other passengers, in the fact that each remains tucked away in his or her coat and in the emotional coldness that guarantees independence, disjunction, and dispersal. He revels in the artificially created diaspora inaugurated by his voluntary emigration. Indeed, one suspects that a will to sever all connections with his homeland, his past, and his heritage is what motivates this migration in the first place. The half-dark ambience of the airplane's passenger cabin anticipates the twilight with which the emigrant Aurach surrounds himself in his studio and his living quarters (236–7/160–1). The situation in which Sebald's narrator voluntarily places himself thereby emulates the conditions under which Aurach lives after his escape to England. Viewed from a psychological point of view, this *choice* to sever all ties with his heritage might be the cause of the youthful narrator's insensitivity to questions about Aurach's past. Just as he himself gives no answer to Gracie's question "And where have you sprung from?," he might project a similar resistance to questions about origin and ancestry on the part of the painter.

As is often the case in Sebald's works, facades can be deceptive, and this is no less true for the life of Max Aurach than it is for Sebald's narrator. Despite the fact that he cherishes the freedom provided by his new life in alien circumstances, this figure is subliminally dogged by a sense of unease and an unconscious wish to reconnect with the homeland from which he fled. This expresses itself in a desire to recapture the comfort and security of his childhood, which emerges around his experience of the teas-maid, a combination alarm clock and tea kettle, that Gracie brings to his room on the first afternoon. The narrator describes the function of this unfamiliar machine and even includes a photograph to verify his depiction (see Figure 5.3):

Die auf einer elfenbeinfarbenen Blechkonsole aufgebaute, aus blitzendem rostfreiem Stahl gefertigte Apparatur glich, wenn beim Teekochen der Dampf aus ihr aufstieg, einem Miniaturkraftwerk, und das Zifferblatt der Weckeruhr phosphoreszierte, wie sich in der hereinbrechenden Dämmerung bald schon zeigte, in einem mir aus der Kindheit vertrauten stillen Lindgrün, von dem ich mich in der Nacht immer auf unerklärliche Weise behütet fühlte. (*Ausgewanderten* 227)
[When I made tea and the steam rose from it, the shiny stainless steel contraption on its ivory-coloured metal base looked like a miniature power plant, and the dial of the clock, as I soon found as dusk fell, glowed a phosphorescent lime green that I was familiar with from my childhood and which I had always felt afforded me an unaccountable protection at night. (*Emigrants* 154)]

Figure 5.3: The comforting teas-maid in the narrator's Manchester room (*Ausgewanderten* 227/154).

The narrator invests enough importance in this strangely English apparatus that it merits representation in the very first illustration for this story. The mechanical perfection of this miniature power-plant is reflected in the gleaming, rust-free steel of its housing, as well as in its unerring operation. The steam it emits anticipates the smoke of the Manchester factories that the young narrator has yet to discover; and its fine-tuned functioning and stable appearance hark back to the heyday of manufacturing in industrial Manchester, thereby serving as a reminder of the city's past. But more telling for the experience of Sebald's narrator is the childhood reminiscence that the phospho-rescent green light of the clock face invokes for him. The final clause of this sentence, which refers to the comfort and protection associated with this light, remains temporally indefinable, so that it is unclear whether it refers to the present time in Manchester, or to the childhood past whose memory it evokes. This indefinability proves important, because it emphasizes the dimension of comfort afforded the narrator by this unfamiliar contraption: it represents an island of domestic relief, contentment, and bonding in the midst of his liberated detachment, his ectopic experience of the alien English environment. Characteristic of Sebald in general is that the relief the teas-maid provides is expressed in terms of light and dark: its phosphorescent glow disrupts and effectively restrains the falling dusk. We are reminded of twilight as one of the dominant motifs of this text, and its anticipation in the epigraph that promises a search for life amidst the twilight of evening (217/147). The fact that this consoling light derives from the face of a *clock* suggests the significance of issues of temporality; and this temporal dimension is further underscored by the ambiguous temporal reference in the final clause. In that sense this passage represents a microcosmic embodiment of this text's time structure in particular, and of Sebald's narratives more generally, in which the narrated past constantly protrudes into the present time of narration.

More than just a redeeming reminder of childhood and the security of home, the teas-maid performs a salvational function for Sebald's narrator. He identifies this machine as a lifeline that rescues him from the boundlessness of his alien detachment:

Darum vielleicht ist es mir, im Zurückdenken an die Zeit meiner Ankunft in Manchester, mehrfach so gewesen ... als sei der von Gracie mir auf mein Zimmer gebrachte Teeapparat, dieses ebenso dienstfertige wie absonderliche Gerät, es gewesen, das mich durch sein nächtliches Leuchten, sein leises Sprudeln am Morgen und durch sein bloßes Dastehen untertags am Leben festhalten ließ damals, als ich mich, umfangen, wie ich war, von einem mir unbegreiflichen Gefühl der Unverbundenheit, sehr leicht aus dem Leben hätte entfernen können. (*Ausgewanderten* 227–8)
[That may be why it has often seemed, when I have thought back to those early days in Manchester, as if the tea maker brought to my room by Mrs. Irlam, by Gracie ...—as if it was that weird and serviceable gadget, with its nocturnal glow, its muted morning bubbling, and its mere presence by day, that kept me holding on to life at a time when I felt a deep sense of isolation in which I might well have become completely submerged. (*Emigrants* 154–5)][32]

In his remembrance of this period in his life, the teas-maid comes to represent the veritable opposite of the autonomy and detachment he otherwise celebrates about his self-imposed exile. In this elaboration on its significance, he expands his association of the light from this machine with his childhood to include the comfort provided by the bubbling sound of the boiling water and, finally, the machine's very presence in his room. If in his experience of total rootlessness he could easily have slipped out of life completely—the language in the

---

32 Hulse's English translation of the final words in this passage does not capture the ominous tone of the German original, which I would render as "I might well have abandoned life completely," suggesting, as does the German, doom and thoughts of suicide.

German original remains vague, but it suggests that he may actually have harbored thoughts of suicide—this machine gives his existence an anchoring point that is quite literally redemptive. Although Sebald's youthful narrator tends to emphasize the liberating mobility that stems from the break with all ties to home and heritage, he is nevertheless haunted by the possibility that this loss of connection with the native context from which he has "sprung" is tantamount to the loss of life itself. The field of seemingly infinite possibilities that opens up before the voluntary exile is simultaneously shot through with a melancholy loss of stability, security, and communal bonds. For the young narrator, the radical break with heritage, with all forms of *Herkunft*, also threatens to cause loss of orientation, lack of direction, and even death.

It is no coincidence that the person who delivers this salvational apparatus is the same one who asks the redeeming question about the narrator's heritage: Gracie Irlam. Although it represents an interpretive stretch to identify her, on the basis of autobiographical resonances with Sebald's life, as a kind of mother-ersatz,[33] the narrator clearly figures her as a vehicle of redemption. This is suggested by the "large photograph" hanging in her office that depicts her as "a pretty Salvation Army girl" ("eine großformatige Fotografie eines schönen Heilsarmeemädchens"; 224/152). Gracie plays the role of the savior of men on multiple levels. Not only does her hotel function as a kind of brothel in which traveling businessmen find solace with "garish women" ("bunten Damen"; 229/155), but she also figures in a mysterious, unexplained way in the life of Max Aurach. When the narrator stumbles upon a painting by Aurach in the Tate Museum, it bears "a title which struck me as both significant and improbable: 'G. I. on her Blue Candlewick Cover'" ("den für mich ebenso bedeutungsvollen wie unwahrscheinlichen Titel *G. I. on her Blue Candlewick Cover*"; 264/177). Although never specified, the letters G. I. are the initials of Gracie Irlam, whom the narrator had earlier associated with the candlewick blankets with which her hotel was replete (224/152, 225/153, 226/153). Aurach's painting of G. I. serves as the structural counterpart to the large-format photograph the narrator sees hanging in her office, and it thereby invokes by association the theme of salvation. But the relationship between Gracie and Aurach remains unarticulated and emerges as a typically luminous

---

33 See Graley Herren, "The Return of the Repressed Mother in W. G. Sebald's Fiction," in *A Literature of Restitution: Critical Essays on W. G. Sebald*, ed. Jeanette Baxter, Valerie Henitiuk, and Ben Hutchinson (Manchester: Manchester University Press, 2013), 234, who interprets the name of the hotel Arosa and Gracie Irlam's "pink" ("rosaroten") dressing gown (*Ausgewanderten* 223/152), along with the date on the photograph of her that hangs in her office, May 17, 1944—the day before Sebald's own birth—as allusions to Sebald's real mother, whose name was Rosa.

Sebaldian coincidence, as *both* "significant" *and* "improbable." We
know, however, that there is a connection between them, since when
the narrator and Aurach have their reunion in 1989, one of their first
topics of conversation is "the flugelhorn player Gracie Irlam" ("die
Flügelhornistin Gracie Irlam"; 269/181), a comment that alludes to the
earlier photograph in which the girl in the Salvation Army uniform
holds a flugelhorn under her arm (224/152). Gracie's first name can
also be read as a suggestion of her redemptive role, as the embodiment
of grace; and perhaps the fact that she is identified with a musical
instrument is indicative of the imbrication of this thematic of salvation
with the operatic rendition of *Parsifal* that assumes such significance
later in the text. Regardless, Gracie represents a redemptive grace
that saves the young emigrant narrator, by providing the rescuing
teas-maid and through the warmth of her candlewick comforters. She
forms a connective link uniting the lives of the two asylum seekers in
Manchester, Aurach and Sebald's narrator. At the time of their 1989
reunion, Aurach points to the parallels between his own life and that of
his interlocutor, noting that the latter has been in exile from his German
homeland for the same amount of time as was Aurach upon their first
meeting in 1966 (270/181).

Max Aurach as Exile by Choice?

Although Aurach and Sebald's narrator seem to be exiles of very
different sorts—the latter *choosing* to leave Germany for the ectopic
liberation provided by an alien land, the former subject to forced
migration in order to escape the Shoah—their status as émigrés shares
certain principal qualities. In London, the first station of his emigration,
Aurach enjoys the company of his Uncle Leo, who preceded him to
England and who provides him with a temporary home and arranges
for Aurach to attend boarding school. During this initial period of
asylum, Aurach remains in contact with his parents via letters. When
this correspondence breaks off in November 1941 as a result of his
parents' deportation, Aurach feels a paradoxical sense of relief, largely
because he can immunize himself psychologically against knowledge of
the torment they have suffered (285/190–1). This radical break with his
heritage allows him to retreat into isolation and attain, as he remarks,
"a certain equability" ("das seelische Gleichgewicht"; 285/191). The
relative peace afforded him by this rejection of his origins increasingly
dissipates as he grows older, so that the pain of remembrance and loss
creates "the shade and dark in recent years" ("meine letzten Jahre so
sehr überschattet und verdunkelt hat"; 286/191). Just a few months
later—in early 1942, when Aurach has the opportunity to move to New
York with his Uncle Leo—he opts to remain in England and begin a
new life by moving to Manchester and commencing his art studies.

The language in which Aurach describes this decision emphasizes his desire for an absolute break with his family lineage and the possibility of a new beginning under the ectopic conditions of a city where he enjoys the freedom of complete detachment:

> Anfang 1942 hat der Onkel Leo ... sich in Southhampton nach New York eingeschifft ... und wir hatten verabredet, daß ich ihm im Sommer, nach Absolvierung meines letzten Schuljahres, nachfolgen würde. Als es soweit war, habe ich mich aber, *weil ich von nichts und niemandem mehr an meine Herkunft gemahnt werden wollte*, entschlossen, statt nach New York unter die Obhut des Onkels allein nach Manchester zu gehen. *Ahnungslos*, wie ich war, glaubte ich, in Manchester ein neues, voraussetzungsloses Leben beginnen zu können, aber gerade Manchester hat mir alles ins Gedächtnis gerufen, was ich zu vergessen suchte, denn Manchester ist eine Einwandererstadt, und eineinhalb Jahrhunderte lang sind die Einwanderer ... in der Hauptsache Deutsche und Juden gewesen. (*Ausgewanderten* 286; emphasis added)
> [In early 1942 ... Uncle Leo embarked at Southampton for New York ... and we agreed that I would follow him in the summer, when I had completed my last year at school. But when the time came I *did not want to be reminded of my origins by anything or anyone*, so instead of going to New York, into the care of my uncle, I decided to move to Manchester on my own. Inexperienced [*Ahnungslos*] as I was, I imagined I could begin a new life in Manchester, from scratch; but instead, Manchester reminded me of everything I was trying to forget. Manchester is an immigrant city, and for a hundred and fifty years ... the immigrants were chiefly Germans and Jews. (*Emigrants* 191; emphasis added)]

The rejection of heritage and ancestry, and the promise of a new life without any limiting presuppositions, constitutes Aurach's primary strategy for forgetting the pain of the past, the suffering of his family, and the fate of the Jewish people more generally. His refusal to join his last remaining blood relative, Uncle Leo, in New York represents his *choice* to live the life of the absolute emigrant, someone who *deliberately* cuts himself off from all bonds with his past and his ancestors. The German words used to describe this decision are telling: his uncle does not simply *remind* him of his heritage, as the English translation indicates; he voices an *admonishment* or *exhortation* about it ("gemahnt"), with all the negative implications of these words. Aurach casts his new life as unconditional and unqualified, possessing the possibility of beginning "from scratch" ("voraussetzungslos") precisely because it frees him of all ties to his prior existence. Only later does he realize that the choice of Manchester, with its large population of German and Jewish émigrés, presents the worst possible conditions for such a radical break. He blames the error of this decision on his own ignorance. He designates this ignorance with the adjective *ahnungslos*, a term that alludes to an etymologically related word with a nearly identical pronunciation, *ahnenlos*, meaning devoid of ancestry. Aurach decides to move to Manchester because he wants to be *ahnenlos*, liberated from his ancestry; but because he is *ahnungslos*, lacking in proper knowledge, his choice of Manchester paradoxically defeats his principal motivation. In Manchester he cannot avoid being reminded—exhorted, admonished—about his heritage, since it is peopled by so many individuals whose heritage he shares. His ancestry thus returns with the uncanny inevitability of Freud's return of the repressed. The city that was supposed to guarantee a connectionless ectopia turns out to be teeming with reminiscences of those very bonds Aurach seeks to sever.

It is worth noting that something very similar can be said for Sebald's youthful narrator. He too, like Aurach, relishes the "deep sense of isolation" ("Gefühl der Ungebundenheit"; 228/155) that the alien atmosphere of Manchester offers. But if the motivation for his voluntary emigration is the absolute autonomy achieved by breaking all ties with his German homeland and the horrors of its recent past, during his own perambulations through the city he is constantly reminded of both the more sordid and the more banal aspects of his native country. His walks take him through the former Jewish quarter of the city, which, as he ominously reports, was abandoned by its inhabitants and all but leveled by the city administration. All that remains is one empty row of houses whose primary characteristics are their broken windows and battered doors (232/157). The allusion to Kristallnacht is unmistakable in this description. The narrator is also haunted by the German-sounding Jewish names he discovers on the sign of an abandoned lawyers' office, "Glickmann, Grunwald und Gottgetreu" (232/157). This is the same narrator who twenty-five years later and twenty-five years older will comment ironically that the Germans probably envied the Jews more for their beautifully poetic German names than for anything else they possessed (335/224). Twisting more toward a caricature of those things traditionally associated with the dark side of German heritage, the architecture of the slaughterhouse in the neighborhood of Ordsall, with its wrought-iron fence and a design that is reminiscent of a Gothic-era German castle, complete with parapets, battlements, turrets, and gates, inexplicably calls to the narrator's mind the names of familiar Nuremberg gingerbread producers (234/159–60). Significantly, it is nothing other than a slaughterhouse—another veiled allusion to the Holocaust—that invokes these reminiscences of the landmark architecture of German history and the baked goods traditionally enjoyed at Christmastime and produced in Nuremberg, the city Hitler and the Nazis celebrated as the capital of their movement. And even if Sebald's narrator is correct to identify this association as a "bad" or tasteless "joke of sorts" ("eine Art von bösem Gespött"; 234/160), surely the joke is on him. For if his—unconscious—aim in emigrating to England was to escape the inherited guilt of second-generation Germans for the atrocities of the Holocaust, then Manchester turns out to be a place full of constant reminders of these events—as it is for Aurach. The operative motto for both Aurach and Sebald's narrator thus might be, "You can run, but you can't hide." The deepest structural affinity between these two characters is their common attempts to evade *Vergangenheitsbewältigung*: coming to terms with the past and the Holocaust. To be sure, they represent different sides in grappling with this past, the one as the offspring of the victims, the other the son of the perpetrators.

Aurach's Art as Deconstructive Representation of Ancestral Ghosts

If Aurach's life in Manchester emerges as a dialectic in which the suppression of heritage is continually countered by its haunting reminder and return, this same dialectic defines the process by which he creates his art. The narrator's description of Aurach's studio and his technique emphasizes the destructive side of this dialectic, highlighting the "Vermehrung des Staubs," the "increase" in "dust" and detritus (238/161), as the true essence of his artistry.[34] Whereas this process of repeatedly drawing and erasing images completely occupies Aurach's work days, at night this dialectical production of dust comes to a standstill:

> Sein heftiges, hingebungsvolles Zeichnen ... dieses Zeichnen und *Hinundherfahren* auf dem dicken, lederartigen Papier sowohl als auch das mit dem Zeichnen verbundene andauernde Verwischen des Gezeichneten mit einem von der Kohle völlig durchdrungenen Wollappen war in Wirklichkeit eine einzige, nur in den Stunden der Nacht zum Stillstand kommende Staubproduktion. (*Ausgewanderten* 238–9; emphasis added)

---

34   Sebald's descriptions of Aurach's studio and his artistic technique draw directly on the portrayal Hughes, *Frank Auerbach*, 13–15, provides of the artist's studio and his method. The final image in Hughes's profusely illustrated monograph, 220, contains a photograph of this studio, complete with piles of paint remnants littering the floor.

[He drew with vigorous abandon ... and that process of drawing
and shading on the thick, leathery paper, as well as the concomitant business of constantly erasing what he had drawn with
a woolen rag already heavy with charcoal, really amounted to
nothing but a steady production of dust, which never ceased
except at night. (*Emigrants* 161–2)]

The stasis that produces a "finished" work does not result from a
teleological process or the achievement of an artistic aim, but instead
marks an accidental interruption in the interminable process itself,
which begins anew the following day. Aurach's technique represents
a nomadic wandering of his charcoal pencil across the canvas: more
than a mere "shading," as indicated by the English translation, the
Hinundherfahren of his utensil suggests an incessant wandering back
and forth, a movement that imitates the fate of his ancestors. Yet
Sebald's narrator cannot disguise his own surprise at what he calls the
"great vividness" of the image that emerges once this process comes
to a standstill: "I marveled to see that Ferber, with the few lines and
shadows that had escaped annihilation, had created a portrait of great
vividness" ("wie Aurach gegen Ende seines Arbeitstages aus den
wenigen der Vernichtung entgangenen Linien und Schatten ein Bildnis
von großer Unmittelbarkeit zusammenbrachte"; 239/162). The paradox
is that a procedure that insists on mediation and remediation somehow
generates a product distinguished by its emphatic immediacy and
vividness, as implied by the German word *Unmittelbarkeit*.

But even such seemingly perfect way-stations in Aurach's never-
ending generation and regeneration of a drawing are subject to
undoing, and only ultimate exhaustion finally causes him to abandon
work on a specific piece:

Entschloß sich Aurach, nachdem er vielleicht vierzig Varianten
verworfen beziehungsweise in das Papier zurückgerieben und
durch weitere Entwürfe überdeckt hatte, das Bild, weniger in der
Überzeugung, es fertiggestellt zu haben, als aus einem Gefühl
der Ermattung, endlich aus der Hand zu geben, so hatte es für
den Betrachter den Anschein, als sei es hervorgegangen *aus einer
langen Ahnenreihe* grauer, eingeäscherter, in dem zerschundenen
Papier nach wie vor herumgeisternder Gesichter. (*Ausgewanderten*
239-40; emphasis added)
[He might reject as many as forty variants, or smudge them back
into the paper and overdraw new attempts upon them; and if he
then decided that the portrait was done, not so much because he
was convinced that it was finished as through sheer exhaustion,
an onlooker might well feel that it had evolved *from a long lineage*

of grey, *ancestral* faces, rendered unto ash but still there, as ghostly
presences, on the harried paper. (*Emigrants* 162; emphasis added)]

The real aim of Aurach's art is not the mimetic reproduction of the
particular object or model his painting is purportedly representing, but
instead an exploration of the very *lineage* of this object's antecedents.
What ends up being depicted on Aurach's canvases hence is not a
static reproduction of the object in all its mimetic accuracy—this, as
we recall, was the basis of the perfection Frohmann achieved with
his successful miniature reproduction of Solomon's Temple. Instead,
what he captures is the historical becoming of the object, the ancestry
and "Ahnenreihe" out of which it emerges.[35] The narrator's language
articulates the problematic of Aurach's art as the troubled depiction
of *heritage*, of that imbrication of present and past, and with tradition,
that his decision to live in Manchester sought to deny. Just as Aurach
is destined to experience this heritage in the constant reminders of his
German-Jewish ancestry that haunt this city, his art instantiates the
reinvocation and recreation of issues of descent. The ashen "ghostly
presences" that haunt his canvases are the ghosts of his own past,
rendered to ash by the Nazi crematoria, which he has otherwise tried
to banish and repress. His artistic practice, like its products, enacts the
problematic of descent at the heart of his trauma and his suffering.

The figures that appear in Aurach's works, like his technique itself,
are explicitly nomadic, constantly on the move, caught up in a process
of emergence and disappearance. In this sense, they are exiles of the
same sort as Aurach, and even Sebald's narrator. Mary McCarthy
distinguishes between exiles and refugees by maintaining that the
former migrate by choice, whereas the latter are forced to emigrate due
to circumstances outside their control.[36] According to this definition,
Sebald's narrator is clearly an exile, while Aurach represents a sort of
hybrid between the exile and the refugee. He is initially driven out of
Germany by forces he neither comprehends nor controls, but he takes
charge of his own displacement when he refuses to follow his Uncle Leo
to New York and opts instead for the isolation provided by the move
to Manchester. But McCarthy outlines a further trait distinguishing

35 The example of Aurach's art printed in the first edition of *Die Ausgewanderten* is
a reproduction of Frank Auerbach's drawing *Head of Catherine Lampert VI* from
1980, and is based on plate 152 from Hughes's biography, *Frank Auerbach*, 186.
The illustration is omitted in the English translation and later German editions,
for reasons of copyright infringement, and also cannot be reproduced here for
the same reasons.
36 Mary McCarthy, "A Guide to Exiles, Expatriates, and Internal Émigrés," in
Altogether Elsewhere: Writers on Exile, ed. Marc Robinson (Boston: Faber & Faber,
1994), 50.

exiles from refugees that is especially applicable to Aurach's existence and his art: refugees are often assisted in resettling, and they are at pains to put down new roots, whereas the whole point of exiles, those who welcome the ectopic autonomy of detachment, is the *refusal* to put down roots and the very celebration of their rootlessness. In her diagnosis, exiles embrace nomadism as the very condition of possibility of their own existence; they are, as she maintains, "more like birds than plants, perching wherever they are," and as a result they "prefer transient accommodations."[37] Aurach's art invokes the roots of heritage, but only to uproot them in the frantic blur of his nomadic technique that depicts presence only as evanescence.

Aurach's preference for "transient accommodations" is concretized most emphatically in the abode he inhabits at the Midland Hotel (348/232). It reflects the paradox that, although he insists on staying in one place, he nevertheless remains a kind of free-floating exile who lives in temporary quarters. This is the paradox of his art, which is nomadic in this same sense, but which nonetheless—or precisely for that reason—interrogates problems of ancestry, heritage, and "roots." His images are, literally, constantly on the move. It is not surprising, then, that immediately following the description of the quasi-nomadism and the hauntings of ancestral ghosts that form the essence of his art, the narrative shifts to a description of Wadi Halfa, the café in which Aurach regularly spends his mornings and evenings, thereby framing the period of concerted work in his studio. Explicitly called a "transport café" (240/162), this establishment embodies the paradox of a nomadism attached to a stable site. The most notable characteristic of this café's physical ambience is the fresco of a caravan in the desert that is painted on one of its walls. This painting creates the illusion that the caravan is approaching the viewer, and according to Sebald's narrator, this difficult perspective and the artist's lack of skill cause this image to flicker as though it were itself a *Fata Morgana* in a desert landscape (243/164). This incandescent quality aligns this image with Aurach's own artistic technique, which reproduces in the *Hinundherfahren*, the wandering of the charcoal across the canvas, the wavering effect of this amateurish painting. The narrator imagines Aurach, himself covered with the dust and detritus of this artistic

37 Ibid., 51. It is a coincidence of Sebaldian proportions that McCarthy names Vladimir Nabokov as the prototype of the exile in this sense, for in his guise as the Butterfly Man he is the ghost who haunts all the stories of *Die Ausgewanderten*. See also Florence Feiereisen and Daniel Pope, "True Fictions and Fictional Truths: The Enigmatic in Sebald's Use of Images in *The Emigrants*," in *Searching for Sebald: Photography after W. G. Sebald*, ed. Lise Patt (Los Angeles: Institute of Cultural Inquiry, 2007), 184, who view Nabokov as a "messenger of hope" because he symbolizes the possibility of life after exile.

process, as integral to this desert fresco: "He seemed to have just emerged from this desert scene, or to belong in it" ("als sei er soeben aus dem Wüstenbild herausgetreten oder als gehöre er in es hinein"; 243/164). He affirms Aurach's self-definition as a paradoxical nomad who is permanently on the move even though he stays put. Like the figures in his paintings, Aurach is running in place.

But the café Wadi Halfa also suggests the other aspect of Aurach's art, its gesture toward problems of heritage and ancestry. The nearly eighty-year-old cook at this establishment is said to be a former Maasai chieftain, who in the post-war years moved to England and gave up his nomadic lifestyle for the more stable profession of a cook (241–2/163). What makes him such a remarkable figure, aside from his height of nearly two meters, is that the numerous waiters in the café, whose ages range from about twelve or thirteen to around sixty years old, are identified as his sons. The workers in Wadi Halfa represent nothing less than a vitally active family lineage, a regenerative chain of ancestry from the living patriarch through several generations of male offspring. Moreover, like the shadowy ancestral figures on Aurach's canvases, they resemble each other to the point that one can scarcely tell them apart:

Da sie alle gleich schlank und gleich groß gewachsen waren und aus ihren ebenmäßig schönen Gesichtern alle mit der gleichen Todesverachtung um sich blickten, konnte man sie kaum auseinanderhalten, zumal sie sich in unregelmäßigen Abständen ablösten und die Kellnerkonstellation dementsprechend in einem fort sich veränderte. (*Ausgewanderten* 242)
[Since they were each as slim and tall as the other, and all displayed the same disdain in their fine, even features, they were scarcely distinguishable, especially as they would take over from each other at irregular intervals, so that the team of waiters currently on duty was continuously changing. (*Emigrants* 163)]

The constantly changing "constellations"—Sebald's German is more precise than the English translation—in which these figures appear are parallel to the kaleidoscopic alterations that emerge on Aurach's canvases through the continual process of representation, erasure, and revision. The identity of these waiters is emphasized by the threefold iteration of the word "gleich" ("equally"), and yet, as in Aurach's works of art, the same is never perfectly selfsame, but instead is always marked by deviation and transformation. Yet one thing sets these waiters apart from Aurach, his artistic representations, and even from Sebald's narrator: their "Todesverachtung," the shared "disdain for death" that Sebald's English translator mysteriously elides in his rendering of this passage. If we ask exactly what instills in them this scorn for mortality, then the most obvious answer is that they defy it due to their integration in a continual line of ancestry, in a heritage and an ongoing chain of descent and descendants. Amidst the dominant nomadic atmosphere of the "transport café" Wadi Halfa, Aurach experiences a paradigmatic example of the redeeming effects of rootedness, filiation, and consanguinity in the domesticated Maasai chieftain and his array of "sons." They represent in the empirical world outside his studio the real possibility of an *Ahnenreihe*, the lineage of ancestry and heritage that Aurach's art depicts in the problematized form of its shadowy ghosts. Perhaps this chieftain and his progeny present an example of life imitating art rather than art imitating life?

Art as *Besinnung auf Herkunft* (Commemoration of Heritage)
The conflict between perennial nomadism, identified with the liberated detachment of an ectopic existence, and confederation in a community of ancestry is characteristic of all three artist figures in this text. The central one is Aurach himself, through whose example we have exposed this dialectic and its inherent problematic. But the same tension informs the existence of Frohmann, the artist in Aurach's dream who represents the paragon of aesthetic success. Significantly, he is also a nomad who travels from ghetto to ghetto. Moreover, he is a textual nomad as well, borrowed from an intertext by Joseph Roth, but who also resurfaces *intratextually* as the war invalid whom Luisa Lanzberg treats in the embedded narrative of her life story (323/215). The artist Frohmann undertakes his nomadic wanderings in order to affirm the threatened confraternity among the Jews of the diaspora: he transports from ghetto to ghetto the perfect resemblance of Solomon's Temple as the *reminder* of this shared origin, heritage, and filiation. He thereby becomes a vehicle for the resurrection of community sensibility. This is clearly not the case for Aurach, who as artist culti- vates the detachment represented by his dark studio, whose artistic representations fail to capture the original with any mimetic accuracy, and who instead invokes a shadowy, ashen ancestry of "ghostly presences" in the composite drawings that spook across his canvases. Only by exploiting this "Pentimento effect," in which ancestry and the vestiges of historical continuity are merely suggested by the presence of temporally prior sketches that underlie and disrupt the most recent one, can Aurach articulate the central problematic of heritage.[38] His

38 Murray Baumgarten, "'Not Knowing What I Should Think': The Landscape of Postmemory in W. G. Sebald's *The Emigrants*," *Partial Answers* 5, no. 2 (2007): 274, discusses Aurach's method and its connection to the Pentimento effect, drawing the illuminating analogy between these images and Francis Galton's

artistic representations exist simultaneously in the present and the past, depicted in the moments of being, disappearing, and becoming. His paintings thus translate Gracie Irlam's fundamental question, "And where have you sprung from?" (224/152), into the medium of visual art. But just as Gracie's question receives no definitive answer, Aurach's paintings pose questions about origin, heritage, and descent without ever indicating any identifiable lineage.

Our final question is whether the same can be said of the last artist represented in this text, namely Sebald's narrator himself. Scholars have often pointed to the way this figure conspicuously stylizes his own act of writing *about* Aurach as a translation of the painter's idiosyncratic technique into his own literary practice: his manuscript reveals, in its prominent erasures, corrections, and constant revisions, the same nomadic quality typical of Aurach's drawings:[39]

> Hunderte von Seiten hatte ich bedeckt mit meinem Bleistift- und Kugelschreibergekritzel. Weitaus das meiste davon war durchgestrichen, verworfen oder bis zur Unleserlichkeit mit Zusätzen überschmiert. Selbst das, was ich schließlich für die "endgültige" Fassung retten konnte, erschien mir als ein mißratenes Stückwerk. (*Ausgewanderten* 345)
>
> [I had covered hundreds of pages with my scribble, in pencil and ballpoint. By far the greater part had been crossed out, discarded, or obliterated by additions. Even what I ultimately salvaged as a "final" version seemed to me a thing of shreds and patches, utterly botched. (*Emigrants* 230–1)]

Just as Aurach's drawings are mere works-in-progress, with a "final" version resulting only from an interruption born of exhaustion and frustration, Sebald's narrator figures his own story as a text-in-process that can never truly "capture" its object or arrive at a satisfactory conclusion. His text, like Aurach's paintings, is portrayed as a palimpsest in which the working drafts reveal the heritage from which the later versions have sprung. But ultimately this comparison is misleading. Aurach's "final" products betray the process of their own generation

---

composite photographs. Galton's procedure of superimposing photographs of blood relations also reveals a connection to ancestry, since these composite photographs sought to distill the hereditary constants out of numerous individual manifestations.

39   Claudia Öhlschläger, *Beschädigtes Leben. Erzählte Risse: W. G. Sebalds poetische Ordnung des Unglücks* (Freiburg im Breisgau: Rombach, 2006), 95–6, and Heidelberger-Leonard, "Zwischen Aneignung und Restitution," 15, discuss this connection between the literary practice of Sebald's narrator and Aurach's painterly technique.

in the shadowy multiplicity of images that are their defining feature, whereas this is decidedly not true for Sebald's (or his narrator's) text, which is printed in its "final" version as a complete work whose earlier drafts either cease to exist or disappear into the literary archive for the perusal of scholars. Sebald's readers are hence dependent on his narrator's *description* of the palimpsest-like character of his manuscripts. The *spatial* art of painting, which renders temporal succession in terms of simultaneous contiguity, has certain advantages in this respect over the *temporal* art of literary narrative. By the same token, the very essence of narrative art is succession and linear development, and the "stories" it unfolds inevitably imply issues of heritage and ancestry.

It is common to discuss questions of temporal succession in narrative in the language of evolutionary development, teleological purpose, and developmental necessity. Yet this concatenation of the prior with the present is precisely what Aurach's paintings both suggest and dispel, so that problems of lineage remain open, suspended in the indeterminate relationships between final rendition and prior drafts. It is much more difficult to achieve this same degree of temporal or teleological uncertainty in narrative art, and that is the challenge confronting Sebald's narrator, if his purpose is to translate the nomadism of Aurach's paintings into narrative form. The primary strategies he employs to approximate the superimposed quality of Aurach's art is the refraction of his themes of heritage and exile through the life stories of three different characters who represent three different generations: the painter Max Aurach, his mother Luisa Lanzberg, and the Sebald-like narrator who recounts their stories. "Max Aurach" thus presents a kind of composite account of the problems of exile, superimposing on the diegetic biography of Aurach's life the autobiography of the frame narrator's search for asylum outside his homeland, as well as the metadiegetic tale of Luisa Lanzberg's alienation from her place of birth. In the structural resonance among these three biographies, "Max Aurach" approximates most closely the "Pentimento" effect characteristic of the painterly technique attributed to the artist Aurach himself. We can view Sebald's text as a palimpsest that overwrites three tales of exile, from various historical periods and with vastly different motivations, in order to render a composite picture of ectopic existence. It is important that these three stories are drawn from distinct historical periods, for they thereby manifest temporal non-identity while at the same time holding open the possibility of historical succession. At this level, Sebald's text interrogates the heritage of ectopic exile under the conditions of modernity without lending this problematic any overly restrictive definition. This composite aesthetic practice, which marries historical references, intertextual resonances, and fictional embellishment to arrive at the "typical," is one of the defining features of Sebald's poetics of history. It represents a tactic that allows him to produce fictional texts that nonetheless retain the "effect of the real."

This brings us to the final challenge that Sebald and his narrator face in their attempt to narratively enact the dynamic of continuity and rupture expressed in Aurach's paintings: the resistance to closure. There can be no closure, of course, in Aurach's paintings, except an ending enforced by the rupture, the breach, or the interruption. The challenge confronting the author W. G. Sebald—and here we must operate on the level of authorial investment—is to find a way to end the unending narrative, to break off the text-in-process, without lending it the sense of completion and closure. This is an art that Sebald masters especially well, and the conclusion of "Max Aurach" presents a prototypical example of a technique that provides formal conclusion, but still choreographs an evocative non-closure in which the story's themes open onto timeless universality. We have already examined the clever art of transition with which this text moves, in its closing pages, from Aurach's situation in Manchester in 1991, to the narrator's dream-like reminiscences about his early days in this city in 1966 and 1967, to the musical examples that bundle together many of the story's cardinal themes, through to the narrator's extended ekphrastic description of photographs from the Lodz ghetto. The deft manner in which the story moves from its recapitulation of Aurach's life to the personal experiences and imaginings of the narrator betokens that confraternity between these figures that the narrative suggests throughout its plot.

This text then concludes—without actually closing—with the narrator's interpretive response to the last photograph he recalls from Genewein's documentation of the Lodz ghetto, the three young women sitting at a loom, weaving a carpet whose geometrical pattern and colors mysteriously remind him of the sofa in his parents' living room: "The irregular geometrical patterns of the carpet they are knotting, and even its colours, remind me of the settee in our living room at home" ("Der Teppich, an dem sie knüpfen, hat ein unregelmäßig geometrisches Muster, das mich auch in seinen Farben erinnert an das Muster unseres Wohnzimmersofas zu Hause"; 355/237). A text that began with the narrator's departure from home and his celebration of a new ectopic existence in an alien land ends with a final reminiscence of the very home he abandoned. He is reintegrated, in his fantasy, with his heritage, represented by the communal space of the family living room. We recall that Aurach's dream of homecoming also transports him imaginatively to his family's living room (262/186), and that when Luisa Lanzberg recalls her childhood home in Steinach, it is the living room that draws her attention and bespeaks communal comfort (291/195). The act of *textile* weaving in which these three women are engaged stands symbolically for the production of this very work as *text*; yet these women produce a *communal* product, the result of a productive collaboration of *three* individuals, and their work thereby also betrays a composite quality. The same can be said about the text of "Max Aurach," which instantiates a narrative collaboration between Sebald's narrator, the painter Aurach—who himself represents a "composite" image based on two historical models, Sebald's Manchester landlord and the painter Frank Auerbach[40]—and the diary of Luisa Lanzberg, which itself is based on a historical document.[41] These three "authors" line up with the three discriminate stories of exile this text laminates together, and the three women in the image from the Lodz ghetto can be seen as symbolic markers for these three tales and their tellers. But more germane for Sebald's art of ending without closure is the gesture by which his narrator first provides these women with names, "Roza, Lusia und Lea" (355/237), thereby stripping away their anonymity and giving them historical faces, only then to elevate them to the level of mythological generality by identifying them with the Parcae, "Nona, Decuma und Morta" (355/237). The implication is that just as these three anonymous women emblematize the fates of historical individuals, their destinies reach beyond questions of historical particularity and stand as representative of universal human problems. The same can be said about the three stories of exile and homelessness presented in Sebald's narrative, which explore this problematic on the examples of three historically discrete individuals, but whose stories acquire universality through the augmenting fictions by which they are combined and enhanced. This is where Sebald's poetics of history, his strategy of creating documentary fictions, or fictionalized documentaries, promises its greatest purchase. But the association of these women with the three fates also reinforces the existential thematic suggested by the Heideggerean theme of Being

---

40 In interviews, Sebald openly identified these two as the models upon whom he based his composite image of Aurach (Schwartz 38–9, 73). On Sebald's reworking of these lives and of the documents in his possession, see Heidelberger-Leonhard, "Zwischen Aneignung und Restitution," 14–15, and Schütte, *W. G. Sebald*, 110.

41 Sebald's file of materials for "Max Aurach" contains his letters from Peter Jordan, as well as photocopies of family documents Jordon shared, including the memoirs of his grandfather Lazarus Frank, a handwritten sketch of the Frank family tree, and two sets of memoirs by Jordan's aunt Thea Gebhardt, née Frank, one on her childhood in Steinach, the other on her youth in Bad Kissingen. These latter documents form the textual basis for Luisa Lanzberg's diary. Klaus Gasseleder, "Erkundungen zum Prätext der Luisa-Lanzberg-Geschichte aus W. G. Sebalds *Die Ausgewanderten*: Ein Bericht," in *Sebald. Lektüren*, ed. Marcel Atze and Franz Loquai (Eggingen: Edition Isele, 2005), 157–75, provides a detailed examination of the relationships between these pretexts and Sebald's adaptation.

as *Besinnung*, as meditation on the origin of our history, with which our deliberations on this story began. As mythological figures these three women exist outside of time, heritage, and destiny; and yet they represent precisely the finitude of *individual* human destiny and the commonality of our shared mortality.

This concluding shift to mythology represents a final invitation to us, Sebald's readers, to interrogate the heritage and lineage not only of these three women from the Lodz ghetto, but also of the characters presented in the text of "Max Aurach." This makes this story an appropriate conclusion for *Die Ausgewanderten*, as a collection of tales about exile. The message of "Max Aurach," and of this collection more generally, is that instead of relishing their lives of ectopic exile and throwing off the ballast of the past, of *Herkunft*, heritage, ancestry, and origins, modern human beings should interrogate this historical lineage as part and parcel of our very existence and our Being. We are reminded of the importance of asking each other and ourselves that central question articulated by Gracie Irlam: "And where have you sprung from?" In embracing this question, perhaps we need to exhibit that "disdain for death" that constitutes the distinguishing, hereditary traits of the sons of the Maasai chieftain who labor in the "transport café" Wadi Halfa—sometimes also known as planet earth.

Six Fabulation and Metahistory: W. G. Sebald and the Problematic of Contemporary (German) Holocaust Fiction

"Writing retraces the contours of the past with a possibly less ephemeral stroke ... it does at least preserve a presence, and it enables one to tell about a child who saw one world founder and another reborn."

Saul Friedlander[1]

Fabulation and Metahistory

The title of this chapter alludes to two classic works of humanistic scholarship, one from the discipline of literary criticism, the other from historiography: namely, to Robert Scholes's *Fabulation and Metafiction* of 1979, and to Hayden White's *Metahistory* of 1973. What joins these two works, aside from the relative proximity of their publication, is an insistence on the significance of poetics as a vehicle for approaching historical reality. For that reason, they provide significant parameters for our understanding of W. G. Sebald's poetics of history, his attempts to approach the representation of historical conjunctures by exploiting fictional and metafictional techniques. Each of these scholars addresses the convergence of poetic discourse and historical facts from different perspectives. Scholes, the literary critic and literary historian, stresses the emphatically self-conscious fabulation of "metafiction," which he describes as a "turning back" of contemporary literature "toward the stuff of history itself," with the purpose of "reinvigorating it with an imagination tempered by

---

1   Saul Friedlander, *When Memory Comes*, trans. Helen R. Lane (New York: Farrar Strauss, 1979), 135.

a decade and more of fictional experimentation."[2] For Scholes, the representational strategies of literary realism are impoverished forms that fail to capture the intricacies of the real: "Reality is too subtle for realism to catch it. It cannot be transcribed directly. But by invention, by fabulation, we may open a way toward reality that will come as close to it as human ingenuity may come."[3] For him the experimental fiction of the 1970s and beyond, based on its fabulative and metafictional tendencies, does not mark a "turning away" of fiction from reality, but instead manifests the seemingly paradoxical attempt "to find more subtle correspondences between the reality which is fiction and the fiction which is reality."[4]

This chiastic formulation is more than just rhetorical play: it highlights the transitional dynamic that joins fiction and reality in a conceptual continuum, an interstitial space in which Sebald's documentary fictions largely operate. Fictional fabulation for Scholes, as for Sebald, represents an avenue that is able to effectively invoke a sense of the real. By the same token, reality itself is often stranger, and at times more horrific and atrocious, than fiction. The Holocaust provides the exemplary instance of a reality that outpaces our wildest nightmares and dwarfs the most gruesome creatures of the imagination. This has led some critics to suggest that in the post-Holocaust world imagination must work overtime to catch up with the rationally choreographed, monstrous reality of Auschwitz and the death camps.[5] Literary fabulation represents but one especially productive instrument for advancing this game of catch-up. If fabulative metafiction ultimately acknowledges the gulf that separates verbal and narrative *representations* of reality from the real itself as factually given, it nevertheless turns toward this reality in an attempt to construct verbal and narrative artifacts that invoke *approximations* of the real. Fiction becomes a lens through which present and past reality can be brought into varied focus. Altering the image by shifting from a metaphorical to a metonymic axis, we can propose that experimental metafiction is a kaleidoscope that configures and reconfigures the "data" of the real in ever changing ways. By doing so, imaginative literature injects the world of the statically "real" with a mobility that fractures any pretenses to historical necessity, opening onto the possibilities of alternative scenarios, reconstructed from the

2   Robert Scholes, *Fabulation and Metafiction* (Urbana: University of Illinois Press, 1979), 4.

3   Ibid., 13.

4   Ibid., 8.

5   Lawrence L. Langer, *The Holocaust and the Literary Imagination* (New Haven, CT: Yale University Press, 1975), 35; Elie Wiesel, "The Holocaust as Literary Inspiration," in *Dimensions of the Holocaust* (Evanston, IL: Northwestern University Press, 1977), 8.

building blocks of empirical experience, that can yet lay claim to being "factual." Language, and fictional writing in particular, have the power to shape if not reality itself, then at least our perception of it. Sebald's poetics of history is especially adept at such a kaleidoscopic reshuffling of historical data and its intermingling with fabulative elements in the service of affirming historical constellations, while challenging us to reconceptualize them and experience them differently.

With this we have arrived at the position of Hayden White, except that the object of his investigation is not twentieth-century fiction, but rather nineteenth-century historical narratives and philosophies of history. For White, the heyday of historiographic realism, much like the parallel development in literary realism, is predicated on a limited— and limiting—set of conventions. The great historians select from among a finite repertory of tropes, discursive arguments, and modes of emplotment in order to create their specific historical narratives.[6] Operating tacitly with a Freudian model that distinguishes the manifest expression of the historical account from the latent rules that serve as its generative grammar,[7] White insists on the *poetic* character of this deep-structural level that inevitably pre-forms all historical narratives. This poetic dimension is precisely what he terms the "'metahistorical' understructure of the historical work." On this latent and formative level of "metahistory," "the historian performs an essentially *poetic* act, in which he *pre*figures the historical field and constitutes it as a domain upon which to bring to bear the specific theories he will use to explain 'what was *really* happening' in it."[8] Metahistory and metafiction hence overlap with regard to their basis in forms of poetic fabulation. The primary difference is that whereas White's historian *unconsciously* relies on a repertory of fabulative techniques, Scholes's metafictional fabulators consciously, indeed *self*-consciously, exploit poetics as a means for disrupting, unsettling, and rewriting accepted narratives about the real.[9] The relationship of metafiction to metahistory is thus similar to that between the Surrealist artistic movement and the Freudian conception of the dream, insofar as the Surrealists consciously manipulated what Freud theorized as the unconscious operations of dream logic. It is no coincidence that one of the pre-eminent American

---

6 Hayden White, *Metahistory: The Historical Imagination in Nineteenth-Century Europe* (Baltimore, MD: Johns Hopkins University Press, 1973), 29.
7 Ibid., x. White makes this Freudian borrowing explicit at the conclusion of his book, 143, where he remarks that the "latent level, considered as linguistic ground" shapes "the manifest level of historical narratives."
8 Ibid., x.
9 For a concise summary of the self-conscious dimension of metafiction, see Patricia Waugh, *Metafiction: The Theory and Practice of Self-Conscious Fiction* (London: Routledge, 1984), 1–19.

practitioners of metafiction, Raymond Federman, dubs this mode of fabulation "surfiction," in explicit analogy to the term Surrealism.[10]

White's position makes clear that there are a handful of "latent rules" that operate below the "manifest content" of the historical text and that function as a kind of generative grammar. Throughout this study our aim is to illuminate those latent literary-aesthetic rules that underpin Sebald's poetics of history. Its central principles are a perspectival narrative approach that ventriloquizes the voices of historical informants through the unitary voice of the first-person narrator, who thereby functions as a "ghostwriter"; closely allied with this, a reliance on intertextual borrowings that transform this seemingly monologic narrative voice into a polyphonic chorus; the constitution of Sebald's works as iconotexts that integrate visual material in a manner that problematizes their illustrative and documentary function; ekphrasis as an alternative descriptive technique for merging text and image; the leitmotif-like structuring of his texts, which generates familiarity out of varied repetition and plays on patterns of historical coincidence; the overlay of diverse models, both real and fictional, to generate composite characters that appear both unique and simultaneously typical; a playful self-reflexivity that metafictionally qualifies the authority of the narrating instance and the text; and finally a combinatory practice that continually selects and reorders historical, fictional, and textual building blocks and that requires inordinate skill at constructing fluid transitions. If *Austerlitz* can be considered Sebald's literary masterpiece, one reason for this is because in this work Sebald demonstrates sovereign control over all these literary tactics. Moreover, in this work Sebald brings these aesthetic practices to bear specifically on the genre of Holocaust fiction, and an exploration of this specific configuration is the aim of the present chapter.

The Complex Problematic of Holocaust Fiction

In the discipline of Holocaust studies, the relationship between fiction and facts, between poetic elaboration and simple insistence on the real, has traditionally been fraught with controversy. As early as 1949, Theodor Adorno gave paradigmatic expression to an absolute interdiction on the application of poetic principles, aesthetic transformation, and fictional representation to the atrocities of the Holocaust. "To write poetry after Auschwitz," he famously maintained, "is barbaric" ("nach

---

10   Raymond Federman, "Surfiction—Four Propositions in Form of an Introduction," in *Surfiction: Fiction Now ... and Tomorrow*, ed. Raymond Federman, 2nd, enlarged ed. (Chicago: Swallow Press, 1981), 7: "Just as the Surrealists called that level of man's experience that functions in the subconscious SURREALITY, I call that level of man's activity that reveals life as fiction SURFICTION."

Auschwitz ein Gedicht zu schreiben, ist barbarisch").[11] He later justified
this proposition by asserting, "The aesthetic principle of stylization ...
make[s] an unthinkable fate appear to have had some meaning; it
is transfigured, something of its horror is removed. This alone does
an injustice to the victims" ("Durchs ästhetische Stilisationsprinzip
... erscheint das unausdenkliche Schicksal doch, als hätte es irgend
Sinn gehabt; es wird verklärt, etwas von dem Grauen weggenommen;
damit allein schon widerfährt den Opfern unrecht").[12] Rightly or
wrongly, Adorno's dictum about the impossibility of poetry—as a
stand-in for poetic elaboration in general—has become a watchword
of Holocaust studies. It has often been overlooked, however, that
Adorno himself later revised this stern judgment, conceding in 1966
that "Perennial suffering has as much right to expression as a tortured
man has to scream; hence it may have been wrong to say that after
Auschwitz you could no longer write poems" ("Das perennierende
Leiden hat soviel Recht auf Ausdruck wie der Gemarterte zu brüllen;
darum mag falsch gewesen sein, nach Auschwitz ließe kein Gedicht
mehr sich schreiben").[13] Especially interesting in Adorno's case is the
change of focus this revision entails. Whereas his initial prohibition
was grounded in the external perspective of aesthetic enhancement,
refinement, or modulation—a position that is consistent with the
formalistic orientation of his aesthetic theory more generally—his later
retraction is based on an implicit doctrine of literature as a mode of
therapeutic expression. In this respect the span of Adorno's positions
already stakes out certain boundaries that traditionally delimit the
terrain of literary representations of the Holocaust. On the one hand,
overwrought aestheticizing, fabulation, and formal experimentation
are viewed with suspicion because they are perceived as strategies
that cover up, redact, or ameliorate the horror of the camps and the
suffering of the victims; on the other hand, and as a corollary to this,
the unmediated, unvarnished testimony of the victims or witnesses
is commonly regarded as the sole adequate vehicle for invoking,

---

11 Theodor W. Adorno, "Kulturkritik und Gesellschaft," in *Kulturkritik und
    Gesellschaft I*, vol. 10.1 of *Gesammelte Schriften*, ed. Rolf Tiedemann (Frankfurt
    am Main: Suhrkamp, 1997), 30; "Cultural Criticism and Society," in *Critical
    Sociology: Selected Readings*, ed. Paul Connerton (Harmondsworth: Penguin,
    1976), 276.
12 Theodor W. Adorno, "Engagement," in *Noten zur Literatur*, vol. 11 of *Gesammelte
    Schriften*, ed. Rolf Tiedemann (Frankfurt am Main: Suhrkamp, 1997), 423;
    "Commitment," trans. Francis McDonagh, *New Left Review* 87–8 (September–
    December 1974): 85.
13 Theodor W. Adorno, *Negative Dialektik*, vol. 6 of *Gesammelte Schriften*, ed. Rolf
    Tiedemann (Frankfurt am Main: Suhrkamp, 1997), 355; *Negative Dialectics*, trans.
    E. B. Ashton (New York: Continuum, 1992), 362.

representing, and transmitting the beastly reality and atrocities of the concentration camps. Critical evaluations of Holocaust literature have thus largely been shaped by a general mistrust of invention, experimentation, and fabulation, and a concomitant privileging of testimony and witnessing grounded in personal experience and with a therapeutic dimension.[14]

The poles of this opposition can perhaps best be elucidated by turning to well-known examples from visual culture. In the late 1970s the NBC mini-series *Holocaust*, which captivated international audiences, may have done more than any other single work to reinvoke the historical significance of the Holocaust for an American and European public diverted from this past atrocity by the more immediate tensions and political animosities of the Cold War. In Germany in particular, where the mini-series aired in 1979, the response was overwhelming, and it played an instrumental role in informing the German public, which had systematically repressed knowledge of the crimes committed against the Jews and other peoples, about these events.[15] Through fictionalized portrayals of two families, one representing the victims, the other the perpetrators, this series coupled the specificity of individual fates with the larger framework of historical evidence. Widely criticized for its tendency to sentimentalize and trivialize historical facts, this work nonetheless elevated popular awareness about the Holocaust. A similar case can be made for Steven Spielberg's cinematic rendition of Thomas Keneally's novel *Schindler's List*, whose release in 1993, along with the opening of the United States Holocaust Memorial Museum in Washington, D.C., incited ABC's news program *Nightline* to declare 1993 "The Year of the Holocaust."[16] Despite its success at raising awareness of the Holocaust in popular consciousness, Spielberg's film was criticized for downplaying the suffering of the victims, valorizing the exceptional instance of a perpetrator turned rescuer, and transforming the history of the Holocaust into what Dominick LaCapra has called a "redemptive narrative" that ultimately displaces the process of mourning, which LaCapra views as a more appropriate and psychologically beneficent engagement with historical atrocity.[17]

---

14 See Sue Vice, *Holocaust Fiction* (London: Routledge, 2000), 3–4; Sidra DeKoven Ezrahi, "Questions of Authenticity," in *Teaching the Representation of the Holocaust*, ed. Marianne Hirsch and Irene Kacandes (New York: Modern Language Association, 2004), 52.

15 Anton Kaes, *From Hitler to Heimat: The Return of History as Film* (Cambridge, MA: Harvard University Press, 1989), 30–1.

16 Michael Rothberg, *Traumatic Realism: The Demands of Holocaust Representation* (Minneapolis: University of Minnesota Press, 2000), 181.

17 Dominick LaCapra, *Writing History, Writing Trauma* (Baltimore, MD: Johns

Fictionalization, especially in such popularizing, easily digestible forms, often gives rise to criticisms of inaccuracy and tranquilizing pacification. The opposite end of the spectrum from these manifestations of Hollywood fabulation and sentimentalism is represented by Claude Lanzmann's monumental testimonial film *Shoah* from 1985. Based solely on interviews with victims and perpetrators, Lanzmann's film evinces an aesthetic austerity and an insistence on evidentiary experience that stands in marked contrast to more popular forms of Holocaust cinema. Not surprisingly, Lanzmann was a vociferous critic of both the NBC mini-series and of Spielberg's *Schindler's List*. Responding to the French broadcast of the *Holocaust* mini-series, he insisted on the uniqueness of the Holocaust as an event that defies translation into any form of artful representation. For Lanzmann, any fictionalization of these events is simply a "transgression," and he calls for a strict "interdiction of representation" with regard to the Holocaust.[18] In his response to *Schindler's List*, Lanzmann likewise attacked the film's fabrication of archives, such as its reconstruction of a gas chamber, as a potential falsification of history through imaginative representation.[19]

But even the immediacy of testimony is anything but unproblematic. Primo Levi was the first to point out that the genuine victims of the Holocaust were those who succumbed to the human degradation and overweening brutality of the camps, whom he referred to as the "drowned"; and he insisted that their testimony represented the only truly authentic witnessing of unimaginable personal trauma, but that their experiences were lost to the historical record.[20] The testimony of those who were "saved," of the survivors, by contrast, is by its very nature incomplete and skewed. The survivors—among whom Levi numbers himself—were those who made accommodations to and compromises with the inhumane conditions with which they were confronted; they were those who, in Levi's word's, "by their prevarications or abilities or good luck did not touch bottom."[21]

Hopkins University Press, 2001), 157.

18 Claude Lanzmann, as quoted in Rothberg, *Traumatic Realism*, 232. Lanzmann's view was shared by his French contemporary Maurice Blanchot, who in the essay "After the Fact," in *Vicious Circles*, trans. Paul Auster (Barrytown, NY: Station Hill, 1985), 68–9, maintains that "there can be no fiction-story about Auschwitz," but also suggests the paradox that the only fiction adequate to representing the Holocaust had to be written prior to—and hence in historical ignorance of—the events themselves.

19 Vice, *Holocaust Fiction*, 5.

20 Primo Levi, *The Drowned and the Saved*, trans. Raymond Rosenthal (New York: Random House/Vintage, 1989), 17, 83–4.

21 Ibid., 83.

Moreover, even the reliability of the testimony presented by those who survived, in his view, must be called into question; for human memory "is a marvelous but fallacious instrument," and those who survived and are willing to testify "have ever more blurred and stylized memories, often, unbeknownst to them, influenced by information gained from later readings or the stories of others."[22] The uncertainty and instability of memory in general and of traumatic memory in particular, and especially of its susceptibility to transmogrifying, falsifying influences from other sources, significantly raises the stakes in the controversy between fabulative and factual representation. It also names a problematic that assumes a privileged status in Sebald's historicizing fictions, one that he already rehearsed, as we have seen, in his very first work of prose fiction, "Beyle." This idea of the *fallibility* of memory introduces the possibility that even purported witness accounts can be unwittingly shaped and manipulated by fictional representations popularized and transmitted through various media. For that reason, it is often impossible to draw a clean line between recorded fact and fiction. Sebald plays with this idea in particular in the intermedial aspect of his works, their inherent constitution as iconotexts that fuse language and documentary image. Moreover, once the historical witnesses themselves can no longer testify—a point that is rapidly approaching—we face a situation in which popular fictions about the Holocaust will necessarily take the place of the evidentiary facts themselves.[23] This is the specter that constantly haunts representations of the Holocaust: the threat of revisionism, the fear that *fictional representations* of the Holocaust could ultimately give way to *the fiction of the Holocaust.*[24] This is the fraught terrain that Sebald attempts to negotiate in his works like *Austerlitz* that deal explicitly with a Holocaust thematic.

If historical events of extreme violence and intense human suffering tend naturally to call forth a demand for what James Young has termed "factually insistent narrative,"[25] there are also oppositional voices that valorize imaginative amplification and fabulative reconstruction as the most viable modality for preserving and communicating the experience of events so horrendous that they seem both unimaginable

22 Ibid., 23, 19.
23 Froma I. Zeitlin, "The Vicarious Witness: Belated Memory and Authorial Presence in Recent Holocaust Literature," *History & Memory* 10, no. 2 (Fall/Winter 1998): 8.
24 Vice, *Holocaust Fiction*, 1.
25 James E. Young, *Writing and Rewriting the Holocaust: Narrative and the Consequences of Interpretation* (Bloomington: Indiana University Press, 1990), 15.

and unspeakable. Recently Ruth Klüger, herself a Holocaust survivor, literary critic, and author of a well-received Holocaust memoir, argued that the most apt aesthetic and literary strategies for portraying the anonymous suffering of Holocaust victims might be drawn from the tradition of literary Modernism, from the experimental techniques employed by such figures as James Joyce and Franz Kafka.[26] The prominent historian of the Holocaust, Dominick LaCapra, has reinforced this view, citing authors such as Kafka, Maurice Blanchot, Paul Celan, and Samuel Beckett as practitioners of a performative mode of writing that models a literature of what he calls "terrorized disempowerment"; for LaCapra, such approaches approximate the experience of traumatized victims without making pretensions to its adequate representation.[27]

It is a fitting irony that this invocation of literary Modernism's poetic innovations brings us back to our point of departure in Adorno: the very aestheticizing features that for Adorno call for an interdiction of Holocaust representation are invoked by Klüger and LaCapra as a potential solution to the dilemma associated with the literary representation of atrocity. To be sure, they have shifted the emphasis from Adorno's position; whereas in this early interdiction he operates exclusively against the backdrop of an aesthetics of production, these latter critics stress an aesthetics of reception, seeking paradigms of literary creation that might re-enact and transmit to contemporary readers the emotional *experience* of traumatized victimhood. The critic who has made the most sustained case for the appropriateness of an imaginative and fabulative approach to the Holocaust is Lawrence Langer. In many respects Langer's view represents a counterargument against Adorno's position that aesthetic embellishment merely "adorns" the horror of Holocaust reality and thereby diminishes and demeans the real suffering of the victims. According to Langer, if imaginative engagement with the facts of the Holocaust manifests an ameliorative strategy, then this has the positive effect of allowing us to confront—*in effigy*, as it were—a reality so monstrous that our immediate inclination is to turn away. In its perfected forms, a literature of atrocity creates alternate fictional worlds that insist on their *affinity* (but not *identity*) with egregious historical events, but also form a kind of palliative that makes this reality approachable and palatable. The literature of atrocity thereby is able, in Langer's words, "to evoke the atmosphere

26 Ruth Klüger, "Dichten über die Shoah: Zum Problem des literarischen Umgangs mit dem Massenmord," in *Spuren der Verfolgung: Seelische Auswirkungen des Holocaust auf die Opfer und ihre Kinder*, ed. Gertrud Hardtmann (Gerlingen: Bleicher, 1992), 211.

27 LaCapra, *Writing History*, 105–6.

of monstrous fantasy that strikes any student of the Holocaust," so that the "result is exempted from the claims of literal truth but creates an imaginative reality possessing an autonomous dignity and form that paradoxically immerse us in perceptions about that literal truth which the mind ordinarily ignores or would like to avoid."[28] This strategy might be termed imaginative indirection; Langer himself employs the phrase "a literature of innuendo" to describe this process of productive aesthetic and fabulative mediation.[29] He also uses the seemingly oxymoronic phrase "imaginative truth" to invoke this notion of a confabulated world that approximates the factual verity of incomprehensible events.[30] But he comes closest to calling attention to one of the most pre-eminent directions of Holocaust literature, the genre of documentary fiction, when he calls for a "wedding of history and innovation."[31] This phrase precisely describes Sebald's approach to the Holocaust, and the overriding techniques of his prose fictions more generally.

Documentary fiction has emerged as one of the privileged genres of Holocaust literature precisely because it manifests an "allusive realism," to cite a phrase employed by Saul Friedlander.[32] This also helps account for the persistent reliance on historical or testimonial intertexts as a distinguishing feature of much Holocaust literature,[33] a facet that is especially prominent in Sebald's works. But as James Young has pointed out, this intermingling of actual events, historical personalities, and testamentary evidence with fictional characters and imaginatively elaborated narrative situations is not without problems. On the one hand, the reference to documentary material allows writers to imbue their fictions with a degree of historical authority; but on the other hand, the fictional and fabulative elements permit the writer to appeal to poetic license and thereby circumvent any obligation to historical accuracy.[34] Documentary fiction thus allows Holocaust writers to have it both ways: they can insist on the imaginative elaboration of historical reality, but at the same time appeal to the facts as a skeleton that vouches for a degree of mimetic accuracy. In the critical reception of such works, this double strategy often opens the writer up either to charges of plagiarism, if adherence to prior documents seems

---

28 Langer, *The Holocaust and the Literary Imagination*, 30.
29 Ibid., 37.
30 Ibid., 8.
31 Ibid., 32.
32 Saul Friedlander, "Introduction," in *Probing the Limits of Representation: Nazism and the Final Solution*, ed. Saul Friedlander (Cambridge, MA: Harvard University Press, 1992), 17.
33 Vice, *Holocaust Fiction*, 2.
34 Young, *Writing and Rewriting the Holocaust*, 52.

too strict, or to taking too many imaginative liberties, if poetic license seems to dominate.[35] Ultimately the key factor may be the writer's ability to balance the factual and the fictional, and to ensure that they mutually enhance one another.[36] One might subscribe for this specific case to the more general dictum once pronounced by Albert Camus: "There is no need of determining whether art must flee reality or defer to it, but rather what precise dose of reality the work must take on as ballast to keep from floating up among the clouds or from dragging along the ground with weighted boots."[37] One of Sebald's accomplishments in the domain of documentary fiction is the critical troubling of this relationship between documentary fact and imaginative fiction: in his works fictions often masquerade as documentary evidence, and facts sometimes appear in the guise of fictions.

One final peculiarity of Holocaust literature needs to be outlined here: the relationship between authorial voice and the depicted events. Literary studies in general have been guided for several decades by a tendency to celebrate the death of the author. Belief in the author's metaphorical "death" has underwritten all those newer directions in literary criticism that parade under the moniker of "textual studies." Even theoreticians of metafiction, such as Raymond Federman, are inclined to derive the advent of playful self-reflexivity in fiction from the dismantling of the two predominant doctrines of classical literary aesthetics, the autonomy of the author and the valorization of originality.[38] In contrast to this, critics of Holocaust literature are often notoriously conservative, holding the work up to the acid test of "factually insistent narrative," and stipulating that the author's biography lend authority to her or his portrayal.[39] Sue Vice designates as one of the three central categories constitutive of Holocaust fiction—and as a primary basis for its critical evaluation—a homology between the empirical author and the textual narrator. She notes that this insistence

---

35 Vice, *Holocaust Fiction*, 1–10, has identified this catch-22 as the basis of the "scandal" commonly called forth by Holocaust fiction.

36 Rothberg, *Traumatic Realism*, 9, 99, employs the term "traumatized realism" to designate the mediation in Holocaust literature between the demands for realism and a suspicion of realism that promotes antirealist tendencies.

37 Albert Camus, as quoted in Langer, *The Holocaust and the Literary Imagination*, 133.

38 Raymond Federman, "Imagination as Plagiarism [An Unfinished Paper ...]," *New Literary History* 7, no. 3 (Spring 1976): 570.

39 See Jonathan Long, "Bernhard Schlink's *Der Vorleser* and Binjamin Wilkomirski's *Bruchstücke*: Best-Selling Responses to the Holocaust," in *German-Language Literature Today: International or Popular?*, ed. Arthur Williams, Stuart Parkes, and Julian Preece (Oxford: Peter Lang, 2000), 62, who has pointed this out for the specific case of Holocaust memoirs: "Far from being dead ... the author in the case of Holocaust memoirs is alive and well."

on ontological identity between author and narrative voice is an inheritance from the genre of Holocaust testimony.[40] In a similar vein, Ruth Klüger maintains that for Holocaust fiction it is not enough to read the text as text; rather, we as readers are invested in having sufficient information about the individuals treated, about the author, and about the relationship between them.[41] LaCapra, finally, refers to a taxonomic grid of Holocaust subject positions, which encompass such roles as victims, perpetrators, collaborators, bystanders, resisters, and those born after the fact. He notes how important it is to break out of this grid-like typology by negotiating subject positions that fall between or outside of these standardized roles.[42] This is a vision that looks ahead to positions typical of Sebald's fictions. Sebald frequently insisted on what he called the ethics of voice, the requirement, as expressed in a 2001 interview with Doris Stoisser, that his readers know something about the narrative presence who is speaking, and that they constantly be made aware that this narrator represents what he describes as "an afflicted consciousness" ("ein betroffenes Bewußtsein"; "*Auf ungeheuer dünnem Eis*" 235–6; cf. Schwartz 169). An alternative to the general recourse to traditional views of the author as the source of authority, and a reflex that is also typical of Sebald's approach to Holocaust narratives, is the identification of the author as a "scribe," a second-order figure who mediates the first-order testimony and memoirs of the victims.[43] But in general, where fictional intervention might compromise the evidentiary authority of Holocaust representation, the ontological authority of the author's or narrator's personal association with this historical event is of central importance.[44]

German-Language Holocaust Fiction

The situation of Holocaust fiction is thus notoriously precarious, confronting authors with complex, often contradictory demands between historical accuracy, authentic depiction, imaginative involvement with the victims, and fabulative elaboration on historical atrocities. Its attempts to negotiate the contested terrain between what one critic has called the "rights of history" and the "rights of

40 Vice, *Holocaust Fiction*, 4.
41 Klüger, "Dichten über die Shoah," 218.
42 LaCapra, *Writing History*, 175.
43 Young, *Writing and Rewriting the Holocaust*, 21.
44 Young, *Writing and Rewriting the Holocaust*, 61. Zeitlin, "The Vicarious Witness," 6–7, has coined the phrase "vicarious witnessing" to designate the mediated testimony of those who never experienced the Holocaust personally, but who reenact the trauma of atrocity by recounting the process by which they take cognizance of it.

imagination" seem doomed to failure from the outset.[45] The result is that Holocaust fiction is commonly greeted in the critical community by heated controversy, even scandal.[46] For obvious reasons, this situation is even more complex for German-language writers, and thus it is understandable that Germans long shied away from fictional engagements with the Holocaust thematic. The primary complication for them, of course, is that they not only need to come to terms with the situation of the victims, asking the general question about how such horrendous, systematically orchestrated acts of violence against humanity were possible at all, but also contend with the guilt and shame of the perpetrators, which means asking how it was possible that *Germans*, with their deeply rooted traditions in Enlightenment rationality, humanistic learning, and cultural-intellectual innovation, could mastermind, organize, and participate in a widespread program of mass human terror and extermination. The psychological consequences of this confrontation with the past, what the Germans call *Vergangenheitsbewältigung*, have often been investigated, and there is no need to rehearse them again here.[47] But it should come as no surprise that there is a dearth of Holocaust testimonials written in German, although in this relative desert two works stand out in particular: the camp memoir *Jenseits von Schuld und Sühne* (Beyond guilt and atonement) by Jean Améry—a persecuted Austrian Jew who abandoned his given name of Hanns Mayer after the war and documented his harassment and torture by the Nazis—and the belatedly published diaries of Romance scholar Victor Klemperer, a Jew who survived in Nazi Germany because he had a non-Jewish German wife, and who detailed the tribulations of day-to-day life for a Jew under these circumstances in a diary he kept carefully hidden. Literary immersion in the events of the Holocaust by German authors at first largely took the form of a strict documentary realism, represented above all in Peter Weiss's *Die Ermittlung* (*The Investigation*) and Rolf Hochhuth's *Der Stellvertreter* (*The Deputy*), which manifested responses to the Eichmann trial in Jerusalem and the Frankfurt Auschwitz trials. The fact that both authors selected the form of documentary theater likely reflects the wish to transform these public legal spectacles, which received worldwide attention, into

---

45   Cynthia Ozick, "The Rights of History and the Rights of the Imagination," *Commentary* (March 1999): 22.

46   Vice, *Holocaust Fiction*, 1–4.

47   The most influential psychological explanation has been offered by Alexander and Margarete Mitscherlich, *The Inability to Mourn: Principles of Collective Behavior*, trans. Beverley R. Placzek (New York: Grove Press, 1975), 23–9. They analyze the Germans' emotional and psychic investment in Hitler as a substitute father-figure, whose tragic loss unleashes a break with the past, the obstruction of memory, and collective trauma.

more limited theatrical spectacles that would allow the German public
to reflect critically on their own involvement in these events. The interrogation of a handful of perpetrators could thereby be extended to the
German public at large, in the hope of circumventing the danger that
the prosecution of *specific* culprits would lead to a more general sense
of exculpation for everyday Germans.

The most renowned piece of German prose fiction from the
immediate post-war era that deals with this historical past and applies
striking metafictional strategies is Günter Grass's *Die Blechtrommel (The
Tin Drum)*. Although it ranks alongside such works as John Barth's *The
Sot-Weed Factor* and Salmon Rushdie's *Midnight's Children* as classic
instances of novels that exploit metafictional operations to explore the
national past, in Grass's case a specific engagement with the atrocities of
the Holocaust is largely absent. Only subsequent to German unification
in 1989 can one speak of a minor boom in German fictional engagements with the Holocaust problematic. There are several reasons for
this. One is the re-emergence of a reunified German national state and
the perceived need to reinterrogate the aberration of previous German
attempts at nation-building. More important is surely the emergence
of a new generation of writers, the so-called second generation, born
during or after the war, whose association with the crimes of the
Holocaust is less direct, whose psychological "baggage" is consid-
erably lighter, and who are hence able to tackle this thematic with less
constraint and more circumspection.

Before we can orient Sebald's works in the landscape of recent
German Holocaust fiction, it is necessary to provide a map—admittedly, a sketchy one—of this terrain. To accomplish this I will briefly
discuss three prominent Holocaust texts, all of which were published
in the same year, 1995, and which represent the crest in this modest
wave of literary involvement with the Holocaust: Marcel Beyer's
Flughunde (The Karnau Tapes); Bernhard Schlink's *Der Vorleser (The
Reader)*; and Binjamin Wilkomirski's *Bruchstücke: Aus einer Kindheit,
1939–1948 (Fragments: Memories of a Wartime Childhood)*. These works
have the advantage that they represent markedly different takes on the
Holocaust thematic, and consequently give a good impression, despite
the relatively small sample, of the diversity in recent German-language
Holocaust literature.

Beyer's *Flughunde* is arguably the most metafictionally complex of
these three works—which perhaps also explains why it has undergone
more muted reception, especially outside of German-speaking Europe.
As is true of all these novels, Beyer's text is structured largely as a
narrative told from the first-person perspective. Its peculiar quirk,
however—and this is a characteristic of Beyer's fiction more generally—
is that it laminates together accounts of the same events—life in Hitler's

bunker near the end of the war—as experienced by two extremely different narrators: the Nazi scientist and functionary, Hermann Karnau, who transfers Nazi racial research to the physiognomy of the voice; and Joseph Goebbels's eldest daughter, Helga, who will ultimately be murdered by her parents as the Nazi state collapses. This structure allows Beyer to juxtapose the views and thoughts of a perpetrator with those of a bystander/victim, one who experiences these events from the proximity of the Nazi inner circle, but who still has the perspective of a child. Interspersed with these dominant but divergent narrative viewpoints is the voice of a nameless omniscient narrator who perceives the narrated events from the outside, thereby lending them a historical frame. What stands out about this novel is Beyer's capacity, through the perspective of Karnau, to examine how a fellow traveler of the Nazi cause develops into a merciless perpetrator, willing to conduct brutal experiments in the name of an ideologically-tainted racial science. When contrasted with the perspective of the child bystander, who is unable to understand the world around her and the motivations of its human agents, Karnau's psychological development assumes grotesque contours.[48] This elaboration, from the inside, of the emerging perpetrator marks Beyer's major (meta)fictional accomplishment.

Bernhard Schlink's *Der Vorleser* scarcely requires an introduction, especially since its filming as a successful and titillating motion picture, *The Reader*, starring Kate Winslet and Ralph Fiennes. The novel itself has been subject to precisely the kind of critical response that is typical of much Holocaust fiction in general, but in particular of German attempts at this genre. Although it received high popular acclaim both in Germany and abroad, academic criticism has been much more circumspect and predominantly critical. The fact alone that a German writer could garner so much popular recognition for a work of Holocaust fiction is a minor accomplishment in itself. One telling symptom of this recognition is the widespread adoption of Schlink's novel for school curricula on the Holocaust in present-day Germany.[49] The novel's first-person narrator, Michael Berg, relates his erotic involvement as a child with an older woman, Hanna Schmidt,

48 Barbara Beßlich, "Unzuverlässiges Erzählen im Dienst der Erinnerung: Perspektiven auf den Nationalsozialismus bei Maxim Biller, Marcel Beyer und Martin Walser," in *Wende des Erinnerns? Geschichtskonstruktionen in der deutschen Literatur nach 1989*, ed. Barbara Beßlich, Katharina Grätz, and Olaf Hildebrand (Berlin: Erich Schmidt, 2006), 44–8, provides a more detailed examination of the narrative voices in this novel and the transformation in Karnau's psychological motivations.

49 Ursula R. Mahlendorf, "Trauma Narrated, Read and (Mis)understood: Bernhard Schlink's *The Reader*," *Monatshefte* 95, no. 3 (2003): 458–9.

who turns out to have been a concentration camp guard and is later put on trial and convicted for her crimes. The work has been alternately either praised for its more nuanced and compassionate portrayal of a perpetrator,[50] or criticized for its marginalization of the real victims of the Holocaust and its tendency to position Germans, both perpetrators and the second generation, as victims of circumstance.[51] Generally the novel has been recognized as an allegory, transposed from the paradigm of parental love to that of impassioned eroticism, for the love–hate bonds characteristic of the relationship between the perpetrator generation and their children. Schlink's primary literary achievement, aside from his ability to create a highly "readerly" and popular work that engages in complex ways with questions of German guilt, responsibility, and shame for the Holocaust atrocities, is the expedient of underpinning this otherwise simple narrative with the structure of detective fiction. His first-person narrator finds himself in the position of having to uncover Hanna's well-concealed secret: the illiteracy that gives rise to profound shame and that plays an obscure role in her development into a perpetrator. The artistry of Schlink's narrative is linked to its capacity to keep this secret in suspense, so that the reader participates in his narrator's process of discovery. This element of suspenseful involvement in unraveling the mystery, based on the strategic dropping of clues and the gradual piecing together of information, accounts for the popular resonance of this work. This surprising linkage of the "serious" problematic of Holocaust responsibility with the low-brow genre of the detective novel might be seen as Schlink's major metafictional innovation.

Binjamin Wilkomirski's *Bruchstücke: Aus einer Kindheit* is similarly steeped in considerable critical controversy, but for reasons that are very different from those associated with Schlink's novel. Originally published under the pretense of being an authentic Holocaust memoir, pieced together in retrospect through the resurgence of childhood memories, this work immediately garnered sustained critical and popular recognition. Indeed, it won several major awards for autobiography in Europe and the United States, including the French Prize for Holocaust Remembrance.[52] Given the paucity of Holocaust testimonies written in German, it is small wonder that Wilkomirski's book

50   Jane Alison, "The Third Victim in Bernhard Schlink's *Der Vorleser*," *Germanic Review* 81, no. 2 (2006): 163.

51   Omer Bartov, "Germany as Victim," *New German Critique* 80 (2000): 34; William Collins Donahue, "Illusions of Subtlety: Bernhard Schlink's *Der Vorleser* and the Moral Limits of Holocaust Fiction," *German Life and Letters* 54, no. 1 (2001): 62; Bill Niven, "Bernhard Schlink's *Der Vorleser* and the Problem of Shame," *Modern Language Review* 98 (2003): 381.

52   Long, "Bernhard Schlink's *Der Vorleser*," 49–50.

was embraced as a major contribution. The problem is that Binjamin
Wilkomirski—as Daniel Ganzfried was the first to reveal—turns out to
be the assumed name of Bruno Dössekker, a non-Jewish Swiss citizen
whose purported autobiography turns out to be a matter of pure
invention. Scholars are currently undecided whether to evaluate this
as a blatant case of literary fraud, or as an instance of psychological
self-deception, in which Dössekker has succumbed to a pathological
identification with the victims of Holocaust trauma.[53] The latter,
more generous view assumes that Dössekker mistakenly integrated
into his own life story—as false memories—information he garnered
from Holocaust memoirs, films, documentaries, and fictions with
which he was fascinated. What makes this case so interesting is that
Wilkomirski's "memoir," and the fluctuation in its critical evaluation,
turns on the central question of whether it is judged as fact or fiction.
Yet even when its factuality has been completely debunked, and hence
its value as Holocaust testimony dispelled, this work can still be taken
as an exemplary model of Holocaust metafiction.[54] Not only does it
play effectively with the central themes of fragmentary memory and
the belated recouping of traumatic experiences, but it also strategically
mimics the randomness of memory recall in the haphazard structure
of its retelling.[55] Above all, Wilkomirski's text and its reception call
attention to one further issue central to Holocaust fiction and the
standard criteria for its critical evaluation: by playing deceptive games
with the ontological identity of author and narrator, it throws open to
controversy the very insistence on an immediate connection between

53 For the complete exposition of Wilkomirski's hoax, see Daniel Ganzfried
and Sebastian Hefti, *Alias Wilkomirski: Die Holocaust-Travestie* (Berlin: Jüdische
Verlagsanstalt, 2002).

54 According to Elena Lappin, "The Man with Two Heads," *Granta* 66 (Summer
1999): 49, the editor of the English translation of this memoir at Schocken Press
asserted that if the book were exposed as a fraud, he would simply reissue it as
fiction. Lappin comes to a peculiarly ambivalent conclusion about Wilkomirski/
Dössekker and his text, 60–1, ultimately arguing that it is most likely fictional,
but simultaneously affirming that the personal anguish he associates with these
events is authentic.

55 On the typically fragmentary and disjointed character of traumatic memories,
see Shoshana Felman and Dori Laub, *Testimony: Crises of Witnessing in Literature,
Psychoanalysis, and History* (New York: Routledge, 1992), 71–3. Wilkomirski's
narrative might be viewed as a conscious attempt to imitate this desultory
quality, especially since his narrator explicitly draws attention to the haphaz-
ardness of his memories, their lack of chronological order and their chaotic
dispersion, and their tendency to occur as isolated images. See Binjamin
Wilkomirski, *Bruchstücke: Aus einer Kindheit, 1939-1948* (Frankfurt am Main:
Jüdischer Verlag, 1995), 7; *Fragments: Memories of a Wartime Childhood*, trans.
Carol Brown Janeway (New York: Schocken, 1996), 4.

authorial personality and the recounted events, a reflex of identity that, as we have seen, constitutes a mainstay of Holocaust literature. Wilkomirski's text, wittingly or unwittingly, breaches what the French scholar Philippe Lejeune calls the "autobiographical pact": the contract writers and readers enter into when they accept autobiographical narrative as predicated on an empirical bond between the author and the narrator.[56] Wilkomirski's faked autobiography crosses this ontological divide and exploits the autobiographical pact as a tool for authenticating the veracity of its inventions. Perhaps this constitutes the ultimate metafictional tactic for documentary fiction.

Holocaust Documentary as the Wedding of History and Metafiction

Since the German publication of *Die Ausgewanderten* in 1992, and its translation into English as *The Emigrants* in 1995, Sebald and his writings have commonly been associated with the Holocaust thematic.[57] Yet the connections between the four biographical tales collected in this volume and the events of the Holocaust are not always obvious. One character is a Lithuanian Jew whose family emigrated to England prior to World War I. Another is a German of mixed Jewish descent who loses his teaching position under the Nazis but serves in the German military during the War. A third is not Jewish at all, but instead an uncle of Sebald's first-person narrator who is presumably homosexual and who emigrates to America long before the Holocaust. The fourth is in fact a Jew who fled the Holocaust as a child and settled in England. What unites these characters more than anything else, as I have argued in previous chapters, is their situation as exiles who are not only physically, but above all emotionally displaced. As we have seen, Sebald's German title for this collection, *Die Ausgewanderten*—rather

---

56   Philippe Lejeune, "The Autobiographical Pact," in *On Autobiography*, ed. Paul John Eakin, trans. Katherine Leary (Minneapolis: University of Minnesota Press, 1989), 12–14.

57   Some critics have expressed reservations about the pervasive identification of Sebald's works as predominantly Holocaust fictions, especially since the realities of the death camps and the fates of their victims only find peripheral mention in his texts. See Jonathan J. Long, "Disziplin und Geständnis: Ansätze zu einer Foucaultschen Sebald-Lektüre," in *W. G. Sebald: Politische Archäologie und melancholische Bastelei*, ed. Michael Niehaus and Claudia Öhlschläger (Berlin: Erich Schmidt, 2006), 220; Adam Zachary Newton, "Place from Place, and Place from Flight: W. G. Sebald's *The Emigrants* and Aharon Appelfeld's *The Iron Tracks*," in *The Elsewhere: On Belonging at a Near Distance: Reading Literary Memoir from Europe and the Levant* (Madison: University of Wisconsin Press, 2005), 69, and Carsten Strathausen, "Going Nowhere: Sebald's Rhizomatic Travels," in *Searching for Sebald: Photography After W. G. Sebald*, ed. Lise Patt (Los Angeles: Institute for Cultural Inquiry, 2007), 475.

than the more common *Die Auswanderer*—contains the implication that these figures are not voluntary emigrants to new worlds, but voluntarily or involuntarily dislocated exiles, or, as I have suggested, "ectopic" individuals. This sense of being permanently out of place haunts their lives and expresses itself as a pervasive melancholy. If these stories present a complexly refracted perspective on the Holocaust on the level of story, this deflection is also incorporated into the narrative structure of the tales themselves: each biography is told by a contemporary first-person narrator who shares a few sparsely presented biographical features with the empirical author Sebald, and with whose first-person voice the embedded first-person voice of each of the informants merges. This embedding of first-person narratives within the context of an overriding first-person narrative framework is one of the distinctive tokens of Sebald's fiction. Developed most fully in *Austerlitz*, this technique constitutes a literary instantiation of the secondary witness, whose "labor of listening and attending" opens the witnessing individual up to empathetic understanding and a muted version of shared trauma.[58]

Sebald was keenly aware of the difficulties attendant upon any literary engagement with the Holocaust. In an interview with Maya Jaggi conducted in 2001, shortly before his death, he pointedly remarked, "I don't think you can focus on the horror of the Holocaust. It's like the head of Medusa: you carry it with you in a sack, but if you looked at it you'd be petrified."[59] For Sebald, the Holocaust represents a historical burden that one can neither set aside nor escape, but with which one must necessarily have an oblique or mediated relationship. We are reminded of Saul Friedlander's assertion that one can only approach the Holocaust by means of "allusive realism," or of Lawrence Langer's claim that "innuendo" is the only proper literary mode for dealing with atrocity. What is unique about Sebald's prose fictions is the pervasive implementation of diverse metafictional techniques in order to accomplish this refraction that permits engagement with the otherwise unspeakable horror of the Holocaust. Sebald's last published work, the prose fiction *Austerlitz*, will be examined here with an eye for the strategic application of such metafictional techniques in a documentary fiction that focuses on a Holocaust thematic.

Not surprisingly, *Austerlitz* has been subject to the same kind of critical controversy that is endemic to Holocaust fiction in general, and German Holocaust fiction more specifically. As Katra Byram has pointed out, this text operates simultaneously in two of the most

---

58 Dominick LaCapra, *Representing the Holocaust: History, Theory, Trauma* (Ithaca, NY: Cornell University Press, 1994), 198.

59 Maya Jaggi, "Recovered Memories," *Guardian*, September 22, 2001, 7.

prominent paradigms of Holocaust literature: in its diegesis, it represents a survivor narrative that relates how the eponymous victim gradually comes to terms with his trauma; in its narrative approach it instantiates the representation of trauma from the perspective of the historical outsider, born after the fact but in the country of the perpetrators.[60] Without recapitulating the critical debates about the ethics of Sebald's text,[61] suffice it to say that whereas the response to the survivor narrative is predominantly positive, the reception of his narrator's ethical stance has frequently been critical, viewed either as overly melodramatic,[62] or as a misappropriation of the Jewish experience of victimhood by the non-Jewish German.[63] My focus here will be on *Austerlitz* as a piece of documentary fiction that exploits metafictional strategies in order to navigate this ethical tension that characterizes the relationship between external narrative stance and the traumatic experiences of the protagonist-victim.

The novel's central character, Jacques Austerlitz, who is also the primary informant for Sebald's anonymous first-person narrator, is another displaced exile like the protagonists of *Die Ausgewanderten*. Born to Jewish parents in Prague prior to the Nazi occupation of Czechoslovakia, he is sent to England with the *Kindertransport*, the small-scale organized operation for rescuing Jewish children from Eastern Europe, and he grows up with Welsh foster parents under the assumed name Daffyd Elias. Only much later is his true identity revealed to him, and he subsequently devotes his life to reconstructing his lost childhood and trying to discover the fate of his parents, who perished in the Holocaust. Sebald's oblique perspective on these events is already evident in this storyline, which focuses not so much on the primary victims of the Nazi terror as on the *collateral trauma* of a survivor whose life has been transformed by events with which he has only a very distant relationship. The character Austerlitz himself and his "fictional" life represent a composite of various historical personalities, as Sebald was quick to admit (*"Auf ungeheuer dünnem Eis"* 196–7). One central component is the story of Susi Bechhofer, who experienced the *Kindertransport* and whose life was retold in the book

60 Katra A. Byram, "A Footnote to History: German Trauma and the Ethics of Holocaust Representation in W. G. Sebald's *Austerlitz*," in *Ethics and the Dynamic Observer Narrator: Reckoning with Past and Present in German Literature* (Columbus: Ohio State University Press, 2015), 192.

61 Ibid., 193–8, provides an excellent summary of this controversy.

62 John Zilcosky, "Lost and Found: Disorientation, Nostalgia, and Holocaust Melodrama in Sebald's *Austerlitz*," *MLN* 121 (2006): 693–7.

63 Brad Prager, "The Good German as Narrator: On W. G. Sebald and the Risks of Holocaust Writing," *New German Critique* 96 (Fall 2005): 85, 89.

Rosa's Child.[64] Another major but hitherto largely unrecognized source was Saul Friedlander's autobiography, of which a heavily annotated copy of the German translation is contained in Sebald's library.[65] Like Austerlitz, Friedlander was born in Prague, lost his parents in the Holocaust, and was raised as a foster child in France, where he (again like Austerlitz) was brought up in the Christian faith. Austerlitz also bears certain traits borrowed from Ludwig Wittgenstein, and this connection underwrites in part this fictional character's architectural interests, since Wittgenstein, among his multiple talents, was also a hobby architect. Sebald's protagonist is thus constructed as a composite of intertextual allusions, combining traits from historically prominent individuals and personal life stories. This has opened this character up to severe objections by some critics, who view him as piecemeal and artificial. One German reviewer even denied that Sebald deserves the name storyteller, calling him instead "a virtuoso of note collection, an imitator of voices, a conversationalist, and an archivist" ("ein Virtuose des Zettelkastens, Stimmenimitator, Konversator und Archivar").[66] Another reviewer criticizes the character Austerlitz for being nothing but "a collection of literary techniques, a paradigmatic showpiece for Sebald's poetic world, and an archival figure of overweening proportions" ("der Sammelpunkt einer literarischen Technik, ein Mustermann für die poetische Welt des Schriftstellers W. G. Sebald, eine Archivgestalt von überdimensionalen Maßen").[67] These reviewers adhere to the principle of "realistically insistent narration," and their critiques allude by way of objection to the prominent application of metafictional strategies in Sebald's text. Yet that is precisely the point of Sebald's technique: the multiple allusions to "real" figures and events invoke what Roland Barthes has called the "reality effect" by bringing the fictional tale into close alignment with real, documented occurrences that are likely to have a ring of familiarity with a wide range of readers.[68] The fiction resides, as is often the case for metafictional texts, in the recombinatory practice that splices together pieces and

---

64 See Jeremy Josephs and Susi Bechhofer, *Rosa's Child: One Woman's Search for Her Past* (London: Tauris, 1996). The history of the *Kindertransport* is retold in Mark Jonathan Harris and Deborah Oppenheimer, *Into the Arms of Strangers: Stories of the Kindertransport* (New York: Bloomsbury, 2000).

65 Saul Friedlander, *Wenn die Erinnerung kommt*, trans. Helgard Oestreich (Munich: Beck, 1998). To the best of my knowledge, Sebald never names this work as a source, but the intertextual resonances are manifold.

66 Iris Radisch, "Der Waschbär der falschen Welt," *Die Zeit*, April 5, 2001, 55.

67 Thomas Steinfeld, "Die Wünschelrute in der Tasche eines Nibelungen," *Frankfurter Allgemeine Zeitung* 67 (March 20, 2001): L 18.

68 See Roland Barthes, "The Reality Effect," in *The Rustle of Language*, trans. Richard Howard (Berkeley: University of California Press, 1989), 145–8, where

fragments from diverse sources to form a quilt that makes pretense to
its own aesthetic totality. Sebald's works are replete with self-reflexive
deliberations on this combinatory practice, which is fundamental to
his narratives in general. In *Austerlitz* we discover self-reflections on
this combinatory structure in the eponymous protagonist's search for
"Familienähnlichkeiten," the "family likeness" in historically diverse
architectural monuments (*Austerlitz* 48/33), or more pointedly in the
game in which he lays out photographs and constantly rearranges
them in order to discover the hidden connections that link them
together (*Austerlitz* 171–2/119). This combinatory practice, as well
as the tendency to self-consciously reflect on the very structures
that fashion the fictional work, are central attributes of metafiction.
Raymond Federman has called the metafictional writer a "plagiarist"
by design, maintaining that for modern writers, imagination does not
create something new, but instead "imitates, copies, repeats, prolif-
erates—plagiarizes in other words—what has already been there."[69]
He insists that such works self-consciously point to the role of the artist
as plagiarist. In *Austerlitz*, Sebald perfects this art of the metafictional
plagiarist and brings it to bear productively on the representation of
the Holocaust victim and the thematic of the Holocaust more broadly.

    We can elucidate the manner in which Sebald creatively appro-
priates metafictional strategies for their application to Holocaust fiction
by examining the narrative structure of this text. Sebald extends and
perfects the Chinese-box structure of embedded first-person narratives
that he employed in his earlier prose fictions, and he adheres to the
practice of constructing a first-person frame narrator who bears certain
points of resemblance with the empirical author Sebald himself. As we
saw in the case of Wilkomirski's *Bruchstücke*, this ontological union
between author and narrator is of crucial importance for the critical
evaluation of Holocaust fiction. This issue of identity is complicated
in Sebald's case, however, because his author/narrator, rather than
representing the perspective of the victim and proffering immediate
testimony, as in Wilkomirski's text, embodies the standpoint of the
personally unaffected outsider. But more importantly, in Sebald's
Holocaust narratives this author–narrator connection is neither
absolutely asserted nor denied; instead, it is consciously suspended
in a web of indeterminacy and innuendo, calculated to raise questions
rather than reinforce certainty. Indeed, Sebald seems to play deliberately on this issue of ontological identification in order to throw it open
as a problem area of Holocaust fiction, or of documentary fiction more

---

he focuses on the role of description in "realistic" narratives and the strategy for
transmogrifying denotation into signification.
69 Federman, "Imagination as Plagiarism," 565.

generally. This issue is compounded in Sebald's text by the fact that his narrator is not the immediate source of the diegetic information, but merely a reporter or witness of someone else's—Austerlitz's— testimony. But this relationship of informant to chronicler is further replicated within the diegetic context of Austerlitz's autobiography, since this character is dependent on other individuals or on written texts and other documents as the sources of information about his own life, his past, and the lives of his parents. He relies, for example, on the testimony of his former nanny Vera for "facts" about his childhood. This structure becomes even more complicated when within Vera's narrative—which is within Austerlitz's narrative, which is within the narrator's narrative—Austerlitz's deceased parents Maximilian and Agáta assume roles as narrators in their own right (*Austerlitz* 242–3/168–9; 249–59/173–80).

Peculiar to this structure of nesting narratives is that each of these narrative voices assumes the position and diction of the first person. As a result, the text unfolds as a series of interlocking testimonials, so that the recovery of the past, and even of one's own personal history, is portrayed in terms of a telescoping structure of testimonial evidence articulated by myriad voices, but ultimately gathered together in the voice of the first-person narrator. By means of this tactic, Sebald mimics on the level of narrative structure the temporal alienation from distant, if influential historical events that is the substance of this story itself, and he highlights the inter-human, indeed the *narrative*, linkages that provide the only approach to these occurrences. In a seeming paradox, while each subsequent testimonial layer gets closer to the experience of the historical source event, it simultaneously adds increasing layers of mediation and hence of potential personal distortion. This technique represents an ideal method for invoking the precarious access to memories and to past historical occurrences. Sebald's text does not merely reflect on the problematic of traumatic memory that is tied to horrendous historical circumstances; rather, it calls attention to the complex problem of historical transmission and our increasingly *mediated* access to critical historical events and the experience of those events. History becomes a matter of hearsay added to hearsay supplemented by hearsay. Sebald thereby aesthetically invokes one of the most critical problems in Holocaust studies in general: how to capture, preserve, and transmit the horrible nature of these events and experiences in all their immediacy, in particular at a time when the generation of victims and primary witnesses is on the verge of disappearing. His text asks on the level of *narrative structure* how we can judge the authenticity of testimony, given this constant narrative refraction of the "facts" through an echo chamber of distinct voices. We are approaching, of course, Hayden White's position that historical accounts are always shaped by certain tropes and strategies of emplotment, so that historical data potentially become as elusive as the Kantian thing-in-itself. Sebald adds an additional complication to this by demonstrating how historical accounts are not simply secondary emplotments of a given set of first-order facts, but instead are tertiary or even fourth-order retellings of prior *narratives*.

One can also view Sebald's peculiar narrative technique from another perspective, one that both reinforces its relevance for the Holocaust thematic and offers a potential solution for the dilemma of historical transmission. Sebald's narrative approach operates by laminating together the structure of witness and testimonial narrative. Each character in the text, be it the anonymous first-person narrator, the character Austerlitz, or even the nanny Vera, performs a double role as both witness to the testimony of others and chronicler of that testimony, on the one hand; and, on the other hand, as testimonial voice of his or her own personal experiences. This is most pronounced on the level of Sebald's narrator, who stands completely outside the life of Austerlitz, to which he is bearing witness via his narrative, but who also operates as a pseudo-autobiographical testifier to his own life experiences, which in part parallel those of Austerlitz. Similarly, Austerlitz, when he takes over the first-person form, functions as an autobiographical self-witness who gives his own personal testimony; but when he passes the first-person position on to others, he shifts positions to become the witness to their testimony. Implicit in this witness–informant interaction is an interpersonal trust or bonding that accepts the accuracy, authenticity, and veracity of the reported testimony. The glue that fuses witness narrative to testimonial account is a profound form of empathy that brings narrator and informant into an emotional union. The interstitial space that marks the divide between witness and informant is infused with a conductive material that permits both personal experiences and their emotive auras to be transmitted between figures.[70] Under such conditions of receptivity, even when the "facts" of historical events are subject to deflections and alienating distortions, their emotional essence or traumatic force can still be transferred. This is the structure Dominick LaCapra calls "empathetic unsettlement," which he is careful to distinguish not only from facile forms of identification, but also from simple appropriation of the other's experience. LaCapra defines this attitude as "a kind of virtual experience through which one puts oneself in the other's

---

70 Sebald's narrative accomplishment might be seen as highlighting the "empathetic projection" that, according to Ezrahi, "Questions of Authenticity," 62, marks a shift in Holocaust literature, in Israel and Germany especially, away from the dominant paradigm of authentic witnessing.

position while recognizing the difference of that position and hence not taking the other's place."[71] This provides an illuminating and apt description for the relationship between witness and informant in Sebald's narrative in general, and between his narrator and protagonist more particularly. Empathetic unsettlement, as the affective bond that links teller and listener in *Austerlitz*, assumes the significant function of a medium by which historical experience is passed on. It is decidedly not a matter of achieving undiluted access to indubitable "facts," but instead of approximating the *emotional valence* associated with how specific human beings *experience* those "facts."

In order to better understand this concept of empathetic unsettlement and the appropriateness of its application to intersubjective relationships in Sebald's *Austerlitz*, it is necessary to draw on another, related conceptual instrument proposed by LaCapra: the distinction between "historical" and "structural" trauma. According to LaCapra, "Historical trauma is specific, and not everyone is subject to it or entitled to the subject position associated with it." Historical trauma relates to the impact a traumatic event has on its immediate victims; it is tied to real experience and its emotional impact.[72] Structural trauma, by contrast, represents a more diffuse, less immediate traumatic experience. It is universal to all people, as opposed to the temporal specificity of historical trauma, and LaCapra correlates it with "trans-historical absence" or "absence of/at the origin."[73] Structural trauma has no immediate source, but rather takes the form of a meta-empirical haunting, a general malaise or discontent predicated on a principal awareness, a persistent but nevertheless mediated consciousness of traumatic historical circumstances. We might view this as the collateral effects of historical traumas that are not subject to empirical experience, but are culturally transmitted. Structural trauma provides a potentially more precise, critically more provocative term for describing what is commonly identified as the "melancholic" tenor of Sebald's texts. It names the *emotional* register of that "natural history of destruction" to which Sebald, his narrator, and his fictional characters frequently allude. Moreover, it highlights the fact that "melancholy" need not imply passive resignation, but can also represent a vehicle of active political-cultural resistance.

From the perspective of this natural history of destruction, the Holocaust takes on the guise of one distinctive episode in a historical linkage of traumatic occurrences. In what was his last interview for a German-language newspaper, first published just days after his death

---

71 LaCapra, *Writing History*, 78.
72 Ibid.
73 Ibid., 77.

in December 2001, Sebald took sides in the debate about the uniqueness of the Holocaust. Although he denies the absolute singularity of these events, he is careful not to minimize or relativize them. Instead, he situates the Holocaust as a historical point of convergence that feeds off the European past, but also plays a determining role in future European history.

> Ich sehe die von den Deutschen angerichtete Katastrophe, grauenvoll wie sie war, durchaus nicht als ein Unikum an—sie hat sich mit einer gewissen Folgerichtigkeit herausentwickelt aus der europäischen Geschichte und sich dann, aus diesem Grunde auch, hineingefressen in die europäische Geschichte. Deshalb sind die Spuren dieser Katastrophe in ganz Europa ablesbar ... Was dahinter stand, war der von der Machtpolitik spätestens seit Napoleon immer wieder verfolgte Traum, aus diesem sehr unordentlichen Kontinent Europa etwas viel Ordentlicheres, Geregeltes, Durchorganisiertes, Machtvolles zu machen. ("*Auf ungeheuer dünnem Eis*" 260)
>
> [I do not view the catastrophe caused by the Germans, as horrendous as it was, as something unique. It developed with a certain logical consequence out of European history, with the result that it subsequently, and precisely for this reason, worked its way into future European history. That's why the traces of this catastrophe are discernible everywhere in Europe ... What stood behind it was the dream, pursued by the politics of power at least since Napoleon, to make of this extremely disordered continent something much more orderly, structured, perfectly organized, and powerful.]

Sebald identifies the Holocaust explicitly as a catastrophe caused by the German people, but one that represents the perverse culmination of a much more general and diffuse European phenomenon, which he identifies—disciple of the Frankfurt School social theorists that he was—with a politics of mastery, underwritten by an intemperate instrumental rationality that seeks to establish sterile order at any cost. For Sebald, as for Max Horkheimer and Theodor Adorno, the affinity of the Holocaust with this greater European political and intellectual-historical tradition renders it even more horrendous than if it were an isolated, unique event. Sebald's awareness of this European history, especially given the purported inevitability with which it produced the gruesome events of the Holocaust, constitutes the fundamental condition of possibility for the experience of structural trauma.

In *Austerlitz*, the aura of this history of Europe as a linked set of devastating acts, committed in the spirit of an aberrant instrumental reason, pervades the consciousness of the first-person narrator. Yet when comprehended as a particularly receptive form of structural trauma, this seemingly "melancholic" demeanor goes beyond fatalism, pessimism, and resignation in the face of overpowering historical forces. It forms the precondition for the narrator's emotional relationship with Austerlitz and is the prerequisite for his own empathetic unsettlement. Austerlitz is an immediate victim of historical trauma: his life has been shaped *in toto* by the displacement from his homeland and the alienation from his family that resulted from the German-caused catastrophe. In the interaction between Austerlitz and the anonymous first-person narrator, Sebald's narrative relates the resonance of the former's *historical* trauma when it strikes the sounding board of the narrator's *structural* trauma. It is indicative of Sebald's metafictional tactics that this productive communicative process is obliquely articulated via an intertextual allusion to a classic work from the German Romantic textual repertoire: Heinrich von Kleist's essay "Über die allmählige [*sic*] Verfertigung der Gedanken beim Reden" ("On the Gradual Formation of Thoughts While Speaking"). Reflecting on his very first meeting with Austerlitz, Sebald's first-person narrator remarks on the aston- ishing manner with which Austerlitz composes his thoughts in the very moment in which he expresses them verbally, and the wording of the German text marks this passage as an intertextual reference to the title of Kleist's essay: "Es war für mich von Anfang an erstaunlich, wie Austerlitz *seine Gedanken beim Reden verfertigte*, wie er sozusagen aus der Zerstreutheit heraus die ausgewogensten Sätze entwickeln konnte" (*Austerlitz* 18; emphasis added). The English rendering is unfortunately unable to recreate this intertextual echo, which I have placed in italics. "From the first I was astonished by the way Austerlitz put his ideas together as he talked, forming perfectly balanced sentences out of whatever occurred to him" (*Austerlitz* 12–13).

The intertextual reference to this essay is key, since one of the primary thrusts of Kleist's argument is that this productive maturation of ideas in the very moment of their articulation can only take place in an explicitly dialogic configuration, where the speaker formu- lates his or her thoughts in the concrete *presence* of an empathetic listener.[74] Kleist argues that in such ideal dialogic circumstances the very face of the listening partner serves as inspiration for the speaker, motivating the discovery and uncovering of his or her most profound

---

74 Heinrich von Kleist, "Über die allmählige Verfertigung der Gedanken beim Reden," in *Erzählungen, Anekdoten, Gedichte, Schriften*, ed. Klaus Müller-Salget (Frankfurt am Main: Deutscher Klassiker Verlag, 1990), 535–6; "On the Gradual Formation of Thoughts While Speaking," in *Selected Prose of Heinrich von Kleist*, trans. Peter Wortsman (New York: Archipelago Books, 2010), 257.

thoughts. "[W]hen speaking, we find a strange source of enthusiasm in the human face of the person standing before us; and from a look that signals comprehension of a half-formulated thought we may often draw the expression needed to find the other half" ("Es liegt ein sonderbarer Quell der Begeisterung für denjenigen, der spricht, in einem menschlichen Antlitz, das ihm gegenübersteht; und ein Blick, der uns einen halbausgedrückten Gedanken schon als begriffen ankündigt, schenkt uns oft den Ausdruck für die ganze andere Hälfte desselben").[75] The very presence of a listener whose countenance betrays comprehending involvement in the thoughts the speaker is attempting to express lends that speaker the necessary wherewithal to formulate his or her ideas in the most complete and articulate fashion. The sympathetic, participatory listener in a dialogic interchange thereby plays an important role as the *facilitator* of the speaker's thoughts and expressions. This is the manner in which Sebald stages the exchange between Austerlitz and his first-person narrator: although the latter largely plays the role of a passive listener for the story of his informant Austerlitz, his concrete presence *as involved listener* forms the condition of possibility of this informant's memory-recall. This dialogic situation is not therapeutic in the strictly Freudian sense; rather, the "empathetic unsettlement" and participatory understanding of the narrator as listener, in all of his physical presence, constitutes the trigger that enables Austerlitz to reconstruct and relate his own (hi)story. It is representative of Sebald's metafictional finesse that this profound characterization of the dialogic interchange in this text is marked only obliquely via an arcane intertextual reference. Sebald's texts often run deepest when they are least explicit. He is an expert at suggesting heavy meaning with an extraordinarily light hand.

I will conclude this analysis of the prominence of metafictional strategies in *Austerlitz* by examining an episode that illuminates more clearly the nature of the empathetic relationship between Sebald's narrator and Austerlitz, but also highlights how Sebald gestures toward this configuration in a roundabout manner through the implementation of metafictional techniques. The passages I will focus on can hardly be called an "episode" in the text; they constitute instead something like a sustained aside or a strategic diversion. I'm referring to the expansive footnote Sebald's narrator introduces when he is just a few pages into his narrative. It is occasioned during his very first discussion with Austerlitz by this informant's remark that the architectural model for the Antwerp train station, in which their conversation takes place, was the train station in Lucerne, Switzerland. At this juncture, an asterisk

---

75 Kleist, "Über die allmählige Verfertigung," 536; "On the Gradual Formation," 257.

interrupts Austerlitz's description in mid-sentence and leads the reader to a discursive footnote that spans three pages in the German edition and includes its own illustration (*Austerlitz* 14–16/10–11). This type of narrative intervention, which disrupts the fictional text by applying a convention borrowed from a divergent discursive domain, namely from academic scholarship, and inserting a passage dominated by extreme narrative self-consciousness, is a common device in certain forms of metafiction. One is reminded, for example, of Vladimir Nabokov's *Pale Fire*, where the commentary on the 999-line poem dwarfs these verses themselves. Similarly, Sebald's footnote in *Austerlitz*—it is the only one—transports the reader into an entirely different discursive register. It begins with a self-reflexive comment by the narrator about something that struck him as he re-read his own text: "In looking through these notes I remember that in February 1971, during a short visit to Switzerland, one of the places I visited was Lucerne" ("Bei der Durchsicht dieser Aufzeichnungen entsinne ich mich jetzt wieder, daß ich im Februar 1971, während eines kurzen Aufenthalts in der Schweiz, unter anderem auch in Luzern gewesen [bin]"; *Austerlitz* 14/10). This footnote is surprising not merely because it so abruptly tears the reader away from the narrative in the very moment it is beginning to gain momentum, but also due to the self-reflexive gesture with which the narrator refers to his own re-reading of this very text and the supplementary thoughts this act of subsequent, secondary reading stimulates. Perhaps we are supposed to take the narrator's productive and interactive engagement with his own text as a model for our own? At any rate, this note goes on to relate how the narrator stood for a long time on the bridge in Lucerne and studied the copula of the train station from a distance. That night, while he was asleep in his hotel room, this station caught fire, and the copula he had earlier admired was almost completely destroyed. At this point the narrator inserts into the footnote an illustration of the burning train station, purportedly taken from the newspaper report about the fire that he read the next day (see Figure 6.1). This image, he claims, stuck in his memory for many weeks, accompanied by "an uneasy, anxious feeling" ("etwas Beunruhigendes und Beängstigendes") that ultimately condensed around the impression "that I had been to blame, or at least one of those to blame, for the Lucerne fire" ("daß ich der Schuldige oder zumindest der Mitschuldige sei an dem Luzerner Brand"; *Austerlitz* 16/11). The footnote concludes with the narrator's confession that even years later he continued to be haunted in his dreams by the image of this flaming copula.

A great deal must be at stake for Sebald's narrator to justify the introduction of this obtrusive footnote at this crucial juncture in his narrative. The associative logic with which he moves from Austerlitz's historical reference about the paradigmatic architecture of the Lucerne

Figure 6.1: Burning Lucerne Train Station (*Austerlitz* 14/10).

station to his own personal experience is central, since it models in miniature the transference that will take place between Austerlitz's narrative and the narrator's own life experiences. Moreover, since it is added to the narrative in retrospect, this footnote performs a general proleptic function, elliptically anticipating in its images of fire and destruction the Holocaust thematic that will turn out to be the source of Austerlitz's historical trauma. This footnote further thematizes the narrator's position as a bystander and seemingly impartial observer; yet his very act of distanced observation, paradoxically, implicates him in the history of what he observes. His regime of objective gazing is transformed into one of involved *looking*, to allude to terminology suggested by Marianne Hirsch.[76] The personal stance described here is one of *affected* observation. There simply is no sensible explanation for why Sebald's narrator feels responsible for the fire in the station whose ornate copula he had previously admired; and ultimately this episode serves primarily as a vehicle for introducing, through a narrative backdoor, the theme of implied complicity for events on which one has had no influence and over which one has no control. The logic of this episode is structured so as to demonstrate how the affected observer is infused with the guilt of the perpetrator.[77]

There are many dimensions to this theme of guilt that Sebald's narrator introduces via this metafictional footnote. It stands for the shame and guilt of second-generation Germans, like Sebald's narrator (and Sebald himself), who cannot avoid sharing the responsibility for the Holocaust, even though they had no direct involvement. But on another level, it also represents the shame and guilt of the survivors among the victims themselves, those, to allude to the words of Primo Levi, who were not drowned, but like Jacques Austerlitz, were saved. Levi devoted an entire chapter of *The Drowned and the Saved* to an exploration of the shame of the survivors, and he subsequently stressed that those who are silent about their traumatic experience are also those who bear the most shame.[78] Austerlitz must struggle to reconstruct the reasons for his expulsion from his family; but throughout his life he is dogged by the belief that he must somehow be to blame for his banishment (*Austerlitz* 66/45, 283/199, 309/216, 326/228). This sense of guilt—the guilt of the victim as survivor, and the guilt of the successor generation of the perpetrators—constitutes at least in part the shared experience that generates the empathy uniting Sebald's German narrator-witness with his Jewish informant-survivor. Regardless of how one interprets the issues of guilt and shame as played out in this text, in the footnote examined here, Sebald conspicuously exploits a metafictional device to broach a series of complex problems that impinge directly upon the Holocaust thematic so central to this text.

One could certainly investigate more of the metafictional techniques Sebald employs in this work for their relevance to the Holocaust problematic. My analysis has largely ignored, for example, one of

---

76 Marianne Hirsch, *Family Frames: Photography, Narrative, and Postmemory* (Cambridge, MA: Harvard University Press, 1997), 15.

77 The only other commentator who deals extensively with this footnote is Byram, "A Footnote to History," 201–3. Her analysis differs from mine insofar as she avoids any discussion of the metafictional dimension of this technique, and because she reads the narrator's consternation primarily as a reflex of his own trauma, which he shares with Austerlitz, rather than as a symptom of his vicarious guilt as a second-generation German.

78 Levi, *The Drowned and the Saved*, 70–87, 149.

Sebald's most widely acknowledged innovations, his inclusion of visual material, such as photographs, diagrams, reproductions of souvenirs or other objects and texts that play a role in the fictional diegesis. On the most general level, these illustrations highlight the tensions between empirical, documentary fact and fabulative fiction that is central for all of Sebald's prose fictions. Like his metafictional strategies in general, these images underwrite his oblique approach to the Holocaust. However, it is not just a matter of discovering a "shield" that allows one to look upon the head of Medusa without being petrified, but also of coming to terms, by means of fictional representations, with the very problems that have been constitutive of Holocaust fiction and its reception from the outset: with themes of guilt, shame, and secondary responsibility; with the crucial problem of empathy and the relationships between victims and the successor generation of the perpetrators; with the insistence, in representations of the Holocaust, on the ontological connections between authors and narrators; and most importantly, with the fundamental issue of how one can best gain access to, preserve in narrative forms, and effectively transmit horrendous incidents from the past with all their traumatic force. Sebald's artistry in *Austerlitz* in particular consists in his ability to demonstrate the relevance of metafictional strategies for the exploration of these crucial problems. This text suggests ways in which the genre of documentary fiction, so significant for an imaginative engagement with the Holocaust, can be transformed into an enhanced form that could go by the name of documentary *metafiction*.[79] Sebald's Holocaust metafiction instantiates a method for transmitting the "structural" trauma of the Holocaust, so as to guarantee that it is passed on, even if in deflected, refracted form, to future generations. Metafiction becomes a method for insuring that the Holocaust stays alive as a traumatic memory; a way of guaranteeing that, even as the historical events recede into an ever-murkier past, humans will continue to experience the requisite "unsettlement" that the reality of such past horrors must evoke—as a necessary admonishment that they must not be repeated in the present or the future.

---

79 Sebald's narratives exemplify the view, expressed over thirty years ago by Alvin H. Rosenfeld, "The Problematics of Holocaust Literature," in *Confronting the Holocaust: The Impact of Elie Wiesel*, ed. Alvin H. Rosenfeld and Irving Greenberg (Bloomington: Indiana University Press, 1978), 20, that Holocaust fiction should not be defined merely by the fact that it takes the Holocaust as its subject matter, but instead by its capacity to discover forms of expression that are appropriate to the representation of extreme dehumanization.

Seven Sebald's Segues: Performing Narrative Contingency in *Die Ringe des Saturn*

"And why should there not be a literary area of history, fictions in which, while respecting the basic givens of history—customs, institutions, mentalities—history would be rewritten by exploiting the role of chance and of particular events?"

Jacques Le Goff[1]

"There is, it would seem, in the dimensional scale of the world a kind of delicate meeting place between imagination and knowledge, a point, arrived at by diminishing large things and enlarging small ones, that is intrinsically artistic."

Vladimir Nabokov[2]

Die Ringe des Saturn represents a pivotal, transitional text in Sebald's oeuvre. First published in 1995, it functions as an important bridge-text between the loosely ordered collections *Schwindel. Gefühle* (1990) and *Die Ausgewanderten* (1992), and the more novel-like form of his last published work, *Austerlitz* (2001). While the earlier books consist largely of independent narratives, loosely tied together by certain shared themes and unified above all by the consistent voice, tone, and perspective of the unnamed first-person narrator,[3] Sebald's

1 Jacques Le Goff, *History and Memory*, trans. Steven Rendall and Elizabeth Claman (New York: Columbia University Press, 1992), 130.

2 Vladimir Nabokov, *Speak, Memory: An Autobiography Revisited*, Penguin Classics (London: Penguin, 2000), 130–1.

3 For reflections on the role of Sebald's narrator as an organizing presence who establishes a coherent narrative voice and tone, see E. L. Doctorow, "W. G. Sebald," in *Creationists: Selected Essays, 1993–2006* (New York: Random House,

last fictional work follows a unitary thread, the self-discovery of its eponymous protagonist in his discursive interactions with the narrator. If the earlier works are constituted as loosely interwoven and interconnected tales, *Austerlitz* is made up of a single storyline, itself structured by an intricate series of subplots, all of which help drive forward the central tale of a fractured life in search of cohesion and a coherent past. That this "novel" ultimately resists any final completion represents a reflection on the necessary incompleteness of the personal history it attempts to reconstruct. Unlike these works, *Die Ringe des Saturn* seems either to have no storyline at all, or to have so many brief, episodic, undeveloped, and seemingly unconnected vignettes that it represents nothing but a motley collection of fragments. The fact that it is Sebald's only work that is divided into chapters signals an attempt to bring order into the apparent chaos. The text mimics those cosmic rings from which it draws its name: like the rings of Saturn, it is composed of narrative debris and the detritus of memory, held together by certain overriding gravitational forces that lend it an appearance of integrity and atomic unity.

It may thus seem paradoxical to claim that *Die Ringe des Saturn* is the first of Sebald's book-length narratives that makes pretense to being an organic whole. Its ten chapters are not designated by names, but are marked simply by roman numerals, indicating at least the possibility of narrative progression. This sense of narrative direction and teleological plan is underscored by the superficial adherence to the generic category of the travelogue or pilgrimage, with its implied structure of way-stations and destinations. This sense of purpose and orientation along a charted course is one force that lends a certain cohesion to Sebald's narrative; but it is constantly counteracted by another force that disrupts this trajectory: the tendency toward spontaneous digression, the temptation to deviate from any given plan based on unforeseen—and unforeseeable—encounters, experiences, recollections, or reflections that register in the narrator's consciousness. Sebald's text is structured around the interactions of these two drives, and the points at which they intersect function as seminal, privileged places in its narrative logic: they build transitions that move the narrative forward at precisely the moment when it is in danger of

2006), 147; Jonathan J. Long, "Disziplin und Geständnis: Ansätze zu einer Foucaultschen Sebald-Lektüre," in *W. G. Sebald: Politische Archäologie und melancholische Bastelei*, ed. Michael Niehaus and Claudia Öhlschläger (Berlin: Erich Schmidt, 2006), 236–7; and Adam Zachary Newton, "Place from Place, and Place from Flight: W. G. Sebald's *The Emigrants* and Aharon Appelfeld's *The Iron Tracks*," in *The Elsewhere: On Belonging at a Near Distance: Reading Literary Memoir from Europe and the Levant* (Madison: University of Wisconsin Press, 2005), 43.

stalling and losing momentum. These points of transition are what I call Sebald's segues, and the purpose of this initial investigation into this work is to investigate the operation of these transitions as the points of cohesion in an otherwise disjointed text. This work stands as a representative microcosm for the art of transition in Sebald's works more generally, insofar as it manifests in its most mature form this practice of shifting radically from one theme to another, without losing the semblance of interconnection.

Anyone who tries to summarize the "plot" of *Die Ringe des Saturn* to someone unfamiliar with the text and its author will immediately become aware of the principal diversity, the centrifugal tendency of this work to break apart into seemingly disconnected and independent episodes. The text consists of a series of distinct and identifiable layers that are laminated onto each other in creative and often surprising ways. These laminations are another way of highlighting the transitional junctures so central to Sebald's narrative, and in this respect this text reflects once again, on the level of its own construction, the rings of Saturn named in its title. These rings exhibit plurality in unity to the extent that they appear as distinct colored bands, which nonetheless abut upon one another and hence seem to be one single, stratified ring. Similarly, Sebald's text consists of a set of discrete narrative dimensions that are contiguous with one another. Like the rings of Saturn, these narrative rings move in a coordinated orbit around a single regulative center. This center is the first-person narrator himself, who serves, like the planet Saturn, as the gravitational force or the nodal point that choreographs the synchronized motion of the various narrative elements.

If one characterizes the structure of *Die Ringe des Saturn* as a series of concentric diegetic circles that move around a narrative core, then it should be possible to identify the nature of these layers and situate them in terms of their proximity to this narrating instance. The outermost layer has already been mentioned: it is constituted by the genre of the travelogue itself, which provides a broad and flexible framework for a course of (narrative) movement that has a sense of direction, without having any precise aim or telos. Sebald highlights this idea of travel along a certain trajectory when he gives his text the telling subtitle "Eine englische Wallfahrt" (an English pilgrimage), a subtitle that is inexplicably left out of the English translation. Pilgrimages traditionally follow a planned-out, charted course, marked by certain stations, and are guided by the larger, abstract or metaphorical goal of facilitating individual salvation. Sebald's narrative signals this idea of trajectory via the recurrent motif of the "Bahn," the course, path, orbit, or track on which something moves, just as the rings of Saturn, according to the passage from the *Brockhaus Enzyklopädie* that Sebald employs as one of

his epigraphs, move "in circular orbits" ("in kreisförmigen Bahnen";
Ringe 5/n.p.) around the planet.[4]

As outermost structural layer, the genre of the travelogue forms a
shell that holds together the varied fragments of Sebald's text. Insofar
as it is marked out by identifiable stops along the path of the larger
journey, the travelogue also helps define the next layer of Sebald's
text: geographical or historical place, as a locus at which certain
documentable events occurred, and which functions as the motivator
of discrete narrative recapitulations. Exemplary of this is the story
of the estate at Somerleyton, which the narrator identifies as "some
kind of no-man's-land" ("quasi extraterritorialen Ort") in which one
completely loses one's geographical, temporal, and even historical
orientation. "Nor can one readily say which decade or century it is,"
the narrator remarks during his experience of Somerleyton, "for many
ages are superimposed here and coexist" ("Auch in welchem Jahrzehnt
oder Jahrhundert man ist, läßt sich nicht ohne weiteres sagen, denn
viele Zeiten haben sich hier überlagert und bestehen nebeneinander
fort"; 49/36). Its stratified historical texture marks the estate as one
of the first examples of an object that operates self-reflexively as an
illustration of the overriding structure of Sebald's narrative itself.

---

4   Aside from its mention in this epigraph, the motif of the "Bahn" is initially
     presented toward the end of the first chapter, when the narrator describes the
     course of history as an arc ("Bahn") that first rises up to a zenith, then falls
     off "into the dark" ("in die Dunkelheit"; 33–4/24). For further occurrences of
     this motif, see *Ringe* 74/55 (the courses, or "Bahnen" followed by the schools
     of herring as they traverse the oceans); 89/68 (the flight of the swallows as
     they circle under the ocean cliffs); 91/69–70 (the empty "Bahn" or course
     the narrator himself follows); 105/81 (the path followed by a man trying to
     evade a persecutor); 107/82 (the "tracks" ("Bahnen") formed by the bolts of
     bleaching fabric in Ruisdael's painting *The Bleach Fields of Haarlem*); 159/126
     (the trajectory of a cannonball as it rips through the crowns of some poplar
     trees); 176/139 (the "Bahnen," or circles that designate the layers of political
     power in the Chinese court); 184/146 (the "Blutbahnen," or streams of blood
     that spell the physical end of the Chinese emperor Hsien-feng); 227/182 (the
     "Laufbahn," or life course of human existence, which is determined by impon-
     derables and inscrutable forces); 233/187 (the "Lebensbahn" or life trajectory of
     an individual); 236/189–90 (the path followed by an automobile in the dream
     vision of Michael Hamburger's wife); 244/195–6 (the trajectory of the rocket
     that destroyed FitzGerald's house during World War II); 251/201 (the crossing
     paths that bring FitzGerald and his lover William Browne together); 318/256
     (bullets that follow a parabolic course); and finally 366/296 (the bolt or "Bahn"
     of black silk produced by a Norwich silk weaver). For an interpretation of this
     metaphor as a rhizomatic narrative structure that mimics trajectories for the
     abuse of power, see Judith Ryan, "'Lines of Flight': History and Territory in
     The Rings of Saturn," in *W. G. Sebald: Schreiben ex patria / Expatriate Writing*, ed.
     Gerhard Fischer (Amsterdam: Rodopi, 2009), 45–60.

The simultaneity of things that are temporally and geographically disparate alludes to the museum-like character of this manor house. As the narrator wanders through its rooms, he is reminded alternately of a "Pfandleihanstalt," a pawn shop in which myriad objects are randomly collected and assembled, or of a "Brockenhaus," an "auction hall" as a place where unused items are collected, repaired, and resold (49/36). This last term functions as a significant nodal point in Sebald's text, a knot at which several dominant themes merge and intertwine. The word "Brockenhaus" itself invokes the famous multi-volume German encyclopedia, the *Brockhaus*, which Sebald cites in the last of his three epigraphs (5/n.p.). This term thereby alludes to the encyclopedic quality of Somerleyton, a classification that also adequately describes the nature of Sebald's text. Furthermore, insofar as a "Brockenhaus" designates a haphazard, chance-like affiliation of textiles and pieces of fabric, this word references a series of themes that stitch together the fragments of Sebald's tattered narrative: specifically, the bolts of bleaching cloth in Ruisdael's painting "Bleach Fields of Haarlem" (106–7/83), but more generally the multiple references to silk that form one of the constitutional leitmotifs of this text. The concept of the "Brockenhaus" also points to a later episode that, like the narrator's experience of Somerleyton, performs a self-referential and self-descriptive function that reflects on the structure of *Die Ringe des Saturn* as a whole: the patchwork fabrics sewn together by the Ashbury sisters out of random scraps of cloth (264–5/211–12).

The third ring of Sebald's narrative is constituted by general reflections on historical events, often triggered by places the narrator visits, or by experiences he has over the course of his journey. One thinks of the extended deliberations on the colonial history of the Congo (147–62/116–28); his recounting of selected historical events in Chinese history, such as the Taiping rebellion and the machinations of the emperor's mother to maintain her own political power and influence (175–93/139–53); the history of the rise and decline of the herring fishery (71–9/52–9); the historical transformation that permanently altered Dunwich Heath (211–18/169–75); and, of course, the history of the Norwich silk industry (345–54/278–86). Sometimes these episodes—as in the last two examples—read like historical summaries of the sort culled from tourist brochures, which strategically highlight the past historical significance of a particular place. This aspect forms a thread that ties these historical digressions to the larger framework of the travelogue.

The next narrative ring is closely related to this one: it is formed by what I call embedded historical narratives. These are accounts of past events provided not directly through the musings of Sebald's narrator, but instead via stories told to him by figures he encounters

on his journeys. At this level we are introduced, for example, to Mrs.
Ashbury's tale about the Irish revolution (267–72/214–19); to Alec
Garrard's (in the English version Thomas Abrams's) history of the
temple in Jerusalem (303–8/244–8); to William Hazel's memories of
the activity at the Suffolk airfields during World War II and his deliberations on the destructive air war on German cities (52–5/38–41);
or even to the discussion about the relationship between the sugar
industry and modern art collecting, as recounted by Cornelis de Jong
(241–3/193–4). These episodes evince one of those characteristics that
are often identified as peculiar to Sebald's prose fictions: the so-called
"periscopic" style that turns his narrator into the medium and mediator
of other people's stories.[5]

Closely related to these second-hand accounts, but existing on a
narrative level decidedly their own, we find another form of embedded
narrative. In contrast to the historical chronicles just discussed, which
are presented to the narrator verbally by characters he meets, this
second class of embedded historical story derives from textual sources.
Here we think above all of how the narrator recounts events from the
life of Algernon Swinburne (200–7/159–66); his reconstruction of the
intertwining lives of Roger Casement and Joseph Conrad, motivated
by his half-conscious reception of a BBC documentary (131–69/103–
34); or the recounting of Chateaubriand's self-exile in England as his
way of escaping the horrors of the French Revolution (311–21/250–9).
As is true of Sebald's embedded narratives in general, these historical
figures often appropriate the voice of the narrator, relating their life
stories with the immediacy of the first person and the present tense. As
in the museum atmosphere of Somerleyton, historical time collapses
as past and present merge, and Sebald's text itself imitates, in its own
narrative structure, the museum-like character of the places and institutions his storyteller visits during his journey. The pilgrimage related
in *Die Ringe des Saturn* is thus not simply geographical in nature: it
is also a *temporal* pilgrimage through the history of modern Europe
and its colonial conquests from the seventeenth through the twentieth

5   Sebald ascribes the development of this form of layered, periscopic first-person
    narration to Thomas Bernhard; see his comments in the interview with Martin
    Doerry and Volker Hage: "Ich würde sein [Thomas Bernhards] Verfahren als
    periskopisch bezeichnen, als Erzählen um ein, zwei Ecken herum—eine sehr
    wichtige Erfindung für die epische Literatur dieser Zeit" ("I would designate
    his [Thomas Bernhard's] technique as periscopic, as narrating as though around
    one or two corners—an extremely important invention for the epic literature
    of this period"; "*Auf ungeheuer dünnem Eis*" 204). See also James Wood, "An
    Interview with W. G. Sebald," *Brick* 59 (1998): 28; and Sebald's discussions with
    Michael Silverblatt (Schwartz 82–3), where he expounds on the innovative
    nature of Bernhard's narrative style and his own desire to imitate it.

century, with special emphasis on the nineteenth century as the age of industrial modernism.

To the extent that this second group of embedded narratives relies on textual models, they are connected with the next narrative ring I will distinguish, which is formed by a diverse set of intertexts in the strict sense. Especially prominent here are the works of Thomas Browne (1605–82) and their thematic and structural analogues, Hans Jakob Christoffel Grimmelshausen's (1621–76) *Der abenteuerliche Simplicissimus* (The adventures of Simplicissimus), and works by Jorge Luis Borges (1899–1986).[6] These intertexts play a role fundamentally distinct from the source-stories of the previous category, since they do not operate on the diegetic level as narratives that can be integrated into the larger framework, but rather as formal or structural models that serve as paradigms for the organizational architecture of Sebald's own text. As such, their integration into the larger narrative is not episodic; rather they occur in the form of leitmotivic patterns that help lend the text a greater sense of cohesion. One quality these structurally-oriented intertexts share is their encyclopedic character. Insofar as they serve a largely structural function, they are related to a further narrative dimension that is especially characteristic of Sebald's prose fictions: the intermedial insertion of illustrations, images, or ekphrastic descriptions that add a supplementary layer to the text. The role of illustrations as forces driving the logic and development of Sebald's narrative can be seen especially well in the examples of Rembrandt's *The Anatomy Lesson of Dr. Nicolaas Tulp* (20–5/12–17) and van Ruisdael's *View of Haarlem with the Bleach Fields* (106–7/82–3). The former is depicted twice as a graphic illustration, while the latter is present only mediately as a detailed ekphrastic elaboration. In this regard, ekphrasis as method—for which Sebald displays a peculiar penchant—constitutes a subcategory in the wider domain of intermedial borrowings.

---

6 Bianca Theisen, "A Natural History of Destruction: W. G. Sebald's *The Rings of Saturn*," *MLN* 121 (2006): 564–76, explores the allusions to Grimmelshausen's novel, but also works out some of the explicit references to the works of Thomas Browne as well as to Shakespeare's *King Lear*. Claudia Albes, "Die Erkundung der Leere: Anmerkungen zu W. G. Sebalds 'englische Wallfahrt' *Die Ringe des Saturn*," *Jahrbuch der deutschen Schillergesellschaft* 46 (2002): 293, stresses the role of intertexts in this work, calling Sebald's narrative "intertextually overdetermined." For more general reflections on the role of intertextuality in this work, see Russell J. A. Kilbourn, "'Catastrophe with Spectator': Subjectivity, Intertextuality and the Representation of History in *Die Ringe des Saturn*," in *W. G. Sebald and the Writing of History*, ed. Anne Fuchs and J. J. Long (Würzburg: Königshausen & Neumann, 2007), 139–62; Martin Swales, "Intertextuality, Authenticity, Metonymy? On Reading W. G. Sebald," in *The Anatomist of Melancholy: Essays in Memory of W. G. Sebald*, ed. Rüdiger Görner (Munich: Iudicum, 2003), 81–7.

The final narrative ring I want to identify is simultaneously the layer that lies closest to the gravitational center of the text, the voice and perspective of its first-person narrator. In the textual topography I am outlining here, this dimension is most proximate with the person and personality of the narrating presence: it circumscribes a larger field that can be associated with issues of autobiography and personal memory. Autobiography by its very nature is structured around a dual temporality, the presence of the narrating self and the past of its narrated persona and experiences. Especially in its early chapters, *Die Ringe des Saturn* highlights this temporal dichotomy by stressing the disparity between the situation of the narrating I—confined to his bed in a hospital room as a physical and emotional consequence of the journey he recounts—and the retelling of his experiences, encounters, and thoughts during the pilgrimage along the Suffolk coast. Throughout these opening sections, the "jetzt" ("now"; 27/18) or "heute" ("today"; 12/5) in which the act of narration takes place is contrasted with the "damals" ("then"/"at the time"; 9/3, 27/18) of the narrated events. This temporal discrepancy is further accentuated by the narrator's proclivity to call attention to the acts of memory through which he accesses these previous experiences, marked by his employment of self-reflexive phrases such as "Genau entsinne ich mich" ("I can remember precisely"; 10/4), "Ich entsinne mich deutlich" ("I still recall"; 26/17), or "Ich erinnere mich" ("I remember"; 267/214). But this dimension of the text is further complicated by the narrator's tendency to incorporate personal memories that have no immediate relation to his journey. One thinks, for example, of his recollections of his deceased colleagues Michael Parkinson and Janine Dakyns (12–17/5–9), or of his recapitulation of the devastating hurricane that occurred in 1987 and its impact on his immediate living environment (326–33/262–8). At certain junctures, such as the section relating the visit to the narrator's friend and colleague Michael Hamburger (219–38/176–90), the outer frame of the travelogue and the inner layer of autobiographical reflection intersect. This episode also provides a telling example of how several of the narrative "rings" converge at certain places in the text, like overlapping Venn diagrams. In the case of Hamburger's personal story about the return to his birthplace of Berlin in 1947, embedded narrative, personal memory, and objective history commingle. One of Sebald's greatest accomplishments in his appropriation of the travelogue genre consists in the subtle manner in which he interweaves subjective history—that is, the *personal experience* of historical events—with the objective history of these factual occurrences. This view of objective history through the personal perspectives of those who experience it represents one of the central principles of Sebald's poetics of history. Due to their mediation through personal experience, otherwise stale facts, such as the destruction of German cities during the Allied air war, the tragedies of the Irish revolution, or even the terror of colonial rule in the Congo, assume the vividness of lived experience. This is a quality *Die Ringe des Saturn* shares with Sebald's other prose works: a capacity to make many facets of a "dead" European history come to life again, so that his reader's imagination is infected by the contagion of visceral memory and memorializing.

Based on this sketch of the multiple dimensions constitutive of *Die Ringe des Saturn*—my list makes no pretensions to being complete—we get a profound sense of this text's complexity and of its multifarious structure. Some critics emphasize precisely the random, disorganized nature of Sebald's narrative, comparing it to such things as the formlessness of the Suffolk coastline the narrator follows,[7] or associating it with the paradigm of the travel odyssey, the "Irrfahrt" or aimless wandering in which the protagonist is buffeted and carried away by events and interventions of chance that are beyond his or her control.[8] Other scholars have sought to identify metaphors or structural models that do justice to the complexity and multiplicity of the text, while at the same time suggesting an underlying order at work in coordinating this mass of fragments into a meaningful pattern. One such model is the rhizomatic configuration, commonly associated with Post-Modern thought and literature, in which certain themes, ideas, or structures lie dormant, in the substructure of the text, only to rise to the surface at irregular and unpredictable intervals.[9] Fundamental to this model is the idea of subliminal or "unconscious" connections that, similar to repressed memories, are triggered and activated by chance occurrences, contingencies, or unexpected combinations. Closely related to this rhizomatic pattern are those models based on the structure of the net or the network, which occurs in several manifestations. One of these is the form of the quincunx,[10] which Sebald's narrator describes and depicts in the first chapter, identifying it as a recurring form that for Thomas

---

7   John Beck, "Reading Room: Erosion and Sedimentation in Sebald's Suffolk," in *W. G. Sebald: A Critical Companion*, ed. J. J. Long and Anne Whitehead (Seattle: University of Washington Press, 2004), 85–6.

8   Jan-Henrik Witthaus, "Fehlleistung und Fiktion: Sebaldsche Gedächtnismodelle zwischen Freud und Borges," in *W. G. Sebald: Politische Archäologie und melancholische Bastelei*, ed. Michael Niehaus and Claudia Öhlschläger (Berlin: Erich Schmidt, 2006), 172.

9   Albes, "Die Erkundung der Leere," 291; Ryan, "'Lines of Flight,'" 52–3; Carsten Strathausen, "Going Nowhere: Sebald's Rhizomatic Travels," in *Searching for Sebald: Photography After W. G. Sebald.*, ed. Lise Patt (Los Angeles: Institute for Cultural Inquiry, 2007), 478.

10 Claudia Öhlschläger, *Beschädigtes Leben. Erzählte Risse: W. G. Sebalds poetische Ordnung des Unglücks* (Freiburg im Breisgau: Rombach, 2006), 162–3.

Browne underlies diverse natural and aesthetic phenomena (*Ringe* 2–30/20–1). Another model that is appropriated from one of Sebald's privileged thematics and applied to his textual structures is that of the railroad network, in which individual tracks that run in discrete directions intersect at certain nodal points, only to diverge once again and head off toward their separate destinations.[11] The central shared feature of all these prototypes, namely the emphasis they place on purely structural configurations, also constitutes their primary short-coming. These models generally either exclude or marginalize the conscious interventions and negotiations enacted by Sebald's narrator, who facilitates, manages, and in many cases *orchestrates* the interconnections that form those points of convergence, thereby allowing this narrative to flow relatively coherently from one episode to the next. In other words, these models tend to stress patterns of movement, recurrence, and intersection that arise as chance happenings, independent of any managing or manipulating narratological consciousness. What they ignore is precisely the *transitional* pivots in Sebald's text, those joints, junctures, or hinges that permit the text to move not only between its diverse thematic interests, but also to maneuver the crossovers between its different structural layers. These transitions require more than just the mechanical operations of impersonal structures; as moments of translation, they demand the spontaneous and deliberate input of a cognizant human subject. Sebald's narrator, in short, is constantly occupied with the work of negotiating the transit among the myriad fragments, themes, and narrative dimensions that make up this text. His role approximates that of a juggler, as David Darby has felicitously suggested,[12] who tries to maintain a sustained interaction among these diverse elements, ensuring that they move together and constitute something that resembles a "story." Sebald's narrator faces daunting challenges in keeping so many elements in play, while simultaneously lending the work as a whole a minimal semblance of cohesion and unity.

As opposed to structural models that write the creative activity of the narrator out of the process of manufacturing connections and

11 Sigurd Martin and Ingo Wintermeyer, "Vorwort," in *Verschiebebahnhöfe der Erinnerung: Zum Werk W. G. Sebalds*, ed. Sigurd Martin and Ingo Wintermeyer (Würzburg: Königshausen & Neumann, 2007), 8; Todd Samuel Presner, "Vienna–Rome–Prague–Antwerp–Paris, The Railway Ruins of Modernity: Freud and Sebald on the Narration of German/Jewish Remains," in *Mobile Modernity: Germans, Jews, Trains* (New York: Columbia University Press, 2007), 251.
12 David Darby, "Landscape and Memory: Sebald's Redemption of History," in *W. G. Sebald: History, Memory, Trauma*, ed. Scott Denham and Mark McCulloh (Berlin: De Gruyter, 2006), 273.

affinities, I will concentrate on a paradigm that amalgamates impersonal structure with an underlying cross-referential and associative
texture that presumes an ordering consciousness: the encyclopedic
collection.[13] Such a compilation is characterized both by a wealth
of diversity—indeed, as encyclopedia, by a pretense to comprehensiveness—as well as by a superficial structural order, such as the
alphabetic principle, which superimposes a sense of interconnection
on these disparate and independent elements. This is also a model to
which Sebald and his narrator refer throughout *Die Ringe des Saturn*,
as when the narrator remarks that he stumbled upon information
about the whereabouts of Thomas Browne's skull while perusing
the *Encyclopaedia Britannica* (*Ringe* 17/9), and encyclopedic structures
also play a salient role in some of the more prominent intertexts that
underpin this text. At the beginning of the final chapter, Sebald's
narrator refers to a literary paradigm that likely serves as a model
for his own textual practice: Thomas Browne's *Musaeum Clausum
or Bibliotheca Abscondita*. He describes this desultory collection of
writings as a

> Katalog merkwürdiger Bücher, Bildnisse, Antiquitäten und
> sonstiger absonderlicher Dinge, von denen dies oder jenes
> tatsächlich Teil einer von Browne selber zusammengetragenen
> Raritätensammlung gewesen sein mag, das allermeiste aber
> offenbar zum Bestand eines rein imaginären, einzig im Inneren
> seines Kopfes existierenden und nur über die Buchstaben auf
> dem Papier zugänglichen Schatzhauses gehörte. (*Ringe* 337–8)
> [catalogue of remarkable books, listing pictures, antiquities and
> sundry singular items that may have formed part of a collection
> put together by Browne but were more likely products of his
> imagination, the inventory of a treasure house that existed purely
> in his head and to which there is no access except through the
> letters on the page. (*Rings* 271)]

Several qualities named in this excerpt—the more detailed
description of Browne's work covers nearly four pages in Sebald's
text (337–40/271–4)—are relevant as self-reflections on the nature of

---

13 For a penetrating analysis of the structure and the history of the encyclopedia,
see Umberto Eco, "From the Tree to the Labyrinth," in *From the Tree to the
Labyrinth: Historical Studies on the Sign and Interpretation*, trans. Anthony Oldcorn
(Cambridge, MA: Harvard University Press, 2014), 18–21, 36–8, where he
emphasizes that the encyclopedia models a labyrinth of rhizomatic outgrowths,
one that makes pretense, like Browne's *Musaeum Clausum*, to subsuming a
wide-ranging diversity of elements joined in an interconnected network.

Sebald's own narrative. The first is its characterization as a catalogue in which disparate elements are collected and collated, from remarkable books—a roundabout allusion to Sebald's intertextual references—to images (Sebald's peculiar use of illustrations), to the description of unusual objects. Sebald's narrator stresses that Browne's textually concretized collection may have a real, non-textual analogue in things Browne himself has assembled in his own cabinet of curiosities, his "Raritätensammlung." Most significant, however, is the ethereal medium that lends this diversity of texts, images, and objects their unity: the imaginative power that spooks through Browne's mind, making his head into a "treasure house" that stores this chaos of disjunctive elements. Browne's mental attitude is dominated by the demeanor of the collector, and his assemblage of unusual artifacts reflects on an empirical level the cognitive collection imaginatively joined together in his own head.[14] Finally, this obsessive drive to assemble things and ideas that are imaginatively linked ultimately expresses itself in textual form, as a combination of graphic letters inscribed on paper. The implication is that the individual elements in Browne's *Musaeum Clausum*, as well as the jumbled fragments that constitute Sebald's text, ultimately assume the cipher-like quality of alphabetic signs, whose multiple assemblage and reassemblage, like an *ars combinatoria*, can produce an infinite number of new ideas and meanings. This suggests that the elements in this stockpile of otherwise unconnected entities are not as important as the manner in which they are combined: the things themselves become secondary to the creative act that discerns affiliations and creates constellations or configurations that generate new significations precisely by means of this act of linkage.[15] In Sebald's *Die Ringe des Saturn*, as in Browne's *Musaeum Clausum*, the distinct narrative elements themselves are not the primary bearers of meaning; rather this role is played by the imaginative syntax that brings them into conjugative relationships. This suggests an alternative critical approach to Sebald's text that, rather than attempting to catalogue and establish hierarchies among its diverse fragments, would focus instead on these transitions and interfaces that constitute

---

14 Klaus R. Scherpe, "Auszeit des Erzählens: W. G. Sebalds Poetik der Beschreibung," *Weimarer Beiträge* 53 (2007): 489, identifies the archival principle as the dominant force behind Sebald's narrative descriptions. Jonathan J. Long, *W. G. Sebald: Image, Archive, Modernity* (New York: Columbia University Press, 2007), 93, 98–9, elaborates on the implications of this "archival consciousness" that stresses the isolation of random bits of information and their resistance to integration.

15 Eco, "From the Tree to the Labyrinth," 37–8, underscores this *inventive*, productive, recombinatory principle as fundamental for the encyclopedic text.

the text as interwoven *text(ure)*. These transitions and interstices are
what I call Sebald's segues.

In terms of textual prototypes for Browne's *Musaeum Clausum*
as well as Sebald's narrative, what comes to mind is the aphoristic
collection or an assemblage of apothegms. This latter form in particular
brings together a highly diverse group of textual elements, from quotations by famous individuals, to stories and anecdotes, to original ideas
and thoughts, through to passages from letters and other sources. The
creative consciousness behind the collection is precisely that of the
imaginative assembler, rather than the individual author of witty, pithy,
or incisive pronouncements, as tends to be the case for the aphoristic
collection. In his description of Browne's *Musaeum Clausum* it is also
possible that Sebald has a specific intertextual allusion in mind, a
text which he as critical scholar knew well and to which he alludes
elsewhere in *Die Ringe des Saturn*: Hugo von Hofmannsthal's "Ein
Brief," his famous letter composed by the fictional Lord Chandos—an
approximate contemporary of the historical Thomas Browne. In this
letter addressed to Francis Bacon, Chandos describes an encyclopedic
work he intended to compile prior to the crisis of expression that
doomed him to silence. He designates this collection of apothegms
as a macrocosmic compilation that encompasses the entire world of
knowledge.

Hier gedachte ich die merkwürdigsten Aussprüche nebenein-
anderzusetzen, welche mir im Verkehr mit den gelehrten Männern
und den geistreichen Frauen unserer Zeit oder mit besonderen
Leuten aus dem Volk oder mit gebildeten und ausgezeichneten
Personen auf meinen Reisen zu sammeln gelungen wäre; damit
wollte ich schöne Sentenzen und Reflexionen aus den Werken
der Alten und der Italiener vereinigen, und was mir sonst an
geistigen Zieraten in Büchern, Handschriften oder Gesprächen
entgegenträte; ferner die Anordnung besonders schöner Feste
und Aufzüge, merkwürdige Verbrechen und Fälle von Raserei,
die Beschreibung der größten und eigentümlichsten Bauwerke
in den Niederlanden, in Frankreich und Italien und noch vieles
andere. Das ganze Werk aber sollte den Titel "Nosce te ipsum"
führen.[16]
[In it I thought of setting side by side the most memorable sayings
which—while associating with the learned men and witty women
of our time, with unusual people from among the simple folk
or with erudite and distinguished personages—I had managed

---

16 Hugo von Hofmannsthal, "Ein Brief," in *Prosa II, Gesammelte Werke in
Einzelausgaben*, ed. Herbert Steiner (Frankfurt am Main: Fischer, 1959), 9–10.

to collect during my travels. With these I meant to combine the
brilliant maxims and reflections from classical and Italian works,
and anything else of intellectual adornment that appealed to
me in books, in manuscripts or conversations; the arrangement,
moreover, of particularly beautiful festivals and pageants, strange
crimes and cases of madness, descriptions of the greatest and
most characteristic architectural monuments in the Netherlands,
in France and Italy; and many other things. The whole work was
to have been entitled *Nosce te ipsum*.[17]]

Thomas Browne's *Bibliotheca Abscondita* and Lord Chandos's assemblage of apothegms display the similar intention of rescuing fragments
of human knowledge from oblivion. In this sense both works operate
as memorial or mnemonic mechanisms, serving as repositories—
archives—of selected aspects of human thought and knowledge. In
Hofmannsthal's case, it is especially striking that this act of collecting
serves the ends of self-definition: the work Chandos is compiling, after
all, is supposed to bear the title "Nosce te ipsum," "Know thyself,"
the admonition of the Delphic oracle. In this encyclopedic form, self-
knowledge is obtained not by means of introspection, but rather by
turning out toward the comprehensiveness of the world. As Peter
Pfeiffer has demonstrated,[18] Hofmannsthal's Chandos letter serves
as an intertext at another place in *Die Ringe des Saturn*, where it is the
prototype for the description of the beetle swimming across the surface
of the water in the well at Michael Hamburger's home, the evocative
image with which chapter seven closes (*Ringe* 238/190). This citation
of Hofmannsthal's text underscores the likelihood that an allusion to
Chandos's apothegmatic assemblage lurks behind Sebald's description
of Thomas Browne's *Musaeum Clausum*. Chandos's characterization
of this work reads, at any rate, like a description of Sebald's own text.

The pseudo-encyclopedic character of Sebald's narrative is also
suggested by one of its most prominent intertexts, Jorge Luis Borges's
short story "Tlön, Uqbar, Orbis Tertius," which deals with—among
other things[19]—the imaginative invention or recreation of a forty-
volume encyclopedia of the fictional planet of Tlön. Although this
encyclopedic tome is not conceived as the product of a single author

17   Hugo von Hofmannsthal, "The Letter of Lord Chandos," in *Selected Prose*, trans.
     Maria Hottinger et al. (New York: Pantheon, 1952), 131–2.
18   Peter C. Pfeiffer, "Korrespondenz und Wahlverwandtschaft: W. G. Sebalds *Die
     Ringe des Saturn*," *Gegenwartsliteratur* 2 (2003): 236.
19   Borges's story itself betrays a kind of encyclopedic structure similar to the
     one it describes. It is analogous to Browne's *Musaeum Clausum* and Chandos's
     collection of apothegms.

or mind, but instead as the collective project of a "secret society" of various scientists, philosophers, and artists, it remains under the governing direction of "an obscure man of genius."[20] The principal task of this mastering intelligence is to subordinate the "inventiveness" of these myriad minds "to a rigorous and systematic plan"[21]—precisely to the encyclopedic system that organizes and orders this knowledge by putting it into a manageable and accessible interrelation. This is exactly the role that Thomas Browne and Chandos play in the organization of their own knowledge collections. Moreover, if the planet Tlön, the object of this compendium of invented knowledge, at first appears to be "a mere chaos, an irresponsible license of the imagination," ultimately it proves to be a coherent "cosmos" whose governing laws "have been formulated, at least provisionally." And if the structure of this imaginative and imaginary world is labyrinthine, it is nonetheless "a labyrinth devised by men, a labyrinth destined to be deciphered by men"—as opposed to reality, which is governed by divine and hence "inhuman" and inscrutable laws.[22] Because the encyclopedia is structured as a labyrinth, its readers struggle, in their very acts of reading, to find their way through the textual meanderings. Umberto Eco highlights this aspect of the encyclopedia, emphasizing how it serves as a "map" that gives readers orientation in the confusing world of knowledge.

> For the reader, the encyclopedia appeared as a "map" of different territories whose edges were jagged and often imprecise, so that one had the impression of moving through it as if it were a labyrinth that allowed one to choose paths that were constantly new, without feeling obliged to stick to a route leading from the general to the particular.[23]

The encyclopedia as map and as labyrinth: it is hard to imagine a pair of concepts that are more appropriate for the peregrinations of Sebald's narrator along the Suffolk coastline, through the history, mentality, and textuality of Western Modernism, as well as for the readers' negotiations of this textual maze as they follow the narrator on this multifaceted journey. The images of labyrinths included in this text do not merely encode the tendency of Sebald's narrator to

---

20 Jorge Luis Borges, "Tlön, Uqbar, Orbis Tertius," in *Labyrinths: Selected Stories and Other Writings*, ed. Donald A. Yates and James E. Irby (New York: New Directions, 1962), 7–8.
21 Ibid., 8.
22 Ibid., 8, 17–18.
23 Eco, "From the Tree to the Labyrinth," 26.

Figure. 7.1: Garden labyrinth as cross-section of brain (*Ringe des Saturn* 216/173).

get lost in material and mental mazes—at one point in his narrative he equates the winding pathways he follows with the sinuosity of his own brain (216/173)—but rather, they also serve as metafictional self-reflections on the encyclopedic makeup and structure of this very text (see Figure 7.1).

Encyclopedias, as Dieter Wrobel has argued in his elaboration of Post-Modern literature, constitute textual spaces at which order and chaos interact in such a way as to create complex systems.[24] On the most superficial level, encyclopedias are organized according to an exogenous structure, the alphabetical system, which aligns individual entries in a paratactic contiguity, placing them in serendipitous proximity or distance from one another based on external questions of alphabetic form. In this organizational scheme, metonymic linkages are established not by intrinsic relationships between elements that are inherently proximate or related, but rather by a more or less arbitrary organizational strategy that imposes systematic order upon these elements from without, based on the coincidence of spelling. Underlying this artificial, fabricated surface-order, encyclopedic knowledge is subject to an alternative internal ordering, a subsidiary system that is endogamous and links the individual elements across textual space by means of thematic and other innate relationships. This

---

24 Dieter Wrobel, *Postmodernes Chaos—Chaotische Postmoderne: Eine Studie zu Analogien zwischen Chaostheorie und deutschsprachiger Prosa der Postmoderne* (Bielefeld: Aisthesis, 1997), 299–300.

is the system of cross-references by which connective lines are drawn internally from one encyclopedic entry to another, what one might call the "*videre*-structure" of internal reference, since it operates in terms of markers that direct the reader to connections that could otherwise pass unnoticed. Sebald calls our attention to this structure in the third epigraph with which he prefaces *Die Ringe des Saturn*, itself derived from an encyclopedic work, the *Brockhaus Enzyklopädie*. This epigraph ends, as does the original entry in the 1973 edition of the *Brockhaus*, with a cross-reference to the entry on the Roche limit "(→ Roch'sche Grenze)" (5/n.p.), dealing with the theory first propounded by the French astronomer Édouard Roche (1820–83) in 1848 that explains, among other things, how the rings of Saturn developed and why they remain in suspension at a certain distance from the planet. The arrow in this citation is the graphic mark for the *videre*-structure of cross-referencing characteristic of the relational suborder common to encyclopedic works. It indicates that there is an intrinsic connection between the entry on the planet Saturn, which Sebald cites in his epigraph, and the entry on the Roche limit. Moreover, if one consults the entry on the Roche limit, one is not only led back by another cross-referencing arrow to the entry on Saturn, but is also encouraged by another cross-reference to examine the entry related to double stars, which is signaled in the *Brockhaus* entry for the "Roch'sche Grenze" as a reference to forms of equilibrium "(→ Gleichgewichtsfiguren)."[25] Thus the system of internal cross-references common to encyclopedic works develops on the pattern of a branching figure, with the stem leading to primary offshoots, and these branching off further into secondary offshoots, with growing intricacy in relation to the initial starting point as one follows the further references. This provides a close approximation of the connective texture that constitutes the thematic and figural interconnections typical of Sebald's narrative. It is indeed a type of network, one that at first blush appears rhizomatic; however, the connective threads are woven by the intervention of an editorial consciousness, as in the case of the encyclopedia, that identifies what linkages are relevant and then marks them as meaningful conjugations.

There is a traditional graphic form that represents this branching syntax of the encyclopedic *videre*-structure: the palmette or anthemion, an ornamental motif found in a wide variety of media throughout history and in diverse cultures. The anthemion is a leaf-like figure, based generally on the form of the palm leaf (hence "palmette"), in which several petals fan out from a single source at the base of the figure (see Figure 7.2).

---

25 *Brockhaus Enzyklopädie*, 20 vols (Wiesbaden: Brockhaus, 1973), 16:27.

Figure 7.2: Anthemion as architectural ornament.

Commonly used, as in the above illustration, in ancient art and architecture as a border or frieze, the anthemion is often related, due to its resemblance to the honeysuckle flower, to notions of fertility and productivity. There is at least one modern attempt to adapt this form for a specific *textual* practice; it occurs in a work Sebald greatly admired and frequently alluded to: Vladimir Nabokov's memoir *Speak, Memory*. In the introduction to this work, Nabokov writes about his various deliberations for appropriate titles, noting that one of them included naming his work after this ornamental figure: "*The Anthemion* which is the name of a honeysuckle ornament, consisting of elaborate interlacements and expanding clusters."[26] Brief as his description is, Nabokov's statement clearly indicates that he conceived this potential title as a reference to the texture by which his memoirs were constructed, as branching lines that form thematic clusters and intersect at unanticipated junctures. Sebald is not only likely to have taken note of this image and its structural application to Nabokov's text, but also to have recognized that Nabokov aligns this pattern of interlacing themes with the operations of human memory. "I witness with pleasure the supreme achievement of memory," Nabokov writes later in this work, "which is the masterly use it makes of innate harmonies when gathering to its fold the suspended and wandering tonalities of the past." And in a related passage he declares, in a formulation that could flow from the pen of Thomas Browne or of Sebald himself, "Coincidence of pattern is one of the wonders of nature."[27] It comes as no surprise that this last remark is heavily underlined in Sebald's copy of Nabokov's memoir.

A pattern resembling the anthemion is also present in another graphic symbol with which Sebald was probably familiar and which

---

26   Nabokov, *Speak, Memory*, 8.
27   Ibid., 134, 123.

has specific thematic connections to *Die Ringe des Saturn*: the figure marking the *Jakobswege*, known in English as the Way of St. James or the Camino de Santiago trail, a network of pilgrimage paths that connect sites devoted to St. Jacob/St. James throughout Europe, from the Baltic states, through Germany, to France and Spain, where they converge at the city of Santiago. The southeast Bavarian branch of this trail system passes through the Allgäu region of Germany where Sebald grew up. In 1987 the European Parliament officially recognized the *Jakobswege* as paths of cultural pilgrimage, designating as their emblem a symbol that looks like an anthemion turned on its side (see Figure 7.3). Although the pilgrimage Sebald undertakes along the Suffolk coast does not cross the Way of St. James, these pathways represent one of the first officially institutionalized networks for religious and cultural pilgrimage in Europe, and its form as network is emblematically represented in the symbol chosen to mark this trail and the monuments it passes. Here we see most clearly how the "digressive" pattern of Sebald's travelogue does not simply follow the aberrant or serendipitous course of the wanderer on foot along the erratic Suffolk coastline, as critics have commonly asserted,[28] but more specifically approximates the planned-out course of the culturally- and historically-oriented pilgrim. Moreover, this pilgrimage displays a pattern, at least in its textual representation, that imitates the *videre*-structure of branching cross-references typical of an encyclopedic work. This cross-thatched texture of internal references defines the nature of Sebald's so-called "coincidences" and contingencies, what he once called a "Koinzidenz des Disparaten," a coincidence of the disparate.[29] The underlying structure of *Die Ringe des Saturn* is adequately characterized by this phrase, provided we acknowledge that the coincidences we discover here are *orchestrated* by the narrator of this text himself. In this regard, they are less coincidences of the disparate than they are "elective affinities and

28 See, for example, Beck, "Reading Room," 85–6; Adrian Daub, "'Donner à Voir': The Logics of Caption in W. G. Sebald's *Rings of Saturn* and Alexander Kluge's *Devil's Blind Spot*," in *Searching for Sebald: Photography after W. G. Sebald*, ed. Lise Patt (Los Angeles: Institute of Cultural Inquiry, 2007), 306–7; Long, *W. G. Sebald*, 19, 142; Lise Patt, "Searching for Sebald: What I Know for Sure," in *Searching for Sebald: Photography After W. G. Sebald*, ed. Lise Patt (Los Angeles: Institute of Cultural Inquiry, 2007), 146.
29 Sebald writes this German phrase in the margin of page 39 in his copy of Hanns Zischler's *Kafka geht ins Kino* (Reinbek: Rowohlt, 1996). The relevant passage in Zischler's text, to which this note refers, contains remarks about the hodgepodge of stories gathered in the newsreel synopses that commonly preceded feature film presentations at European cinema houses during Kafka's lifetime. Sebald obviously saw the format of these newsreel compilations as another analogue for the narrative technique he practiced in *Die Ringe des Saturn*.

correspondences" ("Wahlverwandtschaften und Korrespondenzen"), to cite a phrase that Sebald's narrator employs in reference to the intersecting lines that connect his own life with that of his friend Michael Hamburger, and Hamburger's life to that of the poet Friedrich Hölderlin (*Ringe* 227/182). The figure of the anthemion thus provides a manner of conceptualizing a unifying order for what Silke Horstkotte has termed the "spatio-temporal topography" of Sebald's narrative,[30] a textual form in which the narrator and the reader are not bound to linear time, but can follow a variety of different paths that branch off at random intervals from the primary narrative line.

It might seem like a statement of the obvious to assert that Sebald's *Die Ringe des Saturn* is not strictly speaking either an apothegmatic, anecdotal, or aphoristic collection. It shares with such works a mosaic-like texture in which seemingly autonomous fragments are arranged together by the simple mechanism of juxtaposition and integration into a contained and circumscribed group. But this text has one primary feature that sets it apart: its constitution as an explicitly *narrative* work, which requires that its individual episodes occur in temporal succession, as a series of linear events that somehow flow naturally into one another. The universe of *Die Ringe des Saturn* is largely without plot, at least to the extent that there is no overriding story or *mythos*, aside from the rudimentary frame of the narrator's journey, that lends it cohesion. As James Olney once noted, "In a universe where plot scarcely obtains at all—where, effectively, it either does not exist or is indistinguishable from chaos—there can be no discernible, determinable, or shapeable meaning."[31] Yet Sebald manages to *ascribe* meaning to the unplotted arrangement of events and episodes in his text by establishing a unifying narrative tone, voice, and emotional tenor—commonly designated as melancholic—but also by suturing together seemingly disparate textual fragments by indicating the affinities—elective or otherwise—and correspondences that intrinsically link them. Sebald's narrator constantly faces the challenge either of uncovering or of *inventing* transitions that facilitate the movement from one episode to the next. He is constantly involved in acts of narrative problem-solving, in the sense that he must repeatedly find ways to bridge or plug the gaps in the narrative logic that would otherwise disrupt the cogency of his textual meanderings. Only by creating transitions that superimpose a sequential logic on the otherwise random order of episodes can Sebald's narrative make pretense to

---

30 Silke Horstkotte, "Visual Memory and Ekphrasis in W. G. Sebald's *The Rings of Saturn*," *English Language Notes* 44, no. 2 (Fall/Winter 2006): 127.

31 James Olney, *Memory and Narrative: The Weave of Life-Writing* (Chicago: University of Chicago Press, 1998), 296.

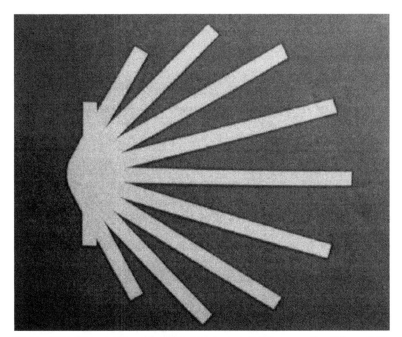

Figure 7.3: The emblem for the European *Jakobswege*, the Way of St. James.

coherence and cohesion. In this respect, as well, the encyclopedic world of Borges's Tlön serves as one of Sebald's prototypes, for the logic of this world, as Borges remarks, is explicitly "successive and temporal, not spatial." As a result, the people of Tlön "conceive the universe as a series of mental processes which do not develop in space but successively in time," and hence for them all relations are constituted by a rudimentary "association of ideas."[32] The world of Tlön is radically *narrative* in character, and its temporal successions, as in Sebald's *Die Ringe des Saturn*, are constructed by means of associative processes that undermine spatial disparity by translating space into temporal sequence. This is precisely how the *videre*-structure of the encyclopedia operates: it draws lines of association, based on ideas, connections, and intrinsic linkages, between elements that have no spatial proximity in the topography of the encyclopedia itself. It links these disparate elements in a logical, a narrative sequence, whose transition is marked by the graphic sign →, the arrow of cross-reference that stands as the symbol for this process of conceptual association.

---

32 Borges, "Tlön, Uqbar, Orbis Tertius," 8–9.

Sebald and his narrator incorporate into their text a prototype for this sort of flexible, mobile, and spontaneous creativity, which selects among a bounty of remnants and disparate fragments in order to piece together finished works: the activity of the Ashbury sisters, Catherine, Clarissa, and Christina, who spend several hours every day in a north-facing room of their estate, "where they had stored great quantities of remnant fabrics" ("wo sie Unmengen von Stoffresten aufgehäuft hatten"). Selecting pieces from among this surplus of odds and ends, they stitch them together to make "multi-coloured pillowcases, counter-panes and similar items" ("vielfarbige Kissenbezüge, Bettüberwürfe und dergleichen mehr"; 264/212). However, like a threefold version of Odysseus's Penelope, they dismantle these quilt-like creations on subsequent days, so that their labors resemble a constant process of construction, deconstruction, and renewed construction, ad infinitum. Speculating about the possible motivations that underlie this seemingly senseless activity, the narrator provides two possible explanations. The first is economic in nature: since there are no buyers for the products they create, the sisters simply take them apart again, bowing to the reality of their economic purposelessness. The second explanation, however, is quite different:

Möglich auch, daß ihnen [den Ashbury Töchtern] in ihrer Phantasie etwas von solch außergewöhnlicher Schönheit vorschwebte, daß die fertigen Arbeiten sie unfehlbar enttäuschten, dachte ich, als sie mir bei einem meiner Besuche in ihrer Werkstatt ein paar der Zertrennung entgangene Stücke zeigten, denn eines davon zumindest, ein aus Hunderten von Seidenfetzchen zusammengesetztes, mit Seidenfäden besticktes oder vielmehr spinnennetzartig überwobenes Brautkleid, das an einer kopflosen Schneiderpuppe hing, war ein beinahe ans Lebendige heranreichendes Farbenkunstwerk von einer Pracht und Vollendung, daß ich damals meinen Augen so wenig traute wie heute meiner Erinnerung. (*Ringe* 264–5)
[It was also possible that in their [the Ashbury daughters'] imagination they envisaged something of such extraordinary beauty that the work they completed invariably disappointed them. At least that was what I thought, when on one of my visits to their workshop they showed me the pieces that had been spared the unstitching. One of them, a bridal gown made of hundreds of scraps of silk embroidered with silken thread, or rather woven over cobweb-fashion, which hung on a headless tailor's dummy, was a work of art so colourful and of such intricacy and perfection that it seemed almost to have come to life, and at the time I could no more believe my eyes than now I can trust my memory. (*Rings* 212)]

According to the logic of this interpretation, the sisters are involved in an ongoing project of aesthetic experimentation. Their aim is to find the perfect combination of remnants that, sewn together according to a prescribed pattern, will realize the extraordinary aesthetic ideal that guides their enterprise. When this is successful, they produce works of such magnificence and beauty that the narrator compares them to nearly perfect works of art. We will examine this example in the next chapter in more detail; germane in the present context is not so much the unusual aesthetic achievement these women attain, but instead the process of trial and error, combination and recombination, that characterizes their creative labors. They proceed by constantly making spontaneous judgments about what remnants best fit together in a manner that will conform to their ideal, and the addition of each new fragment to the evolving whole requires new decisions about which piece of cloth should be the next one added and where it should be sewn together with the others. The work of art is generated by means of a procedure that resembles a kind of strategic game, like moves on a chess board, in which decisions about a new move can only be made once the prior one has been completed and its effects calculated and digested. The remnants of cloth themselves remain throughout this process principally interchangeable, with all aesthetic significance ultimately reducible to their interstices, to the decisions about how they should fit together. What is crucial about the idealized aesthetic entities produced by the Ashbury sisters is precisely the *choosing* and the *stitching*, the acts of transition that bring particular remnants into proximity with others based on intuitions or conscious decisions about their potential "elective affinities and correspondences." The *what* of the aesthetic composition, its substance, has been subordinated to the *how*, the manner and pattern by which the composite elements are put together. My point is that Sebald's *Die Ringe des Saturn* itself represents a mosaic-like narrative of precisely this sort, in which the aesthetic achievement rests not so much on the nature of its individual episodes, but rather on the artistry that builds them into a conglomerate narrative in which the ruptures between disintegrative elements are interlinked and conjoined in meaningful ways. Sebald's art is principally an art of transition, of "sewing" together fragments of textually encoded history—Thomas Browne's "Buchstaben auf dem Papier" ("letters on the page"; *Ringe* 337–8/271)—in such a way that they constitute a composite work of breathtaking artistry and perfection.

In order to exemplify the significant role narrative transitions play in Sebald's text, as well as to expose the complex consideration and profound reflection invested in these segues that weave the disparate episodes into an apparently seamless but nevertheless unplotted storyline, I will chart the course by which a single chapter develops.

The opening chapter of *Die Ringe des Saturn* represents an appropriate object for this exercise, in part because it establishes a pattern for the remainder of the narrative, in part because the path along which it meanders is characterized by unusual diversity and sharp turns in direction. Sebald's text begins with his patented incipit formula, in which the narrator succinctly identifies himself, locates temporally the action of the text in August of 1992, the "dog days" of summer, and names his project as a recounting of the journey he undertook at this time, wandering the Suffolk coastline. His travels are motivated, he notes, by a specific desire, the "hope of dispelling the emptiness that takes hold of me whenever I have completed a long stint of work" ("Hoffnung, der nach dem Abschluß einer größeren Arbeit in mir sich ausbreitenden Leere entkommen zu können"; 9/3). He goes on to indicate the relative success of this endeavor in providing the desired relief, but then reverts to a longer discussion of melancholy as an emotional pathology and the ways in which his experiences during this pilgrimage fueled "das lähmende Grauen," the "paralyzing horror" that overcame him both during and after this trip (9/3). This then leads, by means of a logical sequence that is both causal and metaphorical in nature, to a discussion of the physical condition in which the narrator was dispatched to a hospital exactly one year after beginning his journey: the "paralyzing horror" of what he has experienced results in a physical paralysis (*Lähmung*) that requires medical attention and confines him for a period of time to a hospital bed. The narrator succeeds not only in surreptitiously shifting to a different temporal dimension, to a time post-dating his trip by one year, but also in radically altering the emotional tenor from one of hope to one of utter despair, manifest physically in the contrast between the free mobility of his journey and the absolute paralysis that is one of its consequences. The pivot on which this transformation turns is the phrase "Andererseits jedoch" ("I wonder now, however"; 9/3), with which the third sentence of the text begins. Actively engaging his memory of this stay in the hospital ("Genau entsinne ich mich noch"; "I can remember precisely"; 10/4), the narrator details the situation in his hospital room, the view out his window (which is documented in the text's first illustration), and a comparison between his own physical situation and that of the insect Gregor Samsa in Franz Kafka's short story "Die Verwandlung" ("The Metamorphosis"). This intertextual connection lends the narrator's situation an almost mythic dimension, one that is heightened by a further allusion to an author and work Sebald knew very well: to Thomas Bernhard's novel *Wittgensteins Neffe* (*Wittgenstein's Nephew*), in which the first-person narrator lies immobile in a hospital bed while convalescing from a lung operation and reminisces about his friendship with Paul Wittgenstein, the cousin of the famous philosopher

Ludwig.[33] The narrative situation with which Sebald's text begins thus is constructed as a multilayered intertextual nodal point.

The first major transition in Sebald's narrative comes on the fourth page, when the narrator steps out of his retrospective demeanor and refers to the present moment in which he is composing the final manuscript of this very work, which he locates as a little over a year after his release from the hospital. This temporal marker serves to justify the manner in which the very act of recording his reminiscences reminds the narrator that while he lay in his hospital room, his colleague Michael Parkinson, who is now deceased, was still alive. This thought comes to the narrator "zwangsläufig," in a compulsory manner (12/5), as though this strained associative linkage were mandatory rather than merely serendipitous. And indeed, the contrast between mobility and stasis that characterized the narrator's own transformation builds the link to Parkinson's condition, exaggerated into the juxtaposition between the vitality of life and rigor mortis. From this the narrator moves immediately to a discussion of another former colleague, Janine Dakyns, whose death shortly after that of Michael Parkinson is linked causally with her inability to come to terms emotionally with his unexpected passing (14/7). Mention of her scholarly interest in Flaubert motivates an extended excursus about this writer's scruples regarding his writing and his larger worldview, deliberations that have a certain self-reflective relevance for Sebald's own text. Reminiscing on the times he sat with Janine in her office engaged in these discussions, the narrator provides a detailed description of her "paper universe," the chaos of books, papers, and documents that are on the verge of taking over her office, a chaos that nevertheless seems to be subtended by an inscrutable order (17/9). Janine's name then forms the trigger for the next longer episode, an exposition of the narrator's research into the seventeenth-century Norwich physician Sir Thomas Browne: for Janine was the person who put the narrator in touch with the local authority on this figure, Anthony Batty Shaw. At this point Sebald's text doubles back to make a connection to the recollection of his stay in the Norwich hospital, for this is where Thomas Browne's skull was purportedly once deposited and stored. This, in turn, leads to a meditation on the odyssey to which this skull was subjected, which gives way to reflections on burial rites, Browne's research on the burial urns discovered near Norwich, and a brief sketch of his life (17–20/9–12).

At this point Sebald's text again radically shifts directions, exploiting the temporal parallel between Browne's medical studies and the public dissection of the corpse of the criminal Aris Kindt in Holland as the

---

33 Thomas Bernhard, *Wittgensteins Neffe: Eine Freundschaft* (Frankfurt am Main: Suhrkamp, 1987), 7–8; *Wittgenstein's Nephew* (New York: Knopf, 1989), 3–4.

connective tissue, an event recorded by Rembrandt in his famous painting *The Anatomy Lesson of Dr. Nicolaas Tulp*. This temporal coincidence motivates the extensive discussion of anatomical practices at that time, the critique of these practices inscribed—according to Sebald's narrator—into Rembrandt's painting, and more general critical reflections on the Cartesian marginalization of the body in favor of the ethereal spirit. This latter connection is underwritten by the temporal coincidence between the lives of Rembrandt, Browne, and Descartes, as well as by the speculation that Descartes and Browne might have been present for this dissection (20–5/12–17). At this point the narrative again folds back upon itself, returning, via questions about how Browne might have reacted to this anatomy lesson, to a reference to Browne's remarks about how the English fog is capable of penetrating one's body and enveloping the brain, and shifting from there to autobiographical reminiscences about the "fog" that veiled the narrator's mind while he lay in his hospital bed under the influence of painkilling narcotics (25–6/17). We witness here how Sebald's narrative keeps circling back on itself, tying up loose ends by knotting them together via persistent cross-references to prior episodes. Transitions in Sebald's text thus move in two principal directions: they impel the forward movement of the narrative by splicing one element to another; but they also move backward by connecting subsequent elements with episodes that have gone before. Sebald's segues thus imitate what I have called the *videre*-structure of the encyclopedia, constructing an ever more intricate pattern of narrative branches, but also interlinking these episodic lines by means of retrospective cross-references.

Having returned to his point of departure—the hospital stay that resulted from his journey along the Suffolk coastline—Sebald's narrator documents the fantasies that accompanied his drug-induced stupor, the visions and disconnected sounds that invade his dreams, and the memory of seeing a contrail cut across the portion of sky visible from his hospital window. His inability to discern the airplane that generates this contrail leads to a more general meditation on the "invisibility and intangibility of that which moves us" ("Unsichtbarkeit und Unfaßbarkeit dessen, was uns bewegt"; 27/18), which subsequently allows the narrator to segue back to his consideration of Thomas Browne, who similarly questions the impulses that underlie the world and human motivations. This shift from an empirical observation in one temporal plane, to a general metaphysical speculation, through to a (pseudo-)historical account of Browne's attitudes and opinions can be taken as exemplary of the radical course-changes made possible by Sebald's segues. They allow his narrator to make great thematic and temporal leaps, as though he were wearing narrative seven-league boots, without creating the impression that a rupture has opened up in the narrative logic of the text. The same can be said about the next textual transition, which moves by means of metaphorical association from the floating sensation caused by the narrator's painkillers, to a description of the elevated perspective provided by a ride in a hot-air balloon, to the "elevation," the "Erhabenheit" of Thomas Browne's writing style (28/18). If Browne's style itself is said to operate "with complex metaphors and analogies, and constructing labyrinthine sentences" ("mit weit ausufernden Metaphern und Analogien, labyrinthische ... Satzgebilde"; 28/19), then this simultaneously provides an appropriate self-reflection on the method, procedure, and style employed by Sebald's narrator himself, and represents a commentary on the logic of metaphor, association, and analogy that drives his artful transitions.

This opening chapter continues by supplying further reflections on Thomas Browne's sense of the "order of things" and his belief in an analogical structure that dictates how certain patterns, such as the form of the quincunx, recur in diverse places throughout the natural world (29–32/20–2). This opens onto a summary of Browne's *Pseudodoxica Epidemica*, an encyclopedic work that contains a taxonomy of diverse real and imaginary creatures, and this in turn invokes in the narrator an association with Borges's *Book of Imaginary Beings*. This ultimately gives way, by association, to the figure of "Baldanders," the changeling from Grimmelshausen's picaresque novel *Der abenteuerliche Simplicissimus*, only to culminate in a pessimistic rumination on the "process of consuming and being consumed" and the "shadow of annihilation" ("Prozeß des Fressens und des Gefressenwerdens"; "Schatten der Zerstörung"; 33/23–4) that haunt all things and inhabit all human history. The chapter closes with an extended recounting of motifs from Browne's life and works in which the narrator's melancholic projections and the moroseness of Browne's worldview intermingle to the point of being veritably indistinguishable. To be sure, at its conclusion this chapter returns to the promise of hope and hopefulness with which it began: Browne's faith in the indestructibility of the human soul is juxtaposed with his scientific and medical awareness of the decrepitude of the human body, so that even in the face of natural destruction and decline he looks for "sign[s] of the mysterious capacity for transmigration he has so often observed in caterpillars and moths" ("Spuren der geheimnisvollen Fähigkeit zur Transmigration, die er an den Raupen und Faltern so oft studiert hat"; 37/26). Sebald's text actually practices what Browne preaches: its amazing facility to build transitions and to shift the weight of its thematic concerns among a wide array of individuals, episodes, events, and reflective meditations enacts this transmigration of souls as a transmigration of meanings. The transitions his narrator constructs form the pathways on which these migrations occur: they are the junction boxes that allow the narrative to shift from one element to the next, but that also form nodal points at which various thematic lines converge and intersect. Of course, Sebald's text has much greater depth than this brief summary of its first chapter could hope to plumb. The point is merely to give a concrete illustration of the significant role narrative transitions play as constitutive features of this work, as well as to indicate the great investment of ingenuity that goes into their formulation. It is worth repeating that Sebald's art is an art of transition, an art of the trans-migration and transfiguration of meaning that occurs at the joints at which individual episodes are brought together in a kind of narrative embrace, a meaningful kiss.

I will close this chapter by examining some theoretical models that help to elucidate, describe, or account for Sebald's art of transition. The most obvious prototype—obvious because Sebald himself commented on its significance for his method and mode of thought—is Claude Lévi-Strauss's notion of *bricolage* and its practitioner, the *bricoleur*, terms that Sebald frequently employs either in their French original or in their standard German translations of *Bastelei* and *der Bastler*.[34] In a 1993 interview with Sigrid Löffler, Sebald pointedly remarked, "I operate according to the system of *bricolage*—as it was understood by Lévi-Strauss. It's a form of savage work, of pre-rationalist thinking, where one mucks around long enough among random findings until it all somehow comes together" ("Ich arbeite nach dem System der Bricolage—im Sinne von Lévi-Strauss. Das ist eine Form von wildem Arbeiten, von vorrationalem Denken, wo man in zufällig akkumulierten Fundstücken so lange herumwühlt, bis sie sich irgendwie zusammen-reimen"; *"Auf ungeheuer dünnem Eis"* 84). What stands out about this statement is the experimental, combinatorial practice it depicts: the artist/narrator grubs around in the remnants and fragments he or she has at his or her disposal and repeatedly combines and recombines them until they assume a configuration that appears, for inexplicable reasons, to make sense. This is precisely the practice modeled by the Ashbury sisters. In *Austerlitz*, Sebald has his eponymous character enact this combinatorial practice as a kind of visual game in which he constantly orders and reorders his own photograph collection until the individual pictures fall into "an order depending on their family resemblances" ("eine aus Familienähnlichkeiten sich ergebende

34 On Sebald's affinities with the concept of *bricolage*, see Darby, "Landscape and Memory," 275; Öhlschläger, *Beschädigtes Leben*, 168, 182; and Richard Sheppard, "Dexter—Sinister: Some Observations on Decrypting the Mors Code in the Work of W. G. Sebald," *Journal of European Studies* 35, no. 4 (December 2005): 424.

Ordnung"; *Austerlitz* 172/119). The term "Familienähnlichkeiten" is borrowed from Ludwig Wittgenstein, and it instantiates one of those "hauntings" by Wittgenstein's ghost that spook throughout Sebald's works. Here its significance lies in the fact that this term designates that principle of conglomeration or agglomeration by which Sebald's texts are structured. We can imagine Sebald's narrator in *Die Ringe des Saturn* following a similar procedure, pursuing "family resemblances" as he orders and reorders the episodes of this text into meaningful configurations. The French word *bricolage*, significantly, derives from the game of billiards, where it designates the unpredictable ricochet of a ball given the changing configurations it enters into with the other moving balls on the table and the cushions against which it bounces.[35]

Lévi-Strauss himself chose another metaphor to describe the explicitly combinatorial and fundamentally creative work of the *bricoleur*: that of a kaleidoscope, an instrument that gathers together a set of fragments whose interrelationships can be constantly reconfigured by turning the instrument in one's hand.[36] Although in the case of the kaleidoscope the incessant re-formation of the fragments into new patterns is largely a function of chance—what Lévi-Strauss in another passage calls "objective hazard," relying on a concept first promulgated by the French Surrealists[37]—the intervention of the human subject who manipulates the kaleidoscope itself, and who halts its motion once it generates a pattern that attracts attention, is also a requisite part of this combinatorial practice. In his personal copy of the German translation of Lévi-Strauss's book, Sebald placed two double lines in the margin next to this passage describing the operation of the kaleidoscope.[38] His notes to this text largely focus on matters of *bricolage* and what Lévi-Strauss calls "mythic" or "savage" thought, in particular its opposition to the conceptualizing strategy of the engineer and the natural scientist. In Lévi-Strauss's understanding, mythic thought, for which the process of *bricolage* is representative, expresses a protest against the systematic and rationalistic character of scientific modes of conceptualization. Sebald underlines in his

35 Ursula Renner, "Fundstücke: Zu W. G. Sebalds *Austerlitz*," *Der Deutschunterricht* 57, no. 4 (2005): 24.

36 Claude Lévi-Strauss, *Das wilde Denken*, trans. Hans Naumann (Frankfurt am Main: Suhrkamp, 1973), 50; *The Savage Mind*, trans. George Weidenfeld and Nicolson Ltd. (Chicago: University of Chicago Press, 1966), 36.

37 Lévi-Strauss, *Das wilde Denken*, 34; *The Savage Mind*, 21.

38 Sebald also marked the passage dealing with "objective coincidence," "objektiven Zufall" in the German translation, and he drew a line from this phrase down to the bottom of the page, where he wrote the cryptic collection of English and German words: "Humor / Surprise / Kritik [critique] / Trauer [grief] / Fragen. [inquiry] / neue Metaphysik [new metaphysics]."

text the passage in which Lévi-Strauss asserts the specifically critical function of mythic thought vis-à-vis the ordered hierarchies of scientific thinking: "<u>Mythical thought for its part is imprisoned in the events and experiences which it never tires of ordering and re-ordering in its search to find in them a meaning.</u> But it also acts as a liberator by its <u>protest</u> against the idea that anything can be meaningless with which science at first resigned itself to a compromise" ("<u>Und das mythische Denken ist nicht nur der Gefangene von Ereignissen und Erfahrungen, die es unablässig ordnet und neuordnet, um in ihnen einen Sinn zu entdecken; es ist auch befreiend: durch den Protest</u>, den es gegen den Un-Sinn erhebt, mit dem die Wissenschaft zunächst resignierend einen Kompromiß schloß").[39] The endless reordering of phenomena undertaken by the *bricoleur*, as the modern practitioner of mythic thought, thus represents a critical attempt to destabilize the stagnant and ossified order of rational, taxonomic, systematic thinking. In this regard, *bricolage*, as implemented in Sebald's art of transition and modeled in the artistic practice of the Ashbury sisters (among others), codifies on the level of textual practice the rationality-critical thrust that forms such a prominent subtext to *Die Ringe des Saturn*.[40]

The moment of protest embodied in the combinatorial practice of the *bricoleur* will concern us in more detail in the discussion of Michel de Certeau's conception of the "tactic," emblematic of what he calls "procedures of everyday creativity,"[41] which are similarly intended to subvert the dominant logic and hierarchies of advanced human societies. For the moment, I want to focus on a notion Sebald adopted from Konrad Lorenz's critical archaeology of human cognition, *Die Rückseite des Spiegels* (*Behind the Mirror*), which bears a subtitle that contains a concept central to Sebald's mode of thought, "Naturgeschichte": *Versuch einer Naturgeschichte menschlichen Erkennens* (*A Search for a Natural History of Human Knowledge*). A profusely annotated copy of this text is contained in Sebald's working library, and his marginalia indicate a special interest in the notion of the *fulguratio*, a spark or

---

39   Lévi-Strauss, *Das wilde Denken*, 35–6; *Savage Mind*, 22. The underlining in my citation reflects the underlines Sebald made in his copy of Lévi-Strauss's text.

40   On the critique of "enlightened" thinking that runs throughout Sebald's text, see especially Theisen, "A Natural History of Destruction," 563, who emphasizes how he lambastes forms of knowledge organized into schemas and grids. Anne Fuchs, "'Ein Hauptkapitel der Geschichte der Unterwerfung': Representations of Nature in W. G. Sebald's *Die Ringe des Saturn*," in *W. G. Sebald and the Writing of History*, ed. Anne Fuchs and J. J. Long (Würzburg: Königshausen & Neumann, 2007), 125, also discusses the critique of strategies for rational mastery in Sebald's text.

41   Michel de Certeau, *The Practice of Everyday Life*, trans. Steven Rendall (Berkeley: University of California Press, 1984), xiv.

lightning bolt that suddenly and unforeseeably connects two otherwise unrelated systems or concepts. Lorenz attributes this idea to the medieval theistic philosophers, who used the term to designate any act in which something is created out of nothing.[42] Lorenz does not apply it principally to conscious acts of human creativity; rather, he sees it at work in evolutionary development, where the *fulguratio* manifests itself as an unpredictable quantum leap, an unforeseeable emergence generated at the unexpected junction or juxtaposition of two discrete systems. He writes—and Sebald underlines this passage—"But each act of construction has consisted of a *fulguratio*, a historically unique event in phylogeny which has always had a chance quality about it—the quality, one might say, of something invented" ("Jeder Akt des Aufbaus aber bestand aus einer 'Fulguratio,' die sich in historischer Einmaligkeit in der Stammesgeschichte ereignete, und dieses Ereignis trug jedesmal den Charakter des Zufälligen, wenn man will, den einer *Erfindung*").[43] Lorenz articulates a succinct summary of the Sebaldian notion of coincidence. More important for the arguments pursued here is his association of the fulguration with randomly generated points of transition or spontaneous connections—he uses the metaphor of the short-circuit[44]—that arise when two otherwise independent systems are linked with one another. These newly created pathways do not simply reflect an unconscious creativity, but also have the potential to disrupt more traditional and accepted patterns of thought and behavior. They introduce what Lorenz terms "adaptive modifications" into the evolutionary development of an entire species, and they thereby counteract the inertia of habituation.[45] Lorenz's fulguration thus provides another name for the *videre*-structure of Sebald's narrative transitions: it designates that mode of surprising and creative combination that marks the narrative segues between themes, episodes, and events typical of the compositional texture of *Die Ringe des Saturn*.

If we turn, finally, to Michel de Certeau's conception of the "tactic," we can better discern the process of spontaneous, inventive negotiation in which Sebald's narrator is involved at every narrative juncture in this text, and the fundamentally critical, anti-systematic, deconstructive impulse that underlies this (re)combinatory practice. For Certeau, the

42 Konrad Lorenz, *Die Rückseite des Spiegels: Versuch einer Naturgeschichte menschlichen Erkennens* (Munich: DTV, 1979), 47; *Behind the Mirror: A Search for a Natural History of Human Knowledge*, trans. Ronald Taylor (London: Methuen, 1977), 29. See Judith R. Ryan, "Fulgurations: Sebald and Surrealism," *Germanic Review* 82 (2007): 234, who points to the significance of this concept for Sebald's textual practice.

43 Lorenz, *Die Rückseite des Spiegels*, 55; *Behind the Mirror*, 35 [translation modified].

44 Lorenz, *Die Rückseite des Spiegels*, 49; *Behind the Mirror*, 30.

45 Lorenz, *Die Rückseite des Spiegels*, 89; *Behind the Mirror*, 64.

tactic—like the other so-called "practices of everyday life" he delineates—is a fundamentally improvisational act formulated in response to demands promulgated by "[p]olitical, economic, and scientific rationality." Explicitly referring to Lévi-Strauss's notion of *bricolage*, Certeau defines what he broadly calls "procedures of everyday creativity" as "combinatory or utilizing modes of consumption," or as "an art of combination which cannot be dissociated from an art of using."[46] If social, political, and economic orders and hierarchies deploy "strategies" in order to subjugate individual subjects to an overarching will and calculus of power, individuals, in turn, respond by attempting to subvert, blunt, or appropriate these strategies by turning them to their own critical advantage. These subversive turns are what Certeau calls "tactics." Tactics, Certeau writes, "must constantly manipulate events in order to turn them into 'opportunities.' The weak must continually turn to their own ends forces alien to them."[47] In his further reflections on this process of deflective "turning," by which the strategy imposed by the sociopolitical order is co-opted for the purposes of resistance and protest, Certeau associates it with rhetorical figures in general, but in particular with metaphorical tropes, "turns" of phrase. Rhetorical devices represent "internal manipulations" of the rationally codified system of language, and as such they "inscribe in ordinary language the ruses, displacements, ellipses, etc., that scientific reason has eliminated from operational discourses in order to constitute 'proper' meanings."[48]

In a formulation that seems tailored to the practices Sebald's narrator pursues in *Die Ringe des Saturn*, Certeau defines "tactical trajectories" as the form-giving properties that "according to their own criteria, select fragments taken from the vast ensembles of production in order to compose new stories with them."[49] Based on these cues from Certeau, one could describe Sebald's project in *Die Ringe des Saturn* as a compilation of fragments drawn from the history of Western knowledge, rational practice, and power politics that are creatively recombined so as to form "tactical trajectories" in which they assume a meaning that is at odds with their traditional and accepted interpretations. Sebald's narrator functions not merely as the critical consciousness that selects and privileges certain elements from the repertoire of this history of Western political, economic, and social ascendancy—for which the episodes dealing with Western colonialism are especially emblematic—but also as a creative manipulator in charge of reconfiguring these

46 Certeau, *The Practice of Everyday Life*, xix, xiv–xv.
47 Ibid., xix.
48 Ibid., 23–4.
49 Ibid., 35.

historical fragments into a new "story." In addition, he serves as a spontaneous negotiator who improvises transitions that lend this recombination the guise of a seamless and necessary narrative—that is, he follows a *tactical* trajectory.

Certeau highlights this improvisational quality of everyday critical practices when he compares them with the moves one makes while playing games. For Certeau, games serve precisely as repositories for such tactics insofar as they demand from the game-player not only adherence to a proscribed set of rules—the laws of social and political existence that can only be transgressed under pain of severe punishment—but also spontaneous responses to the specific situations presented by the progression of the game at any given moment, in which we are called upon to apply these rules creatively and selectively so as to ensure the most positive outcome.[50] Sebald's narrator is the tactician or game-player *par excellence* in this sense delineated by Certeau. He practices a brand of impromptu narrative, a form of spontaneous improvisation similar to that performed by certain comedy troupes, such as Chicago's Second City, when they enact ad-lib dramas suggested by immediate cues from their audience. Sebald's narrator is a negotiator of transitions, a master at selecting from and recombining the "remnants" of Western intellectual and political history in order to produce a narrative compilation that, much like the patchwork fabric creations of the Ashbury sisters, achieves a mysterious "Pracht und Vollendung," an unforeseeable "intricacy and perfection" (*Ringe* 265/212). Sebald's text represents a kind of encyclopedically ordered history of modern Western culture, broken into individual fragments that can be reconnected and reordered, by means of creative "fulgurations" or instituted cross-references, into a critically subversive narrative of destruction, desolation, sociopolitical and economic mastery, and brutal subjugation: it is transformed into what Sebald's narrator identifies as a "history of subjugation" ("Geschichte der Unterwerfung"; *Ringe* 24/13). This critical rewriting and recombining of the past represents a salient dimension of Sebald's poetics of history.

At the same time, Sebald's art of transition is notable for its very lack of notability: the transitions he negotiates in order to resplice the remnants of this history appear so smooth and natural as to be veritably transparent—as evidenced by the paucity of critical attention they have attracted. Yet the impression of continuity, completeness, and closure that this text evokes depends fundamentally on the narrator's subtle art of transition. Sebald's segues assume the crucial function of *performing* contingency, of forging connections, creating

---

50 Ibid., 22.

proximities, constructing metonymic and narrative linkages that have the appearance of (un)natural coincidences. The much-vaunted contingencies that dominate Sebald's text are, in fact, *staged* contingencies. The trick is to make them look like they are *not* merely staged. Yet they are the products of conscious intervention on the part of Sebald's narrator, who embodies a manipulating presence, like the editorial genius responsible for the compilation of Borges's encyclopedic universe of Tlön. More than a mere compiler, this narrative consciousness is characterized above all by its capacity to choreograph subtle transitions and cross-references among disparate elements. Perhaps it bears repeating one final time that the essence of Sebald's artistry in *Die Ringe des Saturn* is an art of inventive transitioning, a creative practice that can best be understood as a fusion of revamped encyclopedic strategies, Lévi-Strauss's improvisational *bricolage*, Lorenz's spontaneous fulgurations, and Certeau's shrewdly subversive tactics. The history of Western civilization that emerges from this paratactic reordering and creative remembering (literally and figuratively) of its remnants and fragments is explicitly a *critical* history, one that bears little resemblance to the passive resignation of the chronic melancholic for which Sebald is commonly (mis)taken.

Eight Writing at the Roche Limit: Order and Entropy in *Die Ringe des Saturn*

"Nur diejenige Verworrenheit ist ein Chaos, aus der eine Welt entspringen kann."
["Confusion is chaotic only when it can give rise to a new world."]

Friedrich Schlegel, "Ideen" [Ideas] 71[1]

The Roche Limit, Oppositional Forces, and Historical Preservation

Contrary to the prevailing popular and scholarly view, Sebald's "travelogue" *Die Ringe des Saturn* is not a predominantly melancholic text—neither if we understand the term "melancholy" as a shorthand formula for a singular obsession with decline and destruction, nor if we identify it with unflinching nihilism and a morosely apocalyptic view of history.[2] As Martina Wagner-Egelhaaf has argued, this one-sided

---

1   Friedrich Schlegel, *Charakteristiken und Kritiken I*, vol. 2 of *Kritische Friedrich-Schlegel-Ausgabe*, ed. Ernst Behler and Hans Eichner, 21 vols (Paderborn: Schöningh, 1967), 263; *Philosophical Fragments*, trans. Peter Firchow (Minneapolis: University of Minnesota Press, 1991), 100.

2   This pessimistic take on Sebald's writing has been expressed most radically by Peter Morgan, "The Sign of Saturn: Melancholy, Homelessness and Apocalypse in W. G. Sebald's Prose Narratives," *German Life and Letters* 58, no. 1 (January 2005): 86–7, who locates Sebald in a line of German "romantic nihilists" and believes he subscribes to a heightened "cultural pessimism in which everything is interpreted under the sign of destruction and disorder." Similar views are articulated by Anna Pieger, "Melancholie als Reise- und Schreibbewegung: Zu W. G. Sebalds *Ringe des Saturn*," *Castrum Peregrini* 56, no. 278 (2007): 46, and Thomas von Steinaecker, "Zwischen schwarzem Tod und weißer Ewigkeit: Zum Grau auf den Abbildungen W. G. Sebalds," in *Verschiebebahnhöfe der Erinnerung: Zum Werk W. G. Sebalds*, ed. Sigurd Martin and Ingo Wintermeyer

view of the melancholic temperament represents a short circuit that
elides the more positive, constructive side that always accompanies
its brooding sense of decline. For the melancholic, "order and disorder
are reciprocally related to one another" ("Ordnung und Unordnung
sind wechselweise auf einander bezogen").[3] This assertion holds true
for Sebald's *Die Ringe des Saturn*, in which the focus on destruction and
disorder is continually counterbalanced by an insistence on order and
often extremely subtle forms of organization. Sebald's theme, as well as
the structure of his text, can best be conceived in terms of systems that
tend naturally toward entropy, but which attain relative equilibrium
through the strategic application of specific ordering principles, in
particular repetition, periodicity, and—understood literally—coincidence. These are some of the textual principles that help define Sebald's
literary aesthetics as a poetics of history. In his case, this dynamic of
order and disorder is weighted more toward the negative extreme of
decomposition and decline when he approaches traditional principles
of rational order, because he views them with profound skepticism,[4]
evincing a will to mastery so severe and uncompromising as to

(Würzburg: Königshausen & Neumann, 2007), 119–20. In a more balanced
reading, Claudia Albes, "Die Erkundung der Leere: Anmerkungen zu W.
G. Sebalds 'englische Wallfahrt' *Die Ringe des Saturn*," *Jahrbuch der deutschen
Schillergesellschaft* 46 (2002): 302–3, points to the hope for redemption that
constantly haunts Sebald's text. Maya Barzilai, "Melancholia as World History:
W. G. Sebald's Rewriting of Hegel in *Die Ringe des Saturn*," in *W. G. Sebald and
the Writing of History*, ed. Anne Fuchs and J. J. Long (Würzburg: Königshausen
& Neumann, 2007), 88–9, takes issue with Albes's more positive interpre-
tation, insisting that *Die Ringe des Saturn* evinces a "fixation on decline" that
brackets any redemptive perspective. I am generally in agreement with Ben
Hutchinson, "Die Leichtigkeit der Schwermut: W. G. Sebalds 'Kunst der
Levitation,'" *Jahrbuch der deutschen Schillergesellschaft* 50 (2006): 458, who insists
that although melancholy constitutes a prominent strain in Sebald's fiction,
reducing his work to this represents a monoperspectival distortion. Mark R.
McCulloh, *Understanding W. G. Sebald* (Columbia: University of South Carolina
Press, 2003), 148–9, in my view correctly maintains that although Sebald's take
on history emphasizes the catastrophic, the act of writing itself embodies a
moment of salvation and rescue.

3   Martina Wagner-Egelhaaf, *Die Melancholie der Literatur: Diskursgeschichte und
Textfiguration* (Stuttgart: Metzler, 1997), 117.

4   Several scholars have noted the critique of rationality and instrumental reason
in Sebald's prose narratives, without subjecting it to detailed analysis. See John
Beck, "Reading Room: Erosion and Sedimentation in Sebald's Suffolk," in *W.
G. Sebald: A Critical Companion*, ed. J. J. Long and Anne Whitehead (Seattle:
University of Washington Press, 2004), 75–6; Anne Fuchs, "'Ein Hauptkapitel
der Geschichte der Unterwerfung': Representations of Nature in W. G. Sebald's
Die Ringe des Saturn," in *W. G. Sebald and the Writing of History*, ed. Anne Fuchs
and J. J. Long (Würzburg: Königshausen & Neumann, 2007), 125; and Claudia

promote the very chaos and immanent destruction they are intended
to hold in check. This critical insight motivates a search for alternative
forms of organization that can counteract both entropic dissolution and
the uncompromising stability—the terror—of rational systems.
Sebald was powerfully influenced by Freudian theory, which views
the psychic constitution of the "healthy" individual as a delicate
equilibrium between Eros and Thanatos: an economy in which the
will to union and connection, on the one hand, and a drive toward
aggressive destruction, on the other, maintain a precarious balance in
the face of constant threats to this equilibrium.[5] Another movement that
left an indelible stamp on Sebald's intellectual physiognomy was the
critical theory of the Frankfurt School. He was a careful reader of Max
Horkheimer and Theodor Adorno's *Dialektik der Aufklärung* (*Dialectic of
Enlightenment*), with its incisive analysis of an instrumental reason that
attempts to overcome the irrationality of myth only to fall back itself
into a more barbarous form of mythology.[6] Sebald's worldview appears
so bleak precisely because he attacks those rational strategies developed
in European culture since the Renaissance and Enlightenment, viewing
them as subject to a perverse dialectic that transforms them from tools
for managing chaos into instruments that exaggerate these entropic
tendencies. Similar to Adorno and Horkheimer, however, Sebald
supplements this critical thrust, which diagnoses a reversion of instrumental reason into a destructive totalitarian system, by a perspective
of hope that seeks alternative forms of order and organization capable
of escaping the confines of rational tyranny and authoritarian control.
Walter Benjamin's theme of redemption in the face of historical decline
and natural destruction, as articulated above all in his *Ursprung des
deutschen Trauerspiels* (*Origin of German Tragic Drama*), continually
hovers on the horizon of Sebald's thought and works. Thus, if *Die
Ringe des Saturn* presents a critique of rational strategies for ordering,
organizing, and managing human interactions with the life world,
it also models in its own textual makeup an alternative approach to

Öhlschläger, *Beschädigtes Leben. Erzählte Risse: W. G. Sebalds poetische Ordnung des Unglücks* (Freiburg im Breisgau: Rombach, 2006), 175–91.

5   Sebald's library contains a nearly complete, well worn, and annotated copy of the Freud *Studienausgabe* (Study edition). Sebald was also an engaged reader of Daniel Paul Schreber's *Denkwürdigkeiten eines Nervenkranken* (Memoires of my nervous illness), as evidenced by the heavily annotated copy in his library.

6   Aside from Sebald's profusely annotated copy of *Dialektik der Aufklärung*, numerous other works by Adorno are part of his working library, in addition to many texts by Walter Benjamin. On the impact Horkheimer and Adorno's critique of civilization had on Sebald, and his appropriation of the logic that underwrites the dialectic of Enlightenment, see Ben Hutchinson, *W. G. Sebald: Die dialektische Imagination* (Berlin: De Gruyter, 2009), 5–7.

the cognitive order and organization of things, one that opposes the tendency toward entropic decline and a fall into chaos by introducing constructive forces that inject equilibrium into the system. He offers an alternative to a hyper-rationalist, scientistic, and instrumental reason by developing his own form of *literary* and *textual* reasoning in the very constitution of his works, one that resists patterns of logical necessity and teleological inevitability and deserves the moniker of a *poetics* of history.[7] I will designate this mode of literary composition as a form of writing at the Roche limit.

If Sebald's texts generally evince that Post-Modern tendency to confuse center and periphery,[8] nowhere is this inversion more prominent than in *Die Ringe des Saturn*. This work's very title addresses the relationship between center and periphery, placing emphasis not on the planet Saturn itself, but instead on the rings that, while not constitutive of its planetary core, are its most characteristic feature. The third epigraph Sebald appends to this text focuses attention precisely on Saturn's rings, their purported composition of ice crystals and fragments of a previous moon destroyed by the planet's tidal forces, and the circular paths along which this debris orbits the planet. This epigraph not only identifies the centrality of the peripheral, but also *enacts* it in its own textual movement from center to margin: the quotation ends with a reference to the "Roch'sche Grenze," the Roche limit, the theory of French astronomer Édouard Roche that explains how the rings of Saturn developed and why they remain suspended at a certain distance from the planet. This seemingly marginal reference turns out to be central for the compositional structure of *Die Ringe des Saturn*. The Roche limit demarcates that place of balance where Saturn's tidal forces overwhelm the gravitational self-attraction of one of Saturn's former moons, causing it to break apart. It designates that place where the conflict between two countervailing forces reaches its apogee, but also a precarious equilibrium. At the Roche limit the satellite disintegrates, but its fragments remain in a state of suspension and form orbital rings. Beyond the Roche limit the satellite is able to coalesce due to its own gravitational force, while below the Roche limit it would plummet to final destruction by colliding with the planetary mass. The Roche limit names this point of stability, a state of suspended animation in which the fragments of a former moon are neither subject

---

7   Peter C. Pfeiffer, "Korrespondenz und Wahlverwandtschaft: W. G. Sebalds *Die Ringe des Saturn*," *Gegenwartsliteratur* 2 (2003): 237, comes closest to capturing the essence of Sebald's literary aesthetic when he calls it an "Erlebnisstruktur" ("experiential structure"), ordered according to patterns of correspondence and elective affinities.

8   Albes, "Die Erkundung der Leere," 280.

to ultimate decimation nor able to recoalesce into a single, unified entity.[9] The Roche limit thereby designates a situation in which a once unitary object exists in a nether state between decomposition and reamalgamation, between disorder and order, collapse and coalescence. At the Roche limit, entropy is held in abeyance; but the same can be said for the tendency toward centralizing order. In this sense the rings of Saturn represent an ordered disorder, a loosely organized amalgam of particles that have a discernible mutual relationship and that move in a periodic orbit around a central planetary body.

This is an apt description for the textual structure of *Die Ringe des Saturn*: it is constituted as a loose conglomerate of textual and thematic fragments that display relational affinities and that circulate in a periodic pattern of orbital recurrence.[10] This is the sense in which the compositional strategy of Sebald's text practices a form of writing at the Roche limit: it models a kind of literary composition that operates at the border between dispersion and coalescence, disorder and order, entropy and rigid system. To write at the Roche limit is to embrace the natural entropic tendencies of the universe, but also to pursue a form of non-totalizing organization that counters this trajectory of decline and institutes an equilibrium at which these contrary forces achieve relative stability.

The peregrinations of Sebald's narrator along the coastline of Suffolk emblematically choreograph the traversal of just such a liminal,

9   Neil Christian Pages, "Crossing Borders: Sebald, Handke, and the Pathological Vision," *Modern Austrian Literature* 40, no. 4 (December 2007): 85, points to the possible relevance of Martin Heidegger's distinction, made in *Was heißt Denken?* (*What Is Called Thinking*), between "Zerstörung" ("destruction") as partial ruination and "Verwüstung" as total "devastation." See Martin Heidegger, *Was heißt Denken?*, vol. 8 of *Gesamtausgabe*, ed. Paola-Ludovika Coriando (Frankfurt am Main: Klostermann, 2002), 31; *What Is Called Thinking?*, trans. Fred D. Wieck and J. Glenn Gray (New York: Harper & Row, 1968), 29. In this understanding, the rings of Saturn exemplify a state of incomplete destruction instead of absolute annihilation.

10 Deanne Blackler, *Reading W. G. Sebald: Adventure and Disobedience* (Rochester, NY: Camden House, 2007), 129, acknowledges the dualism of the Roche effect as a paradoxical preservation of the traces of destruction. She also notes, 172, that Sebald's text is structured as a planetary ring in which fragments are brought into a stable configuration. James Chandler, "About Loss: W. G. Sebald's Romantic Art of Memory," *South Atlantic Quarterly* 102 (2003): 242, asserts that the primary theme of *Die Ringe des Saturn* is the patterns formed in the wake of mass destruction. David Darby, "Landscape and Memory: Sebald's Redemption of History," in *W. G. Sebald: History, Memory, Trauma*, ed. Scott Denham and Mark McCulloh (Berlin: De Gruyter, 2006), 277, argues that Sebald's text maintains an alternative order, but he does not identify precisely what it entails.

contested space between the stability of terra firma and the destructive tidal forces of the sea. This is the theme addressed in the second epigraph Sebald appends to his narrative, the quotation from Joseph Conrad's letter to Marguerite Poradowski that invokes the horror of the foot traveler who wanders the coastline and recognizes it as a site of incessant violent struggle.[11] Characteristic of Sebald's method is the way the second and third epigraphs resonate with each other through their proximity, although the subjects they address—foot travel on the coast and planetary history—could hardly be less interrelated. This metonymic connection suggests that when Sebald's narrator traverses the Suffolk coast, he enacts a structural reiteration of the orbital path followed by the rings of Saturn. This pilgrimage takes place at the terrestrial version of the Roche limit, along the seam that marks the conflict between land and sea, relative stability and the forces of change. The shoreline, after all, is the site of elemental struggle at which the most famous work of German literature reaches its culmination, Goethe's *Faust* tragedy. Upon witnessing the *unproductive* but infinite energy of the ocean waves, Faust formulates his plan to gain a fiefdom along the coast, from which he will launch his massive colonial enterprise and his monumental project of mastery over nature, the winning of land from the sea.

Sie [Die Woge] schleicht heran, an abertausend Enden,
Unfruchtbar selbst, Unfruchtbarkeit zu spenden;
...
Da herrschet Well' auf Welle kraftbegeistet,
Zieht sich zurück, und es ist nichts geleistet,
Was zur Verzweiflung mich beängstigen könnte!
Zwecklose Kraft unbändiger Elemente!
Da wagt mein Geist, sich selbst zu überfliegen;
Hier möcht' ich kämpfen, dies möcht' ich besiegen.[12]
[The surging sea creeps into every corner,
barren itself and spreading barrenness,
...
Imbued with strength, wave after wave holds power
but then withdraws, and nothing's been accomplished—
a sight to drive me to despair,
this aimless strength of elemental forces!

---

11   Beck, "Reading Room," 85–6, recognizes the relevance of this analogy between the rings of Saturn and the Suffolk coastline, but he identifies them as sites of random organization rather than as places of vital conflict.
12   Johann Wolfgang von Goethe, *Faust: Der Tragödie erster und zweiter Teil*, ed. Erich Trunz, vol. 3 of *Goethes Werke* (Munich: Beck, 1978), lines 10212–21.

This inspires my mind to venture to new heights,
to wage war here against these forces and subdue them.[13]]

Contrary to Faust, who takes the example of the ocean's power as
inspiration for his own dream of a superhuman will to mastery,
Sebald's narrator feels awed and dwarfed by the omnipotence of the
ocean's might. The impossibility of Faust's aim to establish a utopian
community on the territory reclaimed from the ocean's blind force is
reflected in Sebald's narrative about the history of Dunwich, which but
for a few ruins has been entirely washed away by constant erosion, and
its population displaced:

> Dunwich mit seinen Türmen und vielen tausend Seelen ist
> aufgelöst in Wasser, Sand und Kies und dünne Luft. Wenn man
> von dem Grasplatz über dem Meer hinausblickt in die Richtung,
> wo die Stadt einst gewesen sein muß, dann spürt man den
> gewaltigen Sog der Leere. (*Ringe* 200)
> [Dunwich, with its towers and many thousand souls, has
> dissolved into water, sand and thin air. If you look out from the
> cliff-top across the sea towards where the town must once have
> been, you can sense the immense power of emptiness. (*Rings* 159)]

Sebald's narrator turns to a metaphor from physics in order to invoke
the destruction of this human settlement by the sea's inexorable power:
just as the laws of physics dictate that a vacuum will suck in matter, the
forces of erosion draw the seemingly stable artifacts of civilization into
the suction of their nothingness. Dunwich is an extreme example of
nature asserting its power and reassimilating a domain that had been
colonized by human civilization. The overgrown buildings and dilapidated estates that are mainstays of Sebald's narratives—one thinks of
Prior's Gate in "Dr. Henry Selwyn" (*Ausgewanderten* 8–9/3–4), or the
Ashbury estate and the manor house at Somerleyton in *Die Ringe des
Saturn* (271–2/217–18; 48–50/35–6)—are examples of a more gradual,
less violent reappropriation of cultivated territory and human history
by the forces of nature. Moreover, civilization itself at times mimics this
destructive power commonly ascribed to nature, as exemplified most
palpably in the various projects of political-economic domination that
run like a red thread through the historical accounts of *Die Ringe des
Saturn*, but also in the waves of cultivation that periodically transform
Dunwich Heath. The historical experience Sebald's narrator assimilates

---

13 Johann Wolfgang von Goethe, *Faust I and II*, ed. and trans. Stuart Atkins, vol. 2
    of *Goethe's Collected Works in Twelve Volumes* (Princeton, NJ: Princeton University
    Press, 1994–5), lines 10212–21.

throughout his wanderings along the Suffolk shoreline is exactly
the boom-or-bust periodicity with which places like Somerleyton,
Lowestoft, Southwold, or Dunwich Heath alternately flourish and
decline. As Hans Blumenberg has persuasively argued, the shore as
zone of conflict between firm land and the instable transformative
energy of the sea has commonly assumed a privileged status in the
Western imagination: it marks the place at which human beings, in the
manner of Goethe's Faust, first sense the challenge to self-overcoming
and immoderation.[14] A pilgrimage along the coast is thus ideally
suited—especially when it becomes the springboard for historical
study, as it does for Sebald's narrator—for generating experiences that
stimulate reflection upon the liminal existential position of humanity
and the endless struggle between the civilizing encroachments of
culture and the powerful destructive energies of nature. Sebald's
"natural history of destruction" names this complex space of interactions between civilization and nature.

The Baroque *vanitas* thematic that runs throughout *Die Ringe des
Saturn* forms just one side of this dialectic of inevitable destruction
and countervailing cultural preservation. This theme is woven into
the narrator's reflections on Grimmelshausen's picaresque novel
Simplicissimus, as well as into his deliberations on the writings of Sir
Thomas Browne. Especially in his guise as physician—that is, as an
investigator of the organic world—Browne represents a belief in the
inevitable destruction and disappearance of all natural and cultural
objects. It is logically consistent that after describing the astonishing
mutations of the fantasy figure "Baldanders" from *Simplicissimus*—the
name means "soon other," and hence signifies the process of incessant
transformation—the narrator segues into a commentary on Thomas
Browne's belief that all matter is destined for decline and destruction.

Ähnlich wie in diesem fortwährenden Prozeß des Fressens
und des Gefressenwerdens hat auch für Thomas Browne nichts
Bestand. Auf jeder neuen Form liegt schon der Schatten der
Zerstörung. Es verläuft nämlich die Geschichte jedes einzelnen,
die jedes Gemeinwesens und die der ganzen Welt nicht auf einem
stets weiter und schöner sich aufschwingenden Bogen, sondern
auf einer Bahn, die, nachdem der Meridian erreicht ist, hinunter-
führt in die Dunkelheit. (*Ringe* 33–4)
[Much as in this continuous process of consuming and being
consumed, nothing endures, in Thomas Browne's view. On every
new thing there lies already the shadow of annihilation. For the

---

14   Hans Blumenberg, *Schiffbruch mit Zuschauer: Paradigma einer Daseinsmetapher*
(Frankfurt am Main: Suhrkamp, 1979), 11.

history of every individual, of every social order, indeed of the whole world, does not describe an ever-widening, more and more wonderful arc, but rather follows a course which, once the meridian is reached, leads without fail down into the dark. (*Rings* 23–4)]

The transmutations of Baldanders are conceptualized as absolute inconstancy and—anachronistically—elided with the Darwinian evolutionary theme of a perpetual struggle for survival. Contrary to Hegel's optimistic view of history,[15] the natural course of organic, cultural, and historical development is not an arc that, like a parabola, moves increasingly upward; rather, it follows a trajectory that, like the path of a bullet, initially resists the pull of gravity and rises up, attains a zenith, but then succumbs to gravitational pull and falls back to earth. When he designates this arc as a "Bahn" ("course"), distinguishing it from a "Bogen" ("arc"), Sebald's narrator implicitly links it to the circular "Bahnen," the "orbits" along which the rings of Saturn move: "Die Ringe des Saturn bestehen aus Eiskristallen und vermutlich meteoritischen Staubteilchen, die den Planeten in dessen Äquatorebene in kreisförmigen Bahnen umlaufen" ("The rings of Saturn consist of ice crystals and probably meteorite particles describing circular orbits around the planet's equator"; *Ringe* 5/n.p.). Browne's trajectory of advancement and decline also invokes the recurrent pattern of waves characteristic both of the ocean tides and of the rise and fall of human history. The narrator's summary of Browne's philosophy seems to dispel any hope for permanence, for historical progress, or for escape from the ravishes of time.

Yet this assertion is attributed to the same Thomas Browne who investigates the prehistoric burial urns discovered in Walsingham. The preserved contents of these urns hold out hope for durability, transcendence, and even salvation. For Browne, the "silent expressions" ("das wortlose Zeugnis"; literally, "the wordless testimony") of the evergreen trees used to cremate the bodies whose remains inhabit these urns can be read as "signs of their surviving hope" ("Zeichen ewiger Hoffnung"), allowing him to interpret these ancient rites of cremation as evidence for pre-Christian faith in an afterlife (35/25). The very remnants of these cremated bodies and the artifacts with which they were entombed become signs of a paradoxical permanence that emerges out of acts of destruction. Like the fragments of Saturn's moon that persist and bear witness to this satellite's previous existence, these ashes and preserved artifacts allegorize—in Walter Benjamin's

---

15 On Sebald's implicit critique of Hegel in *Die Ringe des Saturn*, see Barzilai, "Melancholia as World History," 75.

sense—the lives to which they once metonymically belonged. Ashes, teeth, fragments of bones, coins, pieces of armor, jewelry, opals, buckles, even a completely unscathed water glass and a scrap of purple silk: all these objects survive destruction in the burial urns and assume the nimbus of transcendence; they are symbolically numinous entities that escape temporal flux and its trajectory of destruction: "For Browne, things of this kind, unspoiled by the passage of time, are symbols of the indestructibility of the human soul assured by scripture, which the physician, firm though he may be in his Christian faith, perhaps secretly doubts" ("Dergleichen von der Strömung der Zeit verschonte Dinge werden in der Anschauung Brownes zu Sinnbildern der in der Schrift verheißenen Unzerstörbarkeit der menschlichen Seele, an der der Leibarzt, so befestigt er sich weiß in seinem christlichen Glauben, insgeheim vielleicht zweifelt"; 36–7/26).

This remark about the indestructibility promised by *Schrift*, by *script* or *writing*, is tantalizingly ambiguous. In the language of Thomas Browne, this word refers to the Bible as scripture and its New Testament promise of redemption and eternal life. But on a literal level this term alludes to the indestructible, preservationist characteristic of writing (*Schrift*) as such, a theme that is directly addressed at other junctures in Sebald's text. On his visit to the Sailors' Reading Room in Southwold, the narrator leafs through the log book of the ship that once bore the name of this town, and he marvels at the capacity of written signs to preserve events and thoughts from the past and transmit them to future readers. "Every time I decipher one of these entries," he observes, "I am astounded that a trail that has long since vanished from the air or the water remains visible here on the paper" ("Jedesmal, wenn ich eine dieser Aufzeichnungen entziffere, wundere ich mich darüber, daß eine in der Luft oder im Wasser längst erloschene Spur hier auf dem Papier nach wie vor sichtbar sein kann"). He goes on to anoint this miracle as "the mysterious survival of the written word" ("das rätselhafte Überdauern der Schrift"; 120/93). The preserved artifacts and ashes of the Walsingham urns and the suspension of particles of matter in the rings of Saturn both concretize this enigmatic survival that is embodied in the characters of written text. Writing as preservative act, as the creation of traces that invoke and reinvigorate past events and life forms, becomes the paradigmatic example of a suspended animation that promises partial salvation from the downward spiral of temporal decline, historical demise, and material decomposition.

The rings of Saturn emblematize the condition of matter and of meaning generated by this dynamic of opposing forces, of centrifugal and centripetal powers that are at once both destructive and preservative, and that constitute a medium capable of retaining the legible traces of once-existent entities. Writing, like the rings of Saturn, has its proper place in the liminal terrain of the Roche limit. This is the privileged site for the writing of natural history, of *Naturgeschichte* as conceived by Theodor Adorno in his interpretation of Walter Benjamin's philosophy. In the essay "Die Idee der Naturgeschichte" ("The Idea of Natural History"), with which Sebald was surely familiar and which likely helped shape his own notion of a natural history of destruction, Adorno remarks, "For radical natural-historical thought, however, everything existing transforms itself into ruins and fragments, into just such a charnel-house where signification is discovered, in which nature and history interweave and the philosophy of history is assigned the task of their intentional interpretation" ("Unter dem radikalen natur-geschichtlichen Denken aber verwandelt sich alles Seiende in Trümmer und Bruchstücke, in eine solche Schädelstätte, in der die Bedeutung aufgefunden wird, in der sich Natur und Geschichte verschränken, und Geschichtsphilosophie gewinnt die Aufgabe ihrer intentionalen Auslegung").[16] *Die Ringe des Saturn* practices a philosophy of history, and a poetic historiography, in the sense propagated by Adorno and Benjamin, in which the remnants of once-existent Being become the stimulus for a constructive philosophical-historical hermeneutics.

The burial urns of Walsingham allude to one of the central leitmotifs of *Die Ringe des Saturn*: the principle of combustion as a process that dialectically fuses destruction and production.[17] In the extended discussion of natural and human deforestation by means of fire, stimulated by his experience of the treeless Dunwich Heath, Sebald's narrator deliberates on the role of combustion in the eradication of the Amazon rainforests and as an energy resource responsible for the march of civilization.

Die Verkohlung der höheren Pflanzenarten, die unaufhörliche Verbrennung aller brennbaren Substanz ist der Antrieb für unsere Verbreitung über die Erde. Vom ersten Windlicht ... bis zum fahlen Glanz der Bogenlampen über den belgischen Autobahnen ist alles Verbrennung, und Verbrennung ist das innerste Prinzip eines jeden von uns hergestellten Gegenstandes. (*Ringe* 212)
[Our spread over the earth was fuelled by reducing the higher species of vegetation to charcoal, by incessantly burning whatever

---

16 Theodor W. Adorno, "Die Idee der Naturgeschichte," in *Philosophische Frühschriften*, vol. 1 of *Gesammelte Schriften*, ed. Rolf Tiedemann (Frankfurt am Main: Suhrkamp, 1973), 360; "The Idea of Natural History," *Telos* 60 (June 1984): 121.

17 Russell J. A. Kilbourn, "'Catastrophe with Spectator': Subjectivity, Intertextuality and the Representation of History in *Die Ringe des Saturn*," in *W. G. Sebald and the Writing of History*, ed. Anne Fuchs and J. J. Long (Würzburg: Königshausen & Neumann, 2007), 152; McCulloh, *Understanding W. G. Sebald*, 72.

would burn. From the first smouldering taper ... to the unearthly glow of the sodium lamps that line the Belgian motorways, it has all been combustion. Combustion is the hidden principle behind every artefact we create. (*Rings* 170)]

Charcoal becomes the symbol for this union of destruction and production in the process of combustion. As an object that is partially burned so as to become a fuel with more intense combustive properties, it represents a transitional stage between fiery destruction and the preservation of fire's potentially productive energy. Like the coastline and the Roche limit, combustion emblematizes the dialectical inter-action of antithetical forces, the union of destruction and construction.

One final example reinforces the manner in which destruction, preservation, and regeneration are interlinked in the ecological sensi-bility of Sebald's narrator. At the close of the penultimate chapter, he relates the story of the devastating hurricane-like storm that struck the English coast in the autumn of 1987, in which millions of trees were uprooted and destroyed. Sebald's narrator relates a personal experience that communicates the disastrous impact of this natural calamity: looking out of his bedroom window onto the neighboring park formerly populated with magnificent trees, he now perceives only an underworld ("Unterwelt") that conjures up a "ghastly emptiness" ("schauderhafte Leere"; 330/266). Yet even in the wake of this cataclysm, new productive energies begin to transform the natural landscape. The bulldozers that arrive to remove the mutilated tree stumps bring to the surface layers of earth in which the seeds of plant-forms no longer present, but once indigenous to this ecosystem, have lain dormant:

Dadurch kam im wahrsten Sinne das Unterste zuoberst. Der Waldboden, auf dem im Vorjahr noch Schneerosen, Veilchen und Anemonen zwischen Farnen und Moospolstern wuchsen, war nun überdeckt von einer Schicht schweren Lehms. Nur Sumpfgras, dessen Samen wer weiß wie lang in der Tiefe gelegen hatten, ging büschelweise in der bald völlig verbackenen Erde auf. (*Ringe* 332) [Now, in the truest sense of the word, everything was turned upside down. The forest floor, which in the spring of last year had still been carpeted with snowdrops, violets and wood anemones, ferns and cushions of moss, was now covered by a layer of barren clay. All that grew in the hard-baked earth were tufts of swamp grass, the seeds of which had lain in the depths for goodness knew how long. (*Rings* 268)]

The topsy-turvy gesture that brings what was long buried to the surface is reminiscent of the popular Baroque emblem of Fortuna's wheel that symbolizes the vicissitudes of fate and the transience of all things. Yet the seeds of the swamp grass, which due to altered ecological circumstances once again discover ideal conditions for growth, hold out hope for natural rebirth even given the ravages of such senseless ruin. To be sure, the ecosystem of this park has been radically altered: all the plants that thrived in the cool, moist shade of the trees have now been displaced by the grass nourished by the dry soil and unimpeded sunlight. Yet since the seeds of this plant lay buried underground at this very spot, there must have been a previous historical period when it was native, and its resurgence points to the circular dynamic of natural history. Even amid a scene of such utter destruction, Sebald's narrator presents hope for salvation, redemption, and regeneration. Perhaps there is even a ray of hope for the once bountiful herring populations of the North Sea that have been driven to the brink of extinction by overfishing and pollution? Sebald, after all, designates his walking tour of the Suffolk shore as a "Wallfahrt," a pilgrimage, and such journeys are traditionally undertaken as a search for redemption.[18]

Whereas the foregoing examples document the dialectical inter-twinement of destruction and renewal in the realm of nature, there are also instances where this dynamic manifests itself in the domain of culture. One primary example is the activities of the Ashbury family. According to the self-diagnosis of Mrs. Ashbury, she and all her family members are nothing but "fantasists, ill-equipped for life" ("lebensuntüchtige Phantasten"; 274/220); her three daughters, Catherine, Clarissa, and Christina, enact this unfitness for life by devoting themselves to occupations that never generate a finished product or turn a profit. They sit several hours a day in one of the rooms of their manor house sewing together random remnants of cloth to produce "multi-coloured pillowcases, counterpanes and similar items" ("vielfarbige Kissenbezüge, Bettüberwürfe und dergleichen mehr"; 264/212). Their labors have an uncanny effect on the narrator, instilling in him a peculiar anxiety about the fleeting pace of time. The logic behind this association of the three sewing women with the transitory character of the world remains unarticulated. But it is easy to guess that they surreptitiously invoke the image of the Parcae, the three Fates

---

18 Albes, "Die Erkundung der Leere," 285, Christina Kraenzle, "Picturing Place: Travel, Photography, and Imaginative Geography in W. G. Sebald's *Rings of Saturn*," in *Searching for Sebald: Photography after W. G. Sebald*, ed. Lise Patt (Los Angeles: Institute of Cultural Inquiry, 2007), 126, and Anna Pieger, "Melancholie als Reise- und Schreibbewegung: Zu W. G. Sebalds *Ringe des Saturn*," *Castrum Peregrini* 56, no. 278 (2007): 48, insist on the salvational thematic alluded to by the reference in the German subtitle to a pilgrimage.

who spin, draw, and cut the thread of life. Sebald also refers to this myth at the conclusion of "Max Aurach," where he compares the three women weavers in a photograph from the Lodz ghetto to the arbiters of human destiny (*Die Ausgewanderten* 355/237). What stands out about the labors of the three Ashbury sisters, however, is that no matter how much time they invest in their sewing, rarely is anything tangible ever produced, since like Penelope they take apart on one day what they sewed together on another (*Ringe* 264/212). The narrator speculates that the motive behind this act of de-composition might be a lack of customers to purchase the finished items, and that they are economically worthless. This economic irrelevance links the sisters' activity with all the other labors that take place on the Ashbury estate, which is quite literally a place outside of both economic and historical time.

However, the narrator also has an alternative explanation for the futility of their labors and their undoing of almost everything they produce:

> Möglich auch, daß ihnen [den Ashbury Töchtern] in ihrer Phantasie etwas von solch außergewöhnlicher Schönheit vorschwebte, daß die fertigen Arbeiten sie unfehlbar enttäuschten, dachte ich, als sie mir bei einem meiner Besuche in ihrer Werkstatt ein paar der Zertrennung entgangene Stücke zeigten, denn eines davon zumindest, ein aus Hunderten von Seidenfetzchen zusammengesetztes, mit Seidenfäden besticktes oder vielmehr spinnennetzartig überwobenes Brautkleid, das an einer kopflosen Schneiderpuppe hing, war ein beinahe ans Lebendige heranreichendes Farbenkunstwerk von einer Pracht und Vollendung, daß ich damals meinen Augen so wenig traute wie heute meiner Erinnerung. (*Ringe* 264–5)
> [It was also possible that in their [the Ashbury daughters'] imagination they envisaged something of such extraordinary beauty that the work they completed invariably disappointed them. At least that was what I thought, when on one of my visits to their workshop they showed me the pieces that had been spared the unstitching. One of them, a bridal gown made of hundreds of scraps of silk embroidered with silken thread, or rather woven over cobweb-fashion, which hung on a headless tailor's dummy, was a work of art so colourful and of such intricacy and perfection that it seemed almost to have come to life, and at the time I could no more believe my eyes than now I can trust my memory. (*Rings* 212)]

Far from economic irrelevance or superfluity, in this interpretation it is the impossible aesthetic demands they place on their artistic products that dictate their ultimate destruction. The textiles these women produce bear a striking constitutional resemblance to the rings of Saturn: they emerge from an initial act of destruction—the tearing apart of integral pieces of cloth to make a mountain of remnants—and they are generated by a secondary act of cohesion that pieces together selected fragments to reconstitute a structural whole. These textiles, constructed only so that they can subsequently be deconstructed, present a self-reflection on Sebald's own artistic practice. In the story "Max Aurach" this painter's works exist in a constant state of becoming, whereby the charcoal lines and paint applied one day are erased or scratched off the next, so that this process can begin again anew (*Ausgewanderten* 237–9/160–2). Much like the sewing accomplished by the Ashbury sisters, Aurach's paintings are generated by a repetitive process of creation and destruction. Moreover, Aurach is characterized as an artist for whom the *reality* of the material product always falls short of the *ideal* template provided by the aesthetic imagination, and his artistic ambitions conform with the narrator's speculations about the high aims the Ashbury sisters have for their own art. In both instances the inability to realize an aesthetic ideal in the concrete work motivates its constant destruction and reconstitution. This discrepancy between the projections of the creative imagination and the world of mundane reality is one of the subsidiary themes of *Die Ringe des Saturn*, articulated above all in the references to Jorge Luis Borges's story "Tlön, Uqbar, Orbis Tertius," whose narrative trajectory is one in which products of the imagination eventually supplant the empirical world in toto (*Ringe* 91–3/69–71).[19] More significant still is that the narrator of Aurach's story implicitly aligns this painter's method with the paralyzing scruples, the "lähmenden Skrupulantismus," characteristic of his own writing (*Ausgewanderten* 344/230). Just as Aurach and the Ashbury sisters create only to deconstruct, Sebald's narrator fills hundreds of pages with notes that are "crossed out, discarded, or obliterated by additions" ("durchstrichen, verworfen oder bis zur Unleserlichkeit mit Zusätzen überschmiert"; *Ausgewanderten* 345/230). For all of these artists (or artisans), composition and decomposition go hand in hand. All of them create at the Roche limit, at the liminal space formed by the tension between the countervailing principles of destruction and creation.

In all of these instances, preservation also plays a peripheral but significant role. Aurach does eventually produce material works of art, even if these do not conform with the ideal projected by his artistic

19 See Jorge Luis Borges, "Tlön, Uqbar, Orbis Tertius," in *Labyrinths: Selected Stories and Other Writings*, ed. Donald A. Yates and James E. Irby (New York: New Directions, 1962), 17–18.

imagination; Sebald's narrator gathers his documents, prepares his illustrations, and puts his reports and deliberations down on paper in a form transmitted to us, his readers; and even the Ashbury sisters allow certain works to escape the fate of being unsewn and de-composed, like the wedding dress that adorns the headless manikin in their workshop. If we lend credence to the response of Sebald's narrator to this surviving work, it represents an aesthetic accomplishment that betrays such "intricacy and perfection" ("Pracht und Vollendung") that the narrator can scarcely believe his own eyes (265/212). Not only does this work approach the vitality of empirical reality in the vibrancy of its colors; it also approximates that imaginary ideal of aesthetic perfection that the narrator sees as the sisters' aim. As one of the few instances in this text when the narrator actually records and documents an experience of aesthetic reception, it is difficult not to view his response as the ideal he holds out for readers engaged with his own work. This reaction mirrors many of the popular responses to Sebald's works once they began to be widely read, with renowned critics like Susan Sontag identifying them with a possible return of "literary greatness."[20] The analogues to such artistic creations in the world of nature are nothing other than the rings of Saturn: they are similar products of a dialectic of destruction and creation, pieced together out of disparate remnants and fragments, yet exhibiting a discernible form and such an array of colors that they have been observed with awe ever since their discovery.

A similar case can be made for Alec Garrard's (in the English translation, Thomas Abrams's) reconstruction of the temple of Jerusalem, about which Sebald's narrator reports in the penultimate chapter of *Die Ringe des Saturn*. Garrard and his work display many parallels to the Ashbury sisters and the wedding dress that represents the culmination of their artistry.[21] Like the Ashbury family, Garrard has retreated almost completely from the commonplace routines of economic life in a rural community. He has gradually reduced his investments of time and labor in the productivity of his farm so as to devote himself more fully to the—economically speaking—unproductive labor expended on his reconstruction of the Jerusalem temple (302/243). Not surprisingly, this has caused him to be perceived by many, including his

---

20 Susan Sontag, "A Mind in Mourning," *Times Literary Supplement*, no. 5056, February 25, 2000, 3.

21 Pfeiffer, "Korrespondenz und Wahlverwandtschaft," 234–5, points out that this episode also presents an intertextual allusion to Herr Frohmann in Joseph Roth's *Juden auf Wanderschaft* (Wandering Jews), who is likewise building a model of the temple of Jerusalem. As we have seen, Sebald already made reference to this essay in the story "Max Aurach," where the eponymous protagonist dreams about this figure and his perfect representation of the ruined temple (*Ausgewanderten* 262–3/176).

own family, as either peculiarly eccentric or certifiably insane; and even Garrard himself admits that his obsessive labors on this model represent nothing but a "meaningless and senseless project" ("sinn- und zwecklosen Bastelarbeit"; 304/244).[22] The narrator attributed a similar senselessness to the work of the Ashbury sisters. One thing that seems to set Garrard's project apart from theirs, however, is its character as a mimetic reproduction. The wedding dress, although potentially an object intended for use, represents a product of the sisters' collective fancy. Garrard's model of the temple, by contrast, is based on painstaking and ongoing research into the historical substance of the temple as it presumably once truly existed. Furthermore, he has been relatively successful in this project of mimetic reconstruction, since, as he remarks, his model is widely accepted "as the most accurate replica of the temple ever produced" ("als das akkurateste Nachbild des Tempels ... das je geschaffen worden ist"; 303/243).

What does it mean to create an accurate reproduction of something that no longer exists empirically, and whose historical constitution must be reconstructed on the basis of archaeological evidence and religious documents? The temple that serves as the original for Garrard's copy is itself scarcely more than a product of the human imagination:

Unsere ganze Arbeit beruht doch letzten Endes auf nichts als auf Ideen, Ideen, die sich im Verlauf der Zeit andauernd verändern und die einen darum nicht selten veranlassen, das, was man für bereits vollendet gehalten hat, wieder einzureißen und von neuem anzufangen. (*Ringe* 305)
[In the final analysis, our entire work is based on nothing but ideas, ideas which change over the years and which time and again cause one to tear down what one had thought to be finished, and begin again from scratch. (*Rings* 245)]

Garrard's temple, like the textiles made by the Ashbury sisters and Max Aurach's paintings, is another product generated at the dialectical interface of constructive and destructive forces, as are the rings of Saturn and Sebald's *Die Ringe des Saturn*. In Garrard we meet another

22 Garrard's turn from investing in productive agricultural labor, to the monumental efforts devoted to the historical reconstruction of the temple of Jerusalem, has a parallel in Sebald's own life, when he shifts his research and writing away from his breadwinning academic occupation to the seemingly marginal engagement with a peculiar form of semi-documentary, semi-fictional prose narrative. No doubt his family, friends, and acquaintances wondered about the "reason" behind such a reinvestment of his energies. No one could have predicted—least of all Sebald himself—the unanticipated fame this reorientation would eventually bring him.

artist operating at the Roche limit. Despite the fact that it represents a historical reconstruction, his Jerusalem temple is not based on any really existing model, but only on ideas. Insofar as the ideas that serve as the basis for this reconstruction are themselves subject to change and revision, the work itself must be constantly adapted in order to adhere to its author's ambitions for mimetic accuracy. Adequacy of mimetic representation is the motivating force underlying the constant deconstruction and reconstruction of this model—just as it was for the fabrics produced by the Ashbury sisters, as well as for Max Aurach's paintings. Despite all the research and effort that goes into guaranteeing the mimetic accuracy of this miniature, Garrard himself views it as nothing but a "wretched waste of time" ("bloß ein elendes Machwerk"; 308/245), an artistic product that is miserably botched. How could it be otherwise, since by its very nature this work is necessarily in a constant state of flux? As material products, such artistic creations can never be characterized as perfected or complete, but always only as *perfectible* and subject to a process of refining revision—of destruction and reconstruction—that places them on an infinite *trajectory* toward completion. Just as the narrator imagines, as Garrard drives him in his pick-up truck to the neighboring town of Harleston, that this journey *"could go on and on, all the way to Jerusalem"* (309/249), Garrard's labors on the temple will likewise go on and on—perhaps someday actually transporting him to Jerusalem. Even though it lacks ultimate empirical realization and exists only in miniature,[23] Garrard/Abrams expresses the hope that his copy will maintain one decisive advantage over its original: greater durability. "The Temple, Thomas Abrams said as we left his workshop, endured for only a hundred years. Perhaps this one will last a little longer" ("Der Tempel, sagte Alec Garrard, indem wir seine Werkstatt verließen, hat ja nur hundert Jahre überdauert. *Perhaps this one will last a little longer"*; 308/248). The temple of Jerusalem does still exist as an empirical entity, of course; but only as ruins, the golden Dome of the Rock rising above its primary extant fragment. The temple thus has been preserved, but only in the way the rings of Saturn preserve its former moon as agglomerations of dust and shards.

Garrard's artistic project—and this is what aligns it most closely with the strategies of Sebald's narrator and the accomplishments of his prose narratives themselves—aims for a different kind of preservation. It seeks to conserve a *memory* of the original temple of Jerusalem by

---

23 On the role of miniatures in general in *Die Ringe des Saturn*, see Jonathan Long, "W. G. Sebald's Miniature Histories," in *W. G. Sebald and the Writing of History*, ed. Anne Fuchs and J. J. Long (Würzburg: Königshausen & Neumann, 2007), 110–12, where he relates the miniature to issues of perspective and a transcendental overview.

means of careful acts of historical research and diligent reconstruction. This describes perfectly Sebald's poetics of history and what he seeks to accomplish, for example, in the four stories of *Die Ausgewanderten* and in his final prose narrative *Austerlitz*: the resuscitation of the ghosts of the past. But the hope of such adequate reconstruction and preservation can only arise if the project itself remains in flux, as a work in progress, based on constant revision, renewed speculation, and creative ideation. Such reconstructions must remain malleable, constantly open to change and revision. This flexibility constitutes the seminal characteristic of such objects as Garrard's temple reconstruction and the fabrics sewn by the Ashbury sisters, as perfectible (although never perfected) works of art. On the aesthetic and epistemological landscape of Sebald's *Die Ringe des Saturn*, they stand in opposition to artistic products and forms of knowledge that derive from rigid structures or inflexible systems. In Sebald's narrative, the grid and the vanishing point, as forms for rationally organizing visual fields, serve as negative counter-models to the fluid artistic and cognitive practice embodied in the works created by the Ashbury sisters and Alec Garrard, and in Sebald's own ethereal project of ghostwriting.

Grids, Vanishing Points, and Sebald's Critique of Visual-Representational Orders

If the works created by the Ashbury sisters, Alec Garrard, Max Aurach— and by extension, Sebald and his narrator—are valorized as aesthetic creations that exemplify the fluidity of the perpetual work in progress, *Die Ringe des Saturn* also presents a second, more critical discourse on systematized forms of aesthetic (and epistemological) representation. Here Sebald's text follows in the footsteps of Horkheimer and Adorno's *Dialektik der Aufklärung*, exposing how rationalized strategies for perception, representation, and the organization of knowledge manifest *exaggerated* degrees of order that, although deployed in an attempt to resist entropic disintegration, ultimately promote destruction and disorder. This is Sebald's peculiar take on the dialectic of Enlightenment, and it expresses itself in *Die Ringe des Saturn* as a critical examination of the two most prominent organizational strategies introduced into the visual arts in the modern age: the grid as a mechanism for dividing up and parceling out space; and graphic perspective, based on the organizing focus of the vanishing point, as a tool for creating the illusion of three-dimensional depth on a two-dimensional surface. These visual strategies themselves are not the primary focus of Sebald's critique; rather, they stand in for wider epistemological problems related to the rational ordering of thought and knowledge. The age of Enlightenment is dominated, as the moniker itself indicates, by metaphors of light and vision. If sight is the mode of perception privileged by enlightened thinking, Sebald's critique focuses on problems that arise when organizational systems employed for ordering the visual field are taken as models for systematizing knowledge in other spheres, such as politics, history, and epistemology.

Die Ringe des Saturn displays a narrative structure typical of the traditional autobiography, in which a first-person narrator reflects retrospectively on his own prior experiences. In its basic structure, this text presents its narrator as engaged in the project of reconstructing the experiences of the pilgrimage he made along the Suffolk coast in August 1992. His recording of this journey occurs in two primary phases: the composition of a first draft that begins exactly one year after the trip, while the narrator is confined to a hospital bed following an operation on his back (9–10/3–4); and a more amorphous "now" ("Heute," 12/5), a little more than a year after his release from the hospital, in which he is involved with the completion of the final manuscript. The narrative is thus constructed in the form of temporally layered, concentric rings, imitating in its temporal texture the spatial strata of the rings of Saturn. Further layers are added to this elementary structure when the narrator relates incidents from more distant time periods in his own life—such as his visit with the Ashbury family in Ireland and his experience of the hurricane of 1987—as well as by the inclusion of historical events (such as the colonization of the Congo and the Taiping rebellion).[24] The narrator's tale represents a historical reconstruction of the same sort as that pursued by Alec Garrard, except that instead of employing building materials, he works with the less concrete medium of written signs, words, and photographic illustrations. Sebald's narrator is likewise deeply concerned with the adequacy of his conceptualization and representation of this reconstructed past. His deliberations on the act of initial composition, presented at the very beginning of the text, specifically address the difficulty of finding a proper perspective and a suitable organizational structure for the subject matter he seeks to relate:

> Genau entsinne ich mich noch, wie ich, gleich nach der Einlieferung [in das Spital der Provinzhauptstadt Norwich], in

---

24 The narrator's self-awareness of his own stratified narrative technique is reflected in his deliberations on layering in other domains, such as the historical layers legible in the manor house at Somerleyton (49/35–6), the layers in which herring spawn (73/55), or the metaphor of sedimentary strata as applied to memory (221/177). The closest textual analogues are the paper chaos of Janine Dakyn's and Michael Hamburger's studies. Sebald's narrator describes the former with geological metaphors. Silke Horstkotte, "Visual Memory and Ekphrasis in W. G. Sebald's *The Rings of Saturn*," *English Language Notes* 44, no. 2 (Fall/Winter 2006): 123, argues that *Die Ringe des Saturn* is premised on the idea of archaeological strata as a model for memory.

meinem im achten Stockwerk des Krankenhauses gelegenen
Zimmer überwältigt wurde von der Vorstellung, die in Suffolk im
Vorsommer durchwanderten Weiten seien nun endgültig zusam-
mengeschrumpft auf einen einzigen blinden und tauben Punkt.
Tatsächlich war von meiner Bettstatt aus von der Welt nichts
anderes mehr sichtbar als das farblose Stück Himmel im Rahmen
des Fensters. (*Ringe* 10)
[I remember precisely how, upon being admitted to that room
on the eighth floor [in the hospital in Norwich], I became
overwhelmed by the feeling that the Suffolk expanses I had
walked the previous summer had now shrunk once and for all
to a single, blind, insensate spot. Indeed, all that could be seen of
the world from my bed was the colourless patch of sky framed in
the window. (*Rings* 4)]

This passage is immediately followed by the first illustration, a depiction
of the view through the hospital room window onto an amorphous
sky made up of varying shades of gray (see Figure 8.1). The narrator
mentions the strange black netting spanned across this window, without
speculating on what purpose it might serve. This net, which parcels up
the view out of the window into perfect squares, together with the
reference to how the narrator's memories of his journey shrink into a
single blind and insensate point, alludes to the two principal organizing
patterns for representing graphic perspective in the visual arts.

The blind spot is nothing other than the vanishing point, that point
in a three-dimensional perspective representation at which the lines of
sight from the observer appear to converge in the distant background.
Those objects deemed closer to the observing eye are represented
larger, those farther away smaller, with relative distance represented by
gradations in size. The implicit analogy to more distant or proximate
memories is obvious. The black netting alludes to the grid made of
perpendicularly cross-hatched lines, sometimes called a *lucida*, used by
artists as a device to help them render objects faithfully by mapping
them in a regularly delineated space.[25] A famous woodcut by Albrecht

---

25 Several critics have commented on this opening image and the grid that
   organizes the gray of the sky, without exploiting it for an analysis that exposes a
   critique of visual representation. See Blackler, *Reading W. G. Sebald*, 146; Helmut
   Lethen, "Sebalds Raster: Überlegungen zur ontologischen Unruhe in Sebalds
   Die Ringe des Saturn," in *W. G. Sebald: Politische Archäologie und melancholische
   Bastelei*, ed. Michael Niehaus and Claudia Öhlschläger (Berlin: Erich Schmidt,
   2006), 15–16; and Kraenzle, "Picturing Place," 128. Bianca Theisen, "A Natural
   History of Destruction: W. G. Sebald's *The Rings of Saturn*," *MLN* 121 (2006):
   563, recognizes that the critical thrust of Sebald's narrative is the dissection of a
   worldview that reduces everything to patterns of schema and grid.

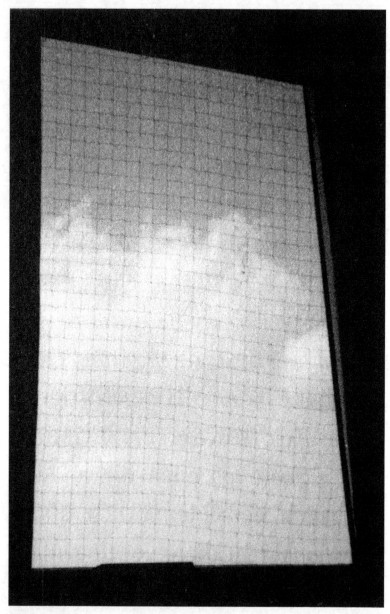

Figure 8.1: Grid and amorphous sky: the view from the narrator's hospital window (*Ringe des Saturn* 10/4).

Dürer, *Man Drawing a Reclining Woman* (1538), depicts a draftsman peering through just such a grid onto the reclining nude he seeks to represent. Before him on his drafting table is a sheet of paper with a complementary grid onto which he transposes the lines of the viewed figure as they intersect those of the grid through which he perceives her (see Figure 8.2). The grid represents a manner for systematically organizing acts of perception and the information they provide. In Dürer's depiction, it additionally manifests a kind of alienating wall that separates the male artist from the potentially lust-engendering reality of the female body he is copying. Its epistemological counterpart is the taxonomy, a rational scheme for systematizing knowledge according to categories, rendering it not only more meaningful but also easier to store and retrieve. What is curious about the initial illustration in *Ringe des Saturn*, however, is that the information upon which this latticework is superimposed remains particularly amorphous: in its various shades of gray one can just barely make out the outlines of clouds against the sky. This very first image in Sebald's text thus juxtaposes the inchoate, depicted as the "grey wasteland" ("graue Einöde") of the sky as seen through the window (11/5), with a medium for regulating this chaos, the grid that apportions this monotone grayness into parsed segments of information that can be more easily managed and processed. This illustration thereby introduces the themes of perspective, point of view, reason, and knowledge that are pursued more fully in the section of the text dealing with Rembrandt's painting *The Anatomy Lesson of Dr. Nicolaas Tulp*, and with Thomas Browne's musings about clarity and obscurity in perception and knowledge (20–5/12–17).

There is one more element in this introductory image that bears examination. On the sill of the window in the lower half of the photograph lies a dark elongated object that can just barely be discerned. In the purposely indistinct reproduction printed in the book, it is difficult to make out its precise nature. This illustration thereby manages to transmit the very problems of perception and exact recognition, addressed in its content, to the readers' engagement with the image itself. It is thus not merely an emblem of traditional historical strategies for organizing visual representations, but also representative of Sebald's own tactic of degrading images in order to problematize their ability to transmit definite visual information. In the original photograph that served as the basis for this illustration, this object is discernible as a book.[26] This suggests that the book, as a different

---

26 The photograph is included in a folder containing illustrations and materials for *Die Ringe des Saturn* at the Deutsches Literaturarchiv, inventory number HS.2004.0001.00022. Although Sebald often possessed sharp original photographs of the images reproduced in his texts, the templates used for his

Figure 8.2: Albrecht Dürer, *Man Drawing a Reclining Woman*.

manner of organizing knowledge, represents an alternative to the more inflexible and schematic arrangement enforced by the grid. The allusion could be to *Die Ringe des Saturn* itself, the book with which Sebald and his narrator are self-consciously engaged in this opening chapter. But one also thinks of Thomas Browne's *Musaeum Clausum or Bibliotheca Abscondita*—a loose collection of diverse bits of knowledge, combining things both real and imaginary—which figures prominently in the final chapter of *Die Ringe des Saturn*, as well as of those works by Borges, "Tlön, Uqbar, Orbis Tertius" and the *Book of Imaginary Beings*, that serve as prominent intertexts. What these works have in common—and what they share with Sebald's narrative—is their pseudo-encyclopedic character, their pretense to approaching a totality through an ad hoc assemblage of desultory fragments, and their refusal to draw distinct lines of demarcation between the worlds of the real and the imaginary, the historical and the fictional. The juxtaposition of book and grid can thus be read in terms of an opposition between two fundamentally distinct manners of ordering and regulating thought and experience. The fact that the grid dwarfs the book, which is on the verge of disappearing into the gray muddle, might be interpreted as a visual instantiation of the dominance instrumental reason wields over alternative modes for arranging knowledge and information.

This illustration is the first in a series of related, grid-like images distributed throughout Sebald's text.[27] These pictures form a sub-class

---

illustrations were often photocopied reproductions that reduced the sharpness of the images and sometimes introduced distortions. On Sebald's common practice of degrading his photographs by photocopying them, see Lise Patt, "Searching for Sebald: What I Know for Sure," in *Searching for Sebald: Photography After W. G. Sebald*, ed. Lise Patt (Los Angeles: Institute of Cultural Inquiry, 2007), 49.

27 Kraenzle, "Picturing Place," 128, notes the connection between the window grid, the caged quail, and the map of Orfordness, but she does not remark on how this matched set articulates Sebald's criticism of visual organization; nor

of illustrations that provide a metacommentary on the text, its structure, and its themes. Later in the first chapter we find the depiction of the quincunx, which for Browne assumes the character of a rudimentary form that recurs throughout various natural entities (28–9/19–20). If in its manifestation as quincunx the grid takes on more positive ramifications, associated with a logic of similitude and the natural signature—similar to what Michel Foucault, in *The Order of Things*, associates with the so-called Renaissance episteme[28]—in its next manifestation the more negative connotations of the grid predominate. This photograph depicts a quail imprisoned in a cage formed of mesh-like fencing (see Figure 8.3). When viewing this image, we not only see the quail staring hopelessly through the fence; we also perceive the entire scene through this barricade, which appears as a blurred lattice in the picture's foreground. In our receptive engagement with this illustration we are placed in a position of those whose perspective imposes an ordering structure upon perception. The fact that the grid itself is blurry, rather than distinct, presents an ironic commentary on such attempts at a rational mapping of perception. And if we had any doubts about the negative implications of this encompassing network, these are dispelled by the accompanying text, which describes the actions of the captured quail and speculates about its sentiments. This bird runs back and forth along the fence of its enclosure, shaking its head, "as if it could not comprehend how it got into this hopeless fix" ("als begreife sie nicht, wie sie in diese aussichtslose Lage geraten sei"; 50/36). The German adjective *aussichtslos* contains a significant pun, meaning both "hopeless," in its common figural sense, and "lacking a view or perspective," in its more literal signification. When read as an epistemological commentary, this photograph suggests that such systematized, grid-like, and rational human engagements with the life world "capture" it in a form that strips it of all vitality. Sebald and his narrator suggest that this approach to life and experience is *aussichtslos*, both hopeless and lacking proper perspective.

The next image in this succession occurs in the narrator's description of his flight from Amsterdam back to Norwich in chapter four. He first ekphrastically describes how, looking down from the plane, he observes how the earth below him is parceled out into a regular, geometric pattern: "Over the centuries the land had been regulated, cultivated and built on until the whole region was transformed into a geometrical pattern" ("Eine über Jahrhunderte sich hinziehende Regulierungs-,

does she acknowledge the parallel group of images that reflect on the vanishing point as another scheme for ordering the visual field.

28 Michel Foucault, *The Order of Things: An Archaeology of the Human Sciences* (New York: Random House/Vintage, 1973), 17–29.

Figure 8.3: Caged quail (*Ringe des Saturn* 50/36).

Kultivierungs- und Bautätigkeit hatte die gesamte Fläche verwandelt in ein geometrisches Muster"; 116/90). Yet these networks that divide the earth into "one lighter and one darker half" ("eine hellere und eine dunklere Hälfte"; 117/91), as does the tractor operating in a field below, are not only employed by humans to organize external reality; these humans themselves are trapped—like the quail in the previous illustration—in the networks they produce.

> Und doch sind sie [die Menschen] überall anwesend auf dem Antlitz der Erde, breiten sich stündlich weiter aus, bewegen sich durch die Waben hochaufragender Türme und sind in zunehmendem Maße eingespannt in Netzwerke von einer das Vorstellungsvermögen eines jeden einzelnen bei weitem übersteigenden Kompliziertheit, sei es so wie einst in den Diamantenminen Südafrikas zwischen Tausenden von Seilzügen und Winden, sei es wie heute in den Bürohallen der Börsen und Agenturen in den Strom der unablässig um den Erdball flutenden Information. (*Ringe* 117–18)
> [And yet they [human beings] are present everywhere upon the face of the earth, extending their dominion by the hour, moving around the honeycombs of towering buildings and tied into networks of a complexity that goes far beyond the power of any one individual to imagine, from the thousands of hoists and winches that once worked the South African diamond mines to the

floors of today's stock and commodity exchanges, through which
the global tides of information flow without cease. (*Rings* 91–2)]

Human beings are imprisoned not only in the concrete honeycombs
of the edifices we build and occupy, and in the mechanical contrap-
tions we invent for exploiting the earth's natural resources, but also
in the more ethereal networks of communication and information
that regulate our bureaucratized, highly administered society.[29] Those
very mechanisms invented to help us simplify and bring order into
a chaotic reality end up, paradoxically, contributing to, rather than
reducing, its complexity. As if seeking to illustrate precisely this
paradox, Sebald interrupts the quoted passage with an illustration
depicting in its foreground a rubble-like landscape of rocks and cliffs,
and in its background a regular series of trees or poles in the distance
(see Figure 8.4). These two focal points of the image are connected by
myriad white lines that look like a mass of electrical wires spanned
between them. The rubble in the foreground is also scored by a similar
set of horizontal lines. These lines appear to be etched onto the photograph in a secondary process, rather than inherent in the photographed
landscape. But instead of infusing the irregular landscape with greater
order and more distinctness, this grid-work makes the image more
obscure, rendering parts of it unrecognizable and indeterminate.

This theme of networks, created with the intent to simplify and
preserve information, but which ultimately confine and unleash death
and destruction, forms a prominent leitmotif throughout *Die Ringe des
Saturn*. It makes itself manifest most poignantly in the fishing nets—not
coincidentally made of silk (75/56)—used to catch swarms of herring,
and which promote such overharvesting that the species itself is
threatened with extinction. These nets, according to the narrator, do not
merely trap the fish, but rather they suffocate them by catching their
gills in the mesh-like webbing. This attribute links the brutally death-
bringing character of the silk fishing nets with the silken rope provided
to the Chinese princes accused of high treason, and with which they
must hang themselves (186/147–8). In keeping with the juxtaposition of
tangible and intangible networks, subsequent references to this theme
stress the ethereal rather than the manifest nature of this meshing.
Yet even when largely immaterial, these nets are no less threatening
or potentially destructive. In the context of the military installations
on the Suffolk coast, the narrator mentions Bawdsey Manor, which
served as "the domicile and research centre of the team under Robert

---

29 This passage and its accompanying image foreshadow the description and illustration of human beings trapped by their industrial machines—in this instance
a weaving loom—presented in the final chapter of *Ringe* (349–51/281–3).

Figure 8.4: Grid-overlaid landscape (*Ringe des Saturn* 117/91).

Watson-Watt that developed radar, which now spreads its invisible net throughout the entire airspace" ("das Domizil und Laboratorium der Forschergruppe, die unter der Leitung von Robert Watson-Watt das Radarsuchsystem entwickelte, das nun mit seinem unsichtbaren Netz den ganzen Luftraum durchzieht"; 283/227). Although ostensibly developed as a strategy for defense and self-protection, this radar network is intimately connected with the weapons of mass destruction named in the very next sentence, with their capacity to transform "whole countries and continents ... into smoking heaps of stone and ash in no time" ("ganze Länder und Kontinente in kürzester Frist ... in rauchende Haufen von Stein und Asche"; 284/227–8). This leads directly to the narrator's observations about the abandoned military research institutes in Orford, among whose inventions for causing mass death is a weapon that shoots out "an invisible web of death-rays" ("ein unsichtbares Netz von Todesstrahlen"; 287/231). As if to reinforce the idea that grid-like networks, strategically planned and executed destruction, and the military installations of Orford inherently belong together, Sebald includes a map of this area that depicts it apportioned into regular quadrants that form a superimposed grid (289/232) (see Figure 8.5). The rational taxonomic order of the network is as all-pervasive as is its potential for prompting massive death and destruction.

Two final illustrations in this series need to be examined, although their connection to the others may not at first appear obvious. These are the images depicting Michael Hamburger's study (*Ringe* 228–9/183–4), and they are especially significant for several reasons. First of all, like

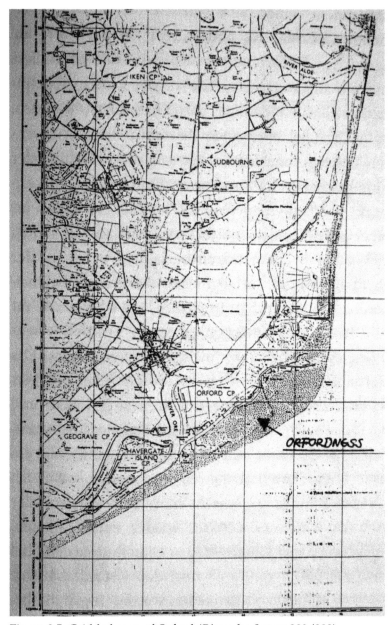

Figure 8.5: Gridded map of Orford (*Ringe des Saturn* 289/232).

Figure 8.6: Michael Hamburger's study (*Ringe des Saturn* 228/183).

the first illustration in this book, they focus on an opposition between rational order and chaotic disorder. As a result, secondly, they help tie this succession of lattice-like representations back to those issues of rational strategies for regulating our perception and experience of the life world, addressed in greatest detail in the opening chapter of *Die Ringe des Saturn*. Finally, and most importantly, they flesh out the idea of an alternative form of order, an inscrutable one that underpins a seeming chaos, an order that is associated with windows, books, mounds of paper, and the written words that grace both of these media (see Figures 8.6 and 8.7).

The first photograph depicts Hamburger's desk, with a jumbled alignment of papers and correspondence strewn across it. These papers form the focal point of the photograph, cutting almost exactly across its meridian. Below them, in the foreground, we see the chair at which Hamburger presumably sits when working at his desk, and above in the background are sets of windows—echoing the gridded window in the book's first illustration—divided into rows of individual panes, thereby forming a *lucida*-like medium through which one perceives the outside world. The opposition between the order of the latticed windows and the disorder of the papers is not as stark in this image as it is in the second one. In this first instance one can imagine that some unknown principle lends these papers a relative order. Still, the rationalized, rigidly ordered perception of the grid-like windows stands in contrast to the relative chaos on the desk. One might make the case that this picture tends to be dominated more by order than by chaos.

This relationship is reversed in the second photograph, in which two stacks of disheveled papers, one especially burgeoning and chaotic, command almost the entire foreground. The left side of the photograph is almost completely occupied by this disordered heap, whereas the right-hand side depicts a doorway into a room whose rear wall, just visible in the background, is made up of the same latticed windows present in the previous photograph. Although the grid-like patterns in this illustration are doubled, the lattice of the windows being repeated in the pattern on the door, they have shrunk in (relative) size and are overshadowed by the confused piles of papers. We recall that when the narrator beholds this study and its apparent disorder, he responds with a sense of identification, as though this were his room and the papers represented a still-life fashioned by his own hand (228–30/183–5). The textual environment deals with "the increasing complexity of our mental constructs" ("die zunehmende Komplexität unserer Geisteskonstruktionen"), and the question whether heightened complexity can truly be identified with advances in knowledge (227/182). These pictures reinforce the idea that there are alternative modes of ordering the world other than by means of the rigidly logical,

Figure 8.7: Paper chaos and grids in Hamburger's house (*Ringe des Saturn* 229/184).

taxonomical, hierarchizing structure of the grid. We can call this alternative a literary or textual reason, insofar as it is associated with books, writing, paper, and manuscripts. The heap of papers in Hamburger's study and hallway are the emblems of Borges's imaginary encyclopedia of Tlön, as well as of Thomas Browne's *Musaeum Clausum*. It also reflects the structure of Sebald's own prose narrative, which is based on chance-like overlap, contingency, and the accident of fortuitous intersections. This is the larger theme that emerges from the episode describing the narrator's visit to Hamburger's home: the "Wahlverwandtschaften und Korrespondenzen" ("elective affinities and correspondences") that ignore logic, causality, and temporality, but that seem to underlie the phenomenal world, even if their precise character cannot be identified and they resist regular and predictable patterns (227/182).

The analogue to Hamburger's rooms stacked with desultory papers is the "paper universe" of Janine Dakyns's study, of which the narrator provides an elaborate description in the opening chapter, and for which he repeatedly relies on geological analogies:

Auf dem Schreibtisch, dem ursprünglichen Ausgangs- beziehungsweise dem Sammelpunkt der wundersamen Papiervermehrung,
war im Verlaufe der Zeit eine richtige Papierlandschaft mit
Bergen und Tälern entstanden, die inzwischen an den Rändern,
so wie ein Gletscher, wenn er das Meer erreicht, abbrach und auf
dem Fußboden ringsum neue, ihrerseits unmerklich gegen die
Mitte des Raumes sich bewegende Ablagerungen bildete. Vor
Jahren bereits war Janine von den immerzu weiterwachsenden
Papiermassen auf ihrem Schreibtisch gezwungen gewesen, an
andere Tische auszuweichen. Diese Tische, auf denen sich in
der Folge ähnliche Akkumulationsprozesse vollzogen hatten,
repräsentierten sozusagen spätere Zeitalter in der Entwicklung
des Papieruniversums Janines. (*Ringe* 15–16)
[On the desk, which was both the origin and the focal point of this amazing profusion of paper, a virtual paper landscape had come into being in the course of time, with mountains and valleys. Like a glacier when it reaches the sea, it had broken off at the edges and established new deposits all around on the floor, which in turn were advancing imperceptibly towards the centre of the room. Years ago, Janine had been obliged by the ever-increasing masses of paper on her desk to bring further tables into use, and these tables, where similar processes of accretion had subse-quently taken place, represented later epochs, so to speak, in the evolution of Janine's paper universe. (*Rings* 8)]

This "paper landscape" does not emerge according to the dictates of logic or causality; it grows due to the unpredictable, oftentimes catastrophic forces of geologic change, such as floods, volcanoes, and calving glaciers. Its order is not one of succession in time, but of layers arranged in space, like the geological layers of the earth—or the rings of Saturn, or the crystallized bough examined in my introductory chapter. If to the outsider this universe of papers seems indeter-minate and lacking all system, Janine insists "that the apparent chaos surrounding her represented in reality a perfect kind of order, or an order which at least tended toward perfection" ("daß die scheinbare Unordnung in ihren Dingen in Wahrheit so etwas wie eine vollendete oder doch der Vollendung zustrebende Ordnung darstelle"; 17/9). One person's chaos is another person's system; and as proof of the method underlying her seeming madness, Janine is able to find immediately whatever she seeks in this ostensibly confused jumble (17/9). She bears in her head a detailed cognitive map that encompasses the entire geography of her "paper universe," permitting her to navigate all its myriad valleys, glaciers, mountains, and crevasses. This tangle of paper is but another of the many labyrinths found in Sebald's text, and Janine provides proof once more that it is impossible to get lost in these labyrinths,[30] at least if they are of one's own making and one takes hold of Ariadne's thread. His encounter with Michael Hamburger forces the narrator to deliberate on the fundamental incomprehensibility of those "imponderables that govern our course through life" ("Unwägbarkeiten, die in Wahrheit unsere Laufbahn bestimmen"; 227/182). Janine's paper universe is structured according to just such "Unwägbarkeiten," imponderable principles; this is why metaphors drawn from the geophysical transformation of the earth are appropriate to its description. Certain laws are surely in operation—like the laws of the Roche limit—but they remain unfathomable, manifesting themselves in the often-unpredictable transformations to which they subject the earth's surface.

The narrator brings this problematic into relation with his own life and sensibilities in a central passage from the first chapter, when he meditates on the meaning of a vapor trail that cuts through the otherwise indistinct sky he perceives through his hospital room window. At first he interprets this "white trail" ("weiße Spur") as a propitious sign; but in retrospect he views it as "the beginning of a fissure that has since riven my life" ("der Anfang ... eines Risses, der seither durch mein Leben geht"; 27/18). The invisibility of the airplane that causes this contrail gives rise to more general meditations regarding the "invisibility and intangibility of that which moves us" ("Unsichtbarkeit und Unfaßbarkeit dessen, was uns bewegt"; 27/18). This theme of inscrutable motives, imperceptible underlying causes, or unfathomable designs forms a leitmotif that runs throughout this text. The examples of Janine Dakyns's and Michael Hamburger's studies indicate that individual human lives can be guided by such imperceptible laws, rather than by consciously formulated, rationally executed plans; indeed, they demonstrate that the flexibility and relative openness of the former often prove to be more orderly and

---

30 I am alluding to John Zilcosky's hypothesis, "Sebald's Uncanny Travels: The Impossibility of Getting Lost," in *W. G. Sebald: A Critical Companion*, ed. J. J. Long and Anne Whitehead (Seattle: University of Washington Press, 2004), 109, that although Sebald's narrators and characters often strive to get lost, their journeys are structured by uncanny returns that ultimately make this impossible. This pattern is just as valid for cognitive pilgrimages as it is for physical journeys.

productive—although not more fathomable—than the rigid taxonomies of rational systems.

A further parallel to the paradoxically chaotic order of Dakyns's and Hamburger's studies is Mrs. Ashbury's carefully preserved assemblage of flower seeds, whose collection bags she hangs up—not coincidentally—in the former library of the estate. "Once they had been taken down, the bags were stored under some inscrutable system on the shelves, which had evidently long since been unburdened of books" ("Die abgenommenen Tüten wurden nach einem undurchsichtigen System verwahrt auf den offenbar vor langem schon von ihrer Bücherlast befreiten Borden"; 263–4/211). Since they are collected in small paper bags, these seeds once more represent a chaotic paper universe—one that replaces the encyclopedic paper universe of the books that once filled the bookcases in this library. The fact that they contain seeds points to their potential for production and dissemination. A peculiar associative logic causes the narrator to move immediately from a description of the impenetrable system ordering this seed collection to the seemingly senseless activity of her three daughters as they sew together (and eventually take apart) random pieces of fabric. As we saw, the wedding dress that survives the process of undoing displays, for the narrator, an "intricacy and perfection" ("Pracht und Vollendung") that defies definition (265/212). The secret and imperceptible system that lends order to Janine Dakyns's paper universe approaches the same kind of perfection: it represents "a perfect kind of order, or an order which at least tended towards perfection" ("eine vollendete oder doch der Vollendung zustrebende Ordnung"; 17/9). Over against the sterile, rigid, rational system of the grid stands another order, one that is imperceptible, unfathomable, flexible, yet nonetheless discernible, and Sebald's narrator champions this latter form of arrangement, manifest above all in paper, books, and written forms—in texts and textiles. If we call this alternative form of cognition and representation "discursive reasoning," then this phrase should not be taken in its narrow philosophical sense as the logical movement from premises to conclusions, but rather in its wider yet more literal signification of wandering from idea to idea, of digressive, seemingly desultory ramblings, as *dis-cursus*. In textual terms, this is what the metaphor of the pilgrimage stands for; and Sebald's *Die Ringe des Saturn* attempts to recreate in its own "dis-cursive" structure the "perfected order" of Janine's paper landscape and the aesthetic splendor of the Ashbury sisters' wedding dress. This represents another dimension of Sebald's poetics of history: what appear to be nothing but disjointed fragments constitute a structural configuration, governed by inscrutable forces, that is as magnificent as the rings of Saturn themselves.

As the preceding arguments have sought to demonstrate, there are good reasons for interpreting Sebald's *Die Ringe des Saturn* as an extended literary elaboration on the epistemological problematic addressed in Michel Foucault's "archaeology of the human sciences," *The Order of Things*. Sebald's narrator alludes to the German title of Foucault's treatise in thoughts attributed to Thomas Browne: "Wir studieren die Ordnung der Dinge, aber was angelegt ist in ihr, sagt Browne, erfassen wir nicht" ("We study the order of things, says Browne, but we cannot grasp their innermost essence"; 28/19). Foucault begins his treatise with a reference to a work by Borges that deals with an impossibly contradictory and disjointed taxonomy of all the possible categories of animals.[31] Sebald and his narrator play out in literary form the critique of rational order Foucault approaches more philosophically. The following passage from the Preface to *The Order of Things* could be taken as a concise summary of the themes raised and expounded upon especially in the first chapter of *Die Ringe des Saturn*:

> Order is, at one and the same time, that which is given in things as their inner law, the hidden network that determines the way they confront one another, and also that which has no existence except in the grid created by a glance, an examination, a language; and it is only in the blank spaces of this grid that order manifests itself in depth as though already there, waiting in silence for the moment of its expression.[32]

Foucault delineates two different orders of order, so to speak: one that is inherent in things and in their relationships to one another; another that is artificially created and imposed upon them from the outside. The first of these remains hidden, like the invisible motives that structure Janine Dakyns's paper universe and Mrs. Ashbury's seed collection. The second is an independent form of organization, a "grid" that is superimposed upon things in the act of their comprehension or perception. We can elucidate this difference by associating it with the Kantian distinction between the phenomenal and the noumenal— although Foucault himself might object to this terminology. The first order is phenomenal in the sense that it resides in the nature and the relational configuration of the things themselves; the second is noumenal insofar as it is a product of our conceptual or perceptual apparatus that is overlain onto objects in the world. The danger, Foucault implies, is that we ultimately confuse the second-order knowledge produced by the imposition of our exogenous conceptual

---

31   Foucault, *The Order of Things*, xv.
32   Ibid., xx.

grid with a *coming to light* of qualities or relationships that exist *latently* or endogenously in the world itself. This is the deception to which *empirical* rationality in particular falls victim; it is the same deception that Kant sought to dispel in his *Critique of Pure Reason*.

If we are inclined to designate the first, inherent, or phenomenal kind of order as "contingency," we must be careful not to confuse this with fortuitousness or accident. Contingency circumscribes those inherent inner qualities and relationships that exist among things; it demarcates those connections and affinities that escape the order imposed by the rational system of the grid or taxonomy. Contingencies are what Sebald's narrator calls the "ghosts of repetition" ("Phantome der Wiederholung"; *Ringe* 233/187), the "chance happenings" or coincidences ("Zufälle"; 233/187), or the "elective affinities and correspondences" (227/182) that, for example, bring the lives of Hamburger, Sebald (or his narrator), and Stanley Kerry into a meaningful constellation. These patterns are not irrational in the strict sense, but they are non-rational in the sense of falling outside of the strict logical framework by which we commonly determine what is "reasonable." Just such a relationship of configuration places the fragmentary particles and the dust from Saturn's former moon into a constellation that forms the relatively stable rings that circle that planet. The same can be said on the level of textual production for Sebald's narrative *Die Ringe des Saturn*: the narrator's peregrinations along the Suffolk coast, functioning like a historical archaeology, uncover diverse elements that stand with one another in recoverable coincidental constellations. This structure is enhanced by the narrator's various reminiscences, which follow up on associative lines that join disparate events from world history with his own personal experiences, creating a resonance that gives both of these dimensions increased depth and richness. If metaphors of sedimentary layers are prominent in the rhetoric of Sebald's text, then this is because they describe the process by which these structural configurations become gradually more multifarious, elaborate, and multifaceted—which is *not necessarily* to say more complex.[33]

Foucault defines his own archaeological project as an attempt to restore "to our silent and apparently immobile [epistemological] soil

---

33 See the passage, examined earlier, in which "the increasing complexity of our mental constructs" is juxtaposed with "the imponderables that govern our course through life" (*Ringe* 227/182). Ben Hutchinson, "'Umgekehrt wird man leicht selbst zum Verfolgten': The Structure of the Double-Bind in W. G. Sebald," *Revista de Filología Alemana* 14 (2006): 108, identifies this passage as an indirect quotation from Claude Lévi-Strauss's *Tristes Tropiques*, another intertext for *Die Ringe des Saturn*.

its rifts, its instability, its flaws,"[34] and this claim could be made for Sebald's *Die Ringe des Saturn* as well. To do so entails not merely establishing a structural order that escapes the logic of the grid, but also presenting a critique of narrowly defined concepts of rational organization. Commenting on the passage from the Gospel of St. Mark in which Jesus banishes evil spirits from a possessed man to the spirits of two thousand pigs—with the consequence that these pigs leap from a cliff to their deaths[35]—Sebald's narrator wonders whether the upshot of this parable is "that human reasoning, diseased as it is, needs to seize on some other kind that it can take to be inferior and thus deserving of annihilation?" ("daß wir unseren kranken Menschenverstand immer wieder auslassen müssen an einer anderen, von uns für niedriger gehaltenen und für nichts als zerstörenswert erachteten Art?"; 88/67). What makes reason pathological is not simply its drive to regulation and order, but its implementation for the purposes of mastery over others, in particular over those we *perceive* as less developed, less rational than ourselves. This perverse logic structures the episodes of colonial and political exploitation invoked by Sebald's narrator as examples of historical catastrophes, brought about by human actions. This "dialectic of Enlightenment" is exposed especially well in the episode dealing with the Dutch colonization of the Congo, in which the so-called civilizing process that unleashes untold death among the natives is guided by a self-aggrandizing ideology that sees itself bringing light into primeval darkness (150/118), replacing the blank spaces on the map of Africa—the blank spots not yet smothered by the grid of reason—with systematically organized knowledge (149/117).[36]

This light–dark dichotomy is first introduced in the opening chapter of Sebald's narrative, in the episode dealing with Rembrandt's *Anatomy Lesson*, in which the materiality of the dissected body is juxtaposed to the rational schema that abstractly maps out the anatomy of the human physique. The public event of the anatomical demonstration marks, according to the narrator, "a significant date in the agenda of a society that saw itself as emerging from the darkness into the light" ("ein bedeutendes Datum im Kalender der damaligen, aus dem Dunkel, wie sie meinte, ins Licht hinaustretenden Gesellschaft"; 20/12). This

---

34 Foucault, *The Order of Things*, xxiv.
35 Mark 5: 1-17.
36 Sebald's text relies heavily on irony to expose the perversity of this colonial ideology. If the aim of colonial intervention is to bring light into darkness, when it fills in the map it reverses this order, making a *"white patch"* into *"a place of darkness"* (149/117–18). This reversal exposes the dialectic by which "enlightened" reason disseminates the darkness of violent mastery—as made explicit in Roger Casement's report on the Congo atrocities, one of Sebald's primary intertexts.

is true because it choreographs the mastery of abstract reason over the materiality of the human body. The narrator's analysis of Rembrandt's painting stresses how the gazes of those following the anatomical lesson focus not on the material body being dissected, but rather on the atlas lying open at the corpse's feet. In an associative linkage that is typical of how this text develops, the narrator connects this privileging of abstract scheme over concrete reality with the Cartesian glorification of the cogito and the denigration of the senses:

> Bekanntlich lehrte Descartes in einem der Hauptkapitel der Geschichte der Unterwerfung, daß man absehen muß von dem unbegreiflichen Fleisch und hin auf die in uns bereits angelegte Maschine, auf das, was man vollkommen verstehen, restlos für die Arbeit nutzbar machen und, bei allfälliger Störung, entweder wieder instand setzen oder wegwerfen kann. (*Ringe* 24)
> [In his philosophical investigations, which form one of the principal chapters of the history of subjection, Descartes teaches that one should disregard the flesh, which is beyond our comprehension, and attend to the machine within, to what can fully be understood, be made wholly useful for work, and, in the event of any fault, either repaired or discarded. (*Rings* 13)]

If Cartesian epistemology represents one of the primary chapters in the history of subjugation, this is because its aim is to subordinate the incomprehensible flesh—Sebald's narrator emphatically chooses a word that invokes the Christian spirit–flesh dichotomy—to the schematic diagram sketched out presumably by divine reason. Many of the themes of the dialectic of Enlightenment converge in this short passage: the subjection of concrete matter to reason; a rejection of what appears incomprehensible in favor of the reductive comprehension proffered by rationality; the debasement of the human body, its reduction to an instrument fit only for productive labor; exploitation of the natural world and of human beings as the means to accomplish rational ends. For Descartes, as for Dr. Tulp in his anatomical research, the study of nature—as the narrator remarks later in this same chapter—aims solely at revealing it to be "a system governed by immutable laws" ("eines vollkommen gesetzmäßigen Systems"; 31/21).

Sebald's narrator portrays the artist Rembrandt as a voice in the wilderness, someone who subtly and clandestinely protests against this rationalist ideology that privileges the machine-like schema of reason over the vitality of the human body and material nature. He accomplishes this by introducing an element into his painting—not coincidentally, this element is a schematic portrayal—that disrupts the required verisimilitude of his representation. The dissected left hand of the victim is not only "grotesquely out of proportion," but also "anatomically the wrong way round" ("grotesk disproportioniert"; "anatomisch gänzlich verkehrt"; 25/16). It seems that Rembrandt has simply substituted for the victim's flesh-and-blood hand the schematic drawing from the anatomical atlas. In this sense, he structures his critique of schematizing reason as an ironic *reiteration* of its own logic, of its tendency to replace the real by its abstract representation. However, in order for this ironic commentary to become recognizable, Rembrandt must deviate from the laws that govern the art of painting in his day: from the law of perspective, which dictates that all objects should be represented in their proper proportions; and from the law of mimetic accuracy, which militates against the anatomical reversal of the hand. This deviation from the prescriptions and norms that obtain in his own discipline underwrites Rembrandt's critical assault. His attack on schematic, abstract reason thereby operates by means of an implicit, displaced criticism of the rules that govern ordered representation in the visual arts. In this regard, he can be seen as a model for Sebald's narrator, who not only seeks to *voice* a critique of reason, but who also *performs* this critique in the aesthetic makeup of his own work. Rembrandt's example demonstrates that this can only be accomplished by rupturing the accepted norms for the artistic medium and genre in which one is operating. Sebald accomplishes this by disrupting the standard features of the classical pseudo-(auto)biographical novel. This helps explain why *Die Ringe des Saturn* exhibits a formal structure reminiscent of one of the founding texts in the German novelistic tradition, Grimmelshausen's *Simplicissimus*—in particular the extensively detailed chapter descriptions contained in the table of contents[37]—a text, moreover, that is historically contemporary with one of Sebald's primary protagonists, Thomas Browne. Grimmelshausen's picaresque novel recounts the wanderings of its protagonist amid the chaos and destruction of the Thirty Years' War. Sebald transmutes this structure by adapting it to the Post-Modern travelogue; his narrator does not immediately experience the ravishes of never-ending war, as does Grimmelshausen's protagonist, but instead revisits the scars left by a more modern, more subtle history of destruction.

As interpreted by Sebald's narrator, Rembrandt's critique of abstract rationality proceeds via strategic ruptures with the rules governing proper representation in the visual arts. One of the laws he transgresses is that of proportionality, dictated by an adherence to the principles of

---

37 Sebald may be imitating the procedure of another famous "Post-Modern" writer, John Barth, who exploits a similar pattern in his historical parody *The Sot-Weed Factor*, a work whose digressive narrative structure displays many similarities with Sebald's *Ringe des Saturn*.

graphic perspective. If Sebald plays out and ironizes the representational and conceptual logic of the grid in a series of illustrations that
highlight the restrictions it imposes upon perception and knowledge,
he proceeds in a similar fashion in order to expose the limitations of
the central organizing principle of graphic perspective, the so-called
vanishing point. It marks the privileged center of any perspective
drawing in the sense that it organizes all the objects in the represented
field according to their relative proximity to the viewer. Objects closer
to the imaginary seeing eye are larger, those farther away are smaller,
and the vanishing point designates, as the English term suggests, that
distant place where the sight lines converge and all objects disappear
from view. The vanishing point represents one among many of the
thematic interests of Sebald's narrator. It is implicit in the dynamic
of center and periphery that governs the distribution of political
power in Sebald's text. According to the narrator, for example, Roger
Casement's position on the periphery of political might, a by-product
of his homosexuality, affords him the capacity to sympathize with the
suppressed, enslaved, and exploited people who are "furthest from
the centres of power" ("am weitesten entfernt ... von den Zentren der
Macht"; 168/134).[38] A position on the periphery—at the margin, at the
limiting point of the coastline—constitutes the condition of possibility
for critical insight into the brutalities promulgated by institutionalized
rational power, as well as for identification with its victims. A similar
gradient in the hierarchies of power is discussed in the episodes dealing
with Chinese history, in which the court of the emperor is described as

---

38 Sebald's suggestion that Casement's homosexuality is the condition of
possibility for his general humanitarian interests is influenced by positions
represented in Freud's essay on the Schreber case, "Psychoanalytische
Bemerkungen über einen autobiographisch beschriebenen Fall von Paranoia
(Dementia paranoides)," in *Zwang, Paranoia und Perversion*, vol. 7 of the
Freud-Studienausgabe, ed. Alexander Mitscherlich, Angela Richards, and James
Strachey (Frankfurt am Main: Fischer, 1973), 185; "Psycho-Analytic Notes on
an Autobiographical Account of a Case of Paranoia (Demetia Paranoides),"
in *The Standard Edition of the Complete Psychological Works of Sigmund Freud*, ed.
and trans. James Strachey, 24 vols (London: Hogarth, 1953–74), 12:61. Freud
asserts "that it is precisely manifest homosexuals, and among them again
precisely those that set themselves against an indulgence in sensual acts, who
are distinguished by taking a particularly active share in the general interests
of humanity—interests which have themselves sprung from a sublimation of
erotic instincts" ("daß gerade manifest Homosexuelle und unter ihnen wieder
solche, die der sinnlichen Betätigung widerstreben, sich durch besonders
intensive Beteiligung an den allgemeinen, an den durch Sublimierung der
Erotik hervorgegangenen Interessen der Menschheit auszeichnen"). In this
volume of the Freud *Studienausgabe* in Sebald's personal library, this passage is
underlined in pencil and marked in the margin with three vertical lines.

the center of authority around which its subordinates orbit (176/139). We should recall that the rings of Saturn also exist on this periphery, and hence provide the proper vantage point for a critical perspective on the center as that place where power is most densely concentrated.

Sebald calls attention to the problematic of the vanishing point and graphic perspective in a series of illustrations that exhibit it, sometimes in exaggerated fashion. This suite of photographs performs a similar function to those that present the grid, serving as a critical metacommentary on a very different order of visual representation. The first illustration in this set occurs in the second chapter. As the narrator describes his entry into the abandoned streets of Lowestoft, he interpolates a photograph showing an avenue with a long line of houses on one side that fade in the distance (55/41) (see Figure 8.8). This image provides a paradigmatic example of graphic perspective and the vanishing point. It is surely not coincidental that it intervenes in the text just after the narrator has described the prison of Blundeston, which he passed along his route: prisons are classic cases of institutions at the periphery of power.

An even more extreme example is introduced toward the end of chapter eight. It depicts the partially dilapidated bridge that leads from the mainland to the abandoned research institutes at Orfordness (292/235) (see Figure 8.9). The horizon between land and sky cuts almost directly across the meridian of this photograph, interrupted solely on the right-hand edge by the pagoda-like building worthy

Figure 8.8: Lowestoft in graphic perspective (*Ringe des Saturn* 55/41).

of its own separate illustration in this same context (294/236). The vanishing point is distinctly marked by what appears as a white rectangle at the very middle of the image, formed by a gate at the other end of the bridge. This rectangle and the two lines of railing posts invoke the structure of the grid and thereby construct an association with the series of illustrations that focus on that figure. The exaggeratedly archetypal character of this image highlights its function as a critical reflection on the principle of perspective, and the textual environment in which it occurs aligns it with a veritable desert of destruction. Wherever he looks, Sebald's narrator perceives nothing but isolation and deterioration; reflecting on the history of this place, he realizes that the buildings, now themselves reduced to rubble, once served as research laboratories for the development of weapons of mass destruction. On the basis of a correlative logic typical of his style of thought, the narrator traces the hillocks of these ruined edifices back to one of the overriding themes of his narrative, rites of burial, linking them with "the tumuli in which the mighty and powerful were buried in prehistoric times with all their tools and utensils, silver and gold" ("Hügelgräber ... in denen in vorge-schichtlicher Zeit große Machthaber beigesetzt worden waren mit all ihren Gerätschaften und all ihrem Silber und Gold"; 293/236). Ultimately all of Orfordness assumes the character of an uncanny "isle of the dead" ("Insel der Toten"; 294/237), which will serve as evidence for subsequent visitors from outer space of the catastrophic destruction that engulfed the civilization that once flourished here. The systematic, hierarchical order of perspective drawing, organized around its single vanishing point, becomes an emblem of the systematic (self-)destruction—the *vanishing* point—of the civilization that invented it. Organized perspectival representation is identified with the will to mastery and devastating weaponry of those one-time power mongers, the "mighty and powerful" ("Machthaber"), for whom these ruins have now become allegorical memorials. The aggressive instinct that transforms rationality into an instrument for the development of ever-more sophisticated weaponry of destruction is revealed, coherent with Freudian theory, as a reflex that culminates in self-destruction.

The final example of an illustration that emphasizes organization of the visual field according to graphic perspective occurs during the discussion of Alec Garrard's model of the temple in Jerusalem (306–7/246–7). This picture is clearly marked as the culmination in this series: it is one of only four in the entire text that completely fills two pages—the others being the reproduction of Rembrandt's *Anatomy Lesson* (22–3/14–15), the picture of the corpses outside the Bergen-Belsen concentration camp (80–1/60–1), and the photograph

Figure 8.9: Bridge at Orfordness (*Ringe des Saturn* 292/235).

documenting pages from Roger Casement's 1903 diary (166–7/132–3).[39] Far from organizing its subject matter into a well-ordered, clearly discernible scheme, this illustration presents its objects as blurred and out of focus. What we have before us is an interior view of the model temple of Jerusalem itself, with its cassette ceiling, columns, and shadow-striped floor converging at the vanishing point of an arched gateway.[40] This illustration verges on parody: while it empha- sizes the theme of graphic perspective as a method for organizing space, its fuzzy character highlights the exact opposite: a lack of distinction that promotes disorientation. The image is almost reduced to a jumble of vertical and horizontal lines, interrupted only by the arched gateway and the obscure human figures that appear to be walking toward it. Instead of peering into a carefully mapped-out space, the eye of the beholder becomes trapped in a visual labyrinth. A representational technique that is intended to provide a lucid systematic overview ultimately—and paradoxically—immerses the

---

39 I exclude the pages from the silk inventory of Norwich (352–3/284–5), since these are separate images that are placed on facing pages, not a single image reproduced on two leafs.

40 I am unable to reprint the image of Garrard's temple here, because one of his wishes upon his passing in May 2010 was that his temple no longer be available for public viewing. His family is honoring this request, and hence has asked that the image not be reproduced here. Interested readers can consult the relevant pages of *Ringe* (306–7/246–7).

viewer in a tangled web. This illustration graphically demonstrates and reinforces a thematic that governs many of the deliberations on visual perspective and representation in this text: the dialectic between the control afforded by a clear-sighted overview and the disorientation of proximate involvement.[41]

The context in which this illustration occurs alludes to this juxtaposition between the presumed clarity of distanced viewing and the obscurity of the close-up perspective. Whereas what we behold is a double-page view of the temple's *interior*, what Garrard/Abrams shows the narrator is, by contrast, a double-page vista that depicts an *overview* of the temple grounds as they look today: "In closing, Thomas Abrams dug out a magazine ... and showed me a double-page aerial view of the Temple precinct as it is today" ("Zuletzt zeigte mir Alec Garrard in einer Illustrierten ... eine doppelseitige Luftaufnahme des Tempelgeländes, wie es heute ist"; 308/248). This juxtaposition between the overview, which the text describes ekphrastically, and the disorienting close-up Sebald presents as illustration, invokes the opposition between a bird's-eye perspective, a "Luftaufnahme" or "aerial view" that affords an all-encompassing field of vision, and the close-up from within, which inhibits the systematic organization of what is perceived and hence invokes a sense of disorientation. If the metaphor for the former is the heightened perspective afforded by the view from above, as from a hot air balloon or a watchtower, the figure for the latter is the labyrinth out of which it is difficult to find one's way.

The prototypical example of the labyrinth in *Die Ringe des Saturn* is the narrator's experience on Dunwich Heath. He is only able to find his way out of this "maze" ("Irrgarten") of undergrowth and myriad, frequently unmarked paths (216/173) when he discovers "a raised area" ("Aussichtsposten") that provides an overview and the possibility of spatial orientation:

Todmüde und schon bereit, mich irgendwo niederzulegen, gelangte ich bei Einbruch der Dämmerung an einen etwas erhöhten Platz, auf dem genau wie in der Mitte des Eibenlabyrinths von Somerleyton ein kleiner chinesischer Pavillon errichtet war. Und als ich von diesem Aussichtsposten hinabblickte, sah ich auch das

---

41 For reflections on this dialectic between overview and entanglement in Sebald's text, see Barzilai, "Melancholia as World History," 75, who describes it as a dichotomy between overview and blindness. Kilbourn, "Catastrophe with Spectator," 155, also stresses the juxtaposition between distanced mastery and helpless immersion; and Carsten Strathausen, "Going Nowhere: Sebald's Rhizomatic Travels," in *Searching for Sebald: Photography After W. G. Sebald*, ed. Lise Patt (Los Angeles: Institute for Cultural Inquiry, 2007), 473–5, contrasts the distanced overview with being lost in a labyrinth.

Labyrinth selber ... ein im Vergleich mit den Irrwegen, die ich
zurückgelegt hatte, einfaches Muster. (*Ringe* 216)
[Dead tired and ready to lie down anywhere, as dusk fell I gained
a raised area where a little Chinese pavilion had been built, as in
the middle of the yew maze at Somerleyton. And when I looked
down from this vantage point I saw the labyrinth ... a pattern
simple in comparison with the tortuous trail I had behind me.
(*Rings* 173)]

The complex confusion of paths that cause the narrator to experience an
odyssey of dead ends and wrong turns is suddenly transformed into a
simple pattern, once the necessary perspective is obtained. Only when
he attains higher ground is the disorienting proximity of the labyrinth
dispelled, giving way to a distinct map that renders it easy to negotiate.
At this point Sebald includes an illustration that documents this transformation: it depicts a garden labyrinth from the air, with its elevated
viewing platform at the center of the photograph (*Ringe* 216/173; cf.
Figure 7.1 in Chapter 7). The paradox of this privileging of a distanced
perspective as more precise is that it seems counterintuitive, reversing,
as it does, the common wisdom that we see things most clearly and
in greatest detail in close proximity, whereas with greater distance the
objects shrink and our view becomes less refined. To be sure, when the
eye or the camera lens get too close to an object, a point is eventually
reached when fine detail gives way to blurred obscurity. The image of
the Jerusalem temple, with its insistence on ordered perspective, on the
one hand, and its obscuring lack of sharpness, on the other, plays with
the dynamic of this turning point where resolution reverts to irreso-
lution and strategies for generating distinctness—be they in the visual
or the epistemological realm—dialectically revert to fuzzy obscurity.
    Sebald is a master of the cryptically suggestive narrative apposition:
the relational configuration of episodes and the tension—the conflict
of gravitational forces—that develops between them often constitutes
the locus of signification. It is telling, then, that after his meeting with
Alec Garrard, and immediately subsequent to the blurry illustration of
the temple—with its dialectical play on perspective, vanishing point,
clarity, and obscurity—the narrator finds himself one final time in a
disorienting labyrinth, the treeless flatlands known as "The Saints":

Ich selber dachte mir beim Dahingehen über die größtenteils
baumlose und dennoch unübersichtliche Ebene, *that I might well
get lost in The Saints*, so oft zwang mich das verwinkelte englische
Fußpfadsystem, die Richtung zu wechseln oder an Stellen, wo
der auf der Karte markierte Weg aufgepflügt oder überwachsen
war, auf gut Glück querfeldein weiterzugehen. (*Ringe* 310)

[My own feeling, as I walked over the featureless plain, was that I might well lose my bearings in The Saints, so often was I forced to change direction or strike out across country due to the labyrinthine system of footpaths and the many places where a right of way marked on the map had been ploughed up or was now overgrown. (*Rings* 249–50)]

Like so many other depictions of the footpaths the narrator travels through coastal Suffolk, this passage represents a self-reflective deliberation on the process of *writing* and *narrating* about this pilgrimage. It is not by chance that his final destination is an area called "The Saints," since this reinforces the suggestion that this journey has the character of a pilgrimage or redemptive quest. The tangled confusion of pathways through this landscape reflects the myriad thematic directions taken by the text. And if the narrator seems to have a map that will help him find his way through this Borges-like garden of forked paths, sometimes his planned-out course is impossible to navigate and he must take a spontaneous detour. Both the narrator's foot journey and his textual meanderings are structured by a dialectic between organized overview and the spontaneous negotiation of a labyrinthine landscape that constantly becomes "unübersichtlich": obscure and unintelligible because one lacks an overview that could help sort out the seemingly "featureless" chaos. Sebald's *Die Ringe des Saturn* is structured by this dichotomy between exaggerated, obfuscating proximity and the clarity of distance: between blind immersion in a landscape or subject matter and a clear-sighted overview; between the centrifugal force of dissolution into isolated fragments and the centripetal thrust toward an organized center; between the chaos of the non-distinct and the hyper-rationality of the well-ordered grid. This is the dizzying divide that Sebald's narrator, and we as readers, must negotiate.

The narrator's oscillation between landscapes that either enforce involved immersion in their materiality or provide the detached isolation of the overview is encapsulated in his experience of the two paintings he studies at the Mauritshuis Museum in The Hague, Rembrandt's *Anatomy Lesson*, which we have already discussed, and Jacob von Ruisdael's *View of Haarlem*.[42] Rembrandt's painting presents

---

42 As Fuchs has pointed out, "Ein Hauptkapitel," 128, Sebald's narrator mistakenly identifies the painting as *View of Haarlem with Bleach Fields*, whereas it is the thematically similar *View of Haarlem* that actually hangs in the Mauritshuis Museum and is described here. In *Die Schmerzensspuren der Geschichte: Zur Poetik der Erinnerung in W. G. Sebalds Prosa* (Cologne: Böhlau, 2004), 216–21, Fuchs provides an extended analysis of Ruisdael's painting and its significance for Sebald's text in terms of a redemptive aesthetics of the natural landscape.

a close-up of the visceral act of dissection, but also the refusal of Dr. Tulp's colleagues to look at the flesh-and-blood victim (21/13). Curiously, when the narrator describes his own experience of viewing this work, he reacts in a like manner: overwhelmed by the materiality of Rembrandt's portrayal, he must flee the gallery and seek refuge in another painting, precisely Ruisdael's *View of Haarlem* (106/82–3). In the distanced, detached overview presented in this work, he finds an antidote to the starkly proximate corporeality of Rembrandt's painting:

> Die gegen Haarlem sich hinziehende Ebene ist aus der Höhe herunter gesehen, von den Dünen aus, wie im allgemeinen behauptet wird, doch ist der Eindruck einer Schau aus der Vogelperspektive so stark, daß diese Seedünen ein richtiges Hügelland hätten sein müssen, wenn nicht gar ein kleines Gebirge. In Wahrheit ist van Ruisdael beim Malen natürlich nicht auf den Dünen gestanden, sondern auf einem künstlichen, ein Stück über der Welt imaginierten Punkt. Nur so konnte er alles zugleich sehen. (*Ringe* 106–7)
> [The flatland stretching out towards Haarlem is seen from above, from a vantage point generally identified as the dunes, though the sense of a bird's-eye view is so strong that the dunes would have to be veritable hills or even modest mountains. The truth is of course that Ruisdael did not take up a position on the dunes in order to paint; his vantage point was an imaginary position some distance above the earth. Only in this way could he see it all together. (*Rings* 83)]

In order to see everything "all together" or *simultaneously*—the temporal modifier is significant—Ruisdael constructs an imaginary vantage point from which to "perceive" Haarlem. In contrast to the overwhelming reality depicted in Rembrandt's painting, and the inclusion of the viewer as an immediate witness to the anatomical operation, Ruisdael's canvas is an imaginative work that provides the narrator with the safe haven of aesthetic artifice. He flees, physically and emotionally, to the artificial, rationalized, carefully mapped representational order that structures Ruisdael's painting. This is the same pattern he will follow subsequent to his experience in the labyrinth of Dunwich Heath, after which he finds solace in the relative comfort and hominess of Michael Hamburger's study. In his description of Ruisdael's *View of Haarlem*, Sebald's narrator emphasizes how it renders spatial depiction as a strategy for mastering temporality: the bird's-eye view the painter imagines and adopts permits him to collapse events that transpire over time into simultaneously occurring episodes in space.

This transposition of temporality into spatiality is the principal feature the narrator recognizes as operative at the Waterloo memorial, a prior visit to which he recalls in the context of his reflections on the Belgian colonial enterprises. This memorial combines in a single monument all those characteristics, both material and immaterial, typical both of graphic perspective and the bird's-eye overview. But it also makes clear how these manipulations of perspective operate as strategies for organizing and mapping out *history*, not just for parceling out and partitioning representational *space*. The memorial itself is constructed as an elevated pyramid with an observation platform from which one can look out over the entire battlefield, and it thereby reiterates the motif of the pavilion-like structures located on hillocks in the labyrinths of Somerleyton and on Dunwich Heath, as well as alluding to the elevated "dunes" from which Ruisdael depicts Haarlem. Inside the rotunda is a panoramic reconstruction of the battle itself, an *imaginary* representation that renders temporal succession as spatial contiguity:

Schließlich kaufte ich mir noch ein Eintrittsbillett für das in einer mächtigen Kuppelrotunda untergebrachte Panorama, in dem man von einer im Zentrum sich erhebenden Aussichtsplattform die Schlacht ... in alle Himmelsrichtungen übersehen kann. Man befindet sich sozusagen am imaginären Mittelpunkt der Ereignisse ... Über die dreidimensionale, vom kalten Staub der verflossenen Zeit bedeckte Horrorszene schweift der Blick an den Horizont zu dem Riesenrundgemälde, das der französische Marinemaler Louis Dumontin im Jahre 1912 ... ausgeführt hat. Das also, denkt man, indem man langsam im Kreis geht, ist die Kunst der Repräsentation der Geschichte. Sie beruht auf einer Fälschung der Perspektive. Wir, die Überlebenden, sehen alles von oben herunter, sehen alles zugleich und wissen dennoch nicht, wie es war ... Stehen wir auf einem Totenberg? Ist das am Ende unsere Warte? Hat man von solchem Platz aus den vielberufenen historischen Überblick? (*Ringe* 157–8)
[At length I bought a ticket for the Waterloo Panorama, housed in an immense domed rotunda, where from a raised platform in the middle one can view the battle ... in every direction. It is like being at the imaginary centre of events ... Across this horrific three-dimensional scene, on which the cold dust of time has settled, one's gaze is drawn to the horizon, to the enormous mural ... painted in 1912 by the French marine artist Louis Dumontin ... This then, I thought, as I looked round about me, is the representation of history. It requires a falsification of perspective. We, the survivors, see everything from above, see everything at once,

and still we do not know how it was ... Are we standing on a
mountain of death? Is that our ultimate vantage point? Does one
really have the much-vaunted historical overview from such a
position? (*Rings* 124–5)]

This passage is worthy of extensive citing because it represents one of
the nodal points in Sebald's text, weaving together many of the visual
metaphors and images we have been analyzing, while elaborating on
their relevance for the construction of our *historical* perspective. Just
as our perception and representation of space are organized around
artificial systems, around grids, vanishing points, elevated perspectives,
and imaginary points of view, so too is our historical understanding
nothing but a representational schematic, a dissimulating panorama
predicated on the assumption of a fictitious and imaginary vantage
point. We envision ourselves at the center of the universe, with an
all-encompassing view that takes in every periphery simultaneously;
and yet we really have no idea what it is (or was) like to experience
those events first-hand. We substitute for the real-life, concrete experiences of the battlefield, for an immersion in the immediate "horrific
scene," the distancing, taming, and comforting—but ultimately falsifying—overview generated by an imaginary vantage point far above
the real events themselves. Neither the "levity" of the balloonist, with
its all-encompassing perspective, nor the "gravity" of the pedestrian,
who for lack of perspective is incapable of finding a way out of the
labyrinthine landscape, presents an ideal situation.[43] History must also
be written at the Roche limit created by the dialectical interaction of
these two forces, and this is what Sebald's poetics of history seeks to
accomplish. Only a strategy that fuses center and periphery, or that
achieves equilibrium between the tidal forces and the power of gravity,
is capable of arriving at a balanced historical understanding.

Early in this text Sebald's narrator presents a paradoxical image
for the fusion of these two perspectives, microscopic immersion in the
details of the concrete and schematizing distance that underwrites a
systematic mastery from afar. While discussing Thomas Browne's style
of writing and philosophy in the first chapter, the narrator imagines
a point of view, no less artificial and imaginary than the bird's-eye
perspective or the vanishing point, that fuses distance and proximity,
detached abstraction and immediate immersion in concrete details.
Speaking in the voice of Thomas Browne, he claims it is as though

---

43 I disagree with Hutchinson, "Die Leichtigkeit," 464–5, 467, who offers a more
optimistic interpretation of "levity" and the bird's-eye view as the possibility of
transcendence. Instead, I see it as a position Sebald criticizes as a questionable
strategy for control and mastery.

one could look *simultaneously* through an inverted telescope, which provides a shrunken but encompassing view, *and* through a microscope, which brings everything closer and homes in on details:

> Je mehr die Entfernung wächst, desto klarer wird die Sicht. Mit der größtmöglichen Deutlichkeit erblickt man die winzigsten Details. Es ist, als schaute man zugleich durch ein umgekehrtes Fernrohr und durch ein Mikroskop. Und doch, sagte Browne, ist jede Erkenntnis umgeben von einem undurchdringlichen Dunkel. Was wir wahrnehmen, sind nur vereinzelte Lichter im Abgrund des Unwissens, in dem von tiefen Schatten durchwogten Gebäude der Welt. Wir studieren die Ordnung der Dinge, aber was angelegt ist in ihr, sagt Browne, erfassen wir nicht. (*Ringe* 28)
> [The greater the distance, the clearer the view: one sees the tiniest of details with the utmost clarity. It is as if one were looking through a reversed opera glass and through a microscope at the same time. And yet, says Browne, all knowledge is enveloped in darkness. What we perceive are no more than isolated lights in the abyss of ignorance, in the shadow-filled edifice of the world. We study the order of things, says Browne, but we cannot grasp their innermost essence. (*Rings* 19)]

Sebald gives voice to the representational ideal that guides his own textual production. Just as one must gain distance from the subjects, experiences, and historical events one seeks to portray, one must also be able to grasp them in immediate detail, as though they were vitally present, even if only as ghosts. Abstracting distance, on the one hand, and close-up immersion, on the other, are fused in this idealized act of perception and representation. Its product is anything but a totalizing, unitary system. On the contrary, the "order of things" laid out by this convergence of a distanced overview and microscopic immersion resembles the configuration of particles contained in the rings of Saturn: every fragment of knowledge is surrounded by a nebula of ignorance. The narrator intones in this context the dark–light dichotomy especially prominent in this chapter, allowing it to resonate as a metaphor for the known and the unknowable. This is the delicate, fragile course pursued by those, like Thomas Browne, Sebald, and his narrator, who attempt to write at the Roche limit, to compose along that field of tension between the opposing forces of proximity and distance, the objective and the subjective, the real and the imaginary, the documentary and the fictional, history and poetics. The immediate context for these reflections on Browne's epistemology are deliberations about his style of writing: the sublimity of his prose, the "ungeheuren Zitatenschatz" ("repertoire of quotations") everywhere evident in his language; the labyrinthine structure of his sentences; the slow, drawn-out cadences of his rhythm; his expansive use of metaphors and analogies (28/19). This is but one more example of how self-reflections about the compositional qualities of *Die Ringe des Saturn* masquerade behind descriptions of the work of others. The juxtaposition between high-flying rhetoric and labyrinth-like sentence structure reiterates on the level of style precisely that opposition between a bird's-eye perspective and the blindness of the labyrinth that we have examined as central for the critical arguments about representation and epistemology put forward in this text. Despite the enormous ballast of this style, Sebald's narrator, like Thomas Browne, is able to lift off and glide "through the circles of spiraling prose" ("auf den Kreisen seiner Prosa"; 28/19), imitating in the circular motion of his writing the movement of Saturn's rings.

The perspective on life, on human interactions with the life world, and on history assumed in *Die Ringe des Saturn* is concretized in the paradoxical aggregation of an inverted opera glass and a microscope. The merger of these two contrary perspectives, conceived in terms of spatial representation, the organization of knowledge, the understanding of history, and as a compositional strategy for writing itself, is the purpose of this narrative. Writing at the Roche limit represents a form of textual composition that emerges at the crosscurrents of these two forces, demanding that the narrator maneuver between the Scylla of heightened abstraction and the Charybdis of blind submergence in immediate reality. Sebald's narrator, like his reader, is constantly on the verge of getting lost in textual, epistemological, and geographical labyrinths; and yet he is repeatedly rescued by a countervailing view that affords a perspectival overview permitting reorientation. But the reverse is also the case: a focus on proximate details rescues him from wallowing in artificial and abstract generalizations.

If gravity and levitation strive toward equilibrium in Sebald's narrative, then so too do melancholy and the hope for salvation. Sebald's general worldview may tend toward a certain pessimism; but this is part and parcel of a Modernist, post-Enlightenment assessment of Western civilization and its historical trajectory. In an essay entitled "Historical Emplotment and the Problem of Truth," Hayden White makes the claim that the Modernist sensibility represents a response to a new sense of history. It emerges, according to White, as

> an anticipation of a new form of historical reality, a reality that included, among its supposedly unimaginable, unthinkable, and unspeakable aspects, the phenomenon of Hitlerism, the Final Solution, total war, nuclear contamination, mass starvation, and ecological suicide; a profound sense of the incapacity of our

sciences to *explain*, let alone control or contain these; and a growing awareness of the incapacity of our traditional modes of representation even to *describe* them adequately.[44]

Sebald's *Die Ringe des Saturn* is a product of, and a response to, this new conception of historical reality. It displays skepticism not only toward the capacity of scientifically systematized reason to account for the acute horrors of the modern world, but also toward the traditional representational strategies we deploy in our attempts to comprehend and represent them. As Sebald himself poignantly remarks in the preface to his essay collection *Die Beschreibung des Unglücks*,

Melancholie, das Überdenken des sich vollziehenden Unglücks, hat aber mit Todessucht nichts gemein. Sie ist eine Form des Widerstands. Und auf dem Niveau der Kunst vollends ist ihre Funktion alles andere als bloß reaktiv oder reaktionär. Wenn sie, starren Blicks, noch einmal nachrechnet, wie es nur so hat kommen können, dann zeigt es sich, daß die Motorik der Trostlosigkeit und diejenige der Erkenntnis identische Exekutiven sind. Die Beschreibung des Unglücks schließt in sich die Möglichkeit zu seiner Überwindung ein. (12)
[Melancholy, the meditation on occurring misfortune, has nothing in common with a fascination with death. It is a form of resistance. And on the level of art, moreover, its function is anything other than merely reactive or reactionary. When melancholy, with its steely gaze, calculates once more how it could possibly have come to this, then it demonstrates that the mechanics of inconsolability and that of knowledge are identical operations. The description of misfortune inherently subsumes the possibility of its overcoming.]

Die Ringe des Saturn manifests this brand of melancholy figured as *resistance to* the general perception of imminent decline and destruction. It incorporates the potential to overcome a debilitating pessimism, not merely by describing the horrific circumstances of historical and contemporary reality, but also by practicing creative representational strategies *for* this description. This is precisely what a form of writing at the Roche limit seeks to accomplish, and where its redemptive potential resides. In this regard, *Die Ringe des Saturn* not only documents a textual pilgrimage, but also enacts what we might call, in conscious allusion

44 Hayden White, "Historical Emplotment and the Problem of Truth," in *Probing the Limits of Representation: Nazism and the Final Solution*, ed. Saul Friedlander (Cambridge, MA: Harvard University Press, 1992), 52.

to the novel by Peter Weiss, one of Sebald's literary lodestars, an "Ästhetik des Widerstandes"[45] ("aesthetics of resistance") that models via the literary text a Modernist sensibility—in accord with Hayden White's proposition—that remains theoretically unfathomable.

---

45 Peter Weiss, *Die Ästhetik des Widerstands*, 3 vols (Frankfurt am Main: Suhrkamp, 1975–81). When asked by Uwe Pralle which post-war German authors had an impact on his own literary production, Sebald named the works of Peter Weiss as especially eye opening (*"Auf ungeheuer dünnem Eis"* 255–6).

Nine Narrating Environmental Catastrophe: Ecopsychology and Ecological Apocalypse in Sebald's Corsica Project

"Das einstmals frohgemute Fortschrittsdenken weicht heute einem katastrophischen Zeitempfinden ... Ozonloch, Grundwasserverschmutzung, Versteppung, Massenmigration, Regenwaldvernichtung ... Ich denke, dieses katastrophische Zeitempfinden wird auch ein neues Erzählen bedingen, im Alltag wie auch in der Literatur." ["Today the once cheerful belief in progress is giving way to a catastrophic sense of time ... ozone hole, pollution of the ground water, desertification, mass migration, destruction of the rain forests ... I believe this catastrophic sense of time will give rise to a new form of storytelling, in everyday life as well as in literature."]

Uwe Timm[1]

The Corsica Project in Sebald's Oeuvre
In early September 1995, just a few months after completing the manuscript of *Die Ringe des Saturn*, Sebald spent two weeks on the island of Corsica, guided by an inchoate vision for a new work of narrative fiction. A full year later, in the first week of September 1996, he made a return trip to Corsica in an effort to further develop this project. But just two months after this second visit, in December 1996, he reports in a letter to a friend that he has abandoned this plan, and that he intends to engage in something new that he hopes will prove

1 Uwe Timm, *Erzählen und kein Ende: Versuche zu einer Ästhetik des Alltags* (Cologne: Kiepenheuer & Witsch, 1993), 104–5.

more successful.[2] After giving up on the Corsica travelogue, Sebald's energies were channeled in two very different directions. Invited to give the poetic lectures at the University of Zurich, he picked up a theme that had concerned him well over a decade earlier, in his previous life as a literary critic: the question about why German literature had remained silent about the catastrophic consequences of the Allied air war.[3] Sebald delivered these lectures between October and December 1997, and they were subsequently published, in revised and expanded form, as the highly controversial book *Luftkrieg und Literatur* (*On the Natural History of Destruction*) in 1999. In an interview with Volker Hage from the year 2000, Sebald indicated that he had decided to re-engage "provisionally" with the problem of the air war because at the time he was unable to move forward with other creative projects (*"Auf ungeheuer dünnem Eis"* 194). He was clearly referring to the Corsica project, and it is a measure of his own dissatisfaction with the development of this material that he felt it could not be resuscitated for the Zurich lectures. By the time of this interview, Sebald's creative energies had already moved in a second direction, toward what would be his final work of creative fiction, the prose narrative *Austerlitz*. In

---

2   Ulrich von Bülow, "Sebalds Korsika-Projekt," in *Wandernde Schatten: W. G. Sebalds Unterwelt*, ed. Ulrich von Bülow, Heike Gfrereis, and Ellen Strittmatter (Marbach am Neckar: Deutsche Schillergesellschaft, 2008), 211. Sebald's precise reasons for jettisoning this project remain largely in the dark, but the few scholars who have broached this question tend to argue that he felt this endeavor replicated too closely what he had accomplished in *Die Ringe des Saturn*. See Judith Ryan, "Sebald's Encounters with French Narrative," in *From Kafka to Sebald: Modernism and Narrative Form*, ed. Sabine Wilke (New York: Continuum, 2012), 131, and Uwe Schütte, *W. G. Sebald: Einführung in Leben und Werk* (Göttingen: Vandenhoeck & Ruprecht, 2011), 177. Graeme Gilloch, "The 'Arca Project': W. G. Sebald's Corsica," in *A Literature of Restitution: Critical Essays on W. G. Sebald*, ed. Jeanette Baxter, Valerie Henitiuk, and Ben Hutchinson (Manchester: Manchester University Press, 2013), 127, offers the most detailed analysis of this abandoned endeavor, comparing it with Walter Benjamin's fragmentary *Arcades* project and viewing it as a storehouse of themes, motifs, allusions, and stylistic experiments that serve Sebald as an incubation chamber. Rüdiger Görner, "Leere Reisekoffer und gedächtnislose Gegenwart: W. G. Sebalds Topographieren im Korsika-Projekt," in *W. G. Sebald: Intertextualität und Topographie*, ed. Irene Heidelberger-Leonard and Mireille Tabah (Berlin: LIT Verlag, 2008), 121, reduces these fragments to the standard themes of mainstream Sebald scholarship, treating the island as an occasion for memory recall, accompanied by the requisite sense of melancholy.

3   Sebald first developed this theme in the essay "Zwischen Geschichte und Naturgeschichte: Versuch über die literarische Beschreibung totaler Zerstörung mit Anmerkungen zu Kasack, Nossack und Kluge," *Orbis Litterarum* 37 (1982): 345–66. The essay was reprinted in the posthumous volume *Campo Santo* (69–100) and is available in the like-named English-language collection (65–95).

this case as well, Sebald was reaching back to material he had been mulling over for several years, and the life of Jacques Austerlitz represents an expanded version of what could have been the fifth biography in *Die Ausgewanderten*. Sebald admitted as much in an interview with Sven Boedecker from 1995, where he remarked that he was mentally occupied with another story that belonged in this context, but that in order to flesh it out he needed time to travel to Bohemia—a clear reference to the background of Austerlitz (*"Auf ungeheuer dünnem Eis"* 119).

Faced with the apparent dead end in which the Corsica material had led, Sebald retreated to topics and themes with which he was more familiar and where he had already achieved both success and public notoriety. This suggests two important things. On the one hand, the Corsica project represented a different, largely untried direction in Sebald's literary pursuits; on the other, he regarded this experiment either as a failure, or as not yet refined enough for public airing. The purpose of the present chapter is to explore what Sebald was attempting to accomplish in his writings on Corsica, and to explain why the project could not be completed at the time. My hypothesis is that with the Corsica travelogue Sebald sought to shift his attention away from issues related to the European catastrophe of the twentieth century, manifest above all in the Holocaust and the Nazi reign of terror, and more toward general considerations about the (self-)destructive proclivities of humankind and their expression in the history of environmental degradation. In the Corsica project, Sebald was trying to expand the focus of what he termed the "natural history of destruction,"[4] by moving away from specific sociopolitical issues and toward broader ecological and ecopsychological concerns. A move in this direction was already initiated in *Die Ringe des Saturn*, where questions about the natural world and the impending environmental catastrophe became significant themes; yet here they were still subordinate to problems of mastery, domination, and exploitation as the primary currents of human cultural and political history. Sebald's manuscripts and background materials for the Corsica project indicate that this balance was about to change: instead of primarily telling the history of catastrophes human beings have perpetrated against other human beings, his emphasis here would be on narrating the history of environmental degradation and the destruction human beings perpetrate against their own life world. But he apparently felt unable to

---

4   The English translation of *Luftkrieg und Literatur* was published under this title, which Sebald borrowed from a planned but unwritten report about the carpet bombing of Cologne by the English military advisor Solly Zuckerman (*Luftkrieg* 38–9/31–2).

develop the necessary rhetorical sensitivity and narrative distance requisite for an effective engagement with this problem—a dilemma he had successfully resolved, in his earlier works and in his final prose fiction *Austerlitz*, by means of a narrative approach structured around a mediated retelling of the lives of those who suffered from exile and displacement. For reasons that need to be explored, the task of narrating *environmental* catastrophe presented him with greater challenges.

Although Sebald bemoaned the largely wasted time and effort invested in the Corsica endeavor, he succeeded in mining the research and draft manuscripts in diverse ways. Some of these sketches morph into episodes that are integrated into the life of his final protagonist, Jacques Austerlitz,[5] while other concerns, in particular the theme of inherent human destructiveness, would be channeled into Sebald's lectures about the Allied air war on Germany and his consternation about the minimal response to this cataclysm in post-war German literature. The only direct fruits of his intensive occupation with the history and natural history of Corsica are two fragmentary extracts he published in his own lifetime, "Kleine Exkursion nach Ajaccio" ("A Little Excursion to Ajaccio") and "Die Alpen im Meer" ("The Alps in the Sea"), along with a completed essay that was discovered among his papers upon his death and subsequently published under the title "Campo Santo."[6] But these published pieces give only a sketchy idea of what Sebald was trying to accomplish in his work on Corsica.

Among Sebald's posthumous papers are two archival boxes with the collected research matter for the Corsica project. These include diverse pages of notes on the politics, history, and natural environment of Corsica; collections of newspaper articles about the island or on topics related to themes Sebald identified with this work; drafts of chapter breakdowns that lay out his changing vision of the work's structure; newspaper pieces collected during his visits to the island; photo-copies of encyclopedia articles and other resources that shaped his background reading; notes from the historical pretexts and intertexts

---

5   Ulrich von Bülow, "Sebalds Korsika-Projekt," 212, 220–1, maintains that the Corsica manuscripts provide the "missing link" between *Die Ringe des Saturn* and *Austerlitz*, and he documents some of the motifs that find their way from this aborted project into Sebald's last work of fiction. Gilloch, "The 'Arca Project,'" 127, denies that the Corsica manuscripts should be located in such an evolutionary scheme, insisting instead that they represent open-ended, "unfinished business." Given Sebald's penchant for returning to ideas and themes that profoundly engaged him, there is good reason to believe he might have revisited the Corsica materials if his life had not been so precipitously extinguished.

6   One can also include among the collateral works associated with the Corsica project Sebald's essay on Rousseau (*Logis* 57–61/41–70).

that influenced his understanding of Corsica and its history; and finally and most importantly, two draft manuscripts that give a general impression of the overall thrust and trajectory of this endeavor.[7] Already the title Sebald gave these manuscripts provides some insight on the nature of the enterprise: "Aufzeichnungen aus Korsika: Zur Natur- und Menschenkunde" (Notes from Corsica: On natural history and anthropology). In particular, his subtitle stresses the intention to explore the ways in which the natural history of the island is interwoven with the character of its human inhabitants. Corsica thus represents for him a locale in which transformations of the natural environment and the mentality of its human occupants are intimately intertwined. These investigations seek to highlight the imbrications between the ecology of the island and the psychology of the human beings who live there. But far from following the traditional tack of gauging how the island's coarse and rugged landscape hardens the character of the islanders, Sebald turns this formula around, focusing on the impact human psychological makeup has had on the long-term environmental devastation marking Corsica's modern history. His focus is explicitly ecopsychological in the very specific sense accorded that term in the recently inaugurated branch of knowledge that defines itself as "ecopsychology." In a 1994 essay that asks why traditional psychology has had so little to say about the impending environmental crisis, David Kidner accuses mainstream psychology of concentrating on a decontextualized individual who stands in absolute isolation from its natural environment, relying on a Cartesian paradigm of human rationality that denigrates the non-human aspects of the natural world, and adopting a cognitive model that suppresses the emotional bonds that tie human beings with the environment.[8] Although he acknowledges the existence of "environmental psychology," Kidner maintains that this sub-field concerns itself solely with the impact particular environmental conditions have on human health and behavior, completely ignoring questions about how and why human behavior could develop in a way that threatens destruction of the life world that

---

7   Ulrich von Bülow published these draft manuscripts under Sebald's working
     title "Aufzeichnungen aus Korsika" (Notes from Corsica). The Corsica
     materials are archived at the Deutsches Literaturarchiv in four folders under the
     heading "Konvolut: Aufzeichnungen aus Korsika," with the inventory number
     HS.2004.0001.00020. Whenever I cite passages from the draft manuscripts that
     have analogues in the published essays, my citations include references to the
     appropriate page numbers of the German and English texts published in *Campo
     Santo*.
8   David W. Kidner, "Why Psychology is Mute about the Environmental Crisis,"
     Environmental Ethics 16, no. 4 (Winter 1994): 362.

sustains the species.[9] He concludes that "environmental destruction is invisible to psychology, which perceives only particular environmental conditions and restricts itself to exploring the effects of these particular conditions on humans."[10] At the time of Kidner's writing in the mid-1990s—the very time Sebald was working on his Corsica project—ecopsychology was just beginning to emerge, above all in the work of Theodore Roszack, whose founding ecopsychological treatise, *The Voice of the Earth*, appeared in 1992.[11] Sebald's Corsica investigations, which operate at the intersection of natural history and anthropology, are fundamentally coherent with this new direction of psychological research.

Why Corsica?

This leads to the question as to why the island of Corsica would suggest itself to Sebald as the appropriate object for such a study. As an island nation whose political history is closely yoked to that of continental Europe and the Mediterranean region more specifically, Corsica represents a microcosm of this larger geopolitical, natural-historical, and anthropological domain. It circumscribes that part of the world that Sebald refers to as the "cradle of our civilization" ("Wiege unserer Zivilisation"; "Aufzeichnungen" 198; cf. *Campo Santo* 39/35). The possessive adjective "our" ("unserer") is significant, since it indicates how Corsica stands as a metonymy, as *pars pro toto*, for the larger abstraction of "Western civilization." As an island, but as representative of this larger geopolitical region and its intellectual-historical traditions, Corsica offers a narrowly circumscribed experimental object from whose study one can extrapolate conclusions about European civilization more generally. It thereby serves the function of the "representative sample" in a scientific experiment that seeks to draw more global conclusions. Corsica also fascinated Sebald as the birthplace of Napoleon, perhaps the most significant political and military mastermind of modern Europe, and a primary exemplar of what he understood as a misguided attempt to impose strict rational

---

9   Ibid., 359.

10   Ibid., 373.

11   Theodore Roszack, *The Voice of the Earth: An Exploration of Ecopsychology* (New York: Simon & Shuster, 1992). Other foundational works of ecopsychology include David Abram, *The Spell of the Sensuous* (New York: Random House/Vintage, 1997), and the essays edited by Theodore Roszack, Mary E. Gomes, and Allen D. Kanner, *Ecopsychology: Restoring the Earth, Healing the Mind* (San Francisco: Sierra Club Books, 1995). For a concise summary of the principles of ecopsychology and the emergence of the field, see Steven Kotler, "Ecopsychology in Ten Easy Lessons: Or How I learned to Become One with a Glacier," *Orion* 31, no. 2 (March–April 2012): 16–25.

order on a world that tends toward the chaotic. In what would be
his very last interview, conducted by Uwe Pralle in December 2001,
Sebald insisted on the continuity of a European politics of mastery
from its inception with Napoleon to its perverse culmination in the
crimes of Nazi Germany. The "traces of this catastrophe," he claims,
"are discernible everywhere in Europe, regardless of whether they are
in evidence in the north of Scotland or on Corsica or Corfu" ("Deshalb
sind die Spuren dieser Katastrophe in ganz Europa ablesbar, ob sie nun
im Norden von Schottland sind oder auf Korsika oder auf Korfu"; "*Auf
ungeheuer dünnem Eis*" 260). He mentions Corsica by name, because
the figure of Napoleon provides a crucial linkage between the political
and human history of the island and the devastating history of modern
Europe more generally. Sebald articulates one of his most prominent
themes, what the Frankfurt School sociologists Max Horkheimer and
Theodor Adorno called the *Dialectic of Enlightenment*.[12] Their well-
known thesis was that attempts to impose reason and order on the
affairs of human life and society ultimately revert to principles of
mastery and coercion that unleash untold destruction. This hypothesis
held an enduring fascination for Sebald, and it expresses itself most
poignantly in his bitter skepticism toward utopian projects aimed at the
reorganization, rationalization, and disciplinary ordering of the natural
and the human worlds.[13]

Equally important is that under the reign of the Corsican nationalist Pasquale Paoli (1725–1807), the island was governed by a
progressive democratic constitution, well before this was the case
either in France or, for that matter, in the colonies of North America.
This point is emphatically made by the German historian Ferdinand
Gregorovius (1821–91), whose history of Corsica Sebald read as part

---

12 On the significance of Horkheimer and Adorno for Sebald, see Ben Hutchinson,
W. G. Sebald: Die dialektische Imagination (Berlin: De Gruyter, 2009), 5–10.

13 Sebald's works are replete with allusions to utopian projects that ultimately
go badly awry. One thinks of the reference in "Paul Bereyter" to Nicholas
Ledoux, who designed a utopian city for the workers at a French salt mine,
and Paul's interpretation of this project as an example of rational systemati-
zation that annihilates natural life (*Ausgewanderten* 67/44–5). A similar reflex
underlies the perverse logic explored in *Austerlitz* via the descriptions of how
fortresses built to defend a nation against external enemies ultimately attract
the very aggression they are supposed to prevent (21–8/14–19). Among the
materials Sebald collected for his Corsica project is an article from *Die Zeit* (May
1991) about Hermann Soergel's (1885–1952) so-called "Atlantropa" project,
which outlined a massive technological design for lowering the water level
of the Mediterranean Sea to gain arable farmland, and building a dam at the
strait of Gibraltar to create the world's largest power plant. Sebald exhibited
ironic skepticism toward the overblown technological optimism that informed
Soergel's plans.

of his background research. Gregorovius emphasizes "that at a time when the great cultured peoples of the European mainland were still in the spell of despotic forms of government, Corsica could produce Pasquale Paoli's democratic constitution, which emerged before America liberated itself and before France began its revolution. Corsica had no slaves, no serfs; every Corsican was free" ("daß zu einer Zeit, als die großen Kulturvölker des Festlandes in despotischen Staatsformen gebannt lagen, Korsika die demokratische Verfassung des Pasquale Paoli erzeugen konnte, welche entstand, ehe Nordamerika sich befreite und ehe Frankreich seine Revolution begann. Korsika hatte keine Sklaven, keine Leibeigenen; jeder Korse war frei").[14] In the photocopy of this text among his research materials, Sebald highlights this passage, and in his manuscript on Corsica he refers to the theme that Paoli's ideal government would be as transparent as crystal, a remark that is contained in this source (Sebald, "Aufzeichnungen" 197).[15]

Sebald first addressed this association of Corsica with utopian political visions in his essay on Jean-Jacques Rousseau, published in the collection *Logis in einem Landhaus* (*A Place in the Country*) and most likely written in conjunction with the greater Corsica project. He reports here on Rousseau's *Projet de constitution pour la Corse*, drafted in 1765 at the request of a Corsican military officer while Rousseau was swept along by the general enthusiasm on the continent for Paoli's democratic project. Sebald summarizes:

> Er [Rousseau] sah in Korsika die Möglichkeit zur Verwirklichung einer Ordnung, die die Übel der Gesellschaft, in der er sich gefangen fühlte, vermied. Seine Abneigung gegen die städtische Zivilisation bewog ihn, den Korsen den Landbau als die einzige Grundlage für ein wahrhaft gutes und freies Leben vorzustellen. Jegliche Hierarchisierung sollte von vornherein verhindert werden durch eine ... in allem auf dem Grundsatz der Gleichheit aufbauende Legislative ... Das ganze auf der Petersinsel umrissene Korsikaprojekt ist somit ein Traum, in welchem der immer mehr auf Warenproduktion, Handel und die Akkumulation von Privateigentum sich ausrichtenden bürgerlichen Gesellschaft in Europa die Rückkehr in unschuldigere Zeiten verheißen wird. (*Logis* 59)
> [He [Rousseau] saw in Corsica the potential for putting into practice an order in which the evils of the society in which he felt

---

14   Ferdinand Gregorovius, *Korsika: Historische Skizzen und Wanderungen im Jahre 1852* (Frankfurt am Main: Societäts-Verlag, 1988), 18.
15   Ibid., 94.

himself trapped could be avoided. His aversion to urban civilization motivated him to suggest the Corsicans adopt agriculture
as the only possible basis for a truly good and free life. All forms
of hierarchy were to be avoided by means of a legal system ...
based on the principle of equality ... The whole Corsica project
outlined on the Île Saint-Pierre is thus a utopian dream in which
bourgeois society, increasingly determined by the manufacture
of goods and the accumulation of private wealth, is promised a
return to more innocent times. (*Place* 56)]

Despite its idealist aims, Rousseau's constitutional project reflects
just one more attempt to impose on society a rational order that
would ultimately revert, following the dialectic of Enlightenment,
into ruinous control and terror. Sebald alludes to this when he cites
Rousseau's fantasy that this small island would surprise Europe by its
progressiveness, only to add that Rousseau would have been shocked
to discover "in what terrifying manner this prophecy was to be fulfilled
within the next fifty years" ("in welch schreckenerregender Weise
diese Prophezeiung sich binnen fünfzig Jahren erfüllen würde"; *Logis*
59/56). The unstated allusion is to the birth and rise of Napoleon, but
surely also to the notorious blood feuds that racked Corsica during
the nineteenth century, which cost thousands of lives and threw the
island into political turmoil.[16] What most fascinated Sebald about
Corsica was this peculiar dynamic that gave it the distinction of
being both the birthplace of liberal democracy and a notorious site of
incessant bloodbaths, caused by irrational internecine and interfamilial
conflict. Corsica represents a microcosm of that paradoxical reflex
Sebald identified with the dialectic of Enlightenment, the inexplicable
amalgamation of a politics of emancipation and a social-psychological
structure that fostered inter-human violence. In his essay on Rousseau,
Sebald suggests that this great democratic thinker, inventor of the
social contract and anti-Modernist emissary for a return to a pastoral
lifestyle, was himself infected by an addiction to the Modernist way
of life he claimed to abhor. He notes the contradiction that although

16 Sebald encountered this ironically skeptical response to Rousseau's ideal-
istic vision already in Gregorovius, *Korsika*, 219, who mocks the notion that
Rousseau's legal reforms would have had any influence on the coarsely
instinctual Corsicans. Sebald was familiar with the history of feuding in Corsica
through the work of his historian colleague at the University of East Anglia,
Stephen Wilson, *Feuding, Conflict and Banditry in Nineteenth-Century Corsica*
(Cambridge: Cambridge University Press, 1988). He also highlighted information about feuds and the vendetta in encyclopedia articles about Corsica,
and in one set of notes he records the statistics about deaths caused by feuding
at diverse junctures of the nineteenth century.

Rousseau was invited to live in exile on Corsica, where he could have realized this pastoral vision, he refused because he was reluctant to sacrifice the comforts of modern civilization (*Logis* 59–60/57). He thus takes Rousseau as emblematic of a "gap between our longings and our rational strategy for living" ("Gespaltenheit unserer Sehnsucht und unseres rationalen Lebenskalküls") that haunts the psychic constitution of all human beings (*Logis* 59/56). This universal sense of tension between ameliorating utopian visions and unfathomable destructiveness was what fascinated Sebald about Corsica.

Sebald also had personal reasons for choosing Corsica as the place to undertake this study of how natural history and human psychology intertwine: with its high mountains and steep ravines and valleys, the island reminded him of the landscape of his own Alpine homeland in the Allgäu region of Bavaria. He marks in his copy of Gregorovius the passage in which this earlier traveler relates the similarities between the plant life of Corsica and that of the European Alps and the Pyrenees;[17] and among Sebald's archival materials one finds extensive lists of plants, trees, and animals that were once found on Corsica, gleaned from Gregorovius and other sources. Far from drawing comfort from this familiarity between Corsica and his own place of origin, it instead instills in Sebald's narrator an uncanny anxiety. When he encounters the open stone outcroppings on the island, he feels "oppressed by the mountains uplifted eons ago, especially since they reminded me of the gloomy valleys of my alpine childhood, above which in winter the sun only appeared around midday in the form of a blue apparition" ("niedergedrückt von dem vor Jahrmillionen aufgeworfenen Gestein, zumal es mich erinnerte an die finsteren Täler meiner alpenländischen Kindheit, über denen im Winter die Sonne nur um die Mittagszeit eine Weile als ein blaues Trugbild erschien"; "Aufzeichnungen" 192). The narrator's descriptions of his hikes through the Corsican landscape similarly highlight this sense of foreboding, unleashed by the feeling of being swallowed up by a limitless landscape that extends in all directions. He notes the paradox that although Corsica is a narrowly circumscribed island, he feels as though he is caught "in the midst of a continent that extends limitlessly in every direction, beyond each of its mountain ranges; as though Corsica were an island only in the sense in which America or Australia are islands" ("mitten in einem nach allen Himmelsrichtungen unbegrenzten, hinter jedem Gebirgszug weiter fortgehenden Kontinent, als sei Korsika eine Insel nur in dem Sinne, in dem letztendlich, auch Amerika oder Australien eine Insel ist"; 192). This experience of Corsica's expansive mountain landscapes does not provide Sebald's narrator with the euphoric awe one might

---

17 Gregorovius, *Korsika*, 134–5.

expect from an ecotourist, whose aim is to experience nature in its most raw and sublime forms. On the contrary, it makes him feel dwarfed, threatened, and imprisoned in a labyrinth in which all attempts to gain orientation remain futile:

> Die Beklemmung, die sich, unfehlbar, wie ich bald feststellte, bei meinen Inselexkursionen auf mich legte, wurde ausgelöst nicht nur von den labyrinthisch um die Gebirgsstöcke sich schlingenden, ein mal ums andere in dunkle Sackgassen hineinführenden Wegen & Straßen, sondern auch von der Tiefe der weithin durch die Täler & über die Rücken der Berge sich ziehenden Wälder, in denen man, insbesondere an grauen Tagen, wenn die Strahlen der Sonne nicht durch die Baumwipfel dringen, ehe man es sich versieht, die Orientierung verliert & wieder das Fürchten lernt, das den Kindern im Märchen, die fernab von ihrem Elternhaus in einer tagelang sich nicht lichtenden Wildnis in die Irre gehen, den Hals zusammenschnürt. ("Aufzeichnungen" 192)
> [The anxiety that—inevitably, as I soon recognized—befell me during my excursions on the island was triggered not merely by the paths & roads that wound their way like labyrinths around the massifs, and that now and again led to dark dead-ends, but also by the depth of the vast forests that stretched through the valleys & across the mountain ridges, and in which one, especially on gray days when the sunbeams do not penetrate the tops of the trees, can quickly lose one's orientation without being aware of it, & due to which one re-experiences that fear that chokes the children in fairy tales, who get lost for days on end in a wilderness without any clearings, far away from their parental home.]

Typical is the way this sentence, which describes how the narrator loses all sense of direction in the dark labyrinth of valleys, mountain ridges, and tree-shrouded paths, itself develops as a labyrinth of intertwining clauses in which readers can also easily lose their bearings. This passage is reminiscent of those sections of *Die Ringe des Saturn*, such as the episode on Dunwich Heath, in which Sebald's narrator describes his total lack of orientation in a landscape that bears no outstanding identifying features (*Ringe* 211–18/169–75). As in that text, here too this experience of being submerged in an underworld is juxtaposed with an overriding perspective from above that unlocks the mystery of the labyrinth and provides rescuing orientation. More significant is the theme of inherent fear and anxiety that is associated with this experience of indomitable nature. By connecting it with the fright of children in fairy tales, who like Hansel and Gretel lose all sense of direction in the vastness of the forest,

Sebald alludes to the fact that on the European continent such untrammeled landscapes exist only in the mythic fantasies of a Romantic past. But he also indicates that this fear of nature's overwhelming expanse, and of the existential power it exerts over human beings, is so deeply ingrained in the human psyche that it plays a leading role in our most popular and widespread cultural myths.[18]

When he returns to this idea of human fear associated with the experience of primeval forests, Sebald no longer invokes their natural grandeur, but instead explains how this human anxiety has led to their eradication. He begins this section of his notes with language that alludes to the opening lines of the traditional fairy tale, thereby cementing the intratextual connection to the earlier passage linking our fear of the forests with the motif of children lost in the woods:

> Es war einmal eine Zeit, da war die ganze Insel von Wald überzogen. Stockwerk um Stockwerk wuchs er Jahrtausende hindurch in einem Wettstreit mit sich selbst bis in die Höhe von fünfzig Metern & mehr, & wer weiß, vielleicht hätten sich größere & größere Arten herausgebildet, Bäume bis in den Himmel hinein, wären die Menschen nicht aufgetreten & hätten sie nicht, mit der für ihr Geschlecht bezeichnenden Angst vor dem Ort ihrer Herkunft, den Wald stets weiter zurückgedrängt. ("Aufzeichnungen" 198; cf. *Campo Santo* 39)
> [Once upon a time the island was entirely covered by forest. Story by story it grew for thousands of years in rivalry with itself, up to heights of fifty meters & more, & who knows, perhaps larger & larger species would have evolved, trees reaching to the sky, if human beings had not appeared & if, with the typical fear felt by their own kind for its place of origin, they had not steadily forced the forest back again. (cf. *Campo Santo* 35)]

Sebald's narrator envisions a natural world that, left undisturbed and free of human interference, would evolve without foreseeable

---

18 Sebald reflects on the inherent inimicality between humans and nature in his essay on Charles Sealsfield in *Unheimliche Heimat*: "Sealsfield conceives of nature as something that is principally foreign, as something that must be broken if one does not wish to be broken by it" ("Sealsfield erfaßt die Natur als das prinzipiell Fremde, als etwas, das gebrochen werden muß, will man nicht von ihm gebrochen werden"). He interprets Sealsfield's perspective on nature as "exemplary for the antagonistic relationship between human beings and nature whose destructive dynamic only became truly virulent in the commodity economy of capitalism" ("Exempel des antagonistischen Verhältnisses zwischen Mensch und Natur, dessen zerstörerische Dynamik durch die kapitalistische Warenwirtschaft erst wirklich virulent wurde"; *Unheimliche Heimat* 35).

limits.[19] But like the once unspoiled forests of Corsica, it is relegated to the domain of fairy tale and myth, to the "once upon a time." This passage opens a central section in Sebald's Corsica manuscript—part of which was excerpted and published as "Die Alpen im Meer" ("The Alps in the Sea")—that describes the ecological devastation of the island since the end of the eighteenth century. One of the attractions the island held for Sebald was precisely the possibility of experiencing ecological decimation in its most immediate and exaggerated forms. In that sense, he pursues a brand of ecotourism motivated more by the desire to experience decline than the pristine recuperation of nature.[20] He once again takes Corsica as a microcosm for a "dialectic of Enlightenment" that exposes how purported advances in human civilization are concomitant with the despoliation of the natural world. But he lends this sociological dialectic a peculiarly psychological, even a Freudian twist: he interprets the human impulse to destroy the primeval forests as a response to our innate fear of the place from which we emanate. He is alluding to a passage in Freud's essay "Das Unheimliche" ("The Uncanny"), in which the psychoanalyst interprets the fear neurotic men experience at the sight of the female genitalia in terms of anxieties about the uncanny return to the place of their birth.[21] Not surprisingly, Sebald's copy of this essay in his personal library is extensively annotated, with this passage marked by three vertical lines in the margin. This shift of the dialectic of Enlightenment into a psychological dimension is one of the distinguishing features of Sebald's investigation of the "natural history of destruction" in the Corsica project. He links the motif of human violence against the natural environment with one of his most prominent themes: *unheimliche Heimat*, the peculiar uncanniness of the homeland, or the

19 This emphasis on the destruction of nature due primarily to human intervention has its parallel in the episode on Dunwich Heath in *Die Ringe des Saturn*, where the narrator attributes the natural decline of this region to the clearing of the primordial forests that began with the appearance of the first human settlers (*Ringe* 211–12/169–70).

20 For an investigation of crossovers between ecotourism and so-called "dark tourism" in Sebald's work, but especially in the Corsica project, see Richard T. Gray, "Reisen in die Vergangenheit (der Natur): W. G. Sebald als Öko-Tourist," *Literatur für Leser* 68, no. 4 (2013): 193–21. For a more general exposition of Sebald's relationship with "dark tourism," see Anne Fuchs, "Von Orten und Nicht-Orten: Fremderfahrung und dunkler Tourismus in Sebalds Prosa," in *W. G. Sebald: Intertextualität und Topographie*, ed. Irene Heidelberger-Leonard and Mireille Tabah (Berlin: LIT Verlag, 2008), 55–71.

21 Sigmund Freud, "Das Unheimliche," in *Gesammelte Werke*, ed. Anna Freud et al., 18 vols (London: Imago, 1940–87), 12:258–9; "The Uncanny," in *The Standard Edition of the Complete Psychological Works of Sigmund Freud*, ed. and trans. James Strachey, 24 vols (London: Hogarth, 1953–74), 17:245.

alienation human beings experience toward their origins or their place of birth. He choreographs the nightmarish aspect of such a return home in the story "Il ritorno in patria" by depicting the return of the exile to his homeland as a decent into hell (*Schwindel* 185–287/171–263). His exploration of this theme in the Corsica project stresses the primordial psychological motivations that underpin the *self*-destructive human proclivity toward annihilating the natural life-world on which our own emergence and survival hinges.

Ecopsychology and Self-Critique

Especially important in Sebald's exploration of this ecopsychological reflex is his narrator's refusal to exempt himself from that fear of nature that motivates our aggressions against it. The passage describing his own loss of orientation and anxiety in the Corsican backcountry implicates him as participating in this vicious circle of fright before, and subsequent violence against one's natural origins. In order to reinforce this self-inculpating critique of the human tendency to intervene aggressively in nature, he relates an episode in which his narrator observes a procession of caterpillars marching in a regimented configuration. After observing this phenomenon for a time, he wantonly removes one of the creatures from this formation, resulting both in the individual caterpillar's death and in the cessation of the procession itself. Sebald's narrator speculates about his own unconscious psychological motivations:

Nachdem ich diese absonderlichen Kreaturen eine zeitlang bereits beobachtet hatte, schob ich, wahrscheinlich aus einer der zerstörerischen Regungen, die die meisten von uns von klein auf in ihrem Herzen tragen, eine der Raupen aus dem Zug heraus, was zur Folge hatte, daß sie tot liegenblieb, offenbar außerstande zurückzukehren an ihren kaum eine Spanne von ihrer jetzigen Position entfernten Platz. Und nicht nur war die aus der Reihe genommene Raupe erstarrt, der ganze Zug rührte sich nicht, machte keine Anstalten, die durch meinen gewaltsamen Eingriff entstandene Lücke zu schließen, sondern hielt einfach nur ein. ("Aufzeichnungen" 195)
[After I had already observed these peculiar creatures for a while, I shoved one of the caterpillars out of this procession, most likely in response to one of those destructive impulses that most of us bear in our hearts from childhood onward, with the result that it just lay there dead, apparently incapable of returning to its former place, which was just inches away. And not only this caterpillar that was removed from its position turned rigid; the entire procession no longer moved, made no attempt to close the gap

that was created by my violent intervention, but simply stopped
dead in its tracks.]

The narrator's action does not follow any rational purpose, but arises
as an inexplicable impulse, as though guided by some inherent will to
experimentation, an urge to wantonly disrupt the orderly movement of
the caterpillars just to see what will happen. As his adjectives indicate,
at the moment of its retrospective retelling the narrator is aware of the
"destructive" and "violent" tendencies that motivate him. He portrays
himself as driven by an obsessive, even morbid curiosity, as indicated
by the extensive period of deliberative observation that precedes
his manipulation. But his own inclination to view this senseless
disruption of a natural process as an act of aggression, one that
"most of us" harbor "in our hearts" from early childhood onward,
lends it a quality of instinctual inevitability. This adds a further
psychological, even psychoanalytic dimension to the human proclivity
toward destructive intervention in the natural world, suggesting that
it is a reflex closely aligned with Freud's aggressive impulse. And
like Freud's theory of Thanatos as an aggression that is directed both
externally against objects in the real world and internally against the
self, instances of environmental disruption paradigmatically exemplify
how object-destruction and self-destruction are interwoven, given the
interdependence of human existence with the biosphere. This episode,
trivial though it may seem, speaks volumes about the unwitting repercussions of even the most seemingly insignificant human actions: with
a kind of domino effect, the violence perpetrated against one single
caterpillar resonates through the entire community and brings their
ritual procession to a standstill. As the narrator discovers when he
subsequently returns to the scene of his crime—he evocatively and
ominously calls it an "Ort des Unglücks" ("place of misfortune")—not
only have the caterpillars failed to move, but their immobility has
caused them to be baked to death by the sun. "To my horror, the caterpillars remained, now as previously, in the very same spot. They had
not budged even an inch, but instead had stood still until, withered
by the sun, they were forced to leave this life one after the other" ("Zu
meinem Schrecken hielten die Raupen nach wie vor an derselben
Stelle. Nicht einen Viertelzoll waren sie weitergerückt, sondern solange
stillgestanden, bis sie, ausgedörrt von der Sonne, eine nach der anderen
lassen mußten von ihrem Leben"; 196). Sebald's narrator is dismayed
by how a seemingly simple act, driven by his own thirst for knowledge,
wantonly disrupts a natural process, culminating in a chain reaction
of death that eventually eradicates an entire community. Through this
simple example, Sebald alludes not only to the inexplicable symbiotic
relationships that govern inter-species dynamics in a vital ecosphere,

but also documents how the most minute acts of intervention can call forth unforeseeably devastating consequences.

This episode is actually borrowed from one of Sebald's historical sources: from Edward Lear's *Journal of a Landscape Painter in Corsica*, where it is related in an appendix that deals with some of the peculiar habits of caterpillars.[22] The primary difference between the intertextual source and Sebald's adaptation is that whereas in Lear's report this episode is related with the dryness and objectivity of the entomologist, Sebald's narrator speculates about his own unconscious psychological motivations and self-critically deliberates on how his action is representative of human proclivities toward wanton violence. In the course of these reflections, he is thrown into such a stupor and so horrified by the unintended consequences of his interference that he fails to notice the arrival of inclement weather (196). A storm forces him to flee the woods in a stumbling rush, and he eventually breathes a deep sigh of relief when he arrives at a café, a "frontier outpost of civilization" ("Vorposten der Zivilisation"; 197) that promises shelter and rescue. Throughout this episode Sebald ironizes the "nature" of human nature itself: the narrator's emotions follow a wild journey, beginning with curious fascination, transmuting into self-reprehensive guilt and horror, with this guilt ultimately giving way, after nature becomes a threat, to the relief provided by a return to the security of civilization.

In Sebald's rendition, this episode follows a trajectory that begins with the human being as overpowering agent who controls nature, depicts the transmutation of this manipulating agent into the fearful victim at the mercy of overweening natural forces, and concludes with a flight into that very civilizing sensibility that turns nature into an object for human mastery in the first place. He takes pains to demonstrate in the example of his own narrator how the anxiety humans harbor toward unvanquished nature underwrites a will to knowledge predicated on control of the natural world—often enough with cataclysmic results. In the thoughts and actions of his first-person narrator he depicts a perversely spiraling psychological logic, grounded in primordial fear, that offers one explanation for human-caused environmental degradation. The indictment Sebald expresses is significant for its

---

22 Edward Lear, *Journal of a Landscape Painter in Corsica* (London: Robert John Bush, 1870), 266–8. The second folder of Sebald's materials for the Corsica project contains a sheet with the heading "Motten/Insekten" ("moths/insects") that includes notes taken directly from this episode. In his manuscript, Sebald translates this incident into German and subsumes it as an unmarked intertext. He plays on the problems of intertextuality itself by embedding within his cloned episode a reference to a similar experience, attributed to a fictional Reverend Barleycorn, which serves to authenticate the narrator's perception of the caterpillars' responses ("Aufzeichnungen" 195–6).

inclusiveness. If Corsica serves as an especially egregious example for the devastation of the natural world based on violent human interventions, the blame for this is not laid at the doorstep of the Corsicans themselves, but rather is diagnosed as a general human psychological reflex. In this sense, Sebald's objective can be seen as an act of narrative consciousness-raising, one that works to bring to thoughtful awareness certain unconscious impulses that underwrite the human tendency to manipulate our natural environment. To Sebald's credit, he displays no naiveté about the complexities of this project of consciousness-raising, demonstrating through the actions of his own narrator the impulse to repress such insight as soon as nature assumes the guise of an imposing existential danger.

Significant segments of Sebald's Corsica manuscript are concerned with documenting the extreme environmental degradation the island has experienced since the end of the eighteenth century, due largely to deforestation and the overhunting of species forced to survive in an ecosystem lacking sufficient resources. But he also addresses the social, political, and inter-human manifestations of violence perpetrated by humans against other human beings. In his source materials, he pays inordinate attention to Corsica's prolonged history of blood feuds, a tradition of foreign colonial rule and bloody rebellions, and an anti-Modernist nationalist movement that relies on brutal acts of terrorism as its chief means of rebellion. In this regard, he once more treats Corsica as a representative microcosm, and his anthropological and natural-historical study of the island occurs against the historical backdrop of the vicious nationalist struggles taking place at that time in the territories of the former Yugoslavia. At one point in his draft manuscript Sebald draws a parallel between the fanatical hunters of Corsica, who ride around the countryside in jeeps, dress in paramilitary clothing, and wreak havoc on the declining animal species on the island, and what he ironically dubs the "Marlboro-style heroes" ("Marlboro-Helden") fighting the civil war in Yugoslavia, who likewise bring about the political and environmental destruction of their own homeland ("Aufzeichnungen" 201; cf. Campo Santo 43/40). In the Corsica project Sebald thus lends his characteristic obsession with the "natural history of destruction" an important ecopsychological turn. He does not abandon the concern with historical acts of social and political violence perpetrated by humans against humans, but rather explores how these actions are offshoots of a greater fear and aggressive instinct that condition human interactions with the natural environment. This linkage is underwritten by a conception of human psychology that embraces the Freudian diagnosis of humans as guided not merely by a libidinal impulse, encouraging them to join together in the shared accomplishments of civilization, but also by an unconquerable aggression, directed not only at human others, but against the natural environment and ultimately against themselves. This psychological perspective lends Sebald's views the pessimistic cast of the inescapable and reveals his characteristic melancholy at its bleakest. For if environmental decimation and violence against our fellow human beings are inherent in our psychic constitution, then how can we rescue ourselves from our current ecological plight, let alone from increasingly violent acts of terror? This is the dilemma Sebald confronts—and arguably fails to resolve—in the Corsica project. Perhaps this is because he painted himself into a psychological and anthropological corner? By the same token, if Sebald's reliance on Freudian theory implies that he shared Freud's cultural pessimism, it also suggests that, like Freud, he held out hope that bringing our plight to conscious attention marks a step toward possible resolution.[23]

Witnessing and Testifying to Human Self-Imposed Exile from Nature

In his critical reception, Sebald has been viewed almost exclusively as a writer whose primary concerns are the past historical catastrophes of (largely) Western civilization and its pursuit of an order-instilling politics of power, culminating in the Nazi-perpetrated Holocaust and the horrors of World War II. Yet the emphatic ecological orientation of his Corsica project demonstrates that this represents but one aspect of a much more complex problematic. Himself a voluntary émigré, Sebald is associated with themes of exile, dislocation, deportation, and the late repercussions caused by the return of memory. It is common to think of him, alluding to an aphorism by the German Romantic Friedrich Schlegel, as "a prophet facing backwards":[24] a writer whose focus on the past is almost obsessive, and whose perspectives on the future are largely bleak. This is consistent with the tendency to align Sebald's conception of history with Walter Benjamin's ekphrastic elaboration on Paul Klee's *Angelus Novus*, in which, in Benjamin's reading, this angel turns its back to the future into which it is interminably driven

---

23 This tension between pessimistic psychological assessment and qualified hope for the future characterizes the concluding paragraphs of Freud's most important contribution to a psychoanalysis of human cultural achievement, *Das Unbehagen in der Kultur*, in *Gesammelte Werke*, ed. Anna Freud et al., 18 vols (London: Imago, 1940–87), 14:505–6; *Civilization and Its Discontents*, in *The Standard Edition of the Complete Psychological Works of Sigmund Freud*, ed. and trans. James Strachey, 24 vols (London: Hogarth, 1953–74), 21:144–5.

24 Friedrich Schlegel, *Charakteristiken und Kritiken I*, Vol. 2 of *Kritische Friedrich-Schlegel-Ausgabe*, ed. Ernst Behler and Hans Eichner, 21 vols (Paderborn: Schöningh, 1967), 176; *Philosophical Fragments*, trans. Peter Firchow (Minneapolis: University of Minnesota Press, 1991), 81.

and looks back in horror at the catastrophic ruins of history that continue to pile up before its backward-directed gaze.[25] This view is consistent with those parts of Sebald's work that deal with problems of exile, displacement, and persecution as the reflexes of a *bellum omnium contra omnes* that manifests itself as a will to political mastery and domination over other human beings. The protagonists of the two works that concentrate most decisively on problems of persecution and exile, *Die Ausgewanderten* and *Austerlitz*, are victims who suffer from the traces of sociopolitical catastrophe—the "marks of pain which ... trace countless fine lines through history" ("Schmerzensspuren, die sich ... in unzähligen feinen Linien durch die Geschichte ziehen"; *Austerlitz* 20/14)—and that are etched into the personal histories of his protagonists. This is one aspect of Sebald's works that has been—justifiably—celebrated: his ability to record with great sensitivity the fates of *individual* victims, whose stories might otherwise be lost in the anonymity of mass death and total annihilation.[26]

One of the most intractable paradoxes in Sebald's thought is his consistent denial that human beings exist as autonomous individuals who are masters of their own fates,[27] even though his literary texts embody a redemptive gesture that depicts the victims of world-historical

25 Walter Benjamin, "Über den Begriff der Geschichte," in *Gesammelte Schriften*, ed. Rolf Tiedemann and Hermann Schweppenhäuser, 7 vols (Frankfurt am Main: Suhrkamp, 1972–91), 1:697–8; "Theses on the Philosophy of History," in *Illuminations: Essays and Reflections*, trans. Harry Zohn (New York: Schocken, 1969), 257–8. For critical reflections on the significance of Benjamin's angel of history on Sebald's worldview, see Julia Hell, "The Angel's Enigmatic Eyes, or The Gothic Beauty of Catastrophic History in W. G. Sebald's *Air War and Literature*," *Criticism* 46 (2004): 361–2, and Richard Crownshaw, "German Suffering or 'Narrative Fetishism'?: W. G. Sebald's *Air War and Literature: Zürich Lectures*," in *Searching for Sebald: Photography after W. G. Sebald*, ed. Lise Patt (Los Angeles: Institute of Cultural Inquiry, 2007), 576–7. Bernhard Malkmus, "Das Naturtheater des W. G. Sebald: Die ökologischen Aporien eines 'poeta doctus,'" *Gegenwartsliteratur* 10 (2011): 214, discusses the relevance of Benjamin's example specifically in the context of Sebald's environmental discourse, as does Gay Hawkins, "History in Things: Sebald and Benjamin on Transience and Detritus," in *W. G. Sebald: Schreiben ex patria / Expatriate Writing*, ed. Gerhard Fischer (Amsterdam: Rodopi, 2009), 169–75.

26 In his interview with Sven Boedecker (*"Auf ungeheuer dünnem Eis"* 106–7), Sebald emphasizes how his protagonists, as individuals, stand out against the anonymous victims of mass catastrophes.

27 See Sebald's interview with Joseph Cuomo (Schwartz 117), or the comments he makes in his discussion with Marco Poltronieri: "Humanity does not consist, as we still hoped in our liberal dreams of the nineteenth century, of emancipated, autonomous individuals. It represents a, to be sure, partially heterogeneous, but principally homogenous mass" ("Die Menschheit besteht nicht, wie wir das im 19. Jahrhundert in unseren liberalen Träumen noch hofften, aus emanzipierten,

forces as sovereign individuals. There is a struggle in his work and his thought between a fatalism that is closely related to Hegel's view of history as a process that transforms even world-historical individuals like Napoleon—or, for that matter, Hitler—into the instruments of its own inscrutable design,[28] and the sensitive elaboration of the individual lives of everyday people who are the victims of history. While the history of civilization appears to evolve behind the backs of human individuals—a view consistent with Benjamin's interpretation of Klee's *Angelus Novus*—Sebald's narrative strategies highlight the salvation of individual victims. His protagonists are freed from the massive and anonymous rubble of catastrophic history by his own acts of writing. The question is whether this redemptive moment can also be identified in Sebald's environmental perspective, which treats the natural world as victim.

There are great differences between these two forms of victimization. Nature itself is anonymous, which may make it more difficult to invoke sympathies for its decimation—hence the central role the fate of the polar bear plays, for example, in attempts to document the disappearing ice sheet. Nature has no empathetic informants—apart from the very human beings who mindlessly perpetuate its destruction—who can tell this story of destruction from the inside. Hence we are perennially thrown back—like the narrator in the episode about the caterpillars—on human testifiers who can present fleeting self-critiques of their own aggressions against non-human nature. This suggests one of the greatest differences between Sebald's ecological and his sociopolitical projects: in the latter, it is relatively easy to segregate perpetrators and victims; whereas in the former, perpetrators and victims are largely indistinguishable. This is one reason why Sebald struggled with the narrative portrayal of environmental catastrophe, whereas he succeeded in developing a narrative stance of empathetic engagement with the victims of sociopolitical terror.

The ecocritical dimension of Sebald's works finds increased articulation in his middle period of production, the years from 1993, just after the publication of *Die Ausgewanderten*, to 1997, when he delivered

---

autonomen Individuen. Sie stellt eine zwar teilweise heterogene, aber prinzipiell homogene Masse dar"; "*Auf ungeheuer dünnem Eis*" 88).

28 Georg Wilhelm Friedrich Hegel, *Vorlesungen über die Philosophie der Geschichte*, Vol. 12 of *Theorie Werkausgabe*, ed. Eva Moldenhauer and Karl Markus Michel (Frankfurt am Main: Suhrkamp, 1970), 42–3; *The Philosophy of History*, trans. John Sibree (New York: Dover, 1956), 29–31. Maya Barzilai, "Melancholia as World History: W. G. Sebald's Rewriting of Hegel in *Die Ringe des Saturn*," in *W. G. Sebald and the Writing of History*, ed. Anne Fuchs and J. J. Long (Würzburg: Königshausen & Neumann, 2007), 73–89, examines the connections between Sebald's and Hegel's views of history.

his lectures about the Allied air war on Germany. He never wavers from his concerted focus on the civilizing process and its paradoxical reversion into violent barbarism; but in these interim years his concerns demonstrate a marked tendency to expand from a concentration on political mastery, to the violence humans direct against the natural environment. This intensifying ecological focus begins to take shape in *Die Ringe des Saturn*, which develops as a pilgrimage through the ecologically and culturally decimated landscapes of Sebald's elective home in East Anglia. Yet throughout Sebald's oeuvre there is a great deal of intellectual commerce that moves between his ecological concerns—his pervasive invocations of environmental degradation at the hands (and the minds) of human beings—and sociopolitical and historical issues—exile, colonialism, the Holocaust, the politics of power more generally. In many respects these are two sides of a single coin. In his middle period the ecological component comes into ever greater prominence, culminating in the Corsica project; but it then goes into remission when Sebald refocuses on sociopolitical matters—which, after all, garnered him his greatest literary successes—in *Luftkrieg und Literatur* and *Austerlitz*. The intertwining of these two critical dimensions is especially manifest in *Die Ringe des Saturn*, which stands out for its imbrication of narratives about political oppression with stories emphasizing nature's submission to the processes of modern industrialization. These two themes even share a common symbolism: the motifs of fire and combustion, which are associated both with the Holocaust and with the human drive toward widespread destruction of the earth's forests. *Die Ringe des Saturn* relates not only the brutal colonization of the Congo by the Belgians and the ravages of the British Opium Wars on China, but also the consequences of long-term deforestation on Dunwich Heath or the staggering reduction of herring stocks due to overfishing. Sebald succeeds in linking these modes of human aggression through such strategies as his oblique association of the extensive killing of herring with the mass murders of the Holocaust. He thus evocatively juxtaposes an image depicting a crowd of fishermen standing among a veritable mountain of dead fish (*Ringe* 73/54; see Figure 9.1) with a picture of human corpses strewn across a wooded landscape (*Ringe* 80–1/60–1; see Figure 9.2), in apparent allusion to what British troops discovered when they liberated the concentration camp of Bergen-Belsen in April 1945. But Sebald's language also reinforces this connection: commenting on a film about the herring fishery he claims to have seen in school, he sarcastically remarks on its portrayal of fishermen who are "working heroically" ("heldenhaft arbeiten"), and how they exemplify "mankind's struggle with the power of Nature" ("Kampf des Menschen mit der Übermacht der Natur"; *Ringe* 72/54). The biophobia that motivates the fishermen

Figure 9.1: Herring catch (*Ringe des Saturn* 73/54).

Figure 9.2: Corpses of Bergen-Belsen (*Ringe des Saturn* 80–1/60–1).

is couched in the bellicose language of Nazi ideology. This connection of overfishing with the politics of the Holocaust is reinforced when Sebald's narrator comments that this film was made in Germany in 1936, and that the fish fulfill their "fate on this earth" ("Schicksal auf dieser Erde") when they are transported, like the Jews to Auschwitz, on "the railway goods wagon" ("die Güterwagen der Eisenbahn"; *Ringe* 73/54).

This same linkage is highlighted in the motif of silk and silkworm cultivation that sutures together the discrete episodes of this rambling, peripatetic narrative. In a 1995 interview, Sebald remarked on how this motif stands as a paradigm for the human drive to exert absolute control over the natural world:.

Diese Seidengeschichte zieht sich durch das ganze Buch und ist für mich ein Paradigma des Übergangs von Natur zu Industrie … An so einem Beispiel kann man gut sehen, wie wahnsinnig das ist, wenn der Mensch etwas in großem Maßstab organisiert. Wie das dann auf und ab ging mit der Seidenindustrie—das ist ein Modellfall für unser Verhalten gegenüber der Natur und für unseren Versuch, die Natur in etwas zu überführen, das wir völlig unter Kontrolle haben. Da wird produziert bis zum Umfallen, dann schmeißen wir's wieder weg, wenn wir's nicht mehr brauchen, und später pflanzen wir wieder sechs Milliarden Bäume. Es ist also *eine* Spezies im Kontext der Natur, die alle diese Dinge anrichtet. (*"Auf ungeheuer dünnem Eis"* 116–17)

[This history of silk runs through the entire book, and for me it represents a paradigm of the transition from nature to industry … On the basis of such an example one can easily recognize how insane it is when human beings organize something on a grand scale. The way things went up and down in the silk industry— that is a paradigmatic case for our behavior toward nature and for our attempt to transform nature into something over which we have absolute control. First we produce until we collapse, and then we throw it all away when we no longer need it, and later on we once again plant six billion trees. There is only *one* species in all of nature that perpetrates such things.]

The silk industry—like the herring fishery—represents the murderous excesses that arise at that human-managed transition between nature and commerce, designed as a form of optimal organization that ensures maximum control over the productive forces of nature. Sebald stresses that this reflex is peculiar to one single species, the human being, and he diagnoses it as a perverse exaggeration of rational proclivities into a form of madness. The model for this dynamic is once again borrowed from Horkheimer and Adorno's *Dialectic of Enlightenment*.

This idea of human beings as an aberrant species runs like a leitmotif throughout much of Sebald's work and is expressed repeatedly in interviews (*"Auf ungeheuer dünnem Eis"* 114, 194, 259). In one instance, he explicitly names as the peculiar quirk of human beings

> daß es uns als Spezies offenbar möglich ist, zur Herstellung von Zerstörung die kompliziertesten und phantastischsten Dinge zu organisieren, aber nicht zur Verbesserung der Gesellschaft oder der Lebensverhältnisse. Das ist ein Paradox, das in sich ein Geheimnis birgt. Und wenn wir hinter dieses Geheimnis unserer inneren Konstitution kommen könnten, wäre einiges gewonnen.
> (*"Auf ungeheuer dünnem Eis"* 187)
> [that it is obviously possible for us as a species to organize the most complicated and fantastic things for the ends of destruction, but not for the betterment of society or our living conditions. That is a paradox that hides a secret. And if we could penetrate this secret of our innate constitution, we would gain a great deal.]

Unraveling the secret that underwrites this paradox in the human psychological makeup forms the crux of Sebald's ecopsychological deliberations in the Corsica project.

Sebald and the Principles of Ecopsychology

This touches the very center of Sebald's reflections on the dynamic of our present-day ecological crises. He locates the paradox of the human situation in the observation that we engage our intelligence and rationality most effectively and efficiently when we invest in strategies of destruction and annihilation. Sebald presents a damning commentary on what ecopsychologist Andy Fisher dubs "technosalvationism," an ideological deception he indicts as the "shared delusion" of our time, and that names the overly optimistic faith that human ingenuity can provide technological resolutions for all the environmental problems, including global warming, that industrialization has wrought.[29] For Sebald the conundrum of our current environmental situation is that human rationality and the technologies it spawns have consistently created new problems, even when striving to solve old ones. He is keenly aware of the ecological paradox that human beings are degrading the environment to such a degree that we are eradicating the conditions necessary for our own survival as a species. In an interview

---

29   Andy Fisher, *Radical Ecopsychology: Psychology in the Service of Life* (Albany: State University of New York Press, 2002), 157.

with Marco Poltronieri from June 1993 he comments incisively on the human condition of self-alienation from the natural world, which he deems responsible for this:

Natur ist der Kontext, in den wir ursprünglich hineingehört haben und aus dem wir sukzessive und in rapidem Maße in den letzten dreißig, vierzig Jahren evakuiert und vertrieben worden sind. Wir haben zwar in unseren organischen Körpern noch eine Erinnerung an die Natur, aber eben nur eine Erinnerung. (*"Auf ungeheuer dünnem Eis"* 94).
[Nature is the context within which we inherently belonged and from which, over the past thirty or forty years, we have been successively evacuated and exiled at a rapid pace. To be sure, in our organic bodies we still have a memory of nature, but precisely only a memory.]

Especially striking is how Sebald formulates our distance from nature in terms of self-imposed exile, and diagnoses a harmonious existence with the natural world as a past condition of which we have only vague memories. This language invokes the themes of the book he had published just prior to this interview, *Die Ausgewanderten*, and gives a first indication that his next literary project, *Die Ringe des Saturn*, will begin to expand the historical and political dimensions of exile by venturing into the domains of nature and ecology. This is more than just a quirk of rhetoric, as evidenced by the similar language Sebald uses three years later in a CBC radio interview with Eleanor Wachtel:

It is a characteristic of our species, in evolutionary terms, that we are a species in despair, for a number of reasons. Because we have created an environment for us which isn't what it should be. And we're out of our depth all the time. We're living exactly on the borderline between the natural world from which we are being driven out, or we're driving ourselves out of it, and that other world which is generated by our brain cells. And so clearly that fault line runs right through our physical and emotional makeup. (Schwartz 56)

He alters the passive-voice formulation, which asserts that humans are "driven out" of nature by some unnamed external force, correcting this to the active-voice, reflexive formulation, which claims we banish *ourselves* from our own natural "homeland." He diagnoses the human condition as disjunction between a physical dependence on the world of nature and a desire to flee into an artificial world "generated by our brain cells." He thereby alludes to the proclivity of humans to excogitate vast utopian schemes for redesigning, reordering, and reorganizing nature. Inevitably such utopias reveal themselves to be dystopias, places of human exile. But he also touches on one of the core thoughts of contemporary ecopsychology: the belief that advances in human intelligence have outpaced our evolutionary adaptation to our natural surroundings. As biologist Edward O. Wilson asserts, human beings represent an "evolutionary chimera": we have "created a Star Wars civilization, with Stone Age emotions, medieval institutions, and god-like technology."[30]

Sigmund Freud was one of the first modern thinkers to highlight the paradox that those cultural and technological innovations humans create in an effort to *prevent* human suffering are frequently responsible for creating new, often more severe forms of misery. In his foundational treatise identifying the malaise humans experience due to conflicts between our psychic constitution and the civilizing processes of cultural accomplishment, *Das Unbehagen in der Kultur* (*Civilization and Its Discontents*), Freud asks why human beings are not capable of finding satisfying resolutions for *social* problems. The human-determined social world should be where we are most capable of regulating suffering and maximizing pleasure—the guiding principles, for Freud, of all human endeavors. He explains the paradox that social institutions create more suffering than they remedy by suggesting that as political and cultural beings, we are infected by "a piece of unconquerable nature" ("ein Stück der unbesiegbaren Natur").[31] This work closes with the pessimistic recognition—Freud was among the first to express it, already in 1929, well before the invention of the atomic bomb—that the human drive for mastery over nature has reached the point where we are capable of exterminating human life completely: "Men have gained control over the forces of nature to such an extent that with their help they would have no difficulty in exterminating one another to the last man" ("Die Menschen haben es jetzt in der Beherrschung der Naturkräfte so weit gebracht, daß sie es mit deren Hilfe leicht haben, einander bis auf den letzten Mann auszurotten").[32]

It is but a small step from this critical insight to the recognition that humans are capable of eliminating not only human life, but the ecological conditions for *all* life on planet earth. However, as historian Dipesh Chakrabarty has reminded us, there is a great difference between abrupt planetary destruction caused by nuclear war and gradual annihilation by climate change. The former represents a

---

30 Edward O. Wilson, *The Social Conquest of Earth* (New York: Liveright/Norton, 2012), 11, 7.

31 Freud, *Das Unbehagen in der Kultur*, 445; *Civilization and Its Discontents*, 86.

32 Freud, *Das Unbehagen in der Kultur*, 506; *Civilization and Its Discontents*, 145.

conscious decision on the part of ruling political elites, whereas the latter is an *unconscious* consequence of human actions more generally.[33] This distinction also describes the two sides of Sebald's "dialectic of Enlightenment," his complementary critiques of human sociopolitical aggression against fellow human beings and of destructive human actions against the non-human environment. Perhaps it also explains why Sebald found it easier to relate the catastrophes caused by consciously implemented sociopolitical programs, than to narrate the unconscious destructive consequences of human actions that are bound up with our psychological constitution. *Intentional* acts of oppression, with identifiable perpetrators, are much easier to analyze and criticize than are *unconscious* behaviors practiced by humans as a species. In the latter instance, any indictment must necessarily also be a critical self-indictment.

As we saw in our examination of the psychological turn Sebald gives to ecological questions, he was fascinated with precisely this extension of Freud's pessimistic vision, and he explored this self-destructive dynamic in its ecological dimensions in *Die Ringe des Saturn* and the fragmentary drafts of the Corsica project. In a discussion with Piet de Moor for a Dutch literary journal in 1992, he responded to a query about the apocalyptic vision at the conclusion of *Schwindel. Gefühle*—which is projected into the year 2013[34]—by commenting on how the final decades of the twentieth century are harbingers of a world in which the very durability and longevity of nature are called into question:

Es ist doch erstaunlich, daß wir in der Schule noch gelernt haben, die Welt wäre ewig und wir alle sehr gut im Gleichgewicht der Natur aufgehoben. Kein halbes Jahrhundert später ist diese beruhigende Gewißheit einfach verschwunden, und eines Tages wird uns die Rechnung präsentiert. Seit wir zu dieser Einsicht gekommen sind, stehen wir unter einem enormen psychischen Druck. Ich glaube, daß uns dadurch das letzte Fundament unserer verbürgten Existenz auf dieser Welt genommen ist. Die theokratischen Stützen sind schon früher weggefallen, danach konnten wir uns mit der Vorstellung trösten, daß man als sterbliches Individuum Teil eines größeren Prozesses ist, der in einer sehr beruhigenden Form abläuft. Inzwischen steht auch

---

33 Dipesh Chakrabarty, "The Climate of History: Four Theses," *Critical Inquiry* 35, no. 2 (Winter 2009): 221.

34 This closing reference to 2013, the (then) future anniversary of Stendhal's crossing the Alps in 1813 and Kafka's sojourn in Riva in 1913, is eliminated in the English translation.

diese Transzendenz nicht mehr fest. (*"Auf ungeheuer dünnem Eis"* 72)
[It is truly amazing that in school we still learned that the world is eternal and that we are safeguarded by our harmonious existence with nature. Less than half a century later this comforting certainty has simply disappeared, and someday soon we will be called to account. Now that we have arrived at this recognition, we stand under enormous psychic pressure. In my opinion this has stripped us of the last foundation of our established existence on this planet. The theocratic supports fell away even earlier, but thereafter we could console ourselves with the idea that as transitory individuals we are at least part of a larger process that operates in a reassuring manner. But in the meanwhile, not even this form of transcendence is guaranteed.]

This statement inevitably reminds one of Freud's famous comment about the three blows that post-Renaissance science has delivered against human narcissism: Copernicus's cosmological blow, which demonstrated that the earth and humanity do not stand at the center of the universe; Darwin's biological blow, which proved that human beings were not an autonomous species, but were related through evolution to other, lower creatures; and the psychoanalytic blow—Freud's own contribution—which demonstrated that, in Freud's celebrated phrase, human beings are not masters in their own house: we are not ruled by reason and deliberate action, but rather by irrational instincts and impulses.[35] Sebald adds a fourth blow to this triumvirate: what we might term the ecological dethroning of the human being, or the insight into the Anthropocene. This ecological blow to our collective narcissism emerges with the growing recognition that modern human beings have disrupted the ecological balance of nature to such an extent that the future existence of life on the planet is compromised. This awareness strips us of that last bit of certainty about the possibility of continued existence in some elemental, or even mental form—that is, in human memory—after our physical deaths. It forces us to abandon the consoling thought that we are part of a larger ecological life world that is pre-programed to evolve into eternity, and that holds out the promise of transpersonal transcendence. In Sebald's diagnosis, not only are we not masters in our own psychic household, but the consequences of our

---

35 Sigmund Freud, "Eine Schwierigkeit der Psychoanalyse," in *Gesammelte Werke*, ed. Anna Freud et al., 18 vols (London: Imago, 1940–87), 12:6–11; "A Difficulty in the Path of Psychoanalysis," in *The Standard Edition of the Complete Psychological Works of Sigmund Freud*, ed. and trans. James Strachey, 24 vols (London: Hogarth, 1953–74), 17:139–43.

irrational actions have disrupted the natural economy of our greater ecological "homeland." The disappearance of this life world banishes any desperate hope for consolation in the face of individual death. This represents the ultimate form of exile—final and irrevocable expulsion from the "garden" of nature, from the last bastion of transcendental consolation. Sebald identifies the tremendous *psychological* pressure this recognition places on contemporary humanity: it challenges us to confront the inherent irrationality of a way of life that undermines the very foundations of life itself, and also suggests that we must seek out and implement appropriate forms of self-therapy. Yet even in this supremely pessimistic remark, Sebald does not abandon all hope; he reserves a small opening for this final form of redemption. It emerges from that very psychic pressure that accompanies the recognition of human beings as *biological* agents and as a *geological* force with the power to transmute ecological conditions on planet earth as a whole.[36]

This is the point where Sebald's thought opens onto a set of ideas that fall under the domain of the relatively recent science of ecopsychology. Based on the belief that a primordial emotional bond ties human beings to the natural environment that sustains them, ecopsychology seeks to adapt both the theoretical and the therapeutic aspects of Freudian and post-Freudian psychology for understanding the reciprocity between humans and the environment. Ecopsychologists operate under the assumption that human beings possess what Edward O. Wilson has termed "biophilia," defined as "the innate affiliation people seek with other organisms, and especially with the living natural world."[37] According to ecopsychologists, the human drive toward dominion over nature, expressed most emphatically in modern technological and industrial innovations, has repressed this primordial sense of our inherent bond with non-human nature. As Roszack has emphasized, our inherent biophilia is offset by an equally innate biophobia, a

---

36 This idea has come to be associated with the thesis of the "Anthropocene" as a new geological age, beginning more or less with the Industrial Revolution around the mid-eighteenth century and characterized as a period in which human beings begin to alter the fundamental constitution of the planet. For an exposition of this thesis and how notions of the Anthropocene are interwoven with Enlightenment traditions of freedom, see Chakrabarty, "The Climate of History," 207–11.

37 Wilson, *The Social Conquest of Earth*, 271. Wilson provides a more detailed exposition of this "biophilia hypothesis" in *Biophilia* (Cambridge, MA: Harvard University Press, 1984). See also Theodore Roszak, "Where Psyche Meets Gaia," in *Ecopsychology: Restoring the Earth, Healing the Mind*, ed. Theodore Roszack, Mary E. Gomes, and Allen D. Kanner (San Francisco: Sierra Club Books, 1995), 4, and the debates in Stephen Kellert and Edward O. Wilson (eds.), *The Biophilia Hypothesis* (Washington, D.C.: Island Press, 1993).

deep-seated fear of nature as threatening and overpowering.[38] In our initial analysis of the self-critical reflex manifest in Sebald's Corsica manuscripts, we observed how he focuses attention on this destructive side of our relationship with the environment and examines how it is fueled by an innate fear of an overpowering nature. Yet despite the modern tendency to emphasize biophobia and repress our deep-seated biophilia, a vague sense of our intimate connection with the earth and its ecosystems lingers in our collective psyche, as an "ecological unconscious"[39] or as what we might call a ghost of untrammeled nature. This ghost continues to haunt us with the persistence of the return of the repressed. This explains what ecopsychologists call the "unspoken grief," the sense of bereavement, or the "ecological despair" we experience when we encounter environmental devastation. Joanna Macy describes this sense of widespread environmental despair in terms very much like those Sebald used in the CBC radio interview from 1997. In her analysis, contemporary humans have lost any feeling of continuity, the certainty that life will go on, a belief that bolstered earlier cultures.[40] Similarly, Dipesh Chakrabarty has emphasized how the current environmental crisis introduces a historical rupture that divorces the past from the future, precisely because it calls into question the very notion of continuity upon which traditional historical sensibilities are based.[41] Using a metaphor that also fascinated Sebald, but applying it to ecological rather than to historical trauma, Macy compares our distress over the decline in biodiversity and the disappearance of major parts of our natural world to a "shadow limb," maintaining that we experience subliminal pain for the parts of our life world that have been "severed" from the whole.[42] This environmental grief is the contemporary, ecologically-nuanced equivalent to the malaise, the *Unbehagen* or "discontent," Freud diagnosed already

38 Roszack, "Where Psyche Meets Gaia," 4.
39 Roszack, *The Voice of the Earth*, 13. As far as I know, he is the first to use this phrase, which has gained currency among ecopsychologists.
40 Joanna Macy, "Working Through Environmental Despair," in *Ecopsychology: Restoring the Earth, Healing the Mind*, ed. Theodore Roszack, Mary E. Gomes, and Allen D. Kanner (San Francisco: Sierra Club Books, 1995), 241. See also Phyllis Windle, "The Ecology of Grief," in *Ecopsychology: Restoring the Earth, Healing the Mind*, ed. Theodore Roszak, Mary E. Gomes, and Allen D. Kanner (San Francisco: Sierra Club Books, 1995), 136–45.
41 Chakrabarty, "The Climate of History," 197–8.
42 Macy, "Working Through Environmental Despair," 258. Sebald first employs this metaphor of the "phantom pain in limbs" ("Phantomschmerz in Gliedern") in an essay on the Austrian-Jewish writer Jean Améry, where it describes that author's relationship to his lost Austrian homeland, "Verlorenes Land: Jean Améry und Österreich," *Text & Kritik: Zeitschrift für Literatur* 99 (1988): 27.

in 1929 as the lingering sense of dissatisfaction we experience with the very civilization that otherwise affords us such overweening comfort. Ecopsychology does not merely attempt to diagnose this persistent sense of mourning we feel when confronted with the mass degradation of the life world; it also seeks to develop means for communicating and raising consciousness about this interrelationship between our psychological malaise and the environmental crisis. Andy Fisher calls these two directions in ecopsychology its "recollective" and "therapeutic" dimensions.[43]

From this perspective, the notorious melancholy in Sebald's works appears in a somewhat different light. That his texts center on problems of "unspoken grief" and issues of memory and recollection of loss has become a critical commonplace. But scholarship has focused largely on how these questions play out in the sociopolitical domain, for which the Holocaust stands as the primary example. Yet as ecopsychology teaches us, similar problems, like a haunting sense of mourning or a feeling of inexplicable loss, inform our human relationship with a non-human natural world that is steeped in ecological crisis. Just as the victims of political trauma must find ways to acknowledge, come to terms with, and articulate the causes of their melancholy in order to overcome it, so too must those suffering from the unconscious grief of ecological despair discover methods for confronting, engaging with, and surmounting environmental catastrophes. Yet therapeutically successful regimes must do more than instill in us a sense of shock and awe or provide solace for irrecoverable loss. Because our unarticulated grief about environmental degradation arises out of complex psychological mechanisms of repression and the unconscious return of the repressed, literary narratives on the order of Sebald's ecocritical travelogues, which seek to raise consciousness about the human psychological reflexes that underpin our ecological crisis, represent necessary first steps toward finding resolutions. Ecopsychology provides a scholarly avenue for approaching Sebald's natural history of destruction and his themes of mourning, loss, and the inability to mourn that emphasizes the redemptive and therapeutic qualities of his melancholic demeanor. In the ecocritical dimension of his oeuvre, Sebald once again emerges as a ghostwriter, but one who seeks to resuscitate the ghosts of non-human nature that have fallen victim to our ecological insouciance.

Yet mere consciousness-raising and invocation of ghosts is inadequate as a narrative strategy, since the human psyche—as Freud never tired of reminding us—has command over extraordinarily effective defense mechanisms, calculated to ward off unpleasant, painful, or

43 Fisher, *Radical Ecopsychology*, 13.

self-incriminating recognitions. For ecopsychologists these reflexes of denial present one of the greatest challenges to any attempt to increase awareness among a wider populace about our self-created environmental crisis. Ecopsychologist Laura Sewall identifies the psychological defense mechanism that prevents us from assimilating the increasingly urgent reports about environmental catastrophe as "psychic numbing." She proposes that we must counter this increasing psychic numbness by cultivating modified perceptual practices that enhance our receptivity for, and our emotional participation in, experiences of environmental crisis.[44] Similarly, environmentalists concerned with the communication of our increasingly dire ecological predicament have begun to question the effectiveness of the standard gloom-and-doom narratives about ecological debasement, projections of the accelerated retreat of the glaciers and ice sheets, the resulting plight of the polar bear, and statistics about carbon dioxide emissions and increases in global warming. They suggest that such depictions trigger a psychological reflex of denial and are blunted by psychic numbing, and hence have meager impact. Lawrence Buell has examined the rhetoric of what he calls "toxic discourse" in terms of strategies such as "pastoral betrayal," predicated on the myth of "betrayed Edens," or "toxic interpenetration," which emphasizes how toxins invade our daily lives. Buell cites Rachel Carson's monumental *Silent Spring* as initiating this fundamental direction of environmental criticism, which pins its hopes for effectiveness on the recognition that the loss of pastoral landscapes and the threat of toxic contamination are problems that menace each and every one of us as individuals.[45] Yet even Buell admits that the "shrill apocalypticism" of antitoxic advocacy can be counterproductive.[46] Theodore Roszack acknowledges the resistance to narratives about environmental catastrophe when he asks, "Is there an alternative to scare tactics and guilt trips that will lend ecological necessity both intelligence and passion?" His answer is simple and straightforward: "There is. It is the concern that arises from shared identity: two lives that become one." He names this bond "love" and "compassion," and he concludes, "This is the link we must find between ourselves and

44 Laura Sewall, "The Skill of Ecological Perception," in *Ecopsychology: Restoring the Earth, Healing the Mind*, ed. Theodore Roszak, Mary E. Gomes, and Allen D. Kanner (San Francisco: Sierra Club Books, 1995), 202–4. According to Macy, "Working Through Environmental Despair," 249, the term "psychic numbing" was first introduced by Robert Lifton in his study of Hiroshima victims, where it describes the psychological effect of witnessing mass annihilation.
45 Lawrence Buell, "Toxic Discourse," *Critical Inquiry* 24, no. 3 (Spring 1998): 645–9.
46 Ibid., 662.

the planet that gives us life."[47] Roszack thus invests wholesale in the cultivation of our inherent biophilia.

The narrator of Sebald's Corsica travelogue is well aware of the psychological resistance-mechanisms that impede our recognition of environmental disasters. Following a detailed description of the catastrophic consequences of the raging human-caused wildfires that beset modern Corsica, he notes:

> Doch wie unwiderruflich die Auswirkungen der Feuer auf die Dauer auch sein mögen, wir gewöhnen uns anscheinend erstaunlich schnell an die Verheerung der Landschaft. Die Zeitungsberichte über die hier & dort dauernd auflodernden Brände, die gegen die mutmaßlichen Verursacher eher halbherzig vorgebrachten Anklagen, die Schadensberechnungen nach Milliarden Francs, die Empörung der Naturschützer, all das hat längst den Charakter eines pflichtschuldigen Kommentars zu letzten Endes unvermeidlichen Ereignissen angenommen. ("Aufzeichnungen" 208)
> [And yet regardless of how irrevocable the consequences of such wildfires might be, we apparently grow accustomed to the decimation of the landscape astonishingly quickly. The newspaper reports about the infernos that constantly flare up here & there, the rather half-hearted accusations brought against the presumed perpetrators, the calculations of damages that run into billions of francs, the indignation of the environmentalists—all of this has long assumed the character of an obligatory commentary about what are ultimately acknowledged as unavoidable events.]

Sebald's narrator radicalizes the conception of psychic numbing by proposing that we not only tune out the constantly repeated news reports about environmental catastrophes, but that we even grow accustomed to the very conditions of environmental degradation itself. His suggestion that admonitions about environmental devastation take on the "character of an obligatory commentary" is strikingly reminiscent of the claim he made in a 1993 interview with Sigrid Löffler about engagements with the Holocaust in post-war Germany, where he maintains that the screening of the English documentary film depicting the liberation of the Bergen-Belsen concentration camp was presented in his high school classroom "without commentary, as a morally obligatory exercise" ("ohne Kommentar, als moralische Pflichtübung"; "*Auf ungeheuer dünnem Eis*" 82). Regardless of whether we are dealing with organized sociopolitical brutality or with violence toward the natural

---

47 Roszack, *The Voice of the Earth*, 39.

environment, humans are reluctant to look these facts in the face, and when we do so, it is only out of a sense of moral obligation. Authors who want to confront their readers with the realities of environmental decline face similar challenges to those who seek to provide genuine emotional access to the horrors of the Holocaust: they must circumvent the "numbing" and the defense mechanisms that prevent their audience from absorbing these human-generated tragedies, and that prevent them from acknowledging their own human culpability.

Sebald's narrator in the Corsica project attempts to win the sympathies of potential readers by shifting from a simple accusation of the perpetrators to a more encompassing perspective that includes accusations against the narrating self. This is also true for the portrayals of psychic numbing to ecological disaster documented in this text. When this narrator describes the dismay one experiences at the sight of a forest recently destroyed by wildfire, but insists that this shock has no long-lasting impact, he supports this abstract observation by relating his own experience:

> Nicht einmal der Schock, der einen beim ersten Anblick einer vom Feuer vernichteten Gegend durchfährt, beispielsweise wenn man mit dem Wagen um einen Felsvorsprung biegt & plötzlich da, wo vor ein paar Tagen noch Buschwald gewesen ist, verbrannt[e], von der Straße bis an den Himmelsrand reichende Hänge vor sich hat, nicht einmal dieser Schock hält, wie ich verschiedentlich an mir selber feststellen konnte, lange vor … Das Auge lernt abzusehen von dem, was es schmerzt, ja vielleicht lernt es die immer graphit-grauer werdende Welt lieben … ("Aufzeichnungen" 208)
> [Not even the shock that comes over one at the first sight of an area destroyed by wildfire, for example when one steers one's car around a rocky outcropping & suddenly sees that there, where just a few days ago there had been brushwood, one is confronted by burned-out cliffs that extend from the road to the horizon—not even this shock lasts very long, as I have witnessed in myself on different occasions … The eye learns to look away from those things that cause it pain, and perhaps it even learns to love a world that is constantly becoming more graphite-gray.]

We begin to understand that the ecopsychological strategy Sebald implements in the Corsica narrative is one of personal confession and shared self-reflection on the emotional experiences of his narrator. This tactic stands in marked contrast to the strategy Sebald implements in his most successful narratives about human exile and the traumas of sociopolitical displacement. In those texts, the first-person narrator has no immediate personal experience of deportation, banishment, or political terror, but rather plays the role either of a concerned and interested outsider who, based on his own research, reconstructs the lives of those who suffered such experiences, or functions as a receptive sounding board who facilitates the memories and recollections of a trauma victim. Whereas in these cases the first-person narrator serves as a witness who gathers and transmits the testimony of trauma victims, in the ecocritical episodes of the Corsica fragments, the first-person narrator himself is relegated to the status of the testifier who must relate the traumas he suffers due to his experiences of human-wrought environmental havoc, and one of the perpetrators responsible for these crimes. Although this narrative stance has the advantage that it invites the reader to participate in both the narrator's trauma and in his gesture of self-accusation and self-implication, it has the disadvantage of being so immediate and penetrating as to call forth the resistance of psychic numbing.

We recall that in his interview with Maya Jaggi from 2001, Sebald remarked on the necessity of approaching topics like the Holocaust in a roundabout, oblique manner: "I don't think you can focus on the horror of the Holocaust. It's like the head of Medusa: you carry it with you in a sack, but if you looked at it you'd be petrified."[48] This insight also applies to narratives about the trauma of environmental disaster, and it goes to the heart of the reasons why Sebald viewed the ecocritical undertaking in the Corsica project as a failure. The dilemma he faced was that in order to render a believable account of the psychological exigencies underpinning human devastation of the natural world, he had to abandon the narrative innovations of this oblique perspective, the "periscopic narration" upon which the successes of his narratives about sociopolitical exile had been built. The notoriously unimpassioned stance of his first-person narrator in these fictions gives way to a rhetorical passion and "apocalyptic shrillness" that can "numb" its audience, thereby undercutting its own admonitions and interfering with the communicative effectiveness of its narrative about ecological catastrophe. In an effort to resolve this problem, Sebald turned to another one of his tried-and-true literary devices: mediation via intertextual resonance.

Literary Intertexts: Exploring the Psychology of Violence Against Nature

If the virtue of Sebald's narratives about exile and displacement resides in a mediated retelling of the repercussions political oppression has on victims and survivors, environmental catastrophe does not offer similar opportunities for a recuperation of its victims' stories. The

---

48 Maya Jaggi, "Recovered Memories," *Guardian*, September 22, 2001, 7.

manifold disappearance of endangered species, the decimated forests, the melting glaciers, the declining ecosystem more generally have no voice of their own and cannot bear testimony to their struggle to survive or recover from ecological degradation. Environmental devastation is also not a completed event whose history can be told in retrospect, as is true of events like the Holocaust, but rather an ongoing process that demands self-critical human reflection and behavioral change. In the Corsica manuscripts Sebald turns to another of his preferred literary strategies in an effort to resolve these inherent difficulties: a reliance on literary intertexts. He recounts Gustave Flaubert's legend of Saint Julian, a work his narrator purportedly discovers accidentally in the nightstand of his hotel room ("Aufzeichnungen" 203). The context for retelling this story of a perversely obsessed hunter is formed by the narrator's critical reflections on the "fever of the chase" ("Jagdfieber") that infects the men of Corsica every autumn, despite the fact that the indigenous animals of the island have been "eradicated almost without trace" ("nahezu restlos ausgerottet"; "Aufzeichnungen" 200; cf. *Campo Santo* 43/39). This episode explores the causes of species decline and extinction, extrapolating from the tale of Saint Julian the more general problematic of the irrational aggression humans harbor against non-human animals, and offering a psychological explanation for its persistence in a modern world where hunting no longer represents an existential necessity. Sebald's narrator interprets the continuance of what has become a senseless activity as an atavistic remnant of our primitive history; hunting represents "the final episode of a story that extends far back into our dark past" ("die Schlußepisode einer weit in unsere dunkle Vergangenheit zurückweisenden Geschichte"; "Aufzeichnungen" 203). The narrator's encounter with the Corsican hunters also invokes reminiscences from his experience of seeing dead animals in his childhood village, and the decorative display of meat in the shop windows of English butchers. This latter phenomenon calls forth the suspicion that the green plastic decorations adorning these packages provide symbolic compensation for the unavoidable guilt we feel for killing these animals in the first place. The very absurdity of these plastic decorations marks them both as signs of hope—since they point to our sense of guilt—and simultaneously of despair—over the fact that we assuage our guilt so easily. They demonstrate "how irrepressibly we desire absolution & how cheap we have always bought it" ("wie unabweisbar der Wunsch nach Versöhnung in uns ist & wie billig wir uns sie von jeher erkauften"; "Aufzeichnungen" 203; cf. *Campo Santo* 46/42). Ecopsychologists are invested in this belief in our need for moral reconciliation with nature, and Sebald's Corsica travelogue expresses a call to embrace this act of redemption in more serious and lasting forms.

Flaubert's Saint Julian stands as a legendary prototype for the paradoxical coexistence of untamed aggression and the desire for reconciliation in one and the same person. He represents a humanity in which "a perverse passion for hunting & a vocation for sainthood do battle in one & the same heart" ("eine perverse Jagdleidenschaft & die Berufung zum Heiligenstand an ein & demselben Herzen reissen [sic]"; "Aufzeichnungen" 203; cf. *Campo Santo* 46/42). Gripped by an irrational fit of aggression, triggered by his killing of a church mouse, Julian sets out on an expedition in which he brutally exterminates every non-human creature he encounters. In the painful dream visions that follow this bout of killing, he imagines himself as an inverse Noah, who attacks the pairs of animals as they stand in line to enter the ark. His story is an allegory not for the rescue of animal life, but for the wanton human eradication of non-human existence in its entirety. The emotional reaction of Sebald's narrator to reading this story is telling, because it models the response Sebald would like to elicit in his own readers: he is "deeply fascinated and disturbed ... by the story, which in itself I approached with reluctance" "[z]utiefst fasziniert & verstört ... von dieser mir an sich widerstrebenden Lektüre" ("Aufzeichnungen" 203; cf. *Campo Santo* 46/42). Sebald's Corsican travelogue is calculated to stimulate our repugnance for the multiple forms of environmental degradation the island has experienced, but also to draw us in as attentive witnesses by engaging our fascination with, and our revulsion for, these acts of wanton destruction.

Flaubert's tale of Saint Julian models a life that is marked by miraculous conversion: haunted by the ghostly spirits of the animals whose lives he has so senselessly extinguished, Julian first wanders aimlessly, driven by his own guilt and pain. Only when he demonstrates compassion for another suffering human being, by sharing a bed with a leprous ferryman, does he find relief from his psychological torment. Just as Julian experiences this sudden "act of grace when the saint is transfigured" ("Gnadenakt der Transfiguration"), Sebald's narrator finds relief from the horror instilled in him by this "utterly *perverse* tale of the despicable nature of human violence" ("von grundauf *perversen* Erzählung über die Verruchtheit der Menschengewalt"; "Aufzeichnungen" 204; cf. *Campo Santo* 48/44). He not only recapitulates in his own emotional transformation the transfiguration that Julian undergoes, but also exhibits the conversion his own readers should experience upon encountering his "perverse narrative" about the infamy of human violence against nature.

Flaubert's Julian is not the sole literary figure who represents wanton destructiveness against nature in Sebald's Corsica fragments; he is joined by another infamous literary animal-killer, the mariner of Coleridge's *Rime of the Ancient Mariner*, whose senseless murder of an albatross calls down punishment against himself and his shipmates. Sebald's narrator remembers having learned by heart the verses of Coleridge's poem for a class in English recitation during his first semester at the university thirty years earlier; and although he thought these lines had slipped from his memory, he discovers that his experiences on the island give rise to almost perfect recall. Indeed, the text of Coleridge's poem haunts him throughout his Corsican travels:

> Während meines ganzen Aufenthalts auf Korsika brachte ich diese Verse [Coleridges] nicht aus dem Sinn, denn überall stieß [ich] auf die Zeichen der von einem zerstörerischen Affekt ausgelösten Verderbnis des natürlichen Lebens, von welcher die Seefahrerballade Coleridges handelt, hörte ich hoch droben zwischen den Felswänden das Echo der Schüsse & sah die verkohlten Stämme und die schwarzen Böden, die das Feuer hinterläßt, wenn es über die Bergseiten eilt. ("Aufzeichnungen" 207).

> [During my entire stay on Corsica I could not get these verses [by Coleridge] out of my mind, for everywhere [I] turned I encountered the signs of a ruination of natural life caused by a destructive affect, of the very sort treated in Coleridge's mariner ballad, I heard high above the cliffs the echoes of shots & saw the charred stumps and the blackened earth left by wildfire as it rushes across the mountainsides.]

Coleridge's mariner, like Flaubert's Saint Julian, represents the irrational destructive instinct and aggressive impulses of human beings more generally, and his action stands symbolically for all the acts of ecological destruction Sebald's narrator experiences on the island. But Coleridge's mariner assumes the role of a *messenger* about the devastation wrought by his own actions: forced to tell his own tale, he invokes a moment of *anagnorisis* in the Wedding-Guest who hears his story, and who comes away from this encounter as a "sadder and a wiser man."[49] We recognize in this episode Sebald's reliance on Freud's theory of the psyche as a tool for explaining why humans strike out randomly and viciously against the life world that sustains them. Freud's aggressive instinct is elided with that more amorphous biophobia proposed by Theodore Roszack. Ecopsychology translates Freud's struggle between the human being's aggressive and erotic impulses, between Eros and Thanatos, into a conflict between our inherent biophilia and an equally

---

49 Samuel Taylor Coleridge, *The Rime of the Ancient Mariner*, in *The Complete Poetical Works of Samuel Taylor Coleridge*, ed. Ernest Hartley Coleridge, 2 vols (Oxford: Clarendon, 1912), line 624.

ingrained biophobia. This ecopsychological perspective offers another way of describing the extreme emotional oscillation of Flaubert's Julian. The tension between his passion for hunting and his call to compassionate sainthood embodies this fundamental instinctual struggle. In the references to Coleridge, aggression and redemption once more operate in a dialectical union, but in this case redemption can only be bought at the price of the mariner traveling the world like an undead ghost and relating his own tragic story. Coleridge's mariner represents but one more manifestation of those wandering revenants, like Kafka's Hunter Gracchus, who play such a privileged role in Sebald's narratives. Coleridge's mariner is quite literally a ghostwriter, or a ghost-narrator, whose tale is intended to have a redemptive impact on his audience. But his story is explicitly one of wanton human cruelty and aggression against "Both man and bird and beast."[50] Sebald's narrator has assumed the subject position and taken over the self-incriminating role of the narrating I that is modeled by Coleridge's mariner, and we, his readers, assume the position of Coleridge's Wedding-Guest.

The intertextual invocation of Coleridge's poem forms the introduction to an extended passage that charts the stages of environmental degradation in the Corsican landscapes: from primeval forest, to mixed woodlands of trees and shrubs, to meadowlands that promise more fertility than they deliver, to wholly unfertile lands, to wastelands whose topsoil is washed away by heavy rains and deposited by the rivers into the sea, until what remains is nothing but a "Steinwüste," a "rocky desert." This is how Sebald's narrator summarizes the environmental history of the island ("Aufzeichnungen" 205). He goes on to describe the catastrophic consequences of the wildfires that devastate ever-increasing swathes of Corsica's remaining forests, but also alludes to the ineffectiveness of those measures implemented to reverse this vicious circle of destruction and desertification. Ultimately his narrator, unlike Coleridge's mariner, comes to a morbidly pessimistic conclusion, even regarding those countermeasures aimed at restoration: they are, he opines, simply further symptoms of this trajectory of environmental decline itself:

> Wie bei jedem Entwicklungsmodell sind auch hier die Versuche, dem in seinem Endstadium mit zunehmender Geschwindigkeit ablaufenden Auflösungsprozess Einhalt zu bieten, von vornherein zum Scheitern verurteilt, ja sie sind, wenn man es genau betrachtet, selber Symptome des Zerfalls. ("Aufzeichnungen" 208)
> [As is true of every developmental model, here too all attempts to halt the process of dissolution, which increasingly gains

---

50 Ibid., line 613.

momentum as it approaches its end stage, are doomed to failure; indeed, they themselves are, if one looks at them closely, nothing other than symptoms of this decline.]

Sebald touches on an extremely timely theme, one that today motivates critics in the debates over global warming: the question of whether, even if radical countermeasures were to be taken immediately, the accumulation of greenhouse gases in the earth's atmosphere has not already reached an irreversible point of radical ecological transformation, portending the future extinction of life.[51] He succinctly summarizes the geometric progression with which environmental decline, once initiated, increasingly hastens toward ultimate demise. Once such a dynamic has been set in motion, even those schemes devised as antidotes to this progressive unraveling become symptoms of the problem itself. The warning Sebald's narrator voices is a familiar one in today's critical environmental circles: we are in danger of passing a point of no return in terms of the degradation of our natural environment—a point beyond which the redemption still left open to Coleridge's mariner, and the *anagnorisis* achieved by the Wedding-Guest who hears his story, will no longer be possible or make any difference.

But lest we accuse Sebald of falling into inescapable pessimism, let us recall that the very choice of the island of Corsica as the object of his ecocritical investigations is linked with the status of the island both as a compact and contained ecosphere of its own, and as a microcosm for Europe and the Mediterranean region more generally. If Corsica serves Sebald as an exaggerated example of how human psychology dictates our destructive intervention in the natural world, then it also functions as an admonition about what can happen, on an even larger scale, if human beings do not enact *timely* strategies for limiting our destructive impact on the life world. Coleridge's mariner, even in the face of Sebald's pessimistic prognosis, still holds out a glimmer of hope and envisions a moment of human *anagnorisis* in which insight generates appropriate *narrative* actions. The challenge Sebald faces in the Corsica texts closely parallels the one faced and successfully resolved by Coleridge's mariner: discovering and implementing a way of effectively narrating the story of human complicity in environmental catastrophe, so that it might lead to transformative insight in his (intra-diegetic) audience.

---

51 James Lovelock, *Gaia: A New Look at Life on Earth*, rev. ed. (Oxford: Oxford University Press, 2000), 38–42, presents a doomsday scenario in which humans irreversibly disrupt the self-regulating homeostasis that controls all life, what he calls Gaia.

Historical Intertexts: Documenting Environmental Loss

Whereas Sebald's *literary* intertexts allow him to investigate the psychological reflexes responsible for the wanton human destruction of the non-human world, as well as providing models for the hope of human redemption, his *historical* intertexts help him document the incremental *loss* in species diversity and forestland that Corsica has suffered over the last 200 years. Among the texts Sebald consulted to reconstruct the island's natural history, three stand out: James Boswell's (1740–95) *An Account of Corsica* from 1769; Gregorovius's *Korsika*, which documents his trip to the island in 1852; and Edward Lear's (1812–88) *Journal of a Landscape Painter in Corsica*, first published in 1870. These texts, along with a series of articles from older encyclopedias, helped Sebald establish a record of historical decline in Corsica's forests and the island's ecological diversity. The theme of loss is a central issue that unites Sebald's focus on sociopolitical oppression with problems of ecological devastation. However, whereas loss can be readily documented in the sociopolitical domain via testimony and memory studies, environmental degradation not only occurs at a much slower pace, but also often lacks witnesses and documentary evidence. Sebald's historical studies serve as sources that chart the degree and pace of ecological demise Corsica has suffered, and he strategically interweaves his own experiences of environmental devastation with the acknowledgment, in these older resources, of Corsica's threatened natural grandeur.

The first chapter of Boswell's *Account of Corsica* is devoted to an almost effusive inventory of the trees that comprise the island's great forests and the richness of the wildlife that inhabits them.[52] Boswell relies on historical accounts by Polybius and Theophrastus to emphasize the continuity of this ecological bounty. But the Corsican woodlands impress him in particular due to the variety, density, and size of the trees he discovers there:

> Trees grow remarkably well in Corsica. There is here almost every sort of forest trees, but it is principally adorned with pines of different kinds, oaks, and chestnut trees. All of these are to be found of a great size; some of the pines in particular, are exceedingly lofty, and the chestnut tree grows to a prodigious bigness.[53]

Sebald was especially interested in such historical accounts relating the grand size of the trees that once characterized the island; among his

---

52 James Boswell, *An Account of Corsica, the Journal of a Tour to That Island, and Memoirs of Pascal Paoli*, 3rd, corr. ed. (London: Edward and Charles Dilly, 1769), 69–80.

53 Ibid., 75.

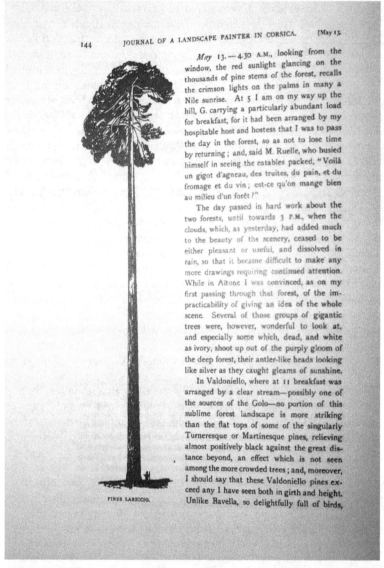

May 13. — 4.30 A.M., looking from the window, the red sunlight glancing on the thousands of pine stems of the forest, recalls the crimson lights on the palms in many a Nile sunrise. At 5 I am on my way up the hill, G. carrying a particularly abundant load for breakfast, for it had been arranged by my hospitable host and hostess that I was to pass the day in the forest, so as not to lose time by returning ; and, said M. Ruelle, who busied himself in seeing the eatables packed, " Voilà un gigot d'agneau, des truites, du pain, et du fromage et du vin ; est-ce qu'on mange bien au milieu d'un forêt ?"

The day passed in hard work about the two forests, until towards 3 P.M., when the clouds, which, as yesterday, had added much to the beauty of the scenery, ceased to be either pleasant or useful, and dissolved in rain, so that it became difficult to make any more drawings requiring continued attention. While in Aïtone I was convinced, as on my first passing through that forest, of the impracticability of giving an idea of the whole scene. Several of those groups of gigantic trees were, however, wonderful to look at, and especially some which, dead, and white as ivory, shoot up out of the purply gloom of the deep forest, their antler-like heads looking like silver as they caught gleams of sunshine.

In Valdoniello, where at 11 breakfast was arranged by a clear stream—possibly one of the sources of the Golo—no portion of this sublime forest landscape is more striking than the flat tops of some of the singularly Turneresque or Martinesque pines, relieving almost positively black against the great distance beyond, an effect which is not seen among the more crowded trees ; and, moreover, I should say that these Valdoniello pines exceed any I have seen both in girth and height. Unlike Bavella, so delightfully full of birds,

PINUS LARICCIO.

Figure 9.3: Drawing of *Pinus Lariccio* from Lear (*Journal of a Landscape Painter* 144).

papers one finds a photocopy of a page from Edward Lear's *Journal of a Landscape Painter* containing a drawing of an especially prodigious representative of *Pinus Lariccio*, a gigantic tree that dwarfs the human figure standing next to it[54] (see Figure 9.3). Boswell's journal, which predates Sebald's other historical sources by several decades, serves as a primary document for recording the natural condition of Corsica in its pristine, pre-modern ecological state.

For Gregorovius, who traveled Corsica almost 100 years later, the island is still distinguished by its natural beauty and a diversity of plants and animals. He presents detailed inventories of natural phenomena, such as lists of geological formations, including the types of rocks and their magical colors, as well as long inventories of typical plant species and their habitats. From Gregorovius's perspective, Corsica still embodies a grandiose landscape, concretized above all in his extended description of his climb of Mt. Rotondo, with its spectacular panoramic views of mountains, ocean, and islands extending all the way to the coast of Italy.[55] Exemplary for his depiction of Corsica's landscape and environment, which for Gregorovius are paradigmatic of the sublime in nature, is his description of an evening climb of a mountain on the outskirts of the town of Bastia, from which he enjoys a panoramic view of the city, the surrounding mountains, and the sea. Gregorovius paints an idyllically pastoral scene:

Ich stieg über Bastia in die nächsten Berge hinauf. Dort ist die Aussicht auf die Stadt, das Meer und die Inseln erfreuend. Wein- und Olivengärten, Orangen, kleine Landhäuschen von den bizarrsten Formen, hie und da eine Fächerpalme, Grabkapellen unter Zypressen, von Epheu [*sic*] ganz erstickte Ruinen, das liegt dort zerstreut … Die Abendsonne ging eben unter, als ich diesen Blick genoß. Der Teich erschimmerte rosenrot, die Berge desgleichen, und das Meer war voll vom Abendglanz, ein einzelnes Schiff glitt darüber hinweg. Die Stille einer großen Natur beruhigt die Seele.[56]
[I climbed the hillsides immediately above Bastia. From this vantage point the view of the city, the ocean, and the islands is pleasant. Vineyards and olive gardens, oranges, little country homes of the most bizarre form, here and there a fan-palm, tombs

54 Lear, *Journal of a Landscape Painter in Corsica*, 144.
55 Gregorovius, *Korsika*, 366–71. Sebald's photocopy of Gregorovius's text displays numerous marginal notations, and his handwritten notes contain a page titled "Aufstieg" ("Ascent"), with details drawn directly from Gregorovius's description of climbing this mountain.
56 Gregorovius, *Korsika*, 125.

among cypresses, ruins choked by ivy are scattered all about …
The evening sun was just sinking as I enjoyed this sight. The pond
gleamed rosy-red, as did the mountains, and the sea was full of
this evening radiance, a single ship went gliding across it. The
stillness of grandiose nature calms the soul.]

With its bird's-eye perspective, its view of city, sea, and pastoral
landscape, and its inclusion of ivy-covered ruins, Gregorovius's
depiction reads like an ekphrastic rendering of a nineteenth-century
painting in which sublime nature is set off against the remnants of
human civilization.

This description caught Sebald's attention, since he places lines in
the margins of his copy and underlines part of the passage. And this
scene resurfaces in his own Corsica travelogue as a hidden intertext,
in which, however, the mood and tone of Gregorovius's original
undergo radical transformation. While Gregorovius emphasizes the
psychological and emotional comfort he derives from this pleasant
pastoral landscape, in Sebald's rendition it culminates in a fantasy of
apocalyptic destruction. Looking out of the window of his hotel room
in Piana, Sebald's narrator enjoys a view of the ocean and the Corsican
mountainsides at sunset:

Die Abenddämmerung verdunkelte schon zur Hälfte das Zimmer.
Draußen aber hing noch die untergehende Sonne über dem Meer
& in dem gleißenden in Wellen von ihr ausgehenden Licht stand
zitternd die ganze von meinem Fenster aus sichtbare & in diesem
Ausschnitt weder von einer Straßentrasse, noch von der kleinsten
Ansiedlung entstellte Welt. Die … aus der Tiefe emporragenden
Felsformationen der Calanches leuchteten in feurigem Kupferrot,
als stünde das Gestein selber in Flammen & gloste aus seinem
Innersten heraus. Manchmal glaubte ich in dem Geflacker die
Umrisse brennender Pflanzen & Tiere zu erkennen oder die eines
zu einem riesigen Scheiterhaufen geschichteten Volks. Sogar das
Wasser drunten im Golf schien zu brennen … Es dauerte eine
geraume Zeit, bis meine geblendeten Augen sich an das sanfte
Zwielicht gewöhnten & ich das Schiff sehen konnte, das aus der
Mitte des Brandes hervorgekommen war. ("Aufzeichnungen"
205; cf. *Campo Santo* 48–9)
[Evening twilight was already darkening half of my room.
Outside, however, the setting sun still hung above the sea & in
the blazing light that rippled from it the whole of that section
of the world visible from my window quivered, & this view
was unspoiled by the line of any road or the smallest human
settlement. The … rock formations of Les Calanques, towering

up from the depths, shone in fiery copper red as if the stone itself
were in flames & glowed from within. Sometimes I thought I
saw the outlines of plants & animals burning in that flickering
light, or the shapes of a whole race of people stacked into a great
pyre. Even the water down below in the gulf seemed to be aflame
… It took my eyes some time to become accustomed to the soft
twilight & before I could see the ship that had emerged from the
middle of the fire. (Cf. *Campo Santo* 44–5)]

What marks this passage as an intertext is not only the gaze upon the
Corsican landscape at sunset, but the mysterious ship that glides across
the observer's vision in both instances. Sebald has stripped the scene
of sublimity, presenting instead the horrific vision of a massive funeral
pyre that engulfs human beings, plants, and animals. Gregorovius's
picture of sublime grandeur, in which human civilization exists harmo-
niously with the natural world, and from which he takes emotional
comfort, has been transmuted into an all-encompassing Holocaust, an
end-of-the-world scenario in which a gigantic inferno encompasses
even the stone formations of the mountains and the sea. Only the ship
that crosses the gulf stands as a sign of possible human survival and
continued existence—until the narrator looks through his telescope
and discovers that there is no living soul on board—"but nowhere
even one single human being" ("aber nirgend auch nur einen einzigen
Menschen"; "Aufzeichnungen" 205; cf. *Campo Santo* 50/46). In the
narrator's fantasy an implicit connection exists between this apocalyptic scene and destructive human behaviors vis-à-vis the natural
world: as he continues to observe this ship after nightfall, he imagines
it inhabited by a single individual, none other than Coleridge's ancient
mariner ("Aufzeichnungen" 205). The transformed intertext from
Gregorovius thereby forms the textual transition between the episode
relating Saint Julian's murderous hunting rampage, and the reflections
on wanton violence against nature intoned in Coleridge's ballad. For
Sebald's narrator, the history of natural destruction characteristic of the
island of Corsica invokes mythic visions of absolute ecological calamity
that culminate in an all-encompassing conflagration on the order of the
biblical Sodom and Gomorrah.

    If Boswell's and Gregorovius's travelogues document a historical
moment prior to Corsica's human-caused ecological decline, Edward
Lear's journey in 1869—a mere seventeen years subsequent to
Gregorovius's visit—marks a turning point at which the signs of the
island's impending environmental demise are already legible. One
of the epigraphs with which Lear introduces his volume addresses
precisely the fast pace by which the natural beauty of the island is
being driven back by the forces of civilization. Taken from a "dramatic

romance" that bears the title *The Corsican Brothers*, this epigraph reads, "So, then, you were determined to come and see Corsica? You have done rightly to hasten your visit, for in a very few years, thanks to the hand of progress and civilisation, they who come to seek for Corsica will not find it."[57] The melancholic tone that runs throughout Lear's travelogue stems largely from this sense that Corsica's imposing natural landscape is on the verge of disappearing. This threat motivates Lear's project of recording, in both words and graphic representations, the natural beauty of the island before it vanishes forever. His text, profusely illustrated with his own etchings of the Corsican landscape and its flora, constitutes an attempt to provide a lasting record of what is about to disappear. Not surprisingly, he remarks repeatedly on the massive wagons that ply the roads through the Corsican forests, loaded with the trunks of enormous trees, and he comments on how the sound of the axe breaks the stillness of the woods.[58] About the forest of Valdoniello he comments that the thinning of the timber is "preluding its downfall";[59] and in the forest of Vizzavona he is disappointed to encounter a landscape that "was ravaged a few years ago by a very destructive conflagration." He goes on to bemoan the "melancholy" impression left by the "black charred trunks of the tall pines," and reflects that this burned-out landscape offers only "the deplorable spectacle of a harsh dead world of naked pine trunks and bristling brown branches."[60] By contrast, he describes the largely intact forest of Bavella as a "never-to-be-forgotten beautiful forest," whose charm resides in a silence broken only by "the cuckoo's notes echoing from the crags, and from the fulness [sic] of melody chanted by thousands of blackbirds." Yet even this pristine forest is threatened by loggers who harvest the immense trees, with the consequence that the particularly slow-moving black and orange lizard indigenous to these woods "frequently gets crushed by the wheels of the great timber carts."[61] Lear is already in tune with the collateral damage the harvesting of the forests has on animal life.

Sebald draws an intertextual allusion to these passages from Lear's journal when his narrator describes a forest hike that leads through a world that has become lifelessly silent:

Auf meinem Weg durch den Wald von Aïtone [sah ich] nicht ein lebendiges Wesen ... weder ein Stück Wild, noch einen einzigen

57 Lear, *Journal of a Landscape Painter in Corsica*, title page.
58 Ibid., 95, 140, 157, 242, 245.
59 Ibid., 141.
60 Ibid., 162.
61 Ibid., 95.

Vogel, noch einen Käfer oder ein anderes wirbelloses Tier. Nicht einmal die lästigen Mücken gab es, die einen sonst meistens beim Gehen umschwärmen. Außerdem mangelte auf dem anscheinend sterilen Nadelboden jeglicher Unterwuchs ... Es war, als sei bis auf die jahrhundertealten Kiefern alles hier ausgestorben vor langer Zeit. Das mich ergreifende Gefühl der Leblosigkeit wurde freilich auch hervorgerufen von einer bedrohlichen Stille. ("Aufzeichnungen" 196) [On my hike through the woods of Aïtone [I saw] not a single living creature ... neither a head of game, nor a single bird, nor a beetle or any other invertebrate creature. There were not even any bothersome mosquitoes, which usually swarm around when one is hiking. Moreover, the sterile needle-strewn ground appeared to lack any undergrowth ... It was as though everything but the century-old pines had died out long ago. To be sure, the feeling of lifelessness that gripped me was also called forth by a threatening stillness.]

As he did with the intertextual reference to Gregorovius, Sebald again radicalizes what in Lear emerges as a simple—if still ominous— warning. Whereas for Lear the stillness of the forest reflects its isolation from the civilized world, and is disrupted only by the melodious sounds of singing birds, what Sebald's narrator experiences is a natural world that is wholly devoid of life. It is as though he were consciously invoking the title of Rachael Carson's landmark book, *Silent Spring*. The "strange stillness" of a landscape without birdsong, which she projects in the "Fable for Tomorrow" that opens her book,[62] is realized concretely by Sebald's narrator on his hike through the Corsican woods. Even the pesky mosquitoes—one of the targets of the widespread spraying of DDT that Carson indicted—are noticeable only because of their absence. These woods also testify to the growing problem of a reduction of species diversity: the centuries-old pines exist as a monoculture in an otherwise sterile landscape. Not surprisingly, Sebald's narrator himself feels haunted by the sensation that he represents the only living creature in an otherwise lifeless world, alluding to the nightmare of an earth devoid of any creatures other than human beings, a scenario invoked earlier in Sebald's manuscript by the pilot Douglas X ("Aufzeichnungen" 173). In Corsica, Sebald's narrator thus becomes witness to a ravaged natural landscape that fits Rachel Carson's predictions of ecological sterility, and the island portends a future world in which human beings are the only remaining species.

---

62 Rachel Carson, *Silent Spring* (1962; rpt. Boston: Mariner Books/Houghton, 2002), 1–3.

Narrating the Apocalypse of Environmental Catastrophe

Sebald's Corsica manuscripts conclude—and I think one can argue that they conclude, rather than simply break off—with a grand rhetorical flourish, covering several pages, that concentrates on the human proclivity for pyromania, graphic depictions of the wildfires that have decimated the Corsican landscape in the last fifty years, and culminating—after some general reflections about how humans measure their might in terms of an ability to stockpile firepower in our weapons arsenals and our production facilities—in a pointedly ironic rhetorical question: "Haven't we even incinerated entire peoples, seen our cities burn down in mile-high firestorms, & haven't we rebuilt everything once again, better & more beautiful than before, & suffered no damage to our soul?" ("Haben wir nicht sogar ganze Völker verbrannt, unsere Städte abbrennen sehen in meilenhohen Feuerstürmen, & haben wir nicht alles wieder aufgebaut, besser & schöner als zuvor, & keinen Schaden genommen an unserer Seele?"; "Aufzeichnungen" 209). The pregnant word "psyche" or "soul"— "Seele"—is the very last one Sebald put to paper for the Corsica project, which had been guided throughout by ecopsychological reflections and speculations. This concluding passage develops the vision of fiery world destruction that Sebald's narrator had invoked, via the transfigured intertextual allusion to Gregorovius, just a few pages earlier, and that introduces the intertextual references to Coleridge's *Rime of the Ancient Mariner*. The implication of the narrator's rhetorical question is that human beings as a species *have indeed* suffered psychic damage, not only from horrific historical events like the Holocaust and the incomparable destruction of the German cities by the Allied bombers during the merciless air war,[63] but also from more long-term, if no less cataclysmic events like the near-eradication of the Corsican forests, which have gradually transformed the island, in Sebald's own words, from a "forested cloak" ("Waldkleid") into a "rocky desert" ("Steinwüste"; 207). No doubt, Sebald envisioned the ecological decimation of Corsica as a harbinger for the fate of Europe and the world.

My sense as to why Sebald found it necessary to abandon this project at the very point at which it reached its rhetorical and argumentative climax has to do with his overriding tendency, throughout his literary work—in marked contrast, one might add, to the tactic he pursued in his literary criticism[64]—to mollify and refract his own opinions, either

---

63 Compare the very similar formulation, in *Luftkrieg und Literatur*, where Sebald ironically notes that the Germans emerged from the annihilation of the Allied air war without any permanent psychological damage (*Luftkrieg* 19/11).

64 On Sebald's peculiarly vociferous voice as a literary critic, see Schütte, W. G.

by putting them in the mouths of fictional characters, or by filtering them through intertextual voices and allusions.[65] When asked in an interview about how he could reconcile his thematic emphasis on the murderous history of the twentieth century with a writing style that harks back to the placid prose of the nineteenth-century realists, Sebald remarked "that the detached narrative style perhaps makes it possible to lend such matters a perspectival alienation, so that as reader one has the feeling that the narrator does not exempt himself from the things that he describes" ("dass der detachierte Erzählstil vielleicht dazu beiträgt, die Sache perspektivisch so zu verfremden, dass man als Leser das Gefühl hat, dass der Erzähler sich nicht schadlos hält an den Dingen, die er beschreibt"; "*Auf ungeheuer dünnem Eis*" 159). In the final pages of the Corsica manuscript, Sebald betrays his own powerful emotional involvement in the environmental disaster he is portraying, as well as in the perverse psychological mechanisms he has diagnosed as their underlying dynamic. In doing so, he falls out of the tone of detachment and calm reportage that is characteristic of his most successful prose fictions, even when they are relating catastrophic events. In another interview, Sebald remarks that the most pressing problem faced by contemporary writers is "how to translate horror into words" ("wie man das Grauen übersetzt in Worte"; "*Auf ungeheuer dünnem Eis*" 123), and he goes on to contend that authors can write about events in a more illuminating manner if they keep them at rhetorical arm's length. He concludes with a kind of definitive statement of purpose:

Das ist mein schriftstellerischer Ehrgeiz: die schweren Dinge so zu schreiben, daß sie ihr Gewicht verlieren. Ich glaube, daß nur durch Leichtigkeit Dinge vermittelbar sind und daß alles, was dieses Bleigewicht hat, auch den Leser in einer Form belastet, die ihn blind macht. (*"Auf ungeheuer dünnem Eis*" 124)
[That is my ambition as a writer: to write about the difficult things in such a way that they lose their gravity. I believe that things can only be communicated by means of levity, and that everything that is as heavy as lead also places a burden on the readers, so that it makes them blind.]

Sebald, 221–42, as well as his *Interventionen: Literaturkritik als Widerspruch bei W. G. Sebald* (Munich: edition text + kritik, 2014), 7–63.

65 Carol Jacobs, *Sebald's Vision* (New York: Columbia University Press, 2015), 101, has emphasized Sebald's proclivity for ending his narratives by speaking through the words or the images of others. If intertextual refraction represents Sebald's formula for successful conclusions, then the absence of such filtering signals one failure of the Corsica manuscripts.

This "levity," this lightly buoyant take on those things that are most "weighty" and emotionally oppressive, is precisely what Sebald was *unable* to accomplish in the Corsica manuscripts: he could not assume a detached, neutral narrative attitude for relating the ways in which the human psychic constitution plays into environmental decimation and human self-destruction. If he was keenly aware that the human eye easily turns away from the things that pain it, then an effective literature that seeks to *mitigate* and raise consciousness about this human proclivity for environmental destruction would also have to mitigate its own rhetoric. Sebald was so passionately invested in the horrors of ecological obliteration during the work on the Corsica project that he found it difficult to attain the detachment and neutrality prerequisite for a successful—that is, psychologically and rhetorically effective—*narrative* recounting of environmental catastrophe. He likely recognized that this work fell short of invoking that moment of *anagnorisis* in its audience that he found modeled in the interaction between the narrating ghost of the ancient mariner and the Wedding-Guest in Coleridge's ballad. If a work like *Schwindel. Gefühle* can end by conjuring a fiery catastrophe that is in many ways similar to the concluding passage in the Corsica manuscripts, in that earlier text this strategy is successful precisely because the narrator's voice is intertextually telescoped through Samuel Pepys's account of the catastrophic fire of London (*Schwindel* 287/262–3). In the Corsica manuscripts, the narrator not only concludes with his own fantasy of an apocalyptic inferno, but also alludes implicitly to the very historical events, the Holocaust and the firestorm over German cities, that preoccupied him throughout his life and works. The Corsica manuscripts end with ironically tinged rhetorical questions aimed directly at the reader. If the narrator's own language imitates his subject matter by developing as a rhetorical conflagration in its own right, this gesture is as off-putting as it is generally out of character with Sebald's mature narrative voice.

Asked by Sven Boedecker in a 1995 interview about the perspective on ecological decline articulated in *Die Ringe des Saturn*, Sebald responded by pointing to the frustration one feels with traditional approaches to this problem:

> Allerdings. Das ist eine Perspektive, über die man kaum nachdenken kann, ohne verrückt zu werden. Es gibt als Reaktion darauf zum einen den Zynismus, andererseits gibt es eine Form wissenschaftlicher Indifferenz. So ist es, und jetzt schaun wir mal, was wir machen können" (*"Auf ungeheuer dünnem Eis"* 116).
> [Indeed. That is a perspective upon which one can hardly reflect without going crazy. One possible reaction to it is cynicism,

another is a form of scientific indifference. That's just the way it is,
and now we have to take a look and see what we can do about it.]

The conclusion of the Corsica draft moves dangerously close to the
very cynicism in matters of environmental catastrophe that Sebald
indicts here. At the same time, these fragments steer clear of the scientific objectivity and emotional "indifference" Sebald names as the other
common extreme into which discourses on ecological destruction tend
to fall. The challenge he faced—and ultimately failed to resolve—in
the Corsica project was precisely the attempt to carve out a narratological position that was objective without being sterilely factual,
but that was also tinged by infectious subjective emotions; a position
grounded in personal experience, but that could still lay claim to
enough psychological universality to provoke searching questions
about the motives that underlie (self-)destructive human behavior
toward the environment that sustains us. The fact that he aborted
this project suggests that he felt he had not—or not yet—been able
to resolve these problems. Whether he would have returned to this
material in some form after the publication of *Austerlitz* remains moot,
since his death brought any future projects to an abrupt end. We do
know that as early as 1991, Sebald the literary critic reflected somewhat
skeptically on the ability of recent Austrian literature to engage productively with the loss of a natural homeland, even though in his view this
same literature largely succeeded in finding a critical voice adequate
to portraying *societal* or *sociopolitical* problems. The Introduction to
his collection of essays on Austrian literature ends with a programmatic statement about the relative success or failure of literature when
dealing with sociopolitical or environmental catastrophes:

> Was … in den repräsentativen Werken der neuen österreichischen
> Literatur … ablesbar wird, das ist die in der angst- und ahnungs-
> vollen Aufzeichnung der Veränderung des Lichts, der Landschaft
> und des Wetters allmählich aufdämmernde Erkenntnis der im
> weitesten Umraum sich vollziehenden Dissolution und Zerrüttung
> der *natürlichen* Heimat des Menschen. Lag die Restaurierung
> der *gesellschaftlichen* Heimat kraft des rechten Wortes immerhin
> noch im Bereich des Möglichen, so scheint es in zunehmendem
> Maße fraglich, ob solche Kunst hinreichen wird, das zu erretten,
> was wir, über alles, als unsere *wahre* Heimat begreifen müssen.
> (*Unheimliche Heimat* 16; emphasis added)
> [What … is legible in the representative works of modern Austrian
> literature … is the gradually dawning insight into the progressive
> dissolution and ruination of human beings' *natural* homeland,
> as recorded in the fearful and apprehensive changes in light, in

landscape, and in weather. If the restoration of the *social* homeland was still within the realm of possibility, based on the employment of the right words, it appears to be increasingly questionable whether this kind of artistry will be sufficient to rescue what we, above all, have to recognize as our *true* homeland.]

The authors he investigates in this study, Sebald suggests, discovered an appropriate literary means for "restoring" and reforming their sociopolitical home; but their artistry was not sophisticated enough to "rescue" the true homeland of *all* human beings, our ecological life world, despite the fact that they registered the subtle symptoms of environmental decline. The question Sebald was interrogating—but ultimately left open—in his Corsica manuscripts was: How do we find the "right words" to rehabilitate the natural world in the face of ever greater devastation caused by human negligence and instinct-driven destructiveness? He sought to confront this dilemma, but was ultimately unable to resolve it to his own satisfaction. Sebald abandoned this project and returned to his engagement with the narration of human-caused sociopolitical catastrophes in part because he was unable to find an adequate literary strategy for narrating environmental catastrophe, and in part because he could return to his own arguably successful and critically acclaimed literary techniques for empathetic portrayal of sociopolitical violence and its psychological consequences. Now it is left to others to seek solutions for the problems Sebald could not resolve. One of the most pressing issues facing critical environmental studies today, not merely in the domain of literary discourse, is the development of adequate, sensitive, and rhetorically effective strategies for narrating environmental catastrophe. In the Corsica project, Sebald made an unfortunately futile attempt to advance down this narrative path.

Bibliography

Abram, David. *The Spell of the Sensuous*. New York: Random House/Vintage, 1997.
Adorno, Theodor W. "Commitment." Translated by Francis McDonagh. *New Left Review* 87–8 (September–December 1974): 75–89.
Adorno, Theodor W. "Cultural Criticism and Society." In *Critical Sociology: Selected Reading*. Edited by Paul Connerton, 258–76. Harmondsworth: Penguin, 1976.
Adorno, Theodor W. "Engagement." In *Noten zur Literatur*. Vol. 11 of *Gesammelte Schriften*. Edited by Rolf Tiedemann, 409–30. Frankfurt am Main: Suhrkamp, 1997.
Adorno, Theodor W. "The Idea of Natural History." *Telos* 60 (June 1984): 111–24.
Adorno, Theodor W. "Die Idee der Naturgeschichte." In *Philosophische Frühschriften*. Vol. 1 of *Gesammelte Schriften*. Edited by Rolf Tiedemann, 345–65. Frankfurt am Main: Suhrkamp, 1973.
Adorno, Theodor W. "Kulturkritik und Gesellschaft." In *Kulturkritik und Gesellschaft I*. Vol. 10.1 of *Gesammelte Schriften*. Edited by Rolf Tiedemann, 11–30. Frankfurt am Main: Suhrkamp, 1997.
Adorno, Theodor W. *Negative Dialectics*. Translated by E. B. Ashton. New York: Continuum, 1992.
Adorno, Theodor W. *Negative Dialektik*. Vol. 6 of *Gesammelte Schriften*. Edited by Rolf Tiedemann. Frankfurt am Main: Suhrkamp, 1997.
Albes, Claudia. "Die Erkundung der Leere: Anmerkungen zu W. G. Sebalds 'englische Wallfahrt' *Die Ringe des Saturn*." *Jahrbuch der deutschen Schillergesellschaft* 46 (2002): 279–305.
Alison, Jane. "The Third Victim in Bernhard Schlink's *Der Vorleser*." *Germanic Review* 81, no. 2 (2006): 163–78.
Améry, Jean. *Jenseits von Schuld und Sühne*. In *Werke*. Edited by Irene Heidelberger-Leonard. 9 vols, vol. 2, 7–177. Stuttgart: Klett-Cotta, 2002–7.
Anderson, Mark M. "The Edge of Darkness: On W. G. Sebald." *October* 106 (2003): 102–21.
Anderson, Mark M. "*Tristes Tropes*: W. G. Sebald und die Melancholie der deutsch-jüdischen Vergangenheit." In *Gedächtnis und Identität: Die deutsche Literatur nach der Vereinigung*. Edited by Fabrizio Cambi, 231–42. Würzburg: Königshausen & Neumann, 2008.
Anderson, Mark M. "Wo die Schrecken der Kindheit verborgen sind: W. G. Sebalds Dilemma der zwei Väter. Biographische Skizze zu einem Portrait des Dichters als junger Mann." *Literaturen* 7/8 (2006): 32–9.
Annan, Gabriele. "Ghosts." *New York Review of Books*, September 25, 1997, 29–30.
Arendt, Hannah. "We Refugees." In *Hitler's Exiles: Personal Stories of the Flight*

from Nazi Germany to America. Edited by Mark A. Anderson, 253–62. New York: Norton, 1998.

Atlas, James. "W. G. Sebald: A Profile." *The Paris Review* 41, no. 151 (Summer 1999): 278–95.

Atze, Marcel. "Koinzidenz und Intertextualität: Der Einsatz von Prätexten in W. G. Sebalds Erzählung 'All'estero'." In *W. G. Sebald.* Edited by Franz Loquai, 151–75. Eggingen: Edition Isele, 1997.

Baker, Kenneth. "W. G. Sebald: Up Against Historical Amnesia." *San Francisco Chronicle,* October 7, 2001, R2.

Barth, John. *The Sot-Weed Factor.* New York: Doubleday, 1960.

Barthes, Roland. *Camera Lucida: Reflections on Photography.* Translated by Richard Howard. New York: Hill and Wang, 1981.

Barthes, Roland. "The Reality Effect." In *The Rustle of Language.* Translated by Richard Howard, 141–8. Berkeley: University of California Press, 1989.

Bartov, Omer. "Germany as Victim." *New German Critique* 80 (2000): 29–40.

Barzilai, Maya. "Facing the Past and the Female Spectator in W. G. Sebald's *The Emigrants.*" In *W. G. Sebald: A Critical Companion.* Edited by J. J. Long and Anne Whitehead, 203–16. Seattle: University of Washington Press, 2004.

Barzilai, Maya. "Melancholia as World History: W. G. Sebald's Rewriting of Hegel in *Die Ringe des Saturn.*" In *W. G. Sebald and the Writing of History.* Edited by Anne Fuchs and J. J. Long, 73–89. Würzburg: Königshausen & Neumann, 2007.

Baumgarten, Murray. "'Not Knowing What I Should Think': The Landscape of Postmemory in W. G. Sebald's *The Emigrants.*" *Partial Answers* 5, no. 2 (2007): 267–87.

Beck, John. "Reading Room: Erosion and Sedimentation in Sebald's Suffolk." In *W. G. Sebald: A Critical Companion.* Edited by J. J. Long and Anne Whitehead, 75–88. Seattle: University of Washington Press, 2004.

Benjamin, Walter. "Theses on the Philosophy of History." In *Illuminations: Essays and Reflections.* Translated by Harry Zohn, 253–64. New York: Schocken, 1969.

Benjamin, Walter. "Über den Begriff der Geschichte." In *Gesammelte Schriften.* Edited by Rolf Tiedemann and Hermann Schweppenhäuser. 7 vols, vol. 1, 691–704. Frankfurt am Main: Suhrkamp, 1972–91.

Bernhard, Thomas. *Der Stimmenimitator.* Frankfurt am Main: Suhrkamp, 1978.

Bernhard, Thomas. *The Voice Imitator.* Translated by Kenneth J. Northcott. Chicago: University of Chicago Press, 1997.

Bernhard, Thomas. *Wittgensteins Neffe: Eine Freundschaft.* Frankfurt am Main: Suhrkamp, 1987.

Bernhard, Thomas. *Wittgenstein's Nephew.* New York: Knopf, 1989.

Beßlich, Barbara. "Unzuverlässiges Erzählen im Dienst der Erinnerung: Perspektiven auf den Nationalsozialismus bei Maxim Biller, Marcel Beyer und Martin Walser." In *Wende des Erinnerns? Geschichtskonstruktionen in der deutschen Literatur nach 1989.* Edited by Barbara Beßlich, Katharina Grätz, and Olaf Hildebrand, 35–52. Berlin: Erich Schmidt, 2006.

Beyer, Marcel. *Flughunde: Roman.* Frankfurt am Main: Suhrkamp, 1995.

Beyer, Marcel. *The Karnau Tapes.* Translated by John Brownjohn. New York: Harcourt, 1997.

Blackler, Deanne. *Reading W. G. Sebald: Adventure and Disobedience.* Rochester, NY: Camden House, 2007.

Blanchot, Maurice. "After the Fact." In *Vicious Circles.* Translated by Paul Auster, 57–69. Barrytown, NY: Station Hill, 1985.

Blumenberg, Hans. *Schiffbruch mit Zuschauer: Paradigma einer Daseinsmetapher.* Frankfurt am Main: Suhrkamp, 1979.

Boehncke, Heiner. "Clair obscur: W. G. Sebalds Bilder." *W. G. Sebald.* Special Issue of *Text + Kritik* 158 (April 2003): 43–62.

Borges, Jorge Luis. "Tlön, Uqbar, Orbis Tertius." In *Labyrinths: Selected Stories and Other Writings.* Edited by Donald A. Yates and James E. Irby, 3–18. New York: New Directions, 1962.

Boswell, James. *An Account of Corsica, the Journal of a Tour to That Island, and Memoirs of Pascal Paoli.* 3rd, corrected ed. London: Edward and Charles Dilly, 1769.

Brockhaus Enzyklopädie. 20 vols. Wiesbaden: Brockhaus, 1973.

Bronfen, Elisabeth. "Exil in der Literatur: Zwischen Metapher und Realität." *Arcadia* 28 (1993): 167–83.

Buell, Lawrence. "Toxic Discourse." *Critical Inquiry* 24, no. 3 (Spring 1998): 639–65.

Bülow, Ulrich von. "Sebalds Korsika-Projekt." In *Wandernde Schatten: W. G. Sebalds Unterwelt.* Edited by Ulrich von Bülow, Heike Gfrereis, and Ellen Strittmatter, 211–24. Marbacher Katalog 62. Marbach am Neckar: Deutsche Schillergesellschaft, 2008.

Byram, Katra A. "A Footnote to History: German Trauma and the Ethics of Holocaust Representation in W. G. Sebald's *Austerlitz.*" In *Ethics and the Dynamic Observer Narrator: Reckoning with Past and Present in German Literature,* 191–220. Columbus: Ohio State University Press, 2015.

Carson, Rachel. *Silent Spring.* Boston: Mariner Books/Houghton, 2002 (1962).

Catling, Jo. "Bibliotheca abscondita: On W. G. Sebald's Library." In *Saturn's Moons: W. G. Sebald—A Handbook.* Edited by Jo Catling and Richard Hibbitt, 265–97. London: Modern Humanities Research Association, 2011.

Catling, Jo. "Gratwanderungen bis an den Rand der Natur: W. G. Sebald's Landscapes of Memory." In *The Anatomist of Melancholy: Essays in Memory of W. G. Sebald.* Edited by Rüdiger Görner, 19–50. Munich: Iudicum, 2003.

Certeau, Michel de. *The Practice of Everyday Life.* Translated by Steven Rendall. Berkeley: University of California Press, 1984.

Chakrabarty, Dipesh. "The Climate of History: Four Theses." *Critical Inquiry* 35, no. 2 (Winter 2009): 197–222.

Chandler, James. "About Loss: W. G. Sebald's Romantic Art of Memory." *South Atlantic Quarterly* 102 (2003): 235–62.

"'Characters, plot, dialogue? That's not really my style …'" *Observer Review,* June 7, 1998, 17.

Coleridge, Samuel Taylor. *The Rime of the Ancient Mariner.* In *The Complete Poetical Works of Samuel Taylor Coleridge.* Edited by Ernest Hartley Coleridge. 2 vols, vol. 1, 186-209. Oxford: Clarendon, 1912.

Corngold, Stanley. "Sebald's Tragedy." In *Rethinking Tragedy.* Edited by Rita Felski, 218–40. Baltimore, MD: Johns Hopkins University Press, 2008.

Craven, Peter. "W. G. Sebald: Anatomy of Faction." *HEAT* 13 (1999): 212–24.

Crownshaw, Richard. "German Suffering or 'Narrative Fetishism'?: W. G. Sebald's *Air War and Literature: Zürich Lectures.*" In *Searching for Sebald: Photography after W. G. Sebald.* Edited by Lise Patt, 558–83. Los Angeles: Institute of Cultural Inquiry, 2007.

Crownshaw, Richard. "Reconsidering Postmemory: Photography, the Archive, and Post-Holocaust Memory in W. G. Sebald's *Austerlitz.*" *Mosaic* 37 (2004): 215–36.

Curtin, Adrian and Maxim M. Shrayer. "Netting the Butterfly Man: The

Significance of Vladimir Nabokov in W. G. Sebald's *The Emigrants*." *Religion and the Arts* 9 (2005): 258–83.

Darby, David. "Landscape and Memory: Sebald's Redemption of History." In *W. G. Sebald: History, Memory, Trauma*. Edited by Scott Denham and Mark McCulloh, 265–77. Berlin: De Gruyter, 2006.

Daub, Adrian. "'Donner à Voir': The Logics of Caption in W. G. Sebald's *Rings of Saturn* and Alexander Kluge's *Devil's Blind Spot*." In *Searching for Sebald: Photography after W. G. Sebald*. Edited by Lise Patt, 306–29. Los Angeles: Institute of Cultural Inquiry, 2007.

Dehairs, Wouter. "Literatur im Kontext? Kontext als Intertext: Analyse von W. G. Sebalds *Schwindel. Gefühle* und dessen Ethik des Erinnerns." In *Rezeption, Interaktion und Integration: Niederländischsprachige und deutschsprachige Literatur im Kontext*. Edited by Leopold Decloedt, Herbert Van Uffelen, and M. Elisabeth Weissenböck, 271–87. Vienna: Praesens, 2004.

Del Litto, Victor. *Album Stendhal, Iconographie*. Paris: Gallimard, 1966.

Doctorow, E. L. "W. G. Sebald." In *Creationists: Selected Essays, 1993–2006*, 143–9. New York: Random House, 2006.

Donahue, William Collins. "Illusions of Subtlety: Bernhard Schlink's *Der Vorleser* and the Moral Limits of Holocaust Fiction." *German Life and Letters* 54, no. 1 (2001): 60–81.

Drews, Jörg. "Wie eines jener bösen deutschen Märchen." *Süddeutsche Zeitung*, October 2–4, 1992, x.

Duttlinger, Carolin. "Traumatic Photographs: Remembrance and the Technical Media in W. G. Sebald's *Austerlitz*." In *W. G. Sebald: A Critical Companion*. Edited by J. J. Long and Anne Whitehead, 155–71. Seattle: University of Washington Press, 2004.

Eco, Umberto. "From the Tree to the Labyrinth." In *From the Tree to the Labyrinth: Historical Studies on the Sign and Interpretation*. Translated by Anthony Oldcorn, 3–94. Cambridge, MA: Harvard University Press, 2014.

Edmonds, David and John Eidinow. *Wittgenstein's Poker: The Story of a Ten-Minute Argument Between Two Great Philosophers*. New York: Ecco/Harper Collins, 2001.

Ehrenstein, Albert. "Der Selbstmörder." In *Gedichte und Prosa*, 95. Neuwied: Luchterhand, 1961.

Elcott, Noam M. "Tattered Snapshots and Castaway Tongues: An Essay at Layout and Translation with W. G. Sebald." *Germanic Review* 79 (2004): 203–23.

The Enigma of Kaspar Hauser. Directed by Werner Herzog. Written by Werner Herzog. Werner Herzog Filmproduktion, 1974.

Ezrahi, Sidra DeKoven. "Questions of Authenticity." In *Teaching the Representation of the Holocaust*. Edited by Marianne Hirsch and Irene Kacandes, 52–67. New York: Modern Language Association, 2004.

Faulkner, William. *Requiem for a Nun*. New York: Vintage, 2001.

Federman, Raymond. "Imagination as Plagiarism [An Unfinished Paper …]." *New Literary History* 7, no. 3 (Spring 1976): 563–78.

Federman, Raymond. "Surfiction—Four Propositions in Form of an Introduction." In *Surfiction: Fiction Now … and Tomorrow*. Edited by Raymond Federman, 5–15. 2nd, enlarged ed. Chicago: Swallow Press, 1981.

Feiereisen, Florence and Daniel Pope. "True Fictions and Fictional Truths: The Enigmatic in Sebald's Use of Images in *The Emigrants*." In *Searching for Sebald: Photography after W. G. Sebald*. Edited by Lise Patt, 162–87. Los Angeles: Institute of Cultural Inquiry, 2007.

Felman, Shoshana and Dori Laub. *Testimony: Crises of Witnessing in Literature, Psychoanalysis, and History*. New York: Routledge, 1992.

Finch, Helen. *Sebald's Bachelors: Queer Resistance and the Unconforming Life*. Oxford: Legenda, 2013.

Fischer, Gerhard. "W. G. Sebald." In *Praktizierte Intermedialität: Deutsch-französische Porträts von Schiller bis Goscinny/Uderzo*. Edited by Fernand Hörner, Harald Neumeyer, and Bernd Stiegler, 265–89. Bielefeld: Transcript, 2010.

Fisher, Andy. *Radical Ecopsychology: Psychology in the Service of Life*. Albany: State University of New York Press, 2002.

Foucault, Michel. *The Order of Things: An Archaeology of the Human Sciences*. New York: Random House/Vintage, 1973.

Freud, Sigmund. *Civilization and Its Discontents*. In *The Standard Edition of the Complete Psychological Works of Sigmund Freud*. Edited and translated by James Strachey. 24 vols, vol. 21, 64–145. London: Hogarth, 1953–74.

Freud, Sigmund. "A Difficulty in the Path of Psychoanalysis." In *The Standard Edition of the Complete Psychological Works of Sigmund Freud*. Edited and translated by James Strachey. 24 vols, vol. 17, 137–44. London: Hogarth, 1953–74.

Freud, Sigmund. *Jokes and Their Relation to the Unconscious*. In *The Standard Edition of the Complete Psychological Works of Sigmund Freud*. Vol. 8. Edited and translated by James Strachey. London: Hogarth, 1960.

Freud, Sigmund. "Psycho-Analytic Notes on an Autobiographical Account of a Case of Paranoia (Demetia Paranoides)." In *The Standard Edition of the Complete Psychological Works of Sigmund Freud*. Edited and translated by James Strachey. 24 vols, vol. 12, 9–82. London: Hogarth, 1953–74.

Freud, Sigmund. "Psychoanalytische Bemerkungen über einen autobiographisch beschriebenen Fall von Paranoia (Dementia paranoides)." In *Zwang, Paranoia und Perversion*, vol. 7 of *Freud-Studienausgabe*. Edited by Alexander Mitscherlich, Angela Richards, and James Strachey, 133–200. Frankfurt am Main: Fischer, 1973.

Freud, Sigmund. "Eine Schwierigkeit der Psychoanalyse." In *Gesammelte Werke*. Edited by Anna Freud et al. 18 vols, vol. 12, 1–12. London: Imago, 1940–87.

Freud, Sigmund. "Screen Memories." In *The Standard Edition of the Complete Psychological Works of Sigmund Freud*. Edited and translated by James Strachey. 24 vols, vol. 3, 301–22. London: Hogarth, 1953–74.

Freud, Sigmund. "Über Deckerinnerungen." In *Gesammelte Werke*. Edited by Anna Freud et al. 18 vols, vol. 1, 529–54. London: Imago, 1940–87.

Freud, Sigmund. *Das Unbehagen in der Kultur*. In *Gesammelte Werke*. Edited by Anna Freud et al. 18 vols, vol. 14, 417–506. London: Imago, 1940–87.

Freud, Sigmund. "The Uncanny." In *The Standard Edition of the Complete Psychological Works of Sigmund Freud*. Edited and translated by James Strachey. 24 vols, vol. 17, 219–56. London: Hogarth, 1953–74.

Freud, Sigmund. "Das Unheimliche." In *Gesammelte Werke*. Edited by Anna Freud et al. 18 vols, vol. 12, 227–68. London: Imago, 1940–87.

Freud, Sigmund. *Der Witz und seine Beziehung zum Unbewußten*. In *Gesammelte Werke*. Vol. 6. Edited by Anna Freud. London: Imago, 1940.

Friedlander, Saul. "Introduction." In *Probing the Limits of Representation: Nazism and the Final Solution*. Edited by Saul Friedlander, 1–21. Cambridge, MA: Harvard University Press, 1992.

Friedlander, Saul. *Wenn die Erinnerung kommt*. Translated by Helgard Oestreich. Munich: Beck, 1998.

Friedlander, Saul. *When Memory Comes*. Translated by Helen R. Lane. New York: Farrar Strauss, 1979.

Fuchs, Anne. "'Ein Hauptkapitel der Geschichte der Unterwerfung': Representations of Nature in W. G. Sebald's *Die Ringe des Saturn*." In *W. G. Sebald and the Writing of History*. Edited by Anne Fuchs and J. J. Long, 121–38. Würzburg: Königshausen & Neumann, 2007.

Fuchs, Anne. *Die Schmerzensspuren der Geschichte: Zur Poetik der Erinnerung in W. G. Sebalds Prosa*. Cologne: Böhlau, 2004.

Fuchs, Anne. "Von Orten und Nicht-Orten: Fremderfahrung und dunkler Tourismus in Sebalds Prosa." In *W. G. Sebald: Intertextualität und Topographie*. Edited by Irene Heidelberger-Leonard and Mireille Tabah, 55–71. Berlin: LIT Verlag, 2008.

Ganzfried, Daniel and Sebastian Hefti. *Alias Wilkomirski: Die Holocaust-Travestie*. Berlin: Jüdische Verlagsanstalt, 2002.

Gasseleder, Klaus. "Erkundungen zum Prätext der Luisa-Lanzberg-Geschichte aus W. G. Sebalds *Die Ausgewanderten*: Ein Bericht." In *Sebald. Lektüren*. Edited by Marcel Atze and Franz Loquai, 157–75. Eggingen: Edition Isele, 2005.

Gfrereis, Heike and Ellen Strittmatter. "Wandernde Schatten: W. G. Sebald's Unterwelt." In *Wandernde Schatten: W. G. Sebalds Unterwelt*. Edited by Ulrich von Bülow, Heike Gfrereis, and Ellen Strittmatter, 7–9. Marbacher Katalog 62. Marbach: Deutsche Schillergesellschaft, 2008.

Gilloch, Graeme. "The 'Arca Project': W. G. Sebald's Corsica." In *A Literature of Restitution: Critical Essays on W. G. Sebald*. Edited by Jeanette Baxter, Valerie Henitiuk, and Ben Hutchinson, 126–49. Manchester: Manchester University Press, 2013.

Goethe, Johann Wolfgang von. *Faust: Der Tragödie erster und zweiter Teil*. In *Goethes Werke*. Vol. 3. Edited by Erich Trunz. Munich: Beck, 1978.

Goethe, Johann Wolfgang von. *Faust I and II*. In *Goethe's Collected Works in Twelve Volumes*. Edited and translated by Stuart Atkins. Vol. 2. Princeton, NJ: Princeton University Press, 1994–5.

Görner, Rüdiger. "Leere Reisekoffer und gedächtnislose Gegenwart: W. G. Sebalds Topographieren im Korsika-Projekt." In *W. G. Sebald: Intertextualität und Topographie*. Edited by Irene Heidelberger-Leonard and Mireille Tabah, 111–23. Berlin: LIT Verlag, 2008.

Görner, Rüdiger. "Los der Ausgewanderten: Literarische Umsetzungen der Exilproblematik." *Neue Zürcher Zeitung*, April 29, 1994, 38.

Grass, Günter. *Die Blechtrommel*. Darmstadt: Luchterhand, 1959.

Grass, Günter. *The Tin Drum*. Translated by Ralph Manheim. New York: Pantheon, 1962.

Gray, Richard T. "Reisen in die Vergangenheit (der Natur): W. G. Sebald als Öko-Tourist." *Literatur für Leser* 68, no. 4 (2013): 193–210.

Gregorovius, Ferdinand. *Korsika: Historische Skizzen und Wanderungen im Jahre 1852*. Frankfurt am Main: Societäts-Verlag, 1988.

Gregory-Guider, Christopher C. "Memorial Sights/Sites: Sebald, Photography, and the Art of Autobiogeography in *The Emigrants*." In *Searching for Sebald: Photography after W. G. Sebald*. Edited by Lise Patt, 516–41. Los Angeles: Institute of Cultural Inquiry, 2007.

Gregory-Guider, Christopher C. "The 'Sixth' Emigrant: Traveling Places in the Works of W. G. Sebald." *Contemporary Literature* 46 (2005): 422–49.
Grimmelshausen, Hans Jakob Christoffel von. *Der abenteuerliche Simplicissimus.* Edited by Alfred Kelletat. Stuttgart: Parkland-Verlag, 1975.
Halbwachs, Maurice. *Das Gedächtnis und seine sozialen Bedingungen.* Translated by Lutz Geldsetzer. Frankfurt am Main: Suhrkamp, 1985.
Halbwachs, Maurice. *On Collective Memory.* Edited and translated by Lewis A. Coser. Chicago: University of Chicago Press, 1992.
Harris, Mark Jonathan and Deborah Oppenheimer. *Into the Arms of Strangers: Stories of the Kindertransport.* New York: Bloomsbury, 2000.
Hawkins, Gay. "History in Things: Sebald and Benjamin on Transience and Detritus." In *W. G. Sebald: Schreiben ex patria / Expatriate Writing.* Edited by Gerhard Fischer, 161–75. Amsterdam: Rodopi, 2009.
Hegel, Georg Wilhelm Friedrich. *The Philosophy of History.* Translated by John Sibree. New York: Dover, 1956.
Hegel, Georg Wilhelm Friedrich. *Vorlesungen über die Philosophie der Geschichte.* In *Theorie Werkausgabe.* Vol. 12. Edited by Eva Moldenhauer and Karl Markus Michel. Frankfurt am Main: Suhrkamp, 1970.
Heidegger, Martin. *Einführung in die Metaphysik.* 2nd ed. Tübingen: Niemeyer, 1958.
Heidegger, Martin. *Introduction to Metaphysics.* Translated by Gregory Fried and Richard Polt. New Haven, CT: Yale University Press, 2000.
Heidegger, Martin. *Was heißt Denken?* In *Gesamtausgabe.* Vol. 8. Edited by Paola-Ludovika Coriando. Frankfurt am Main: Klostermann, 2002.
Heidegger, Martin. *What Is Called Thinking?* Translated by Fred D. Wieck and J. Glenn Gray. New York: Harper & Row, 1968.
Heidelberger-Leonard, Irene. "Zwischen Aneignung und Restitution: Die Beschreibung des Unglücks von W. G. Sebald. Versuch einer Annäherung." In *W. G. Sebald: Intertextualität und Topographie.* Edited by Irene Heidelberger-Leonard and Mireille Tabah, 9–23. Berlin: LIT Verlag, 2008.
Hell, Julia. "The Angel's Enigmatic Eyes, or The Gothic Beauty of Catastrophic History in W. G. Sebald's *Air War and Literature.*" *Criticism* 46 (2004): 361–92.
Herren, Graley. "The Return of the Repressed Mother in W. G. Sebald's Fiction." In *A Literature of Restitution: Critical Essays on W. G. Sebald.* Edited by Jeanette Baxter, Valerie Henitiuk, and Ben Hutchinson, 231–46. Manchester: Manchester University Press, 2013.
Hirsch, Marianne. *Family Frames: Photography, Narrative, and Postmemory.* Cambridge, MA: Harvard University Press, 1997.
Hochhuth, Rolf. *The Deputy.* Translated by Richard and Clara Winston. New York: Grove Press, 1964.
Hochhuth, Rolf. *Der Stellvertreter: Schauspiel.* Reinbek: Rowohlt, 1963.
Hofmannsthal, Hugo von. "Ein Brief." In *Prosa II. Gesammelte Werke in Einzelausgaben.* Edited by Herbert Steiner, 7–20. Frankfurt am Main: Fischer, 1959.
Hofmannsthal, Hugo von. "The Letter of Lord Chandos." In *Selected Prose.* Translated by Maria Hottinger et al., 129–41. New York: Pantheon, 1952.
Hölderlin, Friedrich. *Sämtliche Werke, Briefe und Dokumente in zeitlicher Folge.* 12 vols. Bremer Ausgabe. Edited by D. E. Sattler. Darmstadt: Wissenschaftliche Buchgesellschaft, 2004.

Holocaust. By Gerald Green. Directed by Marvin J. Chomsky. NBC, April 16–19, 1978.

Hoorn, Tanja van. "Erinnerungspoetiken der Gegenwart: Christoph Ransmayr, Reinhard Jirgl, W. G. Sebald." *Der Deutschunterricht* 57, no. 6 (2005): 54–62.

Horkheimer, Max and Theodor Adorno. *Dialectic of Enlightenment.* Translated by John Cumming. New York: Continuum, 1993.

Horkheimer, Max and Theodor Adorno. *Dialektik der Aufklärung: Philosophische Fragmente.* Frankfurt am Main: Fischer Taschenbuch Verlag, 1988.

Horstkotte, Silke. "Pictorial and Verbal Discourse in W. G. Sebald's *The Emigrants.*" *Iowa Journal of Cultural Studies* 2 (2002): 33–50.

Horstkotte, Silke. "Visual Memory and Ekphrasis in W. G. Sebald's *The Rings of Saturn.*" *English Language Notes* 44, no. 2 (Fall/Winter 2006): 117–30.

Hughes, Robert. *Frank Auerbach.* London: Thames & Hudson, 1990.

Hutchinson, Ben. "Die Leichtigkeit der Schwermut: W. G. Sebalds 'Kunst der Levitation.'" *Jahrbuch der deutschen Schillergesellschaft* 50 (2006): 457–77.

Hutchinson, Ben. "'Umgekehrt wird man leicht selbst zum Verfolgten': The Structure of the Double-Bind in W. G. Sebald." *Revista de Filología Alemana* 14 (2006): 101–11.

Hutchinson, Ben. *W. G. Sebald: Die dialektische Imagination.* Berlin: De Gruyter, 2009.

Jacobs, Carol. *Sebald's Vision.* New York: Columbia University Press, 2015.

Jaggi, Maya. "Recovered Memories." *Guardian*, September 22, 2001, 6–7.

Jones, Tom. "Green, Green Grass of Home." By Curly Putnam. Decca Records, 1966.

Josephs, Jeremy and Susi Bechhofer. *Rosa's Child: One Woman's Search for Her Past.* London: Tauris, 1996.

Jurgensen, Manfred. "Creative Reflection: W. G. Sebald's Critical Essays and Literary Fiction." In *W. G. Sebald: Schreiben ex patria / Expatriate Writing.* Edited by Gerhard Fischer, 413–34. Amsterdam: Rodopi, 2009.

Kaes, Anton. *From Hitler to Heimat: The Return of History as Film.* Cambridge, MA: Harvard University Press, 1989.

Kafatou, Sarah. "An Interview with W. G. Sebald." *Harvard Review* 15 (1998): 31–5.

Kafka, Franz. *The Blue Octavo Notebooks.* Edited by Max Brod. Translated by Ernst Kaiser and Eithne Wilkins. Cambridge, MA: Exact Change, 1991.

Kafka, Franz. *Briefe 1913–1914.* Edited by Hans-Gerd Koch. Frankfurt am Main: Fischer, 1999.

Kafka, Franz. *The Castle.* Translated by Mark Harman. New York: Schocken, 1998.

Kafka, Franz. *The Diaries, 1910–1923.* Translated by Joseph Kresh and Martin Greenberg. New York: Schocken, 1988.

Kafka, Franz. *Drucke zu Lebzeiten.* Edited by Wolf Kittler, Hans-Gerd Koch, and Gerhard Neumann. Frankfurt am Main: Fischer, 1994.

Kafka, Franz. "The Hunter Gracchus." In *The Complete Stories.* Edited by Nahum Glatzer, 226–34. New York: Schocken, 1971.

Kafka, Franz. "Der Jäger Gracchus." In *Nachgelassene Schriften und Fragmente I.* Edited by Malcolm Pasley, 305–13. Frankfurt am Main: Fischer, 1993

Kafka, Franz. *Letters to Felice.* Edited by Erich Heller and Jürgen Born. Translated by James Stern and Elisabeth Duckworth. New York: Schocken, 1973.

Kafka, Franz. *Letters to Friends, Family, and Editors.* New York: Schocken, 1990.

Kafka, Franz. *Nachgelassene Schriften und Fragmente II.* Edited by Jost Schillemeit. Frankfurt am Main: Fischer, 1992.

Kafka, Franz. *Das Schloß*. Edited by Malcolm Pasley. Frankfurt am Main: Fischer, 1982.

Kafka, Franz. *Tagebücher*. Edited by Hans-Gerd Koch, Michael Müller, and Malcolm Pasley. Frankfurt am Main: Fischer, 1990.

Kaspar, Judith. "Intertextualitäten als Gedächtniskonstellationen im Zeichen der Vernichtung: Überlegungen zu W. G. Sebalds *Die Ausgewanderten*." In *Wende des Erinnerns? Geschichtskonstruktionen in der deutschen Literatur nach 1989*. Edited by Barbara Beßlich, Katharina Grätz, and Olaf Hildebrand, 87–98. Berlin: Erich Schmidt, 2006.

Kastura, Thomas. "Geheimnisvolle Fähigkeit zur Transmigration: W. G. Sebalds interkulturelle Wallfahrten in die Leere." *Arcadia* 31 (1996): 197–216.

Kellert, Stephen and Edward O. Wilson. *The Biophilia Hypothesis*. Washington, DC: Island Press, 1993.

Kidner, David W. "Why Psychology is Mute about the Environmental Crisis." *Environmental Ethics* 16, no. 4 (Winter 1994): 359–77.

Kilbourn, Russell J. A. "'Catastrophe with Spectator': Subjectivity, Intertextuality and the Representation of History in *Die Ringe des Saturn*." In *W. G. Sebald and the Writing of History*. Edited by Anne Fuchs and J. J. Long, 139–62. Würzburg: Königshausen & Neumann, 2007.

Klebes, Martin. "W. G. Sebald: Family Resemblances and the Blurred Images of History." In *Wittgenstein's Novels*, 87–130. New York: Routledge, 2006.

Kleist, Heinrich von. "On the Gradual Formation of Thoughts While Speaking." In *Selected Prose of Heinrich von Kleist*, 255–63. Translated by Peter Wortsman. New York: Archipelago Books, 2010.

Kleist, Heinrich von. "Über die allmählige Verfertigung der Gedanken beim Reden." In *Erzählungen, Anekdoten, Gedichte, Schriften*. Edited by Klaus Müller-Salget, 534–40. Frankfurt am Main: Deutscher Klassiker Verlag, 1990.

Klemperer, Victor. *Ich will Zeugnis ablegen bis zum letzten: Tagebücher 1933–1945*. 2 vols. Edited by Walter Nowojski and Hadwig Klemperer. Berlin: Aufbau, 1995.

Klüger, Ruth. "Dichten über die Shoah: Zum Problem des literarischen Umgangs mit dem Massenmord." In *Spuren der Verfolgung: Seelische Auswirkungen des Holocaust auf die Opfer und ihre Kinder*. Edited by Gertrud Hardtmann, 203–21. Gerlingen: Bleicher, 1992.

Kochhar-Lindgren, Gray. "Charcoal: The Phantom Traces of W. G. Sebald's Novel-Memoirs." *Monatshefte* 94 (2002): 368–80.

Kotler, Steven. "Ecopsychology in Ten Easy Lessons: Or How I Learned to Become One with a Glacier." *Orion* 31, no. 2 (March–April 2012): 16–25.

Kraenzle, Christina. "Picturing Place: Travel, Photography, and Imaginative Geography in W. G. Sebald's *Rings of Saturn*." In *Searching for Sebald: Photography after W. G. Sebald*. Edited by Lise Patt, 126–45. Los Angeles: Institute of Cultural Inquiry, 2007.

LaCapra, Dominick. *Representing the Holocaust: History, Theory, Trauma*. Ithaca, NY: Cornell University Press, 1994.

LaCapra, Dominick. *Writing History, Writing Trauma*. Baltimore, MD: Johns Hopkins University Press, 2001.

Langer, Lawrence L. *The Holocaust and the Literary Imagination*. New Haven, CT: Yale University Press, 1975.

Lappin, Elena. "The Man with Two Heads." *Granta* 66 (Summer 1999): 7–65.

Laufer, Almut. "Unheimliche Heimat: Kafka, Freud und die Frage der Rückkehr in W. G. Sebalds *Schwindel. Gefühle*." *Naharaim* 4, no. 2 (2010): 219–73.

Lear, Edward. *Journal of a Landscape Painter in Corsica*. London: Robert John Bush, 1870.

Le Goff, Jacques. *History and Memory*. Translated by Steven Rendall and Elizabeth Claman. New York: Columbia University Press, 1992.

Lejeune, Philippe. "The Autobiographical Pact." In *On Autobiography*. Edited by Paul John Eakin. Translated by Katherine Leary, 3–30. Minneapolis: University of Minnesota Press, 1989.

Lethen, Helmut. "Sebalds Raster: Überlegungen zur ontologischen Unruhe in Sebalds *Die Ringe des Saturn*." In *W. G. Sebald: Politische Archäologie und melancholische Bastelei*. Edited by Michael Niehaus and Claudia Öhlschläger, 13–30. Berlin: Erich Schmidt, 2006.

Levi, Primo. *The Drowned and the Saved*. Translated by Raymond Rosenthal. New York: Random House/Vintage, 1989.

Lévi-Strauss, Claude. *The Savage Mind*. Translated by George Weidenfeld and Nicolson Ltd. Chicago: University of Chicago Press, 1966.

Lévi-Strauss, Claude. *Das wilde Denken*. Translated by Hans Naumann. Frankfurt am Main: Suhrkamp, 1973.

Long, Jonathan J. "Bernhard Schlink's *Der Vorleser* and Binjamin Wilkomirski's *Bruchstücke*: Best-Selling Responses to the Holocaust." In *German-Language Literature Today: International or Popular?* Edited by Arthur Williams, Stuart Parkes, and Julian Preece, 49–66. Oxford: Peter Lang, 2000.

Long, Jonathan J. "Disziplin und Geständnis: Ansätze zu einer Foucaultschen Sebald-Lektüre." In *W. G. Sebald: Politische Archäologie und melancholische Bastelei*. Edited by Michael Niehaus and Claudia Öhlschläger, 219–39. Berlin: Erich Schmidt, 2006.

Long, Jonathan J. *W. G. Sebald: Image, Archive, Modernity*. New York: Columbia University Press, 2007.

Long, Jonathan J. "W. G. Sebald's Miniature Histories." In *W. G. Sebald and the Writing of History*. Edited by Anne Fuchs and J. J. Long, 111–20. Würzburg: Königshausen & Neumann, 2007.

Lorenz, Konrad. *Behind the Mirror: A Search for a Natural History of Human Knowledge*. Translated by Ronald Taylor. London: Methuen, 1977.

Lorenz, Konrad. *Die Rückseite des Spiegels: Versuch einer Naturgeschichte menschlichen Erkennens*. Munich: DTV, 1979.

Lovelock, James. *Gaia: A New Look at Life on Earth*. Revised ed. Oxford: Oxford University Press, 2000.

Macy, Joanna. "Working Through Environmental Despair." In *Ecopsychology: Restoring the Earth, Healing the Mind*. Edited by Theodore Roszack, Mary E. Gomes, and Allen D. Kanner, 240–59. San Francisco: Sierra Club Books, 1995.

Mahlendorf, Ursula R. "Trauma Narrated, Read and (Mis)understood: Bernhard Schlink's *The Reader*." *Monatshefte* 95, no. 3 (2003): 458–81.

Malkmus, Bernhard. "Das Naturtheater des W. G. Sebald: Die ökologischen Aporien eines 'poeta doctus.'" *Gegenwartsliteratur* 10 (2011): 210–33.

Mann, Thomas. *Death in Venice*. Translated by Michael Henry Heim. New York: Harper/Collins, 2004.

Mann, Thomas. "Der Tod in Venedig." In *Gesammelte Werke*. 12 vols, vol. 8, 444–525. Frankfurt am Main: Fischer, 1960.

Martin, Sigurd and Ingo Wintermeyer. "Vorwort." In *Verschiebebahnhöfe der Erinnerung: Zum Werk W. G. Sebalds*. Edited by Sigurd Martin and Ingo Wintermeyer, 7–10. Würzburg: Königshausen & Neumann, 2007.

Bibliography   423

McCarthy, Mary. "A Guide to Exiles, Expatriates, and Internal Émigrés." In *Altogether Elsewhere: Writers on Exile*. Edited by Marc Robinson, 49–58. Boston: Faber & Faber, 1994.

McCulloh, Mark R. *Understanding W. G. Sebald*. Columbia: University of South Carolina Press, 2003.

McGuinness, Brian F. "Wittgensteins Persönlichkeit." In *Ludwig Wittgenstein: Sein Leben in Bildern und Texten*. Edited by Michael Nedo and Michelle Ranchetti, i–xv. Frankfurt am Main: Suhrkamp, 1983.

Mitscherlich, Alexander and Margarete Mitscherlich. *The Inability to Mourn: Principles of Collective Behavior*. Translated by Beverley R. Placzek. New York: Grove Press, 1975.

Morgan, Peter. "The Sign of Saturn: Melancholy, Homelessness and Apocalypse in W. G. Sebald's Prose Narratives." *German Life and Letters* 58, no. 1 (January 2005): 75–92.

Müller, Michael. "Kafka und Casanova." *Freibeuter* 16 (1983): 67–76.

Nabokov, Vladimir. *Pale Fire*. New York: Putnam, 1962.

Nabokov, Vladimir. *Speak, Memory: An Autobiography Revisited*. Penguin Classics. London: Penguin, 2000.

Nedo, Michael and Michele Ranchetti, eds. *Ludwig Wittgenstein: Sein Leben in Bildern und Texten*. Frankfurt am Main: Suhrkamp, 1983.

Newton, Adam Zachary. "Place from Place, and Place from Flight: W. G. Sebald's *The Emigrants* and Aharon Appelfeld's *The Iron Tracks*." In *The Elsewhere: On Belonging at a Near Distance: Reading Literary Memoir from Europe and the Levant*, 41–95. Madison: University of Wisconsin Press, 2005.

Niehaus, Michael. "Ikonotext. Bastelei: *Schwindel. Gefühle* von W. G. Sebald." In *Lesen ist wie Sehen: Intermediale Zitate in Bild und Text*. Edited by Silke Horstkotte and Karin Leonhard, 155–75. Cologne: Böhlau, 2006.

Niven, Bill. "Bernhard Schlink's *Der Vorleser* and the Problem of Shame." *Modern Language Review* 98 (2003): 381–96.

Noll, Justus. *Ludwig Wittgenstein und David Pinsent: Die andere Liebe der Philosophen*. Berlin: Rowohlt, 1998.

Northey, Anthony. "Kafka in Riva, 1913." *Neue Zürcher Zeitung*, Fernausgabe No. 93, April 24, 1987, 37–8.

Öhlschläger, Claudia. *Beschädigtes Leben. Erzählte Risse: W. G. Sebalds poetische Ordnung des Unglücks*. Freiburg im Breisgau: Rombach, 2006.

Öhlschläger, Claudia. *"Cristallisation, c'est l'opération de l'esprit": Stendhals Theorie der Liebe und ihre Bedeutung für W. G. Sebalds Poetik der Einbildung*. Paderborner Universitätsreden 98. Paderborn: Universität Paderborn, 2005.

Öhlschläger, Claudia. "Kristallisation als kulturelle Transformation: Stendhal, W. G. Sebald und das Problem der Wirklichkeitstreue." In *Verschiebebahnhöfe der Erinnerung: Zum Werk W. G. Sebalds*. Edited by Sigurd Martin and Ingo Wintermeyer, 105–18. Würzburg: Königshausen & Neumann, 2007.

Olney, James. *Memory and Narrative: The Weave of Life-Writing*. Chicago: University of Chicago Press, 1998.

Ozick, Cynthia. "The Rights of History and the Rights of the Imagination." *Commentary* (March 1999): 22–7.

Pages, Neil Christian. "Crossing Borders: Sebald, Handke, and the Pathological Vision." *Modern Austrian Literature* 40, no. 4 (December 2007): 61–92.

Pasic, Sabina. "W. G. Sebald and the Cinematic Imagination." Ph.D. diss., University of Washington, 2014.

Patt, Lise. "Searching for Sebald: What I Know for Sure." In *Searching for Sebald: Photography After W. G. Sebald*. Edited by Lise Patt, 16–101. Los Angeles: Institute of Cultural Inquiry, 2007.

Perloff, Marjorie. *Wittgenstein's Ladder*. Chicago: University of Chicago Press, 1996.

Pfeiffer, Peter C. "Korrespondenz und Wahlverwandtschaft: W. G. Sebalds *Die Ringe des Saturn*." *Gegenwartsliteratur* 2 (2003): 226–44.

Pieger, Anna. "Melancholie als Reise- und Schreibbewegung: Zu W. G. Sebalds *Ringe des Saturn*." *Castrum Peregrini* 56, no. 278 (2007): 46–64.

Prager, Brad. "The Good German as Narrator: On W. G. Sebald and the Risks of Holocaust Writing." *New German Critique* 96 (Fall 2005): 75–102.

Presner, Todd Samuel. "Vienna–Rome–Prague–Antwerp–Paris, The Railway Ruins of Modernity: Freud and Sebald on the Narration of German/Jewish Remains." In *Mobile Modernity: Germans, Jews, Trains*, 233–83. New York: Columbia University Press, 2007.

Radisch, Iris. "Der Waschbär der falschen Welt." *Die Zeit*, April 5, 2001, 55–6.

The Reader. By Bernhard Schlink. Directed by Stephen Daldry. The Weinstein Company, 2008.

Renner, Ursula. "Fundstücke: Zu W. G. Sebalds *Austerlitz*." *Der Deutschunterricht* 57, no. 4 (2005): 14–24.

Robertson, Ritchie. "W. G. Sebald as a Critic of Austrian Literature." *Journal of European Studies* 41, no. 3–4 (2011): 305–22.

Rosenfeld, Alvin H. "The Problematics of Holocaust Literature." In *Confronting the Holocaust: The Impact of Elie Wiesel*. Edited by Alvin H. Rosenfeld and Irving Greenberg, 1–30. Bloomington: Indiana University Press, 1978.

Roszack, Theodore, *The Voice of the Earth: An Exploration of Ecopsychology*. New York: Simon & Shuster, 1992.

Roszack, Theodore, "Where Psyche Meets Gaia." In *Ecopsychology: Restoring the Earth, Healing the Mind*. Edited by Theodore Roszack, Mary E. Gomes, and Allen D. Kanner, 1–17. San Francisco: Sierra Club Books, 1995.

Roszack, Theodore, Mary E. Gomes, and Allen D. Kanner, eds. *Ecopsychology: Restoring the Earth, Healing the Mind*. San Francisco: Sierra Club Books, 1995.

Roth, Joseph. *Juden auf Wanderschaft*. In *Werke*. Edited by Klaus Westermann. 6 vols, vol. 2, 827–902. Cologne: Kiepenheuer & Witsch, 1990.

Rothberg, Michael. *Traumatic Realism: The Demands of Holocaust Representation*. Minneapolis: University of Minnesota Press, 2000.

Rushdie, Salman. *Midnight's Children*. London: Jonathan Cape, 1981.

Ryan, Judith R. "Fulgurations: Sebald and Surrealism." *Germanic Review* 82 (2007): 227–49.

Ryan, Judith R. "'Lines of Flight': History and Territory in *The Rings of Saturn*." In *W. G. Sebald: Schreiben ex patria / Expatriate Writing*. Edited by Gerhard Fischer, 45–60. Amsterdam: Rodopi, 2009.

Ryan, Judith R. "Sebald's Encounters with French Narrative." In *From Kafka to Sebald: Modernism and Narrative Form*. Edited by Sabine Wilke, 123–42. New Directions in German Studies 5. New York: Continuum, 2012.

Santner, Eric. *On Creaturely Life: Rilke, Benjamin, Sebald*. Chicago: University of Chicago Press, 2006.

Schaefer, Camillo. *Wittgensteins Größenwahn: Begegnungen mit Paul Wittgenstein*. Vienna: Jugend und Volk, 1986.

Schedel, Susanne. *Wer weiß, wie es vor Zeiten wirklich gewesen ist? Textbeziehungen als Mittel der Geschichtsdarstellung bei W. G. Sebald*. Würzburg: Königshausen & Neumann, 2004.

Scherpe, Klaus R. "Auszeit des Erzählens: W. G. Sebalds Poetik der Beschreibung." *Weimarer Beiträge* 53 (2007): 485–502.

Schindler's List. Directed by Steven Spielberg. Universal Pictures, 1993.

Schlegel, Friedrich. *Charakteristiken und Kritiken I*. In *Kritische Friedrich-Schlegel-Ausgabe*, 21 vols, vol. 2. Edited by Ernst Behler and Hans Eichner. Paderborn: Schöningh, 1967.

Schlegel, Friedrich. *Philosophical Fragments*. Translated by Peter Firchow. Minneapolis: University of Minnesota Press, 1991.

Schlesinger, Philip. "W. G. Sebald and the Condition of Exile." *Theory, Culture and Society* 21, no. 2 (2004): 43–67.

Schlink, Bernhard. *The Reader*. Translated by Carol Brown Janeway. New York: Vintage, 1998.

Schlink, Bernhard. *Der Vorleser: Roman*. Zurich: Diogenes, 1995.

Scholes, Robert. *Fabulation and Metafiction*. Urbana: University of Illinois Press, 1979.

Schowengerdt-Kuzmany, Verena. "Into the Funhouse: Modes of Intertextuality in the Works of W. G. Sebald." Ph.D. diss., University of Washington, 2014.

Schütte, Uwe. *Interventionen: Literaturkritik als Widerspruch bei W. G. Sebald*. Munich: edition text + kritik, 2014.

Schütte, Uwe. *W. G. Sebald: Einführung in Leben und Werk*. Göttingen: Vandenhoeck & Ruprecht, 2011.

Schwartz, Lynne Sharon, ed. *The Emergence of Memory: Conversations with W. G. Sebald*. New York: Seven Stories Press, 2007.

Sebald, W. G. *"Auf ungeheuer dünnem Eis": Gespräche 1971 bis 2001*. Edited by Torsten Hoffmann. Frankfurt am Main: Fischer, 2011.

Sebald, W. G. "Aufzeichnungen aus Korsika: Zur Natur- und Menschenkunde." In *Wandernde Schatten: W. G. Sebalds Unterwelt*. Edited by Ulrich von Bülow, 129–209. Marbacher Katalog 62. Marbach am Neckar: Deutsche Schillergesellschaft, 2008.

Sebald, W. G. *Die Ausgewanderten: Vier lange Erzählungen*. Frankfurt am Main: Eichborn, 1992.

Sebald, W. G. *Austerlitz*. Munich: Hanser, 2001.

Sebald, W. G. *Austerlitz*. Translated by Anthea Bell. New York: Modern Library, 2001.

Sebald, W. G. "Berge oder das ..." *Manuskripte* 28, no. 99 (March 1988): 71–8.

Sebald, W. G. *Die Beschreibung des Unglücks: Zur österreichischen Literatur von Stifter bis Handke*. Frankfurt am Main: Fischer Taschenbuch Verlag, 1994 (1985).

Sebald, W. G. *Campo Santo*. Edited by Sven Meyer. Munich: Hanser, 2003.

Sebald, W. G. *Campo Santo*. Translated by Anthea Bell. New York: Random House, 2005.

Sebald, W. G. *Carl Sternheim: Kritiker und Opfer der Wilhelminischen Ära*. Stuttgart: Kohlhammer, 1969.

Sebald, W. G. *The Emigrants*. Translated by Michael Hulse. New York: New Directions, 1997.

Sebald, W. G. "The Law of Ignominy: Authority, Messianism and Exile in *The Castle*." In *On Kafka: Semi-Centenary Perspectives*, 42–58. New York: Barnes & Noble, 1976.

Sebald, W. G. "Leben Ws: Skizze einer möglichen Szenenreihe für einen nichtrealisierten Film." In *Saturn's Moons: W. G. Sebald—A Handbook*. Edited by Jo Catling and Richard Hibbitt, 324–33. London: Modern Humanities Research Association, 2011.

Sebald, W. G. "Literaturfonds." Typescript of an application to the *Deutscher Literaturfonds*. Konvolut "Unterlagen für die Bewerbung um ein Werkstipendium des Deutschen Literaturfonds," file folder 11 of Konvolut "Prosa, Sammlung *Ausgewanderten*," Deutsches Literaturarchiv Marbach, inventory number HS.2004.0001.00011.

Sebald, W. G. *Logis in einem Landhaus: Über Gottfried Keller, Johann Peter Hebel, Robert Walser und andere*. Frankfurt am Main: Fischer, 2000 (1998).

Sebald, W. G. *Luftkrieg und Literatur*. Frankfurt am Main: Fischer, 2001 (1999).

Sebald, W. G. *Der Mythos der Zerstörung im Werk Döblins*. Stuttgart: Klett, 1980.

Sebald, W. G. *Nach der Natur: Ein Elementargedicht*. Frankfurt am Main: Fischer Taschenbuch Verlag, 1995 (1988).

Sebald, W. G. *On the Natural History of Destruction*. Translated by Anthea Bell. New York: Modern Library, 2003.

Sebald, W. G. *A Place in the Country*. Translated by Jo Catling. New York: Random House, 2013.

Sebald, W. G. "Projekt Wittgenstein." Konvolut "Leben Ws: Skizze einer möglichen Szenenreihe für einen nichtrealisierten Film." Deutsches Literaturarchiv Marbach, inventory number HS.2004.0001.00007.

Sebald, W. G. *Die Ringe des Saturn: Eine englische Wallfahrt*. Frankfurt am Main: Eichborn, 1995.

Sebald, W. G. *The Rings of Saturn*. Translated by Michael Hulse. New York: New Directions, 1997.

Sebald, W. G. *Schwindel. Gefühle*. Frankfurt am Main: Fischer Taschenbuch Verlag, 1994 (1990).

Sebald, W. G. "Thanatos: Zur Motivstruktur in Kafkas *Schloss*." *Literatur und Kritik* 66–7 (1972): 399–411.

Sebald, W. G. "Tiere, Menschen, Maschinen—Zu Kafkas Evolutionsgeschichten." *Literatur und Kritik* 205–6 (July/August 1986): 194–201.

Sebald, W. G. "The Undiscover'd Country: The Death Motif in Kafka's *Castle*." *Journal of European Studies* 2 (1972): 22–34.

Sebald, W. G. "Und manche Nebelflecken löset kein Auge auf." *Klagenfurter Texte: Ingeborg–Bachmann–Wettbewerb 1990*. Edited by Heinz Felbsch and Siegbert Metelko, 111–37. Munich: Piper, 1990.

Sebald, W. G. *Unheimliche Heimat: Essays zur österreichischen Literatur*. Frankfurt am Main: Fischer, 1995 (1991).

Sebald, W. G. "Verlorenes Land: Jean Améry und Österreich." *Text & Kritik: Zeitschrift für Literatur* 99 (1988): 20–9

Sebald, W. G. *Vertigo*. Translated by Michael Hulse. New York: New Directions, 2000.

Sebald, W. G. "Verzehret das letzte selbst die Erinnerung nicht?" *Manuskripte* 28, no. 100 (June 1988): 150–8

Sebald, W. G. "Zwischen Geschichte und Naturgeschichte: Versuch über die literarische Beschreibung totaler Zerstörung mit Anmerkungen zu Kasack, Nossack und Kluge." *Orbis Litterarum* 37 (1982): 345–66.

Sebald, W. G., ed. *A Radical Stage: Theatre in Germany in the 1970s and 1980s*. Oxford: Berg, 1988.

Sebald, W. G. and Jan Peter Tripp. *Unerzählt*. Munich: Hanser, 2003.

Sebald, W. G. and Jan Peter Tripp. *Unrecounted*. Translated by Michael Hamburger. London: Penguin, 2005.

Sewall, Laura. "The Skill of Ecological Perception." In *Ecopsychology: Restoring the Earth, Healing the Mind*. Edited by Theodore Roszak, Mary E. Gomes, and Allen D. Kanner, 201–15. San Francisco: Sierra Club Books, 1995.

Sheppard, Richard. "Dexter—Sinister: Some Observations on Decrypting the Mors Code in the Work of W. G. Sebald." *Journal of European Studies* 35 (2005): 419–63.

Sheppard, Richard. "The Sternheim Years: W. G. Sebald's Lehrjahre and Theatralische Sendung 1963–75." In *Saturn's Moons: W. G. Sebald—A Handbook*. Edited by Jo Catling and Richard Hibbitt, 42–106. London: Modern Humanities Research Association, 2011.

Sheppard, Richard. "W. G. Sebald: A Chronology." In *Saturn's Moons: W. G. Sebald—A Handbook*. Edited by Jo Catling and Richard Hibbitt, 619–59. London: Modern Humanities Research Association, 2011.

Shoah. Directed by Claude Lanzmann. New Yorker Films, 1985.

Sill, Oliver. "Aus dem Jäger ist ein Schmetterling geworden: Textbeziehungen zwischen den Werken von W. G. Sebald, Franz Kafka und Vladimir Nabokov." *Poetica* 29 (1997): 596–623.

Sill, Oliver. "Migration als Gegenstand der Literatur: W. G. Sebalds *Die Ausgewanderten*." In *Nation, Ethnie, Minderheit: Beiträge zur Aktualität ethnischer Konflikte*. Edited by Armin Nassehi, 309–30. Cologne: Bölau, 1997.

Sontag, Susan. "A Mind in Mourning." *Times Literary Supplement* 5056, February 25, 2000, 3–4.

Stach, Reiner. *Kafka: The Years of Insight*. Translated by Shelley Frisch. Princeton, NJ: Princeton University Press, 2013.

Steinaecker, Thomas von. "Zwischen schwarzem Tod und weißer Ewigkeit: Zum Grau auf den Abbildungen W. G. Sebalds." In *Verschiebebahnhöfe der Erinnerung: Zum Werk W. G. Sebalds*. Edited by Sigurd Martin and Ingo Wintermeyer, 119–35. Würzburg: Königshausen & Neumann, 2007.

Steinfeld, Thomas. "Die Wünschelrute in der Tasche eines Nibelungen." *Frankfurter Allgemeine Zeitung* 67, March 20, 2001, L18.

Stendhal. *The Life of Henry Brulard*. Translated by John Sturrock. New York: New York Review of Books, 2002.

Stendhal. *Love*. Translated by Gilbert and Suzanne Sale. London: Penguin, 2004.

Strathausen, Carsten. "Going Nowhere: Sebald's Rhizomatic Travels." In *Searching for Sebald: Photography After W. G. Sebald*. Edited by Lise Patt, 472–91. Los Angeles: Institute for Cultural Inquiry, 2007.

Swales, Martin. "Intertextuality, Authenticity, Metonymy? On Reading W. G. Sebald." In *The Anatomist of Melancholy: Essays in Memory of W. G. Sebald*. Edited by Rüdiger Görner, 81–7. Munich: Iudicum, 2003.

Theisen, Bianca. "A Natural History of Destruction: W. G. Sebald's *The Rings of Saturn*." *MLN* 121 (2006): 563–81.

Theisen, Bianca. "Prose of the World: W. G. Sebald's Literary Travels." *Germanic Review* 79, no. 3 (2004): 163–79.

Timm, Uwe. *Erzählen und kein Ende: Versuche zu einer Ästhetik des Alltags*. Cologne: Kiepenheuer & Witsch, 1993.

Triumph des Willens. Directed by Leni Riefenstahl. Universum Film AG, 1935.

Turner, Gordon. "Introduction and Transcript of an Interview Given by Max

Sebald." In *W. G. Sebald: History, Memory, Trauma*. Edited by Scott Denham and Mark McCulloh, 21–9. Berlin: De Gruyter, 2006.

Vice, Sue. *Holocaust Fiction*. London: Routledge, 2000.

Vico, Giambattista. *New Science*. Translated by David Marsh. London: Penguin, 1999.

Wagenbach, Klaus. "Drei Sanatorien Kafkas: Ihre Bauten und Gebräuche." *Freibeuter* 16 (1983): 77–90.

Wagenbach, Klaus. *Franz Kafka: Bilder aus seinem Leben*. Berlin: Wagenbach, 1983.

Wagner, Richard. *Parsifal*. In *The Authentic Librettos of the Wagner Operas, Complete with English and German Parallel Texts*, 429–70. New York: Crown, 1938.

Wagner-Egelhaaf, Martina. *Die Melancholie der Literatur: Diskursgeschichte und Textfiguration*. Stuttgart: Metzler, 1997.

Waugh, Patricia. *Metafiction: The Theory and Practice of Self-Conscious Fiction*. London: Routledge, 1984.

Weber, Markus R. "Bilder erzählen den Erzähler: Zur Bedeutung der Abbildungen für die Herausbildung von Erzählerrollen in den Werken W. G. Sebalds." In *W. G. Sebald: Mémoire. Transferts. Images. Erinnerung. Übertragungen. Bilder*. Special issue of *Recherches Germaniques* 2 (2005): 25–45.

Weber, Markus R. "Phantomschmerz Heimweh: Denkfiguren der Erinnerung im literarischen Werk W. G. Sebalds." In *Neue Generation—Neues Erzählen: Deutsche Prosaliteratur der achtziger Jahre*. Edited by Walter Delabar, Werner Jung, and Ingrid Pergand, 57–67. Opladen: Westdeutscher Verlag, 1993.

Weihe, Richard. "Wittgensteins Augen: W. G. Sebalds Film-Szenario 'Leben Ws.'" *Fair: Zeitung für Kunst und Ästhetik* 7, no. 4 (2009): 11–12.

Weiss, Peter. *Abschied von den Eltern*. Frankfurt am Main: Suhrkamp, 1961.

Weiss, Peter. *Die Ästhetik des Widerstands*. 3 vols. Frankfurt am Main: Suhrkamp, 1975–81.

Weiss, Peter. *Die Ermittlung: Oratorium in elf Gesängen*. Frankfurt am Main: Suhrkamp, 1965.

Weiss, Peter. *The Investigation: A Play*. Translated by Jon Swan and Ulu Grosbard. New York: Pocket Books, 1967.

Weiss, Peter. *The Leavetaking*. Translated by Christopher Levenson. New York: Harcourt, 1962.

White, Hayden. "Historical Emplotment and the Problem of Truth." In *Probing the Limits of Representation: Nazism and the Final Solution*. Edited by Saul Friedlander, 37–53. Cambridge, MA: Harvard University Press, 1992.

White, Hayden. *Metahistory: The Historical Imagination in Nineteenth-Century Europe*. Baltimore, MD: Johns Hopkins University Press, 1973.

Whitehead, Anne. "The Butterfly Man: Trauma and Repetition in the Writing of W. G. Sebald." In *Trauma Fiction*, 117–39. Edinburgh: Edinburgh University Press, 2004.

Wiesel, Elie. "The Holocaust as Literary Inspiration." In *Dimensions of the Holocaust*, 5–19. Evanston, IL: Northwestern University Press, 1977.

Wilkomirski, Binjamin. *Bruchstücke: Aus einer Kindheit, 1939–1948*. Frankfurt am Main: Jüdischer Verlag, 1995.

Wilkomirski, Binjamin. *Fragments: Memories of a Wartime Childhood*. Translated by Carol Brown Janeway. New York: Schocken, 1996.

Williams, Arthur. "W. G. Sebald." *The Literary Encyclopedia*, http://www.litencyc.com/php/speople.php?rec=true&UID=4961 (accessed March 17, 2017).

Wilson, Edward O. *Biophilia*. Cambridge, MA: Harvard University Press, 1984.

Wilson, Edward O. *The Social Conquest of Earth.* New York: Liveright/ W. W. Norton, 2012.

Wilson, Stephen. *Feuding, Conflict and Banditry in Nineteenth-Century Corsica.* Cambridge: Cambridge University Press, 1988.

Windle, Phyllis. "The Ecology of Grief." In *Ecopsychology: Restoring the Earth, Healing the Mind.* Edited by Theodore Roszak, Mary E. Gomes, and Allen D. Kanner, 136–45. San Francisco: Sierra Club Books, 1995.

Wittgenstein, Ludwig. *Briefe: Briefwechsel mit B. Russell, G. E. Moore, J. M. Keynes, F. P. Ramsey, W. Eccles, P. Engelmann und L. von Ficker.* Edited by Brian F. McGuinness and Georg Henrik von Wright. Frankfurt am Main: Suhrkamp. 1980.

Wittgenstein, Ludwig. *Philosophical Investigations.* Translated by G. E. M. Anscombe. Oxford: Blackwell, 2001.

Wittgenstein, Ludwig. *Philosophische Untersuchungen.* In *Schriften,* 279–544. Frankfurt am Main: Suhrkamp, 1963.

Wittgenstein, Ludwig. *Tractatus Logico-Philosophicus.* Bi-lingual German/English edition. Translated by C. K. Ogden. London: Routledge, 1981.

Witthaus, Jan-Henrik. "Fehlleistung und Fiktion: Sebaldsche Gedächtnismodelle zwischen Freud und Borges." In *W. G. Sebald: Politische Archäologie und melancholische Bastelei.* Edited by Michael Niehaus and Claudia Öhlschläger, 157–72. Berlin: Erich Schmidt, 2006.

Wohlleben, Doren. "Poetik des Schwindelns und Verschwindens bei Hartmut Lange, W. G. Sebald und Horst Stern." In *Differenzerfahrung und Selbst: Bewußtsein und Wahrnehmung in Literatur und Geschichte des 20. Jahrhunderts.* Edited by Bettina von Jagow and Florian Steger, 333–53. Heidelberg: Winter, 2003.

Wood, James. "An Interview with W. G. Sebald." *Brick* 59 (1998): 23–9.

Wrobel, Dieter. *Postmodernes Chaos—Chaotische Postmoderne: Eine Studie zu Analogien zwischen Chaostheorie und deutschsprachiger Prosa der Postmoderne.* Bielefeld: Aisthesis, 1997.

Wuchterl, Kurt and Adolf Hübner. *Ludwig Wittgenstein mit Selbstzeugnissen und Bilddokumenten.* Rowohlt Monographien 275. Reinbek: Rowohlt, 1979.

Wünsche, Konrad. *Der Volksschullehrer Ludwig Wittgenstein.* Frankfurt: Suhrkamp, 1985.

Wylie, John. "The Spectral Geographies of W. G. Sebald." *Cultural Geographies* 14 (2007): 171–88.

Young, James E. *Writing and Rewriting the Holocaust: Narrative and the Consequences of Interpretation.* Bloomington: Indiana University Press, 1990.

Zeitlin, Froma I. "The Vicarious Witness: Belated Memory and Authorial Presence in Recent Holocaust Literature." *History & Memory* 10, no. 2 (Fall/Winter 1998): 5–42.

Zilcosky, John. "Lost and Found: Disorientation, Nostalgia, and Holocaust Melodrama in Sebald's *Austerlitz*." *MLN* 121 (2006): 679–98.

Zilcosky, John. "Sebald's Uncanny Travels: The Impossibility of Getting Lost." In *W. G. Sebald: A Critical Companion.* Edited by J. J. Long and Anne Whitehead, 102–20. Seattle: University of Washington Press, 2004.

Zinfert, Maria. "Grauzonen: Das Schreiben von W. G. Sebald: Versuchsanordnung mit schwarzweissen Fotografien." In *"Ein in der Phantasie durchgeführtes Experiment": Literatur und Wissenschaft nach Neunzehnhundert.* Edited by Raul Calzoni and Massimo Salgaro, 321–35. Göttingen: Vandenhoeck & Ruprecht, 2010.

Zischler, Hanns. *Kafka geht ins Kino*. Reinbek: Rowohlt, 1996.

Zischler, Hanns. "Maßlose Unterhaltung: Franz Kafka geht ins Kino." *Freibeuter* 16 (1983): 33-47.

Zisselsberger, Markus. "The Afterlife of Literature: Sebald, Blanchot, and Kafka's Hunter Gracchus." *Journal of the Kafka Society of America* 31-2, no. 1-2 (June 2007-December 2008): 112-29.

Žižek, Slavoj. "Melancholy and the Act." *Critical Inquiry* 26, no. 4 (Summer 2000): 657-81.

Index

The letter *f* following an entry indicates a page that includes a figure

CPSIA information can be obtained
at www.ICGtesting.com
Printed in the USA

9 781501 352614